UNFOLD THE PROBLEM ▸ REVEAL THE LAW ▸ APPLY TO LIFE

CONTRACT
LAW

TT ARVIND

2ND EDITION

OXFORD
UNIVERSITY PRESS

OXFORD
UNIVERSITY PRESS

Great Clarendon Street, Oxford, OX2 6DP,
United Kingdom

Oxford University Press is a department of the University of Oxford.
It furthers the University's objective of excellence in research, scholarship,
and education by publishing worldwide. Oxford is a registered trade mark of
Oxford University Press in the UK and in certain other countries

Public sector information reproduced under Open Government Licence v3.0
(http://www.nationalarchives.gov.uk/doc/open-government-licence/open-government-licence.htm)

Published in the United States of America by Oxford University Press
198 Madison Avenue, New York, NY 10016, United States of America

British Library Cataloguing in Publication Data
Data available

Library of Congress Control Number: 2019933121

ISBN 978–0–19–882926–3

Printed in Great Britain by
Bell & Bain Ltd., Glasgow

Preface

Over the nearly two decades during which I have taught contract law, it has become clear that understanding the context within which contract law functions is essential to a proper understanding of many aspects of contract doctrine. Many features of contract law that, at first sight, appear puzzling become more intelligible when one studies them in the light of the practical problems with which they are intended to deal. Equally, many of the more heated and intricate debates about particular aspects of contract law become more accessible when they are put in the context of how they will affect the practical working of the law. This textbook, accordingly, seeks to take a different approach to the teaching of English contract law from many traditional textbooks, by combining an accessible and thorough discussion of legal rules and concepts with a more contextual analysis of the effect of the rules, and the manner in which they influence the everyday practice of contracting.

The book brings these elements together using a problem-centric approach, a technique drawn from the world of problem-based learning. Every chapter in this book begins with a problem. The chapter briefly introduces the issues the problem poses, why these issues arise, and why they matter in practice. The problems—supplemented throughout by briefer illustrations—are used as 'triggers' to explain doctrinal positions, with the factual base of the problem providing a real-world context within which to explore the principles and concepts we see in contract law.

The key advantage of a problem-centric format is that it introduces students to legal rules, principles, and concepts not in the abstract, but in a real-world context. Contract law as a subject is intensely practical, and approaching it in a contextual way not only gives students a more accessible introduction to the law itself, but also a better sense of the relevance of the law to common life, and the impact and influence which the law has on social practices.

As far as the law itself is concerned, contract law is an ever-changing subject and it continues to be the subject of considerable activity in the Supreme Court. Chapters 16 and 17 in this edition have seen significant rewriting to take account of the judgment of the Supreme Court in *Morris-Garner v One Step (Support) Ltd* [2018] UKSC 20. Chapter 14 now deals with key trends in the case law following *Patel v Mirza*. Chapters 8 and 9 have been updated to deal with recent trends in applying good faith, as well as unilateral discretion clauses. Other chapters have been revised to deal with key cases and statutes up to 31 July 2018. The online resources will provide updates and notes on important cases that are decided after this date.

A major change which will profoundly affect the law of contract in the near future, but whose precise contours are too unclear at the time of writing to permit a detailed consideration of its implications, is the impending withdrawal of the UK from the EU. Significant portions of English contract law are based on EU directives, including virtually all of consumer protection law. Withdrawal from the EU could potentially affect the law in two ways.

First, after withdrawal, the UK will no longer be under any obligation to implement EU directives, or to maintain in force existing laws transposing EU directives. The government has announced its intention to review which laws based on EU directives it will retain after withdrawal. Although early indications suggest an intention to maintain the present state of consumer protection law, the longer term picture remains unclear. The laws may be retained in their present form, they may be amended to make them more market-oriented, or they may be scrapped altogether in favour of home-grown solutions. At the present time, there is no way of telling.

Secondly, and as importantly, even if the directives in question are retained with relatively little change, the UK's courts will no longer be bound by decisions of the European Court of Justice in relation to EU directives. The ECJ's approach has not always been the same as the one initially taken by English courts. Because its decisions up to the date of withdrawal are binding, they trump decisions of English courts. This will not, however, apply to post-withdrawal decisions. It is at present too early to say to what extent English courts will continue to have regard to decisions of the ECJ after Brexit.

As with all academic projects, this book has benefited from support and assistance from far more people than I can hope to thank, but a few stand out for particular mention. My editors at Oxford University Press—Helen Swann, Sarah Viner, Nicola Hartley, Emily Spicer, and Sarah Stephenson—were both graceful and patient with the inevitable slipping of deadlines, and brought a wealth of experience with textbook production without which this book would have been far less accessible and far too wordy. A special word of thanks must also go to Catherine Dale, law librarian at Newcastle University, for her unfailing ability to track down obscure reports of cases at first instance. My wife, Ranveig, and daughter, Siri Vaidehi, were exceedingly patient and understanding, particularly in the later stages when this book took up ever-increasing chunks of evenings and weekends. This project could not have been seen through to completion but for their constant and uncomplaining support.

I would also like to thank the reviewers—students as well as academics—who gave up their time to provide feedback on the book's chapters in draft form: in alphabetic order: Carolyn Abbot, University of Manchester; Jeanette Ashton, University of Brighton; Andrew Baker, Liverpool John Moores University; Christopher Bisping, University of Warwick; François du Bois, University of Leicester; Stephen Bunbury, University of Westminster; Mark Campbell, University of Bristol; Brigitte Clark, Oxford Brookes University; Máiréad Enright, University of Birmingham; John Halladay, University of Buckingham; Patrick Koroma, University of East London; Donal Loftus, University of Salford; Chris Newdick, University of Reading; Alex Nicholson, Sheffield Hallam University; Onyeka Osuji, University of Exeter; Anastasia Tataryn, University of Liverpool; Eliza Varney, Keele University; Chalen Westaby, Sheffield Hallam University; Jeff Young, Oxford Brookes University. Your assistance is deeply appreciated, and has made a considerable contribution to the final shape of this book.

Finally, in my time as an academic I have been fortunate enough to have taught the law of contract with a series of wonderful colleagues to all of whom I owe a deep debt of gratitude—in chronological order, Vanessa Sims, Djakhongir Saidov, Jenny Steele, Phillip Morgan, Deming Liu, Aisling McMahon, Sarah Mackie, Charlotte Ellis, Isra Black, and Liam Kilvington. I owe a debt, too, to the students I have taught over the years. Without the lively debates and reflection that their questions have so frequently prompted, this book would have been neither necessary nor possible.

TT Arvind
York
15 November 2018

New to this edition:

- The chapters on remedies have been fully revised in the light of the Supreme Court decision in *Morris-Garner v One Step (Support) Ltd* (2018).
- The discussion of good faith has been expanded, and includes an outline of key trends in the recent case law.
- A new 'practice in context' feature has been added to Chapter 17 covering spring-board injunctions, an area of growing importance within the law of specific remedies.
- Dozens of new cases and clarifications have been added throughout.

Guide to the Book

Contract Law is a rich learning resource, enhanced with a range of features designed to help you get the most from your studies. This text guides you through problems and scenarios to help you quickly grasp core concepts, identify relevant issues, engage with key debates, and apply your learning to real-life contexts.

Setting the law into its real-world context

> **Problem 9: setting the context**
>
> Consider the following exchange of text messages bet
>
> Hey, hear you're selling your LP collection. How m
>
> I was thinking of around £500.
>
> Oh no. I don't have that much, but I'd really like th

Problem scenarios

Each chapter begins by setting out a hypothetical 'real-life' problem, which will ask you to think about a few questions. You should have these questions in mind as you read the rest of the chapter.

Illustrations

Throughout the chapter, illustration boxes pick up on and expand upon elements of the problem, or invite you to think about different real-life scenarios relating to the topic.

> **Illustration 2.1**
>
> Consider a slight variation on the facts of Problem 2. In were replaced by these messages:
>
> Hi, £185 is fine. Shall we meet in the Square at 4 p
>
> Hi, just saw your message—my phone's been off fo

Together the **'problem'** scenarios and **'illustrations'** frame the topic for the chapter and ground it in real life, helping you to understand how the theory and concepts of contract law apply in practice.

Developing your ability to fully engage with and critically reflect on the law

> **Case in depth:** *Balfour v Balfour* [1919] 2 I
>
> Mr and Mrs Balfour lived in what was then the colony of an irrigation engineer. In 1915, they returned to England a doctor to remain in England for some months as she In August 1916, her husband returned to Ceylon witho cheque for £24, and promised to give her £30 each mo

Case in depth boxes

Case in depth boxes provide detailed discussion of the most influential and important cases in the subject area, to help you to understand how the law has developed and why.

Debates in context boxes

Debates in context boxes highlight areas of the law where commentators and academics disagree, helping you to reflect on the operation of the law and potential future changes in the law.

> **"** **Debates in context: a sword or a sh**
>
> The principle that promissory estoppel cannot be a cau from academics for several decades. The argument ha to the doctrine that requires it to only be a defence, an Other academics have gone further. Professor Atiyah and articles in the 1970s and 1980s calling for consider

> **▶ Practice in context: termination cla**
>
> The legal rules pertaining to breach of contract play a se
> of the contract. Parties can plan for breach, and they o
> provisions to deal with non-performance, or inadequate
> A typical mobile phone contract between a consumer

Practice in context boxes

Practice in context boxes help you to think about the everyday reality of contracts, to give you a practical grounding in the subject.

Supporting you to acquire, reinforce and revise your knowledge of key concepts

Glossary terms

Key terms are highlighted throughout each chapter; you can find a clear, straightforward explanation of what these terms mean in the Glossary at the end of the book.

> situations where a promise or similar statement or
> d upon but where, for some reason, no contract has
> ed **proprietary estoppel** and **promissory estoppel**.
> mation of contracts, these types of estoppel do not
> y require the provision of consideration. They are,
> nore specifically, by **representations** or assurances
> her, on which that other relies.
> ory estoppel share a common structure, they differ

> ### 7.7 In conclusion: applying co
>
> How would the *Investors* rule apply to Problem
> it should not come as a surprise to hear that it is
> court would decide this particular issue. What we
> approach the question, and what it would take in
> In the first instance, *Investors* suggests that the

In conclusion

Each chapter ends with a concluding section, to draw the chapter together, highlight outstanding questions, and apply the discussion back to the problem and illustrations you have considered.

Key points

Following the conclusion, the essential concepts you have studied are summarized in a few bullet points to help you to remember the key points of law covered.

> **Key points**
>
> * Certain promises which are not enforceable as c
>   the doctrine of estoppel. Estoppel operates by
>   something they have asserted, promised, or acc
> * Two types of estoppel supplement the law of c

> **Assess your learning**
>
> You should be able to respond to each of the follov
> can't, then you should revisit the sections listed ag
> Can you:
>
> **(a)** *Identify* the purpose and main approaches to c

Assess your learning

A few questions at the end of each chapter help you to think about what you have learnt, track your progress, and go back to any sections you need to spend more time on.

Further reading

Suggestions for further reading give you a starting point for broadening your knowledge and taking your learning further.

> **Further reading**
>
> PS Atiyah, '*Couturier v Hastie* and the Sale of Non-Ex
> R Brownsword, 'Henry's Lost Spectacle and Hutton's
> (1985) 129 SJ 860.

UNFOLD THE PROBLEM ▸ REVEAL THE LAW ▸ APPLY TO LIFE

Guide to the Online Resources

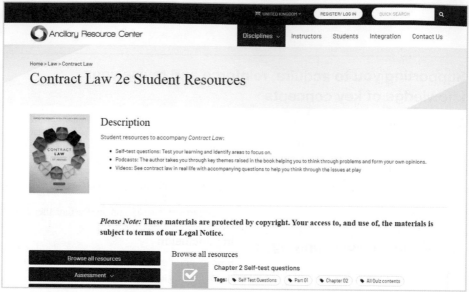

 www.oup.com/uk/arvind2e

Accompanying online resources support your learning and include:

- Self-test questions: test your learning and identify areas to focus on.

- Podcasts: let the author talk you through key themes raised in the book, helping you to think through problems and form your own opinions.

- Video links: apply what you have learnt in the book and see contract law working in real life, with accompanying questions to help you think through the issues at play.

Contents in brief

Detailed contents

Table of Cases

Australia

Canada

New Zealand

Singapore

South Africa

United States of America

European Union

European Court of Justice

Table of Legislation

Introduction

1.1 **The relevance of contract**

The best way to begin studying a subject is by understanding what that subject is about. So let us start by asking a rather basic question. What is the law of contract about, and why does it matter? Why is this branch of law considered important enough to be a compulsory part of the law curriculum?

The answers to these questions are not as obvious as one might initially think. Contracts are ubiquitous, true, but so are horses and dogs. Yet there is no such thing as a 'law of horses' or a 'law of dogs'. What gives the law of contract its importance is not how often we encounter it, but the role which contracting plays in everyday life. Our interests are never going to align perfectly with the interests of those we come into contact with. People disagree with each other all the time, and sometimes these disputes end up in court. Every branch of law, accordingly, has to deal with the potential for dispute that is frequently encountered in social interaction, and to find ways of resolving the problems of conflicting expectations, goals, and interests that underlie most social disputes.

What gives the law of contract its importance is the approach it takes to dealing with this problem. Unlike most other areas of law, the law of contract is, fundamentally, about the freedom of individuals in society to structure their mutual relations in whatever way they deem best, given their individual goals, preferences, and motives. Rather than impose ready-made bundles of rights and duties upon the parties, contract law creates a framework within which parties can define their *own* rights, duties, and powers vis-à-vis each other. To think about legal issues and problems in terms of contract is, therefore, to adopt a very different approach to dealing with the underlying issues.

To illustrate this, consider the following scenario:

Illustration 1.1

The financial crisis that began in 2008 created a prolonged period of low interest rates. Low interest rates helped borrowers, because they had to pay less interest on the loans they had taken out. But low interest rates hurt savers, because they now received a considerably lower return on their savings. Many building societies were troubled by this, because they saw themselves as having a social role in promoting a culture of saving. One of them decided that it would take action to safeguard the position of savers. It announced that it would no longer pass on reductions in the Bank of England base rate to its borrowers. Instead, it would prioritize giving savers a better return. Savers were ecstatic, but borrowers were furious, and challenged the building society's right to act as it had done.

Was the building society right to act as it did in this scenario (which is loosely based on an actual case)?[1] A layperson thinking about the rights and wrongs of the situation might do so in a number of ways. From a moral standpoint, she might ask whether it

---

1. *Alexander (as representative of the 'Property118 Action Group') v West Bromwich Mortgage Co Ltd* [2016] EWCA Civ 496.

was right for a building society to lean so heavily towards a traditional understanding of the virtue of prudence. From a social standpoint, she might ask who the borrowers and savers are, and what their respective means are, in order to determine which of them is best placed to bear the loss. From a more hard-nosed economic standpoint, she might ask what is best for the national economy: a higher savings rate or more spending.

The law of contract does none of these things. The questions it asks are far simpler. Rather than considering the ethical rights and wrongs of the matter, it looks, simply, to the terms on which the parties agreed to deal with each other. The loan which the building society gave its borrowers would have been given under an agreement. What did the terms of that agreement say about interest rates? Did the bank expressly or implicitly promise to link its rates to the Bank of England base rate? Were there other provisions in the agreement that overrode this promise? The answer, in other words, would be based almost exclusively on the terms of the parties' agreement. Broader considerations of right and wrong would play a secondary role, at best.

The resulting freedom given is of foundational importance to a liberal society, and to a liberal economic order. It also means that the framework provided by contract law is flexible and extensible. Contracts are devices by which people buy and sell things, obtain and provide services, and provide and procure necessities and luxuries. But they are also devices by which people organize, govern, and regulate their relationships, determining the terms on which they interact and the claims they have over each other. Parties can use contracts for a simple, one-off transaction of exchange, as when you go into a shop to purchase a soft drink. Or they can use contracts to set out the terms under which they will deal with each other in a complex, long-term commercial relationship, as companies do when they agree to develop and operate a new power plant in a 30-year joint venture. Contracts can also be used to structure and limit the duties and liabilities which one party owes to another, as with the terms and conditions you accept when you sign up for a service like Snapchat or Facebook. Freedom of contract is deeply ingrained in the fabric of everyday life, and we have grown so used to it that we rarely notice it or the role it plays in ordering our lives.

But there are limits to freedom of contract. Consider the following illustration:

Illustration 1.2

Arthur requires an urgent loan, and approaches a local payday lender, Bugsy n' Mack Loans. He has no assets and is unable to offer security. The lender offers to give him a loan at a special reduced rate if he will put up one of his kidneys as security. In the event that he fails to pay the loan when it falls due, the lender will be entitled to surgically remove one of his kidneys and sell it on the organ market.

This is a somewhat extreme example, but its purpose is to illustrate a point: namely, that freedom of contract is freedom under the law and subject to the law. It is not, and cannot be, an unlimited freedom. There are some types of terms that the law will not permit parties to accept, some types of contracts that it will not enforce, and some types of conduct that it will not countenance. The task of contract law is, therefore, not simply to provide a framework within which parties can exercise their freedom of contract. It is, equally, to set bounds to that freedom, police its exercise, and determine the consequences of the parties' exercise of that freedom. We will now turn to examining these tasks in more detail, in section 1.2.

1.2 Working with contract law

1.2.1 The tasks of contract law

The standard legal definition of a contract is that a contract is an agreement enforceable at law. In one sense, this definition is redundant: it tells us nothing at all about what makes an agreement legally enforceable. But in another sense, it encapsulates one of the central roles of contract law. The most obvious legal need which necessitates a role for law is the need for enforcement. Parties may refuse to perform an agreed obligation because they no longer wish to perform or because they are unable to perform (eg because they have run out of money or took on too many commitments). Here, the only way the other party will obtain satisfaction is through the intervention of the courts.

But enforcement is not all contract law is about. If we look to the structure of contract law today, we can see that there are four key tasks which contract law discharges dealing, respectively, with defining *when* a contractual obligation arises, determining *what* the obligation actually requires the parties to do, setting *limits* to freedom of contract, and determining the *consequences* that ensue when one party fails to perform the contract.

Let us start with the first of these: defining when a contractual obligation arises. In legal terms, the law of contract is part of the law of obligations. It forms part of the law dealing with relations between people in society: the duties we owe each other, and the consequences of our failure to discharge those duties. The law of contract deals with one particular type of obligation: namely, obligations created by agreement. This creates a range of issues for the law. Does an agreement exist at all? What must be done for an agreement to be legally binding? What sorts of actions, words, or intention create a contract, and how do these differ from mere negotiations or discussions that did not lead to a concluded contract?

The second task, determining what the contract actually requires of the parties, is also fundamental to contract law. Contracts consist of words. The point of those *words*, however, is to record *acts* which parties must do or refrain from doing. How do we determine what acts a contract required the parties to do? How do we decide whether a contract *required* a particular act to be done? How do we deal with eventualities for which the contract does not provide, either because it was poorly written or because the eventualities in question were unexpected and unforeseen?

The third task is significantly different. Here, we are no longer trying to determine what the parties agreed. Instead, we are trying to determine whether the law permits them to act as they did or to agree on the things they did. Where should the balance between freedom and fairness be struck? To what ends should the law regulate contracting? Should it intervene to protect weaker parties? Should it intervene mainly for the sake of the broader economy?

The fourth task—determining the consequences of breach—puts the focus back on the parties' agreement, but only partially. Agreements sometimes provide what will happen if they are breached, but many do not, and even those that do are rarely comprehensive. It therefore falls to the law to determine what the consequences of the breach are. What remedies are open to the innocent party? How much compensation can they claim, and for what sort of harms?

All rules and doctrines in the modern law of contract are devoted to one or more of these tasks. In studying contract law, it is useful to keep these tasks in mind, and to ask yourself which of these tasks a given rule contributes to, and how it furthers the law's discharge of that particular task.

The focus of this book is to help you understand the rules that comprise the law of contract, not in the abstract, but against the background of these tasks and of the types of circumstances in which the law is called upon to discharge these tasks. Every chapter, accordingly, contains an initial problem and a series of illustrations, in addition to a discussion of the substantive legal rules of contract law in the relevant area. The problem involves a little more complexity than the illustrations. The aim of the problem is to introduce you to the breadth of issues associated with a particular area of contract law. The illustrations are more specific and narrow, and illustrate the purpose and scope of specific *rules* of contract law, rather than the broad areas with which the problems deal.

The problem and illustrations are an essential part of the book. The scenarios presented in them are intended to act as 'triggers'—a set of facts which provide a real-world context that will give you an understanding not just of the principles and concepts we find in contract law, but also of *how* those principles and concepts actually operate in the everyday life of the law. Why do those issues arise? When do they arise? Why do they tend to cause problems which the parties cannot resolve between themselves? Why does the law need to get involved? What are the considerations which the law must balance, and the various competing interests and goals which it must weigh against each other? Working through these questions, and keeping them in your mind as you read the text, will give you a much better understanding of the precise challenges facing the law, as well as the implications of the law taking the approach it does.

1.2.2 **The role of doctrine**

Studying the law of contract involves more than simply studying and learning the rules that are applied in contract cases. Studying some rules is necessary, but it is simply not possible to learn all rules that apply to the law of contract. The leading treatise on contract law, *Chitty on Contracts*, runs to over 4,000 pages, and even so is not wholly comprehensive. Equally, the rules that apply to contracts are not constant. They change as new cases are decided and new statutes passed, and these changes are frequently quite significant.

In the common law system, people often speak of learning 'doctrine'. Learning legal doctrine requires you to learn key rules, concepts, and cases; but it also requires you to go beyond them to understand how the law uses these rules and concepts to deal with actual cases. The key role of legal rules and concepts is to distinguish aspects of a trans-action that have legal significance from those that do not. Should an investment trans-action involving Great Aunt Agatha be treated differently from one involving Rodney, the hotshot City trader? If so, why? Is it because she has less expertise? Because she is likely to be more trusting of those who claim to have expertise? For some combination of these reasons? Or should the differences between them be treated as irrelevant for the purposes of contract law?

To study legal doctrine is to learn to have a feel for how the law of contract approaches questions like this, and to have a sound understanding of the underlying logic of why contract law takes the positions it does. As the points discussed thus far in this chap-ter should indicate, doctrine should be understood not as an abstract set of rules, but as an approach to solving problems that arise in the course of contractual relations. Understanding doctrine fully, therefore, requires paying close attention to the trans-actional context within which disputes arise. To what sort of relations does contract law apply? How do the rules operate in relation to those relations? What aspects of the transaction do they pay attention to, and what aspects do they treat as irrelevant? What consequences flow from taking some aspects into account, but not others? Are these consequences sensible? If not, how can we draft contracts better, so as to avoid the problems which the law creates? These are the sort of questions a contract lawyer must learn to be able to ask and answer through the application of legal doctrine.

Here, too, the problems and illustrations in each chapter will play a central role in your understanding of contract doctrine. Because doctrine is fundamentally about solving practical problems, your understanding of doctrine will be incomplete unless you keep the contexts in which doctrine operates in mind as you study the law. The importance of contract doctrine lies in its relevance to normal life, and the impact and influence it has on social practices. The problems and illustrations that are found throughout every chapter are intended to highlight these aspects of the law: what, precisely, a contract lets people do, the range of flexibility it affords parties, the role contracts play in structuring the relationship between the parties, and the implications of letting such large swathes of our everyday lives be governed by contract.

1.2.3 **The role of debates**

Contract is one of the most pragmatic areas of law. This reflects the fact that a signifi-cant proportion of contract cases involve commercial transactions, particularly at the appellate level. A judge hearing a dispute in relation to a contract for drilling an oil well will have neither the time nor the opportunity to ponder over the finer points of the philosophy of individual responsibility, or of moral responsibility for prom-ises. The focus will, inevitably, be on making pragmatic sense of the parties' contract. This pragmatism has long characterized contract law, and has fundamentally shaped the concepts and rules that the courts use in analysing contracts. English courts thus draw on ideas of 'reasonableness', 'objective meaning', 'business efficacy', 'certainty', and so on, whose role only makes sense against the background of this underlying pragmatism.

Nevertheless, contract law has also been very strongly influenced by what is some-times called 'theory'. Professor Patrick Atiyah, of whom we will hear more shortly, has rightly pointed to the rich vein of theory that runs 'beneath the surface' of the seeming pragmatism of English law.[2] The reason for this is that we are all influenced by our world views. As anthropologists have shown, our world views influence the way in which we perceive problems, and the way in which we evaluate possible solutions to these problems. This is as true of the law as it is of other cultural practices. Judges deciding cases in contract law are inevitably influenced by their views as to what makes contracts important, and what parties seek to achieve through contracting. These views are implicit rather than explicit, and different views have influenced the law in different ways over time.

Debates in contract law are, in essence, attempts to understand what these views are, how they influence English law, and—critically—whether their influence on English law is desirable. What are the things contract law does, and the interests it protects? What interests does it fail to protect, and what are the consequences of this failure?

These issues matter regardless of whether you approach contract law from an academic perspective or a practical perspective. Either way, you will need to understand not just what the doctrinal position is, but also what its limitations are. For academic lawyers, this is an interesting question in and of itself. From a more practical perspective, the utility of these issues lies in their ability to inform effective contract design. Studying the strengths and weaknesses of contract law puts you in a better position to make best use of the tools for contract design which the law gives you, and a better awareness of when it is particularly important to use those tools instead of merely relying on the law.

In studying the law of contract, therefore, it is useful to think in terms of four different aspects of the law with which you should be trying to get to grips. *Doctrine* requires you to understand the most important rules in contract law, but also what they tell us about how the law 'thinks' about transactions. *Application* requires you to work out what the rules actually mean in practice; the problems and illustrations will help you with this. *Critical study* requires you to be able to investigate and analyse the strength and limitations of the positions taken by contract law; the 'debates in context' feature will help you with this. *Practical understanding* requires you to be able to use the rules creatively to design contracts that achieve your objectives; the 'practice in context' feature will help you start to get to grips with the issues involved in doing this.

1.2.4 Unity and diversity in contract law

A final aspect of learning to work with contract law involves learning to work with the considerable diversity that is present within contract doctrine. Let us return to the analogy with horses and dogs at the start of this chapter. We have legal rules applicable to horses and dogs: for example, rules regulating the sale and purchase of animals, rules on animal welfare, rules governing liability for injuries caused by animals, and so on. Yet these do not cohere into anything resembling a 'law of the horse'.

It comes as a surprise to many students to realize that for much of the history of English law, it was the same with contract. It was not until the 18th century that the first treatise on contract law was written, and the idea of 'contract law' as a distinct

---

2. PS Atiyah, *Pragmatism and Theory in English Law* (Stevens and Sons 1987).

branch of law was not firmly established in English law until well into the 19th century. This is not because contracts did not exist before then. Contracts have existed for aeons. Nevertheless, until relatively recently few lawyers or jurists would have thought of a law of contract, much as few today would think in terms of a law of dogs. To the extent that they thought about the law in substantive terms, they would have thought in terms of a law of common carriers, a law of sale and purchase, a law of innkeepers, a law of master and servant, and so on, rather than lumping these together under the head of a law of contract.

Part of the reason for this is that the law of contract encompasses very different types of transactions, ranging from complex financial contracts between banks, which run to thousands of pages, down to the agreement under which you bought or borrowed this book, which in all probability did not even involve a written document. It should be obvious that agreements this different are bound to raise very different issues.

Unsurprisingly, in real life different types of transactions tend to be governed by different legal rules. The legal rules which apply to a consumer loan agreement are very different from those that apply to a joint venture agreement between two multinational companies. The result is that it would be legitimate even today to speak of the existence of a distinct law of consumer credit, a law of sale of goods, a law of construction contracts, a law of electronic contracts, a law of employment agreements, and so on.

This does not mean that there is no longer any point in studying a uniform law of contract, or that we should replace courses on the law of 'contract' with courses devoted to studying the distinct laws of innkeepers, employment, franchises, and consumer credit. Thinking in terms of a law of contract remains useful because it puts the focus on the aspects of relations which the law of contract emphasizes—in particular, the role of consent and what is meant by consent—which continue to play a very significant role in relation to these types of transactions. The focus of this book is, accordingly, on these general rules. Rules applied to specific times of transactions are occasionally referred to illustratively, but they are not the primary focus of the account which this book presents of the law of contract.

1.3 Central issues in contract law

We are now almost ready to begin studying the law of contract. Before plunging into the details of contract doctrine, however, there are a few broad issues we should consider. These issues run through the law of contract, and are of central importance to understanding both why the law sometimes contains the rules it does, and why those rules sometimes come in for the criticism they do. Keeping these in mind as you study the law will, therefore, help you make better sense of the law as well as of the problems which legal rules can sometimes cause in commercial practice and everyday life.

1.3.1 What is a contract, anyway?

When thinking about contracts, the first image that comes to most people's minds is the image of a long document, filled with hard-to-understand clauses written in complicated words, and often printed in a very small font. This is indeed true of some contracts, but the vast majority of contracts do not fit this picture. Indeed, a significant proportion of contracts are not written at all. When you go into a shop and buy something—a newspaper, a pen, a box of ready-made sushi—you are entering into a contract. The contract is never written, and the parties to the contract (you, and the operator of the shop) never discuss anything even remotely like the complex clauses that many people associate with contracts. But none of this changes the fact that in law it is a contract.

What, then, are the essential features of a contract? Although this question may appear to be theoretical, it has very significant practical implications. If, for example, the law is based on the view that the essential feature of a contract is the fact that each party promises to do something for the other, then the rules in relation to when contracts exist, what they require the parties to do, breach, and so on will emphasize requirements that reflect this understanding. Similarly, if we consider contracts to be mainly about commercial transactions, legal rules will emphasize commercial and market-friendly features of contract law.

Given this, it can come as a surprise to discover that there is very little agreement on what contracts are about. This lack of agreement reflects, in a peculiar way, the importance of contract to everyday life. Because contracting is as important as it is—because we depend on contracts for so much of the resources on which we draw in everyday life—judges, lawyers, and academics have for the past two centuries taken contract law very seriously, and have devoted considerable attention to analysing whether it protects the right interests and does the right things, or whether the law is in need of improvement. This section will present a brief survey of the main perspectives about contract that have influenced English law, starting with perspectives that were historically important (but no longer are), before moving on to discuss the theories that dominate modern debate.

1.3.2 Historical views on contract: bargains and the will

For much of the late mediaeval and early modern periods, contracts were seen as being bargains. The typical contract was a contract to buy or sell goods, land, or services. Any such contract necessarily embeds a bargain, where each party gives something to the other which the other person values. The understanding of contracts as being about bargains has left a number of traces in the modern law of contract, including the requirement that each party must provide something of value to the other party for a valid contract to be formed (the doctrine of 'consideration', discussed in greater detail in Chapter 3).

The bargain theory faded from the law in the 18th century, under the impetus of economic change. As industrial and commercial transactions became more complex, new types of contractual transactions emerged which could not be called 'bargains' without severely straining the meaning of the word. A modern contractual document, such as a joint venture agreement or a shareholders' agreement, will typically contain a very wide range of rights, duties, and powers, painstakingly negotiated over an extended period of time. It is difficult to see how terming this a 'bargain' helps with the analysis of contractual problems. The result was the emergence of a new understanding of contracts, grounded in the parties' will. Contracts were, in this understanding, formed through a meeting of minds—described as *'consensus ad idem'*, or 'agreement as to the same thing'. This understanding of contracts—often referred to as the will theory—has also left a lasting influence on contract law, including in the rules on when and how contracts are formed, and in the importance contract law attaches to the intention of the parties to the contract.[3]

The will theory, however, also proved to be limited, and it no longer plays an active role in the modern legal understanding of contract. A key element in its demise was the problem of inequality of bargaining power, or non-negotiated transactions more generally. Parties often ended up having to assent to contracts without any ability to negotiate as to the terms, and without the ability to influence the content of the contract. A number of statutes from the 19th century onwards sought, accordingly, to regulate contracts in order to protect weaker parties. The will theory, however, provided little guidance when it came to how these, more complex, issues should be dealt with. Statutory regulation was clearly independent of the parties' will. Its increasing importance in contract law made the claims of the will theory increasingly less sustainable.

No single understanding of contract has, however, replaced the will theory. Instead, modern discussions about contracts reflect two very different understandings of contracts: one that sees it primarily as a bundle of rights, and one that sees it as a relationship between the parties. In the remainder of this section, we will look briefly at both these approaches to contract, and the light they shed on the issues and concerns with which modern contract law must deal.

1.3.3 Contemporary views on contract: bundles of rights or relationships?

The most influential, and most broadly held, view of contracting today is the view that contracts are bundles of rights and duties created by the parties, and voluntarily accepted by them. This perspective springs from the observation that an important feature which all contracts share is that they concern the obligations of the parties towards each other. In form, they are bundles of rights and duties which each party has consented to assume or grant in relation to their counterparty. There is, accordingly, a significant body of thinking about contract law that puts emphasis on this aspect of contracts.

When parties contract, according to this approach, they in essence agree to formalize some aspect of their relationship, and bind themselves to acting in a particular way. This is embodied in the rights and duties created by their contract. The task of the law is to determine what sort of conduct this formal agreement required of them, and to give effect to it.

This approach stresses the importance of the formal terms of the contract, because those terms are the main source we have for understanding what the parties bound themselves to do. The manner in which the parties behaved once the contract was formed is less relevant. Parties may choose not to insist on their strict legal rights,

---

3. The classic description of the role played by the will theory in contract law is PS Atiyah, *The Rise and Fall of Freedom of Contract* (Oxford University Press 1979).

but as far as the law is concerned it is the strict rights to which effect must be given. Traditionally, this led courts to look at the words of the contract, and at very little else. The words were construed strictly, even if the results were commercially absurd. This approach is usually termed 'formalistic', as it is grounded in a focus on the formal terms of the agreement. Since the 1960s, it has generally been recognized that some more weight must be given to commercial reasonableness, as it is unlikely that sensible commercial parties would actually have intended to produce absurd results. The precise amount of weight that should be given to commercial reasonableness, however, remains the subject of some controversy.[4]

The view that contracts are a bundle of rights is a very orthodox one in English law, and represents the dominant view among commentators on contract law. Many of the authors whose views you will read of in the course of your study of contract law hold to this view of contracting. An author whose views have been particularly influential is Professor Gunther Treitel, formerly Vinerian Professor of English Law at Oxford University, who was for many years considered the leading authority on English contract law.

The relational understanding of contract, on the other hand, takes a very different starting point, which is many ways the antithesis of the view of contracts as bundles of rights and obligations. According to the relational approach (or 'relational contract theory', as it is usually called), contracts are not merely bundles of rights. They are primarily commercial instruments designed to achieve commercial objectives. The focus of the law must, therefore, be on giving effect to these commercial expectations, which may be express or implicit. The formal deal may be expressed in terms of rights and duties, but that is not the main aspect of the contract. The main aspect of the contract lies, instead, in the parties' commercial understanding, and in the joint goals which they seek to pursue through their commercial transaction. The most salient feature of contracts is, therefore, the fact that it creates a relationship between the parties.

Parties create rights and duties in order to try to plan for the future, but those rights and duties are of secondary importance because their planning will neither be perfect nor complete. Much of what they expect each other to do will be implicit in their relationship, rather than explicit in their contract. The law of contract must, therefore, take its starting point in the relationship, rather than in the rights and duties in terms of which it is expressed. The relational theory of contract is particularly closely associated with the work of two American jurists, Professor Stewart Macaulay and Professor Ian Macneil. Professor Macneil likened contracts to a Scotch egg embedded in the middle of a haggis. The haggis was the broader commercial relational context of the transaction. The thick coating of the Scotch egg represented the transaction-specific relations between the parties which are close to the express terms. The rights and duties themselves are the Scotch egg itself. The only proper way to reach and understand what the rights and duties are intended to mean, and the effect they are intended to have, is to go through the outer layers.[5]

---

4. This is discussed in greater detail in Chapter 7 ('Interpreting the terms').

5. IR Macneil, 'Reflections on Relational Contract Theory after a Neo-Classical Seminar' in D Campbell, H Collins, and J Wightman (eds), *Implicit Dimensions of Contract: Discrete, Relational and Network Contracts* (Hart 2003) 208–9.

The relational contract theory was grounded in sociological studies of how business people viewed contracts, and it has powerful academic support. In the UK, its main proponents have been Professor David Campbell, and Professor Hugh Collins, who is currently Vinerian Professor of English Law at Oxford. Professor Collins has called for contract law and contract litigation to be radically altered, so that courts receive more evidence on, and pay closer attention to, the broader commercial context of transactions and the expectations that are implicit in them.[6] Professor Campbell has in a series of articles re-examined cases and doctrines that are considered foundational to contract law, and analysed how their failure to take account of the relational dimensions of contract has led to them defeating, rather than supporting, commercial expectations.[7] Professor Roger Brownsword, one of the leading socio-legal theorists of contract law, has brought relational contract theory together with sociological studies of commercial behaviour to argue that the law must take greater account of parties' implicit expectations and of aspects of commercial transactions which it currently ignores.[8]

Despite its powerful academic support, however, relational contract theory has had very little actual influence on the content of English contract law. For the purposes of learning the law, its greatest relevance lies in the attention it calls to areas where the results produced by contract law diverge most strongly from the expectations of those who enter into commercial and non-commercial contracts. This is useful both for understanding the strengths and weaknesses of contract law, and for alerting us to the areas where it is important to pay particularly close attention to the way in which we design and write contracts. You will see this come up throughout the book, as we look at the way the law functions in practice.

1.3.4 A paternalistic law?

Section 1.3.3 made brief mention of formalistic approaches to reading contracts; that is, a very strict reading of the contract, under the 'bundle of rights' approach to contracts. As that section discussed, the main feature of these formalistic approaches is the emphasis they place on the terms of the contract, and on the importance of giving effect to the terms exactly as agreed to by the parties. In the 1950s and 1960s, this approach began to be challenged by academic scholars and practitioners. The result was the growing influence on contract law of a view—usually termed 'paternalism'—that an important task of the state (and of the laws made by the state) is to protect weaker parties in their own best interests. The law, in this view, should be prepared to be more 'interventionist'—intervening in contracts by refusing to give effect to certain types of terms and even, if necessary, by restricting freedom of contract.

The initial point of challenge was, once again, the issue of unequal bargaining power, and the fact that many parties were left with little choice but to accept the terms that were put to them. These terms were often extremely onerous. Reformers argued

6. H Collins, *Regulating Contracts* (Oxford University Press 1999).
7. See eg D Campbell, '*Arcos v Ronaasen* as a Relational Contract' in Campbell, L Mulcahy, and S Wheeler (eds), *Changing Concepts of Contract: Essays in Honour of Ian Macneil* (Palgrave Macmillan 2013).
8. See especially R Brownsword, *Contract Law: Themes for the 21st Century* (2nd edn, Oxford University Press 2006).

that the law should not accept rules which systematically disadvantaged one side, but should instead intervene to protect the weaker party. Their critiques were particularly sharply focused on a few types of contracts—hire-purchase agreements, consumer credit contracts, clauses limiting liability in contracts to sell goods, and employment contracts. Over the half-century since, these critiques have been increasingly influential, and have led to a number of new statutes being passed which have fundamentally reshaped contract law, away from these strict, formalistic approaches. This has been particularly strong in relation to consumer loans, the supply of goods and services to consumers, employment contracts, and commercial agreements in the construction sector (although this list is by no means exhaustive).

Some commentators have called for an even broader reconsideration of the basic principles of contract law. Foremost among these was Professor Patrick Atiyah, who was Professor of English Law at Oxford during the 1970s and 1980s, and is generally considered one of the leading scholars of contract law. In a lengthy and richly evidenced book titled *The Rise and Fall of Freedom of Contract*, Professor Atiyah argued that many doctrines of contract law simply reflected the earlier prominence of the will theory.[9] The theory was no longer taken seriously, and it was therefore time to reconsider the doctrines that were based on it. The core of the alternative theory he advanced was the idea of reliance: that what mattered most to contracts, and the point to which the law should pay most attention, was that the parties had relied on the other party's assurances. He published a series of essays re-examining central features of contract law, and suggesting how they should be reconfigured to reflect the values which contract law ought to protect.[10] Professor Atiyah's views sparked a lively debate which is still ongoing, but his views have not significantly influenced the actual law. As with the relational theory, their value lies in the fact that they lead us to question and re-examine aspects of contract law whose correctness we might otherwise take for granted; again, look out for this throughout the 'debates in context' features and elsewhere in the book.

The views expressed by Professor Atiyah, as well as those who argued for contract law to take a more proactive role in protecting weaker parties, received a strong response from more traditionally minded scholars. One line of response, which was primarily directed at the debate in the US, but was also influential elsewhere, was that theories calling for greater intervention, or for a reconfiguring of contract law, failed to pay enough attention to the moral importance of the element of 'promise' that underlay contract law. Both the doctrines of contract law and the remedies it provides should, it was argued, be restructured to make them much more focused on the promises the parties make to each other, and to ensuring that these promises are kept.[11]

A very different response came from another set of theorists, closely associated with the University of Chicago. Their argument was that contracts were primarily tools of economic exchange. Given the importance of exchange to society and to the functioning of the commercial system, the law of contract should primarily be oriented

9. PS Atiyah, *The Rise and Fall of Freedom of Contract* (Oxford University Press 1979).
10. PS Atiyah, *Essays on Contract* (Oxford University Press 1990).
11. The classic work is C Fried, *Contract as Promise: A Theory of Contractual Obligation* (Harvard University Press 1982).

towards economic efficiency. This would sometimes require it to take a hard-nosed view towards matters like breach of contract, but such a view could be justified once the role of contract law in supporting the economy was properly understood. This theory is most closely associated with the work of Professor Richard Posner, a US-based scholar of private law and regulation (and now a federal judge). A number of different scholars in England have also drawn upon economic analysis in their work, most notably Professor Anthony Ogus of the University of Manchester.

None of these schools of thought by themselves can account for all of contract law. In an influential article published in 1987,[12] Professor John Adams and Professor Roger Brownsword, both closely associated with the sociological analysis of law (or 'socio-legal studies' as it is also called), argued that contract law had been shaped by different ideologies. The most important trend in the history of contract law was the slow erosion of the ideology of 'formalism' (discussed briefly in section 1.3.2), and its replacement with other more instrumentalist approaches to contract law. An instrumentalist approach sees the law of contract as having a broader social goal, and therefore argues that the rules and doctrines of contract law should be structured to further that goal (rather than simply giving legal effect to the parties' words, as a formalist approach would suggest). Professors Adams and Brownsword suggested that two such approaches had been particularly influential, which they called 'market-individualism' and 'consumer-welfarism'.

Market individualism saw contracts as being about competition, taking place between relatively ruthless participants on a market. Proponents thought that judges (and contract law) should be slow to take on a more interventionist role in relation to these transactions. The focus should, instead, be on promoting security of transactions, and on providing a framework of relatively straightforward and certain rules, so that people who enter into market transactions know where they stand as a matter of law. They contrasted this with 'consumer-welfarism', under which courts see themselves as having a broader role in ensuring that contracts are fair and reasonable. This meant that courts should protect parties against exploitation, ensure a fair deal for consumers, and, in general, favour positions in which commercial businesses bear losses rather than consumers, as businesses are usually in a better position to do so. They argued that there had been a definite tilt in favour of consumer-welfarism within contract law in England, one which was ongoing and likely to continue.

Proponents of the idea of contracts as a relationship, in contrast, take a very different view. The problem with all these approaches to defining the role of contract (market individualism and consumer-welfarism), they suggest, is that they take a top-down approach to the question. This is, they would say, the wrong approach to take. Contract law should not seek to impose external values on a contract. It should, instead, seek to understand the expectations that are inherent in the parties' own understanding of the contract, and give these effect to the maximum extent possible. Exploring how this might be done has been a key issue in much work carried out within relational approaches to contracting, as subsequent chapters discuss in greater detail.

---

12. JN Adams and R Brownsword, 'The Ideologies of Contract' (1987) 7 LS 205.

1.4 **In conclusion: the tasks and goals of contract law**

As we have seen in this chapter, contract law has four key tasks to play in the legal system: determining when contracts are made, determining what they require, setting boundaries to freedom of contract, and providing remedies if contracts are not kept. To study contract law is to study the way in which it goes about discharging these tasks. This involves, to a large extent, the study of contract doctrine and of the transactional context in which doctrine operates. There is no universal agreement on how contract law should go about discharging these tasks, and whether its current approach is an appropriate one.

Underlying these differences is a sharp difference of view on what the goals of contract law are (or should be). This is particularly true when it comes to freedom of contract, but the differences also relate to other aspects of contract law, such as contract remedies. If the law of contracts places heavy reliance on the idea that a contract represents a promise, then legal rules are likely to lean in favour of freedom of contract (with few restrictions). If it places heavy reliance on consumer-welfarism, then legal rules are likely to place more emphasis on fairness, understood according to standards defined by the law.

As the discussion in this chapter has indicated, a key point facing contract law today is how interventionist it should be, and how it should go about resolving conflicting expectations between the parties when disputes arise. How much weight should it assign to the words of the parties' contract? How much weight should be given to the socio-economic context in which transactions take place? Should courts try to make contracts 'fairer' according to an external standard? Should they place weight on unspoken assumptions and practices which deviate from the formal words of the contract? These issues have no easy resolution but they run through legal doctrine and are of fundamental importance to contract practice. You should, therefore, keep them in mind as you study the substantive law of contract in the following chapters of this book.

Forming contracts

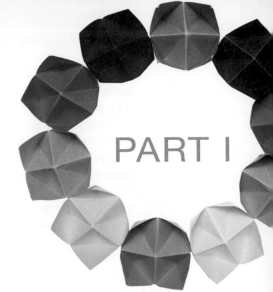

PART I

Introduction

In modern British society, the business of everyday life is suffused with contracting. Imagine this: a typical student wakes up in the morning in a room that she occupies under a contract with a landlord, brushes her teeth with toothpaste acquired through a contractual purchase, and perhaps makes herself a cup of tea in a kettle powered by electricity supplied by a power company under contract. On her way to class, she withdraws money from a cash machine to which she has access under a contract with her bank, possibly buys a sandwich or a drink from a shop thus entering into another contract, and sends a text message to a friend using a mobile network to which she has access under a contract with her phone company.

Most of this is second nature to us. We rarely think consciously about the fact that we are constantly entering into contracts, or relying on contracts already entered into. We therefore pay little attention to the question of when and how a contract comes into being. The law of contract, however, devotes significantly more attention to this question.

Contracts can be entered into in writing, orally (either over the phone or in person), and in a range of other ways. A small number of contracts must, as a matter of law, be in writing. Under s 2(1) of the Law of Property (Miscellaneous Provisions) Act 1989, for example, all contracts involving the sale, or other disposal, of an interest in land must be in writing and signed by the parties. Similarly, under s 5 of the Arbitration Act 1996, any agreement to refer disputes to arbitration must be in writing, or recorded by some other means. But in the absence of special requirements of this type, a contract can be made by any means the parties choose.

Most contracts are not created or accompanied by any formal written document. Text messages, phone calls, emails, and conversations are all perfectly valid ways of entering into contracts. This makes it critical for the law to have clear rules that set out when and how contracts are formed. The question of whether, when, and how a particular contract was formed is often the subject of dispute. Contracts enable us to demand things of other parties that we could not otherwise have demanded. They also let us structure our relations with others as we choose, and according to terms we choose. As a result, one option for a party facing a claim that they have failed to perform a contractual obligation is to argue that there was no contract and, hence, no obligation. Resolving such a situation requires the court to engage with the formation process to determine if the parties actually reached agreement.

English law holds that a contract is formed if the parties reach **agreement** as to something (the subject matter of the contract), supported by **consideration** (something of value given in exchange for the promise) and the **intention to create legal relations**. If any of these elements is not present, then no contract will have been formed. The first three chapters in this Part (Chapters 2, 3, and 4) deal successively with each of these requirements. A key theme underlying the discussion in these chapters is the idea of a 'moment of responsibility'. English law treats contracts as coming into being at a single, identifiable moment, when everything about the contract crystallizes and emerges into its final form. Many of the rules surrounding formation in English law are concerned with attempting to identify that moment, and determining the state of the parties' dealings at that moment. Whilst this approach has clear strengths, it also has some weaknesses, as we will see in greater detail in these chapters.

The fourth and final chapter in this Part—Chapter 5—turns to a slightly different point. Contracts are not the only way in which promises acquire legal effect in English law. Chapter 5 considers the most important of these, a set of rules called **estoppel**, which prevent a party from going back on a promise or assurance in some circumstances, even if that promise or assurance has not crystallized into a contract.

Bargaining and agreeing

Offer, acceptance, and formation

'To bargain is human'[*]

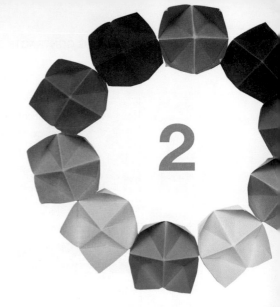

[*] Cf Seneca 'errare humanum est', 'to err is human'.

Problem 2: setting the context

Consider this scenario:

One evening, John, a student, sees this listing on a website selling second-hand goods: flogurstuff.co.uk:

> Used iPhone for sale, in good condition. Screen is clear and scratch-free. Some minor scratches and scuffing to the case. Price £200 ono plus postage, or can meet in person at University of Carmarthenshire. Contact Sam on 07929234491

The following exchange of text messages then ensues:

> Hi, saw the ad about the used iPhone. I'm willing to pay £175, cash on collection. John

> That's too low. But I could go down to £185 if you can pay by 5 p.m. tomorrow. Sam

> Hi, £185 is fine. Shall we meet in the Square at 4 p.m.? John

> That works. See you then! Sam

As you work through the chapter that follows, think about these questions: Was a contract concluded in this scenario? If so, at what stage was it concluded?

2.1 Introduction

'Agreement' does not mean quite the same thing in law as it does more generally. In everyday speech, agreement refers to a subjective mental state, where the parties believe their thoughts, opinions, or intentions to be in accord. The law of contract, however, is not concerned with the subjective question of what the parties thought, believed, or intended. It is concerned with the *objective* question of what they said and did.[1]

---

1. Cf the remarks of Lord Denning in *Storer v Manchester City Council* [1974] 1 WLR 1403, discussed in section 2.2.

'Agreement' as used in law, therefore has a much more technical meaning. Agreement is said to be reached when one party (the 'offeror') makes an **offer** to another proposing certain terms by which he intends to be bound, which that other party **accepts** as made. An agreement will only be taken to have been reached if the acceptance perfectly mirrors the offer (this is often called the 'mirror image' rule). A statement which falls short of mirroring the offer is not an acceptance. Instead, it creates a fresh offer, called a **counter-offer** which only forms a contract if it is itself accepted. Similarly, a statement which does not propose terms or is not certain will not be an offer, but only an **invitation to treat**.

These distinctions can be subtle, but they are important. The precise content of a contract might, for example, depend on whether a particular response during negotiations was an acceptance (thus assenting to the terms proposed by the offeror) or a counter-offer (thus proposing new terms, which the other side would have to accept or reject). This can significantly alter the rights and duties of the parties under the contract.

The traditional approach used in English contract law is to look at the nature and effect of the statements that were made in the process of bargaining. Did any of them satisfy the legal requirements of an offer? Did the response satisfy the legal requirements of an acceptance? If so, a contract was formed at the moment the acceptance was communicated to the offeror.

The tests English law uses are simple and, in theory, apply in all situations of contract formation, whether it involves two individuals haggling over a phone as in Problem 2, or two teams of lawyers engaged in a long negotiation over a contract that runs to several hundred pages, or an individual signing up for an account on Facebook. Nevertheless, as we will see in this chapter, the law of offer and acceptance reflects the way business was done in the 18th and 19th centuries when the tests it uses were formulated. The focus on offer and acceptance, in particular, leads to a focus on trying to identify a single moment—the 'moment of responsibility'[2]—when the contractual bargain emerged. Whilst this works well enough for some transactions, it is an uneasy fit with others, particularly those where the final agreement is the result of a long negotiation, in the course of which a consensus evolves progressively.

We will start this chapter with the relatively straightforward situation of a seller and buyer bargaining over a prospective sale, as in Problem 2. From there, we will move on to seeing how these principles translate to other forms of contracting, focusing specifically on situations involving complex negotiations over detailed sets of terms and conditions, and those involving standard terms and conditions.

2.2 Subjective and objective elements in formation

In order to understand the legal steps that must be taken for a contract to be formed, it is necessary to appreciate an important divergence between legal and commercial understandings of contracting. In commercial terms, the formation of a contract involves the

---

2. This phrase was coined by Hugh Collins. See H Collins, *The Law of Contract* (Cambridge University Press 2003) 158–9.

generation by the parties of a common understanding of what their transaction is about, and a framework of rules to govern their transaction. This process is entirely subjective, depending on their actual intent, motives, and goals. The law, in contrast, treats the process by which the contract is formed as being entirely objective. The central feature of the law of contract formation is its adoption of an objective approach.

The law, for example, repeatedly makes reference to the parties' intent—speaking of the 'intention to be bound' as an important component of the formation process, or of the 'intention to create legal relations' as an essential ingredient of a contract. 'Intention' in these contexts does not refer to what a party may have actually meant or indicated: in contract law, we almost never try to assess a party's actual intention. It refers, instead, to something objective—specifically, to what a reasonable person would have understood as the import of what the party said or did. If a party's intention in saying or doing certain acts was not what a reasonable person would have inferred, the court will give effect to what the reasonable person would have inferred, not what the party intended. For example, if a party writes a letter which a reasonable person would have construed as intending to contract, that party will be bound even if he did not in fact intend to contract, but only saw himself as putting forward a proposal for discussion.[3]

Lord Denning's statement in *Storer v Manchester City Council*[4] is the classic exposition of this point of view:

> In contracts you do not look into the actual intent in a man's mind. You look at what he said and did. A contract is formed when there is, to all outward appearances, a contract. A man cannot get out of a contract by saying: 'I did not intend to contract', if by his words he has done so. His intention is to be found only in the outward expression which his [words] convey. If they show a concluded contract, that is enough.[5]

The objective nature of the legal understanding of contract formation also manifests itself in the law's focus on process in formation. From a commercial point of view, agreement is reached when the parties reach a sufficient degree of common understanding. In law, however, the focus is not on whether the parties have a common understanding of the transaction, but on the two procedural steps of offer and acceptance. Both these manifestations of objectivity are deeply entrenched in English law. In what follows, we will examine both those types of situations in which the current approach works well, and those in which it does not. Our starting point is one particular way in which contracts can be formed; namely, contracts concluded through a fairly straightforward process of bargaining.

2.3 The core paradigm: bargaining

The most obvious way in which a contract can be concluded is through a process of bargaining. Consider Problem 2 at the start of this chapter. The parties start with a particular item—in this case a mobile phone—which one wishes to sell and the other wishes to purchase. They discuss the price, mode of payment, and time and place of

3. For an early example, see *Kennedy v Lee* (1817) 3 Mer 441, 36 ER 170.
4. [1974] 1 WLR 1403.
5. Ibid, 1408.

delivery, and come to an agreement. With minor modifications, transactions of this type occur thousands of times a day up and down the country. They are straightforward and make a good starting point for our study of the process of contract formation.

In law, agreement is reached when one party makes an offer which the other party accepts. We will now proceed to examine what each of these steps means, in the context of a contract concluded through bargaining.

2.3.1 Offers and invitations to treat

Understanding the distinction

Much as with 'agreement', 'offer' has a meaning specific to law. The fact that the parties call something an 'offer' does not mean that it is an offer in the legal sense. In law, an act or statement must have three essential characteristics to be considered an offer. First, it must set out or refer to **terms** on the basis of which the offeror is willing to contract with one or more other persons (the 'offerees'). Secondly, these terms must be sufficiently *certain*—that is, they must be clear enough and broad enough in their scope to form the basis of an enforceable contract. And, finally, the offer must give an indication that the offeror *intends to be bound* without further negotiation as soon as his offer is accepted by the offeree.

A statement which falls short of any of these will be an invitation to treat, and not an offer. In *Harvey v Facey*,[6] Harvey, wishing to purchase a property owned by Facey, sent him a telegram with the words 'Will you sell us Bumper Hall Pen? Telegraph lowest cash price—answer paid.' Facey replied 'Lowest price for Bumper Hall Pen £900.' Harvey immediately replied 'We agree to buy Bumper Hall Pen for the sum of nine hundred pounds asked by you. Please send us your title deed in order that we may get early possession.' To this, the respondent made no reply. The Judicial Committee of the Privy Council held that no contract had been formed. Facey's telegram was not an offer, but only a statement of the price at which he would be prepared to contract. Harvey's reply to this, therefore, was an offer rather than an acceptance. A contract would only have been formed if Facey had then accepted this offer, which he had not done.

The point which the distinction between offers and invitations to treat seeks to capture is practical and simple. Bargaining is an involved process, in the course of which the parties may say and do many things, not all of which will be intended to (or can) have binding legal effect. Invitations to treat are, in essence, statements that are designed to initiate the process of negotiating, without making any commitment that the other party can accept, whereas offers are intended to make a commitment. Consider this statement from Problem 2:

> I'll sell my phone to you for £185, if you can pay me by tomorrow.

This statement is very likely to be an offer: it sets out terms on which the offeror is willing to contract, the terms are certain, and the offeror is willing to be bound by the terms if the offeree accepts. On the other hand, the following statement is unlikely to be an offer.

> I'll sell my phone to you if we can agree on a good price.

---

6. [1893] AC 552 (PC).

The phrase 'a good price' leaves much to the discretion of both parties, because there is nothing that is objectively a good price or a bad price. Such a statement is, rather, typically intended to demonstrate a willingness to negotiate and solicit an offer from the other party. This is precisely the function of 'invitations to treat'.

The extent of the terms which an offer needs to indicate depends on the nature of the transaction. In a simple sale transaction, it is usually sufficient if the price and the goods to be sold are ascertainable from the offer. The terms do not need to be set out in the offer itself. They simply need to be ascertainable. For that reason, a statement in the following form will be an offer.

I'll sell my phone to you at the market price.

This is because the market price is usually something that is ascertainable. Variants of this particular formulation are not uncommon in many types of commercial contracts.

Applying the distinction

Although the test to distinguish between offers and invitations to treat is in theory simple, applying it is often complex. Instances of commercial dealing can often be analysed in more than one way, each of which leads to a different view as to whether a particular step was an offer or an invitation to treat. *Photolibrary Group Ltd v Burda Senator Verlag*[7] serves as a particularly good illustration. Photolibrary had for many years supplied photographic transparencies to Burda Senator Verlag, a German publisher, for use in their magazines. The parties, however, had no general overarching contract governing their relationship. Instead, Burda Senator would from time to time, through its agents in London, send requests for photos matching a particular description to a range of suppliers, including Photolibrary. Photolibrary would then send a selection of pictures matching that description to the agents. These were accompanied by a delivery note, which on its face set out terms of business and on its back set out terms and conditions subject to which it supplied the transparencies. The agents passed the transparencies on to the publisher with their own dispatch note.

One of Photolibrary's terms and conditions related to a fee payable in the event the transparencies were lost. In November 2004, a parcel of 1,865 transparencies belonging to Photolibrary and others were lost in transit between the agents and the publisher. Photolibrary claimed the loss fee payable under its terms of business. The publisher argued that no contract had come into being.

The High Court held that the dealings between the parties could be analysed in two ways, both of which were equally viable.[8] In the first, it was the delivery of the transparencies accompanied by a delivery note that was the offer. The acceptance of the delivery by the agents, and their onward transmission to Germany, constituted the acceptance of the offer. In the second, the request for photos sent by the publisher constituted the offer. The delivery of the transparencies by Photolibrary to the publisher's agents constituted the acceptance. Either way, however, a contract had come into existence.

What is particularly striking about the court's analysis of the parties' dealings is that in the first of the two readings which the court found 'equally viable', the request for

7. [2008] EWHC 1343 (QB), [2008] 2 All ER (Comm) 881.
8. Ibid, [63]–[64].

photos would have been an invitation to treat, whereas in the second, it was an offer. That the court found both accounts equally plausible—holding, in effect, that it was as likely that the request was an invitation to treat as it was that it was an offer—points to how fine the distinction between the two can be in practice, and how difficult it can sometimes be to classify a particular statement as being one or the other.

2.3.2 Acceptances and counter-offers

In comparison with the distinction between offers and invitations to treat, acceptances are more straightforward. An acceptance is a final, unqualified expression of assent to the conditions of the offer as they were put forward by the offeror. Acceptance does not have to take the form of words. The common law has long recognized that acceptance can take the form of conduct or, in some cases, of performance. This is commonly the case in purchases over a shop counter, where the shop attendant's acceptance typically takes the form of handing the goods to the purchaser.

The key characteristics an act or statement must display to be an acceptance are that it must respond to the offer, must be unconditional, and must correspond precisely with the offer's terms. The rule that an acceptance must mirror the offer is sometimes called the mirror-image rule.

The offeree's response to an offer will not necessarily be to accept it. He may reject the offer, or seek to negotiate further by proposing new terms or by seeking to vary the terms of the offer, as Sam did in relation to John's offer in the scenario with which this chapter began. A statement which introduces new terms or attempts to vary the terms of the original offer is not an acceptance, but a counter-offer—that is, a new offer put before the original offeror for his acceptance.

The courts take a fairly rigorous approach to determining whether a response to an offer is an acceptance or a counter-offer. *Jones v Daniel*,[9] which introduced the terminology of 'counter-offer', is a typical example.

> ### Case in depth: *Jones v Daniel* [1894] 2 Ch 332
>
> Daniel made an oral offer, subsequently confirmed in writing, to buy a property in Wales from Jones. After some discussions about the price, Jones's solicitors wrote to Daniel accepting the offer. The letter of acceptance read as follows:
>
> > Mr. W. Jones has considered your offer of £1450 . . . He thinks it very low, but . . . he accepts it, and we enclose contract for your signature. On receipt of this signed by you across the stamp and deposit we will send you copy signed by him.
>
> The enclosed agreement contained the usual conditions of sale, and included provisions specifying a particular date of completion, requiring a 10 per cent deposit, and setting out a temporal limit as to how far back the seller would have to demonstrate his title. Daniel made no reply to this letter. After Jones's solicitors sent two follow-up letters, he returned the
>
>   →

---

9. [1894] 2 Ch 332.

→

agreement unsigned and refused to proceed. Jones sued, arguing that Daniel's letter making the offer and Jones's solicitors' letter accepting it together constituted a contract.

The High Court rejected Jones's argument, holding that no contract had been formed. Romer J found that the agreement prepared by Jones's solicitors contained important conditions, none of which were contained in the original offer. In the earlier case of *Crossley v Maycock*,[10] Sir George Jessel MR drew a distinction between a response to an offer that simply sought to put into more formal terms what had been agreed, and a response that added new conditions that had not previously been discussed or agreed. The former was a valid acceptance, but the latter would not create a contract until those new conditions had been accepted by the original offeror. Applying this principle, Romer J held that the conditions in the agreement prepared by Jones's solicitors were, because of their nature, of the latter type. The letter, he held, in effect meant:

> So far as the price is concerned we are agreed. I now enclose you terms which I require you to assent to. If you assent to them and sign them and pay the deposit, then there will be a binding contract between us, but not till then.

Such a statement was not an acceptance. Instead, it was a 'counter offer of the Plaintiff', which would not create a contract until it itself had been the subject of a valid acceptance. As a result, no contract had come into being and the action failed.

Negotiations in practice often jump back and forth, with parties to the negotiation frequently falling back to previous positions if a negotiating tactic is unsuccessful. The law, however, takes a more rigid position. In law, there can be no automatic return to a previously held position. The effect of a counter-offer is to 'kill' the original offer[11] and render it incapable of acceptance. If a party's counter-offer is rejected, any attempt to return to the original offer is a new counter-offer, which must be accepted by the original offeror for a contract to come into being. This was held in *Hyde v Wrench*,[12] a decision from 1840. Wrench offered to sell his farm to Hyde for £1,200. Hyde rejected the offer. Wrench thereupon wrote to his agent stating that he would 'only make one more offer, which I shall not alter from; that is, £1000 . . .' Hyde responded by offering a sum of £950. After considering the matter for three weeks, Wrench declined Hyde's offer. Hyde then replied stating that he would 'at once agree to the terms on which you offered the farm, viz., £1000 . . . by your letter of the 6th'. Wrench, however, refused to sell. Lord Langdale MR held that in making an offer of £950, Hyde had rejected the offer of £1,000. Having done that, 'it was not afterwards competent for him to revive the proposal of the Defendant, by tendering an acceptance of it'. Consequently, there was no contract.

Returning to Problem 2, therefore, to the extent Sam's reply to John's initial message proposes different terms (here, a different price), it is a counter-offer which destroys John's original offer and requires a fresh acceptance from John in order for there to be

10. (1874) LR 18 Eq 180.
11. *Trollope & Colls Ltd v Atomic Power Constructions Ltd* [1963] 1 WLR 333, 337 (Megaw J).
12. (1840) 3 Beav 334, 49 ER 132.

a contract. But not every statement which seems to deviate from the terms of the offer is a counter-offer. In some cases, it may just be an enquiry as to the finality of the terms or the possibility of negotiation. As always, it is the intention of the party that is key. The case of *Stevenson, Jaques & Co v MacLean*[13] provides a good illustration of this point.

Case in depth: *Stevenson Jaques & Co v MacLean* (1880) 5 QBD 346

Stevenson Jaques were makers of iron and iron merchants in Middlesbrough. MacLean held warrants for iron, which he had purchased from Stevenson Jaques. He asked Stevenson if they could find a buyer for his iron. It was understood that Stevenson would buy the iron from MacLean and sell it on. The market was unsettled, and the price of iron was fluctuating quite rapidly. While Stevenson searched for a buyer, the parties exchanged a number of letters and telegrams concerning the price and terms on which MacLean was willing to sell. On Saturday, MacLean sent a telegram to Stevenson stating that he 'would now sell for 40s., nett cash, open till Monday'. At 9.42 a.m. on Monday, Stevenson sent MacLean the following telegram:

> Please wire whether you would accept forty for delivery over two months, or if not, longest limit you would give.

MacLean made no reply, but sold the iron through a different broker. At 1.25 p.m., he sent a telegram to Stevenson to the effect that he had sold the iron. The telegram reached Middlesbrough at 1.46 p.m. In the meantime, Stevenson had contracted to sell the iron, and telegraphed MacLean to that effect at 1.34 p.m. MacLean refused to deliver the iron to Stevenson, who had to buy iron in the open market at a considerable loss to meet their contractual obligations. Stevenson sued MacLean for non-delivery. MacLean argued that no contract had been entered into, as the telegram Stevenson had sent at 9.42 a.m. amounted to a rejection of the original offer, and a counter-offer.

The High Court rejected MacLean's argument, and held that a contract had been formed. The court pointed out that it was apparent that Stevenson were purchasing the iron not as speculators, but on the basis that they could resell it to someone. Given that, it was reasonable that 'they should desire to know before business began whether they were to be at liberty in case of need to make any and what concession as to the time or times of delivery, which would be the time or times of payment, or whether the defendant was determined to adhere to the terms of his letter'. The result was that there was no counter-offer, and the original offer stood. The telegram was meant 'only as an inquiry, expecting an answer for his guidance, and this, I think, is the sense in which the defendant ought to have regarded it'.

An acceptance must respond to the offer to be valid. Thus if John, in the scenario of Problem 2, had without seeing Sam's advertisement independently made an offer to buy Sam's phone, his statement to Sam would be an offer rather than an acceptance, even if it mirrors the terms of Sam's offer. 'Cross-offers' of this type will not create a contract unless one of them is accepted. This rule can be traced to a single, 19th-century case, the decision of the Exchequer Chamber in *Tinn v Hoffmann & Co*.[14] The rule in *Tinn* has been questioned by Michael Furmston, a leading commentator on contract

---

13. (1880) 5 QBD 346.   14. (1873) 29 LT 271.

law, on the basis that the judges in that case did not agree on the rationale underlying the rule, and that there appears to be no principled reason to refuse to give effect to a contract where both parties contemplate legal relations on an identical basis.[15] Nevertheless, the rule is a fairly strong reflection of English law's focus on assessing offer and acceptance, rather than the broader question of whether the parties were in agreement.

2.3.3 **Communicating acceptance**

> ### Illustration 2.1
>
> Consider a slight variation on the facts of Problem 2. Imagine that the last two text messages were replaced by these messages:
>
> > Hi, £185 is fine. Shall we meet in the Square at 4 p.m.? John
>
> > Hi, just saw your message—my phone's been off for a few hours. I've just sold the phone to someone else. Sorry. Sam
>
> John's text is an acceptance. Was a contract concluded when John sent his text, even if Sam did not actually see it until much later? Answering this question requires us to understand when an acceptance will be said to have been communicated.

The importance of communication

To be valid, an acceptance must be **communicated** to the offeror. A person who receives and decides to accept an offer, but does not tell the offeror this, has not in law accepted the offer. A file note recording a decision to accept an offer does not, for example, operate as acceptance. Acceptance is valid from the moment it is communicated to the offeror, but has no legal effect until it is communicated. Thus in *Kennedy v Thomassen*,[16] the offeree instructed her agent to inform the offerors that she had accepted an offer to purchase two annuities that stood in her name. However, she died before her agent could relay her acceptance to the offerors. It was held that there was no acceptance, since it had not been communicated at the time of her death.

Expressing acceptance

Communicating an acceptance requires the acceptance to have been expressed, and that expression to have been brought to the offeror's notice. A silent acceptance which is not communicated is not ordinarily a valid acceptance in law, and a provision in an offer stating that silence will be treated as acceptance will have no effect. Thus a statement along the lines of 'Unless I hear from you within two days, I will deem you to have accepted' is not legally binding. The logic behind this is that because a contract is a consensual instrument, offers must be voluntarily accepted. Acceptance cannot be forced.

---

15. M Furmston, *Cheshire, Fifoot & Furmston's Law of Contract* (15th edn, Oxford University Press 2007) 71–2.
16. [1929] 1 Ch 426.

In *Felthouse v Bindley*,[17] an uncle and nephew had been discussing a sale of the nephew's horse to the uncle. They parted believing they had agreed a price, but subsequently discovered that they had misunderstood each other. The uncle wrote to the nephew suggesting that they split the difference, and concluded by saying 'If I hear no more about him, I consider the horse mine.'

From what you have seen thus far in this chapter, it should be evident that this statement was a fresh offer, which would have to be accepted in order to form a contract. The nephew made no reply to the uncle, but instructed the auctioneer to leave the horse out of an ongoing auction of his farming assets. The auctioneer forgot his instructions, and sold the horse to a third party. The uncle sued the auctioneer for wrongfully disposing of his property, and the court had to consider whether there was a contract of sale between the uncle and the nephew. It held that although the nephew 'in his own mind intended his uncle to have the horse at the price which he [the uncle] had named . . . he had not communicated such his intention to his uncle, or done anything to bind himself'. Nor could the nephew unilaterally impose a contract by treating an offer as automatically accepted unless expressly repudiated. Consequently, there was no acceptance of the offer, and no contract.

The rule that silence cannot be acceptance is not absolute. The law does in exceptional cases recognize acceptance of an offer by silence.[18] A case in point is *Rust v Abbey Life Insurance Co Ltd*.[19] This case involved an investment by the claimant in property bonds provided by Abbey with a liquidity facility. The claimant had made the investment by handing over a cheque made in favour of Abbey together with an application form. She was subsequently sent the policy, with the detailed terms and conditions. Six months later, she sought the return of a substantial portion of the money, in a manner not permitted under the bonds and facility. She argued that no contract had been concluded in relation to the investment, since she had received the policy after making the investment. The court held that there were two possible routes by which a contract might have been concluded. First, the application form could be said to constitute an offer to invest the money, with Abbey's allocation of units being the acceptance. The dispatch of the policy was a record of the agreement, not the agreement itself. Alternately, if the dispatch of the policy was a counter-offer, then by saying nothing for six months the claimant had implicitly accepted it. In *Re Selectmove*,[20] the Court of Appeal suggested (without conclusively deciding) that if the offeree himself indicated that the offer should be taken as accepted 'if he does not indicate to the contrary by an ascertainable time', that might also be an exceptional case in which silence could constitute acceptance.[21] Nevertheless, exceptional cases of this type are relatively few, and the general rule remains that silence by itself will not ordinarily suffice to accept an offer.

If the offer contains any stipulations about how the acceptance must be expressed, then those stipulations must be complied with. Thus if the offer specifies that the acceptance must be delivered to a specific address, or that it must be in writing and signed, then the acceptance must meet those requirements, or be in a form no less advantageous, to be valid. Sam's statement in the ad in Problem 2 is an example: the

---

17. (1862) 11 CB (NS) 869, 142 ER 1037.
18. *Vitol SA v Norelf Ltd (The Santa Clara)* [1996] AC 800, 812 (Lord Steyn).
19. [1979] 2 Lloyd's Rep 334.   20. [1995] 1 WLR 474.   21. Ibid, 478.

effect of requiring responses to be directed to a mobile number is to preclude the use of email or the post.

The logic behind this rule is to let parties structure the formation process to meet their specific needs. If a party requires a signed documentary record of the formation process, for example, a stipulation that the acceptance must be signed will achieve that. Equally, a party who does not want to run the risk of a letter being lost in the post[22] can obtain a greater degree of security by requiring that the letter be sent by courier or hand delivered.

Stipulations of this type can also extend to other matters, such as setting out the address to which acceptances should be sent. Stipulations as to the form of acceptance may also be implicit, rather than explicit. In *Quenerduaine v Cole*,[23] Cole sent a telegram offering to sell a cargo of potatoes to Quenerduaine. Quenerduaine wrote a letter accepting the offer. By the time the letter arrived, Cole had sold the potatoes to someone else. The court held that there was no contract. The fact that the offer was sent by telegram implied the expectation of a prompt reply. Acceptance by letter was not, therefore, made within a reasonable time.

2.3.4 **The postal rule**

The traditional rule

Acceptance is usually taken to have been communicated to an offeror only when it is brought to their notice. If the parties are speaking face-to-face and the offeree's statement of acceptance is drowned out by an aircraft flying overhead or if the parties are talking on the telephone and the line goes dead or fades out, the acceptance will not have been communicated to the offeror.[24] This does not, however, apply when acceptance is sent by post. If an offer is accepted by post, the acceptance is taken to have been communicated as soon as the acceptance is posted, even though it will be at least a day before the acceptance is received by the offeror (and, in some instances, significantly longer). Controversially, this applies even if the letter is lost in the post and never delivered.[25]

This is called the **postal rule** and has a complex history. The rule is conventionally traced to the early 18th-century case of *Adams v Lindsell*.[26] Lindsell was a dealer in wool, based in St Ives. Adams was a woollen manufacturer, based in Bromsgrove, Worcestershire. On 2 September, Lindsell wrote offering to sell some wool to Adams 'receiving your answer in course of post'. Ordinarily, Lindsell could have expected to receive a reply from Adams by 7 September. However, he had misdirected the letter, sending it to Bromsgrove, Leicestershire. As a result, it did not reach Adams until 5 September. Adams replied immediately, accepting the offer. His letter reached Lindsell on 9 September. Unfortunately, on 8 September Lindsell had sold the wool to a third party since he had not heard from Adams. Adams sued.

---

22. See the discussion in section 2.3.4.   23. (1883) 32 WR 185.
24. *Entores Ltd v Miles Far East Corp* [1955] 2 QB 327, 332 (Denning LJ).
25. *Household Fire Insurance Co v Grant* (1879) 4 Ex D 108.
26. (1818) 1 B & Ald 681, 106 ER 250.

Lindsell relied on the traditional understanding of acceptance, that it was not complete until it was communicated. He argued that they had therefore terminated the offer before acceptance.[27] The court, however, found for Adams. The delay in the acceptance, the court held, arose entirely through Lindsell's error, and had therefore to be taken against him, rather than Adams: had Lindsell not misdirected his letter, the acceptance would have been received on time. The court also observed that if postal acceptances were taken not to be complete until they were received, the effect would be

> that . . . no contract could ever be completed by the post. For if the defendants were not bound by their offer when accepted by the plaintiffs till the answer was received, then the plaintiffs ought not to be bound till after they had received the notification that the defendants had received their answer and assented to it. And so it might go on ad infinitum.[28]

The report of the case is rather brief, as older reports often are. As a result, it is hard to tell from the judgment itself which of the grounds it cites was more important. Nevertheless, the court's observation on the effect of holding that postal acceptances are only complete when received was read as implying that such acceptances were therefore complete when posted. This, rather than Lindsell's fault, was seen as being the main rule in the case. Thus in *Dunlop v Higgin*,[29] where there was no imputation of fault, the offeror was nevertheless held to be bound on the basis of the rule in *Adams v Lindsell*. The House of Lords held that if the offeree 'puts a letter into the post at the right time . . . he has done all that he is expected to do as far as he is concerned'.[30]

The result, therefore, was a new rule that an acceptance that was sent by post was taken to be complete, and would bind the offeror, as soon as it was put in the post. The point, as Alderson B put it in *Stocken v Collin*,[31] was that a party 'is not answerable for the blunder of the post-office'. Such a rule was thought to be a matter of commercial necessity: Lord Cottenham accurately reflected the conventional wisdom of the time in *Dunlop v Higgin*, when he observed that 'Common sense tells us that transactions cannot go on without such a rule.'[32]

It was, for a while, unclear whether this rule only applied to cases where the acceptance was delayed in the post, or whether it also applied to cases where the acceptance was lost in the post and never arrived. In *Dunlop v Higgin* itself, Lord Cottenham had taken the view that it applied to both. Once a party put a letter in the post, 'whether that letter be delivered, or not, is a matter quite immaterial, because, for accidents happening at the Post Office he is not responsible'.[33] The subsequent case law initially took a different view. In *British and American Telegraph Co v Colson*,[34] the Court of Exchequer held that the postal rule would not apply if an acceptance was lost in the post. Distinguishing past authorities, Bramwell B held that as it was the sender of the letter who had chosen to send the letter by post—rather than by some other, more secure, means—it was the

---

27. See section 2.3.5.   28. (1818) 1 B & Ald 681, 683.

29. (1848) 1 HL Cas 381, 9 ER 805. The case was a Scottish appeal, but Lord Cottenham regarded himself as stating principles that were common to English and Scots law (see ibid, 398, 400), and the case was immediately accepted as an authority on English law.

30. (1848) 1 HL Cas 381, 398.

31. (1841) 7 Mee & Wels 515, 151 ER 870. The facts of the case related to a notice rather than an acceptance, but the principle set out in the case influenced subsequent cases on postal acceptances.

32. (1848) 1 HL Cas 381, 400.   33. Ibid, 399.   34. (1871) LR 6 Ex 108.

sender who was responsible for the letter's arrival. The sender could take steps to check whether the letter had been received, whereas the recipient could not, because he did not even know that it had been sent. The situation would only be different if the offer had expressly asked for the acceptance to be posted.[35]

British American Telegraph Co was, however, overruled in *Household Fire and Carriage Accident Insurance Co v Grant*,[36] which established the current rule—that the postal rule applies even when the letter of acceptance is lost in the post and never delivered.

Case in depth: *Household Fire and Carriage Accident Insurance Co v Grant* (1879) 4 Ex D 216

Grant applied for shares in the Household Fire and Carriage Accident Insurance Co. Shares were allotted to him, and a letter was posted to his home address. His name was also entered in the register of members. The letter, however, never reached him. When the company became insolvent, the liquidator applied to Grant for payment of the sum outstanding on the shares. Grant refused, arguing that he was not a shareholder as the contract to subscribe to shares had never been accepted.

The Exchequer Division found that a contract had been concluded when the acceptance was posted, even if it was never received. The court admitted that the postal rule at first sight was hard to reconcile with the requirement that acceptance must be communicated. 'An acceptance, which only remains in the breast of the acceptor without being actually and by legal implication communicated to the offeror, is no binding acceptance.'[37] The way the court found around this was to treat the post office as being the common agent of both parties.[38] Because the post office was not just the offeree's agent, but also the offeror's, handing the letter over to the post office was equivalent to handing it to the offeror. If the post office then lost the letter, it was no different from any situation where an agent lost a letter. If an offeror did not wish to be bound on the acceptance being posted, it was open to him to expressly state in the offer that the acceptance must be received by him by a certain day. *British American Telegraph Co* was overruled as wrongly decided.

Bramwell LJ, who had delivered one of the judgments in *British American Telegraph Co*, dissented in strong terms.[39] There was, he pointed out, no basis for saying that the post office was the offeror's agent. And, if this was indeed the case, then there was no basis for distinguishing acceptances from every type of other communication that might be sent by post—if the postal rule applied to acceptances, it must necessarily apply to everything. The result of this would be to cause a great deal of inconvenience.

Despite Bramwell's dissent, the decision of the majority has come to be accepted as the law. The rule is, however, confined to cases where the letter is posted. It does not apply to delivery by hand, and by extension should not apply to delivery by other means, such as courier services, unless the parties expressly agree that it should. Subsequent cases have also confined the rule to acceptances—it does not apply to other types of

---

35. Ibid, 118–19.   36. (1879) 4 Ex D 216.   37. Ibid, 221.

38. This point was also made in the earlier decision of Lord Romilly in *National Savings Bank Association* (1867) LR 4 Eq 9, 12 (also known as *Hebb's Case*).

39. (1879) 4 Ex D 216, 222–39.

communications that may be made in the course of formation.[40] Whilst there is no authority directly on the point, observations in other cases suggest that it will only apply if the letter is properly addressed, and will not apply if, for example, the offeree puts the wrong address on the letter.[41]

Like the rules on cross-offers, the postal rule reflects the law's focus on the *individual steps* of offer and acceptance, rather than on a broader conception of agreement. Looking at a broader conception of agreement would, surely, require the courts to give weight to whether or not the offeror actually knew that his offer had been accepted. It is only in a framework where that idea of agreement is irrelevant that the courts are able to look at acceptance as an act in and of itself, detached from the broader progress of the parties towards achieving agreement on their transactional framework.

Applicability to modern forms of communication

With the advent of speedier forms of communication such as faxes, emails, and text messaging, the question arose as to when an acceptance communicated by one of these means would be taken to have been received, and what would happen if such a communication was lost and never actually received. The first of these cases was *Entores v Miles Far East Corp*,[42] where a company based in London made an offer by telex to buy 100 tons of copper cathodes from a company based in Amsterdam, which also accepted the offer by telex.[43] The court held that in cases of instantaneous communication, as it held telexes to be, the contract was complete when the acceptance was received, rather than when it was sent. A similar result was reached in the case of *Brinkibon v Stahag Stahl*,[44] which also involved telexes. Lord Wilberforce, however, added a clarification to the rule in *Entores*, to the effect that the rule would not necessarily apply in all circumstances—for example, where messages were sent out of office hours or to persons without authority to act upon them. Cases must, therefore, 'be resolved by reference to the intentions of the parties, by sound business practice and in some cases by a judgement where the risks should lie'.[45]

---

40. *Byrne & Co v Leon Van Tienhoven & Co* (1880) 5 CPD 344. This case is discussed in greater detail in the next section.

41. See *LJ Korbetis v Transgrain Shipping BV* [2005] EWHC 1345 (QB). The case involved a fax that had been sent to the wrong number, rather than a letter that had been sent to the wrong address. However, Toulson J in that case took the view that the position also applied to letters, on the basis that 'Common sense dictates that it is unfair to the intended recipient that he should be bound by something which he is unlikely to receive because of the fault of the sender.' Ibid, [11].

42. [1955] 2 QB 327.

43. Telexes are a now-obsolete technology, but were an early forerunner of the SMS. They allowed persons to send messages in text over a fixed-line telephone network, using a special machine which looked something like a typewriter.

44. [1983] 2 AC 34.

45. Ibid, 42. It should be noted that *Entores* and *Brinkibon* were not directly concerned with the question of *whether* a contract had been completed—it was common ground in both cases that there was a contract—but were instead dealing with the issue of *where* the contract had been entered into. Contracts are, in law, taken to have been entered into at the place where they were concluded. It was this that raised the question of when communication of acceptance was complete—if it was completed when the telex was sent, then the contract would have been concluded in the place where the telex was sent. If it was only completed when the telex was received, the contract would have been concluded in the place of receipt.

This issue assumed relevance in *Thomas v BPE Solicitors*,[46] which considered whether the rule in *Entores* applied to communication by email. One of the issues the court had to consider related to an email which was received by a solicitor in the evening at 6 p.m., but was not read until the next working day because the recipient had gone home. Blair J held that the *Entores* rules did apply to email. The general rule, he said, 'is that the acceptance of an offer is not effective until communicated to the offeror'. The postal rule is 'an anomalous exception . . ., which is limited to its particular circumstances'.[47] Accordingly, an acceptance by email was only communicated when it was actually received. Being received was not, however, the same thing as being read. Instead, an emailed communication was received if it was available to be read, subject to the qualifications relating to office hours and authority set out by Lord Wilberforce in *Brinkibon*. On the facts of the case, given the nature and urgency of the transaction, 6 p.m. was treated as being within office hours, with the result that the communication was taken to have been received at that time.[48]

Text messages are not directly covered by existing rules, but the principles applied are likely to be similar—with the result that, in Illustration 2.1, the contract will have come into being when John's text message was received by the servers on Sam's network for relaying on to his phone, even though his phone was turned off at the time.

Where an acceptance is not received because it was not properly addressed, it is clear that it will not have been communicated to the offeror.[49] There is, as yet, no authority that directly considers the impact of what would happen if such an acceptance were not received, despite having been properly addressed. Many forms of instantaneous communication—including faxes and emails—will inform the sender if the transmission was unsuccessful for some reason. There are, however, instances where this may not happen—due to, for example, a fault in the recipient's email server which results in the message disappearing. The editors of *Chitty on Contracts* have suggested that in such circumstances it would be most appropriate for the acceptance to be held to be effective, as the sender is unlikely to be able to determine whether the acceptance was actually received in an intelligible form.[50] Such a rule would parallel the postal rule in generally favouring the offeree over the offeror, and would also be closer to the original rationale behind the rule in *Adams v Lindsell*, in that the type of situations where instantaneous communication is likely to be lost or garbled will typically either be the fault of the recipient (if, eg, his fax machine is out of order) or of his agents or contractors (eg the email provider).

2.3.5 Revocation and lapse

Revoking offers

Adams v Lindsell and Illustration 2.1 also raise another point. In both cases, the dispute arose because the goods had been sold to another party before the original offeror became aware of the acceptance. This raises the more general question of whether an

---

46. [2010] EWHC 306 (Ch).   47. Ibid, [86].   48. Ibid, [89]–[90].
49. See *LJ Korbetis v Transgrain Shipping BV* [2005] EWHC 1345 (QB), dealing with a fax that had been sent to the wrong number.
50. H Beale (ed), *Chitty on Contracts* (31st edn, Sweet & Maxwell 2012) 2-051.

offeror can change their mind, and withdraw the offer before the contract has been formed. The legal position is that they can; because a contract does not come into being until acceptance is communicated, an offer may be withdrawn or revoked at any time until it has been accepted.

The withdrawal of an offer will not be effective until it has actually been brought to the offeree's attention. Thus the argument in relation to implicit revocation which Lindsell sought to make in *Adams v Lindsell* would in any event not have succeeded, as the purported revocation was not brought to the attention of Adams.

This would also hold for any attempt by Sam to argue that his sale of the phone to a third party implicitly revoked the offer. It is not necessarily the offeror who must bring the revocation to the offeree's attention. It is sufficient if he has knowledge of it, regardless of how he acquired that knowledge. A revocation may, therefore, be effective if it is brought to the offeree's attention by a third party, even if it is not communicated by the offeror. This was the outcome in *Dickinson v Dodds*.[51]

Case in depth: *Dickinson v Dodds* (1876) 2 Ch D 463

Dodds made a written offer to Dickinson to sell a property to him for £800. The offer said that it would be left open until 9 a.m. on Friday. Dickinson decided to accept the offer, but did not immediately respond to Dodds, believing that he had until Friday to do so. On Thursday afternoon, Dickinson was informed by one of his agents, a Mr Berry, that Dodds had been 'offering or agreeing' to sell the property to a third party, a Mr Allan. Dickinson immediately left a formal written acceptance of the offer with Dodds's mother-in-law, with whom Dodds was staying. Berry handed another copy of the written acceptance to Dodds the next morning at 7 a.m., but was told that it was too late as the property had been sold. A few minutes later, Dickinson himself gave Dodds yet another copy of the acceptance, again to be told that he was too late. Dickinson sued, arguing that his acceptance was within time and hence valid.

At first instance, Bacon V-C found for Dickinson, on the basis that for an offer to be withdrawn, that withdrawal must be communicated by the offeror to the offeree.[52] This had not been done in the present case until after Dickinson relayed his acceptance to Dodds, with the result that the withdrawal was not valid.

On appeal, however, this was reversed. The Court of Appeal held, first, that the statement that the offer would be left open until Friday was not binding, because it was made without consideration.[53] Secondly, they held that an offer could be withdrawn at any time until it was accepted. A withdrawal must come to the knowledge of the offeree in order to be effective, but in this case Dodds's withdrawal was very clearly within Dickinson's actual knowledge. It did not matter that the information had not been directly relayed by Dodds, nor was the exact means by which Berry came to know of the withdrawal relevant. It was sufficient that Dickinson had been so informed, and the effect was that the offer was withdrawn and no longer capable of being accepted.

---

51. (1876) 2 Ch D 463.   52. Ibid, 469.
53. We will consider the issue of consideration in some detail in the next chapter.

We will return to the first part of the Court of Appeal's finding—that the promise to leave the offer open until Friday was not binding—in section 2.3.6, when we consider a type of agreement called a 'collateral contract'. In general, however, the rule set out in this case is still good law, and an offer will be successfully revoked as long as it comes to the knowledge of the offeree, even if not from the offeror.

An important point to note in relation to revocation is that the postal rule does not apply to revocation. In such a case, the offer is not revoked until the offeree actually receives the letter of revocation. In *Byrne & Co v Leon Van Tienhoven & Co*,[54] the offerors, who were based in Cardiff, sent a letter on 1 October to the offerees, who were based in New York, offering some goods for sale. The offer was received on the 11th, and accepted the same day by telegram, with a letter confirming the acceptance sent on the 15th. On the 8th, however, the sellers had sent a letter to the offerees revoking the offer. This letter was not received until the 20th. The defendants argued that no contract had been entered into, as the offer had been revoked three days before it was accepted. The court held, however, that unlike acceptances, a revocation was only complete when it was actually received. The postal rule was based on a conception of implicit authority, which did not apply here. Consequently, the offer was accepted before it was revoked, and a valid contract came into being.

An offer can be phrased in terms that make it time-limited ('The offer will be kept open until 9 a.m. on Friday') or that make it contingent on a particular event ('The offer will automatically terminate if our application for planning permission is rejected'). In such cases, any acceptance communicated after that time or event will not bind the offeror. Where there is no express limit on the time for acceptance, the offer must be accepted within a reasonable time, failing which it may lapse and no longer be open for acceptance. In *Ramsgate Victoria Hotel v Montefiore*,[55] the defendant made an offer to buy shares in June. No response was received until November, when the offeree made an attempt to accept the offer. The court held that given the passage of five months between offer and acceptance, the offer had lapsed.

Revoking acceptances

The principles we have been examining thus far apply to the revocation of offers. The revocation of acceptances creates an entirely different set of issues.

The general rule is usually taken to be that acceptances cannot be revoked. This flows directly from the manner in which the common law understands the process of contract formation: because the acceptance is seen as being the 'moment of responsibility' that creates the contract, the contract comes into being as soon as acceptance is communicated. *A concluded contract cannot be unilaterally revoked.* There is, therefore, no room for revoking an acceptance.

Some room for revoking an acceptance may, in contrast, exist where acceptance has been communicated by post: in such a case, it is in principle possible for the offeree to send a communication by a speedier means instructing the offeror to disregard the posted acceptance. Might such a revocation be valid? Whilst there is no case law directly on this point in England, other jurisdictions including New Zealand[56] and

---

54. (1880) 5 CPD 344.   55. (1865–6) LR 1 Ex 109.
56. *Wenkhein v Arndt* (1861) 1 JR 73.

South Africa[57] have taken the view that acceptances cannot be revoked. Some commentators have argued that there is no reason for English courts to follow this rule, and that no harm will be done by permitting acceptances to be revoked in such a case: as the offeror will receive notice of revocation before becoming aware of the acceptance, they are unlikely to suffer any disadvantage as a result. It is, however, unclear what view an English court seized of the matter might take.

The common law position has been subject to a significant degree of statutory modification in relation to distance purchase contracts concluded by consumers. The Consumer Contracts (Information, Cancellation and Additional Charges) Regulations 2013[58] give all consumers who have purchased goods or services under a 'distance contract'—that is, a contract conducted via distance communication up to the moment at which it is concluded[59]—a statutory right (with some exclusions)[60] to cancel the contract by issuing a notice of cancellation within a defined period,[61] usually 14 working days after receipt of the goods for a sale of goods,[62] or from the conclusion of the contract in a contract for services or intangible digital content.[63] The effect of exercising the right is to 'end the obligations of the parties to perform the contract'.[64] Whilst a right to cancel is not precisely the same as a right to revoke acceptance, for most practical purposes the effect is the same.

2.3.6 Structuring the process: auctions, tenders, and collateral contracts

The law of contract gives the parties considerable freedom to structure the process of offer and acceptance to fit with their particular transaction. We have already come across references to some of these. We have seen, for example, that an offeror can prevent the postal rule from applying to a transaction by stipulating that the acceptance must actually be received by him by a particular date or by requiring acceptances to be delivered by a particular means. We have also seen that the offeror can set time limits within which an offer must be accepted. The power of parties to subject the formation process to specific rules, however, goes even further. The rules surrounding auctions and competitive tendering provide a good example.

An auction fits very neatly into the traditional offer–acceptance analysis. The description of an item in an auctioneer's catalogue is not an offer,[65] and is therefore only an invitation to treat. The same is true of the actions and words of the auctioneer before opening bids on the item. Each bid is an offer, and the acceptance comes from the auctioneer when he bangs his hammer down onto his table bringing the bidding to a close.[66] But is an auctioneer bound to accept the highest valid bid? Can the auctioneer, for example, refuse to sell an item that has been listed as not having a reserve price, on the basis that the winning bid is too low? The courts have consistently held that terming

---

57. *A to Z Bazaars (Pty) Ltd v Minister of Agriculture* 1974 (4) SA 392.
58. SI 2013/3134.   59. Ibid, reg 5.   60. Ibid, reg 28.
61. Ibid, reg 29(1).   62. Ibid, reg 30(3).   63. Ibid, reg 30(2).
64. Ibid, reg 33(1)(a).   65. *Harris v Nickerson* (1872–3) LR 8 QB 286.
66. *British Car Auctions Ltd v Wright* [1972] 1 WLR 1519, 1524. This case was a criminal prosecution rather than a contract case, but the court in the course of its decision also made reference to the position in contract law on when a contract was concluded in an auction.

an auction 'without reserve' implies that there is an obligation to sell to the highest valid bidder.[67] The basis of this is the existence of what is called a **collateral contract**.

Collateral contracts sit alongside the main contract, and are typically made to support some aspect of that contract. The collateral contract that was the subject of the auction cases set out the terms and conditions that govern the auction process itself. Its subject matter, in other words, is the process by which the main contract will be formed. Most auction houses publish detailed conditions of sale, setting out the rules in relation to the placing of bids and the determination of which bid has been successful. These rules bind bidders and the auction house, and are a very good example of how collateral contracts can be used to govern the formation process.

Collateral contracts are also used in another type of contracting process, competitive tendering. In tendering, one party issues a public notice (called an 'invitation to tender' or a 'request for tender') inviting bids from suppliers or contractors interested in carrying out the work. The party issuing the tender then evaluates the bids, before selecting one. Invitations to tender are usually invitations to treat rather than offers to sell to the highest bidder.[68] The bids themselves are offers, and the final decision to award the contract to a particular bidder is the acceptance. Nevertheless, the documents that accompany the invitation to tender are frequently treated as creating a collateral contract between the parties, which regulates the process of contract formation in much the same way as do the conditions of sale that are attached to auctions. Thus, for example, tender documents frequently impose special requirements on the form which the tender must take for it to be a valid offer.

In addition, there may also be requirements implied by law. For example, a tender that calls for sealed bids will usually be taken to implicitly rule out referential bids— that is, bids that are phrased with reference to another's bid—unless they are expressly permitted.[69] Similarly, whilst a party usually has free rein in deciding with whom they wish to contract, this may be altered or varied by the terms of a tender. There is, for example, an implied duty in competitive tendering (unless excluded) upon the requestor to actually examine all bids that are received on time. In *Blackpool & Fylde Aero Club v Blackpool Borough Council*,[70] Blackpool Borough Council invited tenders to operate light and heavy aircraft from Blackpool Airport. B&F Aero Club submitted their offer one hour before the bid was due to expire, by depositing it in the council's letter box. Because the council's staff did not empty the box on time, the bid was treated as having been delivered after the deadline, and the contract was awarded to a competitor. The Court of Appeal held that given the wording of the tender documents, it was implicit in the tendering process that any bid delivered on time would be considered. The award of the contract was therefore invalid.

There are also a range of legal tools other than collateral contracts that provide structure, and set limits, to the bargaining process. The law of misrepresentation, for example, provides a set of remedies in the event that one of the parties induces the other

67. *Warlow v Harrison* (1859) 1 El & El 309, 120 ER 925; *Barry v Davies (t/a Heathcote Ball & Co)* [2000] 1 WLR 1962.
68. *Spencer v Harding* (1870) LR 5 CP 561.
69. *South Hetton Coal Co v Haswell Shotton and Easington Coal and Coke Co* [1898] 1 Ch 465; *Harvela Investments Ltd v Royal Trust Co of Canada (CI) Ltd* [1986] AC 207.
70. [1990] 1 WLR 1195.

party to enter into a contract by making a statement that is untrue. Similarly, the law in relation to duress and undue influence sets limits on the type of pressure a party may place on another in the course of bargaining, and provides remedies in the event that those limits are breached. Finally, a range of statutory and contractual devices impose legal duties in relation to the information that must be disclosed to the other side in the course of contracting. These are considered in Part III of this book.

2.4 Beyond bargaining: offer and acceptance in other modes of contracting

Only a minority of contracts actually involve bargaining in this sense through invitations to treat, offers, counter-offers, and acceptances. In other more complex modes of contracting, applying an offer–acceptance analysis becomes a lot less straightforward. We have already seen some examples of this in cases like *Photolibrary Group v Burda Senator Verlag*, where the court noted that the formation process could be analysed in two, mutually incompatible, ways, each of which would have led to different actions being treated as offers and acceptances. We will now consider a broader range of transactions that move beyond bargaining, to examine both the challenges they pose for the traditional offer–acceptance analysis, and the manner in which judges and jurists have responded to these challenges.

2.4.1 Advertisements and unilateral contracts

Illustration 2.2

Consider this notice:

> LOST DOG
>
> White Spaniel/Poodle cross with black patch on ear
>
> Answers to Spot
>
> REWARD
>
> £25
>
> Contact Sarah 07313948723

Is there a contractual obligation to pay the reward to someone who finds Spot?

A significant number of transactions—including tenders, auctions, and most property transactions—begin with an advertisement, as did the scenario in this chapter's problem. Whilst there is no hard-and-fast rule either way, most advertisements are likely to be invitations to treat rather than offers. An offer is valid—and capable of being accepted—by any and every offeree unless it is revoked, and the revocation brought within the actual notice of the offerees. An advertisement such as Sam's advertisement of a used mobile phone for sale, in contrast, is intended to be seen by a large number of people, but the intent of the advertiser is to deal with only one of them. This suggests that advertisements are invitations to treat, rather than offers, and the courts have so held on a number of occasions for precisely this reason. In *Grainger & Son v Gough*,[71] the House of Lords observed that sending price lists for wine to selected potential customers was not an offer but only an invitation to treat:

> If it were so, the merchant might find himself involved in any number of contractual obligations to supply wine of a particular description which he would be quite unable to carry out, his stock of wine of that description being necessarily limited.[72]

Similarly, in *Partridge v Crittenden*,[73] the High Court held that an advertisement offering protected birds for sale was not an 'offer for sale' for the purposes of the Protection of Birds Act 1954, because a public advertisement was only an invitation to treat and not an offer.

This is not, however, an absolute rule. Advertisements can be offers, rather than invitations to treat, if there are special circumstances suggesting an intention to be bound. In the US case of *Lefkowitz v Great Minneapolis Surplus Store*,[74] an advertisement in the newspaper announcing a sale, included the line '1 Black Lapin Stole Beautiful, worth $139.50 ... $1.00. First Come, First Served.' Lefkowitz was the first to arrive, but was turned away on the basis that there was a house rule which said that the offer was for women only. The court held that the advertisement was an offer, which Lefkowitz had accepted and which could not now be altered, because it was 'clear, definite and explicit'.

A more important category of advertisements which can be offers relates to what are called **unilateral contracts**. The classic example of a unilateral contract is a contract offering a reward for an act—for example, for finding a lost dog, as in Illustration 2.2. Typically, a person who finds the dog will not have expressly communicated his acceptance of the offer of the reward. The courts have, therefore, in such cases treated the announcement or advertisement as the offer, and have treated the performance of the requested act as being the acceptance of that offer. Thus in the example of the lost dog, the notice announcing the reward is the offer, which is accepted by actually finding the dog. This captures the key characteristic of unilateral contracts—that the offer is of its nature not designed to be accepted by words, but only by complete performance. Unlike a standard contract, this means that only the offeror is ever bound by the contract. The offeree, in contrast, is at no point of time under an obligation to perform their portion of the contract: until they have performed, there is no contract and hence no obligation. Thus in the example of a reward for finding a lost dog, none of the people to whom the offer is addressed have any obligation to find the dog. Sarah, in contrast, has an obligation to pay them the reward should they successfully find Spot.

The leading case on unilateral contracts is *Carlill v Carbolic Smoke Ball Co*.[75] The Carbolic Smoke Ball Co made carbolic smoke balls, which they marketed as an anti-flu

---

71. [1896] AC 325 (HL). The case was a taxation case rather than a contract case, but the issue was relevant to the final determination.

72. Ibid, 334.   73. [1968] 1 WLR 1204 (QBD).   74. 86 NW 2d 689 (Minn, 1957).

75. [1893] 1 QB 256 (CA).

remedy. They placed an advertisement in a newspaper offering a £100 reward to any person who used their carbolic smoke balls and still got flu, and added that £1,000 was deposited in a particular bank 'showing our sincerity'. Ms Carlill used the smoke balls as instructed, but caught the flu, and claimed £100. The company argued that there was no offer that could have been accepted. The Court of Appeal held that there was a contract, on the basis that the company by their advertisement had shown sufficient intention to be bound, especially by their statement that money had been deposited in a bank.

Special rules apply to the revocation of offers in unilateral contracting. Although the general rule is that an offer can be withdrawn at any time before it is accepted, in relation to unilateral contracts the position would appear to be that an offer cannot be withdrawn once the performance contracted for has started. It is important to distinguish between acts that are merely *preparatory* to performance and those that constitute actual performance. Searching for a lost dog is not performance—it is an act preparatory to performance. Performance would consist of actually finding the dog. In *Errington v Errington*,[76] a father invited his son and daughter-in-law to live in a house he owned, and told them that if they made the mortgage payments, the house would be theirs. After they had made some payments, the father died. It was held that his legal representatives could not revoke the contract as long as the couple continued to make payments on the mortgage, because a unilateral contract could not be revoked once the offeree had 'entered on the performance of the act'.[77]

2.4.2 **Supermarkets, websites, and displays**

Formation processes that commence with the display of goods also pose a challenge for a traditional offer–acceptance analysis. Unlike the situation in Problem 2, no words are exchanged, and the parties' intention must be inferred from the mere fact of display. So, does the display of goods in a shop window constitute an offer of the goods or is it only an invitation to treat? The courts have consistently held that such a display constitutes an invitation to treat rather than an offer. The justification has traditionally been the shop owner's right to refuse to serve or sell to a particular customer. If the display of goods were to be an offer, then a shop owner would be bound to sell the goods to any customer who came in and accepted the offer, calling this right into question. The question first arose in the case of *Timothy v Simpson*.[78] Timothy saw a dress on display in Simpson's shop window, marked 5*s* 11*d*. When he attempted to purchase it, the price turned out to be 7*s* 6*d*. The case itself related to a physical fight that broke out after Timothy insisted on being sold the dress at the price listed. During arguments before Parke B, it was argued for Timothy that 'If a man advertises goods at a certain price, I have a right to go into his shop and demand the article at the price marked.' Parke B disagreed, saying 'No; if you do, he has a right to turn you out.'[79]

This position has since been upheld in a series of cases. In *Fisher v Bell*,[80] the High Court held that the display of a flick knife in a shop window did not violate the prohibition on 'offers for sale' of flick knives in the Restriction of Offensive Weapons Act 1959.

76. [1952] 1 KB 290.   77. Ibid, 295.   78. (1834) 6 C & P 499, 172 ER 1337.
79. Ibid, 500.   80. [1961] 1 QB 394.

The case was a criminal proceeding brought against the shop owner rather than a case in contract per se but, like *Partridge v Crittenden*, it, too, turned on a question of contract law, in this case whether the display was an 'offer'. In *Pharmaceutical Society of Great Britain v Boots Cash Chemists (Southern) LD*,[81] the principle was extended to self-service stores. This, too, was a criminal prosecution, relating to one of the first self-service pharmaceutical stores in the country. Certain medicines were by law required to be sold under the supervision of a registered pharmacist. Boots operated a system where customers picked these medicines off the shelves themselves. The pharmacist supervised the final sale at the cash desk, and had the authority to refuse to sell goods to a customer. The question for the court was whether, in such a system, the sale was effected under the supervision of a registered pharmacist. The Court of Appeal held that it was, on the basis that the display of goods on the shelf was only an invitation to treat. The customer made an offer by taking the goods to the till, and the acceptance came from the assistant in putting the sale through.

As with advertisements, the position that displays are invitations to treat and not offers is not an absolute rule. It comes from the court's assessment of the intention of the parties, seen objectively rather than subjectively. Consequently, if the offeror's outward actions suggest an intention to be bound in displaying the goods, then the display will be held to be an offer. This was the case in *Chapelton v Barry Urban District Council*,[82] where the display on a beach of deckchairs for hire by Barry Council was held to constitute an offer rather than an invitation to treat. Of significance was the fact that the council had placed a signboard with the hire rates near the chairs, and that the issue of a ticket appeared on the facts to be a formality rather than a precondition to hiring the chair.[83] Similarly, in a Scottish case, a sign displayed by the University of Edinburgh warning motorists that the land was private, and that any unauthorized parking would attract a charge of £30 per day, was held to constitute an offer, which the defender in that case had accepted when he chose to park his car there without authorization.[84]

The same principles are also likely to apply to goods sold through websites. In the majority of cases websites will be invitations to treat, rather than offers, unless there are special circumstances pointing to an intention to be bound. The customer makes an offer by clicking on the 'Order' or 'Buy' button. The contract is not complete until the company accepts the order. The primary effect of treating displays—whether physical or online—as invitations to treat rather than offers is in relation to mispricing. We will examine the common law rules on mispricing in greater detail in Chapter 7, but under those rules there are a range of circumstances in which an offeree who was quoted a lower price by mistake will be permitted to insist upon that price.[85] Classifying displays as invitations to treat eliminates this possibility. As with the display of goods, this position can be displaced if something about the website suggests that the website is an offer, rather than an invitation to treat, but most websites are carefully structured to make the customer's order the offer.

81. [1953] 1 QB 401 (CA).   82. [1940] 1 KB 532 (CA).   83. Ibid, 536–7.
84. *University of Edinburgh v Onifade* 2005 SLT (Sh Ct) 63.
85. For one example, see *Centrovincial Estates v Merchant Investors Assurance Co* [1983] Com LR 158.

The display of goods cases are part of a broader category of cases involving the formation of contracts which, unlike in situations of bargaining, are entered into with little or no interaction between the parties. An individual creating an account on Facebook has no ability to negotiate the terms to which he or she agrees—the terms are set out by Facebook, and the individual must assent to them as written. The same is true when it comes to shopping at a supermarket or at Boots. It is also true of, for example, signing up for a mobile phone contract, or with a power company, or taking most forms of public transport, or using a courier. Whilst the courts have managed to fit the offer–acceptance analysis to such contracts, the result is somewhat peculiar in that it is the person with least control over the terms of the offer who is held to be making the offer. In effect, the offeror in these cases is treated in law as making an offer whose terms are dictated by the other party. Partly as a result of the offeror's lack of influence over the terms on which the contract is concluded, these contracts also tend to be heavily regulated by statute—whether it be food safety or product liability laws, or consumer protection and utilities regulation, or laws on privacy and the use of personal data.[86]

2.4.3 Negotiation and the battle of the forms

Illustration 2.3

Consider the following timeline:

11 December: Cropley Structures call Overton Steel asking for a quote for the urgent supply of lubricant-free ball joints, to be shipped on or before 11 January.

13 December: Overton Steel send a quote, along with draft terms and conditions.

19 December: Cropley reply accepting the quote, but requesting deletion of one clause, which puts a cap on Overton's liability if the joints prove defective.

4 January: Overton reply proposing a higher monetary cap, but insisting on the clause.

10 January: Cropley reply agreeing to a monetary cap in principle, but raising a number of issues in relation to the scope of the clause and suggesting wording to address these.

11 January: Overton ship the ball joints to Cropley. They subsequently email Cropley with the shipment details, and voice their concern about the fact that the liability issue is still outstanding. They suggest yet another wording.

21 January: Cropley email Overton confirming receipt and installation, and proposing yet another version of the liability clause.

Has a contract been formed? If so, when?

---

86. See Chapter 13.

Complex, but incomplete, negotiations

The examples we looked at in the earlier sections of this chapter involved either relatively simple bargaining processes, as in Problem 2 for example, or no bargaining at all. A very different set of challenges is posed by instances of contracting where the process leading up to the formation of the contract involves complex commercial negotiations, such as the scenario in Illustration 2.3 involving Cropley and Overton. Complex negotiations can drag on for months, involving the exchange of numerous drafts and redrafts, during which time it is not unusual for parties to begin performing their portion of the deal even as significant portions of the contract remain unagreed and the subject of discussion. This typically happens where parties have agreed on the core commercial terms (eg the price and specifications) but continue to have disagreements on other terms which may commercially be less important even though they are, in a legal sense, of fundamental importance (eg the duration of warranties or caps on the liability of one party in the event of defective performance). 'Agreement' here is a more fluid notion, at least in the commercial sense. It emerges and evolves as the negotiations go on, which makes it difficult, if not impossible, to identify a specific act that can be called the 'offer' and another that can be called the 'acceptance'.

None of this matters if the negotiations are ultimately successful in producing a contract. Difficulties arise, however, where negotiations are incomplete or inconclusive, or end with some issues unresolved. The issue becomes particularly problematic in cases where the parties begin to perform the contract while still negotiating on the precise terms and conditions, and face a dispute before the negotiations are complete. What should the courts do in such a case? What terms should they apply to resolve the dispute? Whilst the problem is generally recognized, courts and academic authorities have been divided on the best way to resolve it.

The traditional approach, which still commands a degree of support both in academic writing and in the case law, is to continue to analyse such cases in terms of offer and acceptance. The question of whether an offer was accepted will be assessed not with reference to a single communication but to the entire course of correspondence. The court 'must consider all these exchanges in context and not seize upon one episode in isolation in order to conclude that a contract has been made'.[87] The essential nature of the question the court asks does not, however, change.

The closely related cases of *Gibson v Manchester City Council*[88] and *Storer v Manchester City Council*[89] present a good illustration of why such an analysis can be problematic in extended formation processes. Both Mr Storer and Mr Gibson were tenants residing in council houses owned by Manchester City Council. In 1970, Manchester City Council, then under Conservative control, set up a scheme to let tenants buy their council houses. Shortly after the scheme began, Labour took control of the council in a local election. One of their first acts was to discontinue the scheme for the sale of council houses, and terminate any contracts that had not proceeded to exchange.

Both Storer and Gibson fell into this category. Both had received letters from the council informing them that the council 'may be prepared to sell the house to

---

87. *Ove Arup & Partners International Ltd v Mirant Asia-Pacific Construction (Hong Kong) Ltd (No 1)* [2003] EWCA Civ 1729, [2004] BLR 49, [64].
88. [1979] 1 WLR 294.   89. [1974] 1 WLR 1403.

you' at a specified purchase price. Both had filled in application forms stating that they wished to purchase their respective houses. Storer had received an agreement for sale for signature, which he had signed and returned. The council had not yet signed the agreement when the scheme was discontinued. Gibson's application did not proceed as far—there had been discussions about the price, as a result of which he had not yet been sent an agreement for sale when the scheme was discontinued. However, the council had taken Gibson's house off the list of houses for whose maintenance they were responsible, and Gibson had carried out some work to the house.

The Court of Appeal held that a contract had been entered into in relation to Mr Storer. The correspondence, together with Storer's signature on the agreement for sale, were held to be sufficient to constitute a contract. In relation to Mr Gibson, however, the House of Lords held that a contract had not come into being, distinguishing his case from Mr Storer's. The initial letter stating that the council 'may be prepared' to sell the house was too uncertain to be an offer, and no subsequent correspondence quite satisfied the conditions of an offer or an acceptance.

From a commercial point of view, the difference in the outcomes of the two cases is peculiar. Negotiation processes can indeed be structured so as to ensure that no agreement emerges until a contract is signed, as we will see in Chapter 4, but no such steps were taken in either of these transactions. The result is also unlikely to reflect the parties' intentions or their expectations: there is very little that would support the suggestion that the stage which Mr Storer's discussions with the council had reached was so significantly different from the stage which Mr Gibson's had reached as to transform the apparent intention of the parties. Rather, the decisions highlight the traditional focus on an objectively identifiable 'moment of responsibility', and the role of identifiable offers and acceptances in establishing the existence of such a moment. The dispatch of the agreement for sale to Mr Storer provided such a moment, thus fitting with the offer and acceptance analysis. The transaction with Mr Gibson, however, had no such moment.

Although the basis on which the House of Lords distinguished Mr Gibson's case from Mr Storer's is therefore intelligible, one can nonetheless question whether this distinction and the approach on which it is based are sensible in the context of extended formation processes. In recent years, some courts have begun to acknowledge that it can be artificial to apply an offer and acceptance analysis to a lengthy commercial negotiation. In *Pagnan SpA v Feed Products Ltd*,[90] negotiations had taken place through an intermediary in a rather complicated process. One of the arguments advanced by the defendants was that there was no contract on a traditional offer and acceptance analysis. The Court of Appeal, however, held that it was 'not helpful' to think in terms of offer and counter-offer in the context of a contract negotiated through a single intermediary. The question was, rather, 'whether there comes a point in time when the intermediary has obtained the agreement of both parties to the same terms'.[91]

90. [1987] 2 Lloyd's Rep 601 (CA).   91. Ibid, 616 (Lloyd LJ).

This reflects a more general principle, which was summed up by Steyn LJ in *G Percy Trentham Ltd v Archital Luxfer Ltd*:[92]

> it is true that the coincidence of offer and acceptance will in the vast majority of cases represent the mechanism of contract formation. It is so in the case of a contract alleged to have been made by an exchange of correspondence. But it is not necessarily so in the case of a contract alleged to have come into existence during and as a result of performance.[93]

In such cases, a contract may have come into being during performance, even if it 'cannot be precisely analysed in terms of offer and acceptance'.[94] *Percy Trentham* itself arose out of a dispute between a principal contractor and a subcontractor. No formal agreement had been signed, although the parties had negotiated, because they were 'jockeying for advantage', as Steyn LJ put it. However, after reviewing the history of the dealings between the parties in great detail, the Court of Appeal found that two subcontracts had, in fact, come into existence. Although there was nothing that could be identified as an offer or an acceptance, the contracts were formed 'partly by reason of written exchanges, partly by oral discussions and partly by performance of the transactions'.

Maple Leaf Macro Volatility Master Fund v Rouvroy[95] shows how far a court may be prepared to go in departing from a traditional offer and acceptance analysis. This case arose out of a multipartite negotiation involving a funding agreement. Several drafts of the agreement were prepared and the question arose as to whether one of the parties, Lion Capital, had assented to the agreement. Lion Capital had seen and commented on one version, referred to as version 8b. The other parties had reached agreement on a later version, version 9, which Lion Capital had received but not responded to. The court held that Lion Capital had nevertheless assented to the agreement, on the basis that version 9 was, in as much as it concerned Lion Capital, substantially the same as version 8b, save for having made a few changes that favoured Lion Capital and for the most part responded to concerns which Lion Capital had raised in its comments on version 8b.[96]

In finding a contract in cases like these, the courts are swayed by the fact that by beginning to perform the contract, the parties have given a strong signal as to their intention to deal with each other—a fact to which Steyn LJ made express reference in his decision in *Percy Trentham*.[97] This makes it seem artificial to hold that there was no agreement, and the courts will look beyond offer and acceptance to the underlying substantive question of whether the parties had reached agreement if necessary to discover what this agreement was. Even so, courts often find that the agreement that had been reached was incomplete because there were, in other words, terms on which the parties had not reached agreement. In these circumstances, whether or not a contract came into existence depends on the nature of the terms. If the terms that have not been agreed render the contract as a whole 'unworkable or void for uncertainty', the

---

92. [1993] 1 Lloyd's Rep 25 (CA).   93. Ibid, 27 (Steyn LJ).   94. Ibid, 29 (Steyn LJ).
95. [2009] EWHC 257 (Comm), [2009] 1 Lloyd's Rep 475. The decision was upheld on appeal: [2009] EWCA Civ 1334, [2010] 2 All ER (Comm) 788.
96. Ibid, [245]–[249], [252].   97. [1993] 1 Lloyd's Rep 25, 27.

court will hold that no contract was formed. Otherwise, the terms on which the parties have reached agreement will be taken to constitute a contract.[98]

The battle of the forms

The willingness to look beyond offer and acceptance has given the courts a flexible set of tools to respond to the problem of contract formation in complex, but inconclusive, negotiations. These tools work well where the parties have actually reached agreement on a substantial set of issues as a result of negotiation. However, the courts have had less success with this approach in situations where the parties have not reached agreement on important issues, due to a failure to negotiate or due to difficulty in finding a common position to which both parties can sign up.

This is more or less what happened in Illustration 2.3, and it occurs surprisingly often in commercial transactions. A commercial sale and purchase of goods, for instance, is often carried through a pro-forma invoice sent by the seller offering goods for sale at a particular price, and an order placed by the buyer accepting the order. In many cases, both have detailed sets of terms and conditions printed on the back, which can differ quite significantly, but the parties never actually discuss whose terms and conditions will govern the contract. Cases of this sort are called instances of the **battle of the forms**, because each party has operated as if their standard form of contract governs the transaction. In such cases, notwithstanding references to the importance of looking to the entire transaction, the courts in practice tend to fall back on a rather conventional offer and acceptance analysis. Their starting point is that where the parties will usually have performed some or all of their contractual obligations, the courts should be reluctant to find that no contract was concluded. They tend, therefore, to hold that a contract was concluded, as a result of the offer having been accepted either by the offeree's conduct or by the offeree's performance.[99]

British Road Services, Ltd v Arthur V Crutchley & Co, Ltd[100] provides a good example. The parties in this case had had a long-standing commercial relationship whereby BRS stored goods in AVC's warehouse. For each set of goods stored, BRS's delivery driver would present a delivery note, which would be stamped by AVC. The delivery note stated that goods were delivered on BRS's standard conditions, whereas the stamp said that the goods were 'Received under AVC conditions'. The two sets of conditions were materially different, but the parties at no time agreed which set of conditions would actually govern the contract. Some crates of whisky delivered by BRS were stolen from AVC's warehouse. AVC's conditions included a clause which capped AVC's monetary liability at a sum much lower than the whisky's actual value. BRS's conditions contained no such limitation. The Court of Appeal held that AVC's conditions were incorporated into the contract, not BRS's. The delivery note was an offer to contract on BRS's conditions. The stamp on the note was a rejection of that offer, and a counter-offer. By placing their goods in the warehouse, BRS had accepted AVC's counter-offer, and the contract was therefore entered into on their terms.

---

98. *Pagnan SpA v Feed Products Ltd* [1993] 1 Lloyd's Rep 25 (CA).

99. See eg *Brogden v The Directors of the Metropolitan Railway Co* (1877) 2 App Cas 666, where it was held that either conduct or performance could serve as acceptance of a contract in such circumstances.

100. [1968] 1 All ER 811 (CA).

The implication of *British Road Services* is that contract formation in a battle of the forms situation follows what has been called the 'last shot rule', under which whoever gets in the last shot before performance will have their terms govern the contract. In a contract for the sale of goods, this will usually be the buyer. This approach was confirmed in *Butler Machine Tool Co Ltd v Ex-Cell-O Corp (England) Ltd*,[101] despite some disagreement amongst the judges hearing that case.

Case in depth: *Butler Machine Tool Co Ltd v Ex-Cell-O Corp (England) Ltd* [1979] 1 WLR 401 (CA)

The plaintiffs, Butler Machine Tool Co Ltd, offered to sell a machine tool to the defendants, Ex-Cell-O Corp, at a set price. The terms included a price variation clause whereby they reserved the right to charge the defendants the price prevailing at the time of delivery. The defendants replied on their own order form which contained no provision for varying the price. The order form had a tear-off acknowledgement slip to be signed by the seller stating that the order was made on the terms set out in the order form. The plaintiffs signed and returned the slip with a covering letter stating that delivery was to be on the terms of its original quotation. Delivery of the machine tool was delayed for 12 months due to the fault of the defendants. The plaintiffs sought to recover a higher price based on the price variation clause.

In the High Court, Thesiger J held that it would be inappropriate to apply a traditional offer and acceptance analysis on these facts. He focused, instead, on the documents that passed between the parties, and held that the price variation clause had been given great importance in the seller's quotation, which stated that it would prevail over any contrary terms offered by the buyers. Given this, he held that it did prevail, and was incorporated into the contract.

Thesiger J's judgment was reversed by the Court of Appeal, which held that the price variation clause was not incorporated. Two of the three judges on the Court of Appeal (Lawton and Bridge LJJ) following a traditional offer and acceptance analysis, holding that the buyers' order was not an acceptance of the sellers' offer but a counter-offer which was accepted by the sellers in signing the acknowledgement slip. The covering letter accompanying that slip could not override the terms of the acknowledgement slip. The contract thus contained no price variation clause.

Denning LJ (as he then was) concurred in the outcome, but used a different reasoning. He agreed with Thesiger J in holding that a traditional offer and acceptance analysis was inappropriate where there was a battle of the forms. Instead, he said, the court should look to all documents passing between the parties, and glean from those what the parties' agreement was. In some cases, the battle would be won by 'the man who fires the last shot'. In others, it would be the person who 'gets the blow in first'. In yet other cases, the terms and conditions of the parties would have to be construed together. And, finally, there would be cases where neither party's terms governed the contract, and where the court had to imply reasonable terms. On the facts of this case, the last shot won, so that the buyers' terms prevailed.

---

101. [1979] 1 WLR 401 (CA).

Lord Denning's more nuanced position parallels the approach that has evolved in relation to complex but incomplete negotiations. However, the law appears to have taken the traditional offer and acceptance route favoured by Lawton and Bridge LJJ. In *Tekdata Interconnections Ltd v Amphenol Ltd*,[102] the Court of Appeal held that a battle of the forms situation should ordinarily be resolved by a traditional offer and acceptance analysis, in the absence of a clear course of dealing between the parties. This approach has attracted criticism, because it imputes an agreement which is not actually there. The reality in cases involving a battle of the forms is that the parties did not agree on the terms that would govern their contract and, in a number of cases, would in all likelihood not have agreed to the terms that the court ultimately held to govern their contract. This is clearly true in the example of Overton and Cropley in Illustration 2.3, but it is also almost certainly true of *Butler Machine Tool* itself. As Thesiger J pointed out, the price variation clause was of extreme importance to the seller in *Butler Machine Tool*, and was unlikely to have been given up in negotiation. The result, therefore, was that he was deemed as a matter of law to have agreed to a contract to which he would never in fact have agreed.

Such an outcome is clearly problematic from a commercial point of view. In addition, the last shot approach also ignores a very important aspect of commercial negotiations. In commercial practice, it is not uncommon for parties to negotiate a higher or lower price depending on the extent of liability they are taking on under a contract. A seller may, for example, charge a higher price in exchange for taking on a higher degree of liability. By adopting the last shot rule that is the natural consequence of an offer and acceptance analysis, the law in effect gives the buyer a contractual advantage which the parties may not actually have agreed he should have, and which may not be reflected in the price.

Finally, the result of the approach in *Butler Machine Tool* is that the outcome of cases can turn on minor variations in the facts which, from a commercial point of view, are mere happenstance. Let us return to the example of the contract in Illustration 2.3. On the version of the facts set out, it is likely that Cropley's draft of 10 January will be held to be the basis of the parties' contract. On an orthodox analysis, Overton's letter of 13 December is the initial offer, with the subsequent proposals constituting one counter-offer after another. By shipping the goods on 11 January, Overton accepted Cropley's counter-offer of 10 January by performance. But it is easy to see how the situation would be completely different if the timeline varied only slightly. If, for example, Overton had sent a revised draft to Cropley *before* shipment of the goods, then it would have been Cropley who would have accepted by performance—in this case, by taking delivery of the goods.

From a commercial point of view, the difference between these cases is a fine one— arguably, too fine to be at all serviceable. The consequence of the use of the offer and acceptance in a battle of the forms situation is that it is on precisely such a fine distinction that the rights, duties, and liabilities of the parties turn. Why, then, does the legal analysis of such situations diverge so significantly from the situation as understood from a commercial perspective? As with other problems with the law of formation

---

102. [2009] EWCA Civ 1209, [2009] 2 CLC 866.

which we have examined in this chapter, the underlying problem in the battle of the forms cases, too, is linked to the fact that the law focuses on the discrete steps of offer and acceptance, rather than the broader question of agreement. To treat the issue as a simple question of offer and acceptance leads, almost inevitably, to an all-or-nothing solution: the terms proposed by one or other of the parties must apply in their entirety, because a contract can only exist if one set of terms constitutes an offer which the other accepted. To treat it as a question of identifying the scope and extent of agreement, in contrast, leads to a focus on understanding how much the parties agreed, and whether that degree of agreement was sufficient to constitute a contract. This is the approach Lord Denning sought to adopt in *Butler Machine Tool* through his menu of four different solutions to a battle of the forms situation. It also closely parallels the approach that the courts have adopted in relation to complex negotiations. The adoption of this approach would be a considerable improvement over the current offer and acceptance analysis.

 Debates in context: 'fuzzy' consent?

The legal rules relating to battles of the forms have attracted a not-inconsiderable amount of academic commentary. One of the more interesting perspectives on why the law seems to have so much difficulty in dealing with this situation was put forward by Professor Ian Macneil, an American contract theorist.[103] Macneil's critique was articulated in the context of US contract law—he was commenting on Article 2-207(1) of the Uniform Commercial Code, and on the jurisprudence that had developed under it—but it applies with equal force to English contract law.

Macneil argued that the issue that gives rise to the battle of the forms problem runs much deeper than most theorists allow. The issue is not that the concepts of offer and acceptance lack sufficient flexibility to deal with battles of the forms. It is, rather, that 'consent' in a commercial sense is rather different from what the common law understands it to be. As lawyers see it, consent is a simple matter of 'yes' or 'no'. You either accept something or you do not. There is no room for partial consent. As a result, if you accept some terms of an offer and reject others, you cannot be said to have consented to the offer. If your answer isn't a clear yes, it can't be anything other than a no. Macneil argued that commercial men, in contrast to the law, do not view consent as being simply about 'yes' or 'no'. Consent, as commercially understood, has room for 'yes, but . . .' and 'yes, kinda sorta' in addition to 'yes' and 'no'. It does not have to take the form of 'we accept'. Commercial consent could equally take the form 'we accept, but do not accept'.[104]

Although Macneil did not put it in precisely these words, the essence of his argument was that consent is often fuzzy. The example he gave was a contract for the sale of 100 widgets for $700, with the delivery to be on or before 30 July. The seller receives a printed purchase order from the buyer, and responds with his own printed sales order. Regardless of the actual

→

103. IR Macneil, *The New Social Contract: An Inquiry into Modern Contractual Relations* (Yale University Press 1980) 72–7.
104. Ibid, 73.

→

words on the order, in commercial terms each party will see the other as consenting on a sliding scale: 99 per cent to the price and quantity, 90 per cent to delivery within a week of the agreed date, 70 per cent to delivery on or before the agreed date, all the way down to 5 per cent for some of the printed terms on their order (eg provisions in relation to liability). The correct way to deal with the consequences of this, he argued, would be to hold that the parties had agreed on only such terms as were found on both documents. As far as other terms went, the court should simply hold that the parties had not agreed, and leave their rights and remedies to whatever the default legal position might be.[105]

Would it make sense for such an approach to be adopted in English law? The idea of consent as being something other than complete is at fundamental odds with English law, and in particular the emphasis it places on certainty,[106] even if it reflects commercial reality. His recommended solution does not, however, depend on treating commercial consent as fuzzy. It is compatible with the approach of focusing on the extent to which the parties had reached agreement on the same set of terms and conditions, which the Court of Appeal took in *Pagnan SpA v Feed Products Ltd*.[107] It is also compatible with the approach which Lord Denning sought to adopt in *Butler Machine Tool*.[108]

It should, however, be noted that the adoption of such an approach to battle of the forms situations will not be uniform, in that it will affect certain types of clauses far more significantly than others. Any clause seeking to limit (or enhance) liability, for example, would be extremely unlikely to be enforced if Macneil's approach were to be adopted. A restrictive warranty, or caps on liability, are amongst the clauses that are least likely to be found in the standard terms of a seller and buyer. But this may be no bad thing, because it would in effect compel parties to obtain express agreement from their counterparties for precisely those clauses that are most likely to be controversial, and to which consent is least likely to be given. It is, in contrast, extremely unlikely to produce the type of result seen in *Butler Machine Tool*,[109] where a party was deemed by law to have consented to a form of contract to which they would have never given actual consent.

Contractless transactions?

As a final point, it is worth briefly considering the consequence of a holding that no contract was formed. If the action was brought by a potential purchaser of goods or services, the finding that no contract existed will in almost all cases leave her without a remedy. If, however, the action was brought by a party who has already supplied goods or services, or rendered some other type of performance, the law may in certain cases give her a remedy for work done even if no contract came into being. The case of *British Steel Corp v Cleveland Bridge & Engineering Co Ltd*[110] is a good illustration.

---

105. Ibid, 73–4.
106. We will discuss the role of 'certainty' in contract in greater detail in Chapter 5.
107. [1987] 2 Lloyd's Rep 601 (CA).   108. [1979] 1 WLR 401 (CA).
109. Ibid.   110. [1984] 1 All ER 504 (QB).

> **Case in depth: *British Steel Corp v Cleveland Bridge & Engineering Co Ltd* [1984] 1 All ER 504 (QB)**
>
> Cleveland Bridge and Engineering were subcontractors for the fabrication of steel work for a building being constructed in Saudi Arabia. The building had an unusual structure, and Cleveland entered into discussions with British Steel to procure steel nodes for the building from them. Because of the time frame, British Steel began casting and delivering nodes while negotiations were still underway. The negotiations proved very problematic, however, and the parties were far apart on issues such as performance bonds, British Steel's liability for consequential damages, and even payment terms. The nodes were delivered behind schedule, and no agreement had been reached when the last batch was delivered. British Steel sued for payment, and Cleveland sued for damages for late delivery.
>
> The court held that although both parties had proceeded at all times on the assumption that a contract would eventually be agreed, in point of fact no contract had been formed. There were no terms to which the parties could at any point of time be said to have agreed, nor did British Steel say or do anything that suggested it intended to be bound.
>
> The result was that the parties were left to their default remedies at law. In the case of British Steel, this meant that it could recover a reasonable price for the nodes it had supplied. Cleveland, however, was left without a remedy for the late delivery.

The remedy in *British Steel Corp* was granted through what is known as a *quantum meruit* claim. *Quantum meruit* claims lie in a range of circumstances, one of which covers cases where a contractor has carried out work at the request of another party but is unable to enforce a contractual claim against that other party because no contract materialized. We will look at the details of *quantum meruit* in Chapter 17. For now, it is sufficient to note the existence of the remedy, and its applicability in cases of formation.

2.5 In conclusion: offer, acceptance, and agreement

In this chapter, we have noted how the courts assess the question of whether two or more parties had reached agreement, using a combination of an objective approach to assessing intention (the '**objective test**'), and a procedural approach to assessing whether and to what extent the parties have actually reached agreement ('offer and acceptance'). As we have seen, this approach has its limitations. There are many cases where there does seem to be an agreement, but where English law does not find an agreement because the parties' discussions do not fit within the traditional offer and acceptance analysis.[111] On the flipside, there have also been cases where English law finds an agreement even though, in commercial terms, the parties had not actually come to an agreement on important issues.

---

111. See eg the cases cited in H Beale (ed), *Chitty on Contracts* (31st edn, Sweet & Maxwell 2012) 2-112, fn 508.

How, then, might this problem be resolved? It would be going too far to say that the traditional offer and acceptance analysis is without use, and should be abandoned. As we have seen, there is a core area of bargaining in which it functions well, and there are other areas in which the courts have, with some straining, managed to make it function relatively well. Yet, as we have also seen, there are a significant number of areas in which it does not function particularly well, and produces results that are not in touch with commercial reality.

Generalizing from the discussion in this chapter, we can broadly speak of three types of processes by which contracts are formed. The first is what I have in this chapter called *bargaining*—situations in which the parties discuss and bargain over a relatively small number of terms, such as the price and the place and time of performance, and reach agreement on them after batting a few offers and counter-offers back and forth. These cases, such as Problem 2 at the start of the chapter, are relatively straightforward, and are the central paradigm upon which the traditional offer and acceptance analysis is based. The second is what we might, adapting US usage, call *adhesion*. Adhesion covers situations in which there is little negotiation or bargaining. The contracting process here, instead, consists mainly of one party agreeing to deal with another on the terms set out by the other. This includes many of the situations we examined in sections 2.3.1 and 2.3.2, and many similar situations in everyday life—including actions such as boarding a bus or train, filling one's car with petrol, or signing up for a Facebook account. The extension of the traditional offer and acceptance analysis to these situations has required some peculiar twists and adaptations, but generally functions fairly well from a pragmatic point of view, particularly when supplemented by a healthy dose of statutory regulation.

The third type of process is what I have called *negotiation*. Negotiation covers situations in which the formation of a contract requires parties to engage in a relatively lengthy process, and to discuss a far broader range of terms and issues. This includes cases involving complex negotiations, where parties actually engage in protracted discussions; situations of a battle of the forms, where parties ought to engage in protracted discussions but fail to do so; and cases like *Gibson* and *Storer*, where the issues are relatively straightforward, but where the number of steps involved in the formation process mean that it lasts for a significant amount of time.

The offer and acceptance approach to formation has little to commend itself in these circumstances. The formation of a contract is always a relational process, and in these cases the relational element comes particularly strongly to the fore. This is at odds with the focus on concrete steps that is characteristic of the traditional offer and acceptance analysis. The result is that far from promoting certainty, the traditional approach in practice contributes to greater uncertainty in these cases. The solution is relatively straightforward. It would require the law to recognize that the true goal of the rules on formation is to discover whether the parties have reached agreement, and to recognize the limitations of offer and acceptance as a test for determining whether they have reached acceptance. This would not require a wholesale revision of doctrine—as we have seen in this chapter, recent decisions of the courts in cases involving complex negotiations, such as *Pagnan SpA* and *Maple Leaf*, have already begun to recognize this principle, and to demonstrate a willingness to look beyond traditional notions of offer and acceptance. A gradual and incremental extension of these to contracts formed through negotiation more generally would address most of the problems caused by the law as it stands today. From a practical point of view, however, the lesson for lawyers is to understand the requirements imposed by the offer and acceptance process as well as the limitations they impose, and to make sure that the things their clients say and do mirror their commercial understanding of the stage at which their transaction is.

Key points

- For a contract to be formed, the parties must have reached agreement.

- English law takes a procedural approach to assessing whether agreement has been reached. Agreement is taken to have been reached if one party makes an offer, which the other party accepts.

- A statement is an offer if it sets out the terms on which the offeror intends to deal, is certain, and discloses an intention to be bound. Otherwise, it is an invitation to treat.

- Intention is always assessed objectively, with reference to what a reasonable observer would have understood from the party's words and deeds. Contract law is not ordinarily concerned with a party's actual intention.

- A response to an offer is an acceptance if it accepts the offer entirely, without any deviations. Otherwise, it is a counter-offer which destroys the original offer.

- An acceptance can take the form of words or of conduct, but either way it must be communicated to be effective.

- Offers can be revoked until accepted. Acceptances cannot usually be revoked.

- Parties have considerable freedom to structure the formation process, and to impose conditions on offers and acceptances, as suits them.

- The rules in relation to offer and acceptance work well in relation to simple bargaining. They work less well in complex negotiations. Here, the courts are sometimes willing to assess whether agreement was reached without relying heavily on offer and acceptance.

Assess your learning

You should be able to respond to each of the following points with a confident 'yes'. If you can't, then you should revisit the sections listed against that point.

Can you:

(a) *Distinguish* between offers, invitations to treat, acceptances, and counter-offers, and *apply* the distinction to the types of contracts you encounter in everyday life? (Sections 2.3.1 and 2.3.2)

(b) *Identify* the role of the objective test in assessing formation, how it differs from a subjective test, and *explain* the rationale behind using an objective, rather than subjective, test? (Section 2.2)

(c) *Understand* the role of communication in relation to acceptances as well as revocations, *identify* the ingredients of communication, and *apply* your knowledge to specific fact scenarios? (Sections 2.3.3 to 2.3.6)

(d) *Explain* how parties can restructure the process of formation using collateral contracts and other devices, and *apply* your knowledge to design special formation processes? (Section 2.3.6)

(e) *Outline* the limitations of the offer and acceptance approach to formation in situations other than simple bargaining, and *identify* the key features of the solutions the courts have found to deal with these limitations? (Section 2.4)

In relation to each of the above, you should be able to:

(i) identify and clearly explain the key rules and principles;

(ii) identify the key cases and statutes, and why they matter;

(iii) apply the principles and cases to specific real or hypothetical fact situations;

(iv) evaluate the limitations, if any, of the law as it currently stands.

Further reading

A De Moor, 'Intention in the Law of Contract: Elusive or Illusory?' (1990) 106 LQR 632.

P Goodrich, 'The Posthumous Life of the Postal Rule: Requiem and Revival of *Adams v Lindsell*' in L Mulcahy and S Wheeler (eds), *Feminist Perspectives on Contract Law* (Routledge 2005).

W Howarth, 'The Meaning of Objectivity in Contract' (1984) 100 LQR 265.

BS Jackson, 'Offer and Acceptance in the Supermarket' (1979) 129 NLJ 775.

E Macdonald, 'Dispatching the Dispatch Rule? The Postal Rule, E-mail, Revocation and Implied Terms' (2013) 19 WebJCLI.

R McClintock, 'Objectivity in Contract' (1988–91) 6 Auckland University Law Review 317.

A Phang, 'Tenders and Uncertainty' (1991) 4 JCL 46.

J Unger, 'Self-Service Shops and the Law of Contract' (1953) 16 MLR 369.

3

Consideration

The requirement of mutuality

'You can't get owt for nowt'

Problem 3: setting the context

Consider the following (fictitious) report from a newspaper:

DUKE PROMISES TO PROVIDE FOR HEROIC RESCUER

Last week, the heroic actions of Ian Wilkins saved the Duchess of Sunderland from near-certain death. But he paid a high price for his heroism. Doctors at the Royal Victoria Institute in Newcastle confirmed yesterday that Ian had suffered paraplegia as a result of a severe trauma to his spinal cord, which he sustained when rescuing the Duchess from the wreckage of her car. The nature of his injury means that he is unlikely to ever regain much functionality in his legs.

Today, the Duke of Sunderland promised to provide Ian and his family with a generous pension for the remainder of his life. This will be at least 50 per cent higher than his current income, increasing annually in line with inflation. 'My wife is alive today thanks to Ian's heroism,' the Duke said. 'My family and I owe him a moral debt which we can never repay. Providing for his material needs is the very least we can do.'

Is an arrangement of this type binding? Is the Duke obliged to fulfil his promise or can he resile from his word and discontinue payments to Ian if he so wishes?

3.1 Introduction

Consider the following snatches of conversation:

Illustration 3.1

   – I have a hamster. I'll sell it to you for £10.

   – Done!

Illustration 3.2

   – Your mum and I are going to buy you a hamster. Would you like that?

   – Yes! Thanks Dad! You're the greatest!

In both instances, the parties have reached agreement. Both involve a person making an offer of a hamster to another, which is accepted on its precise terms. Are they arrangements to which the law should be giving effect? It seems obvious that whereas the first conversation might create a legally binding contract, the second should not: few people, if any, would say that a parent's promise of a pet to a child results in the parent being contractually bound to the child. What, then, is missing in the second example? What more do we need for an agreement to be treated as a legally binding contract?

Virtually all legal systems agree that not every accepted offer creates a contract. Something more is needed. Common law systems have traditionally expressed this additional element in terms of two requirements: that a contract must be supported by **consideration** and that it must be entered into with the intention to create legal relations. The second of these is the subject of Chapter 4. This chapter focuses on the requirement of consideration.

Like the law of formation, the rules relating to consideration are grounded in the idea of a contract as a bargain struck between consenting parties. A bargain, by nature, involves give and take on both sides. Consideration is the price one party pays for the other party's promise or performance. The doctrine of consideration provides, in essence, that a price of some sort must be paid if an agreement is to be enforceable as a contract.[1] The logic underlying this requirement is the logic of exchange: neither party to a contract can, or should expect to, get a free ride. If one party makes a promise, the other party must give something in return for it in order to 'buy' it. An agreement where the obligations are entirely upon one party, with nothing provided in return by the other, is a **gratuitous promise** akin to a gift—a *nudum pactum* or 'naked promise', to use the Latin term—and English contract law does not in general enforce gratuitous promises. Thus in Illustration 3.1, it is obvious that the parties are getting something for something: one party hands over £10, the other hands over a hamster. Illustration 3.2, in contrast, is a classic instance of a gratuitous promise, where nothing is given in exchange. The first agreement is, therefore, supported by consideration, and can give rise to legally binding obligations, whereas the second is not supported by consideration, and therefore does not create a legally binding obligation.

Yet whilst this principle can be stated in relatively simple terms, the actual rules governing the doctrine of consideration are far more complex. To say that 'something' must be provided by each party raises a range of questions. Is anything sufficient? Are there limits on what can and cannot be consideration? Consider a few variations on the hamster example:

Illustration 3.3

– When my hamster has babies, I'll give you one because I like you very much.

– That's great! Thanks!

Illustration 3.4

– Thanks for mowing my lawn. Would you like one of my baby hamsters?

– Yes, please!

---

1. F Pollock, *The Principles of Contract* (3rd edn, Stevens and Sons 1881) 179, quoted with approval in *Dunlop Pneumatic Tyre Co Ltd v Selfridge & Co Ltd* [1915] AC 847, 855 (Lord Dunedin).

> **Illustration 3.5**
>
> – If you feed my hamsters every evening when I'm away, you can have one of the babies when I come back.
>
> – Deal!

> **Illustration 3.6**
>
> – I have a hamster. You can have it if you promise to look after it.
>
> – I promise I'll look after it!

Each of these cases presents a clear example of an offer being accepted by the person to whom it is made. But is the recipient giving **sufficient** consideration in return for the offer to ground a contract? That, in substance, is the question which the rules of consideration seek to answer.

Much as with 'agreement', 'consideration', too, does not mean the same thing in law as it does in everyday parlance. In everyday parlance, we use 'consideration' to mean 'reason' or 'matters taken into account'. We may speak, for instance, of the 'considerations upon which a decision was based' or of giving a proposal 'due consideration'. The legal concept of consideration, in contrast, is a narrower one. At its heart lie two related ideas—the idea of **value** and the idea of **exchange**. Consideration, in law, is something of *value*, which one party gives in *exchange* for the promise made, or performance rendered, by the other party. Much of the body of rules that constitutes the law of consideration can be slotted into one of these two categories. They are concerned with setting out either what constitutes 'value' in legal terms, or when something that is given can be said to be given in 'exchange' for the other party's promise or performance.

As with the rules of formation we studied in the previous chapter, the rules on consideration, too, reflect the law's propensity to view contracts as coming into being at a single 'moment of responsibility', when two parties reach agreement after bargaining over the price. Unsurprisingly, therefore, the rules work very well for transactions which fit that pattern. However, as we saw in Chapter 2 regarding formation, many transactions do not fit this pattern, and here the rules of consideration work less well. This is not a new problem. As far back as 1765, Lord Mansfield, a leading commercial judge, for this very reason attempted to restrict the operation of consideration in *Pillans & Rose v Van Mierop & Hopkins*,[2] but he was overruled by the House of Lords less than 15 years later.[3] Lord Wright called for its abolition in 1935,[4] and in 1937 the Law Revision Committee recommended far-reaching changes to the doctrine.[5] Commentators have

---

2. (1765) 3 Burr 1663.   3. See *Rann v Hughes* (1778) 4 Bro PC 27, 7 TR 350.

4. Lord Wright, 'Ought the Doctrine of Consideration to be Abolished from the Common Law?' (1935–6) 49 Harv L Rev 1225.

5. Law Revision Committee, *Sixth Interim Report: Statute of Frauds and the Doctrine of Consideration* (Cmd 5449, 1937).

continued to call for reform in the years since.[6] Yet every attempt to abolish or restrict the doctrine has failed, and the doctrine remains part of the law.

In this chapter, we will examine the formal rules that make up the doctrine of consideration, before moving on to consider why the doctrine has been so controversial; what, if any, problems it causes; and what can, in practice, be done to mitigate those problems. As we will see, much as with the legal approach to formation, the current form taken by the law of consideration owes much to the continuing influence of a somewhat backward-looking view of contracts as exchange-oriented bargains which achieve concrete shape at a specific 'moment of responsibility'.

3.2 Value

The first requirement imposed by the doctrine of consideration is that the act, forbearance, promise, or commodity given in exchange for the promise should be something of *value*. The legal understanding of value incorporates at least three different conceptual approaches. The first of these approaches is based on the idea of *economic* value. If whatever is given has some economic value, it is good consideration. This approach has a good deal of support in the academic literature as well as in case law, and works particularly well in relation to transactions which involve trade in goods or services.

The second approach asks whether the act or forbearance which is said to be consideration can be said in legal terms to be either a *benefit* to the other party or a *detriment* to the person giving it. This approach is for the most part compatible with the first, and supplements it.

The third approach is much newer, dating to the early 1990s. Its focus is on *practical* benefits, rather than the legal benefits and detriments that are the focus of the second approach. It is not entirely compatible with the other approaches, and for that reason has been controversial amongst commentators as well as the judiciary.

As the law currently stands, any transaction could, in principle, be analysed using any of these approaches. It is therefore important to understand all three, and appreciate the contexts in which each is applied. We will begin with the first approach in the context of a relatively simple transaction, before moving on to the other two approaches and more complex transactions.

3.2.1 Economic value: trading goods and services

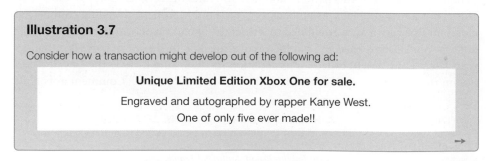

Illustration 3.7

Consider how a transaction might develop out of the following ad:

Unique Limited Edition Xbox One for sale.

Engraved and autographed by rapper Kanye West.
One of only five ever made!!

⟶

6. PS Atiyah, 'Consideration: A Restatement' in PS Atiyah, *Essays on Contract* (Clarendon Press 1986).

→

Being sold to fund textbooks and rent.
Make me an offer!

Contact Paul
01991 492387

As anyone with experience of selling or trading goods on online fora will testify, ads for exotic products tend to attract a range of offers. For a product such as the Xbox in this example, more creative offers might include things like a complete supply of textbooks and rent for the remainder of Paul's education, a guaranteed job on graduation, a lifetime of free beer, and so on. Are these 'value' for the purposes of the doctrine of consideration?

'Sufficient but not adequate'

In transactions for the acquisition or exchange of goods and services, the legal rules concerning 'value' are quite generous. The legal approach to consideration in such cases turns on two key principles. First, the rules of consideration are only concerned with determining whether some value has been given in exchange for the price or performance secured under the contract. The rules are not concerned with the question of whether what is given is commensurate with what is obtained. The price paid for the promise may be fair, outrageously high, or ridiculously low. But for the purpose of determining whether consideration was given, the fairness or unfairness of the bargain is irrelevant. A handful of beans in exchange for a cow, or for that matter an Xbox, is perfectly good consideration in law. The usual way of putting this principle is to say that *consideration must be sufficient, but need not be adequate*. The law is concerned with the existence of value, not with its extent.

This points to an important difference between the legal understanding of value and the way we think about it in everyday life. When we use 'value' in the context of an exchange in everyday life, we tend to associate it with ideas of 'good value' or 'poor value'—with the question of whether what the other side provides is 'worth' what we provide in return. The law of consideration, in contrast, does not concern itself with this question. Its role is to ensure that the transaction reflects an exchange, not that the exchange is a fair one. Some value must be provided, but it doesn't matter how much.

This is not to say that the law of contract is unconcerned with fairness. Although English law does not require a transaction to be fair in general terms, it does include a wide array of rules that assess and enforce fairness in selected aspects of contracting. It is simply that the law relating to *consideration* is not geared towards assessing whether a bargain is fair. The idea that the law should not be drawn into the question of whether the price paid was a fair one is very deeply embedded in English contract law. Thus, for example, consumer protection law gives the courts and the Competition and Markets Authority a broad range of powers to deal with unfair terms in contracts, but not if the unfairness lies in the price that was charged. This distinction has been of fundamental importance to several cases.[7]

7. See Chapter 13.

The rule that consideration need not be adequate is sometimes called a **bright-line rule**—a standard which is unambiguous and clear, with no room for nuance or weighting. If something of value has been given, the courts will treat it as consideration even if the value is nominal, or trivial. The practice of a peppercorn rent—where property is given to a tenant for a nominal rent—has been in existence for centuries and has been consistently upheld. Peppercorn rents, in the modern context, are often ways of creating enforceable contracts where the true motivation behind the contract is natural love and affection. Thus, for example, it is not uncommon for a relative to provide a house or flat to a younger relative for a peppercorn rent. An agreement letting the property for natural love and affection would not be an enforceable contract, and the addition of a peppercorn helps the parties overcome that barrier.

Peppercorn consideration offers a powerful tool to make enforceable agreements which would otherwise have been unenforceable for want of consideration. But it too has limits. If the substance of the transaction does not involve any exchange, there will be no consideration. In *Lipkin Gorman v Karpnale*,[8] the House of Lords was asked to consider whether the provision of gambling chips in exchange for money was a contract supported by consideration. The court held that it was not. Despite its form, in substance the transaction was neither a sale nor a hire of the chips—it was simply a way of providing a means to gamble without directly using money.[9]

'Value in the eyes of law'

Secondly, the question of whether something constitutes consideration does not depend on whether the parties regard it as such. The value that consideration must possess is *'value in the eye of the law'*,[10] not in the eye of the parties. In *Chappell & Co v Nestle*,[11] the House of Lords held that used candy wrappers were capable of being consideration. Nestle ran a promotion in which they offered to send a vinyl record containing the hit single 'Rockin' shoes' by the King Brothers to anyone who sent in three chocolate wrappers along with 1s 6d. The House of Lords had to consider whether an acceptance of this offer created a contract and, if it did, whether the candy wrappers were part of the consideration. It answered both questions in the affirmative. The fact that in *subjective* terms the candy wrappers were of no value to Nestle (they were thrown away) was held to be irrelevant. They had value in *objective* terms, and could therefore be consideration.[12]

The result is that things that the parties may not have consciously thought of as consideration for a promise may nevertheless be treated by the court as good consideration, while things that the parties regarded as consideration may end up not being treated by a court as consideration. The decision of the Court of Appeal in *Pitts v Jones*[13] serves as a good illustration.

8. [1992] 2 AC 548 (HL).

9. Gambling with money was illegal at the time under s 18 of the Gaming Act 1845. This is no longer the case—see Gambling Act 2005, s 334(1)(c).

10. *Eleanor Thomas v Benjamin Thomas* (1842) 2 QB Rep 851.   11. [1960] AC 87 (HL).

12. The case itself was an action for breach of copyright rather than an action in contract. The suit was brought against Nestle by the holders of the copyright in the song. The question of whether an acceptance of Nestle's offer created a contract was relevant for the purposes of determining whether and to what extent Nestle was liable.

13. [2007] EWCA 1301 Civ, [2008] QB 706.

Case in depth: *Pitts v Jones* [2007] EWCA Civ 1301, [2008] QB 706

The defendant, Andrew Jones, was the majority shareholder in a company. The claimants held a minority stake, and also worked in the company. Jones was in the process of selling his shares to a third party, WG Birch Ltd. Birch also agreed to give the claimants the option to sell him their shares six months later. The claimants had a right of pre-emption against Jones (ie the right to buy Jones's shares if he offered them to a third party). The sale would also have had to be approved at an extraordinary general meeting (EGM) of the company, requiring two weeks' notice. The claimants were unhappy about the six-month delay for the sale of their shares. Jones gave them an oral undertaking that he would pay the price of their shares if Birch failed to do so. They thereupon waived the two weeks' notice for the company's EGM, and also waived their right of pre-emption. Birch became insolvent before paying for the claimants' shares, and they sued Jones on his oral undertaking.

One of the arguments in the case related to whether there was consideration for Jones's undertaking. The claimants argued that their cooperation with Jones—specifically, their waiver of their pre-emption rights and of the two weeks' notice for the EGM—was consideration for the undertaking. However, evidence given by the claimants showed that they had not actually thought about withholding cooperation.[14] Counsel for Jones argued that their cooperation could not therefore be consideration. Consideration, he said, had to be the result of 'positive decisions that they would act in a particular way . . . as the result of the promise they had offered'. It could not be given 'subconsciously'.[15]

Smith LJ, delivering the judgment of the Court of Appeal, held that there was consideration. There was, he held, 'so clear a chronological link between the defendant's offer of the undertaking and the claimants' willingness to sign the documents that the natural inference to draw was that the two were directly connected'. This was true 'notwithstanding the fact that the claimants did not consciously realise that by signing the documents they were subjecting themselves to a detriment and were giving consideration for the defendant's undertaking'.[16]

In other words, the question that is asked in determining whether something is consideration is not whether the parties intended their promise or performance to be consideration, or even whether a reasonable person would have concluded that they intended it to be consideration. What matters is the actual nature of what is given, not the parties' motives in giving or receiving it. This is sometimes referred to as the court 'inventing' or 'refusing to invent' consideration,[17] but in reality it simply reflects the fact that consideration, like formation, is judged objectively, not subjectively.

What, then, does the law recognize as being 'value' for the purposes of consideration? Although the courts have never said so in so many words, the general consensus among commentators has long been that 'value' means *economic value*. This makes sense in contracts involving purchasing or bartering goods or services, because the logic of

---

14. Ibid, [15].   15. Ibid, [17].

16. Ibid, [18]. As we will see in Part III, despite having convinced the court that the contract was supported by consideration, the claimants lost the case on a different point.

17. This unfortunate term was coined by Professor Treitel, and has persisted despite well-deserved criticism.

exchange-oriented bargaining is fundamentally economic. In Illustration 3.7, it is evident that the vast majority of offers for the limited-edition Xbox will be of a type that has economic value. This also applies to the hamster examples. Consider Illustration 3.5:

- If you feed my hamsters every evening when I'm away, you can have one of the babies when I come back.
- Deal!

Taking on the responsibility of feeding someone's hamsters clearly has economic value, evidenced, not least, by the fact that there are commercial pet-sitting services which charge money to do precisely this.

3.2.2 Benefit and detriment: transactions beyond trade

If a transaction involves trade in goods or services by way of sale or barter, it is fairly obvious that something of value has been given by each party, in exchange for something of value which they have received from the other party. But what happens with transactions that do not fit this pattern? Consider Problem 3. A rescue is not something to which 'economic value' can be easily attributed. Consider also the fictitious newspaper report in Illustration 3.8.

Illustration 3.8

CORPORATE SCROOGES!

A Yorkshire student has been left stunned after a corporate sponsor refused to pay out on a charitable giving pledge.

Joanna Mickelwick (20), a law student at Three Ridings University, was trying to raise money for Santa Smiles, a charity which provides Christmas presents to children in poverty, by swimming unaided across the English Channel. She attracted over £10,000 in sponsorship pledges, including a pledge of £4,500 from Trucad Bank. Once she had completed her swim, however, she was shocked when Trucad refused to pay the amount it had pledged.

A spokesperson for Trucad said that pressure upon their revenue streams as a result of the financial downturn had forced them into a severe cost-cutting exercise. As a result, they had been left with no choice but to review all outgoings, and severely cut back where there was no legal obligation to pay. This includes most of their charitable giving. 'Whilst we fully support Joanna's work, and hope to be able to support her chosen charities in the future, we are not in a position to do so at this time,' the spokesperson said.

In everyday life, we seldom give much thought to the enforceability of sponsorship arrangements. But *are* they in fact enforceable? What happens if a sponsor refuses to pay once the student has completed the challenge? Does someone who walks from Land's End to John o'Groats, or swims across the Channel, provide 'sufficient consideration' to support a promise of sponsorship?

If this question seems difficult, it is because an arrangement of this type is not an 'exchange' of things having economic value in quite the same way as an agreement to transfer a limited edition Xbox in exchange for five years' worth of free beer. In the latter case, both sides give and receive something which, regardless of whether it is a good or a service, has or can be given a market value, or to which economic value can be attributed with relative ease. When, however, we move away from transactions involving trade to contracts involving things that are *not* commonly traded as commodities—for example, a long walk around Britain—it is not always easy to identify what, if anything, is economically valuable in the transaction.

Partly for this reason, the test which is actually applied in most cases to assess whether consideration is present in a situation is usually articulated not in terms of 'economic value', but in terms of benefit and detriment. Courts ask whether what was provided by the promisee constitutes a '*benefit*' to the promisor, or a '*detriment*' to the promisee. If it does, the courts will usually take it to be good consideration. This doctrine is usually traced to the 1875 decision of the Exchequer Chamber in *Currie v Misa*,[18] where consideration was defined in these terms:

> A valuable consideration in the sense of the law may consist either in some right, interest, profit or benefit accruing to the one party, or some forbearance, detriment, loss or responsibility given, suffered or undertaken by the other.

The language of benefit and detriment is, however, much older. As early as the 1730s, Sir John Comyns had described consideration as something 'for the benefit of the defendant, or to the trouble or prejudice of the plaintiff',[19] and variants on that formulation have been repeated in the years since.

A benefit and detriment analysis can be a very useful way of assessing whether something of value has been given. A good illustration is provided by *Bainbridge v Firmstone*,[20] an early 19th-century decision. The facts of this case are somewhat unusual. Bainbridge owned two boilers 'of great value'. Firmstone asked Bainbridge whether he could borrow the boilers, as he wanted to weigh them. He promised to return them 'in as perfect and complete a condition, and as fit for use by plaintiff, as the same were in at the time of the consent so given by the plaintiff'. However, after dismantling the boilers to weigh them, he refused to reassemble them, leaving them 'in a detached and divided condition, and in many different pieces'. Bainbridge sued, whereupon Firmstone argued that there was no consideration for his promise. The court rejected Firmstone's plea. Lord Denham held that Firmstone 'had some reason for wishing to weigh the boilers', and it was not for the court to enquire what benefit he expected to derive.[21] Patteson J added that regardless of whether Firmstone had a benefit or not, 'there is a detriment to the plaintiff from his parting with the possession for even so short a time'.[22] As a result, there was consideration and Firmstone was liable on the contract.

The decision in *Bainbridge* demonstrates that consideration does not have to simultaneously be *both* a benefit *and* a detriment. It is sufficient if it is either. A detriment assumed at the request of another will almost always be sufficient consideration,

---

18. (1875) LR 10 Ex 153, 162.   19. Com Dig, Action on the Case, Assumpsit, B-1.
20. (1838) 8 Ad & E 743.   21. Ibid, 744.   22. Ibid.

regardless of whether the other person obtains a benefit. The classic example is a contract where one party says to another, 'If you will go to York, I will give you £100.' In such a case, the promise to go to York is clearly a detriment, and for that reason amounts to good consideration.[23] Whilst there are no significant cases directly testing the enforceability of sponsorship agreements, there appears to be little distinction between a promise to pay if a person goes to York and a promise to pay if a person swims across the Channel, as in Illustration 3.8, suggesting that sponsorship agreements, too, may be enforceable.

The ability to separate benefit and detriment makes consideration capable of being extended to cover a range of circumstances—including those where the economic value of the purported consideration is not readily apparent. Returning to Problem 3, Ian's actions clearly constitute a benefit to the Duke, and the injuries he suffers are equally clearly a detriment, thus establishing consideration more clearly than a mere test of economic value could have. The 19th-century case of *Shadwell v Shadwell*[24] provides an excellent example from the body of decided case law.

Case in depth: *Lancelot Shadwell v Cayley Shadwell and another* (1860) 9 CB(NS) 159

Lancelot Shadwell was a young barrister who intended to marry Ellen Nicholl. His uncle, Charles Shadwell, wrote him a letter saying that he was glad to hear of Lancelot's intended marriage, and 'as I promised to assist you at starting, I am happy to tell you that I will pay to you £150 yearly during my life and until your annual income derived from your profession of a Chancery barrister shall amount to 600 guineas'. The uncle paid the money for 12 years, but then stopped. On his death six years later, the nephew sued his uncle's estate for six years' arrears.

The executor opposed the suit, arguing that the uncle's promise was a voluntary one, without consideration. It was plain that it was not intended to be anything more than an act of kindness. As such, there was no contract to enforce. The court was split on the result. The majority opinion, delivered by Earle CJ on behalf of himself and Keating J, held that the nephew's marriage was consideration for the promise to pay. The nephew's undertaking to marry, they held, was both a benefit to the uncle and a detriment to the nephew.

As far as the detriment was concerned, the court held that although 'a man's marriage with the woman of his choice is in one sense a boon',[25] it was also a detriment because it amounted to 'a most material change in his position', in the course of which he 'may have incurred pecuniary liabilities resulting in embarrassments'.[26] It was also a benefit to the uncle, because although a marriage 'primarily affects the parties thereto', there was also a secondary sense in which 'it may be an object of interest to a near relative, and in that sense a benefit to him'.[27]

Byles J dissented. He took the view that the uncle's letter was 'no more than a letter of kindness, creating no legal obligation'.[28] A detriment by itself, he said, should not be treated

→

---

23. See *Great Northern Railway v Witham* (1873) 9 CP 16, 19 (Brett J).
24. (1860) 9 CB (NS) 159.   25. Ibid, 173–4.   26. Ibid, 174.   27. Ibid.
28. Ibid, 178.

> as consideration unless it was either a benefit to the defendant, or had been undertaken at the defendant's request. Neither was true here—the plaintiff's decision to marry was an independent one, with no express or implied request from the defendant.[29] Further, the tone of the letter suggested that by the time it was written, Lancelot had already decided to marry Ellen. This meant that by the time the letter was written, it was past consideration, and hence could not be good consideration.[30]

Shadwell demonstrates the extent to which courts can, if they so choose, stretch the concepts of benefit and detriment. The decision remains controversial. A letter from an uncle to a soon-to-be-married nephew offering to support him financially while his income remains low is not what we would term a contract in everyday parlance—most people would regard such a promise as a conditional gift.

In doctrinal terms, however, it is precisely the expansive view of legal benefits and detriments and the ability to find the existence of one without the other, that makes the doctrine of consideration at all workable outside the area of simple exchange-oriented bargaining.

 Debates in context: 'inventing' consideration

One of the more powerful attacks on the orthodox doctrine of consideration remains that launched by Professor Patrick Atiyah, initially in his inaugural lecture delivered at the Australian National University,[31] subsequently published in an expanded version in a collection of essays.[32]

Atiyah argued that the traditional benefit–detriment understanding of the doctrine of consideration was profoundly flawed. Whilst English law quite clearly did have a law of consideration, it did not mean what the benefit–detriment analysis assumed it to be. In particular, Atiyah argued that consideration was not about reciprocity, and that there was no general rule that a contract had to be reciprocal. Drawing upon cases such as *Shadwell v Shadwell*, he pointed out that the courts regularly enforced contracts that had no element of reciprocity in them, and treated things as consideration which the parties did not regard as such.

Making sense of this, in his view, required a radical reconceptualization of what consideration was about. Consideration as he described it was essentially a pragmatic doctrine—a reason to enforce the promise. Whilst benefit and detriment were ordinarily *sufficient* reasons to enforce a promise, they were not *necessary* reasons. Courts could and did enforce promises for other reasons. *Shadwell* itself, he said, was an example of such a case—a gratuitous promise which the courts chose to enforce because they wanted to protect the nephew, who had relied on continuing to receive his uncle's support.

Professor Guenter Treitel, who was then Vinerian Professor of English Law at Oxford, responded with a strong defence of the orthodox benefit–detriment analysis. The central point

→

29. Ibid, 176–7.   30. Ibid, 177–8.
31. Published as PS Atiyah, *Consideration in Contracts: A Fundamental Restatement* (ANU Press 1971).
32. Atiyah (n 6).

→

of his defence was the suggestion that the presence or absence of consideration did not depend on the parties' intention. Whether the parties themselves had intended something to be consideration was immaterial. What mattered was whether it was a benefit or detriment. If it was, the courts would treat it as consideration. Such an understanding of benefit and detriment, he argued, could explain most of the cases. Treitel termed this 'invented' consideration, to signify the fact that it was the courts, and not the parties, who had chosen to treat the thing in question as consideration. The choice of term was perhaps unfortunate, in that it suggested the courts creating consideration out of thin air, rather than (as Treitel actually meant) picking up on an element of the transaction to which the parties might not have consciously directed their minds, but which was nevertheless capable of constituting consideration.

The current academic consensus is that both sides of the debate had a point. Atiyah's point that the courts seem to be evaluating reasons to enforce or not enforce a contract, rather than conducting a strict enquiry into whether a benefit or detriment was present, is certainly borne out by some of the cases, as we will see. Nevertheless, as we will also see, the courts are frequently influenced by a certain understanding of benefits and detriments when deciding whether a particular agreement is an enforceable contract.

Legal and factual detriments and benefits

One of the issues that *Shadwell* posed was the difficulty of terming Lancelot Shadwell's decision to marry a 'detriment' to him. To term marrying someone of your own choice a 'detriment' is a bit of a stretch, to put it mildly. The court acknowledged this, but held that in legal terms the change in the prospective groom's position was a detriment. What this suggests is that there is a distinctively legal understanding of benefits and detriments, which may exist even if there is no factual benefit or detriment. The editors of *Chitty on Contract* define the legal understanding in these terms:

> Under this notion, the promisee may provide consideration by doing anything that he was not legally bound to do, whether or not it actually occasions a detriment to him or confers a benefit on the promisor; while conversely he may provide no consideration by doing only what he was legally bound to do, however much this may in fact occasion a detriment to him or confer a benefit on the promisor.[33]

Thus the question of whether Lancelot Shadwell's marriage had a beneficial or detrimental effect upon his life is irrelevant. The *legal* detriment comes from his having consented to doing something he was not legally bound to do.[34] If Charles Shadwell's letter had been written to induce Lancelot to formalize his proposed marriage, as the court believed, then the legal detriment Lancelot had incurred consisted of the legal liabilities that flowed from his promise to marry Ellen—even if, in factual terms, the marriage would be to Lancelot's benefit.

In legal terms, any restriction on your personal freedom is a detriment, even if the factual consequences of that restriction are to your benefit. Thus, for example, agreeing

---

33. H Beale (ed), *Chitty on Contracts* (31st edn, Sweet & Maxwell 2012) 3-006.

34. It is worth noting, in this context, that when *Shadwell v Shadwell* was decided, a promise to marry created a binding legal obligation for the breach of which an action in damages lay.

to install a speed monitor in your car will probably be to your benefit, as it is likely to make you drive more carefully. In legal terms, it is nevertheless a detriment, and can therefore constitute consideration for, for example, a promise by your car insurance company to offer you a discount on your premium.

In contrast, the inverse situation, where the benefit or detriment is purely factual and not legal, has proven more problematic, as *White v Bluett*[35] illustrates. This case arose out of a family quarrel. A son was unhappy with his father's plans for the distribution of his property after his death. He made his unhappiness very clear through repeated complaints. The father told him that if he stopped complaining he would release him from liability under a few promissory notes. The son stopped complaining. After the father's death, the executors of his estate sued the son on those promissory notes. The son argued that his father's promise to release him was contractually binding. The court held that there was no contract, because no consideration had been given. The son did not have a 'right' to complain, because the father had absolute discretion in relation to how he chose to distribute his property. A promise to abstain from doing what he had no right to do could not be consideration.

In purely factual terms, it is clear that there was a benefit to the father—namely, the peace and quiet he secured by stopping his son's complaints. Nevertheless, because the son had no 'right to complain', a promise not to complain did not carry with it any benefit or detriment in law. The preference for legal benefits and detriments over purely factual ones also manifests itself in the rule that the discharge of a moral obligation is not good consideration. The leading case on this point is *Eastwood v Kenyon*.[36] Eastwood was the executor of the will of John Sutcliffe. John's heir was his young daughter, Sarah, who was then a minor. Eastwood spent a considerable sum of money on her maintenance and education, and on looking after and managing Sutcliffe's properties, including paying the interest on a mortgage. He incurred a debt of £140 in order to do so, as the estate's funds were insufficient. When she came of age, Sarah Sutcliffe promised to repay the debt, as did the man she married, Kenyon. Kenyon then failed to repay the debt, and Eastwood sued.

Eastwood advanced a number of arguments, some of which were peculiar to the Victorian legal system.[37] One of the arguments, however, was that Kenyon's promise to repay constituted a contract. It was contended that Kenyon was under a moral obligation to repay the debts which Eastwood had incurred in managing Sarah's interests, and that such a moral obligation could be good consideration.[38] The court rejected this argument, and held that Eastwood had provided no consideration. By the time the promise was made, 'the consideration for it was past and executed long before'.[39] Whilst it was true that there may have been a moral obligation to repay Eastwood, the court held that recognizing a moral obligation as consideration 'would be attended with mischievous consequences to society', with suits being multiplied to the prejudice of 'real creditors'.[40]

35. (1853) 23 LJ Ex 36.   36. (1840) 11 Ad & E 438, 113 ER 482.
37. Married women had very limited rights to hold property or assume a legal personality distinct from their husband's in early Victorian England. Some of the issues the court decided therefore concerned technical questions as to the liability of a husband for his wife's pre-marital debts.
38. (1840) 11 Ad & E 438, 451 (Lord Denman).   39. Ibid, 442–3.
40. Ibid, 450–1 (Lord Denman).

Practice in context: maintenance agreements

The refusal to recognize the discharge of a moral obligation as good consideration is intelligible if we accept that benefits and detriments must be legal. By definition, no legal consequences attach to an obligation that is only moral, and its discharge does not therefore in any way alter the legal position of the parties. If the promisor derives any benefit from discharging a moral obligation, it is a factual benefit—the easing of their conscience, the feeling that they have done their duty, and so on—and these do not fit within the understanding of value on which the doctrine of consideration is built. But it causes problems in practice.

A significant proportion of the English cases where the question of legal benefits and detriments is directly implicated deal with maintenance agreements. The typical fact pattern we see in these cases is roughly this. A husband and wife agree to separate. They enter into an agreement under which the husband will pay the wife a certain sum of money every year (or every month). The wife, in consequence, refrains from making an application to the court for a maintenance order. After some time, the husband stops paying the agreed maintenance. Can the wife sue him for breach of contract? There is a long line of cases on this point, in which the question has come down to one of consideration. Has the wife provided consideration for the husband's promise of maintenance?

Looked at in purely factual terms, it would seem clear that the wife has incurred a detriment. She has refrained from doing something she would have been entitled to do. Yet in a number of cases the courts have held there to be no consideration on the basis that in *legal* terms, the ability to apply for maintenance to the court cannot be given up. Any contract which seeks to restrain a person from applying for maintenance under the relevant law—currently, the Matrimonial Causes Act 1973—is void, as the jurisdiction of that court cannot be ousted. As such, no legal detriment has been suffered, and hence no consideration has been given.[41]

There are relatively few cases to the contrary, and those have been very specific to the facts. Thus in *Goodinson v Goodinson*,[42] the court granted a wife's suit for arrears on an agreement of this type, but on the basis that she had provided consideration other than the promise not to sue. More recently, the Court of Appeal in *Soulsbury v Soulsbury*[43] enforced an agreement under which a husband had promised a sum of £100,000 on his death if his wife refrained from enforcing a court order for maintenance of £12,000 a year. This was done on the basis that the contract was a unilateral contract, whose performance the wife had completed: the contract required that she not sue for maintenance while her husband was alive, and she did not.[44] Neither of these are of much assistance to women who have refrained from bringing actions in reliance on their husbands' promises of maintenance, and whose husbands happen to still be alive.

The maintenance cases could have equally been decided on policy grounds—on the ground, that is to say, that public policy demands that courts have the final say on maintenance agreements, and not the parties, as a result of which a private arrangement will not be given binding effect by the courts. And, indeed, several more recent cases have been decided on precisely this ground, rather than on the basis that no consideration was provided. The fact that the absence of consideration argument has been repeatedly invoked, however, points to the entrenchment in English law of the view that purely factual benefits will not ordinarily be consideration.

41. See eg *Bennett v Bennett* [1952] 1 KB 249. 42. [1954] 2 QB 118.
43. [2007] EWCA Civ 969, [2008] 2 WLR 834. 44. Ibid, [49] (Longmore LJ).

Creating commercial relations

In *Witham v Great Northern Railway Co*,[45] Samuel Witham entered into an arrangement with the Great Northern Railway Co, under which he agreed to supply them with iron bars meeting a particular specification, in 'such quantities . . . as the company's store-keeper may order from time to time'. Crucially, the Great Northern Railway Co were not actually required to give Witham any orders: they had the *option* of placing orders, but no *obligation* to do so.

Witham supplied a few orders, but then refused to supply any more. When the railway company sued, Witham argued that because the company were not obliged to order any iron from him, his promise to supply them with iron was not supported by consideration, and hence was not contractually binding. And indeed, in legal terms, it is hard to see how the contract gave any legal benefits to Witham, or placed any legal detriment on the Great Northern Railway Co, under the contract. The contract did not oblige the company to place orders with Witham or even to prefer Witham to other suppliers, and Witham would in consequence have had no legal claim against the company if it had never placed any orders with him,[46] or had unilaterally, and without warning, stopped doing so at any stage.[47]

Nevertheless, the court found that there was a binding contract supported by consideration. The judges appear to have been influenced by the fact that framework contracts of the type entered into between Witham and the company were common in commercial practice (and remain so to this day). They were, as Brett J put it, a 'matter of every day's practice'.[48] But the judges hearing the case were divided on what exactly the consideration was. Keating J was of the view that the company had provided consideration by actually placing an order with Witham.[49] Brett J, in contrast, drew a parallel with unilateral contracts, and cited the example, which we have considered previously, of a person saying 'If you will go to York, I will give you £100.' If that offer could on acceptance give rise to a contract, then so, too, could an offer on the terms 'If you will give me an order for iron, or other goods, I will supply it at a given price.'[50]

Yet it is hard to see how this analogy holds. Walking to York is a detriment in both factual and legal terms, but placing an order for goods that a party actually needs is not a detriment even in legal terms. The reason why this case is not easy to fit within the conventional benefit and detriment analysis becomes clearer if one looks at the commercial nature, effect, and rationale of framework agreements. Ordinarily, if a customer places an order with a merchant, the merchant is at liberty to refuse to fulfil that order. A framework agreement like the one made between Witham and the railway company is in essence a promise by the supplier not to reject orders while the agreement is in effect, but instead to accept all orders that are placed, and to accept them on terms agreed in advance. What consideration, then, could be said to be given for this promise by the supplier?

---

45. (1873–4) LR 9 CP 16.

46. See *Burton v Great Northern Railway Co* (1854) 9 Ex 507, 156 ER 216.

47. See *Baird Textile Holdings Ltd v Marks & Spencer plc* [2001] EWCA Civ 274, [2002] 1 All ER (Comm) 737.

48. (1873–4) LR 9 CP 16, 19.   49. Ibid, 18–19.   50. Ibid, 19.

In commercial terms, the answer to this question is fairly clear. The reason a supplier such as Witham enters into a framework agreement with a large customer, even when the agreement imposes no obligations whatsoever on that customer, is that the supplier expects to profit from the commercial relationship which the framework agreement establishes. If a framework agreement contemplates the supply of goods or services, the supplier typically expects to profit from the agreement because it makes it likelier that the customer will place at least a few orders, even if it is under no obligation to do so—the customer would hardly have gone to the trouble of vetting the supplier and negotiating an agreement if it had no intention of having any further dealings with the supplier. In strictly legal terms, this is not a benefit because there is no 'right' to receive orders (much as there was no 'right to complain' in *White v Bluett*). Nevertheless, such a relationship has commercial significance and commercial value, even though the chance of increased orders is merely a chance, and not a certainty or a legal entitlement.

The relevance of these broader commercial considerations was expressly recognized by the Court of Appeal in *Edmonds v Lawson*,[51] a case decided in 2000. *Edmonds* related to a pupillage contract entered into by an aspiring barrister with a pupil master from the chambers where she had her pupillage. The case had been brought as a test case to see whether a barrister–pupil relationship was governed by employment law, and the parties in that case were not actually in dispute. The key issue it raised of relevance to our present discussion was whether a pupil barrister provides any consideration to her master which is sufficient to ground an enforceable contract. The essence of a pupillage contract, it was argued for the chambers, is that the chambers provide education and training to the pupil, for which the pupil pays no fee. Any work the pupil does on a case is purely for the pupil's own benefit and instruction, and not for the benefit of the pupil barrister. It is not intended or anticipated that the pupil will produce work that is actually useful to any barrister. To the contrary, if a pupil does actually produce work of real value, the barrister who benefits from that work has a professional obligation under the Code of Conduct to pay the pupil for that work, thus placing it entirely outwith the pupil's obligations under the pupillage contract. The result, it was argued, was that a pupil provides no consideration for the training she receives, and a pupillage arrangement is consequently not an enforceable contract.

The Court of Appeal rejected this argument. Lord Bingham's judgment is of particular interest. Pupillage, he held, was not a purely altruistic exercise, but had a strong element of self-interest. Members of chambers 'have a strong incentive to attract talented pupils', because 'their future prospects will to some extent depend on their success in doing so'. If the practice of pupillage was viewed as a whole, it was obvious that chambers would 'see an advantage in developing close relationships with pupils who plan to practise as employed barristers or to practise overseas'. The result was that pupils 'provide consideration for the offer made by chambers such as the defendants' by agreeing to enter into the close, important and potentially very productive relationship which pupillage involves'.[52]

---

51. [2000] QB 501.   52. Ibid, 515 (Lord Bingham CJ).

Lord Bingham's decision represents a very broad approach to the question of what could be a benefit, looking at whether the agreement was in the chambers' self-interest. The court's willingness to recognize as good consideration the commercial value of a relationship and the probabilistic chance that that relationship will produce future benefits, are extremely significant. This will become clearer if we consider the context of the 1990 decision of the Court of Appeal in the case of *Williams v Roffey Brothers & Nicholls (Contractors) Ltd*,[53] which brought a new understanding of consideration into English law, based on the idea of 'practical benefit' which would appear to open the door to treating a very wide range of factual benefits as good consideration. Because of the importance of this case, we will begin by looking in the next section at the context in which it arose, and examine why factual benefits are of particular importance in renegotiations.

3.2.3 Practical benefit: existing duties and renegotiation

Illustration 3.9

Consider the following letter:

Pontifex Bridge Builders
Hawespool Industrial Estate, Mardale, Cumberland

John Thomson
JT Copper
Westmorland Industrial Estate
Westmorland

Dear John,

Following our discussion today, I confirm that we will be prepared to agree to a temporary increase of 5 per cent over the contract price for the copper filaments you're supplying us. This is in recognition of the global increase in the price of copper. The increase will cease to have effect when the LME Copper price returns to within 10 per cent of its price on the contract date. You have agreed that you will continue to supply copper filaments to us in accordance with the schedule set out in our contract of April 16.

Please let me have your confirmation by return fax today, if possible, so we can put this issue to rest.

Best wishes,

Jim

The situation described in this letter—the renegotiation of an agreement to one party's benefit—is very common in commercial practice. But has the beneficiary of the renegotiation provided consideration for the new agreement?

---

53. [1991] 1 QB 1.

This question has long been a difficult one for the law to answer. Renegotiations are extremely common in the commercial world, and also in consumer contracts, but do not fit well with the orthodox doctrine of consideration. What is JT Copper providing in exchange for Pontifex's promise to pay it a higher price? In purely legal terms, nothing. It promises to supply copper filaments in accordance with a particular schedule, but this is something it is already legally obliged to do under an existing contract. Pontifex acquires no benefit to which it is not already entitled, and JT Copper is subject to no new detriment to which it is not already subject. To refuse to enforce such contracts for want of consideration, however, seems commercially unrealistic, if only because they are so common. In English law, this problem is generally described as relating to *pre-existing duties*. If a person is already under a pre-existing obligation to do (or refrain from doing) a particular act, then, so it is argued, a promise to do that very act is not ordinarily capable of being consideration, because it does not involve any benefit or detriment.

This stands in contrast with a case where a party disputes liability—if, for example, JT Copper were to argue that it was not obliged to supply Pontifex the copper because it was entitled to terminate the contract. Here, the transaction involves the *compromise* of a legal dispute, for which each party provides valid consideration in the form of a legal benefit or detriment by giving up their respective legal claims and defences. Such a situation subsists wherever a party honestly believes itself to have a valid legal claim or defence and intends to pursue it, even if the claim or defence was unlikely to have succeeded in court.[54] But where the existence of the duty has been acknowledged by both parties, or where the purported claim or defence is known to be invalid, a person who simply promises to perform that duty provides no legal benefit and incurs no legal detriment.[55]

When stated in these abstract terms, the rule sounds perfectly reasonable. Yet to apply it literally would produce commercial chaos because commercial contracting frequently involves parties entering into precisely such agreements. Price adjustments, as in Illustration 3.9, are a clear example, and there are plenty of others. This problem is an old one, but it is only in the past half-century that English courts have begun to make serious attempts to solve it. These attempts culminated in *Williams v Roffey*, where the court attempted to radically restate the legal position in relation to pre-existing legal duties. The solution it found, however, remains controversial, largely because it is not easy to square with the doctrine of consideration as it is traditionally understood. Because courts have, notwithstanding this, striven to accommodate their solutions within the conceptual framework and language of the doctrine of consideration, those solutions suffer from a range of limitations that restrict their utility and render their precise scope and application uncertain.

The problem of pre-existing duties arises in three types of circumstances. The first of these relates to duties imposed by statute or common law—for example, the duty of the police to maintain law and order or the duty of a parent to maintain his or her children. The second circumstance relates to existing duties imposed under a contract. The third circumstance relates to debts. In the remainder of this section, we will look at each in turn.

54. See eg *Cook v Wright* (1861) 1 B & S 559; *Syros Shipping Co v Elaghill Trading Co (The Proodos C)* [1981] 3 All ER 189, 192 (QB).
55. See *Wade v Simeon* (1846) 2 CB 548.

Circumstance 1: pre-existing duties under common law or statute

It has long been the case that doing or promising to do something that one is already obliged to do by virtue of statute or common law cannot be good consideration. A promise to do more than the statute or common law duty requires, however, can be good consideration. This principle applies to statutory duties imposed upon public officials and agencies,[56] as well as upon private individuals.[57]

The application of this rule to private individuals produces peculiar consequences, which the courts have only been able to circumvent through rather obscure reasoning. In *Thoresen Car Ferries v Weymouth and Portland Borough Council*,[58] Weymouth Borough Council agreed to grant berthing facilities at Weymouth ferry terminal to Thoresen Ferries, so that Thoresen could run a ferry service between Weymouth and Cherbourg, France. Subsequently, the council sought to resile from the contract, and wrote to Thoresen withdrawing the berthing facilities. When Thoresen sued, the council argued that there was no contract because Thoresen had not provided any consideration. Although Thoresen had agreed to pay for the berthing facilities, this could not be consideration because the payment of berthing charges was a statutory obligation under the Harbours, Docks, and Piers Clauses Act 1847.

In strictly legal terms, the council's argument was correct. Yet to accede to it would produce the absurd result that no contract for berthing facilities entered into with a port authority would ever be enforceable. Donaldson J in the High Court therefore held that although Thoresen's promise to pay for the berth could not be consideration, Thoresen had also implicitly promised to use the berth every day—and, through doing so, had both incurred a legal detriment and provided a legal benefit to the council. This promise went well beyond the statutory duty, and hence could be consideration.

Some courts have gone to even further lengths to hold that the claimant has taken on a broader duty than that required under the statute. In *Smith v Roche*,[59] the defendant agreed to pay the mother of his illegitimate children £50 a year in consideration of her undertaking 'the care and nurture' of those children. He failed to pay, and she brought an action on the agreement. The father argued that no consideration had been given for his promise, because statute already imposed an obligation on the unmarried mother of an illegitimate child (but not the father) to care for it until it reached the age of 16. The court rejected this argument. The statutory duty only applied if the mother was not indigent, but the contract was not so qualified because it made no exception for indigence: it bound the mother to care for the child even if she was indigent. As a result, she had taken on a broader duty than that imposed by the statute, and hence had provided consideration.[60]

Ward v Byham[61] provides an even clearer illustration of the lengths to which the courts will go to 'find' consideration in cases involving private individuals and a statutory duty.

---

56. See eg *Collins v Godefroy* (1831) 1 B & Ad 950.
57. See eg *Crowhurst v Laverack* (1852) 8 Ex 208, 155 ER 1322.
58. [1977] 2 Lloyd's Rep 614 (QB).   59. (1859) 6 CB (NS) 223, 141 ER 40.
60. Ibid, 233–4 (Cockburn CJ).   61. [1956] 1 WLR 496.

Case in depth: *Ward v Byham* [1956] 1 WLR 496

The plaintiff and defendant were, respectively, the mother and father of an illegitimate child, a girl called Carol. The defendant had placed Carol in the care of a neighbour, who he paid £1 a week for her maintenance. The plaintiff, a housekeeper, managed to find a job at a house where she would be allowed to have Carol, and asked if she could have Carol and the weekly allowance of £1. The defendant replied with a letter which said:

> Mildred, I am prepared to let you have Carol and pay you up to £1 per week allowance for her providing you can prove that she will be well looked after and happy and also that she is allowed to decide for herself whether or not she wishes to come and live with you.

The mother took Carol with her. She married her new employer some months later, at which stage the defendant stopped the weekly payments of £1. The plaintiff sued. Under the law as it then stood (s 42 of the National Assistance Act 1948), the mother of an illegitimate child was under an obligation to maintain it. The father, however, had no such obligation unless the mother obtained a court order (called an 'affiliation order') against him. The defendant therefore argued that the plaintiff was only doing what she was legally bound to do, and had provided no consideration. The county court rejected his defence and found for the plaintiff.

The decision was unanimously upheld on appeal. Unfortunately, the judges on the Court of Appeal gave differing, and not entirely compatible, accounts of where the consideration lay. Lord Denning took the view that 'a promise to perform an existing duty, or the performance of it, should be regarded as good consideration, because it is a benefit to the person to whom it is given'.[62] He would, in other words, have adopted a broader understanding of what could be a 'benefit' for the purpose of consideration, encompassing a broad range of factual benefits.

Lord Denning's attempt to recognize all promises to perform existing duties as consideration did not win general acceptance. Morris LJ agreed with the outcome, but took the view that consideration lay in the fact that the father was 'animated by a concern for the well-being of the child', and was in effect saying: 'Irrespective of what may be the strict legal position, what I am asking is that you shall prove that Carol will be well looked after and happy, and also that you must agree that Carol is to be allowed to decide for herself whether or not she wishes to come and live with you.'[63] Morris LJ appears to have taken the view that the result was that this was no longer the same as the duty imposed by law, and could therefore be consideration. Parker LJ simply said that the letter 'clearly expresses good consideration for the bargain', without explaining what this was.

Circumstance 2: contractual renegotiation

The law before Williams v Roffey

Until the decision in *Williams v Roffey*,[64] a landmark case already mentioned several times in this chapter, and to be discussed in detail shortly, the generally accepted view was that an existing contractual duty could not be consideration, for much the same reason that an existing statutory duty could not. No detriment is incurred by the

---

62. Ibid, 498 (Lord Denning). He reiterated this in *Williams v Williams* [1957] 1 WLR 148.
63. Ibid, 497–8 (Morris LJ).   64. [1991] 1 QB 1.

promisee because everything they provide in such a situation is something they were already required to provide. Similarly, no benefit accrues to the promisor because everything they receive is something they are already entitled to receive.

The actual case law on which this view was based was, however, somewhat thin, and was based on a line of cases involving sailors. In the 18th and 19th centuries, it was not uncommon for the captain to sometimes promise sailors extra wages in the course of a voyage. This happened for a number of reasons. It might happen, for example, that part of the crew of a ship deserted during a voyage when a ship stopped at an intermediate port, and the captain promised the remaining members of the crew extra money as a way of inducing them not to desert and to bring the ship to its destination. Or it might happen that the ship faced a peril, and the captain promised the crew extra wages if they brought the ship through the peril. The courts were, in consequence, faced with a number of cases where they had to consider the question of whether such a promise was enforceable.

For the most part, the conclusion they reached was that it was not. The reason why they reached this conclusion is not entirely clear. There were no 'official' law reports at the time—cases were collected by private persons, usually barristers, and often for their own use. The accounts of the judgments they contained are not, therefore, entirely reliable. Nevertheless, the majority of the reports suggest that the courts came to this conclusion on the basis of public policy. In *Harris v Watson*,[65] the captain had promised the crew extra wages to get them to exert themselves when the ship was in danger. The court held that the promise was unenforceable, because there was 'a principle of policy', founded on the interests of 'the navigation of this kingdom' against enforcing such agreements. Were they to be enforced, sailors would be in a position to make extravagant demands, permitting a ship to sink if the demands were not met.

Most other cases took a similar line. The exception, however, was *Stilk v Myrick*. Here, the promise of extra wages had been made in the context of a case where some members of the crew had deserted. The captain promised to divide their wages amongst the remaining members of the crew if they brought the ship back into port. When the ship returned, he reneged on the promise. The court held that the promise was unenforceable. The case is reported in two versions, which differ in their account of the reasons given by the court. The shorter report stated that the case was decided on the basis of public policy, just as the earlier cases were.[66] The longer report, in contrast, states that the court considered the public policy ground, but opined that a far better basis for the decision would be to state that the agreement was void for want of consideration, as the crew were already 'bound by the terms of their original contract to exert themselves to the utmost to bring the ship in safety to her destined port'.[67]

The shorter report was prepared by the barrister who had represented the sailors in that case. Nevertheless, it was the account in the longer report that came to be taken as presenting the best account of the ruling in that case. The case was taken as an authority for the proposition that a promise to merely perform an existing contractual duty could not be good consideration. Subsequent case law clarified that if the sailors—or any contracting party—agreed to do something they were not contractually bound to,

---

65. (1791) Peake 102.   66. (1809) 6 Espn 129, 170 ER 851.
67. (1809) 2 Camp 317, 170 ER 1168.

such as sailing an unseaworthy ship, they would have provided consideration,[68] but not otherwise. Until *Williams v Roffey*, which we are about to discuss, this remained the generally accepted position at English law.[69]

Williams v Roffey and 'practical' benefits

Williams v Roffey involved a renegotiation between a contractor (Roffey Brothers) and a subcontractor (Williams) in the context of a building contract. The outcome of the renegotiation was that Roffey Brothers agreed to hike the contractual rates it was paying Williams for the work he was doing. No new obligations were imposed on Williams: he was simply required to perform his duties under the existing contract. When Williams tried to enforce the higher rate, Roffey Brothers refused to pay, arguing that Williams had not provided any consideration for the increase. The Court of Appeal found for Williams, holding that he had provided consideration even though he had not agreed to do anything more than he was already contractually bound to do.

Before we proceed to examine the decision and reasoning in detail, it is useful to start by explaining the commercial context of the case, as it sheds important light on why Roffey Brothers agreed to renegotiate, and why they may initially have been willing to increase the rates they were paying Williams. The dispute in this case arose out of a contract to redevelop a block of flats owned by a housing association. Large construction projects of this type involve multiple parties linked through a complex network of contracts. The site owner engages a lead contractor who has overall responsibility for the project. The lead contractor typically then engages a number of subcontractors, each of whom has responsibility for a specific part of the job. There may, for example, be a subcontractor contracted to do the joinery work, another contracted to do the electrical work, a third to do the final decoration, and so on.

This has a number of consequences, three of which are of particular relevance to the question we are considering. First, in practical terms, the ability of a given subcontractor to do their bit of the work will very often depend on whether another has performed. The decorators will not be able to do their work, for example, until the electricians and plumbers have finished theirs. As a result, even though each subcontract is in legal terms entirely separate from the others, in factual terms their performance is quite closely linked. One subcontractor's failure to perform can, and often does, have a cascading effect on other contracts. Secondly, as far as the site owner is concerned, all responsibility vests with the lead contractor. Even if a failure to meet a deadline, or to produce work of the requisite quality, was due to a subcontractor's default, it is the lead contractor who is on the hook to the site owner. This remains so even if the lead contractor has done everything he possibly can to mitigate the effect of the subcontractor's default. Thirdly, the contract will usually require the lead contractor to pay delay charges if the project is not completed on time. These are calculated on a daily or weekly basis, and can add up to very significant amounts of money if the delay continues. These issues mean that from a commercial point of view, the lead contractor will also have to take on a managerial role, ensuring that the work of the subcontractors is

---

68. *Hartley v Ponsonby* (1857) 7 El & Bl 872, 119 ER 1471.

69. See eg *Atlas Express Ltd v Kafco (Importers and Distributors) Ltd* [1989] QB 833, where the court treated it as self-evident that there would be no consideration if a party was already under an obligation under an existing agreement.

going according to schedule and working to fix problems that arise if any of the subcontractors fall behind schedule.

All of this forms an important part of the background to *Williams v Roffey Brothers*. Roffey Brothers were the lead contractors on the redevelopment project. Williams was one of many subcontractors, his specific task being the carpentry. He had bid an unrealistically low figure in order to secure the contract. He soon ran into difficulty and was unable to complete the work. Williams's failure to complete his work could have had alarming consequences for Roffey Brothers. They therefore found it far more beneficial to increase the amount Williams was paid than to permit Williams to slip into default, as would have happened had they insisted on their strict contract rights.

In the High Court, counsel appearing for Roffey Brothers admitted that they did, in fact, hope to benefit from making these additional payments. But this, he argued, was irrelevant: the benefits they hoped to derive were purely 'practical benefits'. In law, they derived no benefit, as Williams was promising to do no more than he was already bound to do by his subcontract. The question for the court, then, was whether a 'practical benefit' of this type could be consideration, absent a change in the parties' legal position.

The court held that it could. The court took the view that the issue of policy which troubled the courts in *Harris v Watson* and *Stilk v Myrick* was that a party to a contract could use the threat of breach to, in effect, force the other party to pay more. But this issue was far better dealt with through the law of duress—and, in particular, **economic duress**, which had not as yet developed when *Stilk v Myrick* was decided, but which now provided far more appropriate tools to deal with such a contingency. In the absence of duress, coercion, or fraud, it was perfectly legitimate to hold that benefits of the type Roffey Brothers derived in this case could be valuable consideration:

> A gratuitous promise, pure and simple, remains unenforceable unless given under seal. But where, as in this case, a party undertakes to make a payment because by so doing it will gain an advantage arising out of the continuing relationship with the promisee the new bargain will not fail for want of consideration.[70]

From a pragmatic point of view, there was clearly a 'commercial advantage' to both sides in reaching the agreement they did. It was true that Williams suffered no detriment, but where both parties benefited from an agreement, it was not necessary that both should also suffer a detriment.[71]

This decision has significant practical consequences. In the pre-*Williams* dispensation, the agreement between JT Copper and Pontifex in Illustration 3.9 is unlikely to have been enforceable. *Williams*, however, reverses the position, and makes it likely that the renegotiated contract will be enforced. In commercial terms, the consequence is to make enforceable a wide range of renegotiated agreements which, on the orthodox understanding of consideration, would have been unenforceable. Whilst this would seem to be a positive development, it has not been uncontroversial. In *South Caribbean Trading Ltd v Trafigura Beheer BV*,[72] Colman J was deeply critical of the ruling in *Williams*, and declared that he would have refused to follow it were it for the fact that he was bound by it because it issued from a superior court. The decision in *Williams*, he said, was 'inconsistent with the long-standing rule that consideration,

---

70. [1991] 1 QB 1, 19 (Russell LJ).   71. Ibid, 22–3 (Purchas LJ).
72. [2004] EWHC 2676 (Comm), [2005] 1 Lloyd's Rep 128.

being the price of the promise sued upon, must move from the promisee'.[73] To treat a benefit which the promisor secured, but which did not move from the promisee, as good consideration was to adopt 'a completely different principle'.[74] He appeared to take the view that the decision would eventually be overruled by the House of Lords.[75]

For the most part, however, *Williams v Roffey* has been accepted and followed in subsequent cases, and it has become part of the landscape of the doctrine of consideration. Nevertheless, the ruling has its limitations. It does not in any way affect the general rule that gratuitous promises are unenforceable: it simply widens the understanding of what can be consideration. It would not, therefore, have assisted the claimants in *Eastwood v Kenyon*,[76] as in neither case did the promisor seek to 'gain an advantage arising out of the continuing relationship'. And, whilst the decision was based on a shift from a *legal* understanding of consideration to a *factual* understanding of consideration,[77] the courts have been reluctant to extend the ruling beyond the specific type of case in which it arose—namely, agreements to vary existing contracts.

Circumstance 3: pre-existing debts

Illustration 3.10

Consider this letter.

> **Perfect Fitness Gym and Training Centre**
>
> *5 Tyneside Drive, Littleton-upon-Wall, Hexhamshire*
>
> Dear Tom,
>
> This is a confirmation of our agreement on the repayment of £240.00 of membership arrears that are currently outstanding.
>
> a. Your gym membership will be cancelled with immediate effect.
>
> b. You will pay us, through Direct Debit, £30 per month for eight months, due on the 1st of every month (or next working day), starting on the 1st of next month.
>
> c. Subject to clause (d) below, we will waive the penalty charges and interest that are due on your account (currently £124.76).
>
> d. In the event any payment is missed, this agreement will stand cancelled, and the entire amount owing (including interest and penalty charges) will become due immediately.
>
> If this is acceptable, please sign and return the duplicate copy of this letter, along with the enclosed Direct Debit instruction, within seven days to indicate agreement.
>
> Yours sincerely,
> Martin Frazer

---

73. Ibid, [108].   74. Ibid.
75. See the statement at ibid, [109] that '*Williams v Roffey* . . . has not yet been held by the House of Lords to have been wrongly decided . . .'
76. (1840) 11 Ad & E 438, 113 ER 482.
77. Cf R Halson, 'Sailors, Sub-Contractors and Consideration' (1990) 106 LQR 183.

On the face of it, such a situation seems identical to the *Williams v Roffey* scenario. In purely legal terms, Tom is not providing anything in exchange for Perfect Fitness's promise to waive its penalty charges and interest—he provides no legal benefit to Perfect Fitness, nor does he incur any legal detriment in exchange for their promise to grant him extra time and accept a lesser sum. But getting payment without having to incur the expense of litigation is a practical benefit to Perfect Fitness, in the sense of *Williams*.

This is not, however, the view taken by the law. As things currently stand, even if Tom and Perfect Fitness reach agreement, the agreement will be unenforceable for want of consideration. To understand why this is so, we need to start by examining the case law on renegotiation of debts. The pre-*Williams* position on renegotiated debts was far clearer, and subject to far fewer uncertainties, than was true of general contractual obligations. In *Pinnel's case*,[78] a decision from the early 17th century, Lord Coke had held that the payment of a lesser sum where a greater sum was due could not amount to a satisfaction of the debt, even if the creditor while accepting it purported to accept it 'in full satisfaction' of the amount due. If the creditor accepted something other than money that would be good consideration, because 'it shall be intended that a horse, hawk, or robe, &c. might be more beneficial to the plaintiff than the money, in respect of some circumstance, or otherwise the plaintiff would not have accepted of it in satisfaction'.

Pinnel's case spoke of 'satisfaction' rather than 'consideration', reflecting the fact that the legal rules surrounding debt were not quite the same as those that governed other types of contracts in the 17th century. The rule was put into the context of the doctrine of consideration by the House of Lords in 1884 in *Foakes v Beer*.[79]

Case in depth: *Foakes v Beer* (1884) 9 App Cas 605 (HL)

Foakes owed a judgment debt of £2,090 19s to Julia Beer. He asked for more time to pay, and the parties signed an agreement in which he would pay the sum off in instalments over several years. Beer agreed not to take any proceedings on the judgment. Once Foakes had repaid the entire amount, however, Beer did precisely that, bringing proceedings on the judgment to claim interest on the sum. The agreement made no reference to interest.

Counsel for Foakes argued that the proposition that payment of a lower amount could not be good consideration led to perverse results. Few persons who contracted were aware of the rule, and few acted on it. By overruling it, the House of Lords would only 'declare the universal practice to be good law as well as good sense'.[80]

The House of Lords, however, unanimously upheld the rule. A promise to accept a lesser sum in place of a greater one was very clearly a gratuitous promise: nothing of value was received in exchange. The law would quite arguably have been better if such agreements were accepted and enforced, but it was 'impossible, without refinements which practically alter the sense of the word, to treat such a release or acquittance as supported by any new

→

---

78. (1602) 5 Co Rep 117a, 77 ER 237.   79. (1884) 9 App Cas 605 (HL).
80. Ibid, 608.

→

consideration proceeding from the debtor'.[81] If such an agreement were to be enforceable, it had to be entered into as a **deed**.

At least some of the judges realized that their decision ran contrary to commercial practice. Lord Blackburn was particularly troubled by the implications of the decision:

all men of business, whether merchants or tradesmen, do every day recognise and act on the ground that prompt payment of a part of their demand may be more beneficial to them than it would be to insist on their rights and enforce payment of the whole. Even where the debtor is perfectly solvent, and sure to pay at last, this often is so. Where the credit of the debtor is doubtful it must be more so.[82]

Nevertheless, he agreed to the judgment on the basis that he had been unable to persuade the other judges that his arguments in favour of recognizing the contract were satisfactory.

The House of Lords in *Foakes v Beer* clearly recognized that the rule it was approving was problematic. Nevertheless, in the following years the rule grew even more rigid. Lord Coke had indicated in *Pinnel's case* that an agreement to accept a lower amount earlier than the whole was due, or at a different place from that at which it was due, might be good consideration. Cases between *Pinnel's case* and *Foakes v Beer* had held that a payment in a different form, too, might be good consideration. Thus the courts held that payment of a lower amount by cheque,[83] or other negotiable **instrument**,[84] would be good consideration if the original agreement required payment to be in cash. This was clearly an attempt to get around the difficulties of the strict rule in *Pinnel's case*. *Foakes v Beer* cast some doubt on how broadly these cases were applicable, suggesting that they only applied if a new contract had been created. In *D & C Builders Ltd v Rees*,[85] the Court of Appeal took this to its logical conclusion, overruling some of these cases and drastically restricting others. If giving a lower amount in cash would not be good consideration, then neither would giving it by cheque.[86]

Foakes v Beer was not referred to in *Williams v Roffey*, and the position in relation to debt was not expressly considered. In *Selectmove*,[87] the Court of Appeal held that the rule in *Williams* did not apply to cases where the obligation being renegotiated was an obligation to pay a debt, because to so extend the rule would be inconsistent with *Foakes v Beer*, in effect leaving it without any application. *Selectmove* arose out of a tax dispute. Selectmove had failed to pay tax and National Insurance contributions deducted from its employees' salaries to the Inland Revenue as required by law. The company claimed that it entered into an agreement with the tax authorities, through a collector of taxes, to the effect that it would pay its debt off in instalments. The tax authorities nevertheless served a statutory demand, and ultimately had the company

81. Ibid, 613.   82. Ibid, 622.   83. *Goddard v O'Brien* (1882) 9 QBD 37.
84. *Sibree v Tripp* (1846) 15 M & W 23, 153 ER 745.   85. [1966] 2 QB 617.
86. Ibid, 623–4.   87. [1995] 1 WLR 474 (CA).

wound up. Selectmove argued that the tax authorities had contractually agreed to a different payment schedule, as a result of which the statutory demand was invalid. The Court of Appeal held that no contract was entered into as a matter of fact. Even if one had been entered into, it would have been invalid for want of consideration under the rule in *Foakes v Beer*.

Much as the House of Lords had done in *Foakes v Beer*, the Court of Appeal in *Selectmove* acknowledged that the rule produced undesirable results and that the law would be better off if it were different. Nevertheless, they said, avoiding those results would require changing the law, which was a matter for the House of Lords or for Parliament, rather than the Court of Appeal. In *Rock Advertising Ltd v MWB Business Exchange Centres Ltd*,[88] the Supreme Court agreed that *Williams* sat uneasily with *Foakes v Beer*:

> In *Williams v Roffey Bros & Nicholls (Contractors) Ltd*, the Court of Appeal held that an expectation of commercial advantage was good consideration. The problem about this was that practical expectation of benefit was the very thing which the House of Lords held not to be adequate consideration in *Foakes v Beer* ... There are arguable points of distinction, although the arguments are somewhat forced.[89]

The Supreme Court acknowledged that *Foakes v Beer* 'is probably ripe for re-examination',[90] but declined to do so on the basis that the facts did not call for it. It is matter of regret that they did not do so, as the current state of the law causes genuine difficulties in practice. Even if we confine ourselves to debts, when we put the rule in *Pinnel's case* and *Foakes v Beer* alongside English law's tolerance for peppercorn consideration, the results are peculiar, to say the least. Put together, they produce the odd result that a promise to accept £75,000 instead of £100,000 will not be enforceable, whereas a promise to accept a ballpoint pen costing 50p or a used shoe that would otherwise be thrown away, instead of £100,000 is enforceable.

The absurdity of such a position has been pointed out by the courts themselves. In *Couldery v Bartrum*,[91] Jessel MR criticized the rule in acerbic terms:

> According to English common law a creditor might accept anything in satisfaction of his debt except a less amount of money. He might take a horse, or a canary, or tomtit if he chose, and that was **accord and satisfaction**; but, by a most extraordinary peculiarity of the English common law, he could not take 19 shillings and sixpence in the pound; that was *nudum pactum*.[92]

The criticism is not undeserved. It is hard to see what rational purpose such a rule serves, and the peculiarity of the outcomes it produces suggests that there is some problem either with the legal approach to consideration or with the role consideration plays in determining whether a contract should be enforceable.

As a final point, it is worth noting that a party in such a position might have one important defence, under a principle known as **promissory estoppel**, which is discussed in detail in Chapter 5.

---

88. [2018] UKSC 24.   89. Ibid, [18] (Lord Sumption) (citations in quote omitted).
90. Ibid.   91. (1881) 19 Ch D 394.   92. Ibid, 399.

3.3 **Exchange**

Let us now turn to the second aspect of consideration—namely, the requirement of 'exchange'. Consider Problem 3. Could we say that Ian's heroism in saving the Duchess's life constitutes sufficient consideration for the Duke's promise, so as to make it contractually enforceable? When, in general, can something be said to have been given 'in exchange' for something else?

3.3.1 **The ingredients of exchange**

As with many other concepts, the legal understanding of 'exchange' is more narrowly focused than the everyday understanding. In English law, the answer to the question of whether something is given in exchange turns on two rules. First, consideration *must move from the promisee*—that is to say, it must be the promisee under the contract who provides the thing that is said to constitute consideration. Secondly, consideration must be *in respect of the promise*—that is to say, both the promise and the thing that is said to constitute the consideration must be part of the same set of arrangements.

Consideration must move from the promisee

The first of these principles—that consideration must move from the promisee—is fairly straightforward. If the purported consideration is provided by a third party—that is, someone other than the promisee—then there will be no contract. *Crow v Rogers*,[93] a case from 1724, was one of the first cases to enunciate this principle clearly, and serves as a good illustration of its effects. John Hardy owed £70 to Crow, the plaintiff in this case. Hardy told Roger, the defendant, that if Roger paid Crow the £70, then Hardy would give Roger title to a house he owned. Crow and Roger agreed to this arrangement. Roger then failed to repay the £70 to Crow, who sued. The court dismissed Crow's suit, holding that Crow was 'a stranger to the consideration', and could not sue on the agreement.

Similar facts were present in *Price v Easton*.[94] William Price owed £13 to John Price, for a carriage John had sold him. William agreed with Easton that he would work for Easton for a period of time, and that Easton would retain some of his wages and pay them to John. Easton then failed to pay the wages he had retained to John, who sued. The suit was dismissed on the ground, amongst others, that the suit 'does not shew any consideration proceeding immediately from the plaintiff to the defendant'.[95]

These cases indicate a close conceptual connection between the rule that consideration must move from the promisee, and the issue of who the parties to the contract actually are. The underlying logic—which is particularly clear in *Price*—is that one becomes a party to a contract by providing consideration; as such, a stranger to the consideration is a **stranger to the contract** and cannot sue upon it.[96]

---

93. (1724) 1 Str 592, 93 ER 719.   94. (1833) 4 Barn & AD 433, 110 ER 518.
95. Ibid, 435 (Denham CJ).
96. We will return to this issue in Chapter 18, when we consider the question of the rights of third parties who benefit from a contract, but are not parties to it.

Consideration must be in respect of the promise

The second aspect of the legal understanding of exchange is that consideration must be in respect of the promise. Actions or forbearances are not, and cannot be, consideration unless they are done in response to the promise, as the price of the promise. An act or forbearance which is wholly unilateral—which the promisor did not request or want—cannot therefore be consideration. This means that acts or forbearances must usually be done at the express or implied request of the promisor to constitute consideration.

The mere fact that the party acted in a particular way in *response* to a promise does not mean that that act was done in *return* for the promise—for that to be established, it must be shown that the parties agreed, expressly or implicitly, that the act or forbearance in question was the price for the promise. *Combe v Combe*[97] illustrates this rule in action. Mr and Mrs Combe had separated in 1939 after 24 years of marriage. They divorced in 1943. At the time of the divorce, Mr Combe agreed to pay Mrs Combe £100 per annum as a maintenance allowance. He never did. Mrs Combe repeatedly requested payment, but made no application to the High Court for an order of maintenance. Finally, in 1950, she sued to recover the arrears for the previous 6¾ years, arguing that Mr Combe was in breach of contract.

The court had to consider whether she had provided consideration for the defendant's promise to pay £100 each year. It held that she had not, on two grounds. The first was that a promise not to apply to the court for maintenance was unenforceable, because it was against public policy.[98] The second was that the defendant had not actually asked her to refrain from applying to the court. This meant that her actions could not be consideration:

> I do not think an actual forbearance . . . is a good consideration unless it proceeds from a request, express or implied, on the part of the promisor. If not moved by such a request, the forbearance is not in respect of the promise.[99]

This rule makes sense if we view consideration as embodying an understanding of exchange. If a party does something that the other party neither wants nor requests, it is hard to see how there is any exchange involved.

One consequence of this is that natural love and affection will almost never be held to be consideration, because natural love and affection is not given in respect of a promise. Of its nature, natural love and affection subsist regardless of whether or not a promise is given. If the only consideration in a transaction, therefore, is that the promisor bears natural love and affection for the promisee, the transaction is unlikely to be treated as being supported by consideration. Thus, returning to Illustration 3.3:

– When my hamster has babies, I'll give you one because I like you very much.

– That's great! Thanks!

A promise made because the promisor likes the promisee is a classic example of a promise made for natural love and affection. As such, it will not give rise to an enforceable contract.

---

97. [1951] 2 KB 215.   98. See Chapter 14.   99. [1951] 2 KB 215, 226–9 (Asquith LJ).

3.3.2 **Past consideration**

Let us return to Problem 3. Thus far, it might seem that Ian Wilkins would be on solid ground were the Duke to resile from his promise. The consideration clearly proceeded from him, in that he effected the rescue. Equally, his rescue could hardly be said to be something the Duke would not have wanted. There is, however, a second, and more far-reaching, consequence to the rule that consideration must be given in respect of the promise, of which Ian is likely to fall foul. This is that anything provided *before* the promise was made will not be treated as being good consideration, except in a few special cases. This is usually referred to as *past consideration*, because the act, forbearance, or promise is in the past at the time of the promise for which it claimed to be consideration.

The decision in *Re McArdle*[100] illustrates the doctrine. William McArdle died, leaving a life estate in his property to his widow, with the residue to his five children on her death. One of the properties was a bungalow, called Gravel Hill, which was occupied by one of his sons, Montague, and the son's wife, Marjorie. Marjorie carried out a number of repairs and improvements to this bungalow, the cost of which she bore. After the work had been completed, Montague's other siblings signed a document agreeing to proportionately repay Marjorie a sum of £488 for the work she had done once they succeeded to the estate. When William's widow died and the siblings succeeded to the estate, Marjorie claimed the money. The siblings refused to pay, and the case went to court.

The Court of Appeal held that they were not liable to pay, as Marjorie had not provided any consideration in return for their promise. At the time the promise was made, all the work had already been completed. It was, therefore, a 'wholly past consideration', with the result that the agreement to repay £488 was 'a promise with no consideration'. The situation would have been different had any portion of the work remained unfinished at the time the promise was made. In such a case, Marjorie would have provided consideration by promising to complete the work. But she had not, with the result that the promise was unenforceable.

This also applies where the promisor makes two promises, one of which is made after the act that is said to constitute consideration. In *Roscorla v Thomas*,[101] the claimant agreed to buy a horse from the defendant. After the sale was concluded, the defendant told the claimant that he warranted the horse to be sound. The horse turned out not to be sound, and the claimant sued. It was held that the warranty was made without consideration, and hence was unenforceable. It would have been enforceable if it had been given as part of the consideration for the claimant's purchase of the horse, but the purchase was past consideration at the time the warranty was given.

The logic underlying this rule is straightforward. Value must be given in exchange for the promise in order to constitute consideration. Value which is given otherwise than in exchange for the promise is not given in respect of the promise. Consideration, by definition, is the price of the promise, and it is given in exchange for the promise. It is what the promisee does in order to 'buy' the promise. Something done *before* the promise was made will usually have been done for some reason other than 'buying' the promise. For that reason, it will not usually constitute consideration.

100. [1951] Ch 669 (CA).   101. (1842) 3 QB 234.

Consider the hamster example set out in Illustration 3.4:

– Thanks for mowing my lawn. Would you like one of my baby hamsters?

– Yes, please!

The promise of a hamster was not made until after the lawn had been mown. It was, therefore, not in respect of the promise. As such, it is not good consideration for the promise. The same considerations are likely to apply to Ian Wilkins. At the time Ian rescued the Duchess, no promise had been made. His rescue was not, therefore, done in respect of the promise, and cannot therefore be good consideration for it. The result is that there is no contract, and Ian is unlikely to be able to enforce the promise if the Duke should choose to resile from it.

The rule against past consideration has one significant exception. Consider a slight variation on the facts of the example of Ian Wilkins. Assume that the Duke was present at the scene of the accident, and said something along the lines of, 'Someone, please, rescue my wife! I'll reward you!' before Ian rescued the Duchess. Would this make a difference to whether he would be legally bound to stand by his promise of a pension to Ian?

The answer is that it would. The difference here is that the promisee's action—in this case, the rescue—was requested by the promisor, in terms that suggested that the act would be remunerated. Since the 17th century,[102] the courts have consistently held that such a situation is an exception to the usual rule in relation to past consideration, and that a promise made under these circumstances will be enforceable. In *Pau On v Lau Yiu Long*,[103] the Privy Council, in an appeal from Hong Kong, set out three conditions that must be satisfied for this exception to apply.

> The act must have been done at the promisors' request: the parties must have understood that the act was to be remunerated either by a payment or the conferment of some other benefit: and payment, or the conferment of a benefit, must have been legally enforceable had it been promised in advance.

Although this case relates to the laws of Hong Kong, it is generally also taken to be an accurate statement of the position at English law. There is sound logic behind this exception, as the case of *Re Casey's Patents*[104] makes clear.

Case in depth: *Re Casey's Patents, Stewart v Casey* [1892] 1 Ch 104

In 1887, two inventors, J Stewart and T Charlton, obtained patents for improvements they had made to vessels for storing and transporting volatile or inflammable liquids. They entered into arrangements with Casey, the defendant in this case, for commercializing their patents. Casey spent time and money in getting the patents ready for commercial use. In January 1889, they wrote a letter to him which said:

> We now have pleasure in stating that in consideration of your services as the practical manager in working both our patents as above for transit by steamer or for any land

→

---

102. *Lampleigh v Braithwait* (1615) Hob 105, 80 ER 255.   103. [1980] AC 614 (PC).
104. [1892] 1 Ch 104.

> purposes, we hereby agree to give you one third share of the patents above-mentioned, the same to take effect from this date. This is in addition to and in combination with our agreement of the 29th November last.
>
> Possession of the patents was also given to Casey, who was trying to sell them to an interested party. The sale did not come through, and Stewart died shortly thereafter. His heirs and Charlton then sought to recover the patents from Casey who, instead, used their letter of January 1889 to register a share of one-third in the patents. The Stewart heirs and Charlton sued to recover possession of the patents, and to expunge the reference to Casey's interest from the register.
>
> A number of arguments were raised before the court, one of which was that Casey had not provided valid consideration for his promise. At the time the document was signed, counsel for the plaintiffs argued, Casey had already finished rendering the services to which the document referred. This meant that they were past consideration and, thus, not valid consideration.
>
> The Court of Appeal rejected their argument, on the basis that a past service could, under certain circumstances, support a future promise. If at the time the services were rendered there was an implication that 'it was a service which was to be paid for', then a subsequent document containing a promise to pay could be treated as 'a positive bargain which fixes the amount of that reasonable remuneration on the faith of which the service was originally rendered' or, alternatively, as 'an admission which evidences' that sum.[105]

In so holding, the Court of Appeal was drawing on an understanding long established in English law—that a promise of reward made after an act done upon request is not a gratuitous promise, but can be linked back to the original act, if it appears that that was what the parties intended. This principle was relied upon by the court in the case of *Lampleigh v Braithwait*,[106] a decision from the time of James I:

> [A] meer voluntary curtesie will not have a consideration to uphold [a contract]. But if that curtesie were moved by a suit or request of the party that gives the [promise], it will bind; for the promise, though it follows, yet it is not naked, but couples it self with the suit before, and the merits of the party procured by that suit; which is the difference.[107]

The exception to the general rule against recognizing past consideration, in other words, goes some way to recognizing that contracts can be evolutionary, rather than coming into being fully formed at a determinate 'moment of responsibility'. As we saw in Chapter 2, it is common in commercial practice for agreements to emerge piecemeal, and develop over a period of time. The exception, as formulated in *Re Casey's Patents*, and reformulated in *Pao On*, provides for precisely such a situation. The effect is to protect a party who has begun to perform his obligations under a projected contract, even though the parties have not as yet agreed on all the terms that will govern

---

105. Ibid, 115–16 (Bowen LJ).   106. (1615) Hob 105, 80 ER 255.
107. Ibid, 106. The original judgment uses the term '*assumpsit*', rather than 'contract' or 'promise'. *Assumpsit* was the name of the form of action that was historically brought to enforce a contract not under seal. The forms of action were abolished in 1834, and the terminology of *assumpsit* fell out of use thereafter.

the contract, and may not even have agreed on the price, as long as the actions can be shown to be part of an evolving transaction of exchange.

But the *Pao On* rule does not overturn the general rule that past consideration will not be treated as good consideration, and its requirements are strict. If there was no understanding of a reward at the time the act was undertaken, the promise will continue to be treated as an unenforceable gratuitous promise. Thus, for example, in *Mahmoud Assi v Dina Foods Ltd*,[108] a salesman for a bakery, who was working for a low hourly wage, secured an agreement with Waitrose as a result of which the bakery's bread was carried in a large number of Waitrose outlets. This was an extremely lucrative contract for the bakery, and the owner promised the salesman a bonus of £4,000 after the contract had been secured. The court held that although the promise had been made, it was unenforceable because it was a gratuitous promise. The salesman's contract did not promise him a bonus over his salary, nor was any promise of a bonus made in relation to the Waitrose contract until after the contract had been secured.[109] The situation in Problem 3 is precisely analogous, making it unlikely that Ian Wilkins will be entitled to any relief.

 Practice in context: of peppercorns and seals

The rule that the courts will not enquire into the adequacy of consideration, coupled with their willingness to treat nominal consideration as good consideration, makes the humble peppercorn a powerful legal weapon. Whilst peppercorn consideration as a concept is usually associated with rents, there is no legal reason for it to be confined to tenancies. Any contract which might otherwise be unenforceable for want of consideration can be rendered enforceable by including a nominal consideration—the payment of a peppercorn, or a penny, or some other thing of trivial value. This applies across the board. A contract that may be affected by the rule against past consideration, or by the absence of economic value, or by the other issues which we will discuss subsequently in this chapter, can easily be made enforceable through the device of a peppercorn consideration. If a lawyer foresees a potential issue with consideration in the course of drafting a contract, all that needs to be done is to insert a provision where a party provides some form of nominal consideration to the other party. In *Mahmoud Assi v Dina Foods Ltd*, for example, the contract would have been enforceable if the salesman had given a peppercorn in consideration for the bonus of £4,000, as that would not have been past consideration.

The other device by which potential problems with consideration can be overcome is by executing the contract as a deed. Deeds are an old feature of English law, and have been recognized by the legal system since at least the mediaeval period. Deeds are documents in writing, which have been entered into following a particular form specified in law. Until 1990, deeds had to be made under seal. Whilst this is no longer a requirement, the requirements that must be followed before a deed becomes binding are still quite different from those that apply to ordinary contracts.

→

108. [2005] EWHC 1099 (QB).
109. Contrast *Attrill v Dresdner Kleinwort Ltd* [2012] EWHC 1189 (QB), where the promise to create a bonus pool for investment bankers was held enforceable on the basis that it had been created to 'stabilise the workforce' and therefore provided a substantial benefit to the bank.

→

Many agreements are required by law to be made as deeds, but the broader importance of deeds arises from the fact that an agreement made as a deed need not be supported by consideration. To become binding, a deed must be made, executed, and delivered (each of which has a technical meaning in the law relating to deeds).[110] The fact that parties chose to follow this process in entering into their agreement is taken to be sufficient to bind them to it, even if they have not provided consideration.

The effect of these two exceptions is that no party who has access to good legal advice is ever likely to fall foul of the rules on consideration. If an agreement appears to potentially create issues in relation to consideration, all that needs to be done is to enter into it as a deed, or redraft it to provide nominal consideration. The only persons likely to fall foul of the doctrine, therefore, are those who do not have access to, or do not seek, expert legal advice, and who simply expect the law to uphold reasonable expectations.

This raises broader issues about whether the law of consideration is discharging any useful functions within the law of contract. Does it make sense to have a rule whose restrictions produce results that are in many respects contrary to what parties reasonably expect, but which then makes it easy for well-advised parties to get around those very restrictions? We will return to this issue at the end of this chapter.

3.4 In conclusion: consideration, bargaining, and contracts

Let us now draw the threads together, and evaluate the role played in English contract law by the doctrine of consideration. In this chapter, we have seen how the courts use consideration to distinguish agreements that give rise to binding legal obligations from those that do not. The central ideas behind the doctrine of consideration are value and exchange. Just as the rules relating to formation tell us that the idea of a 'moment of responsibility' is central to the legal understanding of how a contract is *made*, the rules relating to consideration tell us that the idea of an exchange for value is fundamental to the legal understanding of what contracts are *about*. Contracts are legally seen as instruments of economic exchange, where each party gets from the other something they value.

Yet as we have also seen, the doctrine of consideration often produces results that are problematic. If the role of the doctrine is to separate agreements to which the law should give effect from those to which it should not, then as cases such as *Foakes v Beer* and *Eastwood v Kenyon* demonstrate, the law fails to give effect to agreements for reasons that are hard to explain or justify. As we have seen in this chapter, both elements that make up the law of consideration—value and exchange—cause problems in transactions that fall outwith its core understanding of value. In relation to the element of value, the focus on benefits and detriments that have *legal* implications—as opposed to those that have purely commercial or factual implications—has led to the

---

110. For an example, see *Silver Queen Maritime Ltd v Persia Petroleum Services Plc* [2010] EWHC 2867 (QB).

law falling out of step with modern commercial practice. The law in relation to renego-
tiating existing duties illustrates the problem particularly well. Creditors who renegotiate loans do so not out of a desire to secure any particular legal advantage, but because
they expect to increase their chance of securing a repayment without having to liti-
gate, or take the debtor into insolvency. This is a gamble—it may or may not come off,
but it is a risk a creditor takes on in the hope of securing a payoff. The fact that the
courts, in cases like *Witham v Great Northern Railway*, have had to resort to what is quite
clearly strained reasoning in order to give effect to perfectly normal and unexceptional
contracts, suggests that the law, as it stands, fails to adequately recognize important
aspects of what precisely it is that motivates parties to contract.

Similarly, in relation to the element of exchange, contracts relating to relationships
that evolve over time are a particular source of difficulty. Continuing relations create a
far broader range of reasons for parties to contract than do more simple transactions of
trade or exchange and, as case law has shown, the doctrine of consideration lacks the
flexibility to deal effectively with these broader factors. The effect of the rules in relation to past consideration, for example, is to require that consideration be provided or
promised at the moment of responsibility. If the two moments—the moment at which
consideration is provided or promised and the moment of responsibility—do not coin-
cide, the courts are unlikely to enforce the contract.

This requirement is problematic where a relationship evolves or emerges over time,
instead of forming at a distinct 'moment of responsibility'. Consider, for example, the
cases of *Re McArdle* and *Eastwood v Kenyon*, which we examined earlier on in this chapter. Seen in their context, both cases were instances of parties attempting to redefine
the nature of their relationship. The claimant's argument in each case was, in essence,
that parties in an existing, *socially* defined relationship had chosen to *legally* redefine
their relationship, and the rights and duties flowing from it. Both actions failed—not
because the court held that the parties had not intended to give their relationship a
legal character, but because the provision of valuable consideration did not accompany
the moment of responsibility which the court identified. *Pao On*, to the extent it partially recognizes the evolutionary character of contractual relations, is clearly a step in
the right direction, but it does not go far enough. *McArdle* and this chapter's problem
show that whether a contract is unenforceable under the rule against past consideration, or enforceable because of a pre-existing promise, can turn on very fine factual
distinctions, and it is questionable whether these very small factual differences should
have the significant consequences they currently have in English law.

The discussion in this chapter has shed some light on these dimensions of contracting, and how the law might be developed to give them appropriate recognition. The
central problem is that the legal understanding of 'benefits' and 'detriments' remains
grounded in conceptions of exchanges, bargains, and moments of responsibility, and
consequently does not capture the extremely wide range of reasons and motives that
actually underlie contract decisions in the real world. This suggests that there is a case
for developing the law in a way that brings a more sound understanding of modern
contracting to the law. Doing this does not require abandoning the idea of consideration, or even a wholesale revision of doctrine. Several recent cases expressly or implicitly
recognize that modern contracting is underpinned by a far wider range of considerations than the mere securing of benefits and detriments. Much attention has been paid

in the academic literature to the idea of 'practical benefit' articulated in *Williams v Roffey*. But the even broader understanding of consideration articulated in *Edmonds v Lawson*[111] is of far greater import. The emphasis of the Court of Appeal in this case was on the fact that the agreement was not altruistic, but served the self-interest of both parties. Whether the contract served a party's self-interest was, in turn, assessed not with reference to its association with any particular form of economic value, but with the extent to which it furthers the party's goals.

This is a far better understanding of consideration than those represented in the standard definitions of 'economic value' or 'benefit and detriment'. Contracting is underpinned by a complex set of factors, but, when boiled down to its essentials, it represents a form of self-interested action taken by a party in the pursuit of definite goals. The tests of economic value, and benefit and detriment, work well as relatively easy ways of ascertaining this in simpler transactions which resemble the understanding of a contract as a bargain. However, they break down in more complex situations, such as those involving renegotiations or those involving gradually evolving relationships or those where a party seeks ill-defined future payoffs that may (or may not) materialize. To the extent cases such as *Pao On*, *Edmonds*, and *Williams* have begun to recognize these broader underpinnings of contracting, and have shown a willingness to move beyond traditional understandings of value and exchange, they represent steps in the right direction. Recognizing the broader principles upon which they are based, and expanding them beyond the narrow areas to which they are currently confined, would go a long way towards addressing the issues that currently make consideration a problematic doctrine.

Key points

- For a contract to be formed, the promisee must have provided consideration to the promisor. Consideration must be something that has value, and which is provided in exchange for the promise.

- 'Value' is defined as being economic value. Economic value is assessed objectively. Any economic value is value in the eyes of the law.

- Value can also be assessed with reference to whether a party provided a benefit to the other, or took a detriment upon himself. Benefits and detriments must be legal benefits and detriments, and not merely factual benefits and detriments.

- Finally, value can be assessed with reference to practical benefits. This is of particular use where the parties have renegotiated a contract, with the result that one party receives something extra for doing work he has already agreed to do.

- Special rules apply to renegotiations for debts.

- 'Exchange' requires consideration to be given in respect of the promise (and not merely in response to the promise). It also requires consideration to move from the promisee, rather than a third party.

- Past consideration is not usually good consideration, save in exceptional circumstances.

111. [2000] QB 501.

Assess your learning

You should be able to respond to each of the following points with a confident 'yes'. If you can't, then you should revisit the sections listed against that point.

Can you:

(a) *Understand* what is meant by 'value' and 'exchange'? (Sections 3.2 and 3.3)

(b) *Explain* the different approaches to assessing value, and *identify* the limitations of the benefit and detriment analysis? (Sections 3.2.1 and 3.2.2)

(c) *Understand* the role of the practical benefit approach to consideration, *identify* the special issues that arise in relation to debts, and *apply* your knowledge to specific fact scenarios? (Section 3.2.3)

(d) *Explain* the rule that consideration must move from the promisee, and be in respect of the transaction, and its significance? (Section 3.3.1)

(e) *Explain* the legal rules governing past consideration? (Section 3.3.1)

In relation to each of the above, you should be able to:

(i) identify and clearly explain the key rules and principles;

(ii) identify the key cases and statutes, and why they matter;

(iii) apply the principles and cases to specific real or hypothetical fact situations;

(iv) evaluate the limitations, if any, of the law as it currently stands.

Further reading

J Adams and R Brownsword, 'Contract, Considerations, and the Critical Path' (1990) 53 MLR 563.

PS Atiyah, 'Contracts, Promises, and the Law of Obligations' (1978) 94 LQR 193.

PS Atiyah, 'Consideration: A Restatement' in PS Atiyah, *Essays on Contract* (Clarendon Press 1986).

JW Carter, A Phang, and J Poole, 'Reactions to *Williams v Roffey*' (1995) 8 JCL 248.

M Chen-Wishart, 'Consideration: Practical Benefit and the Emperor's New Clothes' in J Beatson and D Friedmann (eds), *Good Faith and Fault in Contract Law* (Oxford University Press 1995).

B Coote, 'Consideration and Variations: A Different Solution' (2004) 120 LQR 19.

R Halson, 'Sailors, Sub-Contractors and Consideration' (1990) 106 LQR 183.

N Hird and A Blair, 'Minding Your Own Business—*Williams v Roffey* Revisited: Consideration Reconsidered' [1996] JBL 254.

GH Treitel, 'Consideration: A Critical Analysis of Professor Atiyah's Fundamental Restatement' (1976) 50 Australian Law Journal 439.

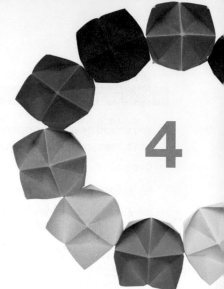

Contracts and informal relations

The intention to create legal relations

'What's law got to do with it?'

Problem 4: setting the context

Consider the following notice:

University of Carmarthenshire Volleyball Club
IMPORTANT NOTICE

Following a number of missed games last year, BUCS have changed their rules on what happens if a team fails to play a game. Games can no longer be rescheduled by mutual arrangement between the teams. All games must take place as scheduled. A team which fails to attend a scheduled game will not be allowed to play in any further games that year—not even friendlies. The only exception is if a team member becomes ill too suddenly to find a substitute.

We will, therefore, with immediate effect be requiring all our team members to COMMIT to playing any game for which they are down on the rota. If you're on the rota for a game, you must be there. No exceptions! We will be asking everyone to sign a declaration agreeing to this. Sorry for being so pushy, but we missed several games last year because of team members being unavailable, and can't afford to run the risk of disqualification if that happens again.

The notice refers to two distinct sets of agreements. First, we have the agreement between the players on University of Carmarthenshire's volleyball team. Secondly, we have the arrangements relating to the conduct of the nationwide volleyball competition, entered into between that team and BUCS (British Universities and Colleges Sport). Do either or both of these have binding, contractual effect? Would the parties have intended to create binding legal relations by making those arrangements? Or are they merely social arrangements, whose breach carries no legal consequence?

4.1 Introduction

Illustration 4.1

Consider the following snippet of conversation. Does it create an enforceable contract?

– Hey, would you like to meet at the pub at 7 today?

– Sure! I'll see you at 7.

In our everyday lives, we very frequently enter into agreements to meet someone at a particular time, drive them to a particular place, engage in a joint activity such as walking or climbing, and so on. We neither intend nor expect these to be legally binding. A person agreeing to meet a friend at the pub would be very surprised if they found themselves liable to be sued for failing to turn up. People see such arrangements as social, rather than legal.

In law, this expectation is translated into the requirement that the parties to a contract must have the **intention to create legal relations**. In the absence of such an intention, a legally binding contract will not come into existence even if the parties reach agreement and provide consideration. The obvious example of cases where parties lack the intention to create legal relations are arrangements which are social or which relate to the family. Illustration 4.1 is one example, as are the many agreements and understandings that characterize families, friends, and acquaintances. But the requirement is relevant to a far wider range of transactions. A wide range of commercial instruments—memoranda of understanding, letters of intent, and so on—are deliberately structured to make it clear that the parties did *not* intend to create legal relations, but were instead recording a commercial understanding. The principle that contracts must be supported by such an intention also affects a range of other transactions, such as collective bargaining agreements between employers and trade unions.

How, then, do we decide whether the parties to a particular agreement had the intention to enter into legal relations? Decisions tend to rely very heavily on the specific facts that are before the court, rather than on rules and principles. In general, English law treats the question as being objective, rather than subjective,[1] and operates by means of rebuttable **presumptions**. If a transaction is familial or social, the courts will presume that the parties to the transaction did not intend to enter into legal relations. But this presumption is rebuttable if a party proves that the parties did, in fact, intend to enter into legal relations. For other types of transactions, such as commercial transactions, the law will presume that the parties did intend to enter into legal relations unless the contrary is proved.

The presumption is based on the character of the *transaction*, not the *parties*. If a transaction is a commercial one, then the fact that the parties to the transaction are close friends is irrelevant. The members of a successful music band may be very good friends, but that does not mean that any agreements they enter into in relation to the division of royalties and other revenues will be presumed to be social or friendly arrangements. The presumption will, on the contrary, be that the transaction *was* intended to be a commercial and binding transaction, unless it is shown that it was not intended to be binding. Likewise, an agreement between two businessmen to go golfing will not be treated as being 'commercial' just because the parties are businesspeople.

In terms of legal rules, this is pretty much all there is. Much of what the courts do in this area is fact-centric, focused on whether the presumptions have been triggered or rebutted. Our focus in this chapter, accordingly, is on understanding how these presumptions work in practice, and what needs to be done to rebut them. In the first half of this chapter, we will consider cases where the presumption is that the parties did *not* intend to create legal relations—that they intended their transaction to be merely friendly or social, rather than legal. In the second half of this chapter, we will move on to commercial transactions, where the presumption is reversed, to examine types of commercial transactions that are structured to place them outside the bounds of legal enforcement.

---

1. See eg *Edmonds v Lawson* [2000] 1 QB 501 (CA).

4.2 'Contractual' and 'friendly' relations: the nature of the distinction

Let us start by examining the nature of the distinction the courts draw. What distinguishes relations that are intended to be 'legal' from relations that are intended to be 'social' or 'friendly'? Consider the following scenarios:

Illustration 4.2

Emma and Tim are a professional couple with a daughter who has recently started attending school. Tim's parents, who are retired, agree to collect their granddaughter from the school every afternoon, and to keep her at their home until either Emma or Tim return from work.

Illustration 4.3

John and Mary are a married couple. Mary's mother is ill and has gone into hospital. Mary's father, a retired joiner, comes to live with them for the duration. He says that he will help them lay a new living room floor while he's there.

Illustration 4.4

Louise and Ian are siblings. Their father has recently been unwell. They are reluctant to put him in a care home, and set up an agreed rota under which each of them will periodically check in on him.

Illustration 4.5

Jane, Cath, and Bill are siblings, who jointly run their family farm. In recent years, they have had a number of disagreements on the direction of the farm (organic or intensive; exotic vegetables or potatoes). They sit down one afternoon and, after several hours of discussion, come to an agreement on: (a) the principles they will apply in running the farm; and (b) a process for dealing with disagreements in relation to the farm's direction.

Illustration 4.6

A group of cousins have recently inherited a large country house from their great-uncle, who died childless. The house has not been well looked-after, and portions of it are in poor condition. The cousins agree on a plan of renovation and modernization, and also on how they will divide the costs of this work. They also agree on a rota for supervising the building work.

Are these arrangements contractual? Most people would—correctly—not regard the first three examples as such, but incline towards the view that the latter two examples *are* contractual. But what, in legal terms, explains why the first three scenarios are not contractual, whereas the last two are?

The courts are in effect asked to choose between two alternative accounts of the transaction. The first treats the transaction as being something that friends, family, and acquaintances do for each other *because* they are family and friends. The second treats it as a different sort of transaction, where one person does something in exchange for something done by the other person, rather than out of friendship, *even though* the people involved are friends and family. The decision of the Court of Appeal in *Balfour v Balfour*[2] illustrates how the courts go about making this choice.

Case in depth: *Balfour v Balfour* [1919] 2 KB 571 (CA)

Mr and Mrs Balfour lived in what was then the colony of Ceylon, where Mr Balfour worked as an irrigation engineer. In 1915, they returned to England on leave. Mrs Balfour was advised by a doctor to remain in England for some months as she was suffering from rheumatic arthritis. In August 1916, her husband returned to Ceylon without her. Before leaving, he gave her a cheque for £24, and promised to give her £30 each month until she returned to Ceylon.

Differences arose between them some months later, and she never returned to Ceylon. The couple eventually separated. She then sued for the monthly payment of £30. The question for the court was whether a binding legal contract had come into being.

In the High Court, Sargant J held that it had. His reasoning was that every husband was under an obligation to support his wife. It was open to the parties to, by contract, define 'the extent of that obligation . . . in terms of so much a month'. The consent of the wife to the arrangement was sufficient consideration (under the benefit–detriment analysis discussed in Chapter 3), and she could therefore sue upon the contract.

The Court of Appeal set aside Sargant J's judgment and held that no contract had come into being. Duke LJ decided the case entirely on the basis that the wife had provided no consideration in return for the husband's promise. The other two judges, however, considered the question of intention to create legal relations in some detail.

Warrington LJ held that there was no enforceable contract because 'these two people never intended to make a bargain which could be enforced in law'.[3] If a contract were to be held to have come into being, he pointed out, the result would be that the wife would be held to have agreed to 'be content with this 30/'[4] regardless of 'whatever happened and whatever might be the change of circumstances'. Similarly, the husband, too, would be held to have bound himself 'to pay 30/ a month for some indefinite period, whatever might be his circumstances'. In the context of a family relationship, this would be an absurd result. The proper conclusion, he thought, was therefore to hold that the husband was 'bound in honour to continue [paying] so long as he was in a position to do so', but was not bound in law.[5]

Atkin LJ (as he then was) agreed. It was quite common for agreements between a husband and a wife to be supported by consideration. But even so, such agreements 'are not contracts

➙

---

2. [1919] 2 KB 571 (CA).   3. Ibid, 575.
4. *l* is an old-fashioned notation for the pound sterling, now superseded by £.
5. [1919] 2 KB 571 (CA).

because the parties did not intend that they should be attended by legal consequences'. The intention, rather, was that the terms of such an arrangement 'may be repudiated, varied or renewed as performance proceeds or as disagreements develop' without regard to whether any of this was in accordance with the common law. This was because in reality 'the consideration that really obtains for [such agreements] is that natural love and affection which counts for so little in these cold Courts'.[6] Neither party to such an arrangement would have expected or contemplated that it would be strictly enforced, or that the wife would be unable to obtain any more than was contractually provided if circumstances changed.[7]

Balfour v Balfour is important not so much in terms of the outcome on the facts of the case as for what it tells us about how the courts distinguish relations that are intended to be legal from those that are not. The first contrast that Warrington and Atkin LJJ drew was between relations that are open-ended, flexible, and intended to change as circumstances change, and relations that have the concreteness and definitiveness that are an intrinsic part of a binding contract. The former are less likely to have been intended to be legal, whereas the latter are more likely to have been so intended. It is in part *because* the Balfours' arrangements would have had to be flexible to be workable—having, for example, the flexibility to increase or decrease the sum of money payable if circumstances changed—that Warrington and Atkin LJJ found it difficult to hold that there was a contract. A binding contractual relationship would mean that the sum of £30 was set in stone, and could not be varied. This could not have been what the parties intended.

Secondly, *Balfour* also implicitly drew a contrast between actions that primarily involve love, concern, or other feelings for the other party, and actions that contain a significant element of self-interest. Atkin LJ held that even if the agreement in *Balfour* on its face involved some valuable consideration, in substance it was 'about' familial relations, and the love and affection inherent in those relations. The acts and obligations assumed under the arrangement were not in 'exchange' for the other party's promise, but out of genuine concern for the well-being of the other person. For that reason, they were seen as being non-contractual.

The importance of the latter point was made even clearer by the decision of the Court of Appeal in *Horrocks v Forray*.[8] The defendant, Mrs Forray, had been the mistress of a man called Sanford for 17 years, from the time she was 15 up until Sanford's death. The two of them had a daughter together. In 1973, a few months before his death in an accident, Sanford bought a house in his own name for Mrs Forray and their daughter. After his death, Mrs Sanford and his executors discovered the existence of Mrs Forray, and sued for possession of the house. The question for the court was whether the agreement under which Sanford had given possession of the house to Mrs Forray was intended to create legal relations.

In *Tanner v Tanner*,[9] the Court of Appeal in somewhat similar facts had held that the parties had intended to create legal relations. In *Horrocks v Forray*, in contrast, the

---

6. Ibid, 579.   7. Ibid, 580.   8. [1976] 1 WLR 230 (CA).
9. [1975] 1 WLR 1346 (CA).

Court of Appeal held that they did not. Scarman LJ distinguished *Tanner* on the basis that it dealt with a relationship that was in the process of coming to an end, where the parties were 'making arrangements for the future at arm's-length'. The man in that case was trying to 'limit and define his financial responsibilities' towards his now-former mistress, while the woman was 'concerned for herself and her children'. This was a 'fertile area' for the growth of a legally binding contract.[10] In *Horrocks*, in contrast, the parties were in a loving relationship. Sanford was making a very generous and luxurious provision for his mistress because 'there was a big place in his heart' for her. This was different from a situation in which the relationship had come to an end making it 'necessary to tie up the bits'.[11] The result was that there was no contract.

From a layperson's point of view, this position might seem somewhat counter-intuitive. Surely a reasonable person takes obligations to someone they love more seriously than obligations entered into when a relationship is in the process of breaking down? The legal approach to contracts, however, is deeply grounded in the idea of an exchange for gain. A transaction that is primarily about mutual affection does not fit this picture, and as a result is not treated as a contract.

When, then, will the courts hold that parties to a family arrangement did actually have the intention to create legal relations? First, as Scarman LJ suggested in *Horrocks v Forray*, and as the outcome of *Tanner* and other subsequent cases demonstrates,[12] if the parties' relationship has broken down, or if they are planning for a time when the relationship may no longer be as affectionate as it currently is, the agreement is no longer primarily 'about' mutual affection, but is at least as much about each party trying to protect their own future position—although, here too, the outcome will depend on the specific facts of the case and the nature of the terms that were agreed.[13]

Secondly, in circumstances where the parties' agreement relates to matters, or entails consequences, which go beyond the bounds of an ordinary family relationship, the courts will usually find that the parties intended to enter into legal relations and create a binding contract. In *Parker v Clark*,[14] the Clarks were an elderly couple who were often unwell. They invited the Parkers to sell their house and come and live with them (Mrs Parker was Mrs Clark's niece), promising to leave the house to Mrs Parker on their death. Unfortunately, once the Parkers had moved in, things did not go well and they ended up leaving in order to avoid being evicted. The court held that the parties had intended to enter into binding legal relations. The arrangement demanded a significant commitment from the Parkers, including selling their cottage, which strongly suggested that the parties must have intended their relations to have a binding character.

On this basis, we can distinguish Illustrations 4.2, 4.3, and 4.4, where there is in all likelihood no intention to create legal relations, from the last two. Unlike the first three, the last two are nor primarily about the parties' natural love and affection. They are, instead, about material gain, and involve the parties' self-interest. Nor do they, of

---

10. [1976] 1 WLR 230, 239.   11. Ibid, 240.

12. See eg *Merritt v Merritt* [1970] 1 WLR 1121; *Soulsbury v Soulsbury* [2007] EWCA Civ 969, [2008] 2 WLR 834.

13. See eg *Harb v HRH Prince Abdul Aziz* [2018] EWHC 508 (Ch), [189]–[207], where the court held that on the facts, the agreement was not intended to create legal relations until one party approved the other's statement withdrawing an allegation.

14. [1960] 1 WLR 286.

their character, involve open-endedness. They are therefore likely to be held to evidence a sufficient intention to enter into legal relations.

4.3 Understanding the presumption: the case of friendly transactions

4.3.1 The logic of the presumption

The principles discussed in the previous section are also applied in determining whether the parties intended to create legal relations in a broader range of contexts than just family transactions. Consider the following example of a transaction at one further step of removal than family transactions; namely, transactions amongst friends.

Illustration 4.7

Gill is a long-standing fan of Cumberland United FC, a Premier League football club. Gill's car has broken down. She has been told that it will need to be at the garage for several weeks. She lives 50 miles from Cumberland United's stadium, and has no easy way of getting there. She sends the following text message to Tom, an acquaintance:

> Hi Tom, can you drive me to the stadium for the next three home games, while my car is being fixed? I'll pay for your petrol and buy you dinner at a place of your choice! Cheers, Gill

Tom sends her this reply:

> Hi Gill, sure I can, no bother at all. Tom

This example differs in an important respect from the example of two friends agreeing to meet in a pub in Illustration 4.1. The benefit which both parties obtain from an arrangement to meet in a pub is purely social—the pleasure derived from time spent in a convivial environment—and not the sort of thing one might obtain commercially. It is easy to see why an arrangement between friends for a purely social benefit will not ordinarily be taken to have been characterized by the intention to create legal relations.

In this example, however, we are dealing with benefits that are *not* purely social, but are more concrete and of the type one could conceivably seek to acquire on the market—the benefit of transport to a venue on the one hand, and the benefit of money and dinner on the other. At one level, therefore, it is tempting to hold that this must be a contract—an offer is made by Gill to Tom of a reward for an act, which the party to whom it is made (Tom) accepts. However, to hold it to be a contract would carry a range of consequences which may not necessarily fit with the parties' understanding of the nature of their relationship. It would mean, for example, that if Tom were to fail to take Gill to one of the next three games, she would have a legal claim against Tom for any loss she suffered, such as the cost of taking a taxi to the game. Is that the sort of relationship the two of them intended to create? Or is the relationship more accurately described as what an anthropologist might term a 'mutual exchange of gifts', where Tom drives Gill to the game not primarily because of the promise of reimbursement and dinner, but because they are friends; and Gill buys Tom dinner not so much in 'exchange' for the lift, but more as one of the many tokens of mutual appreciation which friends regularly exchange within their friendship.

Unlike an arrangement to meet at the pub, this is not the sort of question to which we can give an unequivocal answer. We simply cannot say that parties creating such an arrangement *never* intend to make it binding, and we equally cannot say that they *always* intend to make it binding. Different sets of parties may intend different things in similar circumstances. The question is what the parties to *this* particular transaction intended, to the extent it can be inferred from the surrounding circumstances. The starting point is the presumption that in a transaction of a social character between friends, the parties do not intend to create legal relations. This presumption can, however, be rebutted if there is clear evidence that the parties did in fact intend to create legal relations. This gives the law sufficient flexibility to be able to take account of the specific circumstances of a case in order to determine how binding the parties intended their arrangements to be.

4.3.2 The presumption in action: lifts and car-sharing arrangements

What, then, constitutes clear evidence, sufficient to rebut the presumption that the parties intended their relations to be social rather than legal? The key cases on this question relate to arrangements between friends or acquaintances to give each other lifts or to share cars or other motor vehicles. These cases were mostly brought against insurers in relation to injuries caused in the course of sharing the vehicle, but the question of whether the arrangements were contractual was relevant to the outcome.

Coward v Motor Insurers' Bureau[15] related to an arrangement between Coward and his co-worker, Cole, under which Cole drove both men to work on his motorbike, with Coward making periodic payments to Cole to cover part of the costs of the daily journey. The question was whether these arrangements amounted to a contract. The Court of Appeal held that they did not. It was common for workmen to share transport belonging to one of them with all contributing to its costs, but in the absence of specific evidence such an arrangement was unlikely to have been intended to create a contractual relationship. The ability of the parties to perform their obligations under the agreement were subject to so many uncertainties that it was very unlikely that they actually intended to create a binding obligation.[16]

Connell v Motor Insurers' Bureau[17] involved slightly different facts. Connell used to frequent the same pub as a Mr English. On three occasions, English had driven Connell somewhere at his request, in return for 10s and a drink. The question arose as to whether these arrangements were contractual. The Court of Appeal held that they

---

15. [1963] 1 QB 259 (CA).   16. Ibid, 271 (Upjohn LJ).
17. [1969] 2 QB 494 (CA).

were. The reasoning was that an action for the money would have lain if the trip had been made and the money had then not been paid.[18] Lord Denning MR expressed some doubts about the correctness of *Coward*:

> It is often a very nice question whether there is a legally binding contract when a driver gives a man a lift. I should have thought that, in the ordinary way, when a man agrees to carry a man for payment, there is a contract, albeit informal, no matter whether the payment is by way of contribution to the petrol or a reward for the lift.[19]

Buckpitt v Oates[20] involved an arrangement between two friends, who periodically gave each other rides in their respective cars. The case related to a ride on 10 September 1965, when the claimant had driven both of them from Paignton to Newton Abbot and back. When they returned to Paignton, the claimant asked the defendant if he would drive them both back to Newton Abbot to retrieve something which the claimant had left in a café there. To persuade the defendant, he offered to pay the cost of the petrol, and paid 10s during the journey, which was more than the petrol actually cost. The question was whether this arrangement was contractual. John Stephenson J held that it was not. This specific agreement was simply part of the friendly arrangements between the claimant and defendant, and was not a binding contract. The 10s was not consideration for a contractual bargain. Rather, it was 'a present . . . to the defendant for his help in going back to collect these goods . . . and [there] was no question of any binding promise to carry or to pay'.[21]

This issue came before the House of Lords in *Albert v Motor Insurers' Bureau*.[22] Quirk, a dockworker, regularly carried other dockworkers to and from the docks in his car. He did not always carry the same dockworkers, nor was the arrangement limited to his close friends. The arrangement was, rather, that persons who wanted a lift in Quirk's car would contact him to ask if he could carry them. In return, they either paid sums in cash or in kind (usually beer or cigarettes) although Quirk sometimes let people in financial difficulty travel with him for free.

Four of the five members of the panel hearing the case decided it without considering the question of whether a contract existed. Lord Cross, however, did consider the question, and held that there was a contract. He placed emphasis on two points: that the intention to enter into legal relations can be implicit and does not have to be express, and that parties can intend to enter into legal relations even if they have no intention of taking the other party to court in the event of breach.

The first point Lord Cross made is that the question of whether the parties intended to create legal relations is not a subjective question of what the parties were actually thinking at the time they entered into a contract. Parties can be held to have intended to have entered into legal relations even if they have not, in fact, given any thought to the character of their relations:

> We enter into a contract not because we form any intention to enter into one, but because if our minds were directed to the point we should as reasonable people both agree that we were in fact entering into one.[23]

---

18. Ibid, 504 (Sachs LJ).   19. Ibid, 503.   20. [1968] 1 All ER 1145 (Devon Ass).
21. Ibid, 1147.   22. [1972] AC 301 (HL).   23. Ibid, 339.

Outside the commercial world, parties often enter into contracts without being expressly conscious of the fact that they are doing so. When we board a bus or a train, or use the self-checkout at a supermarket, we seldom consciously think about or turn our minds to the fact that by carrying out this act, we are entering into legal relations with a counterparty. That does not alter the fact that we do, in fact, intend to enter into legal relations. If an officious bystander were to expressly pose the question to us, our answer would be 'yes'.

The second point which Lord Cross's speech in *Albert* highlights is that the key question in determining intention is not whether the parties intended to be able to sue each other, but whether or not they intended to assume legally binding obligations. It may well be that the parties would never so much as consider suing each other in the event of a breach—if, for example, one of Quirk's passengers failed to pay him—and would instead resort to informal, or extra-judicial, remedies, but that does not mean that there is no contract, or that an action would not lie.[24] If Quirk had actually brought an action against a passenger who persistently failed to pay, it is unlikely that any court would deny his suit on the basis that the parties had no intention to contract.[25]

The cases in which the courts found the relationship to have been contractual tended to involve a combination of: (a) benefits that were obviously material; (b) arrangements that were particular; and (c) participation that was not confined to close friends. In *Buckpitt v Oates*, for example, the court appears to have taken the view that the arrangements between the two friends to drive each other in their respective cars were as much about companionship as about specific material goals, and hence were not intended to be contractual.

What implications does this have for the arrangement between Gill and Tom? As the exchange of text messages suggests, the arrangement relates to three future games rather than a single game, and hence involves a commitment which is somewhat more open-ended than the commitments in *Connell* and *Albert*. This might seem to point towards confirming, rather than rebutting, the presumption that it is not likely to have been intended to create legal relations. But the nature of the relationship between Gill and Tom—about which we do not have much information—will also influence the answer. Were Gill and Tom close friends? Classmates? Neighbours? Distant acquaintances? Friends-of-friends? Obviously, the closer their acquaintance, the harder it becomes to argue that the relationship was intended to be legal, rather than merely friendly.

Debates in context: supplementing or replacing consideration?

English law requires agreements to satisfy two entirely separate requirements to be enforceable: the requirement of consideration and the requirement that the parties have the intention to enter into legal relations. The simultaneous existence of these two requirements has caused some debate as to whether we need both, or whether they could not more conveniently be rolled into a single requirement.

→

24. Ibid.   25. Ibid, 340.

The first, and most obvious, proposal would be to eliminate consideration, and make agreements enforceable whenever the parties intended to create legal relations. This is the approach taken in most European legal systems. Outside the common law world, a contract is usually enforceable if the parties intended to enter into legal relations. There is no equivalent to consideration in the laws of most civil law systems (including Scotland). Given the many criticisms that have been levelled against consideration (some of which are discussed in Chapter 3), such an approach has obvious attractions, and it was at one time popular.[26] Nevertheless, it has few supporters in England today. The usual reason given is that the rules governing intention to create legal relations are too poorly developed to do all the work they would be called upon to do if consideration were to be abolished. This was the view taken by Professor Atiyah who was a strong critic of the doctrine of consideration, but who nevertheless did not support replacing it with the requirement of intention.[27] More recently, a similar position has been taken by Professor Ewan McKendrick, Professor of English Private Law at Oxford and a widely published author on contract law, who has pointed out that 'it is not at all obvious that the question whether the parties had an intention to contract will be any easier to answer than the question whether or not there was consideration'—arguing, in other words, that there is no reason to believe that such a change will necessarily improve the law.[28]

Professor Hugh Collins, Vinerian Professor of English Law at Oxford, similarly argued that although the requirement of intention in theory offered the possibility of grounding a contract in the common intention of the parties, in practice the courts were likely to be faced with cases where the parties did not, as between themselves, agree on whether or not the contract was to be legally binding (or may not have considered the issue at all). Here, the court would have to rely on 'hidden policy considerations' in order to decide the question.[29] A similar argument has been made by Professor Steve Hedley, a leading private law theorist, who argued that the decision in *Balfour v Balfour* was in actuality based not on intention but on policy; that in most cases the courts decide the question not with reference to the intention of the parties—which is non-existent—but with reference to their own views of what is fair; and that the main effect of the requirement of intention is to confine contracts to particular commercially oriented domains, while minimizing their role in others (eg matrimonial relations).[30]

A very different position was taken by Professor Bob Hepple, a key figure in social and labour law in the 1970s and 1980s. Professor Hepple called for the requirement of consideration to be preserved, and for the requirement of intention to create legal relations to be abolished. The device, he said, was only attractive because it 'enables the courts to cloak policy decisions in the mantle of private contractual autonomy'. If it was this policy question that was to be decided, then the answer provided by the doctrine of consideration was by far the more satisfactory.[31]

→

26. See eg AG Chloros, 'The Doctrine of Consideration and the Reform of the Law of Contract' (1968) 17 ICLQ 137, 147.

27. PS Atiyah, 'Consideration: A Restatement' in PS Atiyah, *Essays on Contract* (Clarendon Press 1986).

28. E McKendrick, *Contract Law* (8th edn, Palgrave 2009) 101.

29. H Collins, *The Law of Contract* (4th edn, Cambridge University Press 2003) 104–5.

30. S Hedley, 'Keeping Contract in its Place—*Balfour v Balfour* and the Enforceability of Informal Agreements' (1985) 5 OJLS 391, 395–6.

31. BA Hepple, 'Intention to Create Legal Relations' (1970) 28 CLJ 122, 134.

→

It is hard not to have sympathy with authors who have expressed scepticism towards the idea of a broad, all-encompassing principle of intention to create relations. Certainly, it is difficult to see how the tests that have emerged—in particular, the reluctance to enforce long-term, open-ended arrangements, and the reluctance to enforce arrangements grounded in affection—actually speak to the question they claim to test. The mere fact that an agreement was grounded in affection does not mean that the parties to it were less likely to have intended it to have legal consequences.

Nevertheless, the growing trend in international documents which seek to harmonize aspects of commercial law is to ignore the requirement of consideration, and to instead make the test of intention the sole test for the enforceability of an agreement that has been reached between two or more parties. As such, it may very well only be a matter of time before English law is required to give a larger role to the requirement of intention than it hitherto has done.

4.3.3 Applying the presumption

Let us consolidate the principles we have just studied by returning to Problem 4. Competitive sports are a classic example of a situation involving circles of interaction which are wider than personal acquaintances, but which the parties may nevertheless wish to keep within the area of friendly, non-legal relations. They entail the creation of a very wide range of agreements—agreements between players inter se, players' agreements with team owners, the rules to which teams sign up when entering competitions, arrangements with sponsors, and so on. But the question of whether these arrangements are intended to be binding depends entirely on the context.

In high-level sports, such as Premiership football, virtually all agreements that are entered into will be closely negotiated commercial agreements, which are fully intended to be legally binding. At the other end of the spectrum, a group of friends who have agreed to meet every Tuesday afternoon to play five-a-side football may take their agreement and the game very seriously, and they may even be playing for a prize of some sort, but it is extremely unlikely that they will have intended to create legally binding arrangements.

The issue is less straightforward when we are dealing with instances that fall somewhere on the spectrum between these two extremes, as an inter-university volleyball competition does. Nevertheless, the basic approach to resolving this question remains in essence the same as in the car-sharing examples given earlier. For reasons that are substantially similar to those set out by Upjohn LJ in *Coward*, it is unlikely that the arrangements made between the members of a typical amateur college sports team will be taken to evidence the intention to enter into legal relations. The long-term and open-ended nature of the commitment, taken together with the possibilities of conflicts between games and assignment deadlines, or games and presentations, makes it extremely unlikely that individual team members will have intended to enter into binding commitments to attend all matches.

This leaves the second aspect of the transaction—the arrangements between the team and the organizer of the competition. The issue of whether such arrangements evidence an intention to enter into legal relations has come up before the courts on more than one occasion. A comparison of the decisions in *Lens v Devonshire Club, Eastbourne Ltd*[32] and *Modahl v British Athletic Federation*[33] is particularly useful. *Lens* arose out of an amateur golfing competition. A member of the Devonshire Club donated a cup, which was to be competed for by its members in a golf competition. Lens, a member, entered the competition. Following a disagreement about the rules, Lens's name was scratched out of the list of competitors, and his opponent voluntarily withdrew his own name. Lens sued, arguing that the club had acted in breach of a binding contract in removing his name. Scrutton J in the High Court dismissed his suit, holding that no enforceable contract had come into existence, as the parties had not intended to create legal relations. In cases like these, he explained in a later decision, 'no one concerned . . . ever intended that there should be any legal results following from the conditions posted and the acceptance by the competitor of those conditions'.[34]

Modahl v British Athletics Federation, in contrast, involved competition at a higher level, and here the Court of Appeal came to the opposite conclusion, holding that the parties did in fact intend to create legal relations. Diane Modahl was a well-known and successful British medium-distance runner. In the course of a dispute between her and the British Athletic Federation (BAF),[35] the court was asked to decide whether the relationship between the two was contractual. The Court of Appeal held that it was. Athletes accepted that they would be subject to the rules of the BAF when participating in competitions organized by the BAF or the International Association of Athletics Federations (IAAF). Similarly, the BAF accepted the responsibility of administering those rules in relation to everyone who competed in those events, and were subject to its jurisdiction.[36] Whilst it was true that neither side might have given much thought to the fact that they would be liable in damages in the event that they breached their obligations under the contract,[37] it was clear on the facts that the athletes undertook to be bound by the rules, and that the BAF was under the obligation to apply the rules. Both parties, in consequence, demonstrated an intention to enter into legal relations.[38]

Putting these cases side by side, the example we are dealing with would seem to be far closer to *Modahl* than to *Lens*. Unlike *Lens*, the competition is not a small-scale and largely informal affair. We have instead, on the one hand, an association coordinating a large number of teams, accepting responsibility for organizing competitions, and administering its rules. On the other hand, we have teams of individual sportsmen and sportswomen, who agree to subject themselves to these rules in order to participate in the competition. The formality of the process and the arrangements strongly point towards an agreement that the parties intend should have binding effect.

32. The Times, 4 December 1914 (KB).

33. [2001] EWCA Civ 1447, [2002] 1 WLR 1192.

34. See *Wyatt v Kreglinger & Fernau* [1933] 1 KB 793, 806 (CA).

35. Until 1999, the BAF was the body responsible for the governance of athletics events in the UK. In 1999, it went bankrupt—in part due to the high costs of the *Modahl* litigation—and was replaced by United Kingdom Athletics, the current regulator.

36. [2001] EWCA Civ 1447, [50] (Latham LJ).   37. Ibid, [51].   38. Ibid, [52].

4.4 **The commercial context: agreements 'binding in honour only'**

When we move from arrangements between family and friends to commercial agreements, the presumption is reversed. It will now be presumed that the parties did, in fact, intend to enter into binding legal relations, unless one of the parties demonstrates that they did not so intend. *Edmonds v Lawson,*[39] which considered whether a pupillage arrangement was a contract, is a good example. In addition to the issue of consideration, discussed in Chapter 3, the court was also asked to decide whether a pupil barrister and her chambers intended to enter into legal relations when creating a pupillage.

It was argued on behalf of the chambers that the arrangements between the pupil and the chambers were educational in character. Any legal rights and obligations that existed came from the regulatory framework created by the rules of the Bar Council (now replaced in its regulatory role by the Bar Standards Board). Similarly, it was argued that the main redress the parties would pursue against the other would be through the Bar Council, rather than the courts. These, taken together with the absence of written terms and conditions, strongly suggested that the parties did not intend to create legal relations.[40]

The Court of Appeal rejected these arguments, holding that the parties did, in fact, intend to create legal relations. The mere fact that the contract was educational did not mean that it was not intended to be binding. It was perfectly possible to create a binding contract for the provision of education or training. The fact that the parties would not have sued each other for breach was irrelevant—the existence of a binding contract does not depend on whether the parties are likely to sue to enforce it. The arrangements 'had all the characteristics of a binding contract', and would in consequence be treated as being intended to be binding.[41]

As this case suggests, the burden that must be discharged to prove that a commercial contract was not intended to be legally binding is a high one. This does not, however, mean that the burden is impossible to meet. One case in which it *was* met is *Hadley v Kemp.*[42] *Hadley* arose out of arrangements between the members of a group, Spandau Ballet, which was popular in the 1980s. The copyright in the songs and music was owned by a company controlled by one of the members, Gary Kemp, who composed all the songs. The copyright in the recordings was owned by a company controlled by the members of the group collectively. From 1981 to 1987, Gary Kemp paid half the royalties he derived from his copyright on the songs and music (the 'publishing income', as it is called) to the collectively controlled company, for distribution amongst the entire group. In 1988, he stopped making these payments. Three of the other group members sued Kemp, arguing that he was contractually required to make the payments. The court found that there was no intention to create legal relations. From the evidence, the conclusion that it drew was that Kemp was only willing to make the payments on the basis that they were voluntary, and could be suspended or revoked if circumstances changed. He would not have been willing to bind himself to

39. [2000] 1 QB 501.   40. Ibid, [22].   41. Ibid, [23] (Bingham LJ).
42. [1999] EMLR 580 (Ch).

making the payments, and certainly not in perpetuity.[43] As a result, there was sufficient ground to displace the ordinary presumption that the parties to a commercial arrangement would have intended to enter into legal relations.[44]

The parties can also agree that they do not intend to create binding legal relations. Consider the following clause, of the type that one might see in a commercial agreement:

> This Memorandum of Understanding sets out a statement of the mutual intentions of the parties with respect to the transactions it contemplates. It does not constitute obligations that are legal or binding on either side, nor does it create any rights or duties in favour of or against any party.

If an agreement contains a clear clause to this effect, the courts will in general give effect to it, and hold that the parties did not intend to enter into legal relations, even if the transaction is a commercial one. Thus in *Rose & Frank Co v JR Crompton & Brothers*,[45] Crompton manufactured certain products and had appointed Rose & Frank as their sole agents in the US and Canada for the sale of those products. The parties signed an agreement, which included the following clause:

> This arrangement is not entered into, nor is this memorandum written, as a formal or legal agreement, and shall not be subject to legal jurisdiction in the Law Courts either of the United States or England, but it is only a definite expression and record of the purpose and intention of the three parties concerned, to which they each honourably pledge themselves, with the fullest confidence—based on past business with each other—that it will be carried through by each of the three parties with mutual loyalty and friendly co-operation.

When disputes arose between the parties, Rose & Frank sought to sue Crompton for breach of contract. The House of Lords held that no action lay. The clause very clearly provided that it was binding in honour only and, as such, it was unenforceable at law.[46]

There is no set formula of words that parties need to use to make it clear that they did not intend to enter into legal relations. A number of words—including very brief formulations like 'subject to contract'—have been held to have this effect. The words must, however, be clear. If they are not clear, the general presumption that the parties to a commercial transaction intend their contract to be enforceable will prevail.

In *Edwards v Skyways Ltd*,[47] Skyways proposed to make around 15 per cent of its pilots redundant. In negotiations with the pilots' representatives, a number of points were agreed. One of these related to the status of the pilots' pension fund. The agreement reached on the point was that 'to those pilots who are finally declared redundant, the company will make an ex-gratia payment equivalent to their (the company's) own contributions to the provident or pension scheme'. In addition, the pilots would be entitled to withdraw their own contributions. Edwards, who had been made redundant, chose to take this route. The company then sought to withdraw their offer, arguing that as it was stated to be 'ex gratia' it was not binding. The court rejected this argument. 'Ex gratia,' it said, was a phrase commonly used in legal settlements, to

43. Ibid, 612–13.   44. Ibid, 623–4.   45. [1925] AC 445 (HL).
46. Ibid, 454.   47. [1964] 1 WLR 349 (QB).

indicate that a party was willing to pay an amount to settle a claim without admitting that it was under a pre-existing legal liability to do so. This did not mean that the settlement agreement was not intended to be legally enforceable. Given that background, the words did not carry a necessary or even probable implication that the agreement was intended to be without effect.[48]

In drawing a conclusion as to whether the words used in an agreement were intended to signify that the parties lacked the intention to enter into legal relations, the courts may look to the surrounding background to determine what the parties actually intended. *Ford Motor Co Ltd v Amalgamated Union of Engineering and Foundry Workers*[49] provides a good example. This case concerned agreements which were reached between Ford Motors and unions representing their employees. Following a strike, the question arose as to whether the agreements were enforceable. The company argued that they were, whereas some of the smaller unions argued that they were not. The court upheld the unions' argument, and held that the agreements were not enforceable because the parties did not intend them to be binding. The agreements did not themselves say that they were not intended to be binding. Nevertheless, the court was shown a significant amount of evidence—including government reports and guidance—all suggesting that the common opinion of most people involved in the area in England was that agreements between a company and a trade union were not legally enforceable in England, because they were intended to be binding in honour only, not in law.[50] In addition, the court held that a significant number of the provisions of the agreement consisted of 'aspirational clauses drawn in vague terms', or terms whose nature was such that 'the parties cannot really have expected any court to give legal effect to matters couched in that way'.[51] On this basis, the court held that the agreement was not intended to create legal relations.[52]

 Practice in context: establishing the facts

Because the question of intention is so closely tied to the facts specific to a case, the outcomes of cases can sometimes depend much more on the court's appraisal of the evidence that was actually placed before it than on the law. The contrast between the outcomes in two otherwise similar cases—*Simpkins v Pays*[53] and *Wilson v Burnett*[54]—illustrates this rather well.

Simpkins involved an arrangement between three women—Simpkins, Pays, and Pays's granddaughter—who regularly submitted joint entries to a competition run by a newspaper. The entries were submitted in the name of Pays. An entry put together by Pays's granddaughter won a prize of £750. Simpkins claimed that she was entitled to a share in the prize. In evidence, the court found that at the time the arrangements were made, one of the parties had said words to the effect 'We will go shares' which the others had accepted. As a result

→

48. Ibid, 356.   49. [1969] 2 QB 303.   50. Ibid, 325–9.   51. Ibid, 330.
52. This position was subsequently confirmed by statute. See s 179 of the Trade Union and Labour Relations (Consolidation) Act 1992.
53. [1955] 3 All ER 10 (Chester Ass).   54. [2007] EWCA Civ 1170.

➙ of this finding, the court held that the relationship between the parties was 'in the nature of a very informal syndicate so that they should all get the benefit of success', and found Simpkins entitled to a share of one-third.

In *Wilson v Burnett*, in contrast, the court came to the opposite conclusion, holding that there was no intention to create legal relations. Here, Tania Burnett, the defendant, had been at a bingo hall in Plymouth with two co-workers, Stacy Wilson and Abigail Stacey. Burnett had won a prize of over £101,211. Wilson and Stacey sued, arguing that they had contractually agreed to share any prize three ways. The evidence suggested that at the hall itself they had repeatedly pressed Burnett on whether she would share any prize, to the point where Burnett had lost her temper. This, it was held, was inconsistent with the suggestion that the three had agreed in their office to split their bingo winnings, suggesting that any talk before then was just talk, without a clear intention to create legal relations.

The crucial difference between the two cases was that, in the first case, evidence existed which led the court to accept that the parties had agreed that they would 'go shares' and meant it, whereas in the second case the evidence was a lot more ambiguous, leaving it very uncertain what, if anything, the parties had said, and what they meant by it. The main reason for the difference in the results, therefore, was not that the parties' words in the first case had a significance they did not in the second, but that the claimant in the first case was able to *prove* that words had been said at a particular time with a particular import, whereas the claimants in the second case were unable to prove equivalent facts. It was, in other words, primarily a difference as to the quality of the available evidence and the inferences that could be drawn from it, rather than the legal significance of the parties' words.

4.5 In conclusion: the role of intention

The centrality of the presumptions to the requirement of intention means that, unlike the requirements of agreement and consideration, the requirement of intention plays a much more limited role. In commercial transactions, it is not necessary to prove that the intention to create legal relations exists. It will ordinarily be assumed that it does, and it will be for the party alleging that it does not to substantiate that claim. Its main role, instead, is to give the parties flexibility to create documents that record an understanding they have reached, without making that understanding enforceable. In the absence of an express provision to this effect, however, commercial agreements will usually be held enforceable. It is only in very exceptional cases such as *Hadley v Kemp*, or in cases where the practice of treating agreements as not being binding is established as is the case in relation to collective bargaining agreements, that the court will hold that the parties to a commercial transaction did not intend to enter into legal relations.

The primary effect of this doctrine, then, is in areas outside commerce. In particular, it is in the area of relations between friends and family that we see this doctrine operating actively, to exclude significant numbers of arrangements from enforceability on the basis that the parties are not likely to have intended to enter into legal relations. Here, the results of its operation are not always problem-free. The result in *Balfour* itself has been criticized, and the result in cases such as *Horrocks* is also at least somewhat open to criticism. The central rationale underlying the decisions in both cases—the predilection of the courts for holding that arrangements grounded in affectionate relations are not enforceable—is, at the very least, open to question. It is hard to see on what basis the courts have come to the conclusion that parties are *less* likely to want their promises to be legally binding during the currency of a relationship than at the end, when they are dealing with each other in a semi-adversarial way, with a view to protecting their own interests. If one were to have taken the position of the hypothetical officious bystander, proposed by Lord Cross in *Albert v Motor Insurers' Bureau*, and asked the parties in *Horrocks* the question 'Do you intend this arrangement to be binding—in the event, for instance, that Mr Sanford were to die?', it is certainly not obvious that the answer would have been 'no'. It is submitted that more attention needs to be paid to the question of what, precisely, the underlying basis of the presumption is, and why it is applied in the way it currently is in such cases.

Key points

- Contracts are only valid if the parties had the intention to create legal relations.
- This requirement serves two purposes. First, it helps the courts distinguish merely social relationships from legal relationships. Secondly, it lets parties prepare documents which are only commercially binding and not legally binding.
- The law assesses intention to create legal relations through rebuttable presumptions. If a contract is commercial, there is a rebuttable presumption that the parties intended to create legal relations. If a contract is familial, there is a rebuttable presumption that they did not.

Assess your learning

You should be able to respond to each of the following points with a confident 'yes'. If you can't, then you should revisit the sections listed against that point.

Can you:

(a) *Describe* the role played by the intention to create legal relations in contract? (Sections 4.1 and 4.4)

(b) *Identify* the presumptions that apply, *explain* how they can be rebutted, and *apply* your knowledge to specific fact scenarios? (Section 4.3)

(c) *Outline* the key problems with the law of intention to create legal relations? (Section 4.4)

In relation to each of the above, you should be able to:

(i) identify and clearly explain the key rules and principles;

(ii) identify the key cases and statutes, and why they matter;

(iii) apply the principles and cases to specific real or hypothetical fact situations;

(iv) evaluate the limitations, if any, of the law as it currently stands.

Further reading

D Allen, 'The Gentleman's Agreement in Legal Theory and in Modern Practice' [2000] Anglo-American Law Review 204.

I Brown, 'The Letter of Comfort: Placebo or Promise?' [1990] JBL 281.

S Hedley, 'Keeping Contract in its Place: *Balfour v Balfour* and the Enforceability of Informal Agreements' (1985) 5 OJLS 391.

BA Hepple, 'Intention to Create Legal Relations' (1970) 28 CLJ 122.

Non-contractual promises

Promissory and proprietary estoppel

'For I have given my word, and I cannot take it back'[*]

[*] Cf Judges 11:36.

Problem 5: setting the context

Consider the legal issues raised by the following fictional newspaper clipping:

Carrson development in jeopardy as partners descend into acrimony

The high-profile redevelopment of the former Carrson shipyard in Middlesbrough is under threat following a legal dispute between the Carrson family and the intended developers, William Tomlinson Associates. The parties had agreed on a complex transaction structure under which Tomlinson would apply for planning approval. The property would be conveyed to Tomlinson for an agreed price once approval was granted. Tomlinson would carry out the redevelopment at its own risk. If Tomlinson's profits exceeded a certain sum, the excess would be split between the Carrson family and Tomlinson.

Critically, it appears that the agreement was never written down. The parties shook hands over the deal, and each expected the other to stick to their word. Now that planning permission has been granted, the value of the property has risen considerably and the Carrson family are exploiting a legal technicality to say that the agreement is not binding. Both sides are understood to have instructed lawyers, and the dispute appears to be headed for a long and costly lawsuit. . . .

Should the developer have a remedy, even though the agreement failed to comply with the legal requirement that agreements creating interests in relation to land are to be in writing?

5.1 Introduction

Not all agreements are enforceable in law. This could be because the offer was never accepted (Chapter 2), because there was nothing in the transaction that the law would recognize as consideration (Chapter 3), because the law deems the parties not to have intended to enter into legal relations (Chapter 4), or—as in the example above—because the parties did not comply with some sort of legal formality. In this chapter's problem, the formality which was not complied with was the requirement of writing. All agreements which create an interest in property must be in writing.[1] If they are not, they will not be enforceable. The agreement in the scenario above is precisely such an agreement. It should have been reduced to writing. It was not. As a result, it is not a binding contract even though the parties have reached agreement, and even though one party has acted in reliance on that agreement.

But that is not the end of the matter. It is often the case in English law that gaps left by one area of law are filled by another. Where an agreement is unenforceable at contract law because some legal prerequisite or formality has not been met, the gap is filled by the law of **estoppel**. The law of estoppel works by holding a party to be legally

---

1. Law of Property (Miscellaneous Provisions) Act 1989, s 2.

prevented ('estopped') from going back on something she has in the past asserted, promised, or accepted.[2] The effect of estoppel is to hold the person to that past assertion or promise, by preventing her from resiling from it.

Estoppel applies in a very wide range of circumstances, many of which have little or nothing to do with contracting, but it intersects with the law of contract in four types of situations. Two of these apply to statements of existing fact, and are only relevant to contracts that have been properly formed.[3] In this chapter, our focus will be on two forms of estoppel which relate to statements of future intent, rather than existing fact. Both these types of estoppel come into play in situations where a promise or similar statement of future intent has been made and acted upon but where, for some reason, no contract has come into being. These forms are called **proprietary estoppel** and **promissory estoppel**. Unlike the rules in relation to the formation of contracts, these types of estoppel do not require an accepted offer, nor do they require the provision of consideration. They are, instead, triggered by **reliance**—or, more specifically, by **representations** or assurances made or given by one person to another, on which that other relies.

Although proprietary and promissory estoppel share a common structure, they differ in their scope and effect, and in the details of how their elements are applied. Proprietary estoppel only applies to promises relating to an interest in real property, and creates a binding legal obligation which can be enforced in a court. Promissory estoppel, in contrast, can apply to any promise, but is only ever enforced negatively in English law. It can be used as a defence, but not as the basis of an action. The usual way of putting this is to say that promissory estoppel can be a shield, but not a sword. You can use it to defend yourself against claims made by another party, but you cannot use it to launch an action against another party. The significance of this point cannot be stressed enough. Proprietary estoppel can and does create new legal rights. Promissory estoppel does not. It simply creates a temporary bar to the enforcement of existing rights.

Estoppel tends to be invoked in situations such as the one set out in Problem 5, where parties have reached a deal from which one is subsequently trying to withdraw. Intuitively, it appears both morally and legally appropriate to intervene to prevent this, and uphold the honest expectation of the party who acted in reliance on the other's promise. Nevertheless, promissory and proprietary estoppel have been the subject of controversy in recent years. At the heart of these debates lies the uneasy question of the relationship between estoppel and consideration, and the extent to which it is appropriate to enforce promises which are not supported by consideration. Whilst judges in England at one stage favoured the expansion of estoppel, in recent years they have been sceptical about its role.

We will begin by setting out the types of situations in which promissory estoppel is typically engaged, and examine what it is about contract doctrine that leads to these promises not having contractual effect. We will then move on to look at the specific ingredients of promissory estoppel and the effect it has on the rights and obligations of the persons involved. We will then consider proprietary estoppel, and conclude by considering the proper place of estoppel in contracting.

---

2. 'Estopp' is simply an old-fashioned Anglo-Norman way of saying 'stop', equivalent to modern French *etop*.

3. These are estoppel by convention and estoppel by representation.

5.2 The context of promissory estoppel

A plea of promissory estoppel is typically raised in two types of situations. Problem 5 illustrates the first. Here, the parties face a situation where a binding contract has not come into effect. In the problem, this was because the parties did not comply with a legal formality, but the situation could just as easily have arisen if no consideration was provided. Consider, once again, one of the hamster examples discussed in Chapter 3:

Illustration 5.1

  – Thanks for mowing my lawn. Would you like one of my baby hamsters?

  – Yes, please!

As a contract, this promise is unenforceable because the law does not treat **past consideration** as being good consideration.[4] If, however, the person to whom the promise is made relies upon it (eg by buying a hamster cage and hamster food or by paying a vet to have the hamster inoculated), promissory estoppel might come into operation to prevent the promisor from demanding the return of the hamster.

The second, and in the modern context far more common, situation relates to renegotiation. Consideration often creates issues when contracts are renegotiated, because renegotiation very often results in one party agreeing to do more, or accept less, for pragmatic reasons rather than for 'valuable' consideration in the traditional sense. Whilst *Williams v Roffey*[5] deals with renegotiation quite effectively in some cases, not every contractual forbearance is associated with a 'practical' benefit. Promissory estoppel has since at least the 19th century been used to provide the promisee with a remedy in such circumstances. In *Hughes v Metropolitan Railway Co*,[6] Lord Cairns set out what is generally taken to be the classic statement of the role of promissory estoppel:

> if parties who have entered into definite and distinct terms involving certain legal results . . . by their own act or with their own consent enter upon a course of negotiation which has the effect of leading one of the parties to suppose that the strict rights arising under the contract will not be enforced, or will be kept in suspense, or held in abeyance, the person who otherwise might have enforced those rights will not be allowed to enforce them where it would be inequitable having regard to the dealings which have thus taken place between the parties.[7]

In the modern context, promissory estoppel is also used to get around the rule in *Foakes v Beer*[8] which, as you will recall, means that an agreement to accept a lesser sum of money than is due under a contract—for example, a reduced rent or a partial

---

4. See the discussion in Chapter 3, section 3.2.2.   5. [1991] 1 QB 1.
6. (1877) 2 App Cas 439 (HL).   7. Ibid, 448.
8. (1884) 9 App Cas 605 (HL).

payment of a debt—is not enforceable. Here, promissory estoppel can often provide the promisee with a partial defence if the promisor tries to go back on her promise. Consider the scenario set out in the following email:

Illustration 5.2

Dear Santha,

I understand your social enterprise is in financial difficulty as a result of a loss of grant income. We are keen to support the work you are doing. To help tide you over this difficult period, we are prepared to waive half the amount you have borrowed from us. This will reduce your debt to us from £10,000 to £5,000, and your monthly repayment from £250 to £125. We will treat repayment of the £5,000 as being full and final settlement of the entirety of your debt.

Best wishes,
Jim Flanagan
Account Manager
Allendale & District Bank

Foakes v Beer[9] means that any agreement the parties reach will be unenforceable for want of consideration. Yet such a result—which would let the bank withdraw from the renegotiated agreement at will—seems unfair to the borrower, who may have reorganized its affairs in reliance on the bank's promise to waive a portion of its debts. Commerce requires trust and certainty, and permitting a party to resile from a promise in these circumstances arguably cuts against both.

In practice, English courts have therefore been reluctant to allow parties to abandon at will promises or assurances which have been relied upon by the other party, even when those promises are not supported by consideration. The case of *Central London Property Trust v High Trees House*,[10] from which the modern approach to promissory estoppel is taken to derive, serves as a good illustration.

Case in depth: *Central London Property Trust v High Trees House* [1947] KB 130

Central London Property Trust (CLPT) owned a number of properties in London. High Trees House were the lessees of a block of flats on a 99-year lease at a rent of £2,500 per annum. The lease began in 1937. Because of the war, occupancy of the flats was very low, and High Trees were unable to meet their rent. CLPT therefore agreed to halve the rent to £1,250 per annum.

In September 1945, CLPT (who were now in receivership) wrote to High Trees House saying that the full rent was now payable. The receiver also sought the payment of arrears for the entire period, on the basis that the original promise was not supported by consideration.

→

---

9. Ibid.   10. [1947] KB 130.

> →
>
> The parties brought proceedings in the High Court on a 'friendly' basis to ascertain the legal position.
>
> Denning J in the High Court held that CLPT could recover the full rent from the end of the war onwards, but not for the period before then. He agreed that the promise to accept a lower rent was not supported by consideration, and was therefore not enforceable under the rule in *Foakes v Beer*.[11] The law had, however, changed, and now recognized a different ground on which the promise might be upheld:
>
> > There has been a series of decisions over the last fifty years . . . in which a promise was made which was intended to create legal relations and which, to the knowledge of the person making the promise, was going to be acted on by the person to whom it was made and which was in fact so acted on. In such cases the courts have said that the promise must be honoured . . . even though under the old common law it might be difficult to find any consideration for it. The courts have not gone so far as to give a cause of action in damages for the breach of such a promise, but they have refused to allow the party making it to act inconsistently with it. It is in that sense, and that sense only, that such a promise gives rise to an estoppel.[12]
>
> On this basis, CLPT's promise to accept a lower rent was 'a promise intended to be binding, intended to be acted on and in fact acted on' and was therefore 'binding so far as its terms properly apply'.[13] On the facts, this meant that it would apply while the war went on, but not thereafter.

As the judgment in *High Trees* suggests, it was the limitations of the doctrine of consideration more than anything else that was responsible for the use of promissory estoppel in that case and in subsequent cases. If promissory estoppel were to fully plug the holes left by consideration, however, it would in effect become an alternative to consideration—a mode of creating binding legal obligations grounded in reliance, rather than in consideration.

Some commentators have argued for precisely such an outcome, arguing that promissory estoppel represents a 'reliance-based model' for determining when a contract has been concluded, which should be taken at least as seriously as the 'exchange-based' model represented by consideration.[14] The courts have, however, been reluctant to let promissory estoppel go too far into the domain of consideration. Their focus has been, rather, on achieving a balance where promissory estoppel supplements the doctrine of consideration in certain cases, without becoming a full-fledged alternative to it. The balance we see in English law today was, in large part, the work of one judge, Lord Denning, who was responsible for a number of influential decisions in the middle of the 20th century which established both the modern form of the doctrine and its relationship to contract and consideration. We will return to the

---

11. (1884) 9 App Cas 605 (HL).   12. Ibid, 134 (Denning J).
13. Ibid, 136 (Denning J).
14. See esp H Collins, *The Law of Contract* (4th edn, LexisNexis Butterworths 2003) ch 5.

question of how well promissory estoppel addresses the limitations of the doctrine of consideration, and whether it is the best way to respond to those limitations, towards the end of this chapter.

5.3 **The requirements of promissory estoppel**

Let us now move to considering the specific requirements, or ingredients, of promissory estoppel in greater detail. The requirements are easily summarized. For promissory estoppel to arise, there must be a *promise, assurance, or representation*, which is *clear and unequivocal*, to the effect that the promisor will not rely upon a particular *legal right*. The promisee must have *relied* on this promise by changing his behaviour or conduct. Finally, the making of the promise and the reliance on it must take place in circumstances which make it *inequitable* to permit the promisor to resile from the promise. We will now look at each of these elements in turn.

5.3.1 **A promise or representation**

Despite its name, 'promissory' estoppel does not require an express promise to have been made. A person who has by her words or conduct given a clear and unequivocal assurance, or made a clear representation, can also be estopped if that assurance or representation is in the nature of a promise.

In *Robertson v Minister of Pensions*,[15] an army officer was found unfit for general service following an injury. He wrote a letter to the War Office asking whether his disability would be treated as 'attributable to military service' for the purposes of his pension. He received a reply saying that it would be. When he applied for a pension, however, the Minister of Pensions decided that his disability was not attributable to military service. The Court of Appeal held that the letter from the War Office had the effect of estopping the Crown from going back on its promise. Whilst there was no 'promise' as such by the War Office, the assurance it gave Robertson in relation to how his disability would be treated had a similar effect.

An assurance or representation has the nature of a promise if it represents a choice relating to the future. Assurances and representations—whether express or inferred from conduct—which do not look to the future, or do not represent a choice, will not create an estoppel.[16] In *Robertson*, for example, the assurance concerned the manner in which the government would choose to treat Colonel Robertson's injury for pension purposes. In *High Trees*, similarly, the representation related to the way in which CLPT would choose to exercise its right to demand rent. Where, in contrast, the promise or representation did not relate to future conduct, the courts have generally held that the facts do not give rise to promissory estoppel.

In *James v Heim Gallery (London) Ltd*,[17] a landlord decided not to invoke a contractual right to review rent, because he thought he had lost the right through not exercising it on time. Subsequent developments in the case law showed that his belief was

---

15. [1949] 1 KB 227 (CA).
16. *James v Heim Gallery (London) Ltd* (1981) 41 P & CR 269 (CA), 275 (Buckley LJ).   17. Ibid.

false—time was not of the essence in a rent review clause, and failure to exercise the power on time did not extinguish the right. He therefore initiated a rent review. The lessee argued that he was estopped from doing so. The Court of Appeal rejected the lessee's argument. The landlord had not made anything in the nature of a promise pertaining to the future, and his decision did not represent a choice in relation to how he intended to behave. He had simply accepted what he believed to be the position at law. This did not create an estoppel: 'To bow to the inevitable, or the near inevitable, is quite different from agreeing to forego a right.'[18]

Putting this discussion back in the context of the scenarios outlined in this chapter so far, it would seem to be clear that all three meet the requirements of a promise or representation, because all three statements relate to the future. Problem 5 involves an express promise to convey land. Illustration 5.1 involves a promise to transfer ownership of a hamster and Illustration 5.2 involves an assurance that the bank will not seek to recover the entire amount.

5.3.2 Clear and unequivocal

The second requirement that must be met for a claim of promissory estoppel to succeed is that the promise must be 'clear and unequivocal'.[19] Promises and assurances do not have to be expressly given, and can be implied from a person's words or conduct. *Hughes v Metropolitan Railway Co*[20] was such a case. In *Hughes*, a landlord sent a lessee a notice requiring them to carry out repairs to the leased premises. The lessee wrote back asking if they could negotiate a return of the lease to the landlord instead. The negotiations fell through after some months. It was held that by entering into the negotiations, the landlord gave an implicit assurance that he would not require the repairs to be carried out while the negotiations were going on.

Although the promise or assurance does not have to be express, it does have to be clear and unequivocal, or unambiguous. A promise or representation that is inherently vague or uncertain will not be sufficient for the purposes of promissory estoppel, even if it has been relied upon.[21] Nor will promissory estoppel apply to things that are 'mere acts of indulgence' particularly in a commercial context.[22] Just condoning a delay in performance on one occasion, for example, will not create an estoppel waiving the right to object to future delays. The editors of *Chitty on Contracts* have suggested that the promise or assurance must have 'the same degree of certainty as would be needed to give it contractual effect if it were supported by consideration',[23] and the analogy would seem to be sensible given the role promissory estoppel plays in contractual situations. If this view is accepted, an important consequence is that mere silence will not

18. Ibid, 277 (Buckley LJ).

19. *Woodhouse AC Israel Cocoa Ltd SA v Nigerian Produce Marketing Co Ltd* [1972] AC 741 (HL), 755 (Lord Hailsham).

20. (1877) 2 App Cas 439 (HL).

21. *Woodhouse AC Israel Cocoa Ltd SA v Nigerian Produce Marketing Co Ltd* [1972] AC 741 (HL), 755 (Lord Hailsham).

22. *Tool Metal Manufacturing Co Ltd v Tungsten Electric Co Ltd* [1955] 1 WLR 761 (HL), 764 (Viscount Simonds).

23. H Beale (ed), *Chitty on Contracts* (32nd edn, Sweet & Maxwell 2016) 3-090.

ordinarily be sufficiently clear or unequivocal to create an estoppel, just as mere silence does not ordinarily suffice to create a contractual obligation.

5.3.3 **A legal right**

Thirdly, the promise must relate to an existing legal right. The promisor must promise or represent that he will not rely on or enforce a legal right. The right in question does not have to be contractual. It could be any right—whether contractual, proprietary, statutory, equitable, or otherwise. What matters is that 'there is a pre-existing legal relationship which could in certain circumstances give rise to liabilities and penalties'.[24] This gives promissory estoppel a broad scope. In *Robertson v Minister of Pensions*,[25] the doctrine was applied to the legal power of the government to determine whether an injury was suffered in the course of military service. This is clearly not a contractual right, but it is one that can be the subject of promissory estoppel.

Of the three scenarios outlined in this chapter, only one—Illustration 5.2—involves a contractual right. In Problem 5 and Illustration 5.1, the right that is the subject of the promise is a property right. In Problem 5, the property right in question is the one which the Carrson family has in its land, and in the first illustration it is the property right the promisor has in the hamster. All three will, however, satisfy the requirement that the promise concerns an existing legal right.

The emphasis on existing legal rights stands in contrast to Denning J's language in *High Trees*,[26] which seems to emphasize the intention to *create* legal relations, rather than the intention to *alter* existing legal relations. Despite the importance of *High Trees* as a precedent, however, as the law stands today promissory estoppel is not seen as a means of creating new rights and can only be invoked to alter existing legal rights.

5.3.4 **Reliance**

Fourthly, the promisee must have relied on the promise. By 'reliance', we mean that the promisee must have been led to alter his behaviour or conduct by the promise or assurance. If the promisee's behaviour was not influenced by the promise or assurance, the requirement of reliance will not be made out, and estoppel will not apply.[27] Note that the promise or assurance does not have to be the *sole* cause of the alteration. It is sufficient if it is *a* cause. Thus if the promisee altered her behaviour partly in reliance on the promise, and partly as a result of entirely independent circumstances, promissory estoppel can still apply. This approach to causation reflects a general feature of the way contract law treats representations, which we will consider in more detail in Part III when we consider misrepresentations.

The nature of reliance becomes clearer if we apply it to the three scenarios discussed in this chapter. In Problem 5, the fact that Tomlinson spent time and money to obtain planning permission is very clear evidence of reliance. By working to obtain planning permission, Tomlinson altered their behaviour, and did so as a result of the promise of

24. *Durham Fancy Goods Ltd v Michael Jackson (Fancy Goods) Ltd* [1968] 2 QB 839, 847 (Donaldson J).
25. [1949] 1 KB 227 (CA).   26. [1947] KB 130.
27. *Lark v Outhwaite* [1991] 2 Lloyd's Rep 132 (QB).

a conveyance in their favour. Illustration 5.1—the case of the hamster—is somewhat more tricky. Merely taking the hamster is not likely to constitute reliance, in that it does not constitute a change of behaviour. However, if the recipient then proceeds to spend money buying hamster food, or a hamster cage, the purchase is likely to be sufficient to demonstrate reliance. In Illustration 5.2, similarly, if the borrower puts together a budget or spending plans based on the assumption that their debt to the bank has been halved, they will have altered their behaviour as a result of the promise of settlement, and have demonstrated reliance.

Some of the authorities on reliance go further, and suggest that reliance must incorporate an element of detriment.[28] That is to say, it is not sufficient for the promisee to have altered her behaviour. She must have done so in a way that is to her detriment. An alteration that is beneficial, or neutral, is not in this view sufficient reliance for the purposes of promissory estoppel. This position appears to be based on an analogy with estoppel by representation which does require reliance to be detrimental.[29] It may also owe something to the contractual context in which promissory estoppel is increasingly invoked. To speak of 'detriment' creates a parallel with the standard definition of consideration, which can be both useful and attractive when the doctrine is used in a contractual context.

Nevertheless, detriment is not a requirement on which the courts have insisted. In several leading cases where the parties successfully pleaded promissory estoppel—including both *High Trees*[30] and *Hughes v Metropolitan Railway*[31]—reliance arguably operated to the benefit rather than detriment of the promisee. In *High Trees*, the primary effect of the promisees' reliance was to enable them to enjoy a lower rate of rent for an extended period of time. In *Hughes*, it was to let them postpone their contractual obligation to repair the property for several months. It is hard to see how either of these can be termed a detriment. Whilst the suggestion that reliance must be detrimental is still occasionally made in argument and even referred to in decisions,[32] there is good reason to believe that legal doctrine does not require reliance to be detrimental.

5.3.5 **Inequitable**

The final ingredient of promissory estoppel is that it must be inequitable to allow the promisor to go back on her promise or assurance. If it is not inequitable, the courts will not apply promissory estoppel even if the other elements are made out.

It is not possible to come up with a checklist of what makes a particular set of facts 'inequitable'. As with most doctrines with equitable roots, promissory estoppel gives courts discretion to allow or deny relief in response to the specific facts of individual cases. A few general points can, however, be made.

First, the courts will not ordinarily apply promissory estoppel if there has been impropriety on the part of the promisee. The case of *D & C Builders v Rees*[33] provides a

---

28. See eg *EA Ajayi v RT Briscoe (Nigeria) Ltd* [1964] 1 WLR 1326.
29. H Beale (ed), *Chitty on Contracts* (31st edn, Sweet & Maxwell 2012) 3-094.
30. [1947] KB 130.   31. (1877) 2 App Cas 439 (HL).
32. For one recent example, see *Collier v P & MJ Wright (Holdings) Ltd* [2007] EWCA Civ 1329, [36] (Arden LJ).
33. [1966] 2 QB 617 (CA).

good illustration. D&C Builders had carried out building works for Mr and Mrs Rees, who owed them just over £480. Mrs Rees knew that the company was on the verge of insolvency, and told them that she would offer £300 in final settlement of the debt. Because of their financial situation, D&C Builders accepted a cheque for £300, and on Mrs Rees's insistence gave her a receipt saying that the money had been received 'in completion of the account'. They subsequently sued to recover the remaining £180. The Court of Appeal held that they were entitled to recover. Promissory estoppel only applied where it was inequitable to permit the promisor to resile from the terms of the promise. Because Mrs Rees's conduct amounted to intimidation, it was not inequitable to permit D&C Builders to resile from their assurance that their acceptance of a lower sum was in final settlement.

Secondly, the courts will not apply promissory estoppel if it appears that the promisor had good reasons for changing his mind. In *Williams v Stern*,[34] Williams had borrowed money from Stern, and had set up some furniture as security. On the day one of the instalments fell due, Williams asked Stern for extra time. Stern said he would give Williams a week. On the third day, however, Stern discovered that Williams's landlord was about to distrain the furniture for rent in arrears. He immediately seized the furniture. The Court of Appeal held that he was entitled to do so. Given that the goods had been threatened by the promisee's landlord, the promisor was entitled to change his mind.

Finally, although detriment is not a necessary ingredient of promissory estoppel, the fact that no detriment has been or will be caused to the promisee can, in combination with other circumstances, be relevant to the question of whether or not going back would be inequitable. In *The Post Chaser*,[35] the buyers of a consignment of palm oil had by their conduct waived certain defects in the documents of sale. Two days later, they sought to revoke their waiver. Goff J in the High Court permitted them to do so, holding that it was not inequitable for them to insist on their rights. This was because of a combination of the very short time between the waiver and its **revocation**, and the fact that no detriment had been suffered by the promisee in reliance on the representation. Note, though, that it is unlikely that the mere absence of detriment unaccompanied by other factors will by itself be enough.

5.4 **The effect of promissory estoppel**

Two points must be made about the effect of promissory estoppel. The first, which was briefly discussed in the introduction, is that promissory estoppel can only be pleaded as a *defence*. You cannot sue to enforce a promise or representation that is the subject of promissory estoppel, or to recover damages for its breach. The second point is that the effect of promissory estoppel is to *suspend* the right which the promisor promises not to enforce. It does not usually extinguish the right. The right is put into abeyance, and will revive once the circumstances creating the estoppel have passed. We will look at each of these in turn.

---

34. (1879) 5 QBD 409.

35. *Société Italo-Belge Pour le Commerce et L'Industrie SA v Palm and Vegetable Oils Sdn Bhd (The Post Chaser)* [1982] 1 All ER 19, [1981] 2 Lloyd's Rep 695.

5.4.1 **Not a cause of action**

The idea that promissory estoppel can only be used as a defence arises from the principle that it only deals with promises or representations concerning *existing* legal rights, rather than the creation of *new* rights. You cannot use promissory estoppel to enforce the promise or assurance, but you can use it if the promisor seeks to enforce or rely upon the original right in contravention of the promise. Thus, for example, in Illustration 5.1, the promisee of the hamster will not be able to sue for delivery of the hamster if the promisor fails to hand it over. However, if the promisor tries to take the hamster back, the promisee will be able to use the promise as a defence.

The fact that promissory estoppel cannot be the basis of a *claim* does not, however, mean that it cannot be used by a *claimant*. A claimant might, for example, be able to use promissory estoppel to resist a defence raised by the defendant. *Robertson v Minister of Pensions*,[36] which you encountered in section 5.3, was precisely such a case. Robertson's cause of action against the minister was based on his statutory claim for a pension, not on the assurance given by the War Office. Promissory estoppel was used to respond to the minister's defence, which was that Robertson's injury was not attributable to military service.

Robertson is not the only case in which promissory estoppel was successfully used by a claimant. In *Combe v Combe*,[37] Denning LJ cited *Robertson* and a number of similar cases, and then summarized the position thus:

> In none of these cases was the defendant sued on the promise, assurance, or assertion as a cause of action in itself: he was sued for some other cause, for example, a pension or a breach of contract, and the promise, assurance or assertion only played a supplementary role—an important role, no doubt, but still a supplementary role. That is, I think, its true function. It may be part of a cause of action, but not a cause of action in itself.[38]

Underlying Denning LJ's reluctance to permit promissory estoppel to act as a cause of action was the view that this was necessary to protect the position of the doctrine of consideration:

> The doctrine of consideration is too firmly fixed to be overthrown by a side-wind. Its ill-effects have been largely mitigated of late, but it still remains a cardinal necessity of the formation of a contract . . .[39]

The practical implications of this rule can be seen if we return to Problem 5. To succeed against the Carrsons, Tomlinson would have to bring an action on the promise of a conveyance. Because there is no other cause of action available to Tomlinson, the promise cannot play a merely 'supplementary' role. The result will be that Tomlinson will be left without a remedy in promissory estoppel, despite having relied on the promise, because promissory estoppel cannot be a cause of action. This represents a deliberate choice by the English judiciary to the effect that promissory estoppel should supplement the doctrine of consideration, but should not be allowed to subvert it.

36. [1949] 1 KB 227 (CA).   37. [1951] 2 KB 215 (CA).   38. Ibid, 220.   39. Ibid.

> **Debates in context: a sword or a shield?**

The principle that promissory estoppel cannot be a cause of action has come in for criticism from academics for several decades. The argument has been that there is nothing intrinsic to the doctrine that requires it to only be a defence, and that it is illogical to so confine it.[40] Other academics have gone further. Professor Atiyah wrote a number of influential books and articles in the 1970s and 1980s calling for consideration to be abolished altogether, and replaced by a reliance-based test inspired by promissory estoppel. More recently, Professor Hugh Collins has argued that reliance represents an alternative approach to determining when a contract is formed, which deserves to be taken as seriously as the more orthodox approach embodied in the doctrine of consideration.

Courts in several other common law jurisdictions have moved in this direction. The courts in Australia, as well as several US states, have abandoned this distinction, and are now willing to permit claimants to use promissory estoppel as a cause of action. In Australia, the shift came about in the case of *Waltons Stores (Interstate) Ltd v Maher*.[41] Maher owned property, and was in negotiations with Waltons Stores who were interested in taking some of his property on a long-term lease. They said that they would require an existing build-ing to be demolished and replaced by a new one. Maher began carrying out these works, believing—on the strength of Waltons' words—that a contract had been concluded, and that the actual exchange of signed documents was a formality. In reality, a contract had not come into being, and Waltons was under no binding obligation to take the property on lease. Following a retailing review, they decided that they would not proceed with the contract. Maher sued. The High Court of Australia found for Maher, holding that promis-sory estoppel could, in Australian law, be the basis of a cause of action in the same way as proprietary estoppel, both of which should be seen as aspects of a single unified action of equitable estoppel:

> equity will come to the relief of a plaintiff who has acted to his detriment on the basis of a basic assumption in relation to which the other party to the transaction has 'played such a part in the adoption of the assumption that it would be unfair or unjust if he were left free to ignore it'.[42]

Many commentators have argued that English courts should follow the Australian courts, and there have been some signs from the judiciary of willingness to look beyond the tradi-tional division of estoppel into promissory and proprietary estoppel, although no court has as yet sought to restate the law along these lines. The traditional understanding of promis-sory estoppel also has prominent defenders. The editors of *Chitty on Contracts*, for exam-ple, have argued that promissory estoppel is far better understood as a type of forbearance rather than estoppel. As such, it would be a mistake to attempt to turn it into an enforceable cause of action.

The debate continues.

---

40. For an early statement of this view, see D Jackson, 'Estoppel as a Sword' (Parts 1 and 2) (1965) 81 LQR 84 and 223.
41. (1988) 164 CLR 387.   42. Ibid.

5.4.2 **Suspending or extinguishing rights?**

Suspending rights through estoppel

In the majority of cases, the effect of promissory estoppel is to temporarily suspend the right that is the subject of the promise or assurance. The right is not extinguished, and will become enforceable again when the circumstances that gave right to the estoppel have passed. In *High Trees*,[43] for example, the landlord was able to demand payment of the full rent once the war had ended. The promise only suspended full payment while the war was ongoing. Similarly, in *Hughes v Metropolitan Railway*,[44] the tenants' obligation to repair the property did not disappear. It was simply held in abeyance while the parties were negotiating.

In *High Trees*, Denning J linked the suspensory effect of promissory estoppel to the parties' intention. Promises not to enforce a right, including the promise that was the subject of *High Trees*, are typically intended to be temporary. As a result, they should only be treated as suspending the rights of the parties for the intended period, rather than extinguishing them completely. There is also a strong equitable element to the rule that promissory estoppel is ordinarily only suspensory. In the absence of consideration, it is only fair and equitable to permit the promisor to change his mind by giving reasonable notice to the other party.

What, then, is required in order to effectively put an end to a period of suspension? Case law suggests that the promisor is not required to issue a notice expressly terminating the period of suspension, or even making reference to it. All that is needed is 'a clear intimation of a reversal' by the promisor of their previous attitude in relation to the right that was placed in abeyance, and of 'their intention to enforce compliance' with that right.[45] Thus it has been held that filing a claim (ie starting a law suit) or a counterclaim which seeks to assert or enforce the right in question can serve as sufficient notice for the purposes of ending an estoppel.[46]

Extinguishing debts through estoppel

When it comes to debts and the payment of money, a purely suspensory doctrine is of limited utility. Think back to the nature of the problem posed by *Foakes v Beer*[47] and *Selectmove*, where a contract is renegotiated so that one party agrees to accept a lesser sum in place of a greater one. If promissory estoppel were to be purely suspensory, it would mean that the promisor could revive his claim to the greater sum simply by giving notice to the other party. In Illustration 5.2, for example, if the bank could insist on repayment of the full £10,000 at any time simply by giving notice that it had changed its mind, there would be little point to the estoppel. To be of any use in cases involving the part-payment of debts or the payment of lesser sums of money in place of greater ones, therefore, promissory estoppel will need to do more than merely suspend rights. It will need to extinguish them at least in part.

And, in point of fact, the courts have repeatedly treated promissory estoppel as extinguishing a right in cases relating to debts and other payments of money, even while

---

43. [1947] KB 130.   44. (1877) 2 App Cas 439.
45. *Tool Metal Manufacturing Co Ltd v Tungsten Electric Co Ltd* [1955] 1 WLR 761 (HL).
46. Ibid.   47. (1884) 9 App Cas 605 (HL).

claiming to treat it as having no more than a suspensory effect. *High Trees*[48] itself serves as an example. Although Denning J described the effect of the doctrine in that case as suspensory, it was suspensory only in the sense that the right to claim the higher rent for *future* years could be reinstated. The right to claim the higher rent for *past* years was not suspended. It was extinguished. CLPT could not, by giving notice, reinstate the right to demand payment for the years of the war.

On its face, reconciling this with the decision in *Foakes v Beer*[49] appears less than straightforward. *Foakes* was quite unambiguous in holding that an agreement to accept a lesser sum in place of a greater one has no legal effect, and it made no reference to promissory estoppel, or to *Hughes v Metropolitan Railway*,[50] even though it postdates *Hughes*. In historical terms, however, this is readily explicable. *Hughes* was decided in terms of the courts' discretionary power to grant a tenant relief against the forfeiture of a lease. At the time *Foakes* was decided, therefore, *Hughes* would have been seen as a case specifically concerned with the powers of a court in relation to leases, rather than reflecting a more general principle affecting all contracts. It did not come to be seen as representing the same underlying principle as promissory estoppel until the 20th century.

Promissory estoppel, then, should be seen as a later development, which offers one route to mitigating some of the problems created by the doctrine of consideration, and which for that reason does not offend the rule in *Foakes*. The decision in *Collier v P & MJ Wright (Holdings) Ltd*[51] provides a useful illustration of how the courts currently use promissory estoppel in situations that are also covered by the rule in *Foakes v Beer*.

Case in depth: *Collier v P & MJ Wright (Holdings) Ltd* [2007] EWCA Civ 1329

This case related to a commercial loan which Collier, together with two partners, had taken out with P & MJ Wright. Collier and his partners defaulted on the loan. Following a settlement, they began repaying the debt in monthly instalments of £600. Under the terms of the settlement, all of them were liable for the entire loan, so that if any partner failed to pay his share the other partners would have to pay back his share as well.

The other partners got into financial difficulties. Collier began paying monthly instalments of £200 on his own. He claimed that he had a meeting with P & MJ Wright, at which they agreed to release him from liability for the other partners' shares of the loan, leaving him only liable for one-third of the loan. He then continued making monthly payments of £200, until he had repaid this amount. In the meantime, the other partners became insolvent and stopped paying altogether. P & MJ Wright then sued him, demanding repayment of the entire loan.

The facts of the case were disputed—P & MJ Wright denied that they had ever agreed to release Collier from liability for the other partners' shares. However, the case came before the Court of Appeal on a preliminary procedure, which meant that it only had to determine whether there was a 'genuine triable issue'. This turned on two questions. The first was

→

---

48. [1947] KB 130.   49. (1884) 9 App Cas 605 (HL).   50. (1877) 2 App Cas 439.
51. [2007] EWCA Civ 1329, [2008] 1 WLR 643.

→

consideration. On the assumption that P & MJ Wright had in fact promised to release Collier from liability for the other partners' shares, would there have been a valid contract? On this issue, the court held that there was no triable issue—the law was clear that the contract would be invalid under the rule in *Foakes v Beer* because Collier had provided no consideration for that promise.[52]

The second point was the defence of promissory estoppel. Here, the Court of Appeal held both that there was a triable issue and that P & MJ Wright would not be able to claim the residual sum from Collier if promissory estoppel were established. Because the court was not considering the merits, it did not consider the question of whether there was sufficient reliance. Arden LJ suggested that the payment of a lesser sum would in and of itself constitute sufficient reliance, if the debtor was acting on the promisor's assurance in making that payment.[53] Longmore LJ was more sceptical, however, and pointed out that there was no evidence of any alteration of conduct on Collier's part, which would suggest that there was no meaningful reliance.[54] They were not, however, required to decide this point, and they did not do so.

The ruling in *Collier* has been criticized on the grounds that it stretches promissory estoppel further than it ought to be stretched—promissory estoppel, it has been argued, cannot be used to plug every gap in the doctrine of consideration without destroying its coherence.[55] The practical sense behind the ruling can, however, be seen if we relate it back to the scenario set out in Illustration 5.2. If the ruling in *Collier* holds, the effect would be that the bank, once it has given an assurance that it is waiving part of the debt, will not then be able to go back on the assurance.

The exception will be where for some reason it is equitable to allow the bank to resile from its initial assurance. *Collier* does not hold that promissory estoppel is automatically available in all cases where there has been an agreement to accept a lesser sum. The party relying on estoppel will still need to demonstrate that the ingredients of promissory estoppel are made out, including the requirement that resiling from the promise must be inequitable. This gives a degree of protection to the bank, in that it will enable it to change its mind if there is good reason for it to do so, or if there has been some impropriety on the part of the borrower.

The importance of this requirement was highlighted by the Court of Appeal in *MWB Business Exchange Centres v Rock Advertising Ltd*.[56] In that case, a licensor had initially agreed to reschedule payments due from a licensee to enable the licensee to clear arrears under the licence. Two days after the agreement, the licensor changed its mind and sought to cancel the agreement. The Court of Appeal accepted the ruling in *Collier*, but nevertheless unanimously held that the licensor would not be

---

52. Ibid, [23] (Arden LJ).   53. Ibid, [39].   54. Ibid, [46].

55. A Trukhtanov, '*Foakes v Beer*: Reform at Common Law at the Expense of Equity' (2008) 124 LQR 364.

56. [2016] EWCA Civ 553. It is worth noting that the bench hearing this case included Arden LJ, who delivered the lead judgment in *Collier*.

estopped from changing its mind, because going back on its word would not be inequitable. Rock had not suffered any prejudice or detriment as a result of its reliance on the promise, and could easily be restored to the position it had originally occupied.[57] On subsequent appeal, the case was decided on other grounds,[58] but the Court of Appeal's decision nevertheless demonstrates that *Collier* is capable of being applied in a way that achieves a just balance, and thus represents a position that is both necessary and sensible.

5.5 **Proprietary estoppel**

Before we leave the topic of estoppel, we need to briefly consider the other form of estoppel that has relevance to situations where the formation process has failed; namely, proprietary estoppel. Proprietary estoppel differs fundamentally from promissory estoppel in that it creates a cause of action on which proceedings can be brought. To put it in the terms used earlier, it can be a sword. However, as its name suggests, it only applies to a limited set of promises—those pertaining to an interest in real property.

On the face of it, the ability of proprietary estoppel to serve as a cause of action makes it of potential relevance to Problem 5. As we have seen, promissory estoppel is of little assistance to Tomlinson because it can only serve as a defence, and not a cause of action. Can proprietary estoppel, then, help?

The answer is that although proprietary estoppel is, in principle, capable of furnishing a cause of action in such circumstances, it is unlikely to do so in this particular case. The requirements of proprietary estoppel closely parallel those of promissory estoppel, but they are stricter. It is, for example, a clear requirement in proprietary estoppel—unlike promissory estoppel—that reliance must be detrimental and reasonable. The courts have also stressed that the elements of proprietary estoppel 'cannot be treated as subdivided into three or four watertight compartments'.[59]

Instead:

> the quality of the relevant assurances may influence the issue of reliance, that reliance and detriment are often intertwined, and that whether there is a distinct need for a 'mutual understanding' may depend on how the other elements are formulated and understood. Moreover the fundamental principle that equity is concerned to prevent unconscionable conduct permeates all the elements of the doctrine. In the end the court must look at the matter in the round.[60]

In considering the requirements that follow, therefore, it must be kept in mind that the court will treat its enquiry as an integrated one and determine whether proprietary estoppel is made out based on a consideration of all the circumstances of the case, rather than in terms of individual requirements.

---

57. Ibid, [63] (Kitchin LJ).
58. *Rock Advertising Ltd v MWB Business Exchange Centres Ltd* [2018] UKSC 24.
59. *Gillett v Holt* [2001] Ch 210, 225 (Robert Walker J).   60. Ibid.

5.5.1 **A promise or encouragement**

As in promissory estoppel, the first requirement of proprietary estoppel is that there must be something akin to a promise or a representation. This must be of a nature that encourages the defendant to believe that they will be given (or already have been given) an interest in real property, and it must be made by the true owner of the property in question. The property must also be identified: a promise which is vague in terms of the property to which it relates will not give rise to a proprietary estoppel.[61]

5.5.2 **Reliance and reasonableness**

The second requirement is that the promise or encouragement must induce reliance, which must be reasonable. The courts have in recent years placed quite a bit of emphasis on the requirement of reasonableness. The decision of the House of Lords in *Yeoman's Row Management Ltd v Cobbe*[62] provides an excellent illustration.

Case in depth: *Yeoman's Row Management Ltd v Cobbe* [2008] UKHL 55, [2008] 1 WLR 1752

Cobbe was a developer who entered into an oral agreement with Yeoman's Row to develop land owned by Yeoman's Row. Cobbe went to great expense to obtain planning permission for the development. After permission came through, Yeoman's Row sought to increase the price it intended to charge.

Cobbe could not bring an action for breach of contract, because the contract had not been reduced to writing. Instead, he advanced a claim in proprietary estoppel. His claim succeeded in the High Court and the Court of Appeal,[63] but was rejected by the House of Lords.

Lord Scott agreed that the behaviour of Yeoman's Row was unconscionable, but held that that was not sufficient to give rise to a proprietary estoppel.[64] Unlike a domestic claimant, a commercial party such as Cobbe was fully aware of the risks inherent in proceeding without an enforceable agreement:

> It would be an unusually unsophisticated negotiator who was not well aware that oral agreements relating to such an acquisition are by statute unenforceable and that no express reservation to make them so is needed. Mr Cobbe was an experienced property developer and Mrs Lisle-Mainwaring gives every impression of knowing her way around the negotiating table. Mr Cobbe did not spend his money and time on the planning application in the mistaken belief that the agreement was legally enforceable. He spent his money and time well aware that it was not. Mrs Lisle-Mainwaring did not encourage in him a belief that the second agreement was enforceable. She encouraged in him a belief that she would abide by it although it was not. Mr Cobbe's belief, or expectation, was always speculative. He knew she was not legally bound. He

→

---

61. *Capron v Government of Turks & Caicos Islands* [2010] UKPC 2.
62. [2008] UKHL 55, [2008] 1 WLR 1752.
63. See *Yeoman's Row Management Ltd v Cobbe* [2006] EWCA Civ 1139, [2006] 1 WLR 2964.
64. [2008] UKHL 55, [28].

> →
>
> regarded her as bound 'in honour' but that is an acknowledgement that she was not legally bound.[65]
>
> Under the circumstances, Cobbe could not use proprietary estoppel to overturn the result of a risk he had consciously taken: 'conscious reliance on honour alone will not give rise to an estoppel'.[66] Cobbe's action, therefore, failed.

Where the parties are not commercial, however, the courts have tended to be less strict. In *Thorner v Major*,[67] a man had worked without pay on his cousin's farm for several decades, in the expectation—which had been encouraged by his cousin's words and actions—that he would inherit the farm. The House of Lords held that such an expectation was not unreasonable given the facts of the case.

5.5.3 Reliance and detriment

In proprietary estoppel, reliance must be detrimental. That is to say, the promisee must suffer detriment as a result of relying on the promise. Detriment is often clear. In *Thorner v Major*, the detriment was held to lie in the fact that the claimant had worked for no pay on his cousin's farm for over 30 years. Similarly, in *Crabb v Arun District Council*,[68] Crabb had at a meeting with Arun District Council been given an assurance that they would provide him with a right of access to his land through council property. Relying on this assurance, Crabb sold a portion of his land, leaving it with no independent means of access. The council then sought to charge Crabb for the right of access. On Crabb's suit, the Court of Appeal held that the council's assurance and Crabb's detrimental reliance gave rise to a proprietary estoppel in Crabb's favour.

5.5.4 Unconscionability

The final requirement is that it must be unconscionable not to give effect to the expectation of acquiring an interest in real property created by the promisor's actions. Unconscionability by itself is not sufficient to ground an action in proprietary estoppel. If the other elements of promissory estoppel are not made out on the facts of a case, 'however reprehensible the behaviour of the defendant and whatever the court's reaction to it may be, the doctrine of proprietary estoppel will not avail the claimant'.[69]

What, then, is the role of unconscionability in proprietary estoppel? In *Yeoman's Row v Cobbe*,[70] Lord Walker distinguished behaviour that was merely *unattractive* from

---

65. Ibid, [27] (Lord Scott).   66. Ibid, [81] (Lord Walker).
67. [2009] UKHL 18, [2009] 1 WLR 776.   68. [1976] Ch 179.
69. *Capron v Government of Turks & Caicos Islands* [2010] UKPC 2, [40] (Lord Kerr).
70. [2008] UKHL 55, [2008] 1 WLR 1752.

behaviour that was truly *unconscionable*, and explained the nature of unconscionability in these terms:

> [Unconscionability] is being used (as in my opinion it should always be used) as an objective value judgment on behaviour (regardless of the state of mind of the individual in question). As such it does in my opinion play a very important part in the doctrine of equitable estoppel, in unifying and confirming, as it were, the other elements. If the other elements appear to be present but the result does not shock the conscience of the court, the analysis needs to be looked at again.[71]

Returning, then, to Problem 5, it is likely that proprietary estoppel will not come to the rescue of Tomlinson. The transaction between Tomlinson and the Carrson family was a commercial one, and *Yeoman's Row v Cobbe* makes it clear that the requirement that reliance be reasonable will set a high bar in commercial transactions involving property. In such cases, the fact that one party 'chose to stand on her rights rather than respecting her non-binding assurances' is likely to only render that party's conduct unattractive, and not unconscionable,[72] because the promisee entered into the arrangement knowing full well that the obligations only bound the other party in honour.

5.6 In conclusion: estoppel and consideration

Promissory and proprietary estoppel are grounded in the simple principle that a person who gives an assurance on which another person relies should, in some cases, be restrained from going back on that assurance. Because this principle is materially different from the idea that underlies the doctrine of consideration, there is a great deal of scope for the two to productively supplement each other, but also for them to come into conflict.

The use of promissory estoppel in dealing with the problems posed by renegotiations, particularly in relation to debt, is a particularly clear example of the productive role that can be played by promissory estoppel in supplementing the doctrine of consideration. Indeed, as we have discussed in the course of this chapter, it was deliberately nudged in this direction by Lord Denning; and the decision of Arden LJ in *Collier v P & MJ Wright* shows clear signs of being similarly motivated.

Yet, while developing the law of estoppel, the courts have also been keenly aware that estoppel sits somewhat uneasily alongside the doctrine of consideration, and have been reluctant to take steps that will tilt the balance too far in favour of estoppel and against consideration. Throughout his development of promissory estoppel, Lord Denning stressed that promissory estoppel should not be allowed to become a sword, because to do so would be to undermine the role of consideration in contract. Other judges have expressed their concern in more colourful terms. In *Taylor v Dickens*,[73] Judge Weeks QC sitting as a Deputy Judge of the High Court expressed concerns about placing too much store in proprietary estoppel on the fact that one

---

71. Ibid, [92].   72. Ibid.   73. [1998] 1 FLR 806.

party's actions were unconscionable. To do so, he said, would threaten the traditional role of contract, and run the risk of making justice arbitrary:

> In my judgment there is no equitable jurisdiction to hold a person to a promise simply because the court thinks it unfair, unconscionable or morally objectionable for him to go back on it. If there were such a jurisdiction, one might as well forget the law of contract and issue every civil judge with a portable palm tree. The days of justice varying with the size of the Lord Chancellor's foot would have returned.[74]

As things stand, therefore, it appears clear that the English judiciary does not share the enthusiasm some academics have shown for expanding promissory estoppel into a cause of action, to say nothing of replacing consideration with a broader test of reliance. For the present, it would seem that promissory estoppel will remain a tool which supplements consideration and mitigates its shortcomings, particularly in situations involving renegotiated contracts and partly paid debts, without challenging its place in the doctrinal structure of contract law.

Key points

- Certain promises which are not enforceable as contracts may have a limited effect through the doctrine of estoppel. Estoppel operates by preventing a party from going back on something they have asserted, promised, or accepted.

- Two types of estoppel supplement the law of contract: promissory estoppel and proprietary estoppel. The central element in both types of estoppel is reliance.

- Promissory estoppel is a defence, and does not give rise to a cause of action. It suspends rights, but does not extinguish them.

- Proprietary estoppel can be both a defence and a cause of action.

- For promissory estoppel to be triggered, there must have been a promise, assurance, or representation, which was clear and unequivocal and related to a legal right. That promise must have been relied on by the other party, in circumstances making it inequitable for the promisor to go back on the promise.

- To be a promise, a statement must relate to the future. It does not have to be express. It can be implied from a party's conduct.

- A party has relied on a promise if it leads them to alter their behaviour or conduct. Reliance does not have to be detrimental (although some authorities hold otherwise).

- Proprietary estoppel is only available in cases relating to interests in real property.

- It is available if there was a promise or encouragement relating to interests in land. The promise must have been relied on to the promisee's detriment, in circumstances which make that reliance reasonable. The behaviour of the promisor must be unconscionable (and not merely unattractive).

74. Ibid, 820.

Assess your learning

You should be able to respond to each of the following points with a confident 'yes'. If you can't, then you should revisit the sections listed against that point.

Can you:

(a) *Distinguish* between contracts, promissory estoppel, and proprietary estoppel, *identify* the constitutive elements of each, and *describe* the circumstances to which they apply? (Sections 5.2 to 5.5)

(b) *Identify* the role of reliance in establishing promissory estoppel, how it differs from the role of reliance in proprietary estoppel, and the tests for each? (Sections 5.3.4, 5.5.2 and 5.5.3)

(c) *Explain* how promissory estoppel can be used as a shield, *identify* the limitations this places on its use, and *apply* your knowledge to specific fact scenarios? (Section 5.4.1)

(d) *Explain* what it means to say promissory estoppel has suspensory effect, *analyse* how this differs from the effect of a contract, and *apply* your knowledge to design special formation processes? (Section 5.4.2)

(e) *Outline* the way in which promissory estoppel can be used to ameliorate the limitations imposed by the doctrine of consideration? (Sections 5.2 and 5.4.2)

In relation to each of the above, you should be able to:

(i) identify and clearly explain the key rules and principles;

(ii) identify the key cases and statutes, and why they matter;

(iii) apply the principles and cases to specific real or hypothetical fact situations;

(iv) evaluate the limitations, if any, of the law as it currently stands.

Further reading

R Austen-Baker, 'A Strange Sort of Survival for *Pinnel's case: Collier v P&MJ Wright (Holdings) Ltd*' (2008) 71 MLR 611.

E Cooke, 'Estoppel and the Protection of Expectations' (1997) 17 LS 258.

A Duthie, 'Equitable Estoppel, Unconscionability and the Enforcement of Promises' (1988) 104 LQR 362.

R Halson, 'The Offensive Limits of Promissory Estoppel' [1999] LMCLQ 256.

J Mee, 'The Role of Expectation in the Determination of Proprietary Estoppel Remedies' in M Dixon (ed), *Modern Studies in Property Law* (Hart 2009).

J O'Sullivan, 'In Defence of *Foakes v Beer*' (1996) 56 CLJ 219.

A Robertson, 'Reliance and Expectation in Estoppel Remedies' (1988) 18 LS 360.

M Spence, *Protecting Reliance: The Emergent Doctrine of Equitable Estoppel* (Hart 1999).

Keeping contracts

PART II

Introduction

We have thus far been looking at the question of when the law deems a contract to have come into existence. In this Part, we turn to a different issue: the question of how the law determines what the contract requires the parties to do. At one level, the suggestion that the law has any role in this question may seem peculiar. Surely the task of apportioning rights and responsibilities is for the parties to undertake? In practice, legal rules are needed to interpret and fill gaps in contracts. The law's task would be very easy indeed if everyone entering into a contract carefully thought about and recorded their terms. But this is not how contracting works in the real world.

One reason why legal rules are needed is that many contracts are oral. Most contracts are neither written nor signed, and are entered into without parties consciously thinking about the fact that they are contracting, let alone what the terms might be. But even where contracts are written down, they are rarely given the attention one might expect. People have many demands on their time, and reading contractual terms does not strike most people as a particularly productive activity. The result is that contracts are often signed with parties having only a vague idea of what the words say, or how they affect specific situations.

Making a contract comprehensive also takes time and money. A company will soon find itself bankrupt if it tries to anticipate and contractually deal with every situation that every transaction might throw up. As a result, the work that parties put into writing contracts is often insufficient even in more complex transactions. It is common for parties to begin with an existing model contract which they then adapt to the transaction in question. If the model is not completely suitable for the situation in question, the end product can be a lengthy and detailed contract that nevertheless leaves important issues unaddressed, or whose legal terms do not match the parties' commercial goals.

These issues cause little difficulty in the majority of transactions, because parties carry on with their deal as long as it continues to make sense for them. But where the parties find themselves in disagreement, difficult questions are thrown up. First, it is not always obvious what the terms of a contract *are*. Consider a typical contract entered into in a shop. Whilst it is clear that the parties have agreed to sell a particular thing for a particular price, it is not clear what else they have agreed. Will the goods be accompanied by a guarantee? If the customer had a conversation with the shop-keeper about why he wanted the goods, will that form part of the contract? Situations of this kind arise in all types of transactions—commercial and non-commercial. The first challenge courts face in determining what a contract requires the parties to do, therefore, is establishing what the terms of a contract actually are.

A second issue relates to what the terms of the contract *mean*. Contracts are written to achieve particular ends, and to require parties to act in particular ways. However, they are written in words. How do those words relate to what the parties are supposed to do? It is surprisingly common to encounter phrases whose precise meaning is unclear. Making sense of unclear, ambiguous, or contestable wording is the second of the challenges courts face in determining what a contract requires.

The focus of this Part is on how English law deals with these and related questions. English law is marked by a disjunction between legal and commercial perspectives on contracting. Business people take decisions based on commercial considerations, not legal ones. To take an everyday example, if you have a slice of cheese cut for you at the supermarket but then decide not to buy it, most supermarkets will let you do so without worrying about whether your request was an offer or an invitation to treat. In much the same way, commercial parties frequently deal with each other on a relational basis, adjusting and reworking their obligations from time to time regardless of what their contract might strictly require. When parties approach transactional problems, their focus is on the present moment, and on practical ways forward from the present moment.

Courts approach contracts very differently. English courts give effect to the *original* understanding of the transaction. As Part I has discussed, English law treats contracts as crystallizing at a single 'moment of responsibility'. The focus is on the parties' understanding of the transaction at that time. The determination of how risks and responsibilities should be apportioned is made with reference to that moment, not the present. Although transactions evolve dynamically, the contract as the law understands it does not. English courts do not see it as being their role to adjust a contract so that it remains fair in the light of changed circumstances, or takes account of things that may have escaped the attention of one of the parties at the time they contracted.

Chapter 6 begins this discussion by discussing how the courts determine what the terms of the contract are, both where the contract is in writing and where it is oral. Chapter 7 looks at how courts make sense of contracts whose terms are capable of more than one interpretation. Chapter 8 then turns to contracts which leave some issues unaddressed, and looks at the law of implied terms which courts use to deal with such situations. Chapter 9 looks at how parties try to build flexibility into their contracts, and the legal hurdles they face. Chapter 10 concludes the discussion by looking at how the law deals with situations where fundamental changes have occurred, calling into question the assumptions on which the contract was based.

6

Assembling
the contract

Representations, terms, and incorporation

'Sorting the wheat from the chaff'

Problem 6: setting the context

Consider this scenario. As you read, try and work through what you believe the legal implications of each of the statements might be:

Graeme is an avid PC gamer. He decides that he wants to purchase a new gaming rig, and visits GameTyne, the leading builder of custom gaming PCs in the North East. At the shop, he has a long conversation with Ranbir, one of GameTyne's PC builders. At the end of the conversation, he and Ranbir have worked out a configuration for his new PC. Ranbir types up an invoice which sets out the agreed configuration, along with prices. Graeme confirms that he's happy with the price. He pays a 10 per cent deposit, and Ranbir writes an estimated delivery date on the invoice.

The following statements are some of the things Ranbir and Graeme said in the course of their negotiation:

Ranbir: So, what games do you expect to mostly be playing?

Graeme: [Names some games.]

Ranbir: Right, those are pretty high-end games. To be honest, if you want to get the most out of them, my advice as a system builder would be that you're going to need a four-way SLI setup, probably with two dual-GPU cards. You should check the recommended setups for high framerates for those games, but I would think it's probably likely to require something of that order.

. . .

Ranbir: With all these components, you're going to need a very good cooling system. Luckily, I'm a cooling specialist. When building the PC, I'll design a cooling system for you that'll ensure your components won't overheat even if you overclock them aggressively.

. . .

Ranbir: This is a top-notch gaming rig you've put together. Once you see how it performs, I guarantee you won't regret spending all this money on it.

. . .

Graeme: I think I'll go for the [name of video card]. It's best value for money.

Ranbir: For now, yes, but given how resource-intensive games are getting, if you want to future-proof your system, you're better off going for a card one level higher, say [name of alternative video card].

. . .

Graeme: When do you think you'll be able to deliver the system?

Ranbir: It'll be ready for collection on 21 March.

6.1 Introduction: contracting and the identification of the terms

Problem 6 illustrates a common scenario. Rather than a long, written document setting out terms in depth and detail, all we have here is a set of oral discussions between the parties. How, then, do we determine what the terms of the parties' agreement were? Which bits of the parties' discussions were contractual, and which were not?

There are three broad types of cases in which the courts have to answer questions like this. The first is when the parties reach agreement on certain terms in the course of discussions, but do not write them down, or only write some of them down. Problem 6 is an example, and the majority of contracts that people enter into fall into this category. If such a case comes to court, the court has to identify the matters on which the parties reached agreement, and what they actually decided on those matters. This usually involves going through everything the parties said and did, and assembling a contract from that material. The contract the court assembles, needless to say, is not the agreement it thinks the parties *ought* to have reached. It is, instead, the agreement that it believes the parties *actually* reached.

The second situation arises where the parties have produced a written document, but disagree on whether the document was intended to be a complete record of their agreement, ie whether they also reached agreement on other matters, which for some reason or another they did not write down in that document. Here, the main task for the courts is determining what the parties intended. Did they intend the written document to be a complete record of their agreement? Or did they intend it to be only a partial record, supplemented and extended by terms left unwritten?

The third situation is where the parties 'contracted in' to terms that were written elsewhere, and possibly by someone else. Think of a car park or a ticket to a performance. You'll often see a notice saying that your use of the car park, or your attendance at the performance, is subject to the operator's or venue's terms and conditions. These may sometimes be displayed in a notice by the ticket machine or via a hyperlink on the website from which you're buying the ticket. In commercial transactions, you often have situations where parties agree to be bound by a **standard form contract** that is widely used in the industry, but is produced by a third party, such as an industry association. In some sectors of commerce, such as construction, this is the main method of contracting. How does 'contracting in' in this way work? Are there certain minimum criteria that must be met, in terms of notice, for example?

These are the questions we will consider in this chapter. We'll begin, in section 6.2, with unwritten contracts, focusing on oral negotiations, and see how the courts go about the job of separating the wheat from the chaff—of identifying which statements, out of everything the parties said and did, were intended to have contractual force. We will then move on to written documents (section 6.3), and examine what impact the existence of a written contract has on other terms which a party argues were agreed, but which were not written down in the contract. We'll conclude by looking at **incorporation** (section 6.4), and examine the criteria the law sets for holding that external terms were validly incorporated into a contract.

6.2 Unwritten contracts

6.2.1 Types of statements: puff, representations, and terms

Let us start with the first category, unwritten contracts. This is the most common category in everyday life. Most purchases at shops, for instance, are not governed by written terms (with some exceptions, such as furniture or household goods). In such cases, the task for the courts is to look at the things the parties said and did, and extract contractual terms from that material. What did the parties contractually bind themselves to doing, guaranteeing, or achieving?

As with many things in contract law, the courts treat this as a question of the parties' intent. Intention is always assessed objectively: the fact that a party did not actually intend to be bound by a term does not matter if their acts and words indicated that they did. In practice, determining what the parties intended is not always straightforward. In a number of the cases we will study in this section, and elsewhere in this chapter, by the time the case came to court, the parties could no longer agree on what their intention was. In such cases, the court is asked to choose between two alternative accounts of the parties' transaction, each portraying the parties' words and intention in very different lights.

English law approaches this task by sorting out the statements made by the parties into three categories: statements that are '**mere puff**', statements that are factual '**representations**', and statements that are intended to be contractual **terms**. Statements that fall within the first of these categories have no legal effect; statements that fall within the second have some legal effect although they are not contractual; while statements that fall within the third are treated as fully binding contractual provisions.

6.2.2 Mere puff

The first, and lowest, level consists of statements which the law treats as being mere puff. These are the easiest to identify. Statements which are just 'sales talk', which were not intended to be taken literally, and which no reasonable person would have taken literally, are treated as 'mere puff'. Think, for example, about the sort of signs you might see in a typical British tourist town:

Illustration 6.1

We serve the
BEST ice cream
in the world!

The scariest show ever!
Absolute terror
guaranteed!

It will be clear to most people that these claims are not literal statements of fact, and the person making them does not actually promise that they are true. This is precisely what the category of 'mere puff' is intended to capture, and it is for that reason that such statements have no legal effect. The Supreme Court of New Zealand defined 'puffs' as 'extravagant phrasing which would naturally be discounted by sensible persons',[1] which is also a good summary of the position at English law. Thus the courts have held that the words 'strong, holdfast, thiefproof' in relation to a safe,[2] and 'foolproof' in relation to a towing coupling,[3] were mere puff, and carried no legal consequences.

But this is not a hard-and-fast rule. Depending on the facts of the case, the court may hold that a statement that otherwise would have seemed to be puff did, in fact, convey some assurance as to the quality of the goods being sold. In *Osborn v Hart*,[4] for example, the seller had described port as being 'superior old port'. The substance actually sold, however, was of very poor quality, bordering on undrinkable. The court held that the words amounted to a contractual term that the port was superior. In much the same way, a statement that, in isolation, might have seemed like a term or a representation could be held to be puff, if the context suggests that it was not intended to be taken seriously or literally. In *Dimmock v Hallett*,[5] an auctioneer selling a parcel of land described it as 'fertile and improvable'. In reality, part of the land had been abandoned as useless. On the purchaser's suit, the Court of Appeal held that the statement should 'be looked at as a mere flourishing description by an auctioneer'.[6] In the context of an auction, a statement such as this was not intended to be taken as important, and would not carry legal consequences, 'except in extreme cases—as, for instance, where a considerable part is covered with water, or otherwise irreclaimable'.[7]

6.2.3 **Representations and terms**

A representation is a statement of fact, which is made in the course of contracting in order to induce the other party to enter into a contract. However, although it is connected with the contract, it does not actually form part of the contract. Unlike a term, the party making a representation does not promise to ensure that he will secure or has secured the state of affairs set out in the representation. He merely states that he believes it to be true.

The question of whether something is a term or a representation ultimately depends on the intention of the parties, objectively determined. If the parties intended a statement to have contractual effect, it will be treated as a term. If they did not, it will be treated as a mere representation.

---

1. *Turner v Anquetil* [1953] NZLR 952, 957 (Adams J).
2. *Walker v Milner* (1866) 4 F & F 745, 176 ER 773. The safe was, in fact, broken into by a burglar in half an hour using perfectly ordinary equipment.
3. *Lambert v Lewis* [1980] 2 WLR 299, 327 (CA). The House of Lords overruled the decision of the Court of Appeal on another point, but did not disagree with its finding that the statement was puff.
4. (1871) 23 LT 851.   5. (1866–7) LR 2 Ch App 21.
6. Ibid, 27 (GJ Turner LJ).   7. Ibid.

Unlike puffs, both representations and terms are legally binding. However, because representations are not terms of the contract, a breach of a representation does not give you the ability to bring an action for breach of contract. It gives you, instead, an entirely separate action for **misrepresentation** (Chapter 11). Arguing that a particular statement is not a term, but merely a representation, is therefore a legitimate defence to an action for breach of contract. This gives the distinction considerable practical importance.

In assessing whether the parties intended a statement to be a term or a representation, the courts use a combination of three separate factors, which they weigh against the particular facts of each case. These factors are the *importance* of the statement to the parties, the *relative expertise* of the two parties, and whether the party making the statement *assumed responsibility* for its correctness.

Importance

The first factor which the courts take into account is the importance of the statement to the parties. In general, the more important a particular statement was to the parties, the likelier it is that the courts will hold it to be a term of the contract. If the statement is so important that the buyer would not have entered into the contract if it hadn't been made, it is almost certain to be a term of the contract rather than a representation.

The classic case on this point is *Couchman v Hill*.[8] Here, two heifers were being sold at auction. As they were led into the ring, the claimant—who ultimately won the action—asked the auctioneers as well as the sellers if they could confirm that the heifers were 'unserved' (ie that they had never been mated with a bull). Both replied that the heifers were unserved. Two months later, however, a six-month old fetus was removed from one of the heifers. The heifer in question subsequently died because she had carried a calf at a very young age. Clearly, this meant that the heifer was *not* unserved at the time of the auction. The buyer sued. One of the questions that came up for consideration was whether the statement in question was a term or a representation.[9] The Court of Appeal held that it was a term of the contract, in part because of its importance to the claimant.

Similarly, in *Bannerman v White*,[10] a purchaser of hops had asked the seller whether sulphur had been used in treating the hops. He said that he would 'not even ask the price if any sulphur had been used'. The seller replied: 'there was no mould this year, and therefore no occasion to use any sulphur'. It transpired that sulphur had been used on a small proportion of the hops, but these had been so thoroughly mixed with the others that they could not be separated. Here, too, the court held that statement to be a term rather than a representation. Both parties knew that the statement was of such importance to the purchaser that he would not have gone on with the transaction if he had known it was false. As such, it would be contrary to the parties' intention to treat it as a representation.

---

8. [1947] KB 554 (CA).
9. There was also another issue, which we will consider in section 6.3.2.
10. (1861) 10 CB (NS) 844, 142 ER 685.

Special knowledge and expertise

The second relevant factor is the relative expertise of the two parties, or any special knowledge either of them had. If the party making the representation had special skill or knowledge which the other party did not share, the statement is likely to be a term of the contract. If, however, the parties had about the same degree of knowledge, or if the person to whom the statement was made had a greater degree of knowledge, the statement is likely to be a mere representation. The cases of *Oscar Chess Ltd v Williams*[11] and *Dick Bentley Productions v Harold Smith (Motors) Ltd*[12] neatly illustrate how this works in practice.

Case in depth: *Oscar Chess Ltd v Williams* [1957] 1 WLR 370 (CA)

Williams's mother owned an old Morris car, which she had purchased second hand in 1954. In 1955, Williams contracted with Oscar Chess to buy a new car from them, and to give his old car in part-exchange. The car's logbook showed it as having been first registered in 1948, and sold five times between then and 1955. Relying on this, Williams told Oscar Chess's salesman that the car was a 1948 model. The salesman consulted a trade manual which set out valuations for cars made in different years, and gave Williams an allowance of £290 on his new car.

Several months later, Oscar Chess discovered that the car was actually a 1939 model, and was worth no more than £175. The logbook had been forged by a previous owner. Because the external look of the car had not changed in that time, the 1939 model and the 1948 model looked identical. An inspection, even by someone 'with knowledge of motor-cars', would not have shown that it was older than 1948, which was why this had not been spotted earlier. Oscar Chess sued Williams, alleging breach of contract and claiming compensation of £115, the difference in value between what they allowed for the car and what it was really worth.

The majority of the Court of Appeal rejected the dealer's argument, and held that the statement in question was a representation, rather than a term, for two reasons. First, the court held that they were, in essence, faced with a choice between two alternative accounts of the transaction. In the first account, the import of Williams's statement that the car was a 1948 model was this:

> I believe it is a 1948 Morris. Here is the registration book to prove it.

In the second account, its import was this:

> I guarantee that it is a 1948 Morris. This is borne out by the registration book, but you need not rely solely on that. I give you my own guarantee that it is.

The first account would make the statement a representation, whereas the second would make it a term. On the facts, the court held that the first account was likelier to reflect the parties' intention. Denning LJ pointed out that Williams had no personal knowledge of the year

→

---

11. [1957] 1 WLR 370 (CA).   12. [1965] 1 WLR 623 (CA).

> →
>
> in which the car was made, and was just relying on the logbook. As such, he was unlikely to have consented to warranting, as a term of the contract, that the logbook was correct.[13] This meant that it was only intended to be a representation, stating his belief.[14]
>
> Secondly, Denning LJ pointed out it was the purchasers who were the experts, not the sellers. Unlike Williams, who had no way of verifying the age of the car, Oscar Chess could have checked whether the car was a 1948 model, had they so chosen, by noting the engine and chassis numbers and writing to the manufacturers to enquire in which year a car bearing those numbers was made. They had failed to do so, and as a result the loss must lie where it fell.[15]
>
> Morris LJ dissented. He said that on the facts before the court, the statement made by Williams was 'definite and unqualified', not 'a mere expression of tentative or qualified belief'. The result was that the statement was 'adopted as the foundation of the contract' by the parties. It could not be treated as a mere representation, but had to be treated as a term.

We will return to Morris LJ's dissent in a short while, but for the present it is illustrative to contrast *Oscar Chess* with the case of *Dick Bentley Productions v Harold Smith (Motors) Ltd*,[16] where the court came to the opposite conclusion. Harold Smith were car dealers. Dick Bentley had been dealing with them for a couple of years. In 1959, he told Smith that he was interested in buying a 'well-vetted' car. In January 1960, Smith sold him a Bentley car, stating that the car had had a replacement engine and gearbox fitted, and that 'the vehicle had done 20,000 miles since the replacement engine and ancillary parts and gearbox'. The car gave Dick Bentley a lot of problems, and it emerged that the car had been in an accident, and fitted with a new body and gearbox after that accident. The speedometer had also been tampered with, reducing its reading from what should have been over 100,000 miles to 20,000 miles. The Court of Appeal held that Smith's statement was a term of the contract. The leading judgment was again given by Lord Denning, who distinguished this case from *Oscar Chess*. As an expert, he had more knowledge. In addition, because he was a dealer, he was also in a position to obtain the history of the car from its manufacturer, unlike the sellers in *Oscar Chess*. As a result, the statement was a term.[17]

Verification

The third factor that the courts take into account is the question of whether the party making the statement asks the other party to verify its accuracy. If he did, the statement is unlikely to be a contractual term. If, on the other hand, the representor gives an assurance that no verification is necessary, it is likely to be a term.

---

13. A similar point was made by the Court of Appeal in *Routledge v McKay* [1954] 1 WLR 615, which involved the sale of a motorcycle with a similarly forged registration certificate.
14. [1957] 1 WLR 370, 376 (Denning LJ).
15. Ibid, 377.   16. [1965] 1 WLR 623 (CA).   17. Ibid, 627–8.

In *Ecay v Godfrey*,[18] Godfrey sold a boat to Ecay. In the course of the discussions, he told Ecay that the boat was 'sea-going and capable of going overseas, in excellent condition and with a sound hull'. Before the sale went through, however, he also advised Ecay to have the board surveyed. The boat turned out to be in very poor shape (the court described it as 'very dicky') and Ecay sued for breach of contract. The High Court, however, held that the statement in question was a representation rather than a term. Godfrey had asked Ecay to carry out an independent survey of the boat. This suggested that he did not intend Ecay to rely on his statement.

In contrast, in *Schawel v Reade*,[19] Schawel was considering buying a horse from Reade to use as a stud. When Schawel was examining the horse, Reade told him 'you need not look for anything: the horse is perfectly sound', and went on to assure him that there was no need to have the horse fully examined by a vet, as Reade would let Schawel know if anything was wrong with the horse. As it happened, the horse suffered from a hereditary eye disease, which meant that it could not be used as a stud. Schawel sued. The court held that the statement was a term of the contract, on the basis of the strength of the assurance Reade gave Schawel.

6.2.4 **Applying the distinction**

When it comes to an unwritten contract, the essential task for a court is to determine which of the many things the parties may have said or done were intended to have contractual effect. The three factors discussed in section 6.2.3 are not, and should not be seen as, elements in a test which can be applied mechanically. The answer turns, rather, on the parties' intention, assessed with reference to the objective impression that their discussions gave.[20] Was there something in the facts of this particular case that suggested that the parties intended the statement of fact to be something more than a representation—something that would have contractual effect as a term of the contract?[21] The three factors are used by the courts as *indicators* of whether or not this is likely to have been the parties' intention. As a result, there is no set formula in relation to how we fit these factors together. No one factor trumps the others, and the presence or absence of one or more in a given case is never dispositive.

The manner in which this works in practice can be seen by revisiting the statements in Problem 6, and analysing whether they would be treated as terms, representations, or puff.

> To be honest, if you want to get the most out of them, you're going to need a four-way SLI setup, probably with two dual-GPU cards. You should check the recommended setups for high framerates on those games, but I would think it's probably likely to require something of that order.

18. (1947) 80 Lloyd's Rep 286 (KB).
19. [1913] 2 IR 64.
20. *Inntrepreneur Pub Co v East Crown Ltd* [2000] 2 Lloyd's Rep 611, [10] (Ch).
21. See the remarks of Viscount Haldane LC in *Heilbut, Symons & Co v Buckleton* [1913] AC 30, 39 (HL). See also *Routledge v McKay* [1954] 1 WLR 615, 623–4 (CA).

This is likely to be, at best, a representation. Note that Ranbir expressly asks Graeme to check the recommended setup. This, as we have seen, is the type of factor that, typically, makes the statement a representation rather than a term. Ranbir remains responsible for his statement's veracity, but under the law of misrepresentation rather than as a breach of contract.

> I'm a cooling specialist. When building the PC, I'll design a cooling system for you that'll ensure your components won't overheat even if you overclock them aggressively.

This statement, in contrast, is almost certainly a term. First, it has the form of a promise, rather than a statement of fact. Secondly, overheating is a major concern in gaming computers, so the statement is likely to be of importance to Graeme. Finally, Ranbir expressly holds himself out as an expert, and tells Graeme that he can rely on his expertise. These factors, as we have seen, are pretty strong indicators that the parties intended the statement to be a term, rather than a mere representation.

> Once you see how it performs, I guarantee you won't regret spending all this money on it.

This statement is a perfect example of mere puff. It is very obviously sales talk, which is not intended to be taken seriously. Could a seller ever *seriously* intend to make a binding promise that nothing, ever, could make a buyer regret his purchase? This is almost never likely to be the case.

> If you want to future-proof your system, you're better off going for a card one level higher.

This statement is likely to be treated as neither a representation nor a term, but a mere statement of opinion. Ranbir is not asserting any facts, implicitly or expressly. He is, instead, proffering an opinion—a guess—based on his view as to the type of games that are likely to be released in the future. As such, it is unlikely to have legal effect.

> It'll be ready for collection on 21 March.

This is clearly a term. A statement as to a collection date is a promise, which the parties will almost always have intended to have binding effect.

6.3 Written documents

6.3.1 The parol evidence rule

Let us now move on to the second type of situation, where the parties have reduced their agreement to writing. Consider, for example, a variation on Problem 6. Let's say that at the end of the discussion, the salesman, Ranbir, produces the document set out in Illustration 6.2. What is the effect of this document? Is the written document the entire contract, or can the parties still rely on their oral discussions?

Illustration 6.2

GAMETYNE COMPUTING
SALES ORDER

Order details

Sales order number:	CS 0214291/20
Date:	18 April 2019
Salesperson:	Ranbir

Customer details

Name:	Mr Graeme Belkins
Address:	4 Deanside Close
	Newton-upon-Wall
	Hadrianshire
Postcode:	HN1 3LQ
Tel:	0181 397430
Deposit paid:	£156.60
Balance due:	£1408.50
Payment method:	Debit Card
Estimated delivery date:	2 May 2017

System Specifications and price

Component	Description	Price
Processor	Intel Core i7 Extreme 3370K	£250.00
GPU 1	Nvidia GFX 730	£200.00
GPU 2	Nvidia GFX 730	£200.00
Motherboard	MSI GameXtreme 9200i	£175.00
RAM	16 GB Corsair Dual Channel 1600	£250.00
Audio	Soundblaster Gamer FX 32X	£150.00
Case	Coolermaster Overclocker Supercool	£125.00
Fans	6x HiCool Silent	£90.00
Heatsink	Heateater GPU-CPU combo cooling system	£125.00
Peripherals	NONE	£0.00
TOTAL		**£1565.00**

All sales are subject to our terms and conditions, which are printed on the reverse of this slip

Terms and Conditions of Sale

1 Definitions

'Customer' means the person named as the customer on the order form.

'System' means the personal computer assembled by GameTyne and sold to the Customer.

'System Specifications' means the specifications set out on the order form.

2 The system

2.1 GameTyne warrants that the System will be built to the System Specifications as set out on the order form. It is the Customer's responsibility to verify that these are correct prior to placing the order.

2.2 Whilst GameTyne's staff provide an advice service in selecting components, it is the Customer's responsibility to ensure that the System meets the Customer's requirements. GameTyne accepts no responsibility in the event that the Customer finds the System to be unsuitable after delivery.

2.3 It is the Customer's responsibility to ensure that any existing software, accessories or peripherals that he wishes to use with the System are compatible with the System. GameTyne does not guarantee that the System will be compatible with any software, accessories or peripherals that are not sold together with the System.

2.4 Cables, connectors, and other components not specifically mentioned in the System Specifications are not included in the System, and must be separately purchased.

3 Payment and delivery

3.1 The order is not complete until the Customer pays the minimum deposit specified on the order form. Until the deposit is paid, GameTyne reserves the right to revise the price stated on the order form, or to cancel the order.

3.2 Delivery is by collection from GameTyne's premises.

3.3 The Customer acknowledges that whilst GameTyne will endeavour to assemble the System by the estimated delivery date stated on the order form, it does not guarantee that the System will be available for collection on that date. GameTyne will notify the Customer when the System is ready for collection. Unless there are exceptional circumstances, this will be within five working days of the estimated delivery date.

3.4 The balance outstanding must be paid at the time of collection. In the case of payment by cheque, the Customer should allow at least five working days to clear payment. GameTyne will not release the System until it receives cleared funds.

4 Cancellation and returns

4.1 In the event the Customer wishes to cancel the order after placing it, GameTyne will make every effort to cancel the order. The Customer acknowledges, however, that GameTyne may not be in a position to cancel the order if assembly of the System has commenced, or if GameTyne has ordered components for the specific purpose of constructing the system.

4.2 If the Customer suspects that the System is faulty or defective during the guarantee period, he must contact GameTyne for an RMA no later than 96 hours after discovering the suspected fault or defect. GameTyne will at its option either repair any faults or replace the System with one of equivalent specification without cost to the Customer. If no faults or defects are found, the Customer will be liable to pay GameTyne's standard charge for a system check.

4.3 GameTyne also provides a repair service for the System outside the guarantee period. All use of this service will be charged at GameTyne's standard rates.

5 Warranty and liability

5.1 GameTyne warrants that the System will be free of defects for a period of nine months from the date of delivery. This warranty does not apply to any faults arising out of normal wear and tear, negligence by the Customer or any third party, or any failure to follow the operating instructions and recommended operating conditions specified by GameTyne or, if applicable, the manufacturer of any accessory, peripheral or component.

5.2 The warranty will cease with immediate effect in the event of any upgrade, alteration or repair to the System carried out by any party other than GameTyne.

5.3 GameTyne's warranty does not extend to pixel defects in any display supplied as part of the System. These defects are governed exclusively by the manufacturer's terms and conditions.

5.4 The Customer acknowledges that the System has been designed and sold for the Customer's personal use. GameTyne designs systems with an emphasis on gaming, and does not guarantee their suitability for any other purpose, including business purposes. GameTyne will not be liable for any loss the Customer may suffer as a result of the use of the System for any purposes other than gaming.

5.5 To the extent permitted by law, GameTyne's maximum liability to the Customer for any loss, damage or harm caused by any defect or fault in the System is limited to the price of the System. GameTyne disclaims all other liability to the fullest extent permissible by law. In particular, GameTyne will not be liable for any indirect or consequential loss, including without limitation loss of data, goodwill, or software, or for any third party claims.

6 Other terms

6.1 These Terms and Conditions, together with the System Specifications, constitute the entire agreement between GameTyne and the Customer, and supersede all previous discussions and correspondence between them. The Customer acknowledges that GameTyne's staff have no authority to vary the Terms and Conditions of Sale, and that any statements made by staff to the Customer are without legal effect, unless expressly set out in these Terms and Conditions or the System Specifications. To the extent permitted by law, GameTyne excludes all representations and warranties that are not expressly set out here.

6.2 Nothing set out in these Terms and Conditions affects the Customer's statutory rights.

In English law, the starting point in answering these questions lies in a rule called the **parol evidence rule**. 'Parol' is simply an old-fashioned word meaning 'speech' or 'spoken word' (compare modern French *parole*), and the rule originated in the law of evidence. It originally meant that the spoken word could not displace the written word—and, thus, that oral evidence of what the parties agreed on could not displace the evidence of the written contract.[22] In the modern context, however, the rule is a substantive rule and not one of evidence. It states, in effect, that if it appears that the parties intended the terms of a contract to be contained in a single document, then that document will be taken to be an exhaustive statement of the parties' agreement. Terms which are not present in that document, but which may be hinted at in records of other discussions, will not be read into the contract. In practice, this means, first, that the parties' agreement consists of the things that they wrote down and, secondly, that what they wrote down supersedes anything they may have said or done earlier or later.

UK 2000 Ltd v Weis[23] gives us a good idea of the implications of this rule, and the logic underlying it. In this case, the High Court was faced with a dispute arising out of a contract for the sale of land. The property had been sold at auction, and the successful purchaser signed a memorandum of sale. The property contained a *mikvah*—a Jewish ritual bath—with accommodation above it. The vendors' intent was to exclude both the bath and the accommodation above it from the sale. Due to a mix-up, the description of the property in the memorandum that was signed only excluded the bath and not the accommodation. The auctioneer testified that he had, before the auction, said that both the bath and the accommodation were excluded. The court held that the parol evidence rule applied, with the result that it was what was in the written document that prevailed. The auctioneers could have ensured that the description of the property in the memorandum was amended to incorporate the auctioneer's oral statement. If they had done so, the purchaser could have disputed the position and, if need be, withdrawn.[24] But if the written addendum conflicted with the oral statement, it was the addendum that would prevail.

As this suggests, the parol evidence rule—at least in its modern form—is linked to the notion of a 'moment of responsibility', which underlies much of the law of contract. Because the law relies on this idea of a particular single moment when the parties' agreement crystallizes, it is necessarily driven to linking the content of the parties' agreement to a single moment. If the crystallization took the form of a written document, then the content of the parties' agreement, too, will be tied to that document. Things which a party may have believed, but did not put in the document, will not be taken to have been part of the parties' contract.

The parol evidence rule is, therefore, logical; but it is based on an oversimplified understanding of how contracts actually form. As we have seen in Chapter 2, not all contracts come into being at a single, well-defined moment of responsibility. If the parol evidence rule were to be enforced rigidly, therefore, it would have had the potential to cause a significant amount of mischief. Fortunately, the parol evidence rule is not as rigid as it may seem to be at first glance. It has several exceptions, two of which are relevant to our discussion in this chapter.

22. *Goss v Lord Nugent* (1833) 5 B & Ad 58 (KB), 64–5 (Denham CJ).
23. [2004] EWHC 2830 (Ch).   24. Ibid, [52] (Steinfeld QC).

6.3.2 **Exceptions to the rule**

Interpreting a contract

The first exception is that the parol evidence rule does not apply to interpreting a contract. If a court is trying to find out what the terms of a contract *mean*, rather than what they *are*, it can and often will look to other records of the parties' discussions.

We will look at this issue in greater detail in Chapter 7, but the basic point is well illustrated by the case of *Hamid v Francis Bradshaw Partnership*.[25] This case related to the construction of a showroom. The claimant owned the showroom and the defendant was the engineer involved in constructing the showroom. The contract between the two had been written down on headed notepaper and signed by both the parties. It did not, however, make it clear whether the defendant had signed the contract on his own behalf or on behalf of a particular company which he owned and controlled. The claimant said it was on his own behalf, whereas the defendant claimed he'd signed it on behalf of the company.

The court held that the parol evidence rule would not prevent the court from examining other records to determine who the parties to the contract actually were. This was not a question of asking what the terms of the contract *were*, but rather of asking what they *meant* in a situation where it was unclear who they were intended to bind.[26] For much the same reasons, the High Court in *Bunn v Rees*[27] held that the parol evidence rule would not prevent one of the parties from using extrinsic evidence to demonstrate that the parties did not intend to create legal relations, despite having prepared a document setting out terms. Here, again, the question was not what the terms were, but what their significance was.

'Not a complete record'

The relevance of completeness

A more important, but also more difficult, exception is that the parol evidence only applies if the parties intended the written document 'to constitute their contract'.[28] The intention that a written document 'constitutes' a contract entails two things. First, the parties must have intended the written document to record their agreement and, secondly, they must have intended it to be a *complete* record of that agreement.

Both of these elements are vital, and they can be easily illustrated by returning to Illustration 6.2. Assume that the parties only produced the list of specifications at the front of the document, without the footer at the bottom or the terms on the reverse. It is evident that a list of specifications is not intended to be a written contract. It *does* intend to record something of what the parties agreed—namely, a description of the goods that would be made to order—but it is not, in any sense, a record of the agreement. In contracting terms, it is more like a technical appendix to a contract, rather than being the contract itself. As a result, when it comes to the question of what the

---

25. [2013] EWCA Civ 470.

26. In contrast, if it is clear from the agreement who the parties are, the parol evidence rule *will* apply. See *Excalibur Ventures LLC v Texas Keystone Inc* [2013] EWHC 2767 (Comm), [268]–[270] (Christopher Clarke LJ).

27. [2002] EWHC 693 (QB).

28. *Leduc & Co v Ward* (1888) 20 QBD 475, 480 (Lord Esher MR).

terms of the contract actually were, a court will almost certainly look beyond the written document to the parties' discussions, to try and extract the terms of the contract
from those discussions.

But now consider a situation where the document does have the footer and the terms
on the reverse of Illustration 6.2. You can see how this completely changes the legal
significance of the document. The document now contains a lot more than the specifications of the product. It sets out terms which define the respective rights, responsibilities, and obligations of the parties. Here, it is likely that the parties intended the
contract to be a complete record of their agreement. In such a case, it is *unlikely* that
a court seeking to determine the terms will look beyond the written document. The
wording of clause 6—the 'entire agreement' clause[29]—in particular will lend support to
the proposition that this is all the parties wanted to be bound by.

Often, however, we are dealing with situations that fall between these two extremes.
Here, the essential question the court is asking is whether the parties *intended* the
document to be a complete record of their agreement or whether they intended it to
be only a partial record. In the former case, the court will treat the contract as being
completely written, and the parol evidence rule will apply. The parties will not be able
to argue that there were other terms which they did not put in the contract. In the latter case, however, we will have a situation where the contract is partially written and
partially oral, with the oral terms supplementing and varying the written terms. Here,
the parties will be able to argue, based on oral and written evidence, that the contract
contained terms that were not in the written document.

Assessing completeness

How, then, do courts go about determining into which of these two categories a given
situation falls? The first circumstance the courts will take into account relates to the
nature of the document itself. If the document is missing terms that were of importance, or that a complete contract would have needed to cover, it will not be treated
as a complete record of the parties' understanding. The decision of the High Court in
Interoil SA v Watford Petroleum[30] provides a good example. This case involved a complex
transaction spread across multiple contracts and involving, on the side of the claimants,
several companies which belonged to the same group. The defendants sought to argue
that one of the contracts envisaged the involvement of persons who were members of
the same group of companies as the claimant, but who were not actually named on the
document. The court held that the parol evidence rule would not prevent the defendants from seeking to prove this. The defendants' argument was in essence an argument
that the parties had agreed that these persons should have a role, but that a definition
of the role was missing from the contract. If this was correct, then the contract could
not have been intended to be a complete record of the parties' agreement—a complete
record would have set out the roles of all persons involved performing in the contract.[31]

The question is a lot more difficult if the contract on its face looks like a complete
contract and could have been a complete contract, but where one of the parties argues

---

29. See the box 'Practice in context: entire agreement clauses'.
30. [2005] EWHC 894 (Ch).   31. Ibid, [26] (Peter Smith J).

that it was not in fact intended to be a complete record of the parties' understanding. The general approach which the courts take in such circumstances was explained by Lord Russell CJ in *Gillespie Brothers & Co v Cheney, Eggar & Co*:[32]

> although when the parties arrive at a definite written contract the implication or presumption is very strong that such contract is intended to contain all the terms of their bargain, it is a presumption only, and it is open to either of the parties to allege that there was, in addition to what appears in the written agreement, an antecedent express stipulation not intended by the parties to be excluded, but intended to continue in force with the express written agreement.[33]

This means that it is not enough for one party to produce a written agreement. A contract that looks complete creates a strong presumption that it was intended to be a complete record of the agreement, but this is no more than a presumption. If a party alleges otherwise, the parol evidence rule will not stop them from trying to prove their case. The court will, in such a case, look at the facts in their entirety to determine what the parties intended.

The precise nature of what the court is being asked to decide in such cases was explained very well in *Couchman v Hill*,[34] the case of the pregnant heifer discussed in section 6.2.3. The printed conditions of sale provided that the animals being sold were sold 'with all faults, imperfections and errors of description'. The court, therefore, had to also consider the question of whether the sellers' oral statement that the heifers were 'unserved' overrode the written document.

In the Court of Appeal, Scott LJ said that the court was being asked to choose between two alternative, and mutually incompatible, accounts of the transaction. In the first account, favourable to the seller, the question in essence meant this:

> Having regard to the onerous stipulations which I know I shall have to put up with if I bid and the lot is knocked down to me, can you give me your honourable assurance that the heifers have in fact not been served? If so, I will risk the penalties of the catalogue.[35]

The second account, in contrast, would hold that the question meant this:

> I am frightened of contracting on your published terms, but I will bid if you will tell me by word of mouth that you accept full responsibility for the statement in the catalogue that the heifers have not been served, or, in other words, give me a clean warranty. That is the only condition on which I will bid.[36]

If the first account represented the intention of the parties, the oral statement would clearly not have been intended to have contractual effect. If, however, it was the second account that came closer to capturing what the parties intended, then the statement would have been intended to form part of the parties' agreement, even though it expressly contradicted the terms set out in the written agreement.

Which of these accounts is the correct one depends entirely on the facts. In *Couchman* itself, the Court of Appeal held that it was the second account that captured the parties' intent. But, obviously, this will vary from case to case, and the application of the

---

32. [1986] 2 QB 59.   33. Ibid, 62.   34. [1947] KB 554 (CA).
35. Ibid, 558.   36. Ibid.

parol evidence rule is therefore very heavily fact-dependent. The next section considers this issue in more detail.

6.3.3 **The centrality of the facts**

When it comes to actually applying these rules, the mere fact that the parties have signed a written agreement is not, by itself, conclusive. If the facts suggest that it was not intended to be a complete record of their agreement, the courts will not treat it as if it was. *Burley v Joseph W Burley Partners Ltd*[37] is a good illustration. This case involved an agreement between two brothers, Joseph and Kenneth Burley, in relation to the family business. In 1966, Joseph convinced Kenneth to leave his job with the AA, and to instead come and work in the family business—a firm of insurance brokers. Kenneth was not unwilling, but he had a generous final salary pension scheme with the AA which he was reluctant to give up (it would have provided him with a pension of two-thirds of his final salary). Joseph said he would make arrangements to give him the same pension from the family business.

The scheme in which Kenneth was enrolled in the family business, however, was based on the actual returns from investing the amounts that were paid in. The maximum pension payable was capped at two-thirds of his final salary, and he would only have been eligible for that if he had worked for 40 years for the firm. However, the trustee also had the discretion to order the payment of a higher pension than the amount that had accrued.

When Kenneth retired, the pension that had accrued was well below two-thirds of his final salary. Joseph was dead and his successor did not top up the pension beyond what had accrued, on the basis that the written document did not provide for it, and the written document was intended to be the entirety of the parties' agreement. The Court of Appeal rejected this argument. It was perfectly legitimate for the court to go into the question of whether there was an oral agreement as Kenneth alleged. The parol evidence rule was no bar to an argument that the written document was not the entire agreement.[38]

The parol evidence rule does not, in other words, operate as a bar every time there is a written document setting out contractual terms. But the court's willingness to look beyond the written document cannot be taken for granted. It is for the party arguing that the written document was not a complete record to make a case that it was so. If the party cannot adduce sufficient evidence showing this, the courts will apply the parol evidence rule, and treat the written document as a complete record.

In *Techarungreungkit v Alexander Götz*,[39] an antiques gallery had entered into a contract with a prospective seller to buy an antique Buddha statue. As required under the contract, the gallery had given the seller cheques for the purchase price. When the statue was examined by experts, it was pronounced a fake. The gallery then argued that there was an oral understanding between the parties to the effect that the cheques would not be cashed unless the statue was authenticated by the experts. They had been given as a gesture of goodwill and a sign of sincerity, rather than as final payment. The

---

37. [2002] EWCA Civ 1163.   38. Ibid, [17]–[30] (Rix LJ).   39. [2003] EWHC 58 (QB).

court rejected the gallery's argument, on the basis that no evidence had been presented to suggest that the parties had intended the written document to be anything other than a complete record of the parties' agreement.

As these two cases suggest, the question of whether or not a written document was intended to be a complete record of the agreement turns very heavily on the specific facts of the case. The next two cases illustrate just how significant the facts can be. In *National Westminster Bank Plc v Binney*,[40] the court came to the conclusion that the parties intended the written document to be a complete record of their understanding, and consequently rejected the defendant's argument that there was an oral contract that restricted the claimant's ability to exercise its rights under the written document. In *Lloyds TSB Bank Plc v Norman Hayward*,[41] in contrast, the court—on facts that at first glance seem quite similar—came to exactly the opposite conclusion.

Case in depth: *National Westminster Bank Plc v Binney* [2011] EWHC 694 (QB)

Binney, a businessman, was a director and minority shareholder of a company called Kay Management Consultants (KMC). NatWest had extended lending facilities to KMC. KMC's financial position began deteriorating, and NatWest told Binney that it would require a guarantee, or some other security, from him in order to continue lending to KMC. Binney signed a written guarantee for £100,000. Subsequently, Binney also supplied funds of a further £100,000 to KMC. Despite this, KMC went into administration, and NatWest demanded that Binney pay £100,000 under the guarantee.

Binney argued that there had been an oral understanding between him and NatWest that the guarantee would be in place only until he either provided an equivalent amount of funding to KMC directly, or provided some other form of security to NatWest. He said that it had been agreed that once he did this, NatWest would tear up the guarantee. By supplying funds of £100,000 to KMC, he had met this requirement, and the guarantee should therefore be taken as having come to an end.

This understanding, he said, was reached orally between him and his Relationship Manager at NatWest, at the meeting in which he signed the guarantee. It was on the basis of this understanding that he signed the guarantee. NatWest replied by arguing that under the parol evidence rule, this term could not be read into the contract. Binney sought to argue that the parol evidence rule would not apply.

Eder J in the High Court upheld NatWest's argument, and found Binney liable on the guarantee. He held that this would be so regardless of whether or not the parol evidence rule applied. Binney, he said, was 'a highly intelligent, articulate, confident, financially experienced and competent businessman' who 'was used to dealing with banks and to signing financial documents; and had previously signed at least one personal guarantee'. It was 'improbable in the extreme that he would have been prepared to sign the present Guarantee as it stood without qualification if it had been subject to some special term, warranty or assurance amounting to a representation not contained in the Guarantee itself or otherwise confirmed in writing at the time'.[42]

→

---

40. [2011] EWHC 694 (QB).   41. [2005] EWCA Civ 466.   42. Ibid, [52].

> →
>
> Eder J went on to hold that even if, for reasons of time pressure, he initially agreed to sign a guarantee that left out a crucial term (that it would expire when the company was funded), 'a person of Mr Binney's considerable financial experience would have made sure as soon as possible after that meeting that he notified the Bank and confirmed what he now says was the position with regard to the Guarantee'.[43] Binney's explanation, which he put forward in giving evidence, was that he trusted the Relationship Manager with whom he was dealing, and as a result saw no need to insist upon a written document. The court held that this evidence was not credible, as it did not fit with the type of businessman Binney was. As a result, the court held that the only terms that bound the parties were those in the written guarantee, which meant that Binney was liable.

Put simply, the court's view was that when experienced business people are dealing with each other, and when they record their agreement in a detailed written document, they will not usually have intended to be bound by any terms that were not in the document. The fact that a term, which one party alleges they agreed, was not in the document suggests that at least one of the parties did not intend it to be binding, even if it was discussed.

It is tempting to see this decision as setting out a clear rule to the effect that any purported oral agreement that restricts the ability of a bank to invoke a written guarantee will not be enforceable unless it is actually written down. But this is not, in fact, true. Deciding whether something was intended to be a complete agreement is very much a question of fact. This means that cases which, on their surface, look very similar can produce completely different results, simply because of the view the court takes of the facts of each case.

Lloyds TSB Bank Plc v Norman Hayward[44] is such a case, and presents an interesting contrast to *NatWest v Binney*. The case arose out of a set of guarantees given by the shareholders of a football club, AFC Bournemouth, to Lloyds TSB, the club's lenders. At a meeting on 23 November 1994, Lloyds TSB entered into a lending arrangement with AFC Bournemouth, which was recorded in a Facility Letter. Hayward, who was the principal shareholder and chairman, had earlier given Lloyds substantial guarantees in relation to the club's debts, which the Facility Letter continued. In addition, further guarantees were given by Gardiner, the leader of a new consortium of investors who were injecting cash into the club (and who was in the process of replacing Hayward as chairman). However, the meeting continued for several hours after the Facility Letter was signed. Hayward argued that during that time, the parties had orally agreed on further terms that significantly reduced his liability under the guarantees. These, he said, superseded the terms of the Facility Letter.

Counsel for Lloyds urged the court to reject this argument. The argument as made, they argued, would 'seem to have lost sight of the parol evidence rule'. There was a detailed written contract here, and the presumption that it contained all the terms the parties had agreed was very strong. The Court of Appeal agreed with this as a general proposition. However, it held that on the facts there was more than enough ground

---

43. Ibid.   44. Ibid.

to examine whether an oral agreement had been entered into. After a detailed examination of the documentary record—including internal notes in Lloyds TSB's files—it came to the conclusion that the oral agreement urged by Hayward had indeed come into existence, and that it superseded the written terms in the Facility Letter.

Why, then, did the courts come to such a different conclusion of the facts of this case, when compared with *NatWest v Binney*? The judgment suggests that it came down to the facts. In *Binney*, the course of the parties' dealings, taken together with the documentary record and the evidence given by the witnesses, suggested that no oral agreement had been concluded. In *Lloyds v Hayward*, in contrast, the documentary record pointed in the other direction. As these cases suggest, therefore, the question is primarily a factual one, which will be determined by the evidence placed before the court. This will very often come down to the simple question of which of the parties the court believes.

 Debates in context: rule, proposition, or approach?

The fact-specificity of the parol evidence rule has led some commentators to question whether it is a rule at all. The strongest statement of this position came in a report issued by the Law Commission in 1986.[45] Once the cases were considered, the Law Commission said, it became clear 'that there is no *rule of law* that evidence is rendered inadmissible or is to be ignored solely because a document exists which looks like a complete contract. Whether it is a complete contract depends upon the intention of the parties, objectively judged, and not on any rule of law.'[46]

The result, the Law Commission said, was that it was incorrect to call the parol evidence rule a 'rule'. What it was, instead, was a legal *proposition*. In substance, it was no more than a circular statement in this form:

> when it is proved or admitted that the parties to a contract intended that all the express terms of their agreement should be as recorded in a particular document or documents, evidence will be inadmissible (because irrelevant) if it is tendered only for the purpose of adding to, varying, subtracting from or contradicting the express terms of that contract.[47]

The Law Commission's views have attracted support from a range of commentators, including the editors of *Chitty on Contract*. Not everybody, however, agrees. Older case law did quite clearly—and expressly—take the position that it is a rule. Thus in *Jacobs v Batavia and General Plantations Trust Ltd*,[48] the High Court described the parol evidence rule as 'a rule of law' which was 'firmly established'. More recent cases, too, have referred to it as a rule.[49]

A few academic commentators have also dissented. Professor Treitel, one of the leading contract scholars of the 20th century, has taken the view that, contrary to what the Law Commission suggests, the parol evidence rule is very much a rule of law, and cannot be

→

45. Law Commission of England and Wales, *Law of Contract: The Parol Evidence Rule* (Law Com No 154, Cmnd 9700, 1986).

46. Ibid, para 2.17.   47. Ibid, para 2.7.   48. [1924] 1 Ch 287.

49. See eg *Shogun Finance Ltd v Hudson* [2004] 1 AC 919, [49] (Lord Hobhouse).

→

reduced to a circular definition.[50] Treitel's point, in essence, is that the Law Commission assumes that the parties have a common intention on whether or not the written document constitutes a complete record of their agreement. But, he argues, the rule is most often invoked precisely in situations where the parties do *not* have such a common intention. To the contrary, they are in active disagreement about this very point. And the solution the parol evidence rule posits goes well beyond the objective test. The objective test would hold only that the parties cannot rely on unspoken and uncommunicated intent. The parol evidence rule, in contrast, holds that the parties cannot even rely on intent that was spoken, communicated, and agreed, if it does not find a place in the document.[51]

There is certainly merit in Professor Treitel's view. The cases we have seen show that while the parol evidence rule is clearly not a bright-line rule, it nevertheless seems to do some work that goes beyond what the objective test would do. Nevertheless, the extent to which the answers given depend on the facts seems to suggest that it is a lot more content-light than, for example, the rules on offer and acceptance or the rules on consideration.

A better term would be to describe it as an 'approach', rather than a rule in the strict sense or a mere circular proposition, neither of which seem to accurately describe its role. What the parol evidence rule does is to set out how courts go about the task of determining when evidence of an oral understanding is admissible where the parties have also reduced their agreement to writing. This is precisely what the phraseology of 'approach' captures. Thinking about the parol evidence rule as an approach, rather than a rule, goes a long way towards understanding what it stands for, and how it is applied by the courts in actual cases.

 Practice in context: entire agreement clauses

This agreement (together with the documents referred to herein as from time to time amended) constitutes the entire agreement between the parties with respect to the matters dealt with herein and supersedes any previous agreement between the parties in relation to such matters.[52]

Variants of this clause are endemic in commercial contracts. Given what we have just studied in this section, it is relatively straightforward to guess at their purpose. Their aim is to bring the parol evidence rule into operation. By declaring that this document does, in fact, contain the entire agreement between the parties, clauses such as these aim to ensure that a court hearing a dispute does not hold the parties to any terms other than those they have put in their agreement.

Do they work? The answer is 'mostly'.

In general, the courts are very sympathetic to entire agreement clauses. Much may have been said and done in the course of the very lengthy negotiations that can sometimes precede the formation of a contract. It is perfectly understandable that the parties might want to wipe

→

50. E Peel, *Treitel on the Law of Contract* (13th edn, Sweet & Maxwell 2011) 6-013.   51. Ibid.
52. *Sere Holdings Ltd v Volkswagen Group United Kingdom* [2004] EWHC 1551 (Ch).

→

the slate clean, and make it clear that none of those statements have anything at all to do with the written document. The courts have repeatedly stressed the commercial importance this can have. In *Inntrepreneur Pub Co Ltd v East Crown Ltd*,[53] for example, Lightman J explained the rationale behind entire agreement clauses in these terms:

> The purpose of an entire agreement clause is to preclude a party to a written agreement from threshing through the undergrowth and finding in the course of negotiations some (chance) remark or statement (often long forgotten or difficult to recall or explain) on which to found a claim . . .

The courts appreciate that, for this reason, 'entire agreement' clauses are an essential part of the toolkit of contract drafting, and have therefore tended to give effect to them. At the same time, however, the courts have also been at pains to stress that this is not a hard-and-fast rule. The effect of an entire agreement clause will, ultimately, be only what the parties intended it to be. There may well be cases where, on a proper **construction**, the entire agreement clause does not mean what a literal meaning would suggest. This point was emphasized by Moore-Bick LJ in *Ravennavi SpA v New Century Shipbuilding Co Ltd*.[54]

> The effect of an entire agreement clause . . . must depend primarily on its terms, since it is the language chosen by the parties to express their agreement . . . which, construed in its proper context, provides the primary source of their intentions . . . There may be circumstances, of course, in which the court can be satisfied that a clause . . . was not intended by the parties to operate in the way in which its terms would suggest, but any such conclusion must be borne out by the particular circumstances of the case.[55]

It should be noted that there are few reported cases in which the courts have actually read down entire agreement clauses. Nevertheless, the fact that they reserve the power to do so in appropriate cases is significant, and should be borne in mind.

6.4 Incorporation: things referred to

6.4.1 The logic of 'contracting in'

Let us now consider a contract that has been entered into in a manner that is halfway between the two extremes of a completely written contract and a completely oral contract. Look at this transcript of a phone call between two businessmen:

Illustration 6.3

A: So you're happy to accept our quote?

B. Yeah, on the basis of the changes to the schedule of works we've just discussed.

→

---

53. [2000] 2 Lloyd's Rep 611, [7] (Ch). 54. [2007] EWCA Civ 58, [2007] 2 Lloyd's Rep 24.
55. Ibid, [25].

→

A: Yes, that's fine.

B: And we'll be contracting on the basis of the NEC3 Conditions of Contract.

A: Yeah, sure. NEC3 is fine by us.

B: Good. Ask your guys to contact my site engineer, so we can sort out access to the site and you can get started on your portion of the job.

The NEC3 Conditions of Contract are a set of standard form contracts that are very commonly used in the construction industry for large contracts. They are very long and extremely detailed, and have been drafted drawing on decades of experience with managing disputes that arise in construction projects. What the parties are seeking to do here is to *incorporate* these terms into the contract by merely making a reference to them, and agreeing that their provisions will form part of the parties' agreement. This particular example we consider above relates to the incorporation by reference of an elaborate set of standard terms. But it is also possible to incorporate single clauses by reference.

The reason why parties may choose to contract into terms is simple. First, writing a contract takes time and money, and when you're dealing with a contract as elaborate and comprehensive as the NEC3 Conditions of Contract, the cost involved in replicating them is extensive. In such a situation, opting into a ready-made contract is much cheaper. Secondly, contracts drafted by industry bodies tend to be comprehensive, covering things which an individual company might not have thought of, because they draw on the collective experience of an industry. Because they are used extensively in a wide range of situations, their provisions also tend to be tested in court more frequently, with the result that their meaning and effect is a lot more certain than would be the case for a contract specifically drafted for a transaction.

Incorporation is also often used in situations where dealing with a contract physically containing all the terms would be impractical. A contract of carriage is a good example. When you board a coach, or a ferry, or a train, you enter into a contract, but all you receive is a ticket. The ticket will often contain words stating that your agreement with the company is subject to certain standard terms and conditions, a copy of which may be obtained online (or, sometimes, from the ticket office). Here, incorporation by reference is necessary, because it would be impractical in the extreme to give each customer a full, printed copy of all the terms and conditions that apply.

Where the incorporation of external terms is fully and expressly agreed between the parties, both of whom are familiar with the terms being incorporated, incorporation raises no issues. Similarly, if the reference to the terms is contained in a document signed by the parties, the term will almost always be taken to have been incorporated. If a party signs a document of her own free will, she is taken to assent to everything contained in it, including an incorporation of external terms.

Problems, however, arise where the document that effects the incorporation is not a signed contract. Consider the following (fictitious) news item.

Illustration 6.4

They took my iPhone: student's horror experience at festival

For Tim, a 2nd year undergraduate at the University of Carmarthenshire, it seemed like the dream of a lifetime. His favourite bands were playing at a music festival close to his university, and he had managed to get excellent tickets. At the event itself, he found he had a clear view of the stage. Grabbing his iPhone, he began to take hi-res photos.

That was when the dream turned into a nightmare.

Within minutes, Tim had been accosted by two burly security guards who confiscated his iPhone, and ejected him from the event. Tim protested, but was told that entry to the concert was expressly conditional on not taking photos, videos, or any sound recordings. The organizers are now refusing to return his iPhone, saying that it has been confiscated.

Our reporters have since discovered that all tickets to the concert had these words printed on the front: 'Entry subject to conditions. See back for details.' The back of the ticket read, 'By purchasing this ticket, you agree to abide by our terms and conditions for events. The full terms and conditions are available on our website, and from the office.' On checking the website, we found that clause 9 of the terms and conditions says: 'Photography, videos, and audio recordings are strictly prohibited at all events. We reserve the right to confiscate any equipment being used in violation of this term. Confiscated equipment will be forfeited, and will not be returned.'

Tim is having none of it. 'They can't just keep my iPhone. I never agreed to that, and I can't believe they think they can rely on some obscure small print and get away with this.' The venue, however, was unrepentant. 'We've got to take strong action to deter people from making private recordings. Our terms and conditions made it very clear that we would do this, and we intend to enforce our rights strictly.'

A spokesperson for the festival refused to comment, saying that the dispute was a matter for Tim and the venue.

The approach of the courts in such cases is to ask not whether the party in question read and understood the term, but whether the party had the *opportunity* to read the term. If he had, then the term will be taken to be incorporated regardless of whether or not the term was actually read. What, then, constitutes 'an opportunity'? In English law, the courts answer this question not with reference to the actual condition of the person to whom notice is given, but with reference to the steps taken by the person giving notice. If the party seeking to incorporate the clause took 'reasonable steps' to bring the clause to the attention of the other party, the clause will usually be taken to be incorporated. In general, the courts look to three factors to decide whether or not the steps taken were reasonable: the *time* at which notice of the term was given;

the *nature* of the document in which it was given; and the *extent* to which notice was given, that is to say, the amount of attention that was drawn to the term.

We will look in some detail at each of these in the next three sections, but before we proceed to do that, it is worth noting that the approach taken by English law is quite counter-intuitive. Why does the court look at the party *incorporating* the term, rather than the party *receiving* the term? Logically, it would seem that the focus should be on the latter party rather than the former. But the courts have been very clear that this is not the approach taken by English law. The reason for the focus on the incorporator, rather than the person to whose attention the term is supposed to be drawn, becomes somewhat clearer if we return to a point made in Chapter 1—namely, the distinction between viewing a contract as a relationship and viewing it as a bundle of clearly defined and mostly discrete rights and duties. As we saw, the courts tend to take the latter approach. One consequence of this is that they tend to emphasize the need for the law to be certain. By this, they do not mean that the law must be so clear that the outcome of every case can be guessed in advance with a high degree of reliability—this is impossible to achieve. What they mean, rather, is that the law must provide a framework that is sufficiently clear for parties—particularly those engaging in large volumes of commercial transactions—to know what they generally need to do in order to comply with the law.

It is precisely this understanding that the law of incorporation reflects. The reason the focus is on the incorporator, and on the things the incorporator needs to do to have the term incorporated, is that such an approach provides certainty in the sense we have just discussed. A commercial entity seeking to have its transactions governed by a particular type of contract knows, in general, what it needs to do to achieve this outcome. If it does the things that English law considers necessary for 'sufficient notice' to be given, then it will in most cases manage to have the term incorporated. A relational approach, in contrast, would have focused on the reasonable expectations which *both* parties have as to the other's behaviour, thus leading the court to look both at the incorporator's conduct and at the opportunity this actually gave the other party. This is not the approach English law takes.

English law's focus on the incorporator, therefore, makes some sense, but it is nevertheless based on an understanding of contracting that, arguably, leaves out important implicit dimensions of contract. The results can sometimes be quite stark. In *Thompson v London, Midland and Scottish Railway Co Ltd*,[56] a railway company's tickets said, on their face 'see back', and the reverse said that the carriage was subject to detailed terms and conditions, which could be found in the company's timetable. The timetable was not free, and its cost was approximately 20 per cent of the cost of the journey Ms Thompson was undertaking. Ms Thompson herself was illiterate, and could not have read the words on the ticket, or the conditions even if she had access to the timetable. The Court of Appeal held, nevertheless, that the conditions printed in the timetable had been incorporated into the contract, because the company had taken reasonable steps to give notice to its passengers, even if those steps did not actually give Ms Thompson the opportunity to discover the terms of the contract. The situation would only have been different if the company had specific knowledge of Ms Thompson's

56. [1930] 1 KB 41.

disability, which it clearly did not.[57] A modern court hearing this case would probably place a slightly different weighting on the specific facts of the case—it might, for instance, require that the conditions be made available to customers for free—but that is a difference on what sort of conduct is required for 'reasonable' notice to be given. The basic approach remains the same: the court's focus is on the incorporator's conduct, rather than on the actual position of the other party.

With this background, let us now look in more detail at each of the three factors that English law uses to determine whether or not sufficient notice was given on the facts of a particular case.

6.4.2 **Timing**

On the question of timing, the law is both clear and simple. The reference to the terms that are sought to be incorporated must be made at or prior to the time of contracting. If the reference is made after the contract is entered into, the terms will not be incorporated. This is a direct consequence of the importance to English contract law of the idea of a moment of responsibility. Because the contract crystallizes at the moment of responsibility, notice given after that moment cannot give rise to contract terms.

The classic case on this point is *Olley v Marlborough Court*.[58] Mr and Mrs Olley stayed for several months in Marlborough Court, a private residential hotel. When they arrived, they checked in and paid a week's board in advance at reception. They then went to their room. A long notice was displayed in their room. The first paragraph of the notice read as follows:

> The proprietors will not hold themselves responsible for articles lost or stolen, unless handed to the manageress for safe custody. Valuables should be deposited for safe custody in a sealed package and a receipt obtained.

Around six months into their stay, an unknown person stole Mrs Olley's key from the hotel's keyboard when she was out, and took a number of valuable items from her room. The hotel argued that the notice expressly excluded their liability, and had contractual force. The Court of Appeal held that the notice was not part of the contract between the hotel and its guests. The contract was made at the time a guest checked in. This contract was for an indeterminate duration, lasting until terminated by either party. The notice was not seen by Mrs Olley until after the contract was formed. As a result, it was not incorporated into the contract.

6.4.3 **Nature**

The second factor of relevance in determining whether or not a term has been incorporated is the nature of the document in which a reference to that term is made. The courts have consistently held that a document will only incorporate terms to which it refers if the document is of a type that would be expected to have contractual conditions. *Grogan v Robin Meredith Plant Hire*[59] illustrates how this rule works.

---

57. For an example of a case in which the company did have such knowledge, see *Richardson, Spence & Co v Rowntree* [1894] AC 217.
58. [1949] 1 KB 532.   59. [1996] CLC 1127 (CA).

> ## Case in depth: *Grogan v Robin Meredith Plant Hire* [1996] CLC 1127
>
> Robin Meredith Plant Hire (RMP) contacted a company called Triact seeking work. Triact was then laying pipes at a construction site. RMP and Triact entered into an oral agreement, under which Triact would hire a machine and driver from RMP. The parties agreed on the hourly rate that would be payable for the hire, but on no other terms. Every week, RMP's driver presented a timesheet to Triact's site agent, which the site agent signed. The timesheet had as its bottom the following line:
>
> > All hire undertaken under CPA conditions. Copies available on request.
>
> The CPA conditions are a standard form contract, prepared by the Contractors' Plant Association.
>
> In the third week of the hire, an accident occurred. Under the CPA conditions, Triact would have been required to indemnify RMP for any liability they incurred as a result of the accident. The question for the court, therefore, was whether the CPA conditions had been incorporated into the contract.
>
> The court held that they had not.
>
> > Documents such as a time sheet, an invoice or a statement of account do not normally have a contractual effect in the sense of making or varying a contract. The purpose of time sheets is not normally to contain or evidence the terms of a contract, but to record a party's performance of an existing obligation under a contract.[60]
>
> Because timesheets were generally understood to simply be a record of time spent, to be used for accounting purposes, a reference to the CPA conditions on a timesheet had no contractual significance.[61]

Other cases have taken a similar approach. In *Burnett v Westminster Bank Ltd*,[62] the High Court held that a notice on a chequebook did not have contractual effect. What, then, of tickets, such as the one we are dealing with in our example? There have been a number of cases on tickets, with mixed results. Tickets for travel by train[63] and ship[64] have been held to be the sort of documents on which terms may be expected to appear. A ticket for a deckchair on a beach, in contrast, has been held not to be such a document.[65] On the facts of Illustration 6.4, a ticket for an event would appear to be closer to the former, and will therefore in all probability be treated as the type of document on which the appearance of terms will not be unexpected.

6.4.4 Extent of notice

There is one more condition that must be satisfied for a term to be incorporated. Courts look not just to the fact of notice, but also to the extent of notice. If a term is

---

60. Ibid, 1130 (Auld LJ).   61. Ibid, 1131.
62. [1966] 1 QB 742.   63. *Thompson v LM & S Ry* [1930] 1 KB 41.
64. *Hood v Anchor Line (Henderson Bros) Ltd* [1918] AC 837.
65. *Chapelton v Barry Urban District Council* [1940] 1 KB 532 (CA).

unexpected in a particular context, more effort must be made by the party seeking to incorporate it by reference to drawing the reference to the other party's attention.

This principle is an old one, and can be traced back to the Victorian case of *Parker v South Eastern Railway*.[66] Parker had left a bag in the cloakroom of Charing Cross railway station, which at that time was run by the South Eastern Railway (SER). He was given a ticket which said on the front 'see back', and on the back stated that SER would not be liable for the loss of items worth £10 or more. Parker thought the ticket was only a receipt of payment and did not read the clause, though he admitted that he noticed that the ticket contained writing. His bag was lost, and SER sought to rely upon the exclusion clause.

The case was decided at a time when juries were still used in civil trials, so the court's decision consists in large part of deciding the appropriate direction to be given to the jury. Nevertheless, Mellish LJ's decision also contains an important summary of what the court took the law to be. The essence of the court's ruling was that Parker would be bound if he knew of the conditions, or if the ticket was given in a way that amounted to 'reasonable notice'. As to what constituted reasonable notice, Mellish LJ said:

> I am of the opinion . . . that if the person receiving the ticket did not see or know that there was any writing on the ticket, he is not bound by the conditions; that if he knew there was writing, and knew or believed that the writing contained conditions, then he is bound by the conditions; that if he knew there was writing on the ticket, but did not know or believe that the writing contained conditions, nevertheless he would be bound, if the delivering of the ticket to him in such a manner that he could see there was writing upon it, was, in the opinion of the jury, reasonable notice that the writing contained conditions.

As this extract suggests, Mellish LJ linked the reasonableness of the notice to the likelihood that the document contained contractual terms. Early cases continued to follow that line, looking to the nature of the document and the nature of the notice, looking, for example, to issues such as whether the notice was visible and legible.[67] Subsequent cases have, however, taken a different turn. The emphasis now is not just on the nature of the document and notice, but also on the nature of the *term* itself. The more unusual or stringent the term, the greater the lengths to which the person seeking to incorporate it must go to ensure that notice of the term is given. Lord Denning, in typically vivid language, held in *Spurling v Bradshaw*[68] that:

> Some clauses which I have seen would need to be printed in red ink on the face of the document with a red hand pointing to it before the notice could be held to be sufficient.[69]

By contrast, if a term is quite common in a particular trade or business, no special notice of that term will be required: a clause which is usual in a trade is by definition not 'unusually stringent'.[70] The courts have gone to the extent of holding that if the

---

66. (1877) 2 CPD 416.   67. *Sugar v London, Midland and Scottish Railway Co* [1941] 1 All ER 172.
68. [1956] 1 WLR 461.   69. Ibid, 466.
70. See *British Crane Hire Corp Ltd v Ipswich Plant Hire Ltd* [1975] QB 303, where the court was quite strongly influenced by the fact that the clause in question was customary in contracts of that type.

terms in question are 'conditions in common form or usual terms in the relevant business', then it is not even necessary for them to be specifically set out in the document.
A statement along the lines 'subject to our standard conditions of sale, a copy of which
is available on request' is sufficient to incorporate common or usual terms, even if the
specific document has never been seen by the party to whom notice of incorporation
is given.[71]

The distinction between usual and onerous terms has not been free from controversy, with commentators and some judges asking whether it is appropriate for courts
to treat some terms as 'more onerous' and others as 'less onerous'. Nevertheless, courts
have taken this approach more or less consistently since the middle of the 20th century. As things stand, whether a term is onerous or not is a question of fact and not
of law. Onerousness is not capable of precise legal definition, and the question for
the court is whether, given the circumstances of the case[72]—that is, the impact of the
term, and the effort to which the party seeking to incorporate it went to draw it to the
attention of the other party—it would be fair or reasonable to hold that the party was
bound by that term.[73]

 Debates in context: should onerous terms be treated differently?

As we have seen in this section, the requirement of 'sufficient' notice has over the decades
evolved into an approach that distinguishes 'usual' terms and 'onerous' terms, imposing significantly more stringent requirements on parties who seek to incorporate the latter into their
contract by reference. This approach is quite deeply entrenched in English law now, but that
does not mean everybody agrees that the approach is a good thing. A number of academics,
and at least some judges, lean towards the view that the law should not be making such a
distinction, and that 'sufficient notice' should mean the same thing for all types of clauses, as
it did in early cases such as *Parker*.

The clearest summary of the thinking underlying this view is found in a dissenting judgment
by Hobhouse LJ in the case of *AEG (UK) Ltd v Logic Resource Ltd*.[74] Logic Resource ordered
equipment from AEG, which it intended to resell to a customer in Iran. AEG was aware that
the goods had been purchased for the purpose of export outside the UK, although it did not
know the precise destination. AEG responded to the order with a confirmation, on the reverse
of which terms were printed. These terms were not the entire conditions of sale. They were,
instead, an extract from AEG's conditions of sale (the conditions of sale took up two full sides
of paper, in small type), and carried the legend 'A copy of the full conditions of sale is available
on request.' Logic Resource did not request a copy, and never saw the conditions. Some
of the terms were quite onerous, and one in particular became the subject of contention.
Clause 7.5 (which was part of the conditions of sale, but was not printed on the back of the

→

---

71. See eg the remarks of Taylor LJ in *Circle Freight International Ltd v Medeast Gulf Exports Ltd*
[1988] 2 Lloyd's Rep 427, 432 (CA).

72. See the remarks of Hale LJ in *O'Brien v MGN Ltd* [2002] CLC 33, [23].

73. See the remarks of Bingham LJ in *Interfoto Picture Library v Stiletto Visual Programmes Ltd* [1989]
QB 433 (CA).

74. [1996] CLC 265 (CA).

→

confirmation) provided that all defective equipment had to be returned at Logic Resource's cost.

From our study of the battle of the forms in Chapter 2, it should be evident that AEG's 'confirmation' was in reality a counter-offer, because it proposed new terms, and that Logic Resource accepted this counter-offer by conduct, in continuing with the order. It was, therefore, AEG's terms that governed the contract. The equipment in this case turned out to be defective and had to be shipped back from Iran. AEG refused to reimburse Logic Resource for the cost of shipment, and the court had to consider whether or not clause 7.5 had been incorporated. The majority of the Court of Appeal held that it had not, on the basis that it was unusual and onerous, and not standard in this particular trade. Because it had not been printed on the back of the confirmation, AEG had not taken the steps that were required to constitute 'sufficient notice'.

Hobhouse LJ dissented. The majority, he thought, were taking the rule a step too far. The question to be asked, he thought, was not whether the *provisions* of a clause were unreasonable or onerous. The correct question to be asked was whether the clause was of a *type* that one would expect to see on a set of printed terms. It was only where it was not of such a type that an issue in relation to incorporation arose. If, however, it was of such a type, it should be taken to be incorporated no matter how one-sided or onerous its provisions were. On the specific facts of the case, the clause at issue sought to limit liability. It was exceedingly common for parties to commercial contracts to seek to limit their liability. As a result, the clause was validly incorporated. Logic Resource knew full well that sales contracts invariably contained clauses limiting liability. The onus was on them to request a copy of the terms, to determine how AEG had sought to limit its liability. This did not mean that a party would be left remediless if a clause was one-sided or onerous. All it meant was that it was a matter to be dealt with under the legal rules relating to unfair contracts, not the rules relating to incorporation.[75]

Hobhouse LJ's opinion was not accepted by the majority, but it has won support from academic commentators. In a comment published in the Modern Law Review, Professor Bradgate, a contextually oriented scholar, pointed out that the term in question was not unusual—sellers of commercial equipment not infrequently required it to be returned at the purchaser's cost, even if it was defective. The court's decision, Bradgate argued, was only intelligible if it was regarded as a decision on the *reasonableness* of the term: the term was not incorporated because it was unreasonable, and an unreasonable term requires more to be done for it to be incorporated.[76] Professor McKendrick, similarly, has supported Hobhouse LJ's dissent. The question of whether or not a clause is reasonable is dealt with by statute. To add an additional common law rule covering the same ground simply creates legal uncertainty.[77]

There is certainly substance to this point, but the situation is not as clear-cut as these authors' comments might suggest. As Chapter 13 discusses, statutory regulation does not cover all contract types, and leaves certain types of clauses in certain types of contracts untouched. There is a need for common law rules to deal with these cases in a sensible, and principled, way. As we will see in section 6.5, there is a case for saying that the approach represented by cases like *AEG* could form the basis for such a set of rules.

75. Ibid, 274–7.   76. R Bradgate, 'Unreasonable Standard Terms' (1997) 60 MLR 582.
77. E McKendrick, *Contract Law* (8th edn, Palgrave 2009) 154.

6.4.5 **Courses of dealing**

The cases we have looked at thus far involved one-off contracts between the parties. If the parties have a history of dealing with each other, there is one more way in which a term can be incorporated into a contract. Where the parties have an established course of dealing with each other on particular terms, a clause which is usually part of the terms on which they deal will be taken to have been incorporated even if it was not expressly drawn to the other party's attention in the particular transaction that is the subject of dispute. *Spurling v Bradshaw*[78]—the case in which Lord Denning set out the **red hand rule**—is an example. Spurling had a warehouse in East London which Bradshaw had repeatedly used over the years. In this particular transaction, Bradshaw delivered eight barrels of orange juice to Spurling for storage. Some days later, Bradshaw received a receipt for the juice from Spurling. The receipt referred to conditions printed on the reverse. One of these said that Spurling would not be liable for any loss or damage to the goods when in his custody. The barrels of juice were damaged in the warehouse. Bradshaw then refused to pay Spurling's storage charges. Spurling sued Bradshaw for the charges, and Bradshaw counterclaimed for the damage to his goods, alleging breach of contract.

The key issue for the court was whether the clauses printed on the back of the receipt were incorporated into the contract. One of the arguments raised by Bradshaw was that the clause could not form part of the contract, because it was not sent to Bradshaw until well after the contract had been concluded. The Court of Appeal rejected this argument, and found for Spurling. The parties, it was held, had dealt with each other repeatedly over a number of years, as a result of which Bradshaw would have been aware of the terms on which Spurling contracted, including the exclusion clause. The provision was, therefore, incorporated into the parties' contract by reason of their course of dealings, even though in this case it was not received until after the contract was concluded.

This case forms an interesting counter to the decision in *Olley v Marlborough Court*,[79] which we examined in section 6.4.2. On the surface, the facts seem similar. The key difference, however, is that *Olley* involved a single contract: a contract was formed when Mr and Mrs Olley checked into the hotel, and the same contract remained in force until they checked out of the hotel. There was, therefore, no subsequent contract into which the term in question could have been incorporated through a course of dealings. In *Spurling*, in contrast, every consignment stored in the warehouse gave rise to an independent contract. As a result, there were a series of contracts, establishing a course of dealings. Whether the two cases *should* have produced such dramatically different results is, of course, open to question, but it is inevitable given that English contract law treats the formation of a contract as an event taking place at a single moment, in which all terms are crystallized.

A final point to note on the subject of a course of dealings is that the course of dealings must be regular and consistent. If the dealings are inconsistent, such that the term in question is sometimes incorporated into the parties' contract and sometimes not, the court will not, in general, treat the dealings as being sufficiently regular or consistent for the term to be incorporated.[80] Equally, if the dealings are infrequent—for

---

78. [1956] 1 WLR 461 (CA).   79. [1949] 1 KB 532.
80. *McCutcheon v David MacBrayne Ltd* [1964] 1 WLR 125 (HL).

example, four contracts over five years—the courts will not generally treat them as being 'regular'.[81]

Returning to Illustration 6.4, the ticket cases suggest that reference to terms on the back of a ticket is, in principle, sufficient notice, especially if the front of the ticket makes it clear that there are terms on the back. However, there is a clear argument to be made here that the term in question is unusual and onerous. Whilst contracts do commonly prohibit photography and audiovisual recordings at events, a provision allowing confiscation of the equipment will almost certainly be classed as both unusual and onerous.

6.5 Unexpected terms

Before we leave this topic, it is worth stressing a rather important point on onerous terms. The rules we have just studied on onerous terms *only* apply where the term was incorporated by reference. If the term was directly inserted into the parties' contract, English law does not require the party responsible for inserting it to take any steps to draw it to the other party's attention. The term may have been printed in very small print on the back of a form, and it may have been hidden amongst a mass of innocuous and nondescript terms. It may have been wholly unexpected, entirely out of the ordinary, and exceptionally onerous. The common law will take no account of any of these things if it happened to be present in the contract itself. This point is very well illustrated by the decision in *L'Estrange v Graucob*.[82]

Case in depth: *L'Estrange v Graucob* [1934] 2 KB 394

Ms L'Estrange owned a café. Graucob dealt in vending machines. One of their salesmen visited L'Estrange's café, seeking to sell her a cigarette vending machine. L'Estrange was convinced by the sales pitch, and agreed to buy the machine on an instalment plan. She signed a document entitled 'Sales Agreement'. The agreement was written in 'regrettably small print' (the court's description) and included the following provision:

> any express or implied condition, statement, or warranty, statutory or otherwise not stated herein is hereby excluded.

L'Estrange signed without reading the document, and no attempt was made to draw her attention to this term.

Unfortunately for L'Estrange, the machine stopped working within a few months, when L'Estrange still had a good amount left to pay on the instalment scheme. It turned out that the machine could not be fixed, and L'Estrange refused to pay further instalments. She also claimed for the instalments already paid on the basis that the machine was not fit for its intended purpose (an implied term under statute).

→

---

81. *Hollier v Rambler (AMC) Ltd* [1972] 2 QB 71. Contrast *Henry Kendall Ltd v William Lillico Ltd* [1969] 2 AC 31 (HL), where the existence of around 100 contracts over a three-year period was held to constitute a sufficiently regular course of dealings.
82. [1934] 2 KB 394.

> →
> The court held that the contractual clause was valid, and excluded the warranty that would otherwise have been implied. 'When a document containing contractual terms is signed, then, in the absence of fraud, or, I will add, misrepresentation, the party signing it is bound, and it is wholly immaterial whether he has read the document or not.'

Although the case itself is from the 1930s, the English courts take the view that it embodies an important principle of law, which should be upheld. In *Peekay Intermark v ANZ Banking Group*,[83] the Court of Appeal defended the decision in *L'Estrange*, stating that the rule it embodied was:

> . . . an important principle of English law which underpins the whole of commercial life; any erosion of it would have serious repercussions.[84]

The result is that the distinction between onerous terms incorporated by reference and onerous terms directly put into the contract stands, and is unlikely to vanish any time in the near future. The practical implications of this are quite significant, as the following variation on Illustration 6.4 suggests.

Illustration 6.5

Tim buys tickets to a concert using an app on his smartphone. When he clicks on the 'Buy' button in the app, it displays the following screen:

> In order to continue you must accept the following terms and conditions
>
> This agreement is entered into between Fantastic Events plc ('the Company'), and you ('the Customer'). It sets out terms and conditions that govern your attendance at any event you attend which is organized by the Company. As a condition of your purchase of the ticket, you must consent to abide by these terms and conditions.
>
> Page 1 of 74

As anyone who has ever had to accept terms and conditions on a smartphone will attest, reading through the terms and conditions on such a small screen is next to impossible. Nevertheless, as the cases discussed earlier demonstrate, in such a case, unlike the physical purchase discussed above, the term will be valid at common law.

It is hard to see how this distinction makes logical sense. In recent years, the harshest effects of this rule have been mitigated by the rise of statutory regulation, as Chapter 13 discusses in greater detail. Statutory regulation, however, differs from the common law in one significant way: unlike the common law, which is general and applies to all types of contracts, statutory regulation is very specific, and applies only to the specific

83. [2006] EWCA Civ 386, [2006] 2 Lloyd's Rep 511.   84. Ibid, [43].

type of contract and the specific type of term that the statute in question actually covers. If a particular contract term falls outside these bounds, the statute will not help the party affected by the term, no matter how unusual and onerous it is.

Is this position defensible? The standard argument in support of the common law's relatively rigid line is very similar to the reasons Hobhouse LJ gave for dissenting in *AEG*: that this distorts the contractual relationship between the parties, imposes unnecessary burdens upon them, and for that reason is not a step the common law should take. Yet the correctness of this assertion can be questioned. A restriction based on the giving of notice is a procedural requirement, not a substantive one. It does not invalidate clauses because they are unreasonable—it simply requires a party seeking to insert such a clause to tell the other party that he wants the contract to contain a provision that, objectively speaking, is unusually onerous. Imposing such a requirement on all contracts, including those not created by incorporation, would do no more than restrict the parties from trying to sneak unexpected and onerous terms into a contract. As things stand, however, the creation of such a requirement is a step that the common law is extremely unlikely to take.

6.6 **In conclusion: the problem of assembling terms**

In this chapter, we have seen how the courts go about the task of determining what exactly it was that the parties agreed on. If there is a written contract, and the parties intended it to be a complete record of their agreement, things are fairly straightforward. If not, however, things are somewhat more complex. The factors and questions discussed in this chapter are only indicative—the courts have repeatedly emphasized that the real question is determining what the parties objectively intended. It is also important to note that incorporation, construing the significance of oral statements, and considering whether a written document was intended to be a complete record are not entirely separate compartmentalized enquiries. In real cases, the various sources of contractual terms, and the rules relating to them, often run together. Courts will often have to bring together issues in relation to the effect of oral statements, the parol evidence rule, and the incorporation of external terms.[85] The process of assembling the terms of an agreement which have not been reduced to writing is an integrated one, involving looking at many sources, and if necessary drawing on them all.

Underlying all of this, as we have seen, is the desire of the courts to provide a framework of commercial certainty—that is to say, a framework in which commercial parties have a general idea of the steps they need to take if they want to achieve particular objectives. Much of the law relating to defining the express terms of the contract is oriented around this goal—ranging from the rules on incorporation to the effect courts give to entire agreement clauses. Whilst this is a laudable goal, cases such as *L'Estrange v Graucob* suggest that there is certainly room to question whether the courts have taken the idea of certainty too far.

---

85. For an example, see *Mendelssohn v Normand Ltd* [1970] 1 QB 177 (CA).

Key points

- An important task in many contract cases is to determine the terms on which the parties contracted.

- Where contracts are oral or partly oral, the question is whether a statement made by one of the parties was a term. Statements are classified into puff, representations, and terms. Puff contains statements which were not intended to be taken seriously. Representations are statements of fact made to induce the other party to contract, but which do not themselves form part of the contract. Terms are statements intended to be contractually binding.

- In deciding whether a statement is a representation or a term, the courts look to the importance of the statement, the relative knowledge and expertise of the parties, and whether one of the parties took on responsibility for the statement's veracity.

- If the parties have produced a written document recording their understanding, the court will ordinarily presume that they intended that document to record the *entirety* of their understanding. The court will not attach weight to any other supposed terms on which they might otherwise have seemed to have agreed. This is called the parol evidence rule.

- The parol evidence rule will not apply if the document was not intended to be a complete record of the transaction. If either party can show that the document was *not* intended to record the entirety of the transaction, then the court *will* give full effect to any other terms to which the evidence suggests they agreed even if those terms find no place in the written document.

- Parties can also incorporate terms into a contract by referring to them either in oral discussions or in written documentation. Notice of incorporation must be given before the contract is formed. Whether sufficient notice was given depends on the nature of the document that constitutes notice, and the extent to which attempts were made to draw the party's attention to the incorporated term. The more onerous the term, the greater the degree of notice required.

- Notice is not required, however, where the term is contained in a signed document, or a document to which the party expressly agrees (as distinct from being incorporated by reference).

Assess your learning

You should be able to respond to each of the following points with a confident 'yes'. If you can't, then you should revisit the sections listed against that point.

Can you:

(a) *Outline* the distinction between mere puff, representations, and terms, and *apply* the distinction to the facts of specific cases? (Section 6.2)

(b) *Explain* the parol evidence rule, and *identify* the circumstances in which the rule does not apply? (Section 6.3)

(c) *Describe* the main criteria that must be satisfied before a term will be held to have been incorporated by reference into a contract? (Section 6.4)

In relation to each of the above, you should be able to:

(i) identify and clearly explain the key rules and principles;

(ii) identify the key cases and statutes, and why they matter;

(iii) apply the principles and cases to specific real or hypothetical fact situations;

(iv) evaluate the limitations, if any, of the law as it currently stands.

Further reading

M Barber, 'The Limits of Entire Agreement Clauses' [2012] JBL 486.

M Clarke, 'Notice of Contractual Terms' (1976) 35 CLJ 51.

A Corbin, 'The Parol Evidence Rule' (1944) 53 Yale Law Journal 603.

E Macdonald, 'Incorporation of Contract Terms by a "Consistent Course of Dealing"' (1988) 8 LS 48.

E Macdonald, 'The Duty to Give Notice of Unusual Contract Terms' [1988] JBL 375.

D McLauchlan, 'The Entire Agreement Clause: Conclusive or a Question of Weight?' (2012) 128 LQR 521.

E Peden and JW Carter, 'Incorporation of Terms by Signature: *L'Estrange* Rules!' (2005) 21 JCL 96.

SN Waddams, 'Do We Need a Parol Evidence Rule?' (1991) 19 Canadian Business Law Journal 385.

Interpreting the terms

Construction, rectification, and mutual mistake

'Please mind the gap between the parties' words and their intention'

7

Problem 7: setting the context

Read the following letter. What legal issues does it raise?

Happy Coach Trips

7 King's Way, Westerby, Hexhamshire

Dear John,

As you know, we hire out coaches to tour groups. Around six months ago, one of our coaches was involved in an accident due to our driver's negligence. We have admitted liability and are compensating all the passengers for their loss. One of the passengers on the coach, Mr Tom Davis, is a former soldier who lost his left leg at the hip in a wartime incident in Iraq. He wears a permanently fitted bionic prosthetic leg, which combines a motorized knee, ankle, and hip. This leg was destroyed in the accident, and Mr Davis has claimed the cost of purchasing a new one.

We're now in the process of making a claim to our insurance company under our liability insurance policy. The insurer has agreed to cover the claims, but the question that's come up in relation to Mr Davis is whether damage to a prosthetic leg is to be treated as bodily injury or as damage to property under our insurance policy. Our insurers are inclined to take the latter view, on the basis that a prosthetic limb is personal property and not a body part. This is problematic for us, as our insurance policy caps the amount recoverable for lost or damaged property to £300 per item, which is a tiny fraction of the amount we will have to pay Mr Davis. For personal injury, in contrast, the cap is £1,500,000. Unlike ordinary prosthetic legs, Mr Davis's leg was computerized, and adjusts to his gait as well as the terrain. This, taken together with the fact that the leg was not removable, seems to us to create a fairly strong basis for saying that a prosthetic leg was a part of his body.

The insurance policy does not directly address the question of prosthetic legs, whether permanently fitted or removable. To be honest, this is the first time either the insurance company or ourselves have encountered a claim of this type, so it wasn't something we had thought about at the time we agreed the policy schedule. I've attached the relevant provisions of the policy. We would appreciate any advice you may be able to give on the question.

Yours sincerely,

Roy Lloyd

Policy Excerpts

1. DEFINITIONS:

. . .

(h) LOSS OF LIMB(S)—Loss of a hand or foot by permanent severance at or above the wrist or ankle, or any other circumstance that produces total and permanent loss of use of a hand or foot.

→

→

. . .

(s) PERSONAL BAGGAGE—Suitcases and similar containers, their contents, and any other articles carried or worn by passengers (including cameras, spectacles, sunglasses, clothes, jewellery, and watches); but excluding money, stamps, documents, or business goods and samples.

4. PERSONAL INJURY

We will pay the amount of damages for which you are liable at law, and your claim costs, in respect of bodily injury sustained by a passenger during a trip, if the injury is caused solely and directly by an accident involving an insured vehicle during the period of cover. Our liability under this section is limited to bodily injury which:

(a) manifests itself within 12 months of the accident, and

(b) is the sole and direct cause of death, loss of eyes or limbs, or permanent total disablement, or

(c) results in reasonable and necessary medical, hospital, and treatment expenses, or

(d) otherwise creates a legal liability to pay compensation for personal injury.

The amount we will pay you under this head is subject to a maximum limit of £1,500,000 per injured passenger.

. . .

6. PERSONAL BAGGAGE

We will pay the amount of damages for which you are liable at law, and your claim costs, in respect of any loss or damage to personal baggage suffered by a passenger during a trip, if the loss or damage is caused solely and directly by an accident involving an insured vehicle during the period of cover. The amount we will pay you under this head is subject to a maximum limit of £300 per injured passenger.

7.1 **Introduction: the nature of interpretation**

Disagreements between the parties as to what the contract requires of them—as in the letter you have just examined—are a frequent cause of contractual disputes. The disagreement between the insurer and the assured in this problem relates to whether the contract requires the insurer to pay the assured an amount up to the higher cap set out in section 4, or whether the insurer can justifiably refuse to pay any more than the lower cap set out in section 6. The answer to this question turns on the meaning of the contract and, specifically, on what will be considered 'bodily injury' and a 'limb' under the contract. The process of *interpreting* a contract is an attempt to answer questions like these.

Interpretation tends to become an issue if the terms of a contract do not clearly spell out the consequences of a particular event or circumstance. Parties tend to be focused on the practical or commercial aspects of a transaction, not its legal side. The result is that while a lot of time and effort is spent on discussing and working out the commercial terms of a contract, the actual transactors (as opposed to their lawyers) spend relatively little time on the legal terms. In an ideal world, each of the parties signing a contract will read it carefully, work through possible scenarios that might arise in the future, and consider how the contract will apply to those scenarios. If the manner in which a particular situation is dealt with is unsatisfactory, they should then negotiate with the other side to try and deal with it in a more satisfactory way.

In practice, of course, it does not quite happen in this way. Consider the following illustration:

> **Illustration 7.1**
>
> Sam, an undergraduate student, has heard from a friend about an app called 'Yik-Yak', which lets students make funny anonymous comments about lecturers and fellow students during class. Eager to join the fun, he downloads the app, irritatedly clicks through the terms and conditions, and signs up for an account.

This behaviour is typical. Think about how you act when signing up for an online service—say, Facebook or Gmail. Do you read the terms and conditions carefully, work through possible usage scenarios, and think through what outcomes the terms might produce in those usage scenarios before signing up? Or are you more focused on getting access to the service and the benefits you think you will derive from it? For most people, it will be the latter.

This type of behaviour is not unusual when entering into transactions, and it is understandable for the reasons discussed in the introduction to Part II. It does, however, mean that courts are very frequently faced with the task of making sense of contracts whose terms are insufficiently clear either in their meaning or application.

Our focus in this chapter will be on the general approach of the English courts to the interpretation of contractual provisions. As we will see, the approach of English law to interpretation has changed in significant ways in the past two decades. Many of these changes were deeply controversial when they first came about, and some remain controversial today. We will begin by discussing two broad approaches to construing contracts—literalism and contextualism—both of which have influenced English law, and both of which continue to form part of the law (section 7.2). We will then move on to considering the role English law currently assigns to each (section 7.3), and how the courts decide which to apply (section 7.4). Following this, we will examine an alternative remedy—**rectification**—which the courts can deploy to alter the words in a contract if the written words did not reflect the parties' intention (section 7.5). We will conclude by examining how courts deal with situations in which it is impossible to resolve contractual ambiguities because there is no objectively ascertainable meaning to the clause in question (section 7.6).

7.2 Literalism and contextualism: two interpretive techniques

Let us return to Problem 7. There are two ways in which we could interpret the provision at issue in this case. First, we could interpret it in a technical or literal manner. If the parties choose not to define the term 'body' in their contract, then it must mean 'body' as normally understood—that is, a body of flesh, blood, bone, and tissue. If parties want to expand the scope of the term to cover prosthetics, then they should add a term to that effect. If they fail to do so, it is not the court's job to rewrite the contract for them. They must live with the consequences of their failure.

Alternately, we could interpret the provision less strictly and more contextually. Contracting is a purposive act. The interpretation of contracts should therefore try to further the commercial purpose of the transaction. The purpose of a policy insuring a person against bodily harm is to secure against risks of events that incapacitate the assured by impairing their physical functioning. From this point of view, whether the limb in question is real or prosthetic should make no difference. Given the context in which it is used, 'body' should, therefore, be construed broadly.

Which one of these competing readings should the law adopt? It was long thought that English law favoured relatively literal or straightforward readings of contracts. Reading contracts literally has the advantage of certainty. If parties know that the contract will be interpreted in accordance with the ordinary dictionary meanings of its words, they will have a good idea of its legal effect. English courts generally treat certainty as being desirable. Parties to transactions, particularly commercial transactions, should know where they stand so that they can structure their actions accordingly.[1] If an assured (ie an insured person) knows that by default 'bodily injury' will be read narrowly, he can shop around for policies that provide broader coverage, or negotiate special coverage. This should, in theory, also make litigation less likely, as a party who knows he is likely to lose in court has little incentive to incur the time and costs of litigation.

The principal drawback of literalism is that it only works if the parties are equally matched, have skilled lawyers, and pay attention to the intricacies of drafting. If any of these conditions is not met, a literal reading may fail to reflect the outcome the parties wanted to achieve. A contextual approach, in contrast, has the advantage of flexibility, in that it lets the court reach sensible results on the facts of a case. Unlike the literal approach, it does not insist that 'body' can only have one meaning unless the parties expressly redefine it. This flexibility, however, carries a price. If judges have greater discretion in relation to how they interpret contracts, it necessarily means that there will be less certainty in relation to how they will interpret contracts.

The key issues when dealing with questions of interpretation, therefore, are, first, *when* (if at all) a court should look beyond what the contract seems to say to ascertain whether it really means something different; secondly, to *what* types of sources the court should look in order to determine what the contract really means; and, thirdly, *how far* the courts can go in departing from the literal meaning of the contract. As the

---

1. See the comments of Goff LJ in *Scandinavian Trading v Flota Ecuatoriana* [1983] 2 WLR 248, 257.

law currently stands, the courts take a narrow approach to the first question but a very broad approach to the second and third questions. It is only in a relatively narrow set of circumstances that the courts will depart from the ordinary meaning of a contract's words. When they do, however, they will consider a broad range of extra-contractual sources. If need be, they will even depart quite considerably from the words' meaning to read contractual clauses as if they mean something very different from what their words actually say.

This odd combination of narrowness and broadness is a result of the recent history of English law. For much of the 20th century, the received understanding was that English courts would interpret contracts literally, unless the contract, or one of its provisions, was ambiguous. If a contract had a provision that could mean more than one thing, and if it was unclear which of those meanings was intended, the courts would take a contextual approach to construing that provision.

This is no longer true. In the late 1990s, English law began to move decisively away from the strict reading of contracts towards the greater use of contextual readings of contracts. The case that is usually seen as most clearly signalling this shift is the decision of the House of Lords in *Mannai Investment Co Ltd v Eagle Star Assurance*.[2] Mannai Investment were the tenants of an office owned by Eagle Star. The office had been let for a period of ten years, starting on 13 January 1992. Clause 7(13) of the lease gave Mannai a single opportunity to terminate the lease early:

> by serving not less than six months notice in writing on the Landlord or its Solicitors such notice to expire on the third anniversary of the term commencement date.

On 24 June 1994, Mannai tried to exercise its option to terminate the lease by sending a notice that said:

> Pursuant to Clause 7(13) of the Lease we as Tenant hereby give notice to you to determine the Lease on 12 January 1995.

When the termination date arrived, Eagle Star argued that the notice was ineffective, on the basis that clause 7(13) only permitted termination on 13 January 1995. The House of Lords found for the tenant, on the basis that any reasonable person reading the notice would have understood that it did not mean what it literally seemed to say, but was intended to be a notice to terminate on the date permitted by the contract.

At one level, the decision seems obviously right. It is very clear what the tenants meant, and an argument that the notice was invalid because it specified the wrong date seems suspiciously like harping on a technicality. At the time, however, the decision was deeply controversial. It was reached by the narrowest of margins—a 3:2 split—and in the face of a strong dissent by the minority, and it was greeted with outrage. Some commercial barristers were so incensed by the decision that they hoisted a black flag over Lincoln's Inn in protest,[3] and a leading practitioners' journal published an editorial on the case saying that Lord Steyn's speech came close 'to the legal equivalent of blasphemy'.[4]

2. [1997] AC 749 (HL).
3. Lord Steyn, 'The Intractable Problem of the Interpretation of Legal Texts' in S Worthington (ed), *Commercial Law and Commercial Practice* (Hart 2003) 127.
4. Editorial, 'Closing Time from House of Lords' (1997) 18 Property Law Bulletin 14.

Underlying the strong reaction against the decision was the feeling that it was inappropriate to take a contextual approach to interpretation in a situation such as this one, where there was no ambiguity in the language. '12 January' is about as unambiguous a phrase as you can get, and cannot on any theory of meaning be read as actually meaning '13 January'.[5] Nevertheless, the approach taken in *Mannai Investment* was confirmed in *Investor Compensation Scheme v West Bromwich Building Society*,[6] which marked a definitive shift away from a literalist reading of contracts.

> ## Case in depth: *Investor Compensation Scheme v West Bromwich Building Society* [1998] 1 WLR 896
>
> A number of investors had taken out 'Home Income Plans' in the late 1980s, under which they had obtained loans from banks secured by mortgages on their houses, the proceeds of which had been invested in equity-linked bonds. Around the turn of the decade equity yields fell, as did house prices, while interest rates rose, leaving the investors facing heavy losses. Many of them had valid claims for misselling against the financial advisors, banks, or building societies who recommended or sold the Home Income Plans, and possibly also the solicitors who provided advice.
>
> The investors contacted the Investors Compensation Scheme (ICS), a body which had been set up by the government to provide a compensation fund for investors with claims against persons licensed to carry on an investment business. ICS's practice was to compensate the investors directly. The investors would assign their claims to ICS, which would then sue the persons responsible for the misselling. This saved investors the trouble of having to sue the financial advisors, while ensuring that ICS could recover any money it had paid from them.
>
> In this case, however, the claim form which investors signed to assign their rights to ICS had been poorly drafted. It contained a clause that said the following type of claim would be retained by the investor:
>
> > Any claim (whether sounding in rescission for undue influence or otherwise) that you have or may have against the West Bromwich Building Society in which you claim an abatement of sums which you would otherwise have to repay to that Society in respect of sums borrowed by you from that Society in connection with the transaction and dealings giving rise to the claim (including interest on any such sums).[7]
>
> Read literally, this clause was so wide that it would mean that no claims against the building society had been transferred to ICS. This is because just about *any* type of claim could have been used by an investor to set-off (ie 'abate' or reduce)[8] sums he would otherwise have had
>
> →

5. See eg the comments of Sir Richard Buxton in '"Construction" and Rectification after *Chartbrook*' (2010) 69 CLJ 253, 255.
6. [1998] 1 WLR 896.
7. The form is quoted in the speech of Lord Hoffmann: ibid, 909.
8. The use of the word 'abate' in this clause is puzzling, and another example of its bad drafting. 'Abatement' has a technical meaning in the law of nuisance, but not in the law of contract. Here, the House of Lords held that the word seems to have been used simply to mean 'reduce'. Ibid, 903.

→

to repay the West Bromwich Building Society (WBBS). When ICS tried to sue WBBS, WBBS argued that this was what the clause meant, and that the claims against WBBS therefore still vested with the investors, not ICS. The only claims that the clause had transferred were any claims against the solicitors and/or financial advisors.

The House of Lords, by a 4:1 majority, rejected this argument and held for ICS. Lord Hoffmann, speaking for the majority, pointed out that the only persons against whom a claim was realistic were the solicitors and WBBS, and of these WBBS 'would certainly be the prime target'.[9] To construe the clause in a manner that excluded claims against WBBS was, therefore, not commercially sensible. The clause must, instead, have been intended to have a much narrower effect. Lord Hoffmann held that it only excluded claims in rescission—which are not assignable in law—and clarified that if the sum payable was adjusted downwards in the course of rescission, the resulting gain could be retained by the investor.[10] In effect, the clause was construed as if it had read 'Any claim sounding in rescission (whether for undue influence or otherwise) . . .'.

Lord Lloyd dissented in strong terms. There was 'no principle of construction . . . which would enable the court to take words from within the brackets, where they are clearly intended to underline the width of "any claim," and place them outside the brackets where they have the exact opposite effect'.[11] He also disagreed on the point that the result was commercially unreasonable. Not all investors, he argued, had in fact been fully compensated. A number of them had incurred additional expenditure—on legal fees, for example—for which ICS had not compensated them, but which they in law could have recovered from WBBS or the solicitors, if their actions against them were successful. A typical investor had only recovered between half and three-quarters of their losses by way of compensation.[12] Given this, an investor might well have relied on the fact that the wording of the clause seemed to preserve their right of action against WBBS.[13] The fact that over 500 investors had commenced legal proceedings against WBBS and other building societies suggested, in Lord Lloyd's opinion, that the plain meaning of the clause could not be rejected in the manner the majority held it could.[14]

Investors remains good law. The changes it effected in relation to the materials English courts will consider, and the breadth of their power to depart from the literal meaning of contractual provisions, continue to inform the approach of the courts to interpretation. But contextualism should not be taken too far. Although contextualism permits the court to depart quite dramatically from the literal reading, the Supreme Court has subsequently emphasized, in *Arnold v Britton*,[15] that the *triggers* for contextual interpretation should not be overly broad. It is indeed appropriate for the courts to have a very broad discretion when engaged in the process of contextual interpretation, but contextual interpretation should remain the exception. Literal interpretation should be the rule. In what follows, we will first examine how the process of contextual interpretation works, before proceeding to examine when it is appropriate.

9. Ibid, 911.   10. Ibid, 916–17.   11. Ibid, 904.   12. Ibid, 905.
13. Ibid, 902–3.   14. Ibid, 905.   15. [2015] UKSC 36, [2015] 2 WLR 1593.

7.3 **The *Investors* rule**

In order to support the narrower and less literal reading of the contract, Lord Hoffmann advanced five propositions in *Investors*. These five propositions are generally taken to summarize the 'modern' approach to interpreting contracts.

Lord Hoffmann began by distinguishing the 'intellectual baggage' which he associates with the old '"legal" interpretation' from the 'common sense principles' on which the modern approach is based. These principles fundamentally reflect the manner in which 'any serious utterance would be interpreted in ordinary life'. He then set out the following propositions:[16]

(1) Interpretation is the ascertainment of the meaning which the document would convey to a reasonable person having all the background knowledge which would reasonably have been available to the parties in the situation in which they were at the time of the contract.

(2) The background was famously referred to by Lord Wilberforce as the 'matrix of fact', but this phrase is, if anything, an understated description of what the background may include. Subject to the requirement that it should have been reasonably available to the parties and to the exception to be mentioned next, it includes absolutely anything which would have affected the way in which the language of the document would have been understood by a reasonable man.

(3) The law excludes from the admissible background the previous negotiations of the parties and their declarations of subjective intent. They are admissible only in an action for rectification. The law makes this distinction for reasons of practical policy and, in this respect only, legal interpretation differs from the way we would interpret utterances in ordinary life. The boundaries of this exception are in some respects unclear. But this is not the occasion on which to explore them.

(4) The meaning which a document (or any other utterance) would convey to a reasonable man is not the same thing as the meaning of its words. The meaning of words is a matter of dictionaries and grammars; the meaning of the document is what the parties using those words against the relevant background would reasonably have been understood to mean. The background may not merely enable the reasonable man to choose between the possible meanings of words which are ambiguous but even (as occasionally happens in ordinary life) to conclude that the parties must, for whatever reason, have used the wrong words or syntax. (see *Mannai Investments Co. Ltd. v. Eagle Star Life Assurance Co. Ltd.* [1997] 2 WLR 945)

(5) The 'rule' that words should be given their 'natural and ordinary meaning' reflects the common sense proposition that we do not easily accept that people have made linguistic mistakes, particularly in formal documents. On the other hand, if one would nevertheless conclude from the background that something must have gone wrong with the language, the law does not require judges to attribute to the parties an intention which they plainly could not have had. Lord Diplock made this point more vigorously when he said in *The Antaios Compania Naviera S.A. v. Salen Rederierna A.B.* [1985] 1 A.C. 191, 201:

> . . . if detailed semantic and syntactical analysis of words in a commercial contract is going to lead to a conclusion that flouts business commonsense, it must be made to yield to business commonsense.

16. [1998] 1 WLR 896, 912–13.

Two points are worth emphasizing in relation to these five propositions. First, their focus is on the reasonable person, not on the parties themselves. This flows from contract law's emphasis on objectivity. When deciding a question objectively, the court does not ask what the parties actually intended, but what a reasonable person would have made of their words and deeds given the background against which they were said. Secondly, the 'contextualism' implicit in the *Investors* approach has two distinct components: the first relating to the materials at which the courts will look, and the second relating to the extent to which the courts can ignore the plain meaning of the words in the contract. We will now examine each of these components in turn.

7.3.1 **Words and circumstances**

The basic idea of looking at surrounding circumstances in order to interpret contracts did not originate with the decision in *Investors*. As far back as 1877, Bramwell LJ observed that:

> where words are used which would comprehend some other than one necessarily exclusive meaning upon which the judges are to put an interpretation, then . . . all the surrounding circumstances, and the course of dealing between the parties, not only may, but must, be looked at to ascertain the meaning of those words when used in reference to those surrounding circumstances and that course of dealing . . .[17]

There is a long chain of subsequent cases holding that courts must look to the surrounding circumstances in interpreting the law, including two decisions of Lord Wilberforce—*Prenn v Simmonds*[18] and *Reardon Smith Line v Hansen-Tangen*[19]—where he used the phraseology of 'factual matrix' or **'matrix of fact'** which Lord Hoffmann adopted in the second of his five propositions. Lord Hoffmann himself suggested repeatedly that the five propositions he outlined were not particularly new. Lord Bingham, similarly, attempted to demonstrate—extra-judicially—that there was little in the five propositions that was not already present in older authorities.[20]

Nevertheless, Lord Hoffmann's decision was perceived as being radical. Earlier cases tended to concern only situations of ambiguity—that is, situations where the words of the contract lent themselves to more than one meaning. The *Investors* approach liberalizes this in three ways. First, it permits the court to accept interpretations that do not flow from the words of the contract and are not suggested by them. Secondly, it permits recourse to a very wide range of material beyond the contract in constructing these interpretations. And, thirdly, it seems to permit this recourse as a matter of course even if the contract as it stands is not ambiguous, in the sense in which the word was traditionally understood.

In a subsequent case, Lord Hoffmann suggested that the first and third of these were the principal innovations of the *Investors* approach.[21] Commentators were, however,

---

17. *Lewis v The Great Western Railway Co* (1877) 3 QBD 195, 202.   18. [1971] 1 WLR 1381.
19. [1976] 1 WLR 989.
20. Lord Bingham, 'A New Thing Under the Sun? The Interpretation of Contract and the *ICS* Decision' (2008) 12 Edinburgh LR 374.
21. See his comments in *Chartbrook Ltd v Persimmon Homes Ltd* [2009] UKHL 38, [2009] 1 AC 1101, [38].

equally concerned about the second,[22] and with the benefit of hindsight it is easy to see that the courts have in fact routinely begun to look at a much wider range of information than was previously the norm. It has also created a much broader scope for reasonable judges to disagree on what the parties' agreement actually required them to do. The decision in *Employers' Liability Trigger Litigation (BAI v Durham)*[23] illustrates both these points very well.

Case in depth: *Employers' Liability Trigger Litigation* [2012] UKSC 14

This case involved a series of insurance policies insuring employers against liability to their employees for injuries and diseases which the employees had sustained in the course of their employment, and for which the employers would be liable under the rules pertaining to employers' liability in tort.

The policies in question had been issued during the 1950s and 1960s, and were worded in a range of ways. Some applied to 'injuries sustained', while others spoke of 'diseases contracted'. The litigation related to mesothelioma, which is caused by exposure to asbestos, but is a long-tail disease that takes many years after exposure to manifest itself. The question was what 'injuries sustained' meant. Did it mean that the policy only applied if the *disease* manifested itself while the policy was in force (in which case the insurers would not be liable)? Or was it sufficient for the *exposure* to have occurred during the period of cover (in which case the insurers would be liable)?

Examination of witnesses suggested that notwithstanding the difference of wording, the parties operated under the understanding that the policies provided identical coverage.[24] Nevertheless, Stanley Burton LJ in the Court of Appeal held that 'little if any assistance is to be gained by reference to the commercial purpose of [employers' liability] insurance. The commercial purpose was to provide the cover defined in the policy. The cover provided by every policy was defined by the terms of the policy.'[25]

On appeal, the Supreme Court did not agree with Stanley Burton LJ's proposition, and held that the commercial purpose of the policy did matter for the question of how the different wordings were to be interpreted. The testimony of the parties as to what they intended was not in itself particularly useful, since the basic principle in *ICS v West Bromwich* was that a contract would be interpreted as a reasonable person would have understood it, not what the parties actually meant. Nevertheless, the court thought it important to consider the broader commercial purposes for which these policies were issued, and to let that purpose inform the court's reading of the clause. Interpretations that ran contrary to this purpose should be looked at 'with scepticism'.[26] On this basis, the Supreme Court ruled, by a 4:1 majority, that all wordings had the same effect, and covered situations where a disease was caused but did not manifest until later.

→

---

22. See eg M Clarke, 'Interpreting Contracts—The Price of Perspective' (1999) 19 CLJ 18, 19.
23. [2012] UKSC 14, [2012] 1 WLR 867.
24. [2010] EWCA Civ 1096, [2011] 1 All ER 605, [219].   25. Ibid, [333].
26. [2012] UKSC 14, [41] (Lord Mance).

→

Commentators have pointed out that Stanley Burton LJ's decision in the Court of Appeal is difficult to reconcile with the *ICS v West Bromwich* approach to interpreting contracts.[27] The contrast with Lord Mance's decision, quoted above, is particularly striking, and illustrates the extent to which the new approach to interpretation has changed the manner in which courts go about the task of construing contracts.

At the same time, however, it also highlights a significant difficulty with the new approach, namely, that it leaves so much to the discretion of the judge that it makes it difficult to predict what a court will hold a contract to mean; and that it might mean that the parties' rights ultimately depend on which judge and which court a particular case comes before.

The answer to the question of what material the court consider in deciding what the contract means is also broad, but there are two exceptions which Lord Hoffmann emphasized in his third proposition. The first of these, as Lord Mance also pointed out in *Employers' Liability Trigger Litigation*,[28] is that the parties' subjective views are not relevant. Evidence is only relevant to the extent that it speaks to the facts in issue, and the fact in issue is not what the parties subjectively intended but what a reasonable person would have made of the contract. Thus even if it could be shown that Happy Coach Trips wanted cover for prosthetic limbs, or that the insurers would never have agreed to cover for prosthetic limbs, these facts would not be relevant. The question the court asks is not what the *parties* meant but what the *contract* meant.

Secondly, pre-contractual negotiations and discussions are usually excluded. Lord Hoffmann said that this was for reasons of 'practical policy', but did not elaborate. In *Prenn v Simmonds*, Lord Wilberforce said that evidence of this type would usually be unhelpful. Commentators have questioned the basis of this exclusion,[29] but it has been reaffirmed by the Supreme Court in *Chartbrook v Persimmon*[30] and appears unlikely to be disturbed at this point in time. This exclusion only applies to the actual negotiations themselves, and not to facts that were disclosed in the course of negotiation.[31]

7.3.2 Plain meanings and contextual meanings

The second question is how far the court can go in departing from the plain meaning of the contract. The cases have made it clear that the answer is 'very far', if appropriate. The leading case on this point is *Chartbrook v Persimmon*,[32] which was discussed briefly in the previous section. This case involved a contract for the construction of a mixed residential and commercial development by Persimmon on property belonging to Chartbrook. The development agreement provided that Persimmon would make

27. See eg R Merkin and J Steele, 'Compensating Mesothelioma Victims' (2011) 127 LQR 329.
28. [2012] UKSC 14, [41] (Lord Mance).
29. See eg R Buxton, '"Construction" and "Rectification" after *Chartbrook*' (2010) 69 CLJ 253.
30. [2009] UKHL 38, [2009] 1 AC 1101.
31. Ibid, [42]. See also *Oceanbulk Shipping and Trading SA v TMT Asia Ltd* [2010] UKSC 44, [2011] 1 AC 662.
32. [2009] UKHL 38, [2009] 1 AC 1101.

a number of payments to Chartbrook, one of which was an 'Additional Residential Payment' (ARP). The ARP was to be calculated according to a very complex formula. Briefly put, the formula was based on a minimum guaranteed value, and was expressed with reference to the difference between the actual sale price and the minimum guaranteed value. The formula, literally applied, resulted in a payment that was almost five times what Persimmon thought it ought to be. Chartbrook insisted that Persimmon had to pay the amount set out in the contract. Chartbrook's reading of the formula was grammatically the more obvious reading. The calculation urged by Persimmon departed so completely from the wording of the clause that the clause would have had to be completely rewritten to incorporate their formula.

The Supreme Court held that something had gone wrong with the wording of the contract (the fifth of Lord Hoffmann's propositions), and unanimously upheld Persimmon's reading of the contractual formula for calculating payments, even though this involved rewriting the clause, and giving it a meaning which its words could not support. Lord Hoffmann, delivering the main judgment, held that this was unproblematic, and was no different from what had been done in *Mannai Investment*:[33]

> When the language used in an instrument gives rise to difficulties of construction, the process of interpretation does not require one to formulate some alternative form of words which approximates as closely as possible to that of the parties. It is to decide what a reasonable person would have understood the parties to have meant by using the language which they did. The fact that the court might have to express that meaning in language quite different from that used by the parties . . . is no reason for not giving effect to what they appear to have meant.[34]

He then went on to state the rule in terms of what has come to be known as the 'red ink' rule:

> What is clear from these cases is that there is not, so to speak, a limit to the amount of red ink or verbal rearrangement or correction which the court is allowed. All that is required is that it should be clear that something has gone wrong with the language and that it should be clear what a reasonable person would have understood the parties to have meant.[35]

 Practice in context: non-judicial interpretation

We have repeatedly spoken of how a 'court' might interpret a contract, and the sources to which a court might look in interpreting a contract. In reality, a lot of contractual interpretation takes place outside the courts. The first forum where a contract might be interpreted is in an arbitral proceeding. Arbitrators, in theory, apply the law in much the same way as courts do, so this should not be a serious issue. The other forum where contract interpretation might take place is in an attempt to informally resolve a dispute, by negotiations either among the parties' commercial representatives or between their lawyers, or a combination of both. In

→

33. [1997] AC 749 (HL).   34. [2009] UKHL 38, [21] (Lord Hoffmann).
35. Ibid, [25] (Lord Hoffmann).

→ these cases, parties will often look to the contract to try and understand what it means. In negotiation theory, this is seen as being part of the process by which a party tries to understand what its 'Best Alternative To a Negotiated Agreement'—or BATNA—is. The more flexible the rules in relation to interpretation, the less certain a negotiator can be in relation to what a contract really means.

Given the fact that judges themselves have disagreed on what a contract means under the *Investors* approach, it is likely that different negotiators—particularly if they are lawyers—will disagree about the proper interpretation of a contract under the *Investors* approach. This result is that instead of forming a clear base position from which the negotiation starts, the meaning of the contract may end up becoming another argument to be used in a legalized negotiation process. The impact such a change could have on the negotiation process in terms of its cost, duration, and likely outcome has not been studied, but it could potentially be significant. The broader point, though, is that although many rules of contract law (and more generally private law) are formulated on the implicit assumption that they will be applied by detached, non-partisan judges, in reality they are as likely to be applied by hyper-partisan negotiators.

7.4 The threshold for contextual interpretation

7.4.1 The position of literal readings

The freedom which *Chartbrook* gave the courts to depart from a contract's words sparked some alarm. Of particular concern was the emphasis placed in *Chartbrook* on whether a reading made 'commercial sense',[36] which was seen as potentially giving wide and undesirable latitude to judges to rewrite contracts in the interests of fairness, and to making interpretation a very inconsistent process.[37] Partly in reaction to this, the courts have emphasized that the move towards contextualism does not mean that literal readings have been abandoned, and that literalism continues to have a leading role in the process of interpreting contracts. In *Rainy Sky v Kookmin Bank*,[38] for example, the Supreme Court pointed out that although the courts were not bound to strictly give effect to the most natural meaning of the words used in a contract, '[w]here the parties have used unambiguous language, the court must apply it.'[39] In *Wood v Capita*,[40] the Supreme Court went further, suggesting that textualism and contextualism should be seen as complementary, rather than rival approaches:

> Textualism and contextualism are not conflicting paradigms in a battle for exclusive occupation of the field of contractual interpretation. Rather, the lawyer and the judge, when interpreting any contract, can use them as tools to ascertain the objective meaning of the language which the parties have chosen to express their agreement. The

36. Ibid, [93] (Lord Walker).
37. See eg P Clark, 'Business Common Sense' (2012) 76 Conv 190.
38. [2011] UKSC 50, [2011] 1 WLR 2900.   39. Ibid, [23] (Lord Clarke).
40. [2017] UKSC 24, [2017] AC 1173.

extent to which each tool will assist the court in its task will vary according to the circumstances of the particular agreement or agreements. Some agreements may be successfully interpreted principally by textual analysis, for example because of their sophistication and complexity and because they have been negotiated and prepared with the assistance of skilled professionals. The correct interpretation of other contracts may be achieved by a greater emphasis on the factual matrix . . . There may often . . . be provisions in a detailed professionally drawn contract which lack clarity and the lawyer or judge in interpreting such provisions may be particularly helped by considering the factual matrix and the purpose of similar provisions in contracts of the same type.[41]

In *Rainy Sky* itself, the Supreme Court held on the facts that the words at issue were not unambiguous, and construed the clause contextually. In *Wood v Capita*, in contrast, the Supreme Court construed the clause literally. The decision of the Court of Appeal in *Procter and Gamble v Svenska Cellulosa Aktiebolaget*[42] illustrates the factors that led the courts to favour a literal, rather than contextual, reading of the clause.

Case in depth: *Procter and Gamble v Svenska Cellulosa Aktiebolaget* [2012] EWCA Civ 1413

The dispute in this case arose out of a contract for the supply of certain products by Procter and Gamble (P&G) to Svenska Cellulosa Aktiebolaget (SCA). The contract listed prices in euro, but went on to provide for payment in sterling. SCA claimed that the parties had agreed on a fixed exchange rate of £1 = €1.14964, which was to be used to calculate how much had to be paid for any given purchase, regardless of the actual exchange rate. P&G denied this, and said that it was the actual exchange rate that had to be used. The contract said nothing about exchange rates, but SCA produced a 'budget document', which had been used in calculating the prices, and which had an exchange rate notation.

SCA also argued that given the commercial objectives of the parties, a fixed exchange rate made more commercial sense. This argument had substance. SCA had agreed to buy P&G's entire European business for this product line. However, some of the factories—including the one to whose products the supply agreement related—obtained proprietary technology which P&G wanted to remove before transferring them to SCA. The agreement was intended to deal with the transition period. Given that its aim was to give SCA the benefit of supply associated with ownership, SCA argued that from a commercial point of view it made more sense to construe the agreement as providing for a fixed price, regardless of currency fluctuations.

The Court of Appeal rejected SCA's argument, and held that the agreement did not provide for a fixed exchange rate. Moore-Bick LJ agreed that the court should prefer giving a clause a meaning 'which better accords with the overall objective of the contract or with good commercial sense'. This principle, however, only applies where 'a clause is reasonably capable of bearing two meanings (and is therefore ambiguous)'. The court's starting point must always be 'the words the parties have chosen to express their intention', and here those words, considered as a whole, were clear and could not be reasonably construed as providing for a fixed rate of exchange.[43]

→

---

41. Ibid, [13] (Lord Hodge).   42. [2012] EWCA Civ 1413.   43. Ibid, [22].

→

Rix LJ agreed. SCA's argument, he said, was commercially sound and he had much sympathy with it.[44] Nevertheless, it was hard to square with the actual wording of the agreement. Although he was prepared to assume that 'the parties did not in fact intend the serendipity of exchange rate fluctuations to be capable of upsetting the essentially cost based calculation of the prices to be charged', much as SCA had contended, the reality was that 'they failed to deal with that contingency' in the contract.[45] As a result, the provision must be read to mean what it seemed to say, and could not be read to provide for a fixed exchange rate.

This case is not an isolated example. It is not difficult to find cases in which the construing court expressly recognized that the meaning it placed on a contract did not reflect the parties' commercial intention. *Total Gas Marketing Ltd v Arco British Ltd*[46] provides an even starker example. The dispute in that case arose out of what was intended to be a long-term contract for the supply of gas, aiming to last for decades, and related to the question of whether the contract could be terminated because of a delay of a few weeks in the seller signing upstream agreements (which was a formality, and was due to factors entirely outside the seller's control). The House of Lords held that it could. Lord Hope recognized in so holding that this was probably not what the parties had intended to achieve. It was 'most unlikely that the parties to this agreement intended that it should be capable of being terminated by reason only of the non-fulfilment of the condition [relating to the documents being signed]'[47] and that the result 'may be at odds with the commercial purpose of the agreement':[48]

> Long term commercial contracts are made in order to protect the value of the investment. It is disappointing to find that in this case it has not been possible to construe the agreement in such a way as to provide the Seller with the protection which it was designed to achieve.[49]

Nevertheless, even when viewed against the commercial background, the wording of the clause was clear, and must be given literal effect.

This points to an important, but often ignored, aspect of the modern approach to interpreting contracts. Although the courts begin from the premise that most parties to contracts will have intended to create a contract that makes commercial sense, they also recognize that parties are free to enter into contracts that do not seem to make commercial sense, if that is what they want to do. The court will not attempt to second-guess a party who thought a particular contract was worth entering into, even if it seems to the judges that the deal made little sense.

There is a fine balance to be struck here, and the way in which English courts attempt to reach this balance was accurately described by Lord Reid in *Wickman Machine Tools Sales Ltd v Schuler AG*:[50]

> The fact that a particular construction leads to a very unreasonable result must be a relevant consideration. The more unreasonable the result, the more unlikely it is that the

44. Ibid, [25], [31]–[32].   45. Ibid, [37].   46. [1998] 2 Lloyd's Rep 209 (HL).
47. Ibid, 223.   48. Ibid, 224.   49. Ibid, 223.   50. [1974] AC 235, 251.

parties can have intended it, and if they do intend it the more necessary it is that they shall make that intention abundantly clear.

The first part of this quote is very well known, but the second is as important, particularly in its implication that if the parties do make their intention clear, then the court will give effect to it. Policing the boundaries of freedom of contract is not a task the law of interpretation is particularly well placed to do. The importance of not rushing too eagerly into a contextual interpretation was stressed by the Supreme Court in *Arnold v Britton*,[51] where the court upheld a literal interpretation even though the outcome of such a reading was on any view utterly unreasonable. The case arose out of a set of contracts for 99-year leases of holiday chalets, under which the lessees of the chalets agreed to pay the owners of the land a service charge, which was described as 'a proportionate part of the expenses and outgoings incurred by the Lessor'. This started at £90 and was subject to an annual 10 per cent escalation. Because the increase was compounded, the result was that by the expiry of the lease in 2072, the lessees would have been paying an annual service charge of £1,025,004. By contrast, another group of lessees in the same park, with a different escalation clause, would have been paying just £1,900.

The lessees paying the high charge argued that such an outcome was absurd, and ran contrary to the idea that the service charge should be a 'proportionate part of the expenses' actually incurred by the lessor. They argued, accordingly, that the clause should be interpreted as only requiring the payment of a proportionate part of the lessor's actual expenses, subject to a cap computed in accordance with the escalation. The Supreme Court rejected this reading, and held that the clause should be construed literally even though they agreed that the outcome was 'highly unsatisfactory'.[52] Lord Neuberger, delivering the majority judgment, set out seven factors for when contextual readings were appropriate, which should be read as qualifications of the five principles set out in *Investors Compensation Scheme v West Bromwich Building Society*. The first six of these, which are paraphrased below, are of general applicability and emphasize the caution which courts must exercise before deciding to depart from the literal meanings of the words.

(1) Except in very unusual cases, the meaning of the clause will most obviously be gleaned from its language. Commercial common sense, and other similar phrases, are not within the parties' control. The language is, and for that reason it must be respected.

(2) Although it is correct to say that 'the worse their drafting, the more ready the court can properly be to depart from' the natural meaning of words, the court must not search for 'drafting infelicities' in order to justify a departure from the natural meaning.

(3) Commercial common sense should not be invoked retrospectively, and should only be used to determine how matters would have been perceived at the date the contract was made. A contract's wording should not be departed from just because it has worked out badly for one of the parties.

---

51. [2015] UKSC 36, [2015] 2 WLR 1593.   52. Ibid, [66] (Lord Hodge).

(4) Although commercial common sense is important, it should not lead courts to reject the natural meaning of a provision simply because it appears imprudent. Courts should enforce what the parties agreed, not what judges think their agreement ought to have been.

(5) Interpretation must only take account of facts known or reasonably available to both parties, and not facts only known to one party.

(6) Sixthly, in dealing with events which the parties did not intend or contemplate, the court will give effect to what the parties would have intended, if that is clear. The court should not adopt an approach which would defeat the parties' clear objectives, but this in turn should be based on what the parties had in mind when contracting.[53]

7.4.2 The position of contextual readings

Much of the commentary following *Arnold v Britton* suggested that the case represented a step back from cases like *Rainy Sky* and *Chartbrook*, both of which had seemed much more receptive to arguments based on the commercial unreasonableness of a particular outcome. In *Wood v Capita*,[54] however, the Supreme Court suggested that this was based on a misreading of the cases: *Rainy Sky* and *Arnold* 'were saying the same thing',[55] and the cases demonstrated 'continuity rather than change'.[56]

This makes perfect sense if, as discussed in section 7.4.1, we see literalism and contextualism simply as tools to be used in figuring out what a contract actually means, rather than paradigms grounded in policy choices; and it underscores the fact that literalism has never gone away. Two sets of closely related concerns underlie the courts' reluctance to extend contextual readings too far, even when it seems that a literal reading is at odds with the parties' commercial objectives. The first is the view—which is very strongly held—that the task of the courts under English contract law is to give effect to the parties' contract, without taking a view as to its fairness or reasonableness. As Moore-Bick LJ put it in *P&G v Svenska Cellulose*, the court must

> take care not to fall into the trap of re-writing the contract in order to produce what it considers to be a more reasonable meaning.[57]

The consequences of this anxiety not to step over the boundary between merely 'interpreting' and 'rewriting' the contract are evident in *P&G v Svenska Cellulose*. Rix LJ said that to read the clause as providing a fixed exchange rate would have been to stray into rewriting the contract, to create an agreement 'which the parties might, or might not, have arrived at, had they thought of and discussed the problem which has overtaken them'.[58] Lord Hoffmann's speech in *Chartbrook*[59] gives us some sense of the reasoning behind this view. Like Rix LJ, Lord Hoffmann took the view that the mere fact that a contractual term proved particularly unfavourable or onerous upon one party did not and should not sway the court's approach to construing that term. The term, he

---

53. [2015] UKSC 36, [22].   54. [2017] UKSC 24, [2017] AC 1173.
55. Ibid, [14] (Lord Hodge).   56. Ibid, [15] (Lord Hodge).
57. [2012] EWCA Civ 1413, [22].   58. Ibid, [38].
59. [2009] UKHL 38, [2009] 1 AC 1101.

pointed out, might have been agreed in the course of negotiations in exchange for a concession on some other term somewhere else in the contract. Alternately, a party may have just made a bad bargain. In either event, it would be inappropriate for a court to intervene on the side of the affected party.[60]

The second factor underlying the courts' reluctance to extend contextual readings beyond a certain point is the importance attached in English law to the objective approach. Under this approach, as we have seen, the parties' subjective intentions are irrelevant, and the court does not seek to determine what they are. What matters is not the parties' actual intention, but the intention that can be imputed to them from the written document, when considered against the backdrop of the relevant matrix of fact.[61]

The cumulative result of the two factors we have just discussed is that, as Lord Steyn put it in *Total Gas Marketing v Arco British*, 'loyalty to the contractual text viewed against its relevant contextual background is the first principle of construction'.[62] What, then, makes the difference between a case where a contextual reading is appropriate, and one where the court sticks to a literal reading of the contract? The courts have not as yet given us a definitive answer to this question, but the case law suggests that it is helpful to think in terms of three thresholds or triggers, the presence of any of which in a given case makes the courts more willing to adopt a contextual reading. Whilst these are not exhaustive, they represent the main strands within the case law.

Ambiguity

The first of these relates to the type of situation that was discussed in *Rainy Sky* and *P&G v Svenska Cellulose*—namely, those where the clause 'is reasonably capable of bearing two meanings (and is therefore ambiguous)'.[63] As we have seen, the approach of the courts to such cases has been contextual since at least the late 19th century, and whilst the idea of what constitutes an 'ambiguity' has widened in the years since *Prenn v Simmonds*,[64] the essential principle remains much the same.

More difficult questions are raised when we are faced with ambiguity occasioned not by the nature of the clause or provision itself, but by the nature of the circumstances to which it is being applied. The case of *Trafigura Beheer v Navigazione Montanari SpA*[65] provides a good illustration. A cargo of oil owned by Trafigura was being carried on a ship owned by Navigazione Montanari. As the ship lay anchored near Lagos, it was captured by pirates, who forcibly seized a portion of the cargo. The contract provided that the shipowner would be 'responsible for the full amount of any in-transit loss if in-transit loss exceeds 0.5%'. Trafigura argued that this meant that Navigazione Montanari were liable to compensate them for the full amount of oil lost to the pirates.

On a literal reading of the clause, this was obviously correct. The oil was in transit when it was taken, and was therefore an 'in transit loss' in the literal sense of that term. The High Court, however, held that the clause should not be given its literal meaning on the facts of the case. The owners had produced testimony from an expert witness with considerable experience of the carriage of oil. Based on the expert's testimony on

---

60. Ibid, [20].
61. See eg the remarks of Rix LJ in *P&G v Svenska Cellulose* [2012] EWCA Civ 1413, [38].
62. [1998] 2 Lloyd's Rep 209, 218.
63. *P&G v Svenska Cellulose* [2012] EWCA Civ 1413, [38].   64. [1971] 1 WLR 1381.
65. [2014] EWHC 129 (Comm). The decision was upheld on appeal: [2015] EWCA Civ 91.

the commercial background to, and purpose of, these clauses, the High Court came to the conclusion that expressions such as loss in transit:

> connote loss that is incidental to the carriage of oil products, and does not extend to losses such as those that occurred in this case because of the action of the pirates.[66]

Trafigura is a very good illustration of how the courts go about deciding what the impact of a contract is in circumstances where this is not entirely clear. As we will see in the next section, it also gives us very useful guidance on the question of how the courts would approach the terms 'limb' and 'bodily injury' in the example that is the subject of this chapter. Before that, however, we will look at two more types of cases where contextual readings are particularly relevant.

Miswording

The second category of cases consists of those where something has gone wrong with the wording. We have seen examples in *Investors* and *Mannai Investment*. In dealing with such cases, the courts tend to draw a distinction between situations where the contract was badly drafted, and those where it was more carefully drafted. In *Mitsui Construction Co v Attorney General of Hong Kong*,[67] Lord Bridge, speaking of the former category, held that:

> the poorer the quality of the drafting, the less willing any court should be to be driven by semantic niceties to attribute to the parties an improbable and unbusinesslike intention, if the language used, whatever it may lack in precision, is reasonably capable of an interpretation which attributes to the parties an intention to make provision for contingencies . . . on a sensible and businesslike basis.[68]

In contrast, where a contract has been carefully drafted, a strong case must be made out before a court will be persuaded that something has gone wrong with the language, and that it is appropriate to depart from the ordinary meaning of the words used.[69] A formula that the courts often use is that the agreement 'makes no commercial sense'.[70] The burden of demonstrating this is a heavy one, and will not be discharged merely by showing the outcome of a literal reading to be burdensome or onerous. In *Gesner Investments Ltd v Bombardier Inc*,[71] the Court of Appeal was asked to interpret a termination clause in an agreement for the purchase of an aircraft. The termination clause distinguished between 'excusable' breaches and 'non-excusable' breaches. Counter-intuitively, however, a literal reading of the clause meant that it was easier to terminate the contract for an excusable breach than for a non-excusable breach. Counsel for Gesner argued that this was an uncommercial result, which seemed strange. Rix LJ agreed that the literal reading seemed strange,[72] but pointed out that the 'alleged commercial unreality and uncertainty' of the provision were there in the document, and were an uncertain basis 'upon which to demand that what might otherwise be reasonably clear contractual language should be reformulated or glossed'.[73] Although it was

---

66. Ibid, [15].   67. (1986) 33 Build LR 1 (PC).   68. Ibid, 14.
69. See eg the remarks of Lord Hoffmann in *Chartbrook* [2009] UKHL 38, [15].
70. *Sompo Japan Insurance Inc v State Street Bank & Trust Co* [2010] EWHC 1461 (Ch), [23].
71. [2011] EWCA Civ 1118.   72. Ibid, [38].   73. Ibid, [33].

unusual, the provision was not impossible to rationalize from a commercial point of view, and as such it should be given effect as written.

The situation is somewhat easier if the error or mistake is obvious. Here, the courts are ordinarily willing to depart from the literal reading of the contract if two conditions are satisfied:

> first, there must be a clear mistake on the face of the instrument; secondly, it must be clear what correction ought to be made in order to cure the mistake. If those conditions are satisfied, then the correction is made as a matter of construction.[74]

Thus, for example, in *Ulster Bank Ltd v Lambe*,[75] one of the parties had sent the other an offer of settlement which mistakenly proposed a figure of €155,000 instead of £155,000. The High Court of Northern Ireland held that given the history of negotiations between the parties, the defendant 'knew and must have known that the offer in euros was a mistake',[76] and that it was therefore appropriate to interpret the letter as an offer to settle at £155,000.[77]

Changed circumstances

The third type of situation where the courts have shown themselves more willing to depart from a literal reading of a contract relates to changed circumstances. *Lloyds TSB Foundation for Scotland v Lloyds Banking Group plc*[78] provides a good illustration. The Lloyds TSB Foundation was a charitable foundation which had originally been created as part of the process by which the Trustee Savings Bank became a listed company. By a deed signed in 1986, TSB Group was obliged to pay a proportion of its 'group profit before taxation . . . shown in the audited accounts' to the foundation. When Lloyds took over TSB Group in 1997, it succeeded to the group's obligations to make these payments, and a revised deed formalizing the new agreements was executed in 1997, preserving the phrasing of the original.

In 2002, as a result of an EU directive, the manner in which pre-tax profits were stated in the audited accounts was very significantly changed, with the introduction of a new concept of 'negative goodwill' which had to be factored into the accounts. In 2009, this change had a particularly dramatic impact. Lloyds TSB had made a pre-tax operating loss of £10 billion, but after taking negative goodwill into account its audited accounts showed a pre-tax profit of £1 billion. The foundation argued that the phrase 'group profit before taxation . . . shown in the audited accounts' should be held to mean precisely what it said. Lloyds TSB, however, argued that they should be interpreted so as to exclude negative goodwill.

The Supreme Court agreed with Lloyds TSB, and held that it was appropriate to depart from the ordinary meaning of the words, even though they were clear and unambiguous. The new accounting context created by the EU directive was 'unthinkable' in 1986

---

74. *East v Pantiles Plant Hire Ltd* [1982] 2 EGLR 111, 112 (Brightman LJ), approved by the House of Lords in *Chartbrook* [2009] UKHL 38, [22]–[23] (Lord Hoffmann).

75. [2012] NIQB 31.   76. Ibid, 25.   77. Ibid, [28].

78. [2013] UKSC 3, [2013] 1 WLR 366. The case was a Scottish appeal, and hence technically did not involve a decision as to English law. However, English authorities were cited in argument and in the judgment, and the Supreme Court does not appear to have treated Scots law as being any different to English law on the issue of interpretation.

and 1997, when the original and revised deeds were executed.[79] As such, the question for the court was one of how the deed's language 'best operates in the fundamentally changed and entirely unforeseen circumstances in the light of the parties' original intentions and purposes'.[80] On this point, the 'landscape, matrix and aim' of the 1997 deed and its predecessors were clear: their concern was with realized profits and losses before taxation.[81] Negative goodwill fell outside this, and hence should not be taken into account.

7.5 **Rectification**

The flexibility that is inherent in the modern approach to interpretation raises the issue of the boundary, or interface, between interpretation and rectification. Rectification was traditionally seen as a process that was distinct from interpretation. Its origins lie in equity and the jurisdiction of Chancery, unlike interpretation which has always been a common law doctrine. The blurring of the boundary between interpretation and rectification raises questions as to the nature of the relationship between the two remedies. When is it appropriate to deploy rectification, and when is it more appropriate to use interpretation? In this section, we will look in brief at what rectification is, how it remains different from interpretation, and why those differences may matter on the facts of an individual case.

The essential character and requirements of the remedy of rectification were summed up by Slade LJ in *The Nai Genova*[82] in these terms:

> In principle, the remedy of rectification is one permitted by the Court, not for the purpose of altering the terms of an agreement entered into between two or more parties, but for that of correcting a written instrument which, by a mistake in verbal expression, does not accurately reflect their true agreement. It follows that the general rule is that rectification will not be granted unless there has been a mistake in verbal expression *common to all parties*.[83]

Typically, this happens where the parties possess a continuing common intention up to the time the agreement is executed but where, for some reason, the agreement does not conform to that common intention. As long as there is clear evidence (or 'convincing proof')[84] of this, the court has the jurisdiction to 'rectify' the agreement in a way that accurately represents the true agreement of the parties at the time.[85] The rationale behind this was explained by Simonds J in *Crane v Hegeman-Harris Co Inc*:[86]

> it would be a strange thing [otherwise], for the result would be that two parties binding themselves by a mistake to which each had equally contributed, by an instrument which did not express their real intention, would yet be bound by it.[87]

79. Ibid, [46] (Lord Hope).   80. Ibid, [23] (Lord Mance).   81. Ibid, [22] (Lord Mance).

82. *Agip SpA v Navigazione Alta Italia SpA (The Nai Genova and Nai Superba)* [1984] 1 Lloyd's Rep 353 (CA).

83. Ibid, 359.   84. *Crane v Hegeman-Harris Co Inc* [1971] 1 WLR 1390, 1391 (Ch).

85. *The Nai Genova* [1984] 1 Lloyd's Rep 353, 359.

86. [1971] 1 WLR 1390 (Ch). Although the report dates from 1971, the case itself was decided in 1939.

87. Ibid, 1391.

Courts also exercise this jurisdiction if one party knows or must have known that the document, as written, does not express the common intention of the parties but keeps silent.[88]

The existence of this element of mistake is a necessary precondition for the grant of the remedy. In particular, if the mistake is not common to both parties, then the party who was not mistaken must have the element of actual knowledge just discussed. In its absence, rectification will not be granted.

This is obviously a considerable difference between the two. In addition, rectification also differs very significantly from interpretation when it comes to the type of material a court will take into account in deciding whether or not to rectify a contract. In interpretation, as we have seen, the court does not look at pre-contractual negotiations as part of the matrix of fact. No such restriction applies in rectification, where pre-contractual negotiations are routinely examined. The result is that a court in rectifying a contract has a much broader range of material available to it than a court would when merely construing a contract. Given that courts are often asked to do both, this can pose issues for the judge, who must be careful when engaged in interpretation not to be influenced by materials that are relevant to rectification, but not to interpretation.[89]

Given the growing overlap between rectification and interpretation, a number of scholars have argued that this evidentiary distinction no longer makes sense.[90] The evidentiary distinction, however, reflects a fundamental distinction between the two. Interpretation, as we have seen, is not concerned with the actual intention of the parties. It is concerned, instead, with what a reasonable observer would have thought the parties intended, based on what they said and did. Rectification, in contrast, is concerned with the parties' *actual* intentions and knowledge, independent of the written document, and assessing whether, and to what extent, the written document actually reflects the parties' true intention.

For this reason, the evidentiary bar tends to be high in rectification. In *Thomas Bates & Son Ltd v Wyndham's (Lingerie) Ltd*, Brightman LJ explained both the nature and the rationale behind the evidentiary requirements that would have to be met for an action of rectification to succeed:

> The standard of proof required in an action of rectification to establish the common intention of the parties is, in my view, the civil standard of balance of probability. But as the alleged common intention ex hypothesi contradicts the written instrument, convincing proof is required in order to counteract the cogent evidence of the parties' intention displayed by the instrument itself. It is not, I think, the standard of proof which is high, so differing from the normal civil standard, but the evidential requirement needed to counteract the inherent probability that the written instrument truly represents the parties' intention because it is a document signed by the parties.[91]

Scholars have questioned whether, given the broad approach to correcting mistakes taken in *Chartbrook*, rectification will in future be as important as it has been in the

88. *Thomas Bates & Son Ltd v Wyndham's (Lingerie) Ltd* [1981] 1 WLR 505 (CA).
89. See the remarks of Hildyard J in the High Court in *P&G v Svenska Cellulose Aktiebolaget* [2012] EWHC 498 (Ch), [11].
90. See eg R Buxton, '"Construction" and "Rectification" after *Chartbrook*' (2010) 69 CLJ 253.
91. [1981] 1 WLR 505, 521 (CA).

past, given the move to having much of its traditional work done through the process of interpretation.[92]

Debates in context: the 'paper' deal and the 'real' deal

One of the more interesting theoretical debates in relation to the law of contract in recent years has related to the question of the relationship between the parties' commercial understanding and the legal agreement they create. The debate began with sociological studies of contractual practices in the second half of the 20th century. The results of these studies, and in particular those carried out by Steward Macaulay, an American contract scholar, came as a surprise to many lawyers, in that they seemed to suggest that parties did not engage particularly deeply with the legal terms of the contract when the contract was being drafted. They also seemed to ignore the terms after the contract had been drafted, and to instead simply work together in a commercially reasonable way.[93]

This led many contract scholars to conclude that contract law was getting it wrong in its relentless focus on the legal terms of the contract. There was, they argued, a clear distinction between the 'paper' deal which the parties wrote down and then proceeded to ignore, and the 'real' deal which was reflected in their actual contractual practices. In practice, the document representing the 'paper' deal was principally a creation of the parties' lawyers rather than the parties themselves, and did not necessarily represent the way they saw the transaction. If the law of contract is to enforce agreements, then it must enforce the agreements the parties actually see themselves as making, rather than the agreement their lawyers recorded for them. Scholars of this school, such as Hugh Collins and Ian Macneil, have argued for a significant relaxation of rules of relevance, and for the courts to determine outcomes of cases by looking not just at the contract but also at a range of relational circumstances—for example, the extent to which one party depends on another, the extent to which the relationship reflects solidarity between the parties, and so on.[94]

The scholars associated with this school have been influential in academic terms, and some have hailed *Investors* as a partial victory, even if much work still remains to be done. There have also been a number of criticisms of this position. One criticism has come from scholars who have questioned how representative the empirical studies as to contracting behaviour are. Scholars such as Lisa Bernstein have conducted studies of how merchant associations actually resolve disputes that they are asked to arbitrate, and find that they are every inch as formalistic as the courts.[95] Based on this, these scholars have argued that the separation

→

92. See eg H Beale (ed), *Chitty on Contracts* (32nd edn, Sweet & Maxwell 2017) 5-122.

93. S Macaulay, 'Non-Contractual Relations and Business: A Preliminary Study' (1963) 28 American Sociological Rev 55; S Macaulay, *Law and the Balance of Power—The Automobile Manufacturers and Their Dealers* (Russell Sage Foundation 1966).

94. H Collins, *Regulating Contracts* (Oxford University Press 1999); I Macneil, *The Relational Theory of Contract: Selected Works of Ian Macneil* (David Campbell ed, Sweet & Maxwell 2001).

95. L Bernstein, 'Merchant Law in a Merchant Court: Rethinking the Code's Search for Immanent Business Norms' (1996) 144 University of Pennsylvania Law Review 1765; L Bernstein, 'The Questionable Empirical Basis of Article 2's Incorporation Strategy: A Preliminary Study' (1999) 66 University of Chicago Law Review 710.

→

between the enforceable 'legal' deal and the unenforceable 'relational' deal is deliberate, and reflects the fact that parties want to be able to be opportunistic and rigid in situations where their relationship has broken down. If they choose to embody their relationship in a particular way in the legal document, then that must be taken to be a choice they have made, with which the court should not interfere.

Another criticism which has been made of the relational approach to contracting is that it expects too much of the courts. Judges are not trained to understand interpersonal relations, and if they have to base their decisions on fuzzy data about how a relationship has worked in practice, there is a serious danger that they will get it badly wrong.[96]

The debate remains very much alive, and is still ongoing.

7.6 The limits of interpretation: misunderstandings and the law of mutual mistake

Interpretation is a powerful tool in dealing with defects in contracts. Its uses are not, however, unlimited. There are situations in which contractual ambiguities run so deep that they cannot be cured through interpretation. One example is the law of **mutual mistake**. Consider the following scenario:

Illustration 7.2

Uncle Percival is planting a new flower bed in his garden. He calls up the nursery to order a new variety of orchid he heard discussed on a radio programme. He asks the nursery how much that variety costs. He is told 'They cost two fifty per seedling.' Assuming the price to be £2.50, he orders ten seedlings, which he receives and plants. When he receives his credit card statement, he is aghast to discover that he has been charged £2,500 for the plants. When he rings the nursery, the nursery insists he was told on the phone that the price was £250 per plant.

We have here a classic example of a situation in which the parties have completely misunderstood each other. Uncle Percival takes 'two fifty' to mean £2.50, when the nursery actually means £250.00. The words themselves are capable of having either meaning. Which of these sums, then, did the parties contract for?

In English law, situations of this sort are the subject of the rules pertaining to mutual mistake.[97] Mutual mistake deals with cases where an agreement has been reached in

96. J Gava and J Greene, 'The Limits of Modern Contract Theory: Hugh Collins on Regulating Contracts' (2001) 22 Adelaide Law Review 301.

97. In English law, the term 'mistake' is applied to three very different doctrines: mutual mistake (dealt with here), common mistake (dealt with in Chapter 10), and unilateral mistake (dealt with in Chapter 11). All three deal with mistakes made by one or both parties, but their ingredients are very different and they are triggered by rather different events. You should be careful not to conflate them.

semantic terms, in that an offer has been made and accepted on its terms, but not in *substantive* terms. As in Illustration 7.2, the words the parties used to express their agreement were capable of having more than one meaning, and each party assumed that a different meaning was intended. Mutual mistake results in the contract being held to be void. The contract is treated as if it never came into existence.

What, then, are the ingredients of mutual mistake? The first point to note is that 'mistake' as a legal doctrine differs quite significantly from what we may term a 'mistake' in common parlance. In law, the mere fact that one party misunderstood the meaning of a contractual term does not mean that there was a 'mistake'. Instead, mutual mistake is judged through an *objective* test. The objective test for mutual mistake follows the same logic as the objective approach to the interpretation of offers, acceptances, and contractual terms—all of which are interpreted with reference to how a reasonable person would have understood the words the parties used, rather than with reference to what the parties actually intended in using the words they did. However, there is one important difference. The reasonable person we are concerned with in mutual mistake is not a third party observer, but the other party to the contract. The court does not, in other words, ask 'how an entirely detached observer might interpret what each party said or did, but how it would reasonably appear to the other party in the circumstances'.[98]

The first step in this process is to assess whether on an objective interpretation the contract at issue can be given a clear meaning. In relation to Illustration 7.2, for example, the question would be whether either the nursery or Uncle Percival show that any reasonable person hearing the words 'two fifty' would understand them to mean what they claim it meant. If the answer to this question is 'yes', the court will give the clause that meaning. It does not matter that one of the parties actually understood the words differently: if a reasonable party would have taken them to have a particular meaning, that is the meaning the court will give them. It is only where the answer to this question is 'no' that the court will hold the contract to be void for mutual mistake. Here, the substantive disagreement concealed behind the parties' apparent semantic agreement is so great that the parties never reached actual agreement. Neither party can show that their interpretation is the one a reasonable person would have reached, or even that it is the more reasonable one.

In practical terms, this means that to successfully plead mutual mistake, you must be able to show, first, that the clause in question was subject to at least two different and irreconcilable interpretations and, secondly, that neither interpretation is more reasonable than the other: it would have been equally reasonable for a party to have understood the clause either way. *Raffles v Wichelhaus*,[99] the leading case of mutual mistake, illustrates the type of circumstance in which a plea of mutual mistake tends to succeed. Here, the parties had contracted for the purchase of cotton, which the seller was to ship to Liverpool 'ex "Peerless" from Bombay'—that is to say, from Bombay on the ship *Peerless*. As it transpired, there were two ships called *Peerless*, both of which were scheduled to sail from Bombay to Liverpool: the first in October and the second in December. The buyer wanted the cotton to arrive by the first ship, and thought that was what he had contracted for. The seller intended to send the cotton by the second

98. H Beale (ed), *Chitty on Contracts* (31st edn, Sweet & Maxwell 2012) 5-071.
99. (1864) 2 H & C 906, 159 ER 375.

ship, and thought that was what he had agreed to do. The court held that under the circumstances, there was no contract.

Mutual mistake, however, only applies in situations where the parties' words cannot be given a clear meaning through the ordinary process of interpretation. *Ryder v Woodley*[100] is a good illustration. This case arose out of a contract by a Sunderland-based miller to purchase a cargo of 'St. Gilles Marais Wheat'. The cargo which arrived was a mixture of wheat and barley, with the barley being between one-seventh and one-eighth of the total. In evidence, it was shown that St Gilles Marais wheat always contained an admixture of barley. The buyers had thought that it was pure wheat. The judge at first instance held that the buyers did not have to accept the cargo.[101] On appeal, it was held that the phrase had a clear meaning, thus making the buyers liable to accept even though they subjectively believed they were contracting for pure wheat.[102]

Ryder illustrates the point that a clause is not invalid for mutual mistake simply because it might produce results that were unexpected or unanticipated from one party's point of view, or simply because one party misunderstood the import of the words.[103] If the courts, through the processes of interpretation and implication, can find an ascertainable standard by which the parties' conduct or the content of their obligations may be judged, the contract or clause is valid. Thus, the contract in *Ryder v Woodley*[104] was valid because the words the parties used did set a standard for judging whether the wheat was of the correct type: the words had an objective meaning, and that meaning was held to govern the contract even though the buyer had misunderstood them. The contract in *Raffles v Wichelhaus*,[105] in contrast, was void because the parties' words did not give the court any way of deciding which ship was the correct ship.

What, then, will be the position of Uncle Percival's contract with the nursery? As the discussion above suggests, it will turn on whether the words 'two fifty', seen in the context in which they were uttered, were genuinely ambiguous. Are both readings of the words equally reasonable? Seen in the context of garden plants, it would appear that they are: £2.50 is at the low end of what one might expect to pay for flowering plant seedlings, but it is entirely reasonable to expect to find seedlings sold for that price. Similarly, £250 is very much at the high end of what one might expect to pay, but rare species do in fact sell for very high prices. It would seem, then, that this is a genuine case of a mutual mistake, rendering the contract void.

However, this is not necessarily a good outcome for Uncle Percival. If the contract of sale is void for mistake, he no longer has a right to the seedlings and must return them to the nursery. Given that the seedlings have been put into the ground, it may well be that he cannot return them in good condition to the nursery. In such a case, he could

---

100. (1862) 10 WR 294.

101. *Ryder v Woodley, Newcastle Courant*, 2 August 1861, p 2, c 5–6 (Durham Ass).

102. It is unclear from the report whether mistake was actually pleaded in the case; however, subsequent cases have treated it as being an authority on mutual mistake. See *Frederick E Rose Ltd v William H Pim Jnr & Co Ltd* [1953] 2 QB 450 (CA), 460 (Denning LJ); *Harrison & Jones Ltd v Bunten & Lancaster Ltd* [1953] 1 QB 646, 655 (Pilcher J).

103. See *NBTY Europe Ltd v Nutricia International BV* [2005] EWHC 734 (Comm), [26] (Nigel Teare QC).

104. (1862) 10 WR 294.   105. (1864) 2 H & C 906, 159 ER 375.

face a claim of *quantum valebat* for the market value of the plants—which will place him in much the same position as he would have been in had the contract been valid. This issue is discussed in greater depth in Chapter 17 (Non-compensatory remedies).

7.7 In conclusion: applying contextualism

How would the *Investors* rule apply to Problem 7? Based on our discussion thus far, it should not come as a surprise to hear that it is next to impossible to predict how a court would decide this particular issue. What we can identify are how a court would approach the question, and what it would take into account.

In the first instance, *Investors* suggests that the problem cannot be resolved simply by looking at the meaning of the words used in the policy. Approaches akin to those adopted by Stanley Burton LJ in *Durham v BAI*, which seek to detach the wording of an instrument from its context, are unlikely to be held to reflect the modern approach to interpreting contracts. The meaning of the policy would, instead, depend on its commercial purpose. However, as *Investors* and subsequent cases emphasize, this is not the same as what the parties subjectively might have wanted. It refers, instead, to what a reasonable person would have interpreted the contract as covering, given its factual background.

The key to interpreting a contract of this type is, therefore, to assemble the relevant factual matrix. This requires the interpreter to look away from single words and phrases to the document as a whole. What is bodily injury linked to? What heads of loss are recoverable in the event of bodily injury? Are these heads of loss related to the loss of mobility, the loss of the ability to work, or similar things? Here, the definition of 'loss of limb(s)', which expressly includes the 'permanent loss of use of a hand or foot' is potentially of relevance, given that it seems to point to a broader concern in relation to the risk of incapacitation. The size of the caps is also likely to be relevant. If the cap for the loss of personal baggage is so small that it will not cover the bulk of claims for prosthetic limbs—even simple ones—then it would seem to suggest that prosthetic limbs were not personal baggage for the purpose of the contract.

Other relevant questions might include the types of risks the policy deals with, and the specific exclusions it contains. Are there any provisions dealing with incapacity and pre-existing medical conditions? What is the import of those provisions, and what type of risks do they seem oriented towards excluding? How do these link in to the premium payable? On what basis is that calculated? What is the position in relation to excess, and how is that stipulated? What would be the consequence of holding that a loss of this type fell outside the scope of the policy? Would it erect arbitrary divisions between recoverable and non-recoverable loss? Equally, we would have to look to the question of how removable prosthetic devices are treated in other contexts. Are they treated as akin to body parts or to property—for example, by carriers such as ships and airlines?

As these points suggest, the enquiry contemplated by *Investors* is complex. A number of initial reactions to the decision were critical of the decision on precisely this ground. Sir Christopher Staughton, a former Lord Justice of Appeal, writing in the Cambridge Law Journal, said that 'It is hard to imagine a ruling more calculated to perpetuate the vast cost of commercial litigation.'[106] Malcolm Clarke, referring to the 'Hoffmann "school"', feared that its implication was that 'the traditional barrier on the outskirts of a written contract has been largely dismantled'.[107] Underlying these reactions is a broader worry that the contextual approach to interpretation advocated by Lord Hoffmann in *Investors* is inherently uncertain and difficult to apply in comparison with more literal approaches.

The history of cases applying contextualism suggests there is some substance to these complaints. One of the first decisions of the House of Lords applying *Investors* was *BCCI v Ali*.[108] This case involved the interpretation of an agreement entered into between former employees of BCCI, a bank which was forcibly closed and liquidated in 1991 following allegations that it had engaged in criminal activities, and the bank itself. The agreement provided for redundancy and other payments to the employees, who agreed not to pursue any legal claims against their former employer. After the agreement was signed, it was held in *Malik v BCCI*[109] that employees of BCCI could recover 'stigma damages' to reflect the harm done to them through their association with BCCI. The claimants in this case sought to recover stigma damages, and argued that their agreement not to pursue legal claims should be construed as not applying to stigma damages, given that the existence of the action had not been recognized when the agreement was made. The majority of the House of Lords upheld the employees' contention, citing Lord Hoffmann's speech in *ICS* with approval. However, Lord Hoffmann himself—who was on the panel in *Ali*—did not concur with the majority, and delivered a dissent disagreeing with the majority's application of his opinion in *Investors*. His decision would have held that the agreement should be held to preclude an action for stigma damages. Many of the post-*Investors* cases have similarly involved judicial disagreement, whether in the form of dissents in the House of Lords or Supreme Court, or in the form of lower court decisions that differed from the ultimate outcome.

The intent of *Investors* was not, however, to simplify the law, but to keep it from producing results that were technical or absurd. Returning to Problem 7, the *Investors* approach does not aim to make this problem easier to resolve. Instead, it aims to make the resolution less technical and more sensible, even if that makes the process of resolving the dispute harder or more open to disagreement. Accordingly, there is another line of criticism of *Investors* that is levelled on the basis that it does not go far enough. Even after *Investors*, it is argued, the law has not come close enough to erasing the difference between the 'legal' deal and the 'business' deal (see 'Debates in context' in section 7.5). If the purpose of the law is to be to give effect to the legitimate expectations of honest persons,[110] then the law must come far closer to the business deal, and to giving effect to the parties' commercial understanding of their transaction than *Investors* contemplates.

The disagreement between the two sides goes back to the question of the relationship between, on the one hand, the parties' transaction and the commercial understanding

---

106. C Staughton, 'How Do the Courts Interpret Commercial Contracts?' (1999) 58 CLJ 303, 307.
107. M Clarke, 'Interpreting Contracts—The Price of Perspective' (2000) 59 CLJ 18, 19.
108. [2001] 1 All ER 961.   109. [1998] AC 20.
110. Lord Steyn, 'Contract Law: Fulfilling the Reasonable Expectations of Honest Men' (1997) 113 LQR 433.

on which it is built and, on the other, the formal legal terms that the contract embodies. The formalist critique of *Investors*—seen in, for example, the article by Sir Christopher Staughton cited earlier—is based on the position that it is the latter that must be the principal focus of the courts' attention, and that doing so is not commercially unreasonable. The parties are perfectly free to structure this relationship as they choose. If a party could have protected his interests by using a particular form of words but failed to do so, it is not the court's role to give him that protection.

The contextualist critique of *Investors*, in contrast, starts from the position that the courts' focus should be on the commercial deal, not the legal terms. Courts cannot properly understand the transaction if they start with the legal terms—they must, instead, start with an understanding of the transaction as a whole, and aim to give effect to the parties' expectations in the context of the transaction as a whole. This will sometimes require them to give effect to the legal terms as written, but there may be other contexts in which it will require them to go beyond the legal terms.

Investors itself seems to strike a balance between these two extremes, particularly when read in the context of *Arnold* and *Wood*. On the one hand, the courts do begin with the legal document, and they do detach the legal document from the parties' subjective intent. On the other hand, the legal document is construed in the light of the transaction as a whole. Whether this balance has successfully adopted the strengths of both approaches, or whether it has created a test that will suffer from the weaknesses of each approach without their corresponding strengths, is an issue that will only become clear in the coming years as the *Investors* approach entrenches itself in the case law.

Key points

- English law has, in recent years, moved away from a predilection to taking literal approaches to interpreting contract. Courts are now far readier to engage in contextual readings than they once were.

- Engaging in a contextual reading, however, requires certain triggers, or threshold conditions, to be met. The most important of these are ambiguity, miswording, and changed circumstances.

- Contextual interpretation is grounded in the meaning a contractual instrument would convey to the reasonable addressee. This requires reading the instrument as a whole, against the background of the 'matrix of fact'; that is, all the background knowledge available to the parties at the time of contracting. For reasons of policy, material relating to the parties' negotiations is not part of the matrix of fact.

- Contextual interpretation gives considerable discretion to the courts, and recent case law has shown a more cautious approach, with courts emphasizing the need to respect the parties' agreed wording. A contextual reading should not be adopted for the sole reason that it would be more commercially reasonable.

- Courts also have the power to rectify contracts if, due to a mistake in verbal expression, the written instrument deviates from the parties' actual agreement. The evidentiary bar for rectification is very high.

- Where parties have agreed in verbal terms, but have failed to reach substantive agreement because they misunderstood each other, and where the ambiguity cannot be resolved through a literal or contextual reading, the contract is void. This principle is sometimes called 'mutual mistake'.

Assess your learning

You should be able to respond to each of the following points with a confident 'yes'. If you can't, then you should revisit the sections listed against that point.

Can you:

(a) *Identify* the main differences between literal and contextual approaches to interpreting contracts? (Section 7.2)

(b) *Outline* the key elements of contextual readings, including the role of the matrix of fact, and the triggers for engaging in a contextual reading? (Sections 7.3 and 7.4)

(c) *Explain* the remedy of rectification, and the circumstances in which it is available? (Section 7.5)

(d) *Describe* the circumstances under which a contract will be void for mutual mistake? (Section 7.6)

In relation to each of the above, you should be able to:

(i) identify and clearly explain the key rules and principles;

(ii) identify the key cases and statutes, and why they matter;

(iii) apply the principles and cases to specific real or hypothetical fact situations;

(iv) evaluate the limitations, if any, of the law as it currently stands.

Further reading

A Burrows and E Peel (eds), *Contract Terms* (Oxford University Press 2007).

R Buxton, '"Construction" and "Rectification" after *Chartbrook*' (2010) 69 CLJ 253.

S Gee, 'The Interpretation of Commercial Contracts' (2001) 117 LQR 358.

D McLauchlan, 'Contract Interpretation: What is it About?' (2009) 31 Sydney Law Review 5.

G McMeel, *The Construction of Contracts: Interpretation, Implication, and Rectification* (2nd edn, Oxford University Press 2011).

C Mitchell, 'Leading a Life of its Own? The Roles of Reasonable Expectation in Commercial Contracts' (2003) 23 OJLS 639.

C Mitchell, *Contract Law and Contract Practice: Bridging the Gap Between Legal Reasoning and Commercial Expectation* (Hart 2013).

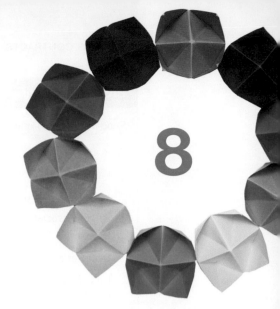

Filling the gaps

Implied terms

'The things we leave unsaid'

Problem 8: setting the context

Read the following letter, and think about the legal issues it raises.

The Surtees Trust
Surtees Hall, Mainsforth, Co. Durham

Rebecca Mainwaring

Furton Associates

Durham

Dear Rebecca,

I'm writing to ask if you can give us some advice on a dispute we're having with the photographer and print-maker Anthony Musgrave.

As you may know, Musgrave rose to prominence in the 1960s and 1970s for his iconic photographs of everyday life in the pit towns of Yorkshire and County Durham. Twenty of these, known as the Fairford Set, are particularly celebrated. In 2007, he released what he said would be a 'limited edition, restricted to 100 copies' of poster-sized prints of the Fairford Set, to be sold on the basis of sealed bids through the auction house Linford's. Because they were announced as being a limited edition, they sold for a very high price. Our bid, which was successful, was for £12 million, and we know it was at the lower end of the successful bids.

To our dismay, in 2012 Musgrave announced that he was going to reissue the same set of 20 prints in a new edition, of 500 copies, this time in a larger size, and once again sold by sealed bids. According to the advance publicity material, the prints are to be made using a superior digital technique, and will be of far higher quality in comparison with the earlier edition. Issuing another edition of the Fairford Set seems to us to be completely contrary to the terms of the previous sale. The description in the sale catalogue of the prints we bought, and the final terms of sale, described it as a 'limited edition, restricted to 100 numbered copies, of poster-sized prints of the Fairford Set'. However, both Musgrave and Linford's claim that neither the catalogue description nor the terms of sale in any way restricted Musgrave's ability to issue further editions in a different size or using a different technique.

We would like your advice on where we stand. As we see it, if a contract describes something as a 'limited edition', then surely it must be implicit in the contract that the artist will not issue future editions of the same material. What sense would there be otherwise in terming anything a 'limited edition'? We think Musgrave is being disingenuous and dishonest, and is in breach of the terms of the sale. We would like your view on the legal position before we take further action.

Yours sincerely,

Thomas Surtees

8.1 Introduction: implicit understandings and contractual gaps

The focus of previous chapters has been on issues, terms, and clauses that parties have actually discussed. But the process of determining the content of a contract will sometimes pose questions relating to matters which the parties' contract does not expressly cover and which they may not even have discussed. In English law, issues of this type are dealt with through **implied terms**.

8.1.1 The nature of implied terms

As the name suggests, implied terms are terms that were not expressly discussed by the parties, but which are nevertheless treated as forming part of the parties' contract. It may at first sight seem counter-intuitive to suggest that a contract could contain terms that the parties did not discuss or reach agreement on, but such terms are in fact a fundamental part of how contracting works in the real world. Consider the following scenario:

Illustration 8.1

You go into a shop to buy a pair of noise-cancelling earphones for your new phone. You find a pair that you like, pay for them, and take them home.

In terms of the formation process, the display of the headphones is an invitation to treat. By taking them to the counter, you make an offer to purchase then, which the person at the counter accepts on behalf of the store. At no stage in the process of offer and acceptance do you discuss or reach agreement on any terms other than the price and the goods that are the subject of the sale. Nor do stores display terms and conditions of sale in the way car parks, for example, do.

Most of us enter into contracts of this sort every day, without discussing any terms other than the price. Does the failure to discuss any other terms mean that none have been agreed? What happens if the headphones turn out to be defective? Does the absence of express agreement mean that selling defective headphones is *not* a breach of contract? Clearly not. That is not what sellers and buyers in such a situation expect, and English law does not hold to a strict understanding of **caveat emptor**[1] in contracts for the sale of goods. Nor should it. A rule that required a buyer to strictly inspect goods and ascertain their every conceivable attribute before committing to purchasing them would make buying and selling things impossible.

Parties frequently leave issues thrown up by their transaction to an *implicit* understanding of what their rights and obligations are. This might be an implicit understanding which the parties share, or it may be one party's understanding of what it expects the law to give it. The latter characterizes consumer transactions. In a scenario such as Illustration 8.1, your contract is grounded on a lot of things you implicitly

---

1. See Chapter 1 for an explanation of this term, and its historical role in English contract law.

assume, but which you are unlikely to expressly discuss with the seller. If you buy headphones in a sealed box, for example, you will usually operate on the assumption that the box actually has headphones in it, that the headphones are as described and similar to the display model, that they will work when plugged in, and so on. People contract without expressly discussing any of this with the shop because they take these things as given. You would ordinarily expect that if you buy headphones without testing them, and they turn out to be faulty, you will be able to insist that the store replace them or give you a refund.

Implicit expectations such as these are also present in commercial transactions. In Problem 8, for example, it seems clear that the parties must have contemplated that the description of the set of prints as a 'limited edition' would impose some sort of limit on Musgrave's legal privilege to make further prints of the set: otherwise the phrase 'limited edition' would be pointless. Yet the contract does not tell us what these limits are and where they lie, and it would not be unusual to find—as in this case—that the parties never discussed them. The law relating to implied terms is concerned with situations such as these. In legal terms, the Surtees Trust is arguing that the contract contained an implied term that Musgrave would not produce future prints of the Fairford Set, based on their implied understanding of what they agreed. The question for the law is when to recognize and give effect to these implicit understandings. The process by which the courts decide what terms to imply and what those implied terms say is referred to as *implication*.

When, then, will the courts imply terms into contracts? And how do we decide what these terms say, and what they require of parties? These questions are the subject of this chapter.

8.1.2 Striking a balance

The process of implication requires the court to strike a difficult balance. To understand the nature of this balance, let us return to Illustration 8.1's example of a person buying a pair of headphones. How does the law decide which, if any, of the many implicit expectations which the parties hold should be protected by the law?

The reason why this question is difficult to answer will become clearer if we consider another, and more specific, example:

> **Illustration 8.2**
>
> Edith verbally agrees with Norman, her neighbour, to pay £100 a year in return for being allowed to drive across a path on his land to get to the main road. A storm causes a tree to fall across the path rendering it inaccessible. Norman asks Edith to pay 75 per cent of the cost of having the tree removed.

Here we are, once again, faced with a minimalistic contract. The parties have not agreed on very much beyond the price, and now face a situation with which the contract does not deal. What, then, are their rights and duties in this situation? Does Norman have to keep the path free of all obstacles? Free of minor obstacles, but not major ones? Or is he under no obligation to do anything, given that the contract does not expressly place him under any?

Situations like these are difficult because they require the courts to tread a fine line between filling gaps in the contract and rewriting the contract. Implication in English law is about the former and not the latter. Implication is not about improving the parties' contract, or making it fairer or more just, or even making it work better. The courts see their task as being to give effect to matters that are implicit in the parties' contract. They will not make a new contract for the parties, nor paternalistically rewrite their contract. The essence of this approach was summarized by Lord Pearson in *Trollope & Colls Ltd v North West Metropolitan Regional Hospital Board*:[2]

> the court does not make a contract for the parties. The court will not even improve the contract which the parties have made for themselves, however desirable the improvement might be. The court's function is to interpret and apply the contract which the parties have made for themselves . . . An unexpressed term can be implied if and only if the court finds that the parties must have intended that term to form part of their contract . . . a term which, though tacit, formed part of the contract which the parties made for themselves.[3]

Much of the law in relation to implied terms is about determining the line between recognizing dimensions implicit within the contract, which the courts will do, and adding things to the contract for the sake of improving it, which they will not do. Courts prefer to err on the side of caution, as the decision of the Court of Appeal in *Fitzhugh v Fitzhugh*[4] illustrates.

Case in depth: *Fitzhugh v Fitzhugh* [2012] EWCA Civ 694

Mr Fitzhugh died intestate, leaving behind a farm amongst other properties. The claimant, Harry Fitzhugh, and the defendant, Anthony Fitzhugh, were his only surviving sons at the time of the litigation. They were joint administrators of Mr Fitzhugh's estate. As administrators, they granted a licence over some fields and outbuildings to Anthony Fitzhugh and his partner, Karen Boddey, in consideration of the payment of an annual fee of £1. This meant that Anthony was both a licensor (in his capacity as joint administrator) and a licensee (in his personal capacity).

The licence provided that it could be terminated on a number of grounds, one of which was the following:

> The Licensee commits any grave or persistent breaches of this Licence and the Licensor having given written notice to the Licensee of such breach or breaches the Licensee fails within such period as the Licensor may specify to rectify such breaches if capable of rectification.[5]

Anthony and his partner failed to pay the annual license fee of £1 for seven years. Harry Fitzhugh, as one of the licensors, then sent them a notice giving them seven days to pay

→

2. [1973] 1 WLR 601.   3. Ibid, 609.   4. [2012] EWCA Civ 694.   5. Ibid, [6].

➡

the fee, but they did not do so. He thereupon brought proceedings seeking possession of the licensed land. Anthony argued that the notice was invalid, as it had to come from all the licensors under the contract, and it had not—Anthony, as a joint licensor, had not consented to its issue.

It was argued on behalf of Harry Fitzhugh that a term should be implied into the contract permitting Harry to act without Anthony's participation where Anthony faced a conflict of interest, as he did here. To do otherwise would be to enable Anthony to take advantage of his own breach. Morgan J, who decided the case at first instance, agreed.[6] His decision was, however, overruled on appeal. Rimer LJ in the Court of Appeal said that the appropriate action for Harry to take would be to invite Anthony to participate in the issue of a notice to himself. If he declined, 'he would be failing in his duties as an administrator of the estate', which meant that Harry could seek to have him removed. Once this happened, Harry would be in a position to issue a notice without Anthony's participation.[7] It was true that this was a cumbersome procedure, which could give rise to practical difficulties and unwanted expenses, but the court would not imply a term into a contract just because the alternative was cumbersome.[8]

Fitzhugh v Fitzhugh demonstrates that the courts will not fill a contractual gap simply because it would be fair or reasonable or normatively better, or even more convenient, to do so. Something more is needed. The case must be brought within one of a small number of categories of cases in which terms will be implied.

8.1.3 The tests for implication

Common law courts tend to imply terms into contracts in two broad types of situations. First, courts may imply a term into a contract based on facts specific to that particular transaction. Here, there is something about that *specific* contract that leads the court to conclude that a particular term should be read into it. In law, we refer to these as **terms implied in fact**, because the court is implying a term on the basis of the specific facts before it, rather than as a general matter of law.

The second category consists of terms that, as a matter of common law precedent or applicable statute, are implied into all contracts of a particular type. These are referred to as **terms implied in law**. Terms implied in law are implied not because of the specifics of a *particular* contract, but because they are seen as belonging in *all* contracts of that type. Unlike terms implied in fact, terms can be implied in law for a range of reasons, including reasons of policy that have little to do with the parties' bargain.

In this chapter, we will study how the law in relation to implied terms functions. We will begin (in section 8.2) with the sort of circumstances that lead courts to imply terms in law, before moving on (in section 8.3) to considering terms implied in fact. Sections 8.4 and 8.5 consider more specific questions of how implied terms can draw on commercial custom, and how they are used in transactions which require the parties to cooperate.

6. [2011] EWHC 3553 (Ch), [89]–[95].   7. [2012] EWCA Civ 694, [17].   8. Ibid, [21].

8.2 **Terms implied in law**

8.2.1 **The context**

Think once again about the example of the purchase of headphones in Illustration 8.1. Now consider the following, similar, examples:

Illustration 8.3

Your bicycle's derailleur keeps slipping the chain when you try to change gear. You take it to the neighbouring bike shop to get it fixed.

Illustration 8.4

Great Aunt Agatha needs a new set of false teeth. She makes an appointment with her dentist, who takes measurements and says that she will arrange to have a new set made.

Illustration 8.5

DJ Bling is a semi-professional DJ, who does regular gigs at clubs and events. One of his clubs is regularly several weeks late with its payments. His contracts with the club consist of one-page letters of engagement issued by the club, which say nothing about the consequences of late payments.

These illustrations share two points in common. First, they are all bare-boned contracts. The parties have discussed, and reached agreement on, only those terms which they regard as important[9]—dates, payment, and so on—which are, primarily, the sort of terms you need if everything in the contract goes *right*. They have neither discussed nor reached agreement on terms that cover situations where things go *wrong*—warranties, consequences of breach, and so on. This happens all the time in the real world. This is not because the parties have been lazy, or failed to spend enough time thinking about their transaction. Rather, it is because the social and commercial context of the contracting process makes the existence of contract gaps inevitable. Dentists and their patients do not haggle over the terms of a contract. A customer in a bike shop, too, does not engage in detailed negotiations in relation to the shop's liability for work poorly done. Doing so would be socially unacceptable.

Secondly, every one of these examples relates to *standard* transactions, of types that are common. Thousands of contracts involving the sale of goods, or the rendering of services, or the making of commercial payments, are likely to be entered into every month. As a result, the vast majority of gaps that arise in relation to these contracts

---

9. Or, in the case of the contract with the club, the terms which one of the parties—the club—regards as important.

also tend to be fairly standard. In contracts for the sale of goods or services, we can be pretty sure that a significant proportion of disputes will relate to the quality of the goods or services—for example, that the headphones fail miserably at reproducing the subtleties of deep basses, that the false teeth are ill-fitting, that the bike was not really fixed, and so on. Similarly, in a contract that involves the making of a commercial payment, many disputes will relate to payment not being made on time.

Terms *implied in law* deal with situations where the nature of the contracting process makes gaps inevitable, and where gaps are relatively easy to predict. Situations involving transactions that are less standard, or gaps that are harder to predict, are dealt with through the rules and process governing the implication of terms in fact (discussed in section 8.3).

8.2.2 Implication by statute

The first and most straightforward type of terms implied in law are statutory implied terms. These are terms that are deemed by primary or secondary legislation to be implicit in all contracts of a particular type.

The paradigmatic example of terms implied by statute are the terms implied by the Sale of Goods Act 1979 into all commercial contracts under which goods are bought or sold, and the similar, but broader, terms implied by the Consumer Rights Act 2015 into all consumer contracts. Let us return to Illustration 8.1, involving a person buying headphones at a shop. The 1979 Act and the 2015 Act flesh out the very basic terms on which the parties have reached agreement. Under both, the following terms, amongst others, are deemed to be implied in any contract under which goods are sold.

- *The right to sell*: the law implies a term into contracts to the effect that the seller has title to the goods at the time of sale—or, to put it differently, that the seller actually has (or will have) the right to sell the goods at the time she sells them.[10] So if you buy a used bicycle, or a car, or a smartphone, there is an implied term in your contract to the effect that the person who is selling the goods to you has the right to sell them. He does not need to be the owner necessarily—he might, for instance, be selling the goods on behalf of, or with the permission of, the owner.
- *Correspondence to samples*: if the goods are sold by sample, then the law will imply a term into the contract to the effect that the goods will correspond to the sample in terms of quality, and that they will be free from defects which would not be apparent on an examination of the sample.[11]
- *Correspondence to description*: if the goods have been sold by *description*, the law implies a term to the effect that the goods will correspond to the description.[12] So, for example, there is an implied term to the effect that a sealed box which says it contains a pair of headphones really will contain headphones, that a phone which is described as having an 'aluminium body' really will be made of that metal (and not merely be painted that colour), and so on. The concept of a sale by description

10. This is called a warranty of title. Sale of Goods Act (SoGA) 1979, s 12; Consumer Rights Act 2015 (CRA), s 17.
11. SoGA 1979, s 15, CRA, s 13.   12. SoGA 1979, s 13, CRA, s 11.

is very broad, but not infinitely broad. Statements that simply relate to the quality of the thing being sold are not considered part of its description.

- *The satisfactoriness of the goods' quality*: if the seller is transacting in the course of her business, the law will imply a term into the contract of sale to the effect that the goods will be of satisfactory quality.[13] 'Satisfactoriness' refers to the state and condition of the goods, and is considered with reference to a range of factors.[14] These include matters such as the goods' safety and durability, their freedom from minor defects, and their appearance and finish. Most importantly, goods will not be of 'satisfactory quality' unless they are 'fit for all the purposes for which goods of the kind in question are commonly supplied',[15] as well as any specific purpose made known to the seller.[16] The description of the goods and their price are also relevant:[17] something branded as a 'premium' product will ordinarily be held to a higher standard than products from the bottom of the bargain bin.

Each of these terms has been the subject of an intricate body of case law, which considers in great detail precisely what they require the parties to do. This is entirely typical of statutory implied terms, whose full ramifications only become clear through studying the case law. In addition, these terms also give significant room to take account of context-specific factors. The result is that this relatively short list of implied terms successfully deals with the vast majority of things that might go wrong in the course of a transaction of sale.

To see this, let us relate these terms back to the illustrations, starting with the headphones. Let's say the packaging describes the headphones in these terms:

Illustration 8.6

Premium high-sensitivity audiophile headphones
- gold plated jack for secure signal transition
- plush cushioned panels for ultimate comfort
- closed over-ear design for superior noise control
- classic black and red design for a premium look

If the headphones turn out to have fairly standard sensitivity (eg 100db), or low sensitivity (eg 90db), or if the jack turns out to have simply had a couple of licks of cheap yellow paint, there will have been a breach of the implied term that the goods will correspond to their description. Similarly, the presence of the words 'premium', 'audiophile', 'comfort', and 'superior noise control' on the packaging will affect what the courts deem to be 'satisfactory quality' (as will the price). If the headphones turn out to be supremely uncomfortable, poking and prodding the ear in all sorts of places, or if they break easily, or produce audio of very poor quality, it is likely that the buyer will have strong grounds to argue that the implied term of satisfactory quality was breached.

13. SoGA 1979, s 14(2), CRA, s 9(1).   14. SoGA 1979, s 14(2B), CRA, s 9(3).
15. SoGA 1979, s 14(2B)(a), CRA, s 9(3)(a).   16. SoGA 1979, s 14(3), CRA, s 10.
17. SoGA 1979, s 14(2A), CRA, s 9(2).

What about Illustrations 8.3 and 8.4—the broken derailleur and Great Aunt Agatha's false teeth? The Sale of Goods Act 1979 does not apply to either of these contracts, because neither is a contract for the sale of goods in the strict sense. Both are, primarily, contracts for services, which incidentally involve the transfer of property in goods. To understand the distinction, it may be helpful to think in terms of a contract with a builder to build an extension onto your house. You would not ordinarily say that the builder is 'selling' you bricks, cement, floorboards, and paint. What you have, instead, is a contract for a builder's services, with property in certain objects being transferred to you in the course of the performance of those services. The situation is much the same with a contract with a dentist for fitting dentures or with a bike shop to repair a bicycle. Property in goods is likely to be transferred in the course of both contracts (property in the false teeth in the first case and property in spare parts in the second case), but neither is a contract for the sale of goods.

In English law, commercial contracts of this type are dealt with under the Supply of Goods and Services Act 1982. The 1982 Act contains three sets of implied terms. The first set deals with goods which are transferred in the course of performing services (and in some other transactions).[18] These terms are substantially similar to the terms implied under the Sale of Goods Act 1979.[19] The second set deals with terms implied into contracts for the hire of goods. These, too, are very similar to the terms implied under the Sale of Goods Act.[20] The third set deals with terms relating to the services themselves. The key term implied into such contracts is that any service provider who is acting in the course of a business will 'carry out the service with reasonable care and skill'.[21]

The Consumer Rights Act 2015, similarly, contains three sets of implied terms dealing with contracts for the sale of goods, contracts for digital content, and contracts for services. Their provisions are substantially similar. The contracts between Great Aunt Agatha and the dentist (Illustration 8.4) and between the bike shop and customer (Illustration 8.3), therefore, will be dealt with in substantially the same way as the contract for the sale of headphones (Illustration 8.1).

Why do we have separate statutes implying similar terms, rather than a single statute? English law tends to eschew broad statements of principle when it comes to implying terms in law, preferring to be quite specific. Implied terms relating to goods transferred under hire-purchase contracts, to take another example, are governed by yet another statute, the Supply of Goods (Implied Terms) Act 1973, whose provisions on implied terms are once again substantially identical to those set out in the Sale of Goods Act 1979.[22] In principle, there is no reason at all why these could not be consolidated into a hypothetical Contracts (Implied Terms) Act. A consolidated statute of this type would certainly make the lives of business people (and even lawyers) easier. However, this is not how English law works. Statutes on implied terms are narrow and particular, because that is how statutes dealing with private law have always been written.

---

18. The Act defines its scope negatively, and excludes contracts for the sale of goods, hire-purchase contracts, contracts intended to operate by way of a security interest, and contracts entered into by deed and without consideration other than the presumed consideration imported by the deed. See Supply of Goods and Services Act 1982, s. 1(2).

19. Supply of Goods and Services Act 1982, ss 2–5.   20. Ibid, ss 7–10.

21. Ibid, s 13.   22. See ss 8–11.

A specific statute also applies to Illustration 8.5—the contract between DJ Bling and the club. Under the Late Payment of Commercial Debts (Interest) Act 1998, there is an implied term in all contracts for the sale or transfer of property in goods, or the carrying out of services,[23] that a debt created under the contract carries with it a right to simple interest at a rate fixed by the government.[24] As a result, DJ Bling will have a right to demand the payment of interest on all fees not paid on time, even if the contract itself makes no mention at all of interest.

The statutes we have considered in this section are not exhaustive—there are far more statutes implying terms into contracts than could be conveniently listed in a textbook. The point to keep in mind is that the statutes which act as a source of implied terms under English law are very varied, cover a wide variety of issues, and tend to be quite specific.

8.2.3 Implication at common law

Let us return now to Illustration 8.2, involving a dispute between Edith and Norman. No statute currently in force contains any implied terms that deal with this situation. However, apart from statutory implied terms, the courts also retain the power to imply terms into contracts as a matter of common law. This process is often referred to as *implication at common law*, to distinguish it from both implication under statute and implication in fact.

As with terms implied through statute, terms implied at common law apply to all contracts of a particular type. Many statutory implied terms began as terms implied at common law before being codified in statute.[25] Unlike statutory implied terms, terms implied at common law are created through precedent, rather than through primary or secondary legislation. We can classify the implication of terms at common law into two broad types: the implication of terms established by precedent and the implication of *novel* terms which have not previously been implied by the courts and which the courts are asked to imply for the first time.

Established terms

The first of these types is relatively straightforward. There is a considerable body of terms which existing precedent requires to be implied into all contracts of a particular type. Employment contracts are a classic example. Case law has established that every contract of employment contains an implied term to the effect that the employee will serve the employer faithfully.[26] Similarly, it also contains an implied term obliging both parties not to act in a manner that damages the relationship of trust and confidence that subsists between employer and employee.[27] Crucially, neither of these terms is set out in statute. They are implied into all contracts of employment because the courts have decided that they should be implied.

---

23. Late Payment of Commercial Debts (Interest) Act 1998, s 2.   24. Ibid, s 1(1).

25. The implied terms set out in the SoGA 1979, eg, are based on terms which emerged in case law over several decades in the 18th and 19th centuries. They were first codified in the Sale of Goods Act 1893, slightly modified by the 1979 Act, and amended again to broaden their scope by the Sale and Supply of Goods Act 1994.

26. *Lister v Romford Ice & Cold Storage Co* [1957] AC 555 (HL).

27. *Malik v BCCI* [1998] AC 20 (HL).

In *Lister v Romford Ice & Cold Storage Co*,[28] the first of these—the implied duty of faithful service—was at issue. Lister, a lorry driver working for Romford, accidentally drove over the foot of a fellow employee (who also happened to be his father) when out on a job. The injured employee was awarded compensation, and an action was brought against Lister by the company's insurers to recover the money from him. In the House of Lords, Lord Tucker set out the following duties of an employee which would be implied into every contract of employment:

(1) the duty to give reasonable notice in the absence of custom or express agreement;
(2) the duty to obey lawful orders of the master;
(3) the duty to be honest and diligent in the master's service;
(4) the duty to take reasonable care of his master's property entrusted to him and generally in the performance of his duties;
(5) to account to his master for any secret commission or remuneration received by him;
(6) not to abuse his master's confidence in matters pertaining to his services.[29]

The result was that Lister was liable to indemnify his employer's insurers for the loss his negligence had caused.[30]

Malik v BCCI[31] related to a different term—the implied duty not to damage the relationship of trust and confidence. Malik worked for a bank, BCCI, which collapsed after regulatory investigations suggested that it had engaged in 'widespread fraud and manipulation', including facilitating money laundering and corruption. He alleged that BCCI's conduct was so egregious that his past employment with BCCI tainted him and adversely affected his employment prospects. The question for the House of Lords was the preliminary one of whether Malik had a cause of action. The House of Lords held that he did, on the basis that BCCI had violated the implied obligation of trust and confidence in an employment relationship.

Common law precedent has similarly established a range of terms that are implied into several types of other agreements, including tenancy agreements, contracts for the carriage of goods, guarantee agreements, contracts with innkeepers, and so on. Once again, there are far more of these terms than a textbook can conveniently discuss. The point to keep in mind is that terms implied at common law are a diverse bunch, covering a wide range of transaction types.

Novel terms

More difficult questions are raised when one party seeks to have the courts imply a new type of term into a particular type of contract. Although any judge has the power to imply a new term at common law, this is not a power which judges exercise frequently.

---

28. [1957] AC 555 (HL). *Lister* is also an important case in relation to vicarious liability in tort law.
29. Ibid, 594.
30. You should note that the case caused an outcry, and the insurance industry eventually voluntarily agreed that it would not in future seek to recover damages against employees where the employer had insured against third party liability. The principles Lord Tucker derived from the duty of faithful service, however, still stand.
31. [1998] AC 20 (HL).

Broadly speaking, the case law suggests that the courts imply novel terms if four relatively stringent conditions are met.

First, the contract must belong to a *'definable category of contractual relationship'*,[32] capable of definition with 'sufficient precision'[33] and of 'common occurrence'.[34] The courts will not in general imply terms at common law into a contract if the category of relationships involved is either too broad or too narrow. In *Ashmore v Corp of Lloyd's (No 2)*,[35] Gatehouse J held that a set of contracts which were identical except for the parties' names was not a sufficiently broad category for terms to be implied at common law: the fact that the contracts were all identical made them *sui generis*. In *Scally v Southern Health and Social Services Board*,[36] in contrast, the court held that a category consisting of employment contracts which were not individually negotiated, and under which the employee had valuable rights of which he was unlikely to be aware, was sufficiently precise and well defined to form the basis for a term implied at common law. The distinction between the two cases lies in the fact that *Ashmore* really just involved one contract, which had been entered into multiple times by different parties, whereas *Scally* involved a category of contracts which had several features in common, but which were not necessarily identical. *Ashmore* did not constitute a 'category' of contracts because a single contract can hardly be said to form a 'category' of its own. *Scally*, in contrast, did.

Secondly, the term must relate to a *matter not dealt with in the contract*. The contract must be one where the parties have not themselves 'fully stated the terms', and where the court is seeking to imply terms to determine what the contract actually is.[37] The courts must be faced with a contract that is only partly in writing, which they have to complete from the materials available to them.[38] In *Liverpool City Council v Irwin*,[39] the contract in question was a tenancy agreement for flats in an apartment block. The signed document was headed 'Conditions of Tenancy' and contained a list of obligations imposed upon the tenant, without mentioning any obligations upon the landlord. The House of Lords held that it would be appropriate to imply terms at common law to determine the scope and extent of the landlord's liability to maintain common areas of the apartment block. A tenancy contract must be mutual, and if the obligations of one side were not set out in the contract the court would have to derive them through the process of implication.

Thirdly, the term that is implied must *flow from the nature of the contract* and the relationship it establishes.[40] It must be a 'legal incident' of that kind of contract or that category of relationship.[41] In *Sim v Rotherham Metropolitan Borough Council*,[42] a group of teachers were taking industrial action, as part of which they refused to provide cover for colleagues who were absent from work. The council argued that their failure to provide cover was in breach of their contract of employment.

---

32. *Scally v Southern Health and Social Services Board* [1992] 1 AC 294, 307 (Lord Bridge).
33. Ibid.   34. *Shell UK v Lostock Garage Ltd* [1976] 1 WLR 1187, 1196 (Lord Denning MR).
35. [1992] 2 Lloyd's Rep 620.   36. [1992] 1 AC 294, 307 (Lord Bridge).
37. *Liverpool City Council v Irwin* [1977] AC 239, 254 (Lord Wilberforce).
38. Ibid, 253 (Lord Wilberforce).   39. [1977] AC 239 (HL).   40. Ibid, 254.
41. *Lister v Romford Ice & Cold Storage Co* [1957] AC 555, 579 (Viscount Simonds).
42. [1987] Ch 216.

The teachers argued that the contract did not impose an express duty to provide cover for absent colleagues. The High Court agreed that there was no express duty, but nevertheless upheld the council's argument by implying a term to that effect. Scott J based his decision on the nature of teachers' professional obligations to their pupils and their institutions. The running of a school requires a framework of administrative rules and an administrative hierarchy, and employment as a teacher therefore carries with it an obligation to cooperate with, and abide by, directions from the head so long as they are not unreasonable. Accordingly, the teachers were in breach of their contracts by refusing to provide cover when directed to do so by their head.[43]

Finally, the term that is sought to be implied must meet the threshold of *necessity*. Necessity has two distinct dimensions. First, it affects respectively the question of *whether* to imply a term into a contract. No term will be implied into a contract unless it is necessary to do so. In *Sim*, Scott J was quite strongly influenced by his view that schools could not operate without clear administrative rules enforced by a clear administrative hierarchy.[44] This made complying with reasonable directives a necessary incident of employment as a teacher. Similarly, in *Scally v Southern Health and Social Services Board*,[45] the House of Lords was influenced by the fact that the employees acquired contractual rights to a full pension only if they made additional contributions, and were unlikely to know this if it was not brought to their attention, thus making action by the employers necessary.

In addition, however, necessity also affects the question of *what* to imply, in that the court will read into the contract *no more* than the nature of the contract implicitly requires.[46] Although the courts have referred to 'wider considerations' and to considerations of policy in deciding whether or not to imply a term, the essential character of the enquiry remains rooted in the incidents arising out of the relationship and transaction in question. Thus in *Liverpool City Council v Irwin*, the House of Lords held that in a tenancy agreement relating to a high-rise building, it was necessary for the landlord to have some obligations in relation to essential facilities such as the staircase and lifts.[47] At the same time, the House of Lords refused to impose an absolute obligation to repair these facilities: to impose such a stringent obligation would go beyond what is necessary. All that was necessary was an obligation 'to take reasonable care to keep in reasonable repair and usability'.[48] Similarly, the House of Lords in *Lister*[49] was unwilling to imply a term to the effect that an employer must indemnify employees against any loss suffered for acts done in the course of employment. Such a term, it was held, did not meet the threshold of being necessary,[50] and would be socially harmful:

> The common law demands that the servant should exercise his proper skill and care in the performance of his duty: the graver the consequences of any dereliction, the more

---

43. Ibid, 247–50.   44. Ibid, 248.   45. [1992] 1 AC 294 (HL).
46. *Liverpool City Council v Irwin* [1977] AC 239, 254 (Lord Wilberforce).
47. Ibid.   48. Ibid, 256.
49. *Lister v Romford Ice & Cold Storage Co* [1957] AC 555, 579 (Viscount Simonds).
50. Ibid, 583 (Lord Morton).

important it is that the sanction which the law imposes should be maintained . . . to grant the servant immunity from such an action would tend to create a feeling of irresponsibility in a class of persons from whom, perhaps more than any other, constant vigilance is owed to the community.[51]

Applying the tests

The manner in which these tests are applied in practice will become clearer if we return to Illustration 8.2. No statutory implied term covers either situation. Will the courts be willing to imply a term at common law to require Norman to keep the path clear—or, alternatively, requiring Edith to contribute to the costs of clearing the path after a storm?

Of the four conditions examined in this section, the first condition is clearly met: a licence agreement to use a path is a common occurrence, and the category of which it is part can be defined with sufficient precision. The second condition, too, is met: the contingency in question—a tree obstructing the path—is not discussed in this contract, and is likely to remain undiscussed in a significant proportion of contracts of this type. The sticking points, however, are the third and fourth conditions. Can it be said that an obligation to clear a path is a 'legal incident' of granting a licence? It is difficult to see how such an argument could be sustained. In *Liverpool City Council v Irwin*, Lord Wilberforce pointed out that keeping an access path clear was often the responsibility of the licensee, and could not be attributed to the licensor unless it was necessary to do so. It is also difficult to see how the implication of a term could be said to meet the two dimensions of the element of necessity, and particularly the second—that the courts will imply no more than is necessary. Under the circumstances, it appears most likely that the courts will not imply a term regarding clearing obstacles into the contract.

The consequence of the refusal to imply a term is that the *loss lies where it naturally falls*. Neither party is under any obligation to the other. It is for the parties to renegotiate their contract if they wish to allocate responsibilities or re-apportion their losses. This means the tree will (literally) lie where it has fallen, with neither party being under any contractual obligation to take any steps to remove it.

In Problem 8, there will be a statutory implied term that the goods sold to the trust—the prints—will correspond with the description 'limited edition, restricted to 100 numbered copies, of poster-sized prints of the Fairford Set'. If the prints were not poster-sized, or not from the Fairford Set, or not part of an edition of 100, Musgrave will have breached the contract. As far as the question at issue is concerned, however, terms implied in law do not help. This is unsurprising. As we saw in this section, terms implied in law tend to be of greatest use where gaps are both relatively standard and easily filled. The point of contention between the trust and Musgrave is neither. In English law, questions of this type are typically resolved by asking whether the situation is one in which a term can be implied in fact. These are discussed in section 8.3.

---

51. Ibid, 579 (Viscount Simonds).

> ## Debates in context: default rules and mandatory rules

Traditionally, all implied terms were treated as being overridden by **express terms**. A term would only be implied into a contract if it did not contradict an express term. If any term— whether implied in law or fact—was contradicted by or incompatible with a term on which the parties had expressly agreed, that term would no longer be implied. For this reason, implied terms were often referred to as *default rules*, indicating that they only applied by default, in situations where the parties had not agreed to the contrary. It was always possible to contract out of an implied term by simply adding a provision in a contract to the effect that that term would not apply. In the 19th century, for example, parties could contract out of all terms implied into a contract for the sale of goods, by providing expressly that they would not apply, or even simply by stating that no warranties in relation to title, condition, or quality were made except to the extent expressly set out in the contract.

This remains true of terms implied in fact, as we will see in the next section. It also remains true of all terms implied at common law, and of a significant proportion of statutory implied terms. But it is no longer universally true. In recent years, there has been a growing tendency for statutes to provide that some or all of the implied terms they contain cannot be excluded by the parties, and that they will prevail notwithstanding anything to the contrary in the contract. Because these laws set out rules that mandatorily apply to all contracts of a particular type even if the parties do not want them to apply, they are called *mandatory rules*.

Many mandatory rules concern contracts entered into between a business and a consumer, and form part of a broader agenda of consumer protection. Here, the idea underlying the use of mandatory, non-derogable implied terms is one of protecting the weaker party. Think back to the discussion in Chapter 2 about the formation process. In terms of the threefold distinction made in that chapter, virtually all consumer contracts are contracts of adhesion. The consumer has neither the opportunity nor the bargaining power to renegotiate contract terms, and is typically in a position of having to take it or leave it when it comes to contractual terms. As a result, there is a growing body of consumer-oriented legislation which implies terms into consumer contracts which the seller cannot exclude. The Consumer Rights Act 2015, for example, sets out several terms which are mandatory and cannot be excluded. In contrast, as far as commercial contracts are concerned, the terms implied by the Sale of Goods Act 1979 are only default rules which the parties can exclude.

Mandatory terms are not confined to consumer contracts. Similar principles are applied to certain types of commercial contracts where inequalities of bargaining power are common. The implied term in relation to interest under the Late Payment of Commercial Debts (Interest) Act 1998 cannot be excluded by the parties, even in commercial contracts, unless they provide for some other effective mechanism that has an equivalent effect. The Housing, Grants, Construction and Regeneration Act 1996, similarly, imposes a large number of restrictions on the types of terms that can be put into a commercial construction contract.

The trend towards the greater use of mandatory rules has divided legal scholars. Most scholars agree with the thesis put forward by Professors Adams and Brownsword, discussed in Chapter 1, that the trend represents a move away from market individualism towards consumer-welfarism. But there are disagreements on whether or not this is a good thing. Some scholars, particularly those writing from a law and economics perspective, argue that

→

→

extensive use of mandatory rules threatens the idea of freedom of contract, and will often be inefficient, leaving all parties worse off.[52] Others argue that some restrictions on freedom of contract are necessary in order to meet broader social and political values that a legal system pursues.[53]

8.3 Terms implied in fact

Unlike implication in law, a court implying a term in fact expresses no opinion as to whether that term belongs in all contracts of a given type. A term is implied in fact into a contract because something about that *specific* contract suggests that it belongs there. If the contract, when properly read and construed, suggests that a particular term was implicitly part of the parties' agreement, then the courts will read that term into the contract as an implied term. The court holds, in effect, that that term formed part of the contract even though the parties did not actually write it into the contract.

As with much of contract law, this principle is simple to articulate but difficult to apply. On what basis do courts hold that a particular term belongs in a contract? In English law, there are two elements to implication in fact. First, much like terms implied at common law, terms implied in fact, too, must meet the threshold test of necessity. Terms are not implied in fact just because they are fair, or because it is reasonable to do so. They are only implied if it is necessary to do so.

Necessity by itself is not sufficient, however. Implication in fact also requires the court to ask whether the proposed term belongs in the specific contract before it. The approach to be taken in answering this question has been articulated in two different ways, both of which are grounded in an objective assessment of the parties' intention: the **business efficacy** approach, which focuses on whether a particular term is necessary to give effect to the parties' commercial intention, and the **officious bystander** approach, which asks whether the term in question would have been regarded by the parties as an obvious part of the contract. Although some attempts have been made in recent years to replace these with an approach which subsumes implication within the broader process of interpretation, this new approach was decisively rejected by the Supreme Court in 2015.[54] In what follows, we will look at the details of each approach in turn.

8.3.1 The test of business efficacy

One of the earliest formulations of the test for implication was set out in *The Moorcock*.[55] The *Moorcock* was a ship owned by the claimants. The defendants owned a wharf, at which the *Moorcock* had docked to discharge its cargo. The ship docked safely, but when it was in dock it hit a concealed ridge as a result of the ebbing of the tide. The

52. AT Kronman and RA Posner, *The Economics of Contract Law* (Little Brown and Co 1979).
53. MJ Trebilcock, *The Limits of Freedom of Contract* (Harvard University Press 1997).
54. *Marks & Spencer plc v BNP Paribas Securities Services Trust Co (Jersey) Ltd* [2015] UKSC 72, [2015] 3 WLR 1843, discussed in greater detail later in the chapter.
55. (1889) 14 PD 64.

claimants sued the wharfingers, arguing that they were contractually obliged to ensure the vessel's safety when docked. The written document contained no such term, so the Court of Appeal had to consider whether there was an implied warranty to that effect.

The court held that there was an implied duty on the wharfingers to ascertain the state of the riverbed, and to warn shipowners of potential hazards. This was not because it was in some inchoate way 'fair' to do so, but because such a duty must have been part of the implied intention of the parties acting as businessmen. In so holding, the Court of Appeal was influenced by the fact that the wharfingers could easily have ascertained whether there were any underwater hazards to docked ships:

> In business transactions such as this, what the law desires to effect by the implication is to give such business efficacy to the transaction as must have been intended at all events by both parties who are business men; not to impose on one side all perils of the transaction, or to emancipate one side from all the chances of failure, but to make each party promise in law as much, at all events as it must have been in the contemplation of both parties that he should be responsible for in respect to those perils or chances.[56]

Bowen LJ's ruling has three limbs: the *necessity* of the term to make the contract work, the *business efficacy* of the contract with and without the term, and the fact that the term must reflect the *intention* of the parties (assessed objectively rather than subjectively). Terms must fit with all three of these to be implied. The test itself came to be known as the business efficacy approach, but it is important not to overstate its breadth. *The Moorcock* did not hold that the courts can imply terms into contracts simply to make the contract more efficacious: the term must also satisfy the tests of intention and necessity. Judges are not trying to decide what would make a contract more efficient, but to ensure that the contract works as the parties intended.

The case law following *The Moorcock* demonstrates how the relationship between these three limbs functions. In *Hamlyn & Co v Wood & Co*,[57] decided two years after *The Moorcock*, counsel for the defendants argued the import of *The Moorcock*'s business efficacy test was that terms should not be implied into contracts 'unless, without such a term, the whole agreement would be frustrated, or there would be a **failure of consideration**'.[58] The bench hearing the case, which included two of the judges who had decided *The Moorcock*, agreed. The point to the decision in *The Moorcock*, Bowen LJ said, was to ask whether the implied term was necessary. If the contract could work with a 'very reasonable effect' even without the implication, no term would be implied.[59] Lord Esher MR was even clearer. In English law, he held:

> the Court has no right to imply in a written contract any such stipulation, unless, on considering the terms of the contract in a reasonable and business manner, an implication necessarily arises that the parties must have intended that the suggested stipulation should exist. It is not enough to say that it would be a reasonable thing to make such an implication. It must be a necessary implication in the sense that I have mentioned.[60]

Subsequent case law continued to read the limbs of *The Moorcock* together. In *Ogdens Ltd v Nelson*,[61] it was cited as authority for the proposition that 'no stipulation or

---

56. Ibid, 68 (Bowen LJ).   57. [1891] 2 QB 488 (CA).   58. Ibid, 489–90.
59. Ibid, 493–4.   60. Ibid, 491.   61. [1903] 2 KB 287 (KB).

agreement which is not expressed ought to be implied, unless it is necessary to give to the transaction the effect or efficacy which both parties must have intended it should have'.[62] Similarly, in *Ellis v Glover and Hobson*,[63] the Court of Appeal pointed out that the parties' intention was central to the test in *The Moorcock*:

> The law implies a contract only for the purpose and with the object of giving such efficiency to the transaction as must have been intended by both parties, to make each party promise in law as much as was in the contemplation of both parties that he should be responsible for.[64]

8.3.2 Obviousness and the officious bystander

In *Reigate v Union Manufacturing Co (Ramsbottom) Ltd*,[65] Scrutton LJ attempted to explain more clearly how the elements of necessity, business efficacy, and intention relate to each other, by introducing a thought-experiment as to how the parties might react if the term were put to them in the process of contracting:

> an implied term is not to be added because the Court thinks it would have been reasonable to have inserted it in the contract. A term can only be implied if it is necessary in the business sense to give efficacy to the contract; that is, if it is such a term that it can confidently be said that if at the time the contract was being negotiated some one had said to the parties, 'What will happen in such a case,' they would both have replied, 'Of course, so and so will happen; we did not trouble to say that; it is too clear.' Unless the Court comes to some such conclusion as that, it ought not to imply a term which the parties themselves have not expressed.[66]

This formulation was taken further by MacKinnon LJ in *Shirlaw v Southern Foundries (1926) Ltd*.[67] MacKinnon LJ was concerned that the language of 'business efficacy' could lead to courts being asked to imply terms 'upon vague and uncertain grounds'.[68] In response, he sought to limit the scope of implication by putting the focus not on the *effect* of the term but on its *obviousness*.[69] A term would be implied, he held, if it was so obvious that it in effect went without saying. To make this point, he came up with an imaginary figure which he called an 'officious bystander'—less politely, a busybody. How would the parties react if such a busybody were to intervene in their negotiations to suggest that they consider adding a particular term? It would only be appropriate to imply the term if—and only if—their response suggested that it went without saying:

> Prima facie that which in any contract is left to be implied and need not be expressed is something so obvious that it goes without saying; so that, if, while the parties were making their bargain, an officious bystander were to suggest some express provision for it in their agreement, they would testily suppress him with a common 'Oh, of course!'

---

62. Ibid, 297 (Lord Alverstone CJ).   63. [1908] 1 KB 388 (CA).
64. Ibid, 400 (Farwell LJ).   65. [1918] 1 KB 592 (CA).   66. Ibid, 605.
67. [1939] 2 KB 206 (CA).   68. Ibid, 227.
69. MacKinnon LJ was drawing on a public lecture he had delivered at the London School of Economics around a decade earlier where he touched on implied terms, and to which he made express reference in the judgment. See F MacKinnon, *Some Aspects of Commercial Law—A Lecture Delivered at the London School of Economics on 3 March 1926* (Oxford University Press 1926) 13.

. . . [I]f a term were never implied by a judge unless it could pass that test, he could not be held to be wrong.[70]

This has since come to be called the *officious bystander* test. Despite MacKinnon LJ's stated intention in *Shirlaw*, it did not replace the business efficacy test. Instead, the two were in practice treated as being alternative formulations of the test for implication, either of which could be used in argument as a reason to imply a term into a contract. As a result, around 40 years later, the Privy Council attempted to consolidate these tests in *BP Refinery (Westernport) Pty Ltd v Shire of Hastings*.[71] The board outlined five factors that were relevant in considering whether to imply a term into a contract:

> (1) it must be reasonable and equitable; (2) it must be necessary to give business efficacy to the contract, so that no term will be implied if the contract is effective without it; (3) it must be so obvious that 'it goes without saying' (4) it must be capable of clear expression; (5) it must not contradict any express term of the contract.[72]

These five factors are not intended to be a cumulative test. They do not represent five boxes that must be checked for a term to be implied. Nor do they represent five alternative approaches to implication. They represent, instead, different ways of articulating the underlying issue with which the court is dealing when considering questions relating to implication—namely, determining the tacit terms on which the parties contracted. Taken together, however, they represent a cautious approach to implication, which seeks to carefully circumscribe the courts' power to imply terms into contracts.

8.3.3 The *Belize* approach

In 2009, the English law on interpretation appeared to undergo a dramatic shift following Lord Hoffmann's judgment in the Privy Council in *Attorney General of Belize v Belize Telecom*.[73] As a Privy Council decision, this case was a decision on the laws of Belize rather than the laws of England. Nevertheless, Lord Hoffmann's decision was almost immediately accepted by the Court of Appeal as also stating the position at English law.[74] The essence of the approach Lord Hoffmann articulated in *Belize* can be pithily summarized. Implication, he held, is an exercise in interpretation. As such, it is a matter of ascertaining the objective meaning of the contract seen in its commercial context. It is not a matter of grafting new terms onto a contract to improve it or make it more robust. For a term to be implied in fact, in addition to being necessary, it must be suggested by the contractual document itself. The process of deciding whether it is so suggested follows the same logic as the *Investors* approach to interpretation: the contract is read as a commercial document set in a commercial context, and its significance and meaning are understood against the background of that context.

This shift was controversial when it happened, and the courts in some common law countries, such as Singapore, unequivocally rejected the link: interpretation, they held, is

---

70. [1939] 2 KB 206 (CA), 227 (MacKinnon LJ).   71. (1977) 180 CLR 266 (PC).
72. Ibid, 282–3 (Lord Simon of Glaisdale).   73. [2009] UKPC 10, [2009] 1 WLR 1988.
74. *Mediterranean Salvage & Towage Ltd v Seamar Trading & Commerce Inc (The Reborn)* [2009] EWCA Civ 531.

an entirely separate process from implication.[75] Nevertheless, the approach was not without logic. Contract gaps arise for much the same reasons as problems of interpretation. Drafting contracts takes time and money, and can be seen by business people as a distraction from the real job of closing and performing the business deal. Contractual clauses can sometimes reflect messy compromises, and parties may simply not foresee everything that might go wrong in the course of a transaction, or may choose to remain silent as a matter of strategy. These circumstances are as likely to create a contractual gap as a misworded or ambiguous clause. As a result, it makes some sense to treat implication and interpretation as being on a continuum, rather than as being two entirely different tasks.

As with the new contextualist approach to interpretation articulated in *Investors*, this approach, too, was not entirely new when it was spelled out in *Belize*. It had long been recognized that the process of implication must always be contextual, and must be related to the express terms of a contract. Well over 100 years ago, the Court of Appeal in *Krell v Henry*[76] observed that:

> one must, in judging whether the implication ought to be made, look not only at the words of the contract, but also at the surrounding facts and the knowledge of the parties of those facts.[77]

More recently, in *Equitable Life Assurance Society v Hyman*,[78] Lord Steyn drew an express parallel between the *Investors* approach to interpretation and what he thought the judicial approach to implication should be:

> If a term is to be implied, it could only be a term implied from the language of [the instrument] read in its commercial setting.[79]

Nevertheless, *Belize* was rightly recognized as marking a very significant shift in the law of implied terms. Prior cases used contextualism within the framework of the tests pertaining to intention—it was, at best, a guide to applying these tests. *Belize* inverted this hierarchy. It is contextualism that provides the framework, the scaffolding, and the conceptual basis of the process of implication.[80] Implication under the *Belize* approach was primarily a textual exercise.[81] The traditional tests were only to be used to the extent that they help answer the core question of the contextual approach to interpretation and implication: what would the contract mean to a reasonable person who reads it against the background of its commercial context.

8.3.4 **The retreat from *Belize***

Over the next six years, the Court of Appeal developed an elaborate jurisprudence around the new approach, centring around the idea of using the 'reasonable addressee' as the basis for implication.[82] The approach was particularly useful in transactions involving

---

75. *Peng v Mai* [2012] SGCA 55.   76. [1903] 2 KB 740 (CA).
77. Ibid, 752 (Vaughan Williams LJ).   78. [2002] 1 AC 408 (HL).   79. Ibid, 459.
80. See *Stena Line v Merchant Navy Ratings Fund* [2011] EWCA Civ 543, [36] (Arden LJ).
81. Ibid, [41] (Arden LJ).
82. See especially *Crema v Cenkos Securities Ltd* [2010] EWCA Civ 1444, [2011] 1 WLR 2066; *Stena Line v Merchant Navy Ratings Fund* [2011] EWCA Civ 543; *Consolidated Finance v McCluskey* [2012] EWCA Civ 1325; *McKillen v Misland* [2013] EWCA Civ 781.

detailed written instruments which recorded the contract either in its entirety or in part.[83] Nevertheless, in 2015 the Supreme Court in *Marks & Spencer v BNP Paribas*[84] rejected the approach altogether, reinstating the distinction between interpretation and implication, and reiterating that it is the business efficacy and officious bystander tests that govern implication. In the course of doing so, they restated the test for implication in what must now be taken to be the definitive summary of the legal approach to implication.

Case in depth: *Marks & Spencer plc v BNP Paribas Securities Services Trust Co (Jersey) Ltd* [2015] UKSC 72

Marks & Spencer had sub-leased four floors in a building in Paddington, owned by BNP Paribas. The lease had a break clause, under which Marks & Spencer could terminate it by giving six months' notice on either of two 'break dates'. The first break date was 24 January 2012. Marks & Spencer gave notice that it would exercise its option to terminate the lease on that date. However, the contract also required it to pay rent in advance every quarter. It could not invoke the break clause if it was in arrears. This meant that at the time of termination on 24 January, it had paid rent for the quarter from 25 December to 24 March, even though the lease was scheduled to be terminated on 24 January. Marks & Spencer argued that it was entitled to a refund of the rent for the period between 24 January and 24 March. The contract had no provision requiring reimbursement, and Marks & Spencer therefore argued that a term to that effect should be implied into the contract.

They succeeded at first instance. Morgan J held, applying *Belize*, that if the lease was read against the relevant background, it would reasonably be read to mean that the rent must be refunded. This was because it used the word 'instalment', which would ordinarily be understood to mean that the lessee should not pay more than the full amount due.[85] The Court of Appeal disagreed, and held that a term should not be implied.[86] The court had to show 'a high level of loyalty to the parties' agreement, read against the admissible background'. A term should not be implied if the party seeking to have it implied only manages to show that it '*could* be a part of the agreement'. To imply a term, the party urging implication must show that it '*would* be part of the agreement'.[87]

Marks & Spencer appealed to the Supreme Court. The Supreme Court upheld the decision of the Court of Appeal,[88] but went much further. Whereas the Court of Appeal had reached its decision by applying the *Belize* approach, the majority of the Supreme Court called the entire approach into question insisting that interpretation and implication were fundamentally different exercises, despite the seeming similarities:

> I accept that both (i) construing the words which the parties have used in their contract and (ii) implying terms into the contract, involve determining the scope and meaning of the contract. However, Lord Hoffmann's analysis in *Belize Telecom* could obscure

→

---

83. For an example of the difficulties posed by a partially oral and partially written contract, see *Crema v Cenkos Securities plc* [2010] EWCA Civ 1444, [2011] 1 WLR 2066, [37]–[38] (Aikens LJ).
84. [2015] UKSC 72, [2015] 3 WLR 1843.   85. [2013] EWHC 1279 (Ch), [35].
86. *Marks & Spencer plc v BNP Paribas Securities Services Trust Co (Jersey) Ltd* [2014] EWCA Civ 603, [24].
87. Ibid, [24].   88. [2015] UKSC 72, [2015] 3 WLR 1843.

→

the fact that construing the words used and implying additional words are different processes governed by different rules.[89]

The result was that in implication it was the traditional tests of business efficacy and the officious bystander that should be applied. *Belize* should not be seen as having changed 'the law governing the circumstances in which a term will be implied into a contract', even though the court acknowledged that the case 'has been interpreted by both academic lawyers and judges as having changed the law'.[90]

The judges were not uniform on this point. Lord Carnwath agreed that no term should be implied, but took the view that the *Belize* approach was 'a valuable and illuminating synthesis of the factors which should guide the court', whose continuing authority should not be questioned.[91] He was, however, in a minority, and it is Lord Neuberger's judgment that now represents the law.

In the course of his judgment, Lord Neuberger offered six comments on the approach to be taken to implication, which should be seen as supplementing the five factors set out above (section 8.3.2) in *BP Refinery (Westernport) Pty Ltd v Shire of Hastings*:[92]

- 'the implication of a term is "not critically dependent on proof of an actual intention of the parties" when negotiating the contract . . . one is not strictly concerned with the hypothetical answer of the actual parties, but with that of notional reasonable people in the position of the parties at the time they were contracting.'
- 'a term should not be implied into a detailed commercial contract merely because it appears fair or merely because one considers that the parties would have agreed it if it had been suggested to them. Those are necessary but not sufficient grounds for including a term.'
- 'it is questionable whether . . . reasonableness and equitableness, will usually, if ever, add anything: if a term satisfies the other requirements, it is hard to think that it would not be reasonable and equitable.'
- 'business necessity and obviousness can be alternatives in the sense that only one of them needs to be satisfied, although I suspect that in practice it would be a rare case where only one of those two requirements would be satisfied.'
- 'if one approaches the issue by reference to the officious bystander, it is vital to formulate the question to be posed by [him] with the utmost care.'
- 'necessity for business efficacy involves a value judgment . . . the test is not one of "absolute necessity" . . . It may well be that a more helpful way of putting [it is] . . . that a term can only be implied if, without the term, the contract would lack commercial or practical coherence.'[93]

Despite the attractions of *Belize*, the return to orthodoxy in *Marks & Spencer v BNP Paribas*[94] is welcome. Treating the question of implication as a question of interpretation requires the courts to ascribe an intention to parties which they could not possibly have

89. Ibid, [26] (Lord Neuberger).   90. Ibid, [24] (Lord Neuberger).
91. Ibid, [74].   92. (1977) 180 CLR 266 (PC).
93. [2015] UKSC 72, [21].   94. [2015] UKSC 72, [2015] 3 WLR 1843.

had, in that it necessarily assumes that the answer to the point at issue can be found in the written document if we just read it in the right way. The court is in effect seeking to discover a solution that is ostensibly already present in the contract, even though the parties never intended to actually provide that particular solution. Such an approach may work well in transactions involving lengthy and complex documents, but is considerably less useful in transactions with oral contracts, or brief written contracts.

Relating this back to Problem 8, under the approach restated in *Marks & Spencer v BNP Paribas*, the court will begin by looking at what the commercial purpose of the contract was. If the court comes to the conclusion that the commercial purpose was simply to sell a small number of prints, it will leave the trust in the position in which it finds itself. It is only if it finds that the commercial purpose of the contract, judged with reference to what the parties must objectively be taken to have intended, included an element of exclusivity, that it will imply a term into the contract (under the *Moorcock* approach), and even then only if such an implication is necessary to give effect to the contract. Similarly, it will also only imply such a term (under the officious bystander approach) if it believes that the parties at the time of contracting would have treated it as obvious that the words 'limited edition' applied to future editions as well as the present edition.

 Practice in context: implication and the civil litigation process

In order to understand how implied terms function in English law, it is useful to keep the nature of the English civil litigation process in mind. As you should be aware, the civil litigation process in common law jurisdictions is adversarial. This has ramifications for how terms are implied into contracts in the course of adjudication. It means that, in practice, a judge does not of her own accord look at the contract and work through possible terms that might be implied into the contract. Instead, she is dealing with terms suggested, and forcefully argued for, by lawyers for every side involved in the litigation (in complex disputes, there may be more than two sides).

The terms that are implied into contracts, and which we see in reported case law, therefore do not usually originate from the court, and it is not the court's job to formulate them. The terms originate from the parties' lawyers, and the court's role in practice is to decide which, if any, of the rival terms that are urged upon it should accept. From a judge's point of view, therefore, the process which the rules of implication are intended to guide and support is not one of *drafting* or *formulating* implied terms, but of *choosing between* rival formulations of implied terms (or, indeed, having no implied terms at all).

Judicial statements in relation to implication—and, indeed, the caution with which common law courts approach the task of implication—make far more sense when considered against this background. Some judges—most notably, Lord Denning—sought to broaden the type of circumstances in which they could imply terms into contracts, to encompass all situations in which it would be *reasonable* to do so.[95] These attempts were strongly resisted by their colleagues, who took the view that to give courts such a wide power would be 'dangerous'. The more appropriate position would be to imply terms only when it was *necessary* to do so.[96]

→

95. *Liverpool City Council v Irwin* [1977] AC 239 (Lord Denning).   96. Ibid, (Lord Wilberforce).

→

The reason the courts emphasize the importance of necessity as heavily as they do, for example, is that it is relatively easy for a well-paid and skilled lawyer to make an argument that a contract would work *better*, or more smoothly, if a particular term were implied. It is, in contrast, significantly harder for even a skilled lawyer to argue that a term is necessary. In the latter case, what needs to be shown is not that the contract would work *badly* without the term, but that it will not work *at all* if that term were not implied. This is obviously considerably more difficult than merely demonstrating that it would be inconvenient or inefficient. This is also true of the requirement that the term be capable of clear formulation. This rule is not just a guideline for judges, but also for the lawyers who actually propose draft terms for implication into contracts.

The link between pleading practice and the strictness of the test for implication has been made by the courts themselves. In *Shirlaw v Southern Foundries (1926) Ltd*,[97] MacKinnon LJ described the 'occasional impatience' of judges with the very broad use that lawyers sought to make of the ruling in *The Moorcock*,[98] and added that he thought Bowen LJ would have been 'rather surprised' to see how his decision had become a 'favourite citation' of lawyers seeking to have a term implied into a contract. It was this underlying concern that led him to seek an alternative, and less easily stretched, formulation. The focus on necessity and certainty, and the willingness of the courts to hold the parties to a position which is inconvenient or a contractual framework which works badly, is therefore at least in part a pragmatic response to the aggressive litigation strategies that lawyers adopt, particularly in high-stakes commercial cases.

8.4 Implication by custom

A third way of implying terms into a contract is through implication by custom. Under this approach, a term will be implied into a contract if it is part of standard usage or custom in the field or market within which the parties are operating. As with all classes of implied terms, the onus of establishing the conditions for implication is on the party seeking to have the term implied into the contract. In relation to **customary implied terms**, this requires producing evidence that the custom or usage in question actually exists, and that it has general acceptance. It is insufficient to show that there was a trade practice to that effect, or even that it was regarded as best practice. The practice must be shown to be invariable to be regarded as custom or usage, and it must be sufficiently certain to form the basis of an implied term.

Implication by custom can seem similar to implication in law, because the term in question is implied into all contracts of a particular type, unless excluded by the parties. However, there are two important differences. First, in implying a term by custom, the court itself expresses no opinion on whether the term belongs in contracts of that type. The term is implied because the commercial world tends to put it into contracts of that type. As a result, unlike implication in law or fact, there is no need to prove that the term is necessary. All that needs to be shown is the existence of a custom or usage regarding that term.

97. [1939] 2 KB 206 (CA).   98. (1889) 14 PD 64.

Secondly, unlike terms implied in law, there is no such thing as a 'mandatory' term implied in custom. Terms implied in custom, like all terms implied in fact, can be excluded by the parties. The most obvious way of doing this is to insert an express provision to that effect, but a term implied by custom will also be taken to have been excluded if it can be shown that the parties' decision not to include that term was deliberate, or if it is inconsistent with an express term of a contract.

The result is that customary terms will not be implied if they contradict the terms of the contract. That said, the courts do not take a very literal approach to assessing whether a customary implied term is in conflict with an express term. In *Peter Darlington and Partners Ltd v Gosho Co Ltd*,[99] the claimant and defendant had contracted for the sale of canary seed. It was an express term of the contract of sale that the seed would be 'pure'. The seed which the seller supplied under the contract was 98 per cent pure. The purchaser refused to accept it, on the basis that it was not pure. In court, however, the seller adduced evidence to demonstrate that in the birdseed trade, 'pure' canary seed was understood as meaning canary seed which was 'almost pure'. The court held that there was an implied term in the contract permitting the canary seed to be almost pure, which was implied as a result of custom.

Let us relate this to the context of Problem 8—the dispute between the Surtees Trust and Anthony Musgrave—to understand how it actually works. Here, the court will begin by asking whether there are any customs in the art community, or the community of producers and collectors of prints, that pertain to the releases described as 'limited editions'. Are there any customs in relation to limited edition prints? Is there any customary understanding of the nature and role of describing a particular run as a 'limited edition'? If the answer to these questions is 'yes', and if the court is satisfied that parties to such contracts invariably treat that term as a part of their contract, the court will imply that term into the parties' contract, unless there is an express term which is inconsistent with it.

As should be evident from this description, implication by custom is likely to be relatively uncommon, because it is quite rare for parties to be able to show that persons engaged in that particular type of transaction always treat a particular term as being part of their contract. In most cases, no such custom exists.

8.5 Good faith and cooperation

8.5.1 Good faith

The implied terms we have looked at thus far have been narrow and specific. Historically, English law did not imply general duties into contracts. Other jurisdictions, however, did, particularly those associated with the civil law. In Germany, for example, all contracts are subject to an implied duty of 'good faith and fair dealing' (*Treu und Glauben*), which has been construed as being of very broad application. Some common law jurisdictions have also been willing to imply duties of good faith into commercial contracts. In the US, the duty of good faith is expressly recognized both in the Uniform Commercial Code[100] and in the *Restatement (Second) of Contracts*[101] as a

---

99. [1964] 1 Lloyd's Rep 149.   100. §1-304.   101. S 205.

general principle applicable to all commercial contracts. Others, such as Australia, have recognized it as a duty applied to specific types of commercial contracts.

English law, in contrast, has long resisted recognizing a broad duty of good faith. In *Walford v Miles*,[102] the House of Lords expressly rejected it as being incompatible with English contract law's commitment to individualism.[103] More recently, however, the High Court and the Court of Appeal have both indicated that English law may now be more favourably disposed to good faith as an idea. In *Yam Seng v International Trade Corp*,[104] Leggatt J in the High Court suggested that the courts would be willing to imply duties of good faith into contracts, not as general, overarching duties applicable to all commercial contracts or even to all contracts of a particular type, but as terms implied in fact based on the specifics of a particular transaction.

The contract in *Yam Seng* involved a distribution agreement for Manchester United branded toiletries (mainly perfumes). The contract was brief, and failed to set out the parties' duties in any level of detail, probably because it had been drafted by the parties rather than their lawyers. ITC failed to supply the merchandise it had contractually agreed to supply, with the result that Yam Seng was unable to meet its obligations under contracts it had entered into with retailers. ITC sought to explain its failures, but over time Yam Seng came to the view that its explanations were false. In court, Yam Seng argued that ITC had behaved dishonestly, and that the court should read in an implied term requiring them to behave in good faith.

Leggatt J agreed that a duty of good faith could and should be applied to that case. He was influenced by the fact that the contract in question was a long-term contract, which would have to be able to deal with circumstances that were potentially very different from anything that the parties might be able to anticipate at the time of contracting. He was also influenced by a growing practice where parties sometimes insert an express duty of good faith into a contract. This, he felt, suggested that the idea had commercial meaning, which the law should be capable of recognizing and where necessary implying into a contract. He was also influenced by the experience of the law with the duty of cooperation which the courts have been able to interpret and apply sensibly as an implied term. This meant that English law could now accommodate an implied duty of good faith.

The duty is not a general duty because it is qualified by two conditions. First, it does not apply to all contracts. The question of whether or not a contract is subject to a duty of good faith is a question to be resolved according to the standard tests for implying a term in fact. Secondly, the duty of good faith does not have a uniform content. What it requires in any given case will depend entirely on the facts of that case, on the commercial context established by the contract,[105] and on the presumed intention of the parties.[106] A duty of good faith will not mean the same thing in every contract into which it is implied. In *Yam Seng* itself, the conclusion to which the court came was that the duty in the context of that contract implied an obligation, first, to honestly provide accurate information to the other party and, secondly, not to authorize sales that would undercut the agreed prices. ITC was not in breach of the second duty, but it had failed to honestly explain to Yam Seng the causes and nature of its inability to provide

---

102. [1992] 2 AC 128 (HL). The case is discussed in greater detail in Chapter 9.
103. Ibid, 138 (Lord Ackner).   104. [2013] EWHC 111 (QB).
105. Ibid, [147].   106. Ibid, [131].

timely supplies, as a result of which it was in breach of the first duty. In a different case, however, the duty could have a very different meaning.

Good faith, in this sense, is arguably not so much a single, consistent implied *term* as it is an *approach* to determining the content of terms implied in fact. Once the court decides, on standard principles of implication, that the contract was subject to an implied duty of good faith, the court will use the context of the transaction to determine what that duty actually entails. The idea of principles underlying implication is not a new one. In *The Moorcock* itself, Lord Esher MR thought that the term implied into that contract was grounded in the principle of honesty in business dealings, an approach that is not fundamentally different from that taken in *Yam Seng*.[107] Where *Yam Seng* differs is in its attempt to work through the implications of treating this as a more generalized approach, capable of productive use in a broad range of cases.

Subsequent cases considering *Yam Seng* have taken a cautious approach to good faith, emphasizing that the courts should not routinely imply such a term. Commercial parties will not ordinarily intend to oblige one party to subordinate its interests to further the competing interests of the other,[108] and an implied term of good faith can only be implied subject to the usual requirements, including necessity[109] and consistency with the express terms.[110]

Where a contract is relational, involving 'a longer term relationship between the parties [to] which they make a substantial commitment', the courts have been more willing to imply a term of good faith, in recognition of the fact that these contracts

> may require a high degree of communication, cooperation and predictable performance based on mutual trust and confidence and involve expectations of loyalty which are not legislated for in the express terms of the contract but are implicit in the parties' understanding and necessary to give business efficacy to the arrangements.[111]

In such contracts, the courts are relatively more willing to find an implied term of good faith, particularly in situations where its main import is a requirement of honesty, restraining the parties from engaging in conduct 'that would be regarded as "commercially unacceptable" by reasonable and honest people'.[112]

Given how recent this development is, it is too early as yet to predict how significant its effect will be. For the present, it is sufficient to note that early indications suggest it may play an important role in the process of implying terms into a contract.

8.5.2 Cooperation

Much as with good faith, there is no general duty in English law requiring parties to cooperate with each other. The ethos of individualism which is said to underlie English law places the responsibility for looking after a party's interests squarely on that party

---

107. (1889) 14 PD 64, 67.
108. *Hamsard 3147 Ltd v Boots UK Ltd* [2013] EWHC 3251 (Pat), [86], [92] (Norris J).
109. *Carewatch Care Services Ltd v Focus Caring Services Ltd* [2014] EWHC 2313 (Ch), [105]–[112] (Henderson J).
110. *Knatchbull-Hugessen v SISU Capital Ltd* [2014] EWHC 1194 (QB).
111. *Yam Seng v International Trade Corp* [2013] EWHC 111 (QB), [142].
112. *Bristol Groundschool Ltd v Intelligent Data Capture Ltd* [2014] EWHC 2145 (Ch). [196]. See also *D&G Cars Ltd v Essex Police Authority* [2015] EWHC 226 (QB).

themselves. Nevertheless, the courts will sometimes imply a term imposing a duty of cooperation. A development project which requires planning permission, for example, will require quite a bit of collaboration and cooperation between the site owner, the developer, the project promoters, and other parties. Similar issues arise in relation to contracts to manufacture specialized items, such as a yacht. Judges have implied a duty of cooperation in circumstances like these since the 19th century,[113] and they continue to do so.

In general, the case law suggests that a duty of cooperation will not be implied merely because cooperation would be desirable, or because its absence would make the contract cumbersome. It must actually be required for the contract to be performed. In *Mackay v Dick*,[114] the claimants had agreed to sell a mechanical excavator to the defendants. The sale was subject to the condition that the machine could excavate clay at a particular rate on a 'properly opened up' face. The purchasers refused to provide a properly opened up face for testing the machine, and instead tried it on a face that was not properly opened up. The court held that the purchasers were subject to an implied duty to cooperate, and were therefore contractually bound to provide conditions in which the machine could be fairly tested:

> where in a written contract it appears that both parties have agreed that something shall be done, which cannot effectually be done unless both concur in doing it, the construction of the contract is that each agrees to do all that is necessary to be done on his part for the carrying out of that thing, though there may be no express words to that effect.[115]

As with the emergent duty of good faith, the duty of cooperation thus implied will not usually be a wide one, because questions of its scope and extent remain subject to the test of necessity. In *Swallowfalls Ltd v Monaco Yachting and Technologies SAM*,[116] the Court of Appeal was asked to consider the existence and scope of an implied term of cooperation in a shipbuilding contract (in that case, for a luxury yacht). Longmore LJ's discussion of the scope of the duty of cooperation shows that its actual content was quite heavily coloured by the practical exigencies of shipbuilding, and the specificities of the structure of that particular contract:

> since . . . the builder only earns a stage payment when the buyer's representative signs a certificate that the relevant stage or milestone has been achieved . . . [if] the relevant milestone has in fact been reached, the buyer must so certify as part of his implied obligation to co-operate in the performance of the contract. Similarly if the buyer proposes a variation and the builder notifies the buyer of the impact in price, performance and delivery, the buyer must co-operate to agree, propose an alternative solution or abandon the proposed variation.[117]

Similarly, in *Hudson Bay Apparel Brands LLC v Umbro International Ltd*,[118] Umbro had granted Hudson Bay Apparel an exclusive licence for the sale of off-field soccer-based clothing in the US. The contract prohibited Hudson Bay from marketing licensed clothing without obtaining Umbro's written approval in relation to the designs. The

113. *Mackay v Dick* (1881) 6 App Cas 251 (HL).   114. Ibid.
115. Ibid, 263 (Lord Blackburn).   116. [2014] EWCA Civ 186.
117. Ibid, [32].   118. [2009] EWHC 2861 (Ch).

dispute arose because Umbro had withheld its approval for one line of potentially lucrative clothing. Hudson Bay argued that there was an implied duty of cooperation, which required Umbro not to unreasonably withhold approval for a line of clothing. The court agreed that there was an implied duty of cooperation, but refused to give it as broad a meaning as Hudson Bay argued. Instead, it implied a more limited duty of cooperation, under which Umbro was not permitted to refuse or fail altogether to consider products or materials submitted for approval.[119] As with the emergent duty of good faith, therefore, the idea of cooperation is better seen as a principle underlying commercial conduct, which will occasionally (but not regularly) lead to a specific duty being implied into a contract.

8.5.3 Contractual discretion

A final term of this type is implied into contracts that give one of the parties the discretion to make determinations or decisions that affect the other party's position. Contracts of this type are common, both in the consumer context and the commercial context. A bank, for example, will usually have the ability to determine the interest rate charged on loans to domestic and commercial customers.[120] Social media sites have very broad discretion to suspend accounts or delete content. Committees of organizations have discretion in determining the cut-off date for membership for the purpose of internal elections.[121] Contracts rarely expressly limit these discretionary powers. Should the law imply a term to do so?

Over recent decades, English courts have tentatively begun to answer this question with a 'yes'. Early cases linked it to fairness. In *The Vainqueur Jose*,[122] where the courts were required to decide on whether there were any implied fetters on the powers of a Protection and Indemnity club (a type of marine insurance organization) to determine deductions on payments to a member, the High Court held that the exercise of discretion was governed by common law principles, including 'fairness, reasonableness, bona fides, and absence of misdirection in law'. However, in *The Product Star (No 2)*,[123] the Court of Appeal held that the concept of 'fairness' was of little help. What mattered, rather, was that the discretion 'must not be exercised arbitrarily, capriciously or unreasonably', in addition to being exercised 'honestly and in good faith'. This flowed from the commercially sensible presumption that 'where A and B contract with each other to confer a discretion on A, that does not render B subject to A's uninhibited whim'.

Later cases have drawn more heavily on an analogy with the concept of *Wednesbury*[124] unreasonableness in administrative law, which holds that a decision is unreasonable (or irrational) if no reasonable decision-maker would have reached it.[125] This analogy was drawn with some reluctance, recognizing that administrative law and contract law

---

119. Ibid, [122] (Mark Herbert QC).
120. *Paragon Finance v Nash* [2001] EWCA Civ 1466, [2002] 1 WLR 685.
121. *Evangelou v McNicol* [2016] EWCA Civ 817.
122. *CVG Siderurgicia del Orinoco SA v London Steamship Owners Mutual Insurance Association Ltd (The Vainqueur Jose)* [1979] 1 Lloyd's Rep 557 (QB).
123. *Abu Dhabi National Tanker Co v Product Star Shipping (The Product Star) (No 2)* [1993] 1 Lloyd's Rep 397 (CA).
124. *Associated Provincial Picture Houses Ltd v Wednesbury Corp* [1948] 1 KB 223.
125. *Gan Insurance Co Ltd v Tai Ping Insurance Co Ltd (No 2)* [2001] EWCA Civ 1047.

serve different purposes, and subject to the proviso that 'the scope of an implied term will depend on the circumstances of the particular contract'.[126]

In *Braganza v BP Shipping Ltd*,[127] the Supreme Court broadly endorsed this approach, and added the clarification that the implied term would include both limbs of the *Wednesbury* test: in addition to the outcome-focused test cited earlier, the decision-maker would also be required to take the right matters into account in making the decision. The precise scope, however, will depend on the context of the specific contract that is at issue in a given case.

It is important that you do not see these duties as having a moral content, or as holding the conduct of commercial parties to a standard of morality. They have a far narrower scope, as can be seen if we relate them back to Problem 8. In principle, this approach—engaging with underlying principles of commercial conduct—on its face comes closest to capturing the actual nature of the trust's discontent; namely, its feeling that Musgrave has been less than honest in its dealings with the trust. Nevertheless, it is unlikely that such a duty will be implied on the facts of this case. In *Yam Seng*, Leggatt J was particularly influenced by the fact that that contract was a long-term contract. There is little in his decision to suggest that the courts will be willing to imply a duty of good faith into shorter-term contracts. This also applies to the duty of cooperation. The case law suggests that it only applies where cooperation is necessary for a contract to actually work. It is not a means of making the contract fairer or more reasonable. That a party's conduct may have been unethical or undesirable or excessively self-serving is not a reason to imply a term of good faith or cooperation into the contract. To do so would be to cross the line into rewriting the parties' contract, which the courts will not generally do.

8.6 In conclusion: words, intentions, and objectivity

Let us now try and pull the threads of our discussion together. As we have seen, English law incorporates several routes by which a court can imply a term into a contract.

There are three key characteristics shared by the approaches to implication. First, there is a preference in English law for precise implied terms over broad, generic duties. We saw, for example, that terms implied in law are only implied into contracts of a particular defined class, which tend to be quite specific. Terms in relation to the quality of goods are the best example of this trend, but as we saw it also applies to terms implied at common law. This also applies to terms implied in fact, where the courts have in more than one case refused to imply a term in fact on the basis that it is broad and insufficiently precise. For this reason, broader terms that seek to prescribe general standards of conduct rather than specific acts that should be done or not done remain controversial in English law. The clearest example of this is the continuing reluctance of the English courts to recognize a general duty of good faith, and the

126. *Paragon Finance v Nash* [2001] EWCA Civ 1466, [2002] 1 WLR 685, [41] (Dyson LJ).
127. [2015] UKSC 17, [2015] 1 WLR 1661.

emphasis they place on giving such a duty a specific, contextual content in those cases where it is implied.

Secondly, implication in English law is closely tied to the court's understanding of the nature of the parties' contract. It is for this reason that courts have emphasized that terms implied at common law must be grounded in the natural incidents of the type of transaction or type of relationship into which the parties have entered. Although courts continue to speak of 'policy' and 'wider considerations', the case law shows that these play, at best, a secondary role. The courts' understanding of the natural incidents of the contract remains the key determining factor.

Thirdly, there is a growing preference in English law to avoid filling contractual gaps, unless there is something out of the ordinary about the transaction in question. As we have seen, the courts have expressly stated time and again that the ordinary result of a contract gap should be that the loss lies where it falls. They have backed this up by refusing to imply terms even where it makes the contract quite inconvenient for the parties. An unfair or unfortunate result is not sufficient to trigger implication.

In practical terms, the lesson is to ensure that contracts are properly thought through, and drafted with sufficient express terms to cover not just the issues that might go right, but also the issues that might go wrong. In particular, it is critically important not to trust the courts to impose appropriate standards of conduct on the parties—particularly in long-term contracts—and to incorporate expressly any broader duties such as duties of cooperation which the parties believe to be important. As Chapter 9 discusses in greater detail, such duties can and do play a productive role in commercial contracts.

Key points

- English law implies terms into contracts through law, fact, and custom.
- Terms are implied in law if statute requires them to be implied. They are also implied in common law if they have been recognized in prior cases, or if they meet the four tests for novel terms: (1) they must belong to a definable category of contractual relationship which is of common occurrence and capable of definition with sufficient precision; (2) they must relate to a matter not dealt with in the contract; (3) they must be a legal incident of that kind of contract or that category of relationship; and (4) the term must meet the threshold of necessity.
- Terms are implied in fact if they are necessary, and if they satisfy the test for determining that they belong in that particular contract. This test is articulated in terms of an 'officious bystander' or in terms of 'business efficacy'.
- Terms can also be implied by custom if that term is part of standard usage or custom in the field or market within which the parties are operating.
- In recent years, courts have begun to recognize the possibility of implying terms imposing duties of good faith and cooperation, and restricting the exercise of contractual discretion. Unlike in civil law systems, however, these terms are implied in fact in response to circumstances specific to the contract before the court.

Assess your learning

You should be able to respond to each of the following points with a confident 'yes'. If you can't, then you should revisit the sections listed against that point.

Can you:

(a) *Identify* the most important statutory sources of terms implied in law, and *outline* the main terms that they imply? (Section 8.2.2)

(b) *Identify* the four tests that the courts use to determine whether to imply a novel term into a contract at common law? (Section 8.2.3)

(c) *Explain* the differences between terms implied in law and terms implied in fact, and *discuss* the tests that courts use to decide whether to imply terms in fact? (Section 8.3)

(d) *Describe* the role played in commerce by terms implied through custom? (Section 8.4)

(e) *Outline* the circumstances in which, and effect to which, courts imply duties of good faith and cooperation in commercial contracts? (Section 8.5)

In relation to each of the above, you should be able to:

(i) identify and clearly explain the key rules and principles;

(ii) identify the key cases and statutes, and why they matter;

(iii) apply the principles and cases to specific real or hypothetical fact situations;

(iv) evaluate the limitations, if any, of the law as it currently stands.

Further reading

R Austen-Baker, *Implied Terms in English Contract Law* (Edward Elgar 2011).

AJ Bateson, 'The Duty to Co-operate' [1960] JBL 187.

H Beale and T Dugdale, 'Contracts Between Businessmen' (1975) 2 British Journal of Law and Society 45.

JF Burrows, 'Contractual Co-operation and the Implied Term' (1968) 31 MLR 390.

A Kramer, 'Implication in Fact as an Instance of Contractual Interpretation' (2004) 63 CLJ 384.

G McMeel, *The Construction of Contracts: Interpretation, Implication and Rectification* (2nd edn, Oxford University Press 2011).

E Peden, 'Policy Concerns Behind Implication of Terms in Law' (2001) 117 LQR 459.

A Phang, 'Implied Terms, Business Efficacy, and the Officious Bystander: A Modern History' [1998] JBL 1.

TD Rakoff, 'Implied Terms: Of "Default Rules" and "Situation Sense"' in J Beatson and D Friedmann (eds), *Good Faith and Fault in Contract Law* (Oxford University Press 1995).

Flexible terms

Uncertainty, vagueness, and incompleteness

'The best-laid schemes o' mice an' men . . .'[*]

[*] Robert Burns, 'To a mouse' 39.

Problem 9: setting the context

Consider the following exchange of text messages between two friends:

> Hey, hear you're selling your LP collection. How much do you want for them?

> I was thinking of around £500.

> Oh no. I don't have that much, but I'd really like them.

> I don't need the cash straight away. How about you pay for a few LPs every month, depending on what you can afford?

> Great, but what if I don't have money one month?

> We'll talk about it then and sort something out. Don't worry!

> Brilliant! Deal!

Have the parties reached a binding agreement? What legal effect do you think the parties' agreement has in terms of the things it requires each party to do or not do?

9.1 Introduction: certainty and the complex transaction

When we think of contracts, we tend to think of terms that are clear and straightforward. Terms may require a party to do a specific *act*, for example a tenant's duty to pay the rent by a particular date. Alternatively, they may require a party to achieve a particular *outcome*, such as a tenant's duty to ensure that the house is in the same condition at the end of a lease as it was at the start. Terms of this type are straightforward because their wording clearly sets out what each party is required to *do* for the other under a contract, and precisely what each party is entitled to *expect* from the other under the contract.

But not all contracts are this clear, as Problem 9 illustrates. The parties have obviously reached some form of agreement, in that they've agreed on a purchase price and on the goods to be sold. Yet you can see that the agreement is horribly incomplete. Which LPs will be sold each month? They won't all be worth the same, so how do you decide how much to pay for them? What happens if the buyer offers to pay an amount which the seller rejects as being too low? And what does an agreement that the parties will 'talk about it and sort something out' actually mean, in concrete terms?

You can see why the parties couldn't really have concluded the agreement on any other terms, given the uncertainties in relation to the buyer's means in any month. Nevertheless, these gaps mean that it is far from clear what the contract actually requires the parties to do in any given month. What happens if there is a month in which the parties never manage to agree on which LPs will be transferred and for how much? Are they both in breach of contract? What is each party entitled to expect from the other? The language of the agreement itself does not answer any of these questions.

Open-ended clauses like this one are not confined to friendly transactions as seen in Problem 9. They are also increasingly common in commercial contracts. Many modern transactions are complex and multi-layered. Unlike a sale of goods transaction, complex transactions involve so many factors that it is virtually impossible to provide for even the *types* of situations that may come up in the course of performing the transaction. Richard Epstein, an American theorist of private law, suggested that non-instantaneous transactions always have a large number of 'unknown unknowns'—things which are so unforeseeable that the parties cannot sensibly say anything about them beyond being aware that the unforeseeable may happen.[1]

In everyday relations, we tend to deal with the presence of these 'unknown unknowns' on the basis that if something unexpected happens, everyone will sit down and figure out a solution. Yet it can be surprisingly difficult to draft a legally enforceable clause which says, 'if something unexpected happens, we will sit down and figure out a solution that works for everyone concerned'. In English law, clauses of this type run up against two related doctrines: **vagueness** and **incompleteness**, both of which render the clause or contract void in law. Issues relating to vagueness typically arise where the parties have reached some form of agreement, but have recorded it in terms that are so unclear, or so open-ended, that they do not yield a clear meaning, and give no real way of deciding what the parties are required to do and whether they have done it. 'Incompleteness' arises where the parties have failed or forgotten to deal with an important issue in their contract. A contract is incomplete if it fails to deal with a matter which is so fundamental that the transaction cannot be performed without agreement being reached on it.

Vagueness and incompleteness are closely related to the requirement of **certainty** in contracting, which crops up in a number of different areas of contract law. This requirement reflects the view that judges should not rewrite contracts by adding new terms to them. If a clause's meaning is so uncertain that a judge will, in effect, be required to write a new, clearer term to enforce it, he or she should refuse to do so.

The difficulty with this view is that it is not always easy to write a clause that injects enough flexibility into the contract to cope with 'unknown unknowns' while preserving enough certainty to keep the clause enforceable. Compare the following two clauses, the first of which (Illustration 9.1) is taken from a straightforward sale of goods, while the second (Illustration 9.2) is taken from a more complex transaction.

Illustration 9.1

The seller shall ensure that the Product complies with all regulatory standards that may be applicable. It shall be the duty of the buyer to notify the seller of any use to which the buyer intends to put the Product, which may result in such requirements becoming applicable.

---

1. R Epstein, 'In Defense of the Contract at Will' (1984) 51 University of Chicago Law Review 947.

Despite the formality of the language in which this clause is drafted, the commercial objective of the parties is very clear, as is the mechanism they have adopted to attain that objective. The commercial objective is to ensure that the product in question meets all regulatory requirements, for example product safety standards. The clause puts this in legal terms, setting out the *outcome* which the seller is required to achieve (produce goods which comply with all applicable regulatory requirements), as well as the *acts* which the buyer is required to do (telling the seller what it plans to do with the goods). As a result, the clause is straightforward to apply. It is easy to figure out what each of the parties is required to do, and to decide whether they have done it.

The clarity and specificity of this clause contrasts sharply with the broader and more open-ended character of the clause in the next illustration:

Illustration 9.2

The parties will use their best endeavours to obtain all approvals that may be necessary to achieve the objectives set out in this contract.

The commercial objective of the parties is as clear in this clause as it was in Illustration 9.1. The parties want to ensure that they work together, so that the contract succeeds commercially. Because they cannot currently identify what problems their transaction might encounter, they have tried to achieve this objective through a clause which sets out a broad, non-specific duty of cooperation.

Clauses of this type are common. However, they are inherently far less certain than the more specific clause set out in Illustration 9.1. It is a very simple matter to decide whether a party has notified another about a proposed use of the product. It is less simple to decide whether a party has used 'best endeavours' to achieve the objectives set out in a contract. How can a court even make a start in deciding whether the endeavours a party used were the 'best' it could have used?

Questions such as these have come to increasing prominence in the past two decades, as the growing complexity of commercial transactions has made flexible clauses increasingly important. The courts tend to be reluctant to declare contracts to be unenforceable, particularly in commercial transactions where the parties have acted on the assumption that their agreement was legally binding. Nevertheless, flexible clauses have posed a range of difficulties for the courts, particularly when it comes to clauses designed to get parties to sit down and work out a solution to an unexpected problem. Poor design can end up making flexible clauses unenforceable. Studying the doctrines of vagueness and incompleteness gives us an understanding of how contracts can be designed to be both flexible and legally valid.

We will begin our survey of this area by examining the contours of the doctrine of certainty as it applies to contractual terms, starting with a survey of the law pertaining to vagueness (section 9.2), and then moving on to incompleteness (section 9.3). We will conclude by evaluating how well English contract law deals with the issues that arise from the need for flexibility in complex transactions (section 9.4).

9.2 Unclear terms: vagueness and open-ended clauses

Let us begin with a slightly absurd example. Imagine that Google's former motto, 'don't be evil' were to become a clause in a contract:

Illustration 9.3

12. Conduct: The parties agree that they will not be evil in performing their obligations under this contract.

Would a court enforce such a clause, awarding damages against a party on the basis that it had been 'evil'? The answer would self-evidently appear to be that it will not: there is something faintly ridiculous about the idea of a civil court in England using the concept of 'evil' as the basis of a decision. But what might be the *legal* basis for such a refusal?

In the standard doctrinal account, the refusal to enforce clauses like the one in Illustration 9.3 is explained with reference to the clause's vagueness—the fact that its wording is so imprecise and open-ended that it could mean everything and anything. At one level, this appears instinctively right. It is far from clear what standard we could apply to decide whether a party has been 'evil' without, in effect, scratching out the word 'evil' and replacing it with other, less vague, words. On this account, courts refuse to give legal effect to vague provisions because they are reluctant to replace the parties' words with words of their own devising, as vague clauses require them to do.

This reluctance is not, however, absolute. As section 9.1 of this chapter discussed, a certain degree of vagueness is inevitable in most commercial contracts, and English courts do not invalidate clauses or contracts lightly, particularly in a commercial context. In many cases, an English court will use interpretation, implication, and the objective test to give a seemingly vague clause some enforceable content, rather than holding it to be invalid. As a practical matter, therefore, whether a clause is too vague to be enforced is usually a matter of degree rather than reflecting a binary divide between terms that are perfectly clear and those that are perfectly unclear.

As with other matters of interpretation and implication, this enquiry too is a contextual one. Whether a clause can be made to work, and the meaning it will be given if it can, is a function not just of the specific words that are used in that clause, but also of the type of transaction to which it relates, and the specific duty that is at issue in the dispute. Broadly speaking, two sets of contextual factors can be used to give enforceable content to a clause that is drafted in non-specific, and somewhat vague, language; namely, contextual factors which are specific to the facts of a case, and general commercial usage of the term or phrase in question. In this section, we will study each in turn, before concluding with more general observations about the implications of the doctrine of vagueness for the law and practice of modern contracting.

9.2.1 The role of case-specific contextual factors

Consider the following two clauses:

Illustration 9.4

This order is given on the understanding that the balance of purchase price can be had on hire-purchase terms over a period of two years.

Illustration 9.5

The loading time shall be 36 running hours, on terms of usual colliery guarantee.

Both clauses are taken from decided cases. On the face of it they have a lot in common. Both contemplate that the contract will be subject to some external set of terms, but neither actually tells us *what* these external terms are. Contrast this with Illustration 9.6, which is a more typical example:

Illustration 9.6

This contract is subject to the Infrastructure Conditions of Contract Minor Works Version (August 2011), jointly published by the Association of Consulting Engineers and the Civil Engineering Contractors Association.[2]

In comparison with Illustration 9.6, the terms in Illustrations 9.5 and 9.4 are vague. No two sets of hire-purchase terms are the same. Which precise terms govern the contract? Equally, what precise document does the phrase 'usual colliery guarantee' in Illustration 9.5 refer to?

Despite these seeming similarities, however, when the clauses actually came to court, only the contract in Illustration 9.4 was held to be void. The contract in Illustration 9.5, in contrast, was held to be fully enforceable. The reason for the difference lay in the commercial context of each case. The clause in Illustration 9.4 was the subject of *Scammell v Ouston*.[3] The decision of the House of Lords in this case is generally taken to be the leading statement of the law on the topic of vague terms in contracts, and is worth considering in some detail.

---

2. The reference in this clause is to one of two 'suites' or sets of contract terms that are commonly used in large-scale building contracts in the UK. The other suite is the NEC3 contract suite published by the Institution of Civil Engineers.

3. [1941] AC 251 (HL).

Case in depth: *Scammell v Ouston* [1941] AC 251 (HL)

Scammell v Ouston involved the acquisition of a goods vehicle[4] by HC & JG Ouston from Scammell & Son, an automobile dealer. Discussions took place in person in November and December 1937. At a meeting on 6 December, the parties agreed a price of £268 for the van. They also agreed that Ouston would provide an old lorry—described as a 1935 model—in part-exchange, and receive a rebate of £100. The balance of the price was to be 'had on hire purchase terms over a period of two years'. This was confirmed by an exchange of letters on 7 and 8 December 1937.

In a hire-purchase transaction, the buyer does not contract with the dealer. He contracts, instead, with a third party financier. The third party was not identified in the contract, but it was understood by both parties that it would be the United Dominions Trust Co Ltd, and Scammell obtained the consent of the United Dominions Trust for the hire purchase.[5]

Before the hire-purchase agreement was signed, however, Scammell asked to inspect the vehicle Ouston provided as part-exchange. After inspection, Scammell rejected the vehicle. They claimed (as it turned out, wrongly)[6] that it was a 1934 model rather than a 1935 model, and that it was in poor condition. On that basis, they said they would be unable to pay the rebate. Ouston sued for breach of contract. In the course of the hearing, Scammell dropped its claims as to the condition of Ouston's vehicle, and defended the action on the basis that no contract had been concluded.

Scammell's lawyers' argument was simple. They contended that the parties' intention was clearly to only transact through a tripartite hire-purchase agreement. Such an agreement would need a number of terms in order to be enforceable, none of which had been agreed. The parties had not even agreed on the rate of interest, the amount of each monthly instalment, or the precise structure of the hire-purchase transaction.[7] The contract, as a result, was void for uncertainty.[8]

The High Court, as well as the Court of Appeal, held that the contract was not void. All essential terms had been agreed, including the price, the rebate, and the model of the van being sold. Whilst the terms of the hire-purchase agreement had not been agreed, that was only 'the method of financing the transaction'. Its effect was to impose an obligation on one of the parties to find a financier who would provide the purchase price on a hire-purchase arrangement.[9]

On appeal, the House of Lords found for the defendant, and held unanimously that the phrase 'on hire purchase terms' was too uncertain to be enforceable. The phrase, as Viscount Simon put it, was 'so vaguely expressed that it cannot, standing by itself, be given a definite meaning'. The reasoning of the House of Lords was that there was no such thing as a standard set of hire-purchase terms. Unlike certain other kinds of contracts which were invariably concluded on the basis of certain 'usual terms', hire-purchase contracts were characterized by a great

→

---

4. The vehicles involved in this case are described both as a 'lorry' and a 'van' in the judgment of the Court of Appeal, and a 'van' in the judgment of the House of Lords. At the time, the terms were somewhat more interchangeable than they are today. In modern terminology, the vehicles in question are closer to trucks than vans.

5. [1941] AC 251, 262 (HL).

6. See the judgment of the Court of Appeal: *Ouston v Scammell* [1940] 1 All ER 59, 62 (Slesser LJ).

7. Ibid, 60.   8. Ibid, 61.   9. Ibid, 64 (Slesser LJ), 66 (MacKinnon LJ), 67 (Goddard LJ).

deal of diversity not just in the specific terms, but also in the way they were structured.[10] It required 'further agreement to be reached between the parties before there would be a complete *consensus ad idem*',[11] because there was no way of identifying from the contract what sort of terms or structure were contemplated. At least five very different structures, with very different obligations, had been suggested by various judges and lawyers involved in this case, all of which were consistent with the agreed terms.[12] The contract did not even set out whose responsibility it was to obtain hire-purchase finance. Lord Wright pointed out that in the Court of Appeal itself, one of the judges had appeared to take the view that finding a financier was Ouston's responsibility as the buyer, whereas another judge took the view that it was Scammell's responsibility as the seller.[13] As a result, it was impossible to say what the parties' rights and obligations under the contract were, and the contract was accordingly void for uncertainty.

The House of Lords in *Scammell v Ouston* treated the case as an example of an **agreement to agree**.[14] In an agreement to agree, the parties have not actually agreed on the terms. They have merely noted that they expect, at some stage, to reach agreement on a set of terms. Such a contract is not ordinarily enforceable. *Scammell v Ouston* remains good law on this point, and there continue to be cases in which the courts refuse to give effect to contracts on the basis that they are uncertain and/or agreements to agree. Nevertheless, the courts have in later cases stressed that cases like *Scammell v Ouston* are rare.[15] If the courts can identify the scope of the parties' rights and obligations through interpretation, implication, and incorporation, then that should be the preferred approach. *Shamrock Steamship Co v Storey & Co*[16]—in which the clause in Illustration 9.5 was held enforceable—is a typical example.

The dispute in *Shamrock* arose out of a contract for the sale of coal, to be loaded at Grimsby. The parties' agreement had a contract to the effect that the loading time would be '36 running hours, on terms of usual colliery guarantee'. The dispute in this case related to the question of when the 36 hours referred to in the clause began to run. The contract was silent on this point, leaving matters to the 'usual colliery guarantee'. Unfortunately, the contract did not explain what guarantee this was, and it was shown in evidence that there were three different forms of colliery guarantee that were used at Grimsby. None of them was more commonly used than any other, and none had any better claim to be regarded as more 'usual' than the other.

The defendants argued that this meant the clause was void for uncertainty, because it was impossible to determine which of these three different sets of terms governed the parties' contract. The court rejected the defendants' argument, and held the clause to be enforceable. Although there were three different forms of colliery guarantee, all three contained exactly the same provision on the point that was at issue in this case; namely, when the loading time was said to start. As a result, it did not matter that a

10. [1941] AC 251, 257 (Viscount Maugham).   11. Ibid, 254.
12. Ibid, 259–60 (Lord Russell).   13. Ibid, 265 (Lord Wright).
14. Ibid, 261 (Lord Russell).
15. See eg *Scammell v Dicker* [2005] EWCA Civ 405, [2005] 3 All ER 838, [41] (Rix LJ).
16. (1899) 81 LT 413, (1899) 16 TLR 6 (CA).

particular guarantee could not be identified as the applicable one. On the dispute at hand, the parties' contractual rights and duties were clear, because the time would have begun to run at the same moment under all three sets of terms and conditions.

What, then, accounts for the difference in outcome between *Scammell v Ouston* on the one hand and *Shamrock v Storey* on the other? The answer lies in the relationship between the obligation whose breach was in question and the term that was alleged to be vague. Although there were many matters on which the three sets of colliery guarantees differed, the dispute in *Shamrock* related to one of the relatively few points on which all three were in agreement. In *Scammell v Ouston*, in contrast, Scammell's obligation to 'deliver' the vehicle to Ouston would have entailed very different things under each of the five structures which the phrase 'on hire purchase terms' might have meant. In some it would have entailed delivery to and payment by the financier, in others it would have entailed delivery to Ouston. As a result, it was far from clear what Scammell was required to do in order to comply with the clause.

The question of vagueness is therefore not decided in the abstract. It is decided with reference to the specific circumstances of the case, and to the significance the words at issue have in the context of those circumstances. Equally, as *Shamrock* also indicates, the ordinary consequence of a clause being uncertain is that that particular clause will be invalid. The rest of the contract, insofar as it can be severed from the affected clause, will continue in full force and effect. It is only in cases where the issue affects the contract as a whole or where the clause in question is so critical to the contract that the contract cannot work without it, as was the case in *Scammell v Ouston*, that the entire contract will be unenforceable.[17]

The courts also distinguish between clauses that are vague and clauses that are hard to apply. A clause is only vague if the words themselves do not yield a clear meaning. A clause whose words are clear and have an intelligible meaning in law is enforceable, even if it is hard to apply. In *Arkady Gaydamak v Lev Leviev*,[18] the High Court was faced with a contract that had been drafted by two businessmen, in relation to a transaction involving Angolan diamonds. The transaction had a very complex structure and was deliberately designed to obscure the true ownership and control of the venture. The following clause is typical of the type of terms found in that agreement:

> The positioning of Leviev in front of the business community, as the owner and controller of those assets and activities, has been made for convenience purposes only. As long as Leviev is in front, he is regarded vis-à-vis the abovementioned share of Gaydamak in the assets and activities as a trustee in favour of Gaydamak.[19]

One of the arguments taken by the defendants was that the agreement was too uncertain to be enforced. Vos J rejected this contention, holding that the mere fact that the words were difficult to construe did not make a contract uncertain:

> The terms may be hard to construe, and may even invite litigation, but they do clearly provide a number of intelligible mutual obligations. Difficulties of construction do not in themselves deprive an agreement of its enforceability.[20]

17. For a more recent example, see *Nigel Cayzer v Robert Beddow* [2007] EWCA Civ 644, where the Court of Appeal conceded that some terms had been agreed, but nevertheless held the entire contract to be void for uncertainty because the terms that were vague were central to the agreement.
18. [2012] EWHC 1740 (Ch).   19. Ibid, [79].   20. Ibid, [217].

This reflects the fact that even on the most expansive interpretation, the rules relating to certainty do not seek to *police* contracts and ensure that parties write them properly. They seek, rather, to insulate the courts from being drawn into the task of *writing* contracts to cover for the parties' failure to do so properly. The mere fact that a contract was badly drafted does not make it uncertain. It is only uncertain if it fails to create intelligible mutual obligations. As we will see in the next section, this acquires particular importance when it comes to dealing with flexible terms that are open-ended, but have a particular significance in commercial usage.

9.2.2 **The role of commercial usage**

Contracts frequently contain terms that on their face appear to be vague or uncertain, but which are nevertheless commonly used in commercial practice. In general, if the courts are dealing with terms that have a clear commercial meaning or significance, they tend to give effect to those terms on the basis of their commercial meaning, even if they seem vague in laypersons' terms. A common instance of such a term is the idea of 'reasonableness', which is used very frequently in contract law as well as in commercial contracts. Although terms such as 'reasonable quality' or a 'reasonable price' are imprecise, the idea of reasonableness has developed a clear meaning in common law, drawing on commercial usage.

'Best endeavours' clauses, such as the one in Illustration 9.2, are another example. These clauses usually reflect attempts to solve what economists call a commitment problem. Commitment problems reflect the possibility that one of the parties will grow less committed to the contract if changed circumstances make the contract less profitable for that party. Best endeavours clauses—and their variant, the reasonable endeavours clause[21]—seek to deal with such a situation by requiring the party in question to make serious efforts to work towards a goal, even if that goal is no longer as attractive to him as it originally was. As such, they have been used in a range of contracts since at least the early 20th century.[22]

As Illustration 9.2 indicates, however, best endeavours clauses only impose a requirement to *attempt* to achieve an outcome, not to actually achieve it. This raises issues in relation to certainty. The clause in Illustration 9.2 is clearly less precise than a clause that, for example, requires all steel plates used in a machine to be 9mm thick. How do we decide what it requires a party to do, and whether a party has complied with it?

The courts' response to best endeavours clauses has been to generally hold that they are *not* inherently vague and may be capable of being enforced, as long as the objects which the endeavours are supposed to be directed to pursuing are certain.[23] If, however, the objects themselves are uncertain—if, in other words, the contract does not make

21. A clause requiring reasonable endeavours is generally understood as imposing a less stringent obligation than a clause requiring the use of 'best endeavours'. The phrase 'all reasonable endeavours', which is sometimes used, is usually equated with an obligation to use best endeavours. See *Rhodia International Holdings Ltd v Huntsman International LLC* [2007] EWHC 292 (Comm), [2007] 1 CLC 59.

22. The earliest reported case on a best endeavours clause was decided in 1911. *Sheffield District Railway Co v Great Central Railway Co* (1911) 27 TLR 451.

23. *R & D Construction Group Ltd v Hallam Land Management Ltd* [2010] CSIH 96.

it clear what the best endeavours are supposed to be directed towards achieving—the courts will generally refuse to give effect to the clause.[24] The question of what the clause actually requires the parties to do is treated as a contextual one, to be decided with reference to the factual and contractual context within which the clause occurs.[25] The decision of the Court of Appeal in *Jet2.com v Blackpool Airport*,[26] a case involving a best endeavours clause, provides a particularly good illustration of how courts draw on commercial usage and the commercial context to give content to a flexible term that, taken in isolation, may seem to be vague.

Case in depth: *Jet2.com v Blackpool Airport* [2012] EWCA Civ 417

In this case the Court of Appeal was faced with a dispute between Jet2.com, a low-cost airline, and Blackpool Airport, relating to the scope and enforceability of a best endeavours clause. In 2005, Jet2.com entered into an agreement with Blackpool Airport Ltd (BAL), setting out the terms on which Jet2.com would operate its flights from Blackpool Airport (BA) for the next 15 years. Clause 1 of the agreement provided as follows:

> Jet2.com and BAL will co-operate together and use their best endeavours to promote Jet2.com's low cost services from BA and BAL will use all reasonable endeavours to provide a cost base that will facilitate Jet2.com's low cost pricing.[27]

To keep Jet2.com's costs low, BAL began permitting it to schedule flights to arrive and depart from the airport outside the airport's ordinary opening hours. The agreement did not expressly require BAL to do this, and in 2010 as part of a cost-cutting exercise, BAL informed Jet2.com that it would no longer permit flights to take off and land outside the airport's usual opening hours. Jet2.com sued for breach of contract. Jet2.com's argument was that although the contract did not expressly require BAL to open the airport outside the usual opening hours, it was nevertheless required to do so as a result of its duties in clause 1, to use best endeavours to promote Jet2.com's services and provide a cost base facilitating low-cost pricing. BAL, in reply, argued that clause 1 was unenforceable for vagueness. Alternately, if clause 1 was enforceable, it did not require BAL to act contrary to their own commercial and financial interests.[28]

The Court of Appeal found for Jet2.com. The obligation to use best endeavours to promote Jet2.com's business, it held, required BAL to 'do all that it reasonably could do to enable that business to succeed and grow'.[29] This included enabling aircraft to operate early in the morning and late at night, without which the low-cost aircraft model was unviable. On the point of BAL's commercial interests, the court held that 'whether, and if so to what extent, a person who has contractually taken on the duty of using best endeavours can have regard to his own financial interests will depend very much on the nature and terms of the contract in question'.[30] In some cases, it may well be the case that the person's own financial interests

→

---

24. *Bower v Bantam Investments Ltd* [1972] 1 WLR 1120.
25. *Phillips Petroleum Co (UK) Ltd v Enron (Europe) Ltd* [1997] CLC 329.
26. [2012] EWCA Civ 417, [2012] 1 CLC 605.   27. Ibid, [6].
28. The airport was chronically loss-making at the time, and it eventually closed in 2014 after its owners were unable to continue funding it.
29. [2012] EWCA Civ 417, [31] (Moore-Bick LJ).   30. Ibid, [32] (Moore-Bick LJ).

take precedence, but this will depend on the context in which the contractual commitment was made.[31] On the facts of this case, BAL could not contractually refuse to permit flights to land or depart outside its ordinary opening hours only because it incurred a loss as a result.

Lewison LJ dissented. He held that the obligation in clause 1 was so 'open-textured' that it could create potentially unlimited obligations on the part of BAL. The dispute in this particular case concerned flight times, but nothing in the clause restricted it to flight times. It could just as easily have applied to the provision of check-in staff and other matters. 'Would it, for example, require BAL to provide enhanced passenger lounges for Jet2.com's departing passengers; or to offer them complimentary refreshments while they wait?'[32] Given these uncertainties, he would have held the clause to be void for uncertainty.

Despite Lewison LJ's dissent, most cases on best expectations have been along the lines as the decision of the majority in *Jet2.com v BAL*. In *IBM United Kingdom Ltd v Rockware Glass Ltd*,[33] the Court of Appeal was asked to decide the effect of a clause which required Rockware to 'use its best endeavours' to obtain planning permission for a proposed development. Rockware applied for planning permission, but when permission was refused it let the matter drop without pursuing the statutory appeal to which it was entitled. IBM successfully sued Rockware for breach of contract. The Court of Appeal held that in this context, the obligation to use best endeavours required Rockware to 'take all those steps in their power which . . . a prudent, determined and reasonable owner' would take.[34] In failing to pursue an appeal, it had breached this obligation.

9.2.3 **Vagueness and enforceability**

As the discussion in this section should have shown, although vague clauses are not in general enforced in English law, the courts also go to some lengths to uphold the validity of language which reflects common commercial usage even if it is somewhat vague. It is this that underlies the position we see in English law, under which a clause that requires the parties to be 'reasonable', or to use 'best endeavours', or to 'cooperate' with the other party,[35] are enforceable, whereas a clause that requires a party not to be 'evil' is likely to be void for uncertainty.

One way to approach this area is to see it as providing a toolkit which commercial parties and lawyers can use in designing flexible contractual clauses. 'Best endeavours', 'reasonable endeavours', 'collaboration', 'good faith', and other similar phrases become, in this understanding, different building blocks which can be used by a skilled lawyer to put together a contract that is both flexible and enforceable. As the analogy of a toolkit also suggests, however, straying beyond these established types of clauses can lead to the contractual provisions in question becoming unenforceable. If the court comes to the conclusion that the words used by the parties were too vague and uncertain to be enforceable, as it did in *Scammell v Ouston*,[36]

---

31. For an example, see *Terrell v Mabie Todd & Co Ltd* [1952] 2 TLR 574.
32. [2012] EWCA Civ 417, [52].   33. [1980] FSR 335 (CA).   34. Ibid, 349.
35. On cooperation clauses, see Chapter 8.   36. [1941] AC 251 (HL).

the clause in question will be void. Best endeavours clauses are no exception to this rule. The cases discussed in section 9.2.2 demonstrate that courts can and will give legal effect to best endeavours clauses in a way that is quite closely connected with their commercial purpose. Nevertheless, courts remain cautious in doing so, and the requirement of certainty has not gone away. If, for example, the objectives that the endeavours are intended to further are unclear, the clause is likely to be void for uncertainty.

From this perspective, the agreement in Problem 9 provides an excellent example of what happens when parties stray beyond these established categories in crafting their contract. Given the discussion in this section, it is clear that the agreement is vague on a number of points. What does it mean to say that 'a few LPs' will be paid for each month, and that both the number and the identity of the LPs sold will depend on what the buyer 'can afford'? How are any of these to be assessed? Yet, as the discussion in this section has also demonstrated, the parties could, with only a little bit of work, have made an agreement that was fully enforceable. It would, for example, have been open to the parties to agree that the buyer would pay '£25 per month', that the LPs transferred to the buyer every month would represent a 'reasonable price' for that sum (or that they would be transferred in some determinate order), and that the buyer would make 'best endeavours' to pay the agreed sum every month, but would be entitled to miss (for example) up to six payments over the life of the agreement.

The result, however, is somewhat peculiar. A party who is advised well by a skilled lawyer would have been able to craft an enforceable agreement, but a party who did not would find herself caught short. Is such a situation desirable? And why does the law adopt such an approach, given that even commercial parties will not infrequently draft agreements without taking legal advice, and without fully realizing the consequences of adopting the precise form of words they have chosen? We will return to this issue in section 9.4.

9.3 Missing terms: incompleteness and agreements to agree

Incompleteness, as it is conventionally described, covers contracts which are missing essential terms. The category of 'essential' terms is, however, narrower than one might think. The existence of a body of rules in relation to filling contract gaps, whether by implying new terms (Chapter 8) or interpreting unclear terms (Chapter 7), means that many terms that may be missing from the contractual *document* are not missing in terms of contract *law*. Consider the following example. What would your response be if you were asked which of the following terms are essential in a contract for the sale of a refurbished mobile phone: the price, a description of the phone's physical condition, and a statement as to whether the phone is in working order? Most people would assume that at least the price was essential, but the correct answer is that none of these terms are essential because every single one of these gaps can be filled either by implication or by interpretation. If a contract to sell something fails to set out the price the law implies a term into the contract to the effect that that thing was to be sold at a reasonable price.[37] If it fails to describe the condition of the thing being sold, the law implies a term into the contract either to the effect that the goods will be of satisfactory quality (if the seller is a business)[38] or to the effect that they are sold as is (if the seller is not a business).[39] Likewise, the use of the word 'refurbished' to describe the phone will ordinarily be interpreted to mean that the phone is in working order, even if the contract does not expressly say so.

The law works similarly in relation to a range of other types of common terms and types of contracts, filling gaps that might on the face of things appear to have left the contract incomplete. The result is that, in practice, incompleteness usually becomes an issue only in a relatively narrow set of circumstances, primarily relating to what are commonly called framework agreements. Framework agreements, as their name suggests, set out a broad framework for a transaction but leave many details unaddressed. They tend to be used where the parties have reached agreement on broad principles but have not as yet thrashed out the nitty-gritties. Problem 9 provides precisely such an example in the context of an everyday arrangement between two friends, but situations of this type are not uncommon in the world of commercial contracting.

Broadly speaking, the courts have taken two very different approaches to dealing with incompleteness in framework agreements. The first approach is to enforce these agreements by filling the gaps left by the parties' words. This is usually done by implying a term of 'reasonableness' into them. The clauses discussed in the hypothetical mobile phone contract are a typical example of this approach in practice. The second approach, in contrast, is to treat the agreement as an 'agreement to agree' and, hence, as having no legal effect. In such cases, the court in effect holds that the contract cannot be enforced simply by interpreting the parties' words: it will, instead, require the court to rewrite the contract in order to make it work. As such, the contract is unenforceable as written.

Both approaches remain in use, and it is therefore important to understand what leads to an agreement being put in one category rather than the other. In summary, the essence of the distinction appears to lie in the difference between incomplete agreements whose missing terms can be dealt with through *unilateral action* by a party or some form of objective determination, which the courts will enforce, and agreements which require *cooperative action* between the parties or some form of subjectively negotiated determination, which the courts will not enforce. The difference, to put it another way, is between frameworks for *action*, which are enforceable, and frameworks for *discussion*, which are not. In the remainder of this section, we will consider the nature of this distinction in more detail, before coming back to its broader implications for commercial practice.

9.3.1 Frameworks, mechanisms, and incompleteness

The modern form of the doctrine of incompleteness in contracts began with the case of *May and Butcher v The King*,[40] decided by the House of Lords in 1929.[41]

---

37. Sale of Goods Act 1979, s 8(1).   38. Ibid, s 14(2).   39. Ibid, s 14(1).
40. [1934] 2 KB 17 (HL).
41. The case went unreported when it was decided. However, it was printed five years later as a note to the report of a subsequent case, *Foley v Classique Coaches* [1934] 2 KB 1 (CA). The decision in *Foley* is discussed in more detail later in this section.

Case in depth: *May and Butcher v The King* [1934] 2 KB 17 (HL)

The end of the First World War left the government with a lot of surplus military equipment, which the government began to sell. May and Butcher entered into a contract with the Disposals Board in June 1921, under which the government agreed to sell them all old tentage that the government sold as surplus to requirements. The agreement was to run until December 1921. In January 1922, the contract was extended for a further period up to 31 March 1923.

In relation to price and quantity, the contract provided as follows:

> The price or prices to be paid, and the date or dates on which payment is to be made by the purchasers to the Commission for such old tentage shall be agreed upon from time to time between the Commission and the purchasers as the quantities of the said old tentage become available for disposal, and are offered to the purchasers by the Commission.[42]

The contract also contained an arbitration clause, providing that any disputes between the parties would be resolved by arbitration.

In August 1922, disputes arose between the parties as a result of a change of personnel at the Disposals Board. The previous practice had been to sell goods by communicating their specifications to the purchaser, who could then accept the specifications or inspect the goods if he chose. The new head of the Disposals Board discontinued the practice of supplying specifications, and instead left it to the purchaser to inspect the goods to determine their specifications and condition. May and Butcher were unhappy with the new arrangement, and after some discussions the Disposals Board declared that it was no longer bound by the agreement.[43] May and Butcher sued the board for breach of contract.[44]

The Disposals Board argued in court that no agreement had come into being. Key issues had not been agreed, including fundamental matters such as price, date of payment, and period for delivery. As such, all the parties had agreed on were certain clauses, which would govern the actual contracts for the sale of tentage as and when those were made. Those contracts would not, however, be made until price, date of payment, and period for delivery were agreed on.

Rowlatt J in the High Court, and Sargant LJ and Eve J in the Court of Appeal, found for the Disposals Board, and held that the contract had never come into being.[45] The House of Lords upheld their decisions. The House of Lords acknowledged that the Sale of Goods Act provided that if the price is not determined by a contract, a reasonable price will be assumed. Nevertheless, they held, in this case the parties had in fact created a mechanism to set the price; namely, their mutual agreement. As a result, the terms they

→

---

42. [1934] 2 KB 17.   43. Ibid, 18–19.

44. Because of the structure of English civil procedure at the time, any claim in contract against a government department had to be brought by way of a special process called a 'petition of right', with the king (or queen, as the case may be) being the defendant. The case is for that reason expressed as having been brought against the king, although it was in reality against the Disposals Board.

45. Scrutton LJ dissented in the Court of Appeal, as is discussed in more detail in section 9.4.

> →
> had produced merely constituted an agreement to agree, rather than a contract, and was unenforceable.[46] The presence of an arbitration clause did not help matters, because that presupposed the existence of a valid and binding agreement. There was 'nothing in the arbitration clause to enable a contract to be made which in fact the original bargain has left quite open'.[47]

Much as in *Scammell v Ouston*,[48] the House of Lords in *May and Butcher* suggested that the law of incompleteness is grounded in the common law principle that agreements to agree are not enforceable. Yet the supposed antipathy to 'agreements to agree' has never been an absolute rule in English law. Consider the following illustration:

Illustration 9.7

In the event of any deviation or change of voyage, it is hereby agreed to hold the assured covered at a premium to be arranged.

It is hard to think of a clearer instance of an agreement to agree than a contract which explicitly states that the premium is 'to be arranged'. Nevertheless, clauses of this type, called 'held covered' clauses, are very common in insurance policies, and are fully enforceable in English law.[49] They are read as being an agreement to provide insurance cover for a 'reasonable premium', rather than as contemplating a course of negotiations leading to the parties agreeing on a premium. The question of what is 'reasonable', of course, is a question of fact which the courts have long been prepared to settle if the parties are unable to themselves reach agreement.

As the example of 'held covered' clauses suggests, the strictness of the rules on incompleteness is tempered by the fact that the courts will give effect to clauses that have the form of agreements to agree, but which are in substance frameworks for action, and are capable of being implemented without any further concord being required of the parties. Within a few years of the decision in *May and Butcher*, two further decisions demonstrated how such an approach can apply to salvage contracts that might otherwise be held to be void for incompleteness. The first of these was the decision of the House of Lords in *WN Hillas & Co Ltd v Arcos Ltd*[50] which came less than three years after *May and Butcher*.

---

46. [1934] 2 KB 17, 20 (Lord Buckmaster).
47. Ibid, 21 (Lord Buckmaster).
48. [1941] AC 251 (HL).
49. On 'held covered' clauses generally, see J Davey, 'The Reform of Insurance Warranties: A Behavioural Economics Perspective' [2013] JBL 118, 129–37.
50. [1932] All ER Rep 494, (1932) 147 LT 503 (HL).

Case in depth: *WN Hillas & Co v Arcos Ltd* [1932] All ER Rep 494, 147 LT 503

Hillas & Co had contracted with Arcos in May 1930 for the purchase of 22,000 Russian softwood timber standards 'of fair specification' during the 1930 timber season. The contract also gave Hillas an option to buy a further consignment of softwood from the 1931 season. The material portion of the clause read as follows:

> Buyers shall also have the option of entering into a contract with the sellers for the purchase of 100,000 standards for delivery during 1931. Such contract to stipulate that, whatever the conditions are, buyers shall obtain the goods on conditions and prices which show to them a reduction of 5 per cent on the f.o.b. value of the official price list at any time ruling during 1931.

In November 1930, Arcos contracted with a third party to sell them the entirety of the timber they imported into the UK during the 1931 season. Rumours appeared in trade journals, and Hillas asked Arcos whether they had taken steps to reserve the 100,000 standards covered by the option for them. On being told that Arcos would be unable to supply softwood to Hillas, in December 1930 Hillas notified Arcos of their intention to exercise their option to purchase the softwood standards from the 1931 timber season. Arcos refused to supply the timber to Hillas, who sued for breach of contract.[51]

Arcos initially argued that the option had been revoked by the parties in July 1930.[52] When that line of argument failed, they adopted a new argument to the effect that no contract had come into being between them and Hillas.[53] All they had was an agreement to agree. The wording of the option itself contemplated a subsequent contract, and the option was missing important particulars including the actual specifications of the timber, the place, manner and time of shipment, and sizes and quantities. All of these matters were important, and until agreement was reached on them, no contract could come into existence.[54]

The House of Lords rejected Arcos's argument, and found in favour of Hillas. *May and Butcher*, they held, should not be seen as setting out a universal approach that applied to all cases of contractual interpretation. Each case should be decided based on the construction of the contract at issue in that case. With reference to the contract at issue in *Hillas*, the House of Lords laid much emphasis on the words 'of fair specification', and held that these words had a clear commercial meaning, which meant that the contract was not incomplete or uncertain. 'Fair' in this context did not mean 'fair as between the interests of buyer and seller', but simply 'a fair selection from the seller's stock of wood available for sale in that season'.[55] The result was that the contract had all the terms it needed, and was enforceable.

---

51. The clearest account of the facts of the case are in the report of the High Court proceedings. *WN Hillas & Co Ltd v Arcos Ltd* (1931) 40 Lloyd's Rep 106 (KB), 106–7.

52. Ibid, 106–8.

53. See *WN Hillas & Co Ltd v Arcos Ltd* (1931) 40 Lloyd's Rep 206 (KB), 207.

54. See esp the proceedings in the Court of Appeal, and the observations of Scrutton LJ: *WN Hillas & Co Ltd v Arcos Ltd* (1931) 40 Lloyd's Rep 307 (CA), 310.

55. *WN Hillas & Co v Arcos* [1932] All ER Rep 494 (HL), 502 (Lord Thankerton).

The rationale underlying the decision in *Hillas v Arcos* was explained by Lord Wright in his speech in that case:

> it is clear that the parties both intended to make a contract and thought they had done so. Business men often record the most important agreements in crude and summary fashion; modes of expression sufficient and clear to them in the course of their business may appear to those unfamiliar with the business far from complete or precise. It is, accordingly, the duty of the court to construe such documents fairly and broadly, without being too astute or subtle in finding defects . . . [This], however, does not mean that the court is to make a contract for the parties, or to go outside the words they have used, except in so far as there are appropriate implications of law, as, for instance, the implication of what is just and reasonable to be ascertained by the court as matter of machinery where the contractual intention is clear but the contract is silent on some detail.[56]

In *Foley v Classique Coaches*,[57] the Court of Appeal considered the question of how *Hillas v Arcos* was to be reconciled with *May and Butcher*. The leading judgment was given by Scrutton LJ who, as it happened, had also been on the benches of the Court of Appeal which decided both *Hillas* and *May and Butcher*. Scrutton LJ acknowledged that the two 'are not easy to fit in with each other'.[58] The lesson to be drawn, however, was that 'each case must be decided on the construction of the particular document',[59] with significance being attached to the parties' belief that they had a binding contract, as well as to the presence of mechanisms to settle disputes or failures to agree, such as an arbitration clause.[60] The final decision as to whether the contract was valid or void for uncertainty must be based on reading the contract as a whole, including any terms implied into it.[61]

Neither *Hillas* nor *Foley* abolished the category of agreements to agree. They sought, instead, to link this category much more closely to the parties' intention. If the parties genuinely intended their arrangement to be non-binding, such that each had the right to accept or reject the other party's offer, it would be legitimate to treat it as an agreement to agree. If, however, the parties appeared to have intended to create a binding agreement, the courts should be hesitant to declare the agreement void for uncertainty. This is not, however, the form which the doctrine takes in modern English law. As we will see in section 9.3.2, this is because subsequent cases rejected an important component of the approach put forward by Lord Wright in *Hillas v Arcos*—namely, the primacy it gives to the parties' intention—in favour of an approach that focuses less on the parties' intention and more on the objective character of the clause. The result of this has been the creation of several categories of agreements which are, in law, treated as non-binding agreements to agree, even though the parties themselves intended to impose binding obligations upon each other.

9.3.2 Frameworks for discussion: the problem of agreements to agree

In the course of his decision in *Hillas*, Lord Wright discussed what the position might have been if the clause in *Hillas* had, in fact, done no more than set out a duty to

---

56. Ibid, 503–4.   57. [1934] 2 KB 1 (CA).   58. Ibid, 9.   59. Ibid, 10.
60. Ibid, 10–11 (Scrutton LJ).   61. Ibid, 16 (Maugham LJ).

negotiate. Even here, he said, it was possible to hold that the parties had created a binding agreement:

> There is then no bargain except to negotiate, and negotiations may be fruitless and end without any contract ensuing; yet even then, in strict theory, there is a contract (if there is good consideration) to negotiate, though in the event of repudiation by one party the damages may be nominal, unless a jury think[62] that the opportunity to negotiate was of some appreciable value to the injured party.[63]

In *Courtney and Fairbain Ltd v Tolani Brothers (Hotels) Ltd*,[64] however, a bench of the Court of Appeal expressly rejected this position as being 'bad law'.[65] Any such contract, it was reasoned, would be 'too uncertain to have any binding force':

> No court could estimate the damages because no one can. tell whether the negotiations would be successful or would fall through: or if successful, what the result would be. It seems to me that a contract to negotiate, like a contract to enter into a contract, is not a contract known to the law.[66]

This applies not just to a contract to negotiate in the strict sense, but also to contracts which on a true construction appear to *contemplate* further negotiation. The contract in *Courtney v Tolani* itself was of the latter kind. The dispute in this case arose out of a contract between a site owner and a developer to redevelop a site in Hertfordshire. Through an exchange of letters, the parties reached a commercial agreement. The letter included this paragraph in relation to the price:

> Accordingly I would be very happy to know that, if my discussions and arrangements with interested parties lead to an introductory meeting, which in turn leads to a financial arrangement acceptable to both parties you will be prepared to instruct your quantity surveyor to negotiate fair and reasonable contract sums in respect of each of the three projects as they arise. (These would, incidentally be based upon agreed estimates of the net cost of work and general overheads with a margin for profit of 5 per cent.) which, I am sure you will agree, is indeed reasonable . . .

Shaw J in the High Court held that the exchange of letters had created a binding agreement, interpreting the contract as providing for a price equal to a 'fair and reasonable cost' with overheads, incremented by a margin of 5 per cent. The Court of Appeal reversed his decision, and held that the contract was void for uncertainty. The price was of fundamental importance, and a contract which contemplated further negotiation was a mere agreement to negotiate, which was not enforceable.[67]

The view that agreements contemplating further negotiation are void was accepted in some subsequent cases, which also accepted the position that Lord Wright's statements on agreements to negotiate in *Hillas* were bad law.[68] Although some judges

62. At the time *Hillas* was decided, juries were still used fairly frequently in civil cases. In the modern context, we would substitute 'unless the court thinks' for 'unless a jury think'.
63. [1932] All ER Rep 494, 505.   64. [1975] 1 WLR 297 (CA).
65. Ibid, 302 (Diplock LJ). Although the Court of Appeal was bound by the decisions of the House of Lords, the judges took the view that Lord Wright's observations on the enforceability of an obligation to negotiate were *obiter dicta*.
66. Ibid, 301 (Denning LJ).   67. Ibid, 301 (Denning LJ).
68. See eg *Mallozzi v Carapelli SpA* [1976] 1 Lloyd's Rep 407 (CA).

continued to enforce such clauses even after *Courtney v Tolani*, on the basis that this question was one which had to be decided on a case-by-case basis,[69] that route was closed off by the House of Lords in *Walford v Miles*,[70] which approved the stricter position taken in *Courtney v Tolani*. The parties in the *Walford* case had been negotiating a possible acquisition by Walford of the Miles's business. It was agreed that if certain conditions were fulfilled, Miles would 'terminate negotiations with any third party or consideration of any alternative with a view to concluding agreements' with Walford. The parties further agreed that even if Miles 'received a satisfactory proposal from any third party before close of business on Friday night he would not deal with that third party and nor would he give further consideration to any alternative'.[71] Such a clause is sometimes called a 'lock-out' clause or an 'exclusive negotiations' clause. Its purpose is to get the parties to commit to negotiating exclusively with each other, and not with third parties, in relation to a particular transaction. Clauses of this type are very common in commercial practice, and *Walford v Miles* was not in any way unusual. Miles entered into discussions with a third party in breach of this agreement, and eventually agreed a sale with that party. Walford sued.

In the House of Lords, it was argued by Walford's lawyers that an agreement to negotiate should be enforceable in much the same way as a best endeavours clause. A best endeavours clause does not impose an obligation to achieve a result, but it does impose obligations in relation to how the parties should behave, and the extent to which they must have regard to the other party's interests. An agreement to negotiate, it was argued, could be given effect in much the same way: there is no obligation to actually reach agreement, but there is an obligation to do something akin to taking best endeavours which they characterized as an implied duty of good faith.[72] The House of Lords rejected this argument. Lord Ackner, who delivered the judgment of the court, held that negotiations were *inherently* adversarial. To require the parties to act in good faith while negotiating was therefore repugnant to the very idea of negotiating:

> Each party to the negotiations is entitled to pursue his (or her) own interest, so long as he avoids making misrepresentations. To advance that interest he must be entitled, if he thinks it appropriate, to threaten to withdraw from further negotiations or to withdraw in fact, in the hope that the opposite party may seek to reopen the negotiations by offering him improved terms.[73]

This does not mean that lock-out clauses are never effective, but their effectiveness is limited. Lord Ackner identified two important limitations in his speech in *Walford v Miles*. First, he held that the effect of such a clause can only be negative, in that whilst it can preclude a party from contacting or dealing with others, it cannot impose a requirement that he actually engage in negotiations or actually try to reach agreement. Secondly, a lock-out clause will need to set out a specific duration in order to be enforceable. A lock-out clause which does not have an expiry date lacks the certainty that it needs to be enforceable. The courts will not imply a term holding the clause to apply for a 'reasonable term', as to do so would indirectly impose a duty to negotiate in good faith.[74]

---

69. See eg *Donwin Productions Ltd v Emi Films Ltd* [1984] Lexis Citation 01 (QB).
70. [1992] 2 AC 128 (HL).   71. Ibid, 133.
72. On implied duties of good faith generally, see Chapter 8 on implication.
73. [1992] 2 AC 128 (HL), 138 (Lord Ackner).   74. Ibid, 139–40 (Lord Ackner).

Subsequent cases have confirmed and extended this rule. In *Phillips Petroleum v Enron*,[75] the parties had attempted to get around *Walford* by adding a 'reasonable endeavours' clause (which is generally enforceable, as section 9.2 discussed). The contract in question was a long-term contract for the sale of natural gas, and at the time of contracting it was not clear how much gas would be needed at a given point of time. The contract, accordingly, provided that the parties 'shall use reasonable endeavours to agree' on the date on which deliveries would begin, the quantities that each party would take, and a range of other matters including a commissioning date for the plant and a date for a run-in test.[76] Gas prices fell before a commissioning date could be agreed, and the buyer thereafter steadfastly refused to agree on any commissioning date or test date even though the plant was ready to be commissioned. The seller sued for breach of contract, arguing that the buyer had failed to use reasonable endeavours to agree. The Court of Appeal held that the agreement was void, as a mere agreement to agree. The words 'reasonable endeavours' did not create an objective standard to be applied in relation to the conduct of the parties in reaching agreement.[77] An obligation of this type was unenforceable because there were no criteria 'on the basis of which a third party can assess or adjudicate the matter in the event of dispute'.[78]

Similarly, in *Shaker v Vistajet*,[79] the parties had entered into a Letter of Intent in relation to the sale of an aircraft. The Letter of Intent required the buyer to 'proceed in good faith and to use reasonable endeavours' to reach agreement by a particular cut-off date, and also provided for the payment of a deposit by the buyer. Agreement was not reached, and the sellers sought to retain the deposit arguing that the buyer had not complied with the obligation to act in good faith and use reasonable endeavours to agree. They argued that this was a condition precedent to the return of the deposit, so that the deposit would only be returned if the buyer acted in good faith and used reasonable endeavours. Teare J held that even if the seller's construction of the Letter of Intent were correct, the condition precedent would be unenforceable in law, as it would be a mere agreement to agree, which could not be enforced unless the contract also specified objective criteria that could be used in the absence of agreement.[80]

In contrast, where the term relates to a dispute within a contractual relationship, the courts have shown some willingness to uphold a duty to negotiate in good faith to seek to resolve the dispute. In *Emirates Trading Agency LLC v Prime Mineral Exports Pte Ltd*,[81] a contract for the sale of iron ore provided that if any disputes arose between the parties, 'the parties shall first seek to resolve the dispute or claim by friendly discussion'. Citing *Yam Seng v International Trade Corp*,[82] Teare J held that this clause not only created an enforceable obligation to resolve disputes by friendly discussions, but also necessarily imported an obligation 'to seek to do so in good faith'.[83] *Walford v Miles* did not apply to a dispute resolution clause, where the good faith obligation has 'an identifiable standard, namely, fair, honest and genuine discussions aimed at resolving a dispute'.[84]

---

75. *Phillips Petroleum Co UK Ltd & ors v Enron Europe Ltd* [1997] CLC 329 (CA).   76. Ibid, 332.
77. Ibid, 337, 340–2 (Kennedy LJ).   78. Ibid, 343 (Potter LJ).
79. *Charles Shaker v Vistajet Group Holding SA* [2012] EWHC 1329 (Comm).
80. Ibid, [17]–[18].   81. [2014] EWHC 2104 (Comm), [2015] 1 WLR 1145.
82. [2013] EWHC 111 (QB). See the discussion in Chapter 8, section 8.5.1.   83. Ibid, [51].
84. Ibid, [64].

9.3.3 **Actions, discussion, and enforceability**

As the introduction to section 9.3 suggested, the effect of the decision in *Walford v Miles* is to create a dichotomy between agreements that create a framework for action, which are enforceable, and agreements that create a framework for discussion, which are not. A framework for action is a framework which contains requirements that are objectively determinable, even if they are vague. The requirements do not have to be obligations to achieve particular outcomes—they can equally be obligations to act in a particular way (eg 'reasonably') or to be held to a particular standard (eg your endeavours must be the 'best' you can do). The key is that it must be possible for courts to decide what the terms mean and what they require, drawing if necessary on commercial usage and practice.

A framework for discussion, in contrast, is one that contemplates some form of collective decision-making by the parties. The process it involves is necessarily mutual, requiring the participation of both parties to determine its outcome. Such a framework is treated as inherently unenforceable in English law. The courts will not enforce any aspect of the framework—not even requirements that seek to set out standards to which the parties will adhere in their negotiations.

What, then, are the implications of this distinction for practice? Consider, once again, Problem 9. On the basis of the discussion in this section, it is easy to see that the parties' agreement will be void for uncertainty. The agreement fails to provide any objective basis on which to determine which LPs will be sold in which month and for how much. Equally, as the penultimate message makes clear, the parties have not even reached agreement on the frequency at which the LPs will be sold. There is a clear understanding that it is not necessarily going to take place on a monthly basis, but they have given no indication beyond that. The parties appear to be operating on the assumption that they will 'work things out' as and when required, but as we have seen that is not an assumption which the courts are prepared to legally recognize. Given that no cut-off date for completion has been agreed, the ruling in *Walford v Miles* precludes the courts from reading the agreement as containing an enforceable lock-in. The consequence is that the agreement is void, whether or not a dispute actually arises. There is nothing to stop the seller from disposing of the remaining LPs at any stage in the performance of the transaction.

9.4 **In conclusion: cooperation, competition, and the limits of flexibility**

Let us now put the pieces together, and consider the fuller implications of the points that have emerged from the discussion in this chapter. The discussion thus far has shown that the agreement in Problem 9 is legally unenforceable. The idea of an agreement to buy a 'few LPs every month' depending on what one party can afford is both too vague and too subjective to be enforceable. Equally, a term to the effect that the parties will 'sort something out' is a classic example of an agreement to agree.

That a court will not fill such gaps is understandable. Nevertheless, there are unspoken, implicit dimensions to the agreement that a court could easily have enforced—that, for example, the LPs will not be sold to a third party unless the two parties are unable to reach agreement as between themselves, or that the parties will make genuine (and not perfunctory) efforts to reach agreement. Why, then, do English courts choose not to give effect to these implicit and unspoken understandings?

A fundamental issue faced by modern contract law, which this chapter has touched on, is that two threads run through the practice of contracting, both of which also run through the case law on certainty: one that sees contracts as being about collaboration and cooperation by the parties acting jointly, and the other that sees contracts as being about self-interested action by the parties acting individually. Resolving the tension between these two threads is not easy, because the reality is that contracting necessarily involves both types of behaviour. Finding a balance that accommodates both has been a major theme in contract litigation in recent years, and is likely to continue to be an issue for the courts for some time to come.

The rules pertaining to the doctrine of certainty make most sense when viewed against the backdrop of this debate. The current state of English law suggests that it leans very strongly towards the latter at the expense of the former. It is, typically, clauses which rely too much on vaguely defined collaborative action that are struck down by the courts as being insufficiently certain 'agreements to agree'. Thus, for example, whilst the courts will generally give effect to a best endeavours clause, they will not enforce a clause that calls upon the parties to make best endeavours to reach agreement, even if it is blindingly obvious that a defendant wilfully sabotaged the negotiation or totally failed to engage with it.[85] Whilst the courts have justified this approach on the basis that an adversarial approach is inherent in negotiation, this is not in fact true. There is a rich theoretical and practical literature on negotiation strategy, which has shown that negotiation can be about collaborative joint problem-solving as much as it can be about adversarial action.[86] From this perspective, the aim of a clause that imposes an obligation to use best endeavours to reach agreement, or to negotiate in good faith, is to seek to ensure that the negotiation process is structured as a process oriented towards joint problem-solving, rather than about adversarial action. There is no reason why parties should not be free to do this, as the laws of many countries other than England recognize.

This gives some context to the other aspect of the law in relation to uncertainty which we have discussed in this chapter. A common theme running through many of the cases we have examined here—including *May and Butcher, Hillas v Arcos, Phillips Petroleum v Enron*, and *Scammell v Ouston*—is that the disputes in those cases did not arise out of the supposed uncertainty that was cited as having made the contract void. In *Phillips Petroleum*, the underlying issue was the shift in the oil price, rather than anything directly concerning the commissioning of the plant. In *May and Butcher*, the underlying issue was the disinclination of the Disposals Board to release the specifications of tents, rather than an actual failure to agree on the price of the tents. In *Scammell v Ouston*, the underlying issue was that the seller no longer wished to accept the buyer's van in part-exchange. It had nothing to do with the hire-purchase agreement, the purported

85. The Court of Appeal expressly said so in *Phillips Petroleum v Enron* [1997] CLC 329, 342–3 (Potter LJ).

86. The classic introduction to this field is R Fisher and W Ury, *Getting to Yes: Negotiating an Agreement Without Giving In* (Random House 1981) which first introduced the notion that negotiation could be about joint problem-solving.

reason why the agreement was void. In each of these cases, therefore, the effect of the court's decision was to let a party behave strategically, challenging a contract to obtain an entirely unrelated advantage. Such a position presupposes a framework in which contracts are viewed as being almost entirely about competition rather than cooperation.

This propensity of English law to view contracts as about competition, and its disinclination to recognize the element of cooperation in them, has been criticized by some contract theorists,[87] and supported by others.[88] One possible solution is to focus the law more closely on the intention of the parties rather than on the certainty or uncertainty of the contract's language, and to examine whether those intentions are sufficiently evident from the contract to give effect to them. Such an approach would have changed the outcome of a number of the cases that have been considered in this section. In *Scammell v Ouston*, for example, such an approach would have suggested that the intention of the parties was to get hire-purchase financing from the Dominion Trust Co Ltd on its standard terms, and the agreement would therefore have been treated as enforceable if such consent was forthcoming. Such an approach would also lead to a much greater willingness to enforce clauses that set out a 'best endeavours' obligation to reach agreement than is presently the case.

Whether such an approach would be better or worse than the current approach is a question on which opinions are bound to differ, but for present purposes it is sufficient to note that there do not appear to be any signs that the law is likely to move in this direction in the near future. From a practical point of view, therefore, the lesson is that it is of critical importance to stick strictly to the toolkit the law offers us to embed flexibility within the contractual framework, because parties who depart from it do so at their peril.

Key points

- The terms of a contract must be certain for the contract to be enforceable.
- An 'agreement to agree'—where the parties leave core terms undecided—is not enforceable.
- An agreement will also not be enforceable if the terms are vague. Terms will not be treated as being too vague if a contextual reading can make it clear what the parties' rights and obligations are. The vagueness of an individual term will not make the entire contract void, unless the contract cannot function without that term.
- Certain types of terms, which might on their face seem vague, are valid because they have a recognised meaning in commercial usage. This includes phrases such as 'best endeavours' and 'reasonable'.
- A contract which is missing an essential term will be treated as incomplete, and will not be enforced. This frequently occurs where parties try to leave a contract open-ended to make it flexible. If the agreement is flexible through permitting unilateral action by a party,

---

87. See esp H Collins, *Regulating Contracts* (Oxford University Press 1992).

88. See eg J Gava and J Greene, 'Do We Need a Hybrid Law of Contract? Why Hugh Collins is Wrong and Why it Matters' (2004) 63 CLJ 605.

or through the use of objective criteria, the courts will enforce it. If the agreement is flexible through requiring cooperative action, or through the use of subjective criteria, it will not be enforced.

- Clauses which require negotiation in good faith will not ordinarily be enforced.

Assess your learning

You should be able to respond to each of the following points with a confident 'yes'. If you can't, then you should revisit the sections listed against that point.

Can you:

(a) *Identify* the main forms which the requirement of certainty takes in English law? (Section 9.1)

(b) *Outline* what makes a clause vague, and *explain* the role of contextual readings and commercial usage in determining whether a clause is vague? (Section 9.2)

(c) *Describe* the types of clauses which are treated as unenforceable for incompleteness, and *discuss* the position of agreements to negotiate in good faith? (Section 9.3)

In relation to each of the above, you should be able to:

(i) identify and clearly explain the key rules and principles;

(ii) identify the key cases and statutes, and why they matter;

(iii) apply the principles and cases to specific real or hypothetical fact situations;

(iv) evaluate the limitations, if any, of the law as it currently stands.

Further reading

I Brown, 'The Contract to Negotiate: A Thing Writ in Water' [1992] JBL 353.

R Buckley, '*Walford v Miles*: False Certainty About Uncertainty: An Australian Perspective' (1993) 6 JCL 58.

N Cohen, 'Pre-Contractual Duties: Two Freedoms and the Contract to Negotiate' in J Beatson and D Friedmann (eds), *Good Faith and Fault in Contract Law* (Oxford University Press 1995).

J Cumberbatch, 'In Freedom's Cause: The Contract to Negotiate' (1992) 12 OJLS 586.

P Giliker, 'Taking Comfort in Certainty: To Enforce or Not to Enforce the Letter of Comfort' [2004] LMCLQ 219.

JM Paterson, 'The Contract to Negotiate in Good Faith: Recognition and Enforcement' (1996) 10 JCL 120.

P Tochterman, 'Agreements to Negotiate in the Transnational Context—Issues of Contract Law and Effective Dispute Resolution' (2008) 13 Uniform Law Review 685.

Fundamental changes

Frustration and common mistake

'Things fall apart, the contract cannot hold'*

* Cf WB Yeats, 'The Second Coming', line 3.

Problem 10: setting the context

Read the following (fictional) press clipping, and think through the legal and commercial issues it raises.

Hundreds of jobs in jeopardy as nuclear contractor faces uncertain future

MARYPORT, 12 OCT 2011: Hundreds of people are facing potential redundancy as one of Cumbria's leading employers teeters on the verge of insolvency following a major policy shift by the German government.

In 2010, Kernkraftwerk GmbH, a leading German nuclear power company, awarded Nuclear Solutions plc a ten-year maintenance contract for Kernkraftwerk's three oldest plants. Nuclear Solutions won the contract because of their experience with Sellafield. The contract was to start running from this November. Over the past 11 months, Nuclear Solutions have invested millions of pounds in recruiting staff, setting up offices, and preparing for the start of the contract.

The future looked rosy, but the transaction came to a sudden halt this March when the German government, responding to popular protests against nuclear power after the Fukushima accident in Japan, ordered the closure of all three plants that Nuclear Solutions was contracted to maintain. The closure was initially expected to be temporary, but in August the German chancellor announced that none of the plants would be permitted to reopen. Some compensation is likely to be paid to Kernkraftwerk, but they have refused to commit on sharing it pro rata with Nuclear Solutions. Nuclear Solutions is facing significant losses as a result of the failure of this contract, and its very survival is understood to be in question.

10.1 Introduction: contracts and unplanned contingencies

10.1.1 Contract law and the 'unknown unknowns'

All contracts involve planning. When parties agree on a term that relates to the future, they are coming up with a plan as to how they will deal with future risks and contingencies. When you buy a gaming controller with a 12-month guarantee, you and the seller have agreed on a plan to manage a specific risk; namely, that something might go wrong with your gaming controller in the coming 12 months. In determining what the content of a contract is, the court is trying to determine what the parties' plan for dealing with a particular risk was.

But there are always 'unknown unknowns'—which, as Chapter 9 discusses in greater detail, include risks which are so completely unforeseeable, and have such a dramatic impact on the contract, that the ordinary techniques of interpretation and implication cannot deal with them. Consider the following examples:

Illustration 10.1

In 2010, Roe the Day, a specialist sushi restaurant, entered into a contract with a rice farm in Miyagi, Japan, for the annual supply of several tonnes of short-grained 'hitomebore' rice. In 2011, following the Tohoku earthquake and tsunami, two-thirds of the farm's acreage was covered with mounds of salty sludge and detritus from the tsunami, leaving it unusable for cultivation. Roe the Day found an alternative supplier, but had to pay a much higher price and suffered a huge loss as a result.

Illustration 10.2

Uncle Percival engages a builder to replace his gas fireplace with an open wood-burning fire. After the contract has been signed, he discovers to his horror that his house is in a smoke control area, and that it is against the law for him to use an open wood-burning fire. The builder has by this time purchased materials for the fireplace, and insists on proceeding because he cannot return them and cannot bear the loss.

In both illustrations, the parties' plan has fallen apart. They find themselves faced with circumstances which are unexpected, and have fundamentally changed the character of the transaction, but for which their contract did not plan. In Illustration 10.1, the change has left the farm entirely unable to perform its obligations under the contract, and the restaurant holding what is potentially a significant loss. In Illustration 10.2, performance remains possible—there is nothing stopping the parties from *building* the fireplace—but has been rendered pointless from Uncle Percival's point of view in that the fireplace cannot be legally used. The unplanned-for contingency has affected his ability to enjoy the benefit of the contract.

Fundamental changes such as those discussed in the two illustrations above and in Problem 10 face the law with a difficult choice. On the one hand, it is difficult to mitigate their effects through implied terms or implication without rewriting the parties' contract. Yet to hold that contracts remain binding as written, despite the fact that things have fundamentally changed, also seems absurd. Is it commercially realistic to hold that a person entering into a contract to supply rice must do so even if his crop is destroyed by a natural disaster? Likewise, in Illustration 10.2, both parties have clearly messed up, in that neither realized that the law prohibited the use of that type of fireplace at Uncle Percival's address. Should the law hold that contracts must proceed even if the parties were operating under a fundamental misconception as to how things stood? Or should the law take a more nuanced position?

Some civil law jurisdictions, such as Germany[1] and the Netherlands,[2] as well as international documents such as the UNIDROIT Principles,[3] give courts broad powers to respond to unplanned contingencies by 'adjusting' the contract to take account of the changed circumstances, their effect upon the commercial purpose or 'foundation' of the transaction, and the contractual allocation of risks. English law does not; nor do most common law systems. Because common law courts are reluctant to be drawn into the task of rewriting the parties' contract, the law takes a more rigid approach to unplanned contingencies. The choice in English law is between holding the parties to the contract as written, and treating the contract as having come to an end because of the unplanned contingency. English law does not recognize the intermediate position of adjusting the contract, which one finds in continental legal systems.

How, then, do courts determine whether an unplanned contingency brings a contract to an end, or lets it continue in full force and effect? English law contains two different doctrines to deal with this issue: **frustration** and **common mistake**. Frustration and common mistake deal with situations where the parties find themselves in uncharted territory, which is far beyond the range of possible contingencies they had in mind at the time of contracting. The severity of the damage caused by the 2011 tsunami (the subject of Illustration 10.1) took everyone by surprise, and few if any contracts had provided for the possibility of such an event. The German government's abrupt abandonment of nuclear power (the subject of Problem 10) was similarly unexpected. The doctrines thus ask courts to determine the *limits* of a contract, the point where the contractual framework runs out, leaving the parties in a no-man's land where things have fallen apart and the contract no longer holds.

10.1.2 Frustration and common mistake: understanding the distinction

Despite their similar function, frustration and common mistake are different doctrines. The question of which covers a particular case depends on whether the unplanned contingency relates to the past or the future. Frustration covers cases where the parties mispredicted the future. Here, something happens *after* the contract was entered into that changes the contract's character (eg the tsunami in Illustration 10.1). This is usually termed the *'frustrating event'*. The effect of frustration is to **discharge** the contract—that is, to terminate it with effect from the occurrence of the frustrating event. If the parties have already started performing the contract, the law gives the courts a range of powers to undo the partly performed transaction and restore the parties to their pre-contractual position, or as close to it as is possible.

Common mistake, in contrast, covers cases where the parties were unaware of or misunderstood *existing* facts, so that they expressly or implicitly assumed that something was true, and only discovered that it was not after the contract was entered into (eg the existence of a smoke control zone in Illustration 10.2). Because their common

---

1. § 313 BGB.   2. Art 6:258 lid 1 BW.
3. UNIDROIT Principles of International Commercial Contracts (2010 edn), Art 6.2.3.

assumption was false, they now find that the contract is radically different from what they thought it would be. The effect of common mistake is to render the contract *void in law*. The contract is treated as having been vitiated by the mistake, with the result that in law it was stillborn, and never came into being.

The nature of the distinction between situations that are dealt with by common mistake and frustration can be illustrated by considering two very similar situations, which relate to very similar risks but are governed by different doctrines.

Illustration 10.3

You are selling your old laptop. You have agreed a price and date for sale with a buyer. As you are crossing the street, you are knocked down by a car which jumps a red light. The laptop is smashed beyond repair in the accident.

Because the laptop was destroyed *after* the contract was entered into, English law treats the issue as being one of whether the contract remains valid notwithstanding the radical change in circumstances. The parties' rights and obligations in this case will, accordingly, be determined with reference to the doctrine of frustration.

Illustration 10.4

You are meeting a buyer who has expressed interest in buying your old laptop. The two of you agree on a price, and you go home to fetch the laptop to hand it over. When you return home, you discover that a heavy wind that morning has caused a tree branch to crash through your bedroom window, smashing the laptop beyond repair.

Here, because the laptop was destroyed *before* the contract was entered into, English law treats the issue as being one of whether a valid contract even came into being. The parties' rights and obligations will, accordingly, be determined with reference to the doctrine of common mistake.

From a commercial point of view, this distinction is somewhat artificial. Whether a court applies common mistake or frustration, it is doing the same thing: responding to a risk or contingency for which the parties did not plan, but which has now eventuated. For this reason, many legal systems—and in particular the civil law systems of continental Europe—do not distinguish between the two. Instead, they deal with them under the same doctrine[4] or under doctrines which carry substantially the same remedies.[5] In English law, however, the distinction is quite significant. Whilst both doctrines put an end to the contract, they do so in different ways and the result that the remedies that a court will actually award differ depending on whether the case is

---

4. This is the case in German law. See § 313 II BGB.

5. This is the case in Dutch law. Compare Art 6:228 lid 1 sub c and Art 6:230 lid 1 (common mistake) with Art 6:258 lid 1 (unforeseen circumstances) of the Burgerlijk Wetboek.

one of common mistake or frustration. The requirements of frustration and common mistake are also expressed differently in law, even though they build on a similar basis, and different factors are relevant in each type of case.

The artificiality of the distinction between common mistake and frustration has led some authors in England and the US[6] to treat them as two aspects of the same underlying principle. The doctrines do have a lot in common. Both apply where the parties find themselves faced with circumstances that are radically different from those they expected to face and planned for, and where this fundamentally alters the character of the contract. Both also have similar effects, in that the parties' obligations under the contract are brought to an end. Equally, both are exceptional doctrines. A contract is only discharged by frustration, or void for common mistake, if the changed circumstances in which the parties find themselves are unexpected, extremely serious in terms of their impact upon the contract, and outside the province of both parties' responsibilities under the contract. Otherwise, the contract remains valid, with the result that the parties must either perform the contract as written, notwithstanding the changed circumstances, or pay compensation for breach of contract.

Despite these similarities, the distinction between the two is well entrenched as a matter of legal doctrine and they are unlikely to converge further. We will therefore consider them in separate sections in this chapter, starting with frustration (section 10.2) and moving on to common mistake (section 10.3).

10.2 **Frustrating events**

10.2.1 **'A thing radically different': the context of frustration**

Let us start with frustration, which deals with post-contractual changes. A contract is frustrated if changes render its performance 'a thing radically different' from what had been contracted for.[7] This will only happen if the event in question was truly unforeseen and unforeseeable. A contract will not be discharged by frustration, even for fundamental changes, if the parties had expressly or implicitly *allocated* the risk of the event that is alleged to have frustrated the contract, or if the event was within the *control* of one of the parties. Many cases on frustration accordingly relate to dramatic events: marauding soldiers during the English Civil War,[8] disruption of shipping by German U-boats during the First World War,[9] the closure of the Suez Canal during the Suez War,[10] buildings destroyed by fire,[11] and so on.

Given the importance the English legal system attaches to contracts, it is perhaps unsurprising that judges approach the task of fixing a contract's limits with some

---

6. S Macaulay, J Kidwell, and W Whitford, *Contracts: Law in Action, Vol II: The Advanced Course* (2nd edn, LexisNexis 2003) 579–80.

7. *Davis Contractors v Fareham UDC* [1956] AC 696 (HL), 729 (Lord Radcliffe).

8. *Paradine v Jane* [1647] Aleyn 26, 82 ER 897.

9. *Pacific Phosphate Co Ltd v Empire Transport Co Ltd* (1920) 4 Lloyd's Rep 189.

10. *Tsakiroglou & Co Ltd v Noblee Thorl GmbH* [1962] AC 93 (HL).

11. *Taylor v Caldwell* (1863) 3 B & S 826, 122 ER 309.

reluctance. Early cases took a rigid view, and tended to hold that contracts contin-ued to be valid and binding even if circumstances had changed beyond recognition. *Paradine v Jane*,[12] which took place against the backdrop of the English Civil War, provides a good example. Jane had leased land from Paradine. In 1643, soldiers in the service of Charles I took possession of the land and did not return it to Jane's possession until 1646, when the Royalist army surrendered. Paradine then brought an action in debt, demanding payment of the rent for the period between 1643 and 1646. The court held that Jane was liable to pay rent even though he had at the rel-evant time been forcibly ousted from the land by an army. If he had wanted to be exempted from paying the rent in times of war, he should have inserted a clause to that effect in the contract. In the absence of an exempting clause, he would be liable for the rent even if the land had been completely destroyed. The court would not protect a party if the contract did not:

> the rent is a duty created by the parties upon the reservation, and had there been a cov-enant to pay it, there had been no question but the lessee must have made it good, not-withstanding the interruption by enemies, for the law would not protect him beyond his own agreement . . . [A]s the lessee is to have the advantage of casual profits, so he must run the hazard of casual losses, and not lay the whole burthen of them upon his lessor . . . though the land be surrounded, or gained by the sea, or made barren by wild-fire, yet the lessor shall have his whole rent . . .

Underlying this case is a view of contracts that refuses to countenance the possibil-ity of the contractual framework ever running out. If an unforeseen risk eventuates, and if the contract does not expressly provide for it, then the parties must simply continue to perform the contract they have made. The fact that this leads to a party being stuck with grossly disproportionate obligations, for example paying rent for land that has fallen into the sea as a result of coastal erosion, is irrelevant. It was open to the party to protect himself against a particular contingency by incorporat-ing a contractual provision to that effect. If he fails to do so, the court will not come to his rescue.[13]

The courts no longer take such a rigid view. There is a general recognition today that contractual frameworks are not all-encompassing. Some contingencies are so far beyond anything the parties planned for that the only sensible way of dealing with them is to hold that they have taken the parties outside the bounds of the contract, with the result that the contract is discharged and the parties no longer bound by it. A major impetus to this rationalization of doctrine was the outbreak of the First World War, which not only severely disrupted shipping, but led to the government assuming emergency powers to requisition ships as well as plant, machinery, and labour. The result was the wholly unforeseeable disruption of a vast number of commercial con-tracts. Under these conditions, seeing the earlier fragmentary case law as representing a single approach to unforeseen and radically altered conditions was both attractive and useful.

---

12. [1647] Aleyn 26, 82 ER 897.

13. Note the similarity with the dissent of Lord Goff in *Mannai Investment Co Ltd v Eagle Star Assurance* [1997] AC 749 (HL), discussed in Chapter 7 ('Interpreting the terms').

Despite the recognition of the possibility of frustration, however, the attitude seen in *Paradine v Jane* has not wholly disappeared. The courts remain reluctant to disturb negotiated contracts. In particular, they will not intervene in a contract merely because it has become more onerous or expensive for one of the parties. *Davis Contractors v Fareham Urban District Council*,[14] from which the language of 'a thing radically different' comes, is a classic example. Davis Contractors had agreed to build 78 houses for Fareham UDC. The contract was supposed to take eight months and the agreed price was £94,425. Due to a shortage of skilled labour, the work ended up taking 22 months and costing £115,234. Davis Contractors argued that the contract had been frustrated by the lack of availability of labour. The House of Lords held that it was not frustrated. The mere fact that 'there has been an unexpected turn of events which renders the contract more onerous than the parties had contemplated' was not sufficient to frustrate a contract.

Virtually all cases where frustration has been successfully pleaded tend to relate to one of three relatively narrow sets of circumstances, or *frustrating events*. The first of these, which also accounts for the vast majority of cases where frustration was successfully pleaded, is where performance of the contract has become *impossible* by reason of a supervening event. The second category covers cases where performance has not become impossible *in perpetuum*, but has had to be temporarily *suspended or delayed* due to the change in circumstances. The third category covers situations where performance remains technically possible, but where the change in circumstances has made it impossible to achieve the commercial purpose of the contract, a purpose which was shared between the parties. The scope of this third category, which is sometimes referred to as *frustration of purpose*, is particularly narrow, and it has only been successfully pleaded in a very small number of cases. In the discussion that follows, we will begin by examining these three frustrating events (section 10.2.2), before moving on to look at the relationship between frustration and provisions of the contract (section 10.2.3), and the remedies that are generally available for frustration (section 10.2.4).

10.2.2 Frustrating events

Impossibility

On the face of it, it seems uncontroversial to say that parties will not be held to a contract whose performance has become 'impossible'. In practice, however, things are not so straightforward. The question of whether performance of a contract is, indeed, impossible or simply more onerous is not always easy to answer. Consider the following illustrations:

> **Illustration 10.5**
>
> Farmer Maggot agrees to sell his prize bull Tarmund to Farmer Giles. Two weeks before the sale is to take effect, the bull falls ill and dies.

Here, it is obvious that performance of the contract has become impossible. The thing that was actually contracted for, the delivery of a specific live bull named Tarmund, no

---

14. *Davis Contractors v Fareham UDC* [1956] AC 696 (HL), 729 (Lord Radcliffe).

longer exists. The delivery of a partially decomposed carcass, which is the only thing that can still be delivered, will self-evidently be 'a thing radically different'.

But compare this with the situation presented in the following news clipping:

Illustration 10.6

Hedge Betty concert cancelled

Hundreds of fans of the band Hedge Betty have been left distraught after the band abruptly cancelled the concert scheduled for next Saturday at the Waterfront, Norwich. Our reporters have learned that the cancellation was prompted by the illness of the band's drummer, who has come down with flu and is reportedly running a high fever. The owners of the venue are likely to be left holding a significant loss, as they have promised a full refund to all ticket-holders.

Here, it is not obvious that the performance by the band of its contracted obligations has become impossible.[15] Does the drummer's illness *really* mean that they cannot perform? Has her flu made it impossible (rather than merely onerous) for the band to hold a concert? Can performing with a replacement drummer or an ill drummer really be termed 'a thing radically different'? Issues of this sort are not uncommon in practice, and it is these issues that make frustration a challenging area of law.

Destruction of the subject matter

Illustration 10.5 presents what is arguably the easiest case of impossibility, namely situations where the subject matter of the contract has been destroyed due to the eventuation of a risk for which the contract did not provide. The leading case on such situations is the decision of the Court of King's Bench in *Taylor v Caldwell*,[16] which is now seen as having begun the move away from the strict approach in *Paradine v Jane*.[17]

Case in depth: *Taylor v Caldwell* (1863) 3 B & S 826

Caldwell & Bishop owned a popular venue called the Surrey Music Hall and Gardens. Taylor & Lewis entered into an agreement with them to take the hall for four days in June, July, and August 1861, to hold a series of concerts and fêtes. A week before the first of these events was to take place, the music hall was completely destroyed by an accidental fire. Taylor had by then spent a lot of money printing advertisements and otherwise preparing for the concerts. They sued Caldwell & Bishop for breach of contract, arguing that the contract required them to provide Taylor with the use of the hall, which they had failed to do.

In court, Taylor's argument was simple. *Paradine v Jane*[18] had held that the court would not protect a party facing difficulty as a result of an accident if the contract did not. As a result,

→

15. Note that the band's obligations will be owed only to the venue, with whom the band will have contracted, rather than the ticket-holders. For further details, see Chapter 16.
16. (1863) 3 B & S 826, 122 ER 309.   17. [1647] Aleyn 26, 82 ER 897.   18. Ibid.

→

the destruction of the premises by fire should not 'exonerate the defendant from performing their part of the agreement'.[19] In reply, Caldwell's lawyers did not challenge the correctness of *Paradine v Jane*. They argued, instead, that there was a 'general custom of the trade and business' in the entertainment industry under which a contract was treated as automatically coming to an end. That term was an implied condition in this agreement, and the destruction of the hall by fire therefore had the effect of bringing the agreement to an end.

Blackburn J upheld Caldwell's plea, and held that the contract was subject to an implied condition, and had consequently come to an end when the hall was destroyed:

> There seems no doubt that where there is a positive contract to do a thing, not in itself unlawful, the contractor must perform it or pay damages for not doing it, although in consequence of unforeseen accidents, the performance of his contract has become unexpectedly burthensome or even impossible . . . But this rule is only applicable when the contract is positive and absolute, and not subject to any condition either express or implied: and . . . where, from the nature of the contract, it appears that the parties must from the beginning have known that it could not be fulfilled unless when the time for the fulfilment of the contract arrived some particular specified thing continued to exist, so that, when entering into the contract, they must have contemplated such continuing existence as the foundation of what was to be done; there, in the absence of any express or implied warranty that the thing shall exist, the contract is . . . subject to an implied condition that the parties shall be excused in case, before breach, performance becomes impossible from the perishing of the thing without default of the contractor.[20]

In the modern context, *Taylor v Caldwell* is taken to be an authority for the proposition that the destruction of the subject matter of a contract will frustrate the contract. This is largely a result of subsequent case law and commentary. *Taylor v Caldwell* did not use the language of frustration, and the language of the decision suggests that the court saw itself as doing no more than applying orthodox rules in relation to the implication of terms. As the passage quoted above shows, Blackburn J was at pains to stress that the general rule continued to be that stated in *Paradine v Jane*; namely, that contractual obligations continue to be binding even if their performance has become impossible. This is not, however, how the law is viewed today.

The most important difference between the approach taken in *Taylor v Caldwell* and the modern approach is that under *Taylor v Caldwell* a contract could only be discharged for impossibility if it contained an express or implied term to that effect. In the absence of such a term, the parties would not be released from their obligations even if performance had become impossible. In the modern context, in contrast, frustration is seen as being grounded in a *legal* rule, not a contractual rule. A contract comes to an end on the occurrence of a frustrating event because the law says that it does.[21] The

---

19. (1863) 3 B & S 826, 831.   20. Ibid, 833–4 (Blackburn J).

21. Cf the speech of Lord Radcliffe in *Davis Contractors v Fareham UDC* [1956] AC 696 (HL): 'frustration occurs whenever the *law* recognises that . . . a contractual obligation has become incapable of being performed . . .' (ibid, 728) (emphasis added).

terms of the contract are relevant for the purpose of determining whether a *particular* event is serious enough to frustrate the contract, but the *principle* that contracts are discharged by frustrating events does not depend on the court being able to find a term in the contract which says so. In sharp contrast to the reasoning in cases like *Taylor v Caldwell*, modern courts are very clear that in applying frustration, they are disrupting the contractual allocation of risks and duties in the interests of justice, and not simply giving effect to the parties' implicit intention (as *Taylor* suggested):

> the doctrine [of frustration] is one of justice, as has been repeatedly affirmed on the highest authority. Ultimately the application of the test cannot safely be performed without the consequences of the decision, one way or the other, being measured against the demands of justice. Part of that calculation is the consideration that the frustration of a contract may well mean that the contractual allocation of risk is reversed . . .[22]

The intellectual history of this shift is more complex than is usually supposed. As far back as 1916, well before case law abandoned the language of an 'implied condition', secondary sources had begun to describe frustration in terms akin to the modern approach, as covering cases where 'the impossibility arises from a cause that neither party can reasonably have contemplated when the contract was made, and as to which the terms of the contract make no provision'.[23] The shift in the case law, therefore, appears to have been the result of a broader shift in the way lawyers thought about the law, rather than being a judicially led change.

In conceptual terms, however, the significance of this shift is profound. *Taylor v Caldwell* was decided on the basis that an implied term in the contract had, in fact, dealt with the risk of the event that had now occurred. In the modern approach, in contrast, the rules of frustration only apply when the express and implied terms of the contract *fail* to deal with the risk of the event in question. If the contract deals with the event, the case is seen as falling within the scope of interpretation and implication, and outside the scope of frustration.[24] It is only where the event is entirely unplanned for, and has placed the parties in a situation that is outside the boundaries of the contract framework, that it could potentially fall within the scope of the doctrine of frustration. This point was very clearly put by Lord Reid in *Davis Contractors Ltd v Fareham UDC*:[25]

> there is no need to consider what the parties thought or how they or reasonable men in their shoes would have dealt with the new situation if they had foreseen it. The question is whether the contract which they did make is, on its true construction, wide enough to apply to the new situation: if it is not, then it is at an end.[26]

The current approach to frustration thus, in effect, inverts the logic of *Taylor v Caldwell*. Although this shift has little practical effect on cases relating to the destruction of the subject matter, there are other types of cases in which the modern approach does make a difference, as we will see in the course of this chapter.

22. *Edwinton Commercial Corp v Tsavliris Russ (The Sea Angel)* [2007] EWCA Civ 547, [2007] 2 Lloyd's Rep 517, [112] (Rix LJ).
23. Board of Trade, *Report of the committee appointed by the Board of Trade to consider the position of British manufacturers and merchants in respect of pre-war contracts* (Cd 8975, 1918) p 4.
24. See section 10.2.3 (Planned contingencies).
25. [1956] AC 696 (HL).   26. Ibid, 721.

Returning to the situation that was the subject of Illustration 10.5, the contract in that case will quite clearly be discharged for frustration regardless of which of these two approaches is adopted. A similar outcome will result if the subject matter has not been destroyed but has been rendered unavailable, for example because it has been stolen. Consider the following variation on the facts of Illustration 10.5:

Illustration 10.7

Farmer Maggot agrees to hire his prize bull Tarmund out to Farmer Giles for use in the following breeding season. Two weeks before the bull is due to be delivered to Farmer Giles, it is stolen and is not recovered until well after the breeding season has ended.

Although the bull has not been 'destroyed' in this case, its theft nevertheless makes performance of the contract impossible. The issue giving rise to impossibility here is not *impossibility* as much as it is *unavailability*. The courts have, in general, been willing to treat situations of unavailability as frustrating the contract, if the unavailability makes the contract's performance impossible.[27] The effect of the theft of the bull, to the extent it is an unforeseen contingency, will therefore be to frustrate the contract.

This is not, however, an absolute rule. The principles we have been discussing thus far apply to *unallocated* risks; that is to say, to the risk of contingencies for which the parties have failed to provide in their contract. It is open to the parties to alter the outcome by expressly or implicitly allocating the risk, or by imposing an obligation on one party to take steps to prevent its eventuation. Thus in Illustration 10.7, it is open to the parties to provide in their contract that the risk of theft rests with Farmer Maggot (in which case he will be liable under the contract even if the bull is stolen), or to require Farmer Maggot to take measures to reduce the likelihood of theft (in which case he would be liable under the contract if he failed to take those measures). Secondly, the principles discussed in this section only apply if performance is truly impossible. If, to return to Illustrations 10.5 and 10.7, the contract required the supply of *a* bull without naming a particular bull, the death or theft of Tarmund may well not frustrate the contract, on the basis that it can still be performed by supplying a different bull. We will return to both these points in section 10.3.

Key individuals and impossibility

The language of 'destruction' of the subject matter works well when we are dealing with contracts involving things. But what happens in contracts involving *people*, for example a contract relating to a music gig, as in Illustration 10.6?

English law draws a distinction between contracts where performance is required to be personal and those where it is impersonal. In a personal contract, you contract to have a particular individual render certain services to you. In an impersonal contract, you contract for a particular set of services, rendered with a particular level of care and skill, but you are indifferent when it comes to the question of who it is who actually renders the services. Early cases articulated the difference in terms of 'a relationship of

---

27. See *Gamerco SA v ICM/Fair Warning (Agency) Ltd* [1995] 1 WLR 1226.

confidence'[28] or 'a contract which no deputy could perform'.[29] The essential character of the difference is illustrated by the contrast between the following two scenarios:

Illustration 10.8

Olivia has just finished her law course at Three Ridings University. She hires Constantine Movers to transport her possessions back to her hometown. On the day of the move, Constantine Movers tell her that the driver she was allocated has died following a heart attack. As a result, they will no longer be able to transport her goods.

Illustration 10.9

Three Ridings University engages Perfect Portraits plc to have a portrait of their Vice-Chancellor painted by the rising young artist Lucy Young. Three days before the sittings are to commence, Lucy Young tragically dies of a heart attack. Perfect Portraits contact Three Ridings University to cancel the contract.

It should be evident that the identity of the person involved matters in the latter case of Illustration 10.9 but not in the former of Illustration 10.8. Generally speaking, people who engage movers or delivery men care about the quality of the service not the identity of the delivery men. A person who engages a portrait artist, however, will usually care about the identity of the artist.

The law of frustration incorporates this distinction. If the contract was intended to be personal, as in Illustration 10.9, and if the person concerned, by reason of death or disability, is no longer physically able to perform the contract, then the contract will be treated as having been frustrated by reason of that death or disability.[30] In *Hall v Wright*,[31] Pollock CB explained the logic behind the legal position:

> [A] contract by an author to write a book, or by a painter to paint a picture within a reasonable time, would, in my judgment, be deemed subject to the condition that, if the author became insane, or the painter paralytic, and so incapable of performing the contract by the act of God, he would not be liable personally in damages any more than his executors would be if he had been prevented by death.[32]

Pollock CB used the same language of an 'implied condition' and 'act of God' as *Taylor v Caldwell* had done. In the modern context, a court would reason in terms of frustration without resort to either of these devices, but the outcome would be much the same.

Returning, then, to the situation that was the subject of Illustration 10.6 (the Hedge Betty concert), the first question that arises is whether the identity of the drummer matters to the contract, such that her absence frustrates the concert. There is no single

---

28. *Stubbs, Administrator v Holywell Railway Co* (1866–7) LR 2 Ex 311, 314 (Martin B).
29. *Robinson v Davison* (1870–1) LR 6 Ex 269 (Bramwell B).
30. See the observations of Martin B in *Stubbs, Administrator v Holywell Railway Co* (1866–7) LR 2 Ex 311, 314.
31. [1859] El Bl & El 746, 120 ER 695.   32. Ibid, 793.

answer to this question. It will, instead, depend on how important the drummer is to the band. If the drummer is a central figure, such that the band cannot work with a different drummer on short notice, the contract is likely to be frustrated. If, however, the band is of a type where the use of substitute drummers is common, the drummer's illness will not frustrate the contract.

Does it matter that the drummer's illness is temporary, and does not involve the permanent disabilities Pollock CB discussed in *Hall v Wright*? The answer is that it does not. Much as with contracts involving property, a temporary circumstance can also frustrate the contract if it affects the day on which, or period in which, performance fell due. In *Robinson v Davison*,[33] a well-known pianist by the name of Arabella Goddard had agreed to play at a concert in Gainsborough on 14 January 1871. Very shortly before the concert, she fell seriously ill and would not have been able to perform without putting her life in danger. The concert was cancelled and the organizers sued her to recover their losses. The court held that the fulfilment of the contract depended on Ms Goddard being 'in a state of health to attend and play at the concert on the day named'.[34] Given that she was seriously ill and unfit to play on that day, the contract was discharged.

As with the law relating to the destruction of the subject matter, this, too, can be altered by the parties' contract. In *Robinson*, Bramwell B stressed that whilst the contract in that case was brought to an end by the pianist's ill health, it was always open to the parties to provide otherwise: 'the parties might expressly contract that incapacity should not excuse'.[35] If a risk has been expressly or implicitly allocated by the contract, its eventuation will not frustrate the contract, as we will see in greater detail in section 10.3.

Legal impossibility

The third key circumstance in which a contract is frustrated by reason of impossibility is where the contingency is a consequence not of physical changes, but of a change in the law which makes performance either unlawful or impossible. In Problem 10, the issue is not that performance of the contract has become physically impossible. It is that a change in the law has made it impossible to perform the contract without violating the law. In situations of this sort, the common law has long held that the contract is frustrated by reason of *supervening illegality*. Supervening illegality applies where a contract was legal when it was made but subsequently becomes illegal as a result of a change in the law.[36]

Many cases of supervening illegality relate to war or sanctions. *Denny, Mott & Dickinson Ltd v James B Fraser & Co Ltd*[37] is a typical example. Here, the parties in 1929 entered into a long-term contract for the lease of a timber yard and the purchase of timber. In 1939, on the outbreak of the Second World War, the government issued an order severely restricting transactions in timber. The House of Lords held that this order had made further transactions between the parties impossible, with the result that the contract was frustrated. Likewise, in *Fibrosa SA v Fairbairn Lawson Combe Barbour Ltd*,[38]

33. (1870–1) LR 6 Ex 269.   34. Ibid, 275 (Kelly CB).   35. Ibid, 277–8.
36. A contract which was illegal from the outset is not covered by the rules on frustration. Instead, contracts of this type are dealt with under the rules relating to illegality (not 'supervening' illegality), which are discussed in greater detail in Chapter 14.
37. [1944] AC 265 (HL).   38. [1943] AC 32 (HL).

a contract for the sale of machinery to a Polish company was held to have been frustrated following the German invasion of Poland and the British declaration of war on Germany, which had turned what was originally a perfectly legal transaction into one which involved trading with the enemy.

Supervening illegality does not have to involve high policy. *Any* governmental action, including the action of municipal bodies or regulators, can frustrate a contract if it has the effect of making performance illegal (although a mere requirement for regulatory approval will not frustrate a contract, if it is actually possible to obtain that approval[39]). A contract can also be frustrated by government action which does not directly prohibit performance, but nevertheless makes performance impossible. The requisition of ships during wartime—which made them unavailable for contracted charters—has produced many such cases over the years, but there are also more everyday examples of low-level municipal action. The classic example is *Gamerco v ICM/ Fair Warning (Agency) Ltd*,[40] which arose out of regulatory problems in connection with a European tour by Guns N' Roses, a hard rock band that was wildly popular in the late 1980s and early 1990s. One of the proposed performances in the tour was at the Vicente Calderon Stadium in Madrid. Four days before the concert was to take place, engineers discovered structural problems with the stadium. Madrid City Council banned its use the next day; 44,500 tickets had been sold and significant losses were incurred. In litigation between the band, the tour organizers, and the Spanish promoters, it was held that the contract had been frustrated by the actions of Madrid City Council. Although Madrid City Council had not prohibited the concert, banning the use of the stadium was a frustrating event as there were very few venues in the city which could have accommodated 44,500 people.[41]

Finally, there is some authority which suggests that a contract may be frustrated if government action materially alters the terms on which the contract was to be performed, even if that alteration does not make performance impossible. In *Levenshulme Urban District Council v Manchester Corp*,[42] the parties had entered into an agreement which was to be embodied in an Act of Parliament. The parties prepared a draft bill, but in the course of its passage the terms were altered to impose a range of conditions that the original contract did not contemplate. The court held that under the circumstances, the contract was frustrated.[43]

Whether a contract is frustrated on this basis is a question of degree. *Brauer & Co v James Clark (Brush Materials) Ltd*[44] involved a contract for the export of goods from Brazil. The Bank of Brazil refused to grant an export licence unless the goods were valued at a higher price than that stipulated in the contract. The bank's condition did not require the contract price to be changed. It would have been met if the seller had bought the goods at a higher price, and sold them on to the buyer at the original contract price. This would have required the seller to make a moderate loss on the transaction which, unsurprisingly, he was unwilling to do. The buyer sued for breach,

---

39. See *DVB Bank v Melli Bank* [2013] EWHC 2321 (Comm).
40. [1995] 1 WLR 1226 (QB).   41. Ibid, 1233.   42. (1908) 72 JP 470.
43. Note that the outcome would have been different if the court had come to the conclusion that either of the parties had taken on the risk of the contract's terms being altered in the course of their passage through Parliament.
44. [1952] 2 All ER 497, [1952] 2 Lloyd's Rep 147 (CA).

and the seller argued that the regulatory action had frustrated the contract. The Court of Appeal held that on the facts the bank's actions were insufficient to frustrate the contract. They had made the contract more onerous for the seller, but only a high degree of onerousness would frustrate the contract. For example, if circumstances made it impossible 'to obtain a licence without incurring a cost a hundred times as much as the contract price', the contract might well be frustrated.[45] In such a case, it would have become 'a thing radically different'. But a smaller change would not have this effect.

Delay and temporary impossibility

The cases we have discussed thus far have involved situations where the impossibility applied to the entire period of performance. In *Taylor v Caldwell*, the destruction of the hall affected every one of the days on which performances were to take place. Likewise, in *Gamerco*[46] and *Robinson v Davison*,[47] the circumstances affected the entirety of the only scheduled performance. But what happens if the circumstances only affect a portion of the contract, for example if Arabella Goddard in *Robinson* had been contracted to give five recitals, only one of which was affected by her illness? And, similarly, what happens if the circumstances only operate to *delay* performance rather than prevent it altogether, for example if Guns N' Roses in *Gamerco* had only been required to delay their concert by two weeks, rather than cancel it altogether?

A significant proportion of the cases on this point have involved shipping contracts, and have in consequence turned on relatively specialized matters such as the distinction between voyage charters and time charters, or the construction of 'restraint of princes' clauses,[48] which are well beyond the scope of an introductory book on contract law. Over the years, however, a fairly consistent approach has evolved, which has now crystallized into what the courts term a 'multifactoral' approach.

The origins of the multifactoral approach go back to the 'War Cases', involving the requisition of commercial ships by the Royal Navy during the First World War. Requisitioned ships were not held indefinitely and compensation was usually paid for their use. Nevertheless, their requisition meant that they were no longer available for commercial shipping, and a number of cases arose in which the courts had to consider whether ship charters were frustrated by the temporary requisition of the ships. Earlier cases had suggested that the answer to this question depended on the length of the delay or unavailability,[49] and the courts hearing the War Cases for the most part followed this lead,[50] as did later cases on temporary impossibility for reasons other than delay. In *Pioneer Shipping Ltd v BTP Tioxide Ltd*,[51] a series of strikes at a port meant that a ship would have been able to carry out less than half the voyages for which it had

---

45. [1952] 2 All ER 497, 500 (Singleton LJ).
46. *Gamerco v ICM/Fair Warning (Agency) Ltd* [1995] 1 WLR 1226 (QB).
47. (1870–1) LR 6 Ex 269.   48. *Bank Line v Capel* [1919] AC 435 (HL).
49. See *Jackson v Union Marine Insurance Co Ltd* (1874) LR 10 CP 125, which involved a ship which ran aground causing a delay of eight months in the performance of the contract.
50. See eg *Tamplin v Anglo-Mexican Steamship Co* [1916] 2 AC 397 (HL); *Bank Line v Capel* [1919] AC 435 (HL).
51. [1982] AC 724.

been chartered. The court held that under the circumstances the contract had been frustrated.

The facts of these cases meant that the length of the delay, or the extent of the disruption, was a good proxy for deciding whether the agreement had been rendered 'a thing radically different' by reason of that delay or disruption. More recently, however, the courts have been faced with cases where the facts were not so straightforward, and involved a range of other circumstances. The multifactoral approach seeks to take account of these broader circumstances. In *The Sea Angel*,[52] Rix LJ elaborated on the character of this test, and its relationship to the general principle underlying frustration that performance must have become a thing 'radically different':

> In my judgment, the application of the doctrine of frustration requires a multifactorial approach. Among the factors which have to be considered are the terms of the contract itself, its matrix or context, the parties' knowledge, expectations, assumptions and contemplations, in particular as to risk, as at the time of contract, at any rate so far as these can be ascribed mutually and objectively, and then the nature of the supervening event, and the parties' reasonable and objectively ascertainable calculations as to the possibilities of future performance in the new circumstances. Since the subject matter of the doctrine of frustration is contract, and contracts are about the allocation of risk, and since the allocation and assumption of risk is not simply a matter of express or implied provision but may also depend on less easily defined matters such as 'the contemplation of the parties', the application of the doctrine can often be a difficult one. In such circumstances, the test of 'radically different' is important: it tells us that the doctrine is not to be lightly invoked; that mere incidence of expense or delay or onerousness is not sufficient; and that there has to be as it were a break in identity between the contract as provided for and contemplated and its performance in the new circumstances . . . If the provisions of a contract in their literal sense are to make way for the absolving effect of frustration, then that must, in my judgment, be in the interests of justice and not against those interests. Since the purpose of the doctrine is to do justice, then its application cannot be divorced from considerations of justice.[53]

Rix LJ's words are wide, and appear to have been intended to set out an approach that applies to *all* cases of frustration. Whilst subsequent cases on delay have adopted and applied the multifactoral approach,[54] it has not as yet been applied to cases of impossibility. As such, as things stand, it appears to have established itself as the principal way of dealing with situations of temporary frustration and delay, but not more widely within the doctrine of frustration.

Frustrated purposes

The final type of frustrating event occurs where performance remains technically possible, but in a context which is so radically altered that the purpose of performance

52. *Edwinton Commercial Corp v Tsavliris Russ (The Sea Angel)* [2007] EWCA Civ 547, [2007] 2 Lloyd's Rep 517.
53. Ibid, [111]–[112].
54. See *Bunge SA v Kyla Shipping Co Ltd* [2012] EWHC 3522 (Comm), [2013] 1 Lloyd's Rep 565; *Islamic Republic of Iran Shipping Lines v Steamship Mutual Underwriting Association (Bermuda) Ltd* [2010] EWHC 2661 (Comm), [2011] 1 Lloyd's Rep 195.

has been frustrated. The existence of this category is justified with reference to a line of cases arising out of the cancellation of the coronation of King Edward VII due to his illness. This cancellation gave rise to pleas of frustration, as individuals who had booked rooms or organized events sought to unwind their contracts.

The key case is *Krell v Henry*,[55] which involved the hire by the defendant of a flat owned by the claimant. The defendant intended to view the coronation procession from the flat. A deposit was paid. After the coronation was cancelled, the defendant refused to pay the balance and the flat-owner sued. Arguments in the Court of Appeal revolved around two issues. The first was whether the parties' bargain was for the *flat*, with an incidental view of whatever happened to be going on outside the window (as the claimant argued), or for a *view* of an event which just happened to be situated in a flat (as the defendant argued).[56] The second was whether the risk of the procession's cancellation had passed to the defendant (as the claimant argued) or whether the contract was grounded on 'the absolute assumption of both parties' that the procession would pass below the window (as the defendant argued). The Court of Appeal, applying *Taylor v Caldwell*, held that there was a common assumption that the coronation would take place. The result was that 'the object of the contract was frustrated by the non-happening of the coronation and its procession on the days proclaimed'.[57]

Krell v Henry was controversial when it was decided, and other coronation cases went the other way. In *Herne Bay Steam Boat Co v Hutton*,[58] the defendant had hired a steam boat from the claimants to take passengers to view the naval review that was to accompany the coronation, and also to cruise around the fleet. When the coronation was cancelled, the defendant refused to take the boat or pay for it, and the plaintiff sued. The case was heard by the same bench of the Court of Appeal as *Krell v Henry*, but produced the opposite outcome. The Court of Appeal held that the naval review was not a 'foundation of the contract', and the fact that it was cancelled did not therefore frustrate the contract. They also pointed out that the fleet remained anchored, and that it remained possible to cruise around the fleet. Such a cruise would attract fewer passengers than one to see the coronation naval review, but that was the defendant's risk under the contract.

Krell appears to have influenced the decision in *Minnevitch v Café de Paris (Londres) Ltd*.[59] Minnevitch and his band had been engaged by the Café de Paris to put on comedic acts, and were paid per performance. On 20 January 1936, King George V died, and the café cancelled the band's performance without payment. The café was closed for mourning on 21 January, and the band's performances were cancelled by the café for the rest of the week. The band sued for their wages. Macnaghten J partially allowed their claim, holding that the performances on 20 and 21 January had been frustrated by the death of the king but not the other performances that week. Apart from *Minnevitch*,[60] few subsequent cases have followed *Krell v Henry*, and it is unlikely that they will. In *Larrinaga & Co, Ltd v Société Franco-Américaine des Phosphates de Medulla*,

---

55. [1903] 2 KB 740 (CA).   56. Ibid, 745.   57. Ibid, 754 (Vaughan Williams LJ).
58. [1903] 2 KB 683 (CA).   59. [1936] 1 All ER 884 (KB).
60. *Minnevitch* itself does not cite *Krell*, but a note in the All England Reports suggests that it was seen as applying the principle laid down in the coronation cases.

Paris,[61] Viscount Finlay in the House of Lords said that he doubted the extension of the *Taylor v Caldwell* rule to the coronation cases, specifically singling out *Krell v Henry* for criticism. In *Maritime National Fish Ltd v Ocean Trawlers Ltd*,[62] Lord Wright in the Privy Council cited Viscount Finlay's words with approval, and added that *Krell v Henry* also had the potential to reallocate losses without any clear justification for why those losses were being reallocated.[63]

Even apart from this criticism, which is bound to have a persuasive effect on any court hearing an argument based on *Krell v Henry*, it is hard to see how the mere frustration of a commercial purpose could render performance under a contract 'a thing radically different', save in the most exceptional circumstances. In *Krell v Henry*, the Court of Appeal seem to have thought that the contract was frustrated because the parties had contracted for a view rather than for a room. Yet this was a product of the specific facts of that case. Given the way in which the courts have in recent times articulated the test for frustration and their reluctance to disturb commercial contracts, *Krell* is unlikely to be treated as representing a broader principle. Hardship by itself will not frustrate a contract.

The implications of this can be seen by relating the discussion back to Problem 10. The issue Nuclear Solutions is facing in their losses is as a result of German government action. Yet it is not the losses that will frustrate the contract. What will frustrate the contract, and render it a 'thing radically different', is that the German government's actions in compelling the closure of the plant amount to a classic example of supervening illegality. The losses, and consequent hardship, are entirely irrelevant: the supervening illegality frustrates the contract regardless of whether either party has suffered any losses or hardship as a result.

10.2.3 Frustration and the contractual framework

Frustration is not intended to interfere with contracts where the parties have provided for a particular risk or contingency in one way or another. If the contractual framework can be stretched to cover the contingency through the ordinary techniques of interpretation and implication, then it is the contractual framework that will govern the case, not the rules of frustration. The centrality of the contract was stressed in *Davis Contractors v Fareham UDC*:[64]

> frustration depends . . . on the true construction of the terms which are in the contract, read in the light of the nature of the contract and the relevant surrounding circumstances when the contract was made.[65]

In other words, the courts start by determining the 'thing' the parties contracted for by reading the contract against the background of the 'matrix of fact'. Having done this, they compare that with the position in which the parties now find themselves, to determine whether the events in question are so completely outside the scope of the contract as to frustrate it. The result is that there are a range of circumstances in which the rules of frustration give way to the provisions of the parties' contract.

---

61. [1923] All ER Rep 1 (HL).   62. [1935] AC 524 (PC).   63. Ibid, 529.
64. *Davis Contractors v Fareham UDC* [1956] AC 696 (HL).   65. Ibid, 720 (Lord Reid).

Planned contingencies

The first, and most obvious, type of circumstance where the courts will treat the contingency as being within the contractual framework is where the parties have expressly or implicitly allocated the risk of the contingency in question in their contract or otherwise planned for it.

One way in which parties might plan for a particular contingency is through a broadly phrased duty imposed on one of the parties. In *Dany Lions Cars v Bristol Cars*,[66] the parties entered into a contract under which the defendants undertook to convert the claimant's Bristol 405 car to accommodate an automatic gearbox. Fitting an automatic gearbox proved to be impossible without drastically impairing the car's functionality, and the defendants refused to do so. The claimant sued, and the defendants argued that the contract was frustrated by reason of impossibility. The court rejected the argument on frustration. The defendants had 'assumed a positive liability to achieve a result', and their failure to achieve that result could not be excused by reason of frustration.

An allocation of risk can also be implicit. In *CTI Group Inc v Transclear SA*,[67] CTI Group was trying to break a Mexican cement cartel. Transclear knew this, and agreed to sell cement to it, but were unable to find a supplier: every supplier they contacted was pressurized to withdraw by Cemex, who were the driving force behind the cartel. Transclear argued that the contract was frustrated. The Court of Appeal held that the contract was not frustrated, as the sellers had implicitly taken on the risk of being unable to find a supplier.

A 'strategic silence', in which the parties foresaw a risk but chose to remain silent about it, is usually taken as prima facie evidence of an implicit allocation which is sufficient to exclude frustration. But this is only a prima facie inference. The mere fact that a risk was *foreseeable* does not absolutely exclude the application of frustration in the absence of evidence that one of the parties assumed the risk in question. For foreseeability to exclude frustration, the risk must be such that 'any person of ordinary intelligence would regard [it] as likely to occur'.[68] In *The Sea Angel*,[69] Rix LJ suggested that foreseeability was a matter of degree: the less foreseeable an event, the more likely it is that its foreseeability will be a factor in determining whether or not it was frustrating.[70]

A third way in which parties may plan for a contingency is by creating a contractual mechanism dealing with a broad *class* of risks. Classic examples are price-adjustment clauses or delay clauses. These clauses provide for changes in the parties' rights and obligations if certain events take place (eg a change in the costs of components or a delay due to circumstances beyond the reasonable control of the parties). The eventuation of such an event, then, will not operate to frustrate the contract.

Clauses of this type are examples of flexible contracting (Chapter 9). Their scope is not absolute, however. If the clause, properly construed, does not cover a particular

---

66. [2013] EWHC 2997 (QB).   67. [2008] EWCA Civ 856, [2008] 2 CLC 112.

68. H Beale (ed), *Chitty on Contracts* (31st edn, Sweet & Maxwell 2012) 23-061.

69. *Edwinton Commercial Corp v Tsavliris Russ (The Sea Angel)* [2007] EWCA Civ 547, [2007] 2 Lloyd's Rep 517.

70. Ibid, [127].

type of event or risk, that clause will not prevent frustration. In *Metropolitan Water Board v Dick Kerr and Co Ltd*,[71] the parties had contracted to construct a reservoir. The contract provided that the Water Board's engineer had the power to extend the time for construction in the event of delay, and obliged the contractors to apply to the engineer for an extension. The contract was interrupted by the First World War, when the contractors were required to stop work and sell their equipment to the government. The House of Lords held that the delay clause was only designed to cover temporary circumstances, and was therefore inapplicable to such a fundamental change. The result was that the contract was frustrated.

Election, fault, and alternative ways of performing

The second set of circumstances where the provisions of a contract will prevent its frustration is where there are different ways in which a contract might be performed. If there is more than one way in which a contract can be performed, then the fact that one of them is frustrated will not lead to the frustration of the contract. Instead, the outcome will ordinarily be that the party is contractually bound to perform the contract in one of the other possible ways. In *Blackburn Bobbin Co v TW Allen & Sons*,[72] a seller had agreed to supply the buyer with Finnish timber. The seller's practice was to have the timber shipped directly from Finland. He held no stocks himself. When the First World War broke out, shipping in the Baltic Sea was severely disrupted, and the seller was no longer able to source timber from Finland. The court held that the contract was not frustrated. The buyer did not know, and had no way of knowing, where the seller obtained his timber. If the seller had chosen a supply chain that was vulnerable to disruption, that was his choice, and he must bear the risk of it.

Similarly, in a series of cases involving the Suez crisis and subsequent war, the courts held that the closure of the Suez Canal did not frustrate an ordinary shipping contract where a precise route was not stipulated. Unless the goods were extremely perishable, it remained possible to send them around the Cape of Good Hope. Whilst that would make shipping costlier, that by itself was not a frustrating event.[73] In *The Eugenia*,[74] the ship ended up trapped in the Suez Canal for several days during its closure. The Court of Appeal held that that, too, did not frustrate the contract. The charterer had made an express choice to sail through the Suez Canal rather than around the Cape, at a time when there were clear signs that the crisis might escalate. As such, he must bear the consequences of his choice.

In *Maritime National Fish Ltd v Ocean Trawlers Ltd*,[75] the defendants chartered a ship with an otter trawl from the claimants, intending to use it for fishing. Under Canadian law, fishing with an otter trawl required a licence from the government. The defendants applied for licences for five trawlers, but only three were granted. They selected three trawlers, excluding the one they had chartered, and argued that the charter had been frustrated by their failure to obtain a licence. On appeal, the Privy Council held

---

71. [1918] AC 119 (HL).　　72. [1918] 2 KB 467.
73. *Tsakiroglou & Co Ltd v Noblee Thorl GmbH* [1962] 2 AC 93.
74. *Ocean Tramp Tankers Corp v V/O Sovfracht (The Eugenia)* [1964] 2 QB 226.
75. [1935] AC 524 (PC).

that there was no frustration, as the only reason the trawler was unlicensed was that the defendants chose not to nominate it. A contract would not be frustrated by an event which was within the control of one of the parties.

Similarly, in *The Super Servant Two*,[76] J Lauritzen had contracted for Wijsmuller to carry an oil rig on either of two barges, *Super Servant One* and *Super Servant Two*. Wijsmuller decided to use *Super Servant Two*, and allocated *Super Servant One* to other contracts. A few months before the rig was to be carried, *Super Servant Two* sank. Wijsmuller argued that the contract was frustrated. The Court of Appeal held that the loss of *Super Servant Two* would be a frustrating event only if the contract required the rig to be carried on *Super Servant Two*. Because it did not, the contract was not frustrated, and Wijsmuller was in breach.

The availability of alternative modes of performance is particularly salient where generic goods are involved. The fact that the seller's warehouse burned down is not usually a defence to a contract for a sale of wheat, for example, because the seller would be expected to procure substitute wheat on the market. This does not, however, apply if a specific source is stipulated. In *Howell v Coupland*,[77] the parties contracted for the purchase of 200 tonnes of potatoes that were to be grown in a designated field. Through no fault of the seller, the crop in the field failed and only 60 tonnes could be delivered. It was held that the contract was frustrated by reason of impossibility, because it required the crop to come from that field.

 Debates in context: an overly broad doctrine?

Most of the cases where frustration was successfully pleaded have involved physical impossibility or supervening illegality, whether permanent or temporary. Whilst there is nothing inherent in the language of being 'radically different' that links it to these particular categories, that is where judicial reasoning appears to have led. On its face, this approach would seem to take a *narrow* view of the things that are relevant in determining the legal response to a fundamental change. Nevertheless, scholars have long argued that even this narrow approach goes too far. In a critique of the War Cases written in 1918, Professor AD McNair, an eminent legal scholar who would later become the first President of the European Court of Human Rights, argued that frustration should remain oriented around implied conditions.[78] The difficulty with reasoning in terms of 'impracticability' or 'commercial purpose', he argued, was that the courts, 'by aiming at being too business-like' tended 'to do the true interests of business a great disservice':

> Is it suggested that if in *Taylor v Caldwell* the plaintiff had hired the defendant's Surrey Gardens for an entertainment to be given in the open air, and a deluge of rain had made the concerts 'impracticable', the plaintiff would have been excused?[79]

For much the same reason, he also stressed that frustration should remain grounded in an implied condition based on the officious bystander test (discussed in Chapter 8). An event

➡

---

76. *J Lauritzen AS v Wijsmuller BV (The Super Servant Two)* [1990] 1 Lloyd's Rep 1.
77. (1876) 1 QBD 258.
78. AD McNair, 'War-Time Impossibility of Performance of Contract' (1919) 35 LQR 84.
79. Ibid, 95.

→

should only be treated as a frustrating event if the parties would, had the possibility of that event been mentioned to them at the time of contracting, have responded 'Oh, of course, if that happened, it would knock the bottom out of our bargain.'[80]

Professor McNair's concerns have been echoed by modern scholars—most notably, by Sir John Smith, an extremely distinguished commentator on contract law—who argued powerfully for frustration to be subsumed into the processes of implication and interpretation.[81] George Triantis, a leading North American scholar of contract and commercial law, has similarly pointed out that the concern with seeking to protect parties from unexpected losses sits uneasily with the general trend in contract law, which is relatively unconcerned with whether a party makes a gain or loss as a result of a contract being performed.[82]

The growing importance assigned to contractual allocations of risk in the modern law should, thus, be seen as an attempt to accommodate these concerns. The debate as to whether it does so adequately, or whether it strays too far in its pursuit of 'the interests of justice', as Rix LJ put it, is a matter on which debate is likely to continue.

10.2.4 Consequences of frustration

Discharge

Frustration automatically discharges the contract. The contract comes to an end as soon as the frustrating event occurs. If the parties have not yet started work on the contract, then discharge fully unwinds the transaction. Neither party has incurred any expenditure or provided any benefit to each other, so there is nothing more to unwind. The situation is less straightforward if the parties have begun working on the contract, or partially performed their contractual obligations. In such a situation, it is entirely conceivable that one or both parties have incurred expenditure in preparing for the contract, and possibly even provided the other party with benefits through part performance. Here, the frustrating event will cause loss to one or both parties. Unwinding such a transaction is more complex, because it raises questions on whether and how to divide these losses.

Before 1943, the common law's approach was simple and brutal. Frustration brought the contract to an end, but the only remedy that flowed from that was that the parties were released from future performance of the contract. If a payment, but not performance, had fallen due when the contract was frustrated, the party making the payment was not discharged and had to pay, but the party rendering performance was discharged and did not have to perform. In effect, this meant that if a deposit or advance had been paid for something, the party receiving the deposit could keep it without having to render any performance in return. In *Chandler v Webster*,[83]

---

80. Ibid, 99.
81. JC Smith, 'Contracts: Mistake, Frustration, and Implied Terms' (1994) 110 LQR 400.
82. GG Triantis, 'Contractual Allocations of Unknown Risks: A Critique of the Doctrine of Commercial Impracticability' (1992) 42 University of Toronto Law Journal 450.
83. [1904] 1 KB 493.

the court was faced with facts that were substantially the same as those of *Krell v Henry*. As in *Krell*, the contract was held to have been frustrated by the cancellation of the coronation procession. However, the hirer in this case had paid a significant advance, and the remainder had fallen due before the procession was cancelled. The court held that the hirer could not recover the amount he had paid, and was also liable to pay the remainder of the hire charge even though the contract had been frustrated.[84]

If performance, but not payment, had fallen due when the contract was frustrated, the party who had performed would be entitled to nothing, even if they had provided substantial benefits to the other party and incurred significant expenses in doing so. As it is quite common for contracts to provide for payment 'on completion', this meant that parties often ended up with a windfall benefit for which they had to pay nothing.[85]

The law did provide some limited remedies to those affected by these rules. In some cases where a deposit or advance had been paid, the party could recover it under the law of **restitution** if there had been a total failure of consideration.[86] Similarly, in some cases, a party who had provided a benefit to the other could recover the fair market value of that benefit through an action in *quantum meruit*.[87] Overall, however, the result was a law which not infrequently gave one party an undeserved windfall.[88] The legal rules were likened to a guillotine, falling 'with faultless precision but often with ruthless effect'[89] and were the subject of strong criticism from the judiciary.

The Law Reform (Frustrated Contracts) Act 1943 was passed to deal with these issues, by putting in place a rule that was less arbitrary than the existing rules of law. Section 1(2) of the Act changed the law in relation to money paid before the contract was frustrated and s 1(3) changed the law in relation to goods or services supplied before the contract was frustrated.

Money already paid or due

Section 1(2) creates a new set of rules in relation to money that was paid, or fell due for payment, before frustration.

If money has already been paid by one party to the other, s 1(2) says that it can be claimed back by the party who paid it. The right is not, however, absolute. The proviso to s 1(2) states that where the person receiving the advance has incurred expenses for the purpose of performing the contract, the court may, 'if it considers it

---

84. In *Krell v Henry*, the claimant was held to be legally entitled to retain the deposit that the defendant had paid, even though the contract had been discharged for frustration.
85. See *Appleby v Myers* (1867) LR 2 CP 651.
86. In non-technical language, a total failure of consideration arises where the party gets nothing of what they had bargained for. See *Fibrosa SA v Fairbairn Lawson Combe Barbour Ltd* [1943] AC 32 (HL).
87. See *Bush v Whitehaven Town and Harbour Trustees* (1888) 52 JP 392 (CA). *Quantum meruit* is discussed in brief in Chapter 2.
88. In *Cantiare San Rocco, SA v Clyde Shipbuilding and Engineering Co, Ltd* [1924] AC 226 (HL), Lord Shaw described the rule as the 'something for nothing doctrine'. Ibid, 258.
89. Law Revision Committee, *Seventh Interim Report: Rule in Chandler v Webster* (Cmd 6009, 1939) p 3.

just to do so', allow him to retain some or all of the advance, up to the actual amount of his expenses.

Similarly, if a payment had fallen due before the contract was frustrated, but has not yet been paid, s 1(2) provides that it does not need to be paid. However, if the person to whom the sum was payable has incurred expenses for the purpose of performing the contract, the court may permit her to recover some or all of the advance, up to the actual amount of her expenses.

In both cases, the precise amount that is payable is left to the court's discretion. The Act does not contain any guidance in relation to how the court's discretion is to be exercised, and there has been very little case law under this section. The first significant case in which a court had to consider how the section was to be applied was *Gamerco*,[90] discussed in section 10.2.2. The promoters had paid an advance of $412,000 to the group and the organizers, and had incurred additional expenses of around $450,000. They sought to recover the advance, relying on s 1(2). The defendants said that they had incurred expenses of $50,000, but were unable to produce evidence of their expenses.

Garland J in the High Court took the view that the overriding objective of the section was to permit the court to do justice, with a view to mitigating 'the possible harshness of allowing all loss to lie where it has fallen'. Given the vastly disproportionate expenses incurred by the two sides, and the inability of the defendants to substantiate their expenses, he ordered that the entire advance should be returned. The defendants were not allowed to retain any portion of the advance to meet their own expenses.

Garland J's decision has been criticized for going beyond the scope of the discretion allowed to him by the Act. Carter and Tolhurst, for example, have argued that once a party proves that they have incurred expenses, the court must award them something to defray their expenses.[91] With respect, it is hard to see how this follows from the statute. The court's power to allow the retention of an advance under s 1(2) is worded in permissive, not mandatory, language; and is given to the court to exercise 'if it considers it just to do so'. The discretion this gives to a court is certainly wide enough to let it order the return of the entire advance, if that is the outcome the judge believes just.

Performance rendered before frustration

Prior to the Act, there was no general right to recover payment for benefits conferred by one party upon the other before frustration, although an action in *quantum meruit* would lie under some circumstances. Section 1(3) now gives a party who has provided another party with a valuable benefit a right to recover a sum as payment for the benefit. The Act gives the court a broad discretion to determine how much is recoverable, depending on what the court considers just. However, it provides, first, that the amount recoverable should not exceed the value of the benefit and, secondly, should take into account any expenses which the party *receiving* the benefit spent on

90. [1995] 1 WLR 1226.
91. JW Carter and GJ Tolhurst, 'Gigs N' Restitution: Frustration and the Statutory Adjustment of Payments and Expenses' (1996) 10 JCL 264.

performing the contract (note: not *providing* the benefit) and the effect of the frustrating event on the benefit.

In *BP Exploration Co (Libya) v Hunt*,[92] the House of Lords approved a two-stage approach to calculating payments under s 1(3), which had originally been formulated by Robert Goff J in the High Court.[93] In the first stage, the court identifies whether any valuable benefit has been conferred by the claimant upon the defendant and, if so, what the value of that benefit is. This value then forms the upper limit of the sum that a court may award under s 1(3). In the second stage, the court decides how much it would be appropriate to award, keeping in mind the factors s 1(3) asks the court to consider. The basic measure would be 'the reasonable value of the plaintiff's performance' which would be a *quantum meruit* in relation to services or a *quantum valebat* in relation to goods. Where the benefit had not been requested by the defendant, recovery would be rare save in cases where the defendant had been incontrovertibly benefited.

As interpreted in *BP v Hunt*, s 1(3) appears to have done very little to change the law. Recovery under the section is linked to the provision of a benefit, and to the techniques of quantification associated with *quantum meruit*. Yet, as we have seen, the remedy of *quantum meruit* was available even before the Act. If that is the only effect of the statute, then it would seem not to have done very much and, indeed, most of the pre-Act cases on pre-frustration benefits would be decided in exactly the same way under the Act.[94]

The Act in consequence fails to deal satisfactorily with expenditure incurred in connection with a frustrated contract. In Problem 10, for example, the frustration is problematic only because Nuclear Solutions has spent money on the contract. Yet the law of frustration, as it stands, does not provide any remedy in such a case. Whilst s 1(2) of the Act does deal with contractual expenditure, it only provides a remedy where the contract provides for the payment of an advance. The contract in Problem 10, in common with many other contracts of that type, makes no such provision. As such, Nuclear Solutions can recover nothing, even though it has spent significant amounts of money in preparation for the contract. Section 1(3) will not be of much avail. The section does not deal with expenditure at all: its sole focus is on providing redress commensurate with the value of the benefits that were provided by one party to the other. Because value is defined with reference to the situation after the frustrating event has occurred, the work done by Nuclear Solutions is unlikely to be seen as having conferred any valuable benefit upon Kernkraftwerk.

This gap has not passed unnoticed, and in 1955 there was some discussion within the government of passing legislation to allow broader recovery of expenses, but nothing came of it.[95] Nevertheless, it remains possible to design contractual clauses that expressly deal with splitting losses in the event of frustration; and it is advisable to do so where such frustration is a possibility.

92. [1983] 2 AC 352 (HL).   93. [1979] 1 WLR 783.
94. This includes *Appleby v Myers* (1867) LR 2 CP 651.
95. TNA LCO 2/5430, Memorandum recommending that the principles of s.1(2) of the Act should be extended to contracts where no prepayment is required before completion (1955).

10.3 Common mistake

10.3.1 'A thing essentially different': the context of common mistake

Let us now turn to common mistake. Common mistake, like frustration, deals with situations where the parties find themselves in an unforeseen situation. Unlike frustration this is not because things have changed, but because they contracted based on a shared misunderstanding of how things actually are.

Illustration 10.10

Consider the following small variation to the facts of Problem 10.

> The contract between Nuclear Solutions and Kernkraftwerk was entered into not before, but *after* the suspension by the German government of its nuclear programme. Both parties incorrectly believed that the suspension was only temporary.

Here, the impact on the contract of the parties' misunderstanding will be dealt with through the rules on common mistake rather than frustration. The test applied in common mistake is to consider whether the mistake renders performance of the contract 'essentially different' from what was contemplated. If it does, the contract will be void. Unlike frustration, which only operates prospectively, common mistake operates retrospectively. The contract will be treated as if it never came into existence.

Although the test of 'essentially different' is strikingly similar to the test of 'radically different' used in frustration, in practice common mistake is a significantly more limited doctrine than frustration. There are two reasons for this. First, parties to commercial contracts are expected to do their research. If they enter into a contract under a mistake because they have failed to do so, that cannot be a ground to avoid the contract. They are bound by what they have put in the contract.[96] Secondly, English law does not impose duties of disclosure on parties negotiating a contract. Save in exceptional circumstances, parties are free in negotiations to withhold important information from the other party, as long as they do not make false statements.[97] The policy underlying this rule would be undermined if parties could challenge contracts every time they made a mistake as to the facts. Anyone in possession of a material fact would be compelled to disclose the fact to the other side if they wanted to have certainty regarding the validity of the contract.

The categories of common mistake that make contracts void are, therefore, exceptions to the general rule that mistakes do not ordinarily affect the validity of a contract. Only three types of common mistake render the contract void: mistakes as to the existence of the subject matter, mistakes as to the possibility of performance, and

---

96. See eg the remarks of Wright J in *Bell v Lever Brothers* [1930] 1 KB 557, 563.
97. See Chapter 11, section 11.2.1.

certain types of mistakes as to the quality of the subject matter. In addition, as with frustration, these only apply if the underlying risk has not been allocated by the contract. It is this, more than anything, that limits the scope of common mistake even in comparison with frustration: in a typical contract, most facts about which the parties might be mistaken will be covered by a contractual warranty or condition. In this section, we will look at the scope of each of these in turn, considering both the types of situations to which they apply and how they are affected by implied or express terms in the contract, before turning to the legal consequences of common mistake.

10.3.2 Mistakes as to the existence of the subject matter

The rules in relation to common mistakes as to the existence of the subject matter are very similar to the rules dealing with frustration on the basis of destruction of the subject matter, save only that frustration applies where the subject matter was in existence when the contract was formed, whereas common mistake applies when it had already ceased to exist at the moment of formation. In essence, if both parties at the time of formation mistakenly believe that the subject matter exists, when in reality it has been destroyed or has ceased to exist (sometimes termed 'res extincta'), the contract will be void for common mistake.

The classic case is *Couturier v Hastie*.[98] Here, the parties had contracted for the sale of a cargo of corn which was on board a ship. Unknown to the parties, the corn had begun deteriorating on the ship, and had been sold by the master of the ship to prevent it from deteriorating further. The question before the court was whether the buyer had to proceed with the purchase. The seller argued that the buyer did in fact have to proceed with the purchase, even though the corn no longer existed. The buyer would not be left remediless: he would receive the sum for which the corn had been sold by the master. The House of Lords held, however, that the buyer was not liable, because the contract was premised on the existence of the goods:

> looking to the contract itself alone, it appears to me clearly that what the parties contemplated . . . The contract . . . plainly imports that there was something which was to be sold at the time of the contract, and something to be purchased.[99]

Because there was no such thing capable of being sold at the time of the contract, the buyer was not liable.

The House of Lords did not use the terminology of mistake, or even declare the contract void, and the judgments in all four courts where the case was heard[100] treated the question as being predominantly one of contract interpretation.[101] Subsequent cases and statutes,[102] however, treated the case as having established a legal rule, which came to be incorporated into the law of mistake. Other cases have applied the rule in

---

98. (1856) 5 HLC 673.   99. Ibid, 681–2.

100. In the court system of the day, the case was first heard at *nisi prius*, from which it was appealed to the Court of Exchequer ((1852) 8 Ex 40), from which it was appealed to the Exchequer Chamber ((1853) 9 Ex 102), from which it was appealed to the House of Lords.

101. See esp the decision in the Exchequer Chamber: *Hastie v Couturier* (1853) 9 Ex 102, 107 (Coleridge J).

102. See Sale of Goods Act 1979, s 6.

contexts other than the sale of goods. In *Strickland v Turner*,[103] it was applied to a contract of annuity (a type of life insurance policy) taken out on the life of a person who had died before the policy was taken out. In *Galloway v Galloway*,[104] it was applied to a separation agreement between a man and woman who believed that they were married to each other when, in fact, the man's first wife was still alive meaning that the second marriage was invalid.

But the scope of this principle is severely limited by the fact that a contract may itself allocate the risk of the unforeseen eventuality to one or the other party. If, for example, a contract on its proper construction contains an express or implied term warranting that the subject matter exists, then the risk of its non-existence will be taken to have been allocated by the contract. The contract will be valid, and the party warranting the existence of the subject matter will be liable in breach of contract. In the Australian case of *McRae v Commonwealth Disposals Commission*,[105] the Commission, an Australian government agency, had granted McRae a contract to salvage a shipwrecked tanker located on a reef described as 'Journaund Reef' at a given location. McRae fitted out a salvage expedition, but found neither tanker nor reef at the location. It transpired that the tanker had never existed and the Commission had confused it with a barge shipwrecked 12 miles away. McRae sued for damages. In defence, the Commission argued that the contract was void for common mistake. The High Court of Australia held that the contract was valid. The Commission had acted solely on rumour, in a manner that was 'reckless and irresponsible',[106] and by its actions it had provided an implied assurance that the tanker existed. This assurance was an implied term, and the Commission was liable for its breach.[107] The import is that the law of common mistake is trumped by the terms of the contract, and it is therefore essential before applying mistake to first construe the contract to see whether there is an express or implied term covering the point at issue.[108]

10.3.3 Mistakes as to the possibility of performance

A contract can also be void for common mistake if its performance will require an act which is physically impossible or legally impossible, but which the parties wrongly believed to be possible. *Sheikh Brothers v Ochsner*[109] was a case of physical impossibility. Ochsner had contracted with Sheikh Brothers to harvest and process crop grown on Sheikh Brothers' land. He was contractually obliged to deliver an average of 50 tonnes per month. In fact, the nature of the land made it impossible to produce that quantity. The Privy Council held that the contract was void for mistake.

But this does not apply if one of the parties has contractually assumed the risk of impossibility. Whether it has done so is a matter of construction. In *Dany Lions v Bristol Cars*,[110] which was discussed in section 10.2.3 in relation to frustration, Bristol

---

103. (1852) 7 Ex 208.   104. (1914) 30 TLR 531.

105. (1951) 84 CLR 377.   106. Ibid, [7].   107. Ibid, [19].

108. See *Great Peace Shipping Ltd v Tsavliris Salvage (International) Ltd* [2002] EWCA Civ 1407, [80]–[83] (quoting *McRae* with approval).

109. [1957] AC 136 (PC). The case was an appeal from Kenya, where the law of contract had been codified, but it is generally taken to also reflect the position under English common law.

110. [2013] EWHC 2997 (QB).

Cars also pleaded common mistake, arguing that the contract was void because both parties had wrongly believed that the car could be modified to accommodate an automatic gearbox. The court rejected this defence. On a proper construction of the contract, Bristol Cars had contractually warranted that it was possible to modify the car to accommodate an automatic gearbox. This meant that it had contractually taken upon itself the risk of impossibility, and was therefore liable.[111]

In contrast, in *Credit Suisse AG v Up Energy Group Ltd*,[112] the court held that the risk of impossibility had arguably not been contractually assumed. The contract in that case contained an option giving Credit Suisse the right to require Up Energy Group to purchase certain securities from it. The terms under which the securities were issued, however, prohibited transfer to persons connected with the issuer. The defendant was connected with the issuer, and the transfer contemplated by the agreement was therefore impossible. The court held, on an application for summary judgment, that although the Up Energy Group had given certain contractual warranties, it was not clear that these covered the specific issue with transferability. Further, given Credit Suisse's role in structuring the transaction, this was a risk it ought to have foreseen, but did not. As a result, it was arguable that the contract was void for common mistake, and the case should proceed to trial.

This also applies where the impossibility arises from a legal rule rather than physical or contractual impossibility. In *Cooper v Phibbs*,[113] Cooper had agreed to take a lease of a fishery from Phibbs, his uncle. Both parties believed that Phibbs owned the fishery. As it turned out, the fishery was trust property and Cooper was already entitled to an equitable life interest. The court held that the agreement should be set aside for mistake: an agreement to sell property to someone who already owned it was impossible to perform. The facts of this case, which related to a situation where it was legally impossible for the *purchaser* to take the property, should be distinguished from a case where it is legally impossible for the *seller* to sell the property because of a defect in title. The latter situation will typically be covered by an implied warranty of title,[114] and will therefore be a breach of contract by the seller rather than a common mistake.

10.3.4 **Mistakes as to quality**

The issue is far more complex where the mistake relates to a quality of the subject matter, rather than to its existence or to the possibility of performance. Consider Illustration 10.2, relating to the installation of a fireplace in an area subsequently discovered to be subject to a smoke control order. Here, the subject matter of the contract still exists, and performance remains possible. What has been discovered to be impossible is *using* the fireplace as Uncle Percival intended. Such a mistake is the precise sort that falls within the scope of the rules relating to mistakes as to a quality of the subject matter.

Courts are reluctant to set aside contracts on the basis of a mistake as to the quality of the subject matter, much as they are reluctant to discharge contracts for frustration of purpose. Mistakes as to quality will only very rarely be sufficiently fundamental to render the performance of the contract 'essentially different'. The leading case is

---

111. Ibid, [24]–[28].   112. [2013] EWHC 3611 (Comm).
113. (1867) LR 2 HL 149.   114. See Chapter 8, section 8.2.1.

Bell v Lever Brothers,[115] which demonstrates very clearly why judges are reluctant to give a wide scope to mistakes as to quality (in much the same way as they are reluctant to give a wide scope to frustration of purpose).

Case in depth: *Bell v Lever Brothers* [1932] AC 161 (HL)

Bell and Snelling were approached by Lever Brothers in 1923, who wanted them to turn around a loss-making company called the Niger Company. Their terms were to run until 1933. They were extremely successful, turning a loss-making business into a very profitable one. Partly as a result, in 1929 the Niger Company merged with its main competitor on very favourable terms, which earned hundreds of thousands of pounds for Lever Brothers. The merger, however, meant that Bell's and Snelling's roles no longer existed. As their contracts still had four years to run, Lever Brothers entered into agreements with them to pay them substantial sums of money for loss of office (£30,000 to Bell and £20,000 to Snelling).

Subsequently, it transpired that Bell and Snelling had engaged in trading cocoa on their own account. This was a breach of their fiduciary duty as directors. It represented a potential conflict of interest (the Niger Company also traded in cocoa) and it also opened the Niger Company to liability for breach of two 'Pool Agreements'. These breaches meant that Lever Brothers would have been entitled to sack both Bell and Snelling without paying any compensation. Some months after it had paid them the loss of office payments, Lever Brothers discovered this. It sued Bell and Snelling for the return of the money, arguing that the money had been paid under a mistake. The mistake was the belief that Bell and Snelling had a continuing right of employment under their contract, and that their employment could only be terminated with their consent. This belief was a mistake because it was not true: Bell and Snelling could have been sacked for breach of contract. The agreements to pay loss of office payments were therefore void for common mistake.[116]

Unlike today, in British business culture at the time it would not have been unusual to fire a senior manager on a point of principle for failing to adhere to 'a strict sense of business honour',[117] even if the misconduct had not caused the company any loss, and even if the employee in question had in fact earned considerable profits for the company. The jury, accordingly, found that Lever Brothers would as a matter of principle have terminated Bell and Snelling without paying any compensation. The question for the court was whether the mistake was sufficient to avoid the contract.

The judges who heard the case were deeply divided both on the outcome and on the correct approach to take in answering the question. On one side were the three judges in the majority in the House of Lords (and whose view is now the law), who held that the contract was not void. On the other side were the judges who heard the case in the High Court and Court of Appeal, as well as the two dissenting judges in the House of Lords (all of whom would have held the contract void for mistake).

→

---

115. [1932] AC 161 (HL).

116. The terminology used to describe mistake was somewhat different in the 1930s, and the arguments and judgments use the term 'mutual mistake' rather than 'common mistake'. Today, 'mutual mistake' means something completely different (see Chapter 7), and we would describe a *Bell v Lever Brothers* situation as 'common mistake'.

117. [1930] 1 KB 557, 569 (Wright J).

→

We will start with the latter. At first instance, Wright J held that the contract was invalid because of the parties' common mistake. The test he applied looked at whether the mistake related to facts which 'constitute the underlying assumption without which the parties would not have made the contract they did'.[118] The evidence in the case suggested that, had the parties known of Lever Brothers' right to terminate the contract, they would have used that right instead of agreeing to pay compensation. This meant that the mistake went 'to the root of the whole matter', and the contract was accordingly liable to be set aside.[119]

The Court of Appeal, and the dissenting judges in the House of Lords, agreed with Wright J. Drawing a parallel with frustration, Scrutton LJ held that the key issue was whether the contract rested on an implicit understanding that the validity of the contract depended on the existence of a particular state of facts, which were the foundation to the contract, 'essential to its existence', and 'a fundamental reason for making it'.[120] Here, it was obvious that the existence of an effective contract between the parties was such a foundation for *both* parties: Lever Brothers was hardly likely to be willing to make a large payment to terminate a contract if it could have terminated it for nothing, and Bell and Snelling could not honestly have negotiated for such a payment. Lord Warrington, who dissented in the House of Lords, also agreed with this reasoning, and held that the distinction to which the court ought to direct its mind was that between mistakes as to facts that were merely *material* and mistakes as to facts that affected 'the substance of the whole consideration'.[121]

The majority of the House of Lords, however, took a very different approach. Instead of focusing (as the courts below had done) on the relative importance of the mistake to the parties' mutual *decision* to contract, the majority focused on the relationship of the mistake with the *subject matter* of the contract. The question whether 'the mistake . . . is as to the existence of some quality which makes the thing without the quality essentially different from the thing as it was believed to be'.[122] This is a very different question from that asked by the judges in the courts below (and Lord Warrington in his dissent), and the outcome was accordingly also different. If the focus is on the decision to enter the settlement agreement, as it was for the judges in the Court of Appeal, then the distinction between an employment contract that has been breached and one that has not will have foundational significance. If, however, the focus is on the subject matter of the settlement agreement, then an agreement to terminate a broken contract is not 'essentially different' from an agreement to terminate a contract that has not been breached. In both cases, the same agreement is being terminated.[123]

Lord Atkin specifically rejected the intention-oriented tests proposed by the Court of Appeal, and the language of 'basis', which he thought were misleading. Although the test was attractive on paper ('few would demur to this statement'),[124] to extend common mistake to any 'fundamental reason' for making the contract would allow judges 'liberty to construct for the parties contracts which they have not in terms made by importing implications which would appear to make the contract more businesslike or more just'.[125] The narrower test of looking at whether the 'new state of facts makes the contract something different in kind from the contract in the original state of facts' would, in contrast, avoid this danger.[126]

118. Ibid, 564.   119. Ibid, 568.   120. Ibid, 585 (Scrutton LJ), 595–6 (Greer LJ).
121. [1932] AC 161, 207.   122. Ibid, 218 (Lord Atkin).   123. Ibid, 223–4 (Lord Atkin).
124. Ibid, 225 (Lord Atkin).   125. Ibid, 226 (Lord Atkin).   126. Ibid.

Subsequent cases have confirmed that common mistake as to quality will very rarely operate to make a contract void. In *Leaf v International Galleries*,[127] the parties had contracted to sell a painting of Salisbury cathedral which both believed to have been painted by Constable. The Court of Appeal held that the contract was not void for mistake, because the contract was for the sale of a particular painting which had in fact been sold. The fact that it was by a different artist did not render it essentially different. Similarly, in *Kyle Bay Ltd v Underwriters Subscribing Under Policy Number 019057/08/01*,[128] the parties had settled an insurance claim arising from the destruction of a nightclub by fire. The claim had been settled for £205,000, with both parties believing that the policy provided a particular (relatively low) level of cover. It was subsequently discovered that the policy provided a higher level of cover, and that a considerably larger sum of money would have been payable. The owners of the nightclub sought to have the settlement agreement set aside for common mistake. The court held that it would not be set aside, as the mistake did not render the settlement agreement 'a thing essentially different'.

Associated Japanese Bank (International) Ltd v Crédit du Nord SA[129] provides a rare example of a successful plea of common mistake as to quality. The case arose out of a transaction for the sale and leaseback of four machines, which the claimants had funded and which the defendants had agreed to guarantee. It was subsequently discovered that the transaction was fraudulent and the machines never existed. The claimant and the defendant were both innocent of the fraud, which had been carried out by the purchaser. Because the subject matter of the guarantee was the debt, rather than the machines themselves, the case was not one of non-existent subject matter. The court held that the guarantee was void for common mistake, as a guarantee of obligations under a lease with non-existent machines was 'essentially different' from a guarantee of obligations under a lease with four machines which existed.

In so deciding, Steyn J was significantly swayed by the fact that the situation was closely analogous to one of non-existent subject matter.[130] It is unlikely that the defence would have succeeded but for this analogy. These decisions, therefore, highlight the significance of the distinction between the narrower test favoured by Lord Atkin and the intention-oriented test that the minority in that case would have adopted. On the intention-oriented approach to mistake, it is very likely that the contract in *Kyle Bay*, and possibly *Leaf v International Galleries*, would have been set aside. In both cases, the mistakes arguably affected 'the substance of the whole consideration', and were 'a fundamental reason' for the contract. The effect of placing the focus away from the parties' intention, and instead on the impact of the mistake on the performance, is to substantially reduce the ability of courts to intervene to reallocate risks to which a party unexpectedly finds itself subject.

10.3.5 Remedies for common mistake

The consequences of common mistake can be briefly and pithily stated. Common mistake renders the contract void. In law, the contract is treated as if it never came into

---

127. [1950] 2 KB 86 (CA).   128. [2007] EWCA Civ 57.
129. [1989] 1 WLR 255.   130. Ibid, 269.

being. A court has no remedial flexibility or discretion—it cannot, unlike frustration, make orders for sharing expenses or paying for benefits. A party who has provided a benefit to another may have a remedy in *quantum meruit* for the fair value of the benefit,[131] but a party who has incurred expenses in reliance will have no remedy.

For a while, the courts attempted to get around the narrowness of this position by relying on a separate, and broader, doctrine of mistake that had existed in equity. The equitable doctrine was not as restrictive as the common law doctrine. Additionally, it rendered the contract voidable rather than void, which gave courts discretion to order a party to pay for benefits provided to it by the other party. This discretion was used in cases like *Cooper v Phibbs*,[132] where the nephew was ordered to pay the uncle for the value of improvements made to the property.

In *Solle v Butcher*,[133] the Court of Appeal held that this doctrine had not been affected by *Bell v Lever Brothers*, and that courts could continue to invoke their discretionary powers under the equitable doctrine of mistake. However, the Court of Appeal in *The Great Peace*[134] held that this was inconsistent with the actual ruling in *Bell*. The case related to a contract under which the *Great Peace*, a ship, was engaged to assist another ship, the *Cape Providence*, which was in trouble. The parties wrongly believed the ships to be closer to each other than they actually were. When the owners of the *Cape Providence* realized the true position, they cancelled the contract. The owners of the Great Peace sued for breach, and the defendants argued that the contract was void for common mistake. Under the rule in *Bell v Lever Brothers*, the contract was not void. The *Great Peace* would still have arrived on time to assist the ship, just not as quickly as was thought. This meant that performance was not 'essentially different'. Under the broader equitable rule, however, the contract could have been set aside. The Court of Appeal held that the equitable rule had not survived the decision in *Bell v Lever Brothers*. The contract was, therefore, valid. The result is that courts no longer have remedial discretion in relation to common mistake, and can neither refuse to set aside the contract nor make any orders to mitigate the hardship that setting aside the contract may cause.

10.4 In conclusion: hardship and the basis of the transaction

What, then, does the discussion in this chapter tell us about the strengths and limitations of the doctrines of frustration and common mistake? A key issue facing the law is the tension between the *commercial* needs that lead people to seek legal redress and the *doctrinal* approach that the law deploys in response to those needs. The *commercial* need underlying frustration and common mistake is changed circumstances. A party finds that they are performing the contract in circumstances they did not expect or intend, and as a result are finding themselves facing a burden they did not agree to take on, or holding losses they were not contractually intended to bear. The law, however, does not deal with fundamental changes in *circumstances*, only with fundamental changes in the *subject matter* of the transaction. Although a change in the subject matter is almost

131. See Chapter 17, section 17.4.2.   132. (1867) LR 2 HL 149.   133. [1950] 1 KB 671.
134. *Great Peace Shipping Ltd v Tsavliris Salvage (International) Ltd* [2002] EWCA Civ 1407.

always a result of a change in circumstances, the law is not responding to the change in circumstances itself, but only to the effect it has had upon the subject matter of the contract. It does not ask the question: 'Was it intended that this party would bear these losses?' The question which it asks is, instead, 'Is this—the performance that can actually be delivered—what the parties contracted for? Is this the thing that, metaphorically speaking, they intended to "buy" and "sell"?' The law will only intervene if the answer to this question is 'No, this is a radically different thing.' It will not intervene otherwise.

This focus on the subject matter also runs through the remedies that English law grants in the event of frustration or common mistake. The all-or-nothing character of the remedy, focusing on upholding, discharging (frustration), or annulling (common mistake) the contract, makes perfect sense if we see the law as being concerned with upholding the integrity of the subject matter of the contract, but not if we see it as being concerned with the allocation of unallocated losses. Similarly, the focus on fairly valuing benefits in s 1(3), and the lack of any power to assess and fairly distribute losses in either frustration or common mistake, also makes sense in the context of a focus on the subject matter, rather than the contractual allocation of risk.

A more explicit focus on losses and hardship would certainly make the law more commercially realistic, and would not require the courts to be any more interventionist or paternalistic than they already are. Cases such as *Davis Contractors Ltd v Fareham UDC*[135] would be decided precisely the same way as they already were under such an approach, albeit for a different, and more commercially sensible, reason: that in a works contract it is almost always the parties' intention that the contractor bear the risk of fluctuations in the price of labour. That said, there is little indication of any impending shift in the courts' approach to frustration, and the current problems are likely to continue to exist for the foreseeable future.

This does not mean that the law of contract leaves parties without any way of dealing with fundamental changes in circumstances. It provides a number of tools which enable the parties to design clauses and mechanisms which have precisely this effect. *Force majeure* clauses, for example, almost always deal with changes in circumstances, not the subject matter. Price adjustment clauses, discussed in Chapter 9, are another and more precise way of dealing with a more limited set of changes in circumstances. English law has little difficulty with giving effect to such clauses. The point to take away, therefore, is that English law puts the onus of designing ways of coping with changes in circumstances on the parties. If they fail to do so, the court will not do so either: the parties will be held bound to perform the contract as written.

Key points

- English law recognizes two distinct ways of dealing with unplanned contingencies: frustration and common mistake. Frustration applies to situations where circumstances have changed after the contract was formed, whereas common mistake applies where the parties mistakenly assumed something to be true which was subsequently discovered to be untrue.

135. [1956] AC 696 (HL).

- Both doctrines are narrow, and will only be applied in exceptional circumstances. They will not apply unless the impact on the contract is fundamental—rendering it a thing 'radically different' (frustration) or 'essentially different' (common mistake). They will also not apply if the risk was expressly or implicitly allocated by the contract.

- Frustration is largely confined to three types of circumstances: impossibility, super- vening illegality, and frustrated purposes. The last of these, in particular, is kept within very narrow bounds by the court. Frustration discharges a contract with effect from the date of the frustrating event. The parties no longer have any contractual obliga- tions to each other, but the court has the discretion to order payment for benefits that have already been provided, and to make some allowances for expenses that have been incurred.

- Common mistake is largely confined to three types of mistakes which are shared by the parties: mistakes as to the existence of the subject matter, mistakes as to the possibil- ity of performance, and mistakes as to a quality of the subject matter. The last of these is a very narrow one, which is rarely successful. Common mistake renders a contract void. A court has no remedial discretion. A party who has paid a deposit or provided benefit may have an action in restitution, but a party who has incurred expenses has no remedy.

Assess your learning

You should be able to respond to each of the following points with a confident 'yes'. If you can't, then you should revisit the sections listed against that point.

Can you:

(a) *Identify* the circumstances under which a contract will be frustrated? (Section 10.2.2)

(b) *Outline* the consequences of frustration, and *describe* the remedial powers available to a court making an order to discharge a frustrated contract? (Section 10.2.4)

(c) *Identify* the circumstances under which a contract will be void for common mistake? (Sections 10.3.1 to 10.3.4)

(d) *Outline* the consequences of a contract being void for common mistake? (Section 10.3.5)

(e) *Explain* the relationship between frustration and common mistake, and the manner in which their application is influenced by the terms of the parties' contract? (Sections 10.1, 10.2.3, and 10.3.1)

In relation to each of the above, you should be able to:

(i) identify and clearly explain the key rules and principles;

(ii) identify the key cases and statutes, and why they matter;

(iii) apply the principles and cases to specific real or hypothetical fact situations;

(iv) evaluate the limitations, if any, of the law as it currently stands.

Further reading

PS Atiyah, '*Couturier v Hastie* and the Sale of Non-Existent Goods' (1957) 73 LQR 340.

R Brownsword, 'Henry's Lost Spectacle and Hutton's Lost Speculation: A Classic Riddle Solved?' (1985) 129 SJ 860.

JW Carter and GJ Tolhurst, 'Gigs n' Restitution: Frustration and the Statutory Adjustment of Payments and Expenses' (1996) 10 JCL 264.

S Hedley, 'Carriage by Sea: Frustration and *Force Majeure*' (1990) 49 CLJ 209.

C Macmillan, 'How Temptation Led to Mistake: An Explanation of *Bell v Lever Brothers Ltd*' (2003) 119 LQR 625.

C Macmillan, *Mistakes in Contract Law* (Hart 2010).

E McKendrick, 'The Consequences of Frustration: The Law Reform (Frustrated Contracts) Act 1945' in E McKendrick (ed), *Force Majeure and Frustration of Contract* (2nd edn, Informa Law 1995).

JP Swanton, 'The Concept of Self-Induced Frustration' (1990) 2 JCL 206.

G Treitel, *Frustration and Force Majeure* (3rd edn, Sweet & Maxwell 2014).

Regulating contracts

PART III

Introduction

An important aspect of the law of contract, which the book has hinted at but not as yet discussed in detail, is the way in which it responds to the presence of power and inequality in contracting. As we saw in Chapter 2, in the real world, a very significant proportion of contracts are not freely negotiated. Instead, the terms are imposed by one party on the other. This has profound normative implications. Consider your experience in signing up for an account with Facebook—or, for that matter, any other online service. You are required to agree to detailed terms and conditions to sign up, but you have no ability to influence those terms. Nor can you request information that you may need to make an informed decision. You cannot, for example, obtain information as to which types of advertisers Facebook sells your personal data to, how those advertisers use that data to build up a profile on you, or even what their internal guidelines are as to acceptable use of that data.

This happens because the formation process is very often one-sided. The *benefits* flowing under the contract are not one-sided. The services Facebook provides may be free, but they are not gratuitous. Facebook needs your personal data at least as much as you require their services in your social life, and both parties therefore get something of value out of the contract. However, Facebook does not need *you* as a specific individual to sign up for their services. They require a critical mass of individuals, certainly, but whether a given person does or does not sign up is a matter of indifference. Their customers are entirely fungible. You have very little bargaining power as far as they are concerned. They, in contrast, have a considerable amount of bargaining power over you: if you want their services, you need to accept their terms.

Issues of this type are particularly salient in the world of consumer contracting, but they also occur in commercial contracts. In the construction sector, for example, project managers are often spoiled for choice when it comes to finding subcontractors. Subcontractors have far less choice and, consequently, far less bargaining power.

The fact that many, if not most, contracts are characterized by inequality of bargaining power raises a number of issues for the law. Should the law take account of it? Does it matter at all that one party 'had the other over a barrel' while negotiating, to use a figure of speech which recurs in the case law, or that one party was told to 'take it or leave it'?

As with most issues in English law, these matters cannot be reduced to black and white. The question is not *whether* the law should intervene, but *when* it should do so, and to what *end*. Notwithstanding the rhetoric of freedom of contract, and the persistence of the idea of '*caveat emptor*'—that protecting himself is the buyer's responsibility, not the law's—English law regulates contracts and has done so for centuries. Some rules of English law regulate the bargaining process by setting standards in relation to the flow of information in bargaining, and by setting limits to the pressure which one party can put the other under. Other rules regulate the terms of the contract themselves, by creating mandatory duties which the parties cannot contract out of, and by creating mechanisms to ensure that the public interest is protected.

In this Part, we will look at each of these in turn. The first two chapters examine the regulation of the bargaining *process*, looking respectively at how English law deals with the problem of untrue statements (Chapter 11) and how it sets limits to hard bargaining and the application of pressure (Chapter 12). The next two chapters look at how the law regulates contract *terms*, starting with rules that are intended to protect weaker parties (Chapter 13) and concluding with rules that are intended to protect the public interest (Chapter 14).

11

Untrue statements

Misrepresentation and unilateral mistake

'For truth is precious and divine;
Too rich a pearl for carnal swine.'*

* Samuel Butler, *Hudibras* II:2:257.

Problem 11: setting the context

Consider the facts set out in the following scenario:

Student anger as college's dodgy practices exposed

Students at Sarum College are up in arms after the college's graduate earnings claims were shown to be riddled with serious inaccuracies.

In its most recent prospectus, the college painted a rosy picture of its students' employment prospects, citing government studies in relation to the premium a typical graduate could expect to earn over the course of their career. A substantial number of students at the college have confirmed that this statement played an important role in their decision to study there.

Now, however, documents leaked by a whistle-blower have suggested that these figures bear little resemblance to the actual earnings of the college's graduates.

Last year, the Institute for Economic Research and Analysis (IERA), an independent think tank, carried out a study of the earnings of graduates working in England. It found that graduates of a number of institutions earned (on average) less than non-graduates. The IERA did not publish the names of these institutions, although individual institutions were informed of its findings. Documents which we have seen show that Sarum College is one of the institutions whose graduates earn less than non-graduates. Shockingly, it appears that the college decided that it would not alter its marketing material in any way, despite the IERA's findings.

A spokesperson for the college would neither confirm nor deny the accuracy of the leaked documents, but insisted that the college had acted appropriately. She said that the prospectus was based on government data, and pointed out that it made no specific claims in relation to its graduates' earnings.

Student representatives, however, have declared themselves 'entirely unsatisfied' with the college's statement. They are understood to be demanding a substantial refund of their fees on the basis that the college induced them to enrol under false pretences.

This problem presents a classic situation where one party enters into a contract relying on the other party's statements, which subsequently turn out to be somewhat misleading. But how much of an obligation should a party have to place the truth before the other party? When does a statement become too misleading to be justifiable? And what recourse should this give rise to?

11.1 Introduction: the problem of information asymmetry

When we decide to enter into a contract, we invariably base our decision on our **knowledge**, beliefs, and impressions about the things we are contracting for, and the persons we are contracting with. Consider how we as consumers decide to buy a particular brand of smartphone (eg an iPhone) rather than another (eg a Samsung). We form an impression about the characteristics of each phone from independent reviews, advertisements, our friends' feedback, and the sales pitch we encounter in store. On the basis of that impression, we come to a decision as to which phone better suits our needs. Businesses work in a similar way. A company deciding which supplier it wants to use will also form an impression about the desirable and undesirable characteristics of each supplier on its shortlist based on information it gathers, and come to a final decision based on those impressions.

A significant portion of this information comes from the person with whom we are contracting. The phraseology used in the law of contract can often make it seem that the law assumes all parties to the contract to have the same set of background factual information. The legal rules on interpretation, for example, speak of 'the information available to the parties', in the plural, as if the information available to party A is the same as the information available to party B.[1] But this is not usually true. It is almost always the case that one party knows things the other does not, and that the only source of information you have for some facts is the other party. Problem 11 at the head of this chapter presents one example, but the majority of the transactions we enter into on an everyday basis are similar. Consider the following scenario:

Illustration 11.1

You go into a used electronics shop intending to buy a second-hand smartphone. A salesman in the shop shows you a number of different phones, and tells you a little bit about the condition of each phone.

In this example, you know nothing at all about the condition of the phones you see. You do not know whether they are in working order, whether the battery holds charge, or for that matter even whether the shop has put a completely different set of innards into the case of a phone. More importantly, you have no practicable way of ascertaining any of these things. Even if you had the necessary technical skill, the shop is unlikely to let you disassemble the phone or subject it to tests to satisfy yourself as to its condition. You are entirely dependent on the information provided to you by the shop.

Situations like this are not exceptional. Economists describe them as involving 'imperfect knowledge', or 'information asymmetry'.[2] The vast majority of contractual transactions involve some measure of information asymmetry. Information asymmetry creates the scope for things to go wrong in at least two ways. First, a party may fail to disclose important information which would have swayed the other party's decision had she known of it. The survey data in Problem 11 is a clear example. So too is Illustration 11.1, where a sales assistant could easily show you a phone without telling you that it had a cracked screen, which the shop has replaced with a non-original

---

1. See the discussion in Chapter 7 ('Interpreting the terms').

2. The classic paper in economics on this issue is G Akerlof, 'The Market for "Lemons": Quality Uncertainty and the Market Mechanism' (1970) 84 Quarterly Journal of Economics 488. George Akerlof, Michael Spence, and Joseph Stiglitz, were jointly awarded the Nobel Prize in Economics in 2001 for their work on information asymmetry.

third-party screen. Secondly, a party may provide incorrect information, by telling the other party something that is not in fact true.

In some cases, the parties deal with the problem directly by incorporating appropriate provisions in their contract. It is, for example, possible for the parties to agree a term under which one party takes on a contractual obligation to ensure that the information is true.[3] Where the parties have done this, the legal position is straightforward. If the information is false, the party who has taken on the contractual obligation is in breach of contract, and will face the consequences that follow from breach.[4] But where the parties fail to include a term, the task of dealing with the problems posed by information asymmetry falls to the law. In these cases, the phenomenon of information asymmetry poses a threefold problem.

The first problem is figuring out *when* to assign significance to information asymmetry. In everyday transactions, information asymmetry is often irrelevant. Consider the following advertisement:

Illustration 11.2

The London and South-Western Railway Company
The cleanest railway toilets in England!

The toilets on our trains are cleaned three times as often as the toilets on any other train company's services.

The train company clearly knows a lot more than you do about how often their toilets are cleaned. But their superior knowledge will typically have little, if any, relevance to your decision to contract. A commuter's decision to take a train will be determined more by their schedule than by the frequency at which the toilets are cleaned. In other situations, however, including those described in Illustration 11.1 and Problem 11, the information asymmetry and the party's statements do, in fact, profoundly affect the decision to contract. The task for the law is to establish a sensible basis on which to distinguish situations where information asymmetries matter from those in which they do not.

The second problem is one of figuring out *how* to deal with information asymmetry. What should happen if a court finds that information asymmetry did, in fact, matter in a particular situation—that, for example, the phone in Illustration 11.1 did not hold more than half-an-hour's charge? What remedies should the parties have? Should the affected party be able to get out of the contract? Should the court order the payment of compensation?

The third problem is one of figuring out *how broad* a duty the court should impose. Should the law take a 'do not conceal' approach, in which it imposes an affirmative obligation on the parties to disclose all relevant facts to each other (thus requiring the seller in Illustration 11.1 and the college in Problem 11 to make a clean breast of the

---

3. See Chapter 6 ('Assembling the contract').
4. See Chapters 15 ('Breach of contract') and 16 ('Compensatory remedies').

facts)? Or should it take a much lighter-touch 'do not lie' approach, where it merely imposes an obligation to ensure that the things you do say to your counterparty are accurate (thus requiring the seller in Illustration 11.1 and the college in Problem 11 to answer all questions honestly, but not to volunteer information unless requested)?

There is no easy answer to these questions, and different legal systems take different approaches to solving the underlying problem. Some legal systems, particularly civil law systems such as Germany, deal with the problem of information asymmetry directly and explicitly. German law deals with information asymmetry by imposing a pre-contractual duty of good faith, which prevents a party having superior knowledge from using that superior knowledge to the detriment or disadvantage of the other party. English law takes a very different approach. There is no general duty to disclose relevant information in English law, nor are there any general principles specifically directed to the problem of information asymmetry. Instead, as we will see in greater detail in this chapter, it deals with the problem of untrue or misleading statements through three different doctrines. Two of these, **misrepresentation** and **mistake**, apply to all transactions. The third, *unfair commercial practices*, creates special rules that only apply to consumer transactions. Misrepresentation is by far the broadest and more generally applicable doctrine. We will therefore begin by examining how the law of misrepresentation works, the sort of situations in which it applies, and the remedies it provides (section 11.2). We will then move to briefly examine the law of mistake (section 11.3), followed by an outline of two specific unfair practices related to untrue statements; namely 'misleading actions' and 'misleading omissions' (section 11.4). We will conclude with a comparative assessment of how well English law deals with the underlying problem of information asymmetries and the duties of the parties in pre-contractual discussions.

11.2 Untrue statements: the law of misrepresentation

In conceptual terms, misrepresentation is the simplest and most direct way of dealing with the problem of untrue pre-contractual statements. The basic principles of the law of misrepresentation can be stated pithily. If one party makes a statement of fact to another (a *'representation'*), and that statement turns out to be untrue, that party has made a misrepresentation. If the misrepresentation contributes to the other party's decision to enter into the contract, it is said to have *induced* the contract. A party who was induced to enter into a contract as a result of a misrepresentation has two remedies. First, he has the remedy of *rescission*, which gives him the option to rescind or cancel the contract by giving notice to the other party. Secondly, he can in some cases claim damages for the loss caused by the misrepresentation. If the misrepresentation did not induce the contract, in contrast, the contract remains fully valid and no consequences flow from the misrepresentation.

Despite its conceptual simplicity, the details of the law of misrepresentation are somewhat complex, especially on the question of the parties' remedies. As with many areas of English contract law, the legal rules pertaining to misrepresentation represent a complex mixture of common law, equity, and statute. More unusually, several aspects of the remedies for misrepresentation are derived from tort law rather than contract, and remain subject to overlapping actions in tort. This has left the law with a number of peculiar features, which the courts and Parliament have only been partially successful at ameliorating.

The source of this complexity lies in the fact that dealing with information asymmetries always involves a balancing act. Acquiring and verifying information can be onerous even for the person making the representation. Consider, once again, Illustration 11.1, and the specific position of a seller who makes a representation that a phone is in full working order. A phone can be used in a lot of ways—ranging from emulating vintage gaming consoles to aiding medical surgery—not all of which a seller will be able to test. How much does the seller have to do to verify what he is saying before making a representation? Can he defend himself against a charge of misrepresentation by saying that he carried out all the tests that a reasonable person would have, and honestly believed his statement? Equally, can the college in Problem 11 defend itself by saying that it based its statement on one of two possible data sets?

Where we set the boundary of liability depends on which of two views we take of the purpose of misrepresentation. The first sees it as being about setting standards of conduct for *representors*. It focuses on the state of mind of the representor, and determines the boundaries of liability with reference to whether she made the representation honestly and after having exercised some care to ascertain its veracity. The second sees it as being about protecting *representees* who have relied on representations. It focuses on the representation's impact on the party to whom it is made, and consequently tends towards imposing liability whenever the misrepresentation played a role in the decision to enter into a contract.

English law has traditionally followed a combination of both. The law divides misrepresentations into three classes: those that are *fraudulent*, those that are *negligent*, and those that are *innocent*. Until the 1960s, these distinctions—which reflect a focus on the representor's conduct—were of fundamental importance to the law on misrepresentation. Since then, English law has increasingly tilted towards protecting representees. Whilst the distinction between the three types of misrepresentation has not been abolished, it has been significantly eroded, particularly in relation to remedies and the position of innocent misrepresentation. The growing focus on representees permeates all aspects of the law of misrepresentation, as we will see in greater detail in this section.

11.2.1 **False statements**

A party makes a misrepresentation if he makes a statement which is factually false. In English law, this rule has three elements: the absence of general duties to disclose relevant facts, an objective approach to construing ambiguous statements, and a distinction between statements of fact and statements of opinion. In this section, we will look at each of these in turn.

Duties to disclose

The first point to note is that misrepresentation is triggered by false *statements*. For an action of misrepresentation to be maintainable, there must have been either a statement or conduct that was equivalent to a statement. The courts may imply a representation from conduct if a reasonable person would naturally assume from the other party's conduct that 'the true state of facts did not exist and that, if it did, he would necessarily have been informed of it'. But that does not dilute the requirement that the implication must be based on clear words or clear conduct of the representor.[5] Silence is not misrepresentation, and an action is not maintainable simply because a party failed to disclose a relevant fact. In *Fletcher v Krell*,[6] Fletcher had been engaged by Krell to act as a governess for a family in Argentina. She signed her name as 'Margaret Fletcher, spinster'. Before she was due to leave for Argentina, the family discovered that she had been divorced, and Krell informed her that her services would not be required. She sued successfully for breach of contract. The court held that she had not been under a duty to disclose the fact that she had been divorced, and had not misstated her status in describing herself as a spinster.

As this suggests, there is no general duty to disclose relevant facts, and parties are free to conceal facts as long as they do not lie. To this general rule, four exceptions have been carved out by case law and legislation, which we will now briefly examine.

Contracts *uberrimae fidei*

First, some types of contracts are held to be contracts of utmost good faith (or, to use the legal term, *uberrimae fidei*). Here, parties must deal with each other in good faith and make a full declaration of all material facts. Insurance contracts are the classic example of contracts which are *uberrimae fidei*, and at common law as well as statute,[7] a party taking out a policy must disclose all material facts and risks to the other party. This principle is narrow. It is confined to types of contracts that have already been recognized as contracts of utmost good faith. Courts are reluctant to widen the category any further. In *Fletcher v Krell*, one reason the court gave for refusing to hold that there had been a misrepresentation was that doing so would, in effect, turn contracts of employment into contracts of utmost good faith, and that was not a step they were willing to take.

True statements that become untrue

Secondly, a duty to disclose changed circumstances may arise at common law, if its result is to render untrue a statement that was true when it was made. The leading case is *Davies v London & Provincial*.[8] An agent of London & Provincial (L&P) had retained some money belonging to L&P. L&P believed this to be criminal embezzlement and instructed the police to arrest him. They then were advised that the actions were not criminal and they withdrew the instructions. The agent's friends in the meantime approached L&P's officials, and attempted to negotiate a settlement. The officials referred to the 'embezzlement' and said that the agent would not be arrested before Tuesday. They did not, however, disclose that he could not be arrested at all. The

---

5. *Property Alliance Group Ltd v Royal Bank of Scotland plc* [2018] EWCA Civ 355, [2018] 1 WLR 3529, [132].

6. (1873) 28 LT(NS) 105, (1873) 42 LJ QB 55.   7. See eg Marine Insurance Act 1906, s 18(1).

8. (1878) 8 Ch D 469.

agent's friends arranged for £2,000 to be deposited with trustees for the security of the company. Upon learning that the agent could not have been arrested, they sought to have the agreement set aside.

The court held that L&P had a duty of disclosure in this case. Apart from contracts *uberrimae fidei* and fiduciary relations (where equity imposes similar duties), a duty of disclosure also arose to correct a previously true statement which was no longer true:

> If a statement has been made which is true at the time, but which during the course of the negotiations becomes untrue, then the person who knows that it has become untrue is under an obligation to disclose to the other the change of circumstances.[9]

Similarly, in *Spice Girls Ltd v Aprilia World Service BV*,[10] the Spice Girls, a popular girl band, had been hired by the defendants to promote their products. After the contract was entered into, one of the members made it clear that she intended to leave the group. The group failed to disclose this to the defendants, even though it would have prevented the contract from being carried out. It was held that their action amounted to a misrepresentation.

Duties imposed by law or contract

Thirdly, duties of disclosure may be imposed by law. Financial regulation imposes significant duties of disclosure on financial intermediaries dealing with consumers. Consumers also have broad rights of information under legal rules dealing with unfair trading. These are discussed in section 10.4.

Finally, parties may also impose duties of disclosure on other parties by including a provision in their contract requiring the other party to disclose all material facts, or warrant that it has disclosed all material facts. Provisions of this type are common in contracts ranging from complex commercial transactions to contracts to buy and sell houses. Thus whilst the general principle remains that there is no general duty to disclose, they can in practice be imposed in a number of ways.

The role of reasonableness

The second point to note, following on from the duty to disclose, is that in determining whether a statement is true or false, the court will construe it objectively, and in context. It does not matter that the person making the statement had no intention to deceive, and genuinely believed it to be true. The court is concerned with the objective truth of the statement, not the representor's subjective belief.

Where a statement is capable of having more than one meaning, the courts will adopt a test of reasonableness to determine which meaning was intended. This is illustrated by the decision of the Court of Appeal in *Foster v Action Aviation*.[11] Foster was interested in buying an aircraft made by a company called Emivest. Action Aviation offered to sell him an 'as new' aircraft that had been used for demonstration. Foster asked the chairman of Action Aviation whether the aircraft had ever been in an accident. The chairman replied: 'No, I bought the aircraft new; it's never been in an accident.' As it happened, the aircraft had suffered a hard landing after which it had had

---

9. (Fry J).   10. [2002] EWCA Civ 15.   11. [2014] EWCA Civ 1368.

to be repaired. This accident was logged and reported to Emivest and the insurers. It was not, however, reported to the aviation authorities because it was not reportable under the rules. Foster bought the aircraft, but was unhappy with it and resold it at a considerable loss. When he discovered the accident, he sought to claim damages on the ground of misrepresentation. In evidence, it was found that the chairman had no intention to deceive Foster, and had genuinely believed that an unreportable incident did not amount to an accident. Nevertheless, the court held that there had been a negligent misrepresentation by the company:

> however much the incident did not have to be reported to the FAA it was still an accident in the sense used by Mr Foster in his question and Mr Harding should have appreciated that was the way in which his negative answer should be understood.[12]

In other words, a representor will have made a misrepresentation if he failed to disclose a fact covered by a reasonable reading of what the question asked. The fact that he understood the question differently is irrelevant.

Similarly, in *Burki v Seventy Thirty*,[13] the claimant had subscribed to a matchmaking service on the basis of representations by the service provider as to the number of men who were on its database. The database included men who were active subscribers as well as men who had been subscribers in the past but were no longer so. The High Court held that the statement was a misrepresentation. Any reasonable person would have understood the statement as being about 'the numbers of wealthy, actively engaged paying members' as opposed to former members who were still on the books.[14]

Applying this to Problem 11, the key issue will be whether the college's representation regarding employment prospects would have been understood on a reasonable reading to refer to its graduates specifically (as the students claim) or to the national picture (as it claims). This will turn on the precise wording of the statement and the context in which it appears, but it should be evident that the position is in any event not as straightforward as either the college or the students make it. Where the representation is framed in words that are ambiguous, the reasonable reading is not always easy to ascertain objectively.

The fact/opinion distinction

Thirdly, following the duty to disclose and the test of reasonableness, the statement must be *factually* false. This excludes two types of statements. First, it excludes statements which are 'mere puff', for example a claim that a café serves 'the best coffee in town'. These are not intended to be claims of objective fact and hence will not give rise to a misrepresentation.[15] Secondly, it distinguishes statements of *fact* from statements of *opinion*. A statement of opinion does not ordinarily give rise to a misrepresentation. Only a statement of fact does.

The exclusion of statements of opinion is, in principle, both logical and necessary. In everyday life, we frequently make statements that are intended to articulate a view rather than to assert the existence of a state of facts. But the divide between fact and

---

12. Ibid, [23].   13. [2018] EWHC 2151 (QB).   14. Ibid, [136].
15. See Chapter 6 ('Assembling the contract').

opinion is not a sharp one, and it can create difficulties in a range of circumstances. Consider the following example:

Illustration 11.3

> You are planning a summer break in southern Europe with your flatmates. You are unsure whether to book your holiday in Ibiza or Skiathos. You visit a travel agent, who says to you: 'You'll have more fun with our Ibiza package.'

At first sight, this might appear to be clearly a statement of opinion rather than of fact. 'Having fun' is not an objectively measurable quantity, and it is not generally possible to assess 'likelihood of having fun' in objective factual terms. But consider the following sequel:

> You arrive in Ibiza. On arrival, you are horrified to find that the travel agent has booked you into a run-down hotel which is 12 miles from the nearest bars and nightclubs, without any transport links.

Let us, for the moment, set aside the question of whether this is a breach of contract.[16] Were the agent's words 'you'll have more fun with our Ibiza package' a misrepresentation? Even though they are phrased in the form of an opinion, there is a strong case for saying that they are. In English law, the fact/opinion distinction is qualified in three different ways. First, the distinction is *contextual* rather than literal. The representor's words are not looked at in the abstract. They are looked at in the context in which they were said. Words that in one context would appear to be a statement of fact may well be treated as a statement of opinion in another context. Secondly, any statement of opinion must be of an opinion that was *honestly held*. If you express an opinion that you do not actually hold, then your statement is a misrepresentation even if it is phrased as an opinion. Thirdly, statements of opinion can sometimes contain an *implicit assertion of fact*. If that implicit assertion is false, the statement will be a misrepresentation.

Let us look at each of these in turn, starting with the contextual character of the distinction. The decisions in *Bisset v Wilkinson*[17] and *Esso Petroleum v Mardon*[18] illustrate how the transactional context can influence whether a statement is seen as a matter of fact or opinion.

Case in depth: *Bisset v Wilkinson* [1927] AC 177 (PC)

This case arose by way of appeal to the Privy Council from New Zealand. Bisset owned land in New Zealand, which he agreed to sell to Wilkinson and Alexander. The land was to be used for sheep farming. While some of it had been used for sheep farming in the past, portions had

→

---

16. The remedies you might have for breach of contract in this sort of situation are discussed in greater detail in Chapter 16 ('Compensatory remedies').
17. [1927] AC 177 (PC).   18. [1976] 1 QB 801 (CA).

lain fallow after being abandoned by a previous occupier and had never been used to farm sheep. Before the purchase was agreed, the farm had been inspected by the purchasers and by Wilkinson's father, an experienced sheep farmer. In the course of discussions, Wilkinson asked Bisset about the carrying capacity of the farm (ie how many sheep it could support through the winter). It was conceded at trial that Bisset said it could support 2,000 sheep, if it were worked as he had worked it with a six-horse team.[19]

Wilkinson and Alexander purchased the property in 1919. The agreement provided for a down-payment, with the balance to be paid on 1 May 1924. The defendants attempted to use the property for sheep farming, but were unable to support anywhere near 2,000 sheep on the property during the winter in 1920. In 1921, the sheep price collapsed due to market fluctuations, and the defendants shifted from sheep farming to cropping and dairy farming. When the final payment fell due in 1924, the defendants refused to pay and sought to rescind the contract for misrepresentation.

Sim J in the Supreme Court at Dunedin held that the contract was not voidable for misrepresentation, on two grounds.[20] First, he held that the statement as to the carrying capacity of the farm was one of opinion rather than fact. This was because of the peculiar circumstances of the case. Ordinarily, a statement about the carrying capacity of a farm would indeed be a statement of fact. In this case, however, the purchasers knew that a portion of the farm had not previously been used for sheep farming, and they also knew how many sheep the farm was carrying when it was sold because they had inspected it. As such, they were not justified in 'regarding anything said by the plaintiff as to the carrying capacity as being anything more than an expression of his opinion on the subject'.[21] An opinion could only be a misrepresentation if it was not honestly held, and on the facts this opinion was honestly held. He held further that the true carrying capacity of the farm had not been proved, as the farm had not been used for sheep farming for long enough. This meant that the purchasers had failed to show that the statement was false.

On appeal, the Court of Appeal of New Zealand reversed Sim J, and held that the statement was a misrepresentation. They rejected the argument that the statement was merely one of opinion, on the basis that saying that a seller 'was giving only an opinion' when asked about the carrying capacity of a farm was 'improbable and contrary to what takes place in bargaining about a sheep farm'. Given that Bisset had been expressly asked what the carrying capacity of the farm was, the logical reading of his response was that he was answering the question, and not simply stating his opinion.[22]

On further appeal, the Privy Council reversed the Court of Appeal and restored the judgment of Sim J. As with Sim J, they placed emphasis on the fact that a portion of the farm had lain fallow and not been used for sheep farming by anyone. This fact, they held, was 'most material', and meant that any statement as to the farm's carrying capacity could only be one of opinion.[23] They also concurred with Sim J's finding that the true carrying capacity of the farm had not been proved.

---

19. The precise wording of his answer was disputed, but the form of words did not influence the final decision.

20. (1925) 26 GLR 329.   21. Ibid, 330.   22. Ibid, 334 (Stout CJ).

23. [1927] AC 177 (PC), 183–4.

Bisset v Wilkinson is important because it illustrates how much cases in misrepresentation are influenced by the views of individual judges as to which facts are more salient. An important reason why the Court of Appeal's decision differed from the other two courts was that the Court of Appeal placed emphasis on the general transactional significance of the statement. In the context of buying and selling a sheep farm, any statement as to the carrying capacity of the farm would be received as a statement of fact. Sim J and the Privy Council, in contrast, stressed the specific transactional context of that particular sale. Because all parties knew that a portion of the farm had never been used for sheep farming, any statement as to its carrying capacity could not be received as anything other than a statement of opinion. As the final outcome shows, it is this latter context that is now the salient one.

Bisset v Wilkinson involved a statement that appeared to be one of fact, but which was ultimately held to be one of opinion because of the surrounding facts. *Esso Petroleum v Mardon*,[24] in contrast, involved a statement that, at face value, seemed to be one of opinion, but was ultimately held to be one of fact. Esso Petroleum wanted a new petrol station in Southport, and located a site on a busy street in the centre of the town. They calculated that it would have a throughput of 200,000 gallons a year. Unfortunately, the council insisted in the course of granting planning approval that the station be built back-to-front, so that only the showroom was seen from the street and not the petrol pumps themselves. It was obvious that this would have a negative impact upon the petrol station's throughput, as a casual passer-by on the main street would no longer see the pumps. However, Esso failed to revise its estimated throughput even after it had built the station back-to-front.

Esso then offered a tenancy of the station to Mardon. In evidence, it was found that:

> Mr. Mardon was told that Esso estimated that the throughput of the [site] would amount to 200,000 gallons a year . . . Mr. Mardon then indicated that he thought 100,000 to 150,000 gallons would be a more realistic estimate, but he was convinced by the far greater expertise of, particularly, Mr. Leitch.[25]

In actual fact, the throughput was only 78,000 gallons and Mardon made losses. The parties attempted to renegotiate the contract, but the concessions Esso were willing to make were insufficient to make the business profitable. Esso cut off Mardon's petrol and sued for possession. Mardon gave up the site, and counterclaimed for damages for misrepresentation. Counsel for Esso relied heavily on *Bisset v Wilkinson*, arguing that the cases were indistinguishable.[26] The Court of Appeal, however, held that this case was very different from *Bisset*. In *Bisset*, because the land had never been used for sheep farming, both parties were 'equally able to form an opinion as to its carrying capacity'. Here, however, Esso had special knowledge and skill, in that they knew the patterns of traffic in the town, the throughput of comparable stations, and overall had better experience and expertise. As such, they were in a much better position than Mardon to make the forecast, and were liable accordingly.[27]

Put differently, what the court was in effect saying was that *Bisset v Wilkinson* did not involve any information asymmetry, while *Esso v Mardon* did. All parties in *Bisset*

24. [1976] 1 QB 801 (CA).   25. Ibid, 815 (Lord Denning MR).   26. Ibid, 810.
27. Ibid, 818 (Lord Denning MR).

were equally ignorant of the carrying capacity of the farm, and furthermore the parties knew that they were all equally ignorant. Under the circumstances, the statement could not reasonably have been construed as a representation. In *Esso v Mardon*, in contrast, Esso *did* know more than Mardon. Both parties knew this, and they also knew that Mardon was in fact relying on Esso's superior knowledge. As a result, the reasonable reading of Esso's statements was that they were representations made with a view to inducing the contract.

This brings us to the second limb of the exception, which is that the exception only applies if the opinion is honestly held. Honest belief is not a defence if the statement in question is one of fact, as the case of *Foster v Action Aviation*, discussed earlier, shows. It is a defence if the statement is one of opinion, but the requirement of honesty is important. A person who claims to hold an opinion or intention which she does not actually hold is making a fraudulent statement. This is a misrepresentation even if it is a statement of opinion. In *Edgington v Fitzmaurice*,[28] a company issued a prospectus offering debentures to the public. The prospectus stated that the directors intended to use the debentures to expand the company's business. This was untrue. The directors in fact intended to use them to pay off the company's debts. The claimant, who had subscribed to shares after having read the prospectus, sued for misrepresentation. The court held that the words were a misrepresentation, on the basis that 'the state of a man's mind is as much a fact as the state of his digestion'.

It is not always easy, however, to establish that a person was being dishonest in this sense when expressing an opinion. The state of a man's mind is a hard thing to prove. The evidentiary burden is, however, somewhat ameliorated by the third limb of the exception. This states that an opinion may be held to contain an implicit representation that the representor knows of facts that justify holding the opinion. In *Smith v Land and House Property Corp*,[29] a property offered for sale was described as 'let to a most desirable tenant'. In point of fact, the tenant was in arrears with the rent and went bankrupt shortly after the sale. The court held that the statement was a misrepresentation even though it was couched as an opinion. This was because in stating it, the representor implicitly also represented that he knew facts justifying the opinion.

Let us now return to Illustration 11.3. The discussion above should have given you a good sense as to why the statement by the travel agent is almost certain to have been a misrepresentation. First, the travel agent does have superior expertise, as in *Esso Petroleum v Mardon*. Unlike *Bisset v Wilkinson*, both parties are not equally able to formulate an opinion at the time of contracting, because you as a holidaymaker have not actually seen the hotel or its location. Secondly, the opinion is unlikely to be held to have been honestly held. At the least, the travel agent will be held to have implicitly represented that he knew of facts justifying his opinion that you would have 'more fun' in the place he had found for you, much as in *Smith v Land and House Property Corp*. These cumulatively suggest that the statement will be held to have been a misrepresentation.

What about the college's statement in Problem 11? A statement as to graduate earnings in a prospectus differs from the situations we have been considering so far. Although the college has superior expertise, if the statement is clearly linked to a

---

28. (1885) 29 Ch D 459.   29. (1884) 28 Ch D 7.

specific body of evidence (eg a government study), it is unlikely that it will be held to also implicitly represent that the college knows additional facts going beyond that body of evidence. If, however, the statement was phrased more broadly—for example, a more general statement of its graduates' prospects that are not specifically tied to the government study, then it is likely that it *will* be held to represent that the college knows facts justifying that opinion.

As this suggests, applying the fact/opinion distinction often involves drawing lines which are not easy to draw. As the cases discussed in this section show, the courts tend to draw the line based on their view as to the significance of statements and the manner in which they would have been received, which they examine against the background of the factual context of that specific transaction. This process is not dissimilar to that used in relation to interpretation (discussed in Chapter 7), and reflects the same underlying principle of contextual objectivity.

11.2.2 **Materiality**

For a misrepresentation to be actionable, it must be material in the sense that it must induce the contract. To put it differently, it must play a role in bringing about the contract. However, it does not have to be the sole factor or even the decisive factor which motivated the representee to enter into the contract. It is sufficient if it is *a* cause, or one factor among many, even if it is not *the* exclusive cause. Recent cases have tended to express this by saying that the misrepresentation must play a 'real and substantial part' in the representee's decision to enter into the contract, but not necessarily a 'decisive part'.[30] In *Edgington v Fitzmaurice*,[31] discussed in the previous section, the claimant had been induced to subscribe to the debenture partially by the misrepresentation and partially by his own misreading of the prospectus. The court held that the contract could be rescinded for misrepresentation, as the misrepresentation was one of the factors that had induced the contract. Applying this to the facts of Problem 11, the import is that Sarum College will be liable even if a student was induced to choose Sarum College due to a combination of factors—for example, the misrepresentation as well as the fact that she could live at home while studying there.

The bar imposed by this requirement is not a very high one. Nevertheless, the requirement is a real one. The mere fact that an untrue representation was made is insufficient. If the representee treated it as irrelevant, the misrepresentation will not be actionable. In *JEB Fasteners v Marks Bloom*,[32] the claimant had taken over a company after inspecting its accounts. The accounts had been inaccurately prepared, in circumstances that meant that they constituted a misrepresentation. In evidence, however, it was shown that the purpose of the takeover was to secure the services of two directors of the company, and that it would have proceeded even if accurate accounts had been presented. The court held that the claimant had no remedy for misrepresentation, as the misrepresentation did not induce the contract. Returning to Problem 11, if a student read the information in the prospectus and immediately dismissed it as 'just

---

30. *Avon Insurance plc & ors v Swire Fraser Ltd & anor* [2000] CLC 665, [18] (Rix J); *Dadourian Group International Inc v Simms* [2009] EWCA Civ 169, [2009] 1 Lloyd's Rep 601, [99].
    31. (1885) 29 Ch D 459.   32. [1983] 1 All ER 583.

exaggeration', it is extremely unlikely that she will be able to claim that the misrepresentation played a material part in her decision to contract.

If the representee has taken steps to try and verify the representation, the court may hold that the representee was induced by the information she gathered, rather than by the representation.[33] But the representor cannot argue that the representee could have discovered the true state of affairs if she had carried out reasonable checks. In *Redgrave v Hurd*,[34] the claimant told the defendant that his law practice had an income of £300 a year. This was in fact untrue. The claimant also gave the defendant papers which showed an income of under £200 a year, along with papers showing a small amount of additional business. The defendant did not examine these papers. He signed the agreement and paid a deposit on the strength of the representation. When he discovered the true position, he refused to proceed with the transaction and sought to have the contract set aside. It was held that he was entitled to have the contract set aside:

> If a man is induced to enter into a contract by a false representation it is not a sufficient answer to him to say, 'If you had used due diligence you would have found out that the statement was untrue. You had the means afforded you of discovering its falsity, and did not choose to avail yourself of them.'[35]

In Problem 11, therefore, Sarum College will not be able to defend itself by saying (for example) that IERA's report was widely reported in the press or that it was available on the website. The fact that accurate information was available elsewhere does not excuse a misrepresentation.

The representee does not have to entirely believe the representation. If the representee has doubts about the truth of the representation, but is unable to find evidence to verify or rebut it, she is entitled to act on the representation. If the representation then turns out to be false, she will be entitled to sue in misrepresentation notwithstanding her initial doubts.[36]

11.2.3 Remedies

If a misrepresentation has induced a contract, the representee has a range of remedies against the representor. The default remedy is **rescission**, that is, the ability to have the contract annulled on the basis that it was induced by misrepresentation. In addition, the representee may in some cases also have the right to claim **damages** for loss caused by the misrepresentation. Claiming one does not bar the other: a party is free to claim both rescission and damages.

Rescission

Setting aside the contract

The standard remedy for misrepresentation is rescission. The representee has the option of choosing to rescind the contract by giving notice to the other party. The

33. See eg *Atwood v Small* (1838) 6 Cl & F 232.
34. (1881) 20 Ch D 1. See also *Peekay Intermark Ltd v Australia and New Zealand Banking Group Ltd* [2006] EWCA Civ 386.
35. (1881) 20 Ch D 1, 13 (Sir George Jessel MR).
36. See *Hayward v Zurich Insurance Co plc* [2016] UKSC 48.

effect of rescission is to set the contract aside for all purposes, prospectively as well as retrospectively. In legal terms, the contract is treated as if it never was, and the court will seek to restore the *status quo ante*. That is to say, it will seek to put both parties in the position they would have been in had the contract never been entered into.

It is important to note that rescission is only an *option* available to the representee. The representee can also elect to affirm the contract, and have it remain valid notwithstanding the misrepresentation. Rescission is also not an absolute right. The law recognizes three bars to rescission, whose effect is that the representee loses the right to rescind the contract. The court also has a broad discretion to refuse to permit a party to rescind a contract, and to instead award *damages in lieu* if the judge believes that it would be more appropriate to do so.

Bars to rescission

The first of the bars to rescission is lapse of time. A representee will lose the ability to rescind a contract for misrepresentation if there has been undue delay in bringing an action. What constitutes 'undue delay' appears to depend on whether the misrepresentation was innocent, negligent, or fraudulent. In *Leaf v International Galleries*,[37] a gallery sold a painting as being a Constable when it was not in fact by Constable. The purchaser did not discover this until five years after the sale. The misrepresentation in this case was innocent, as the gallery honestly believed the painting to be by Constable and was not negligent in so believing.[38] The Court of Appeal held that rescission was barred by lapse of time. The five-year delay was an undue delay, even though the buyer had not known of the misrepresentation for much of that time. In contrast, in *Salt v Stratstone Specialist Ltd*,[39] a car was sold as brand new when in reality it had been in the showroom for two years and had suffered an accident in that time. The past history was not discovered until three years after the purchase. The Court of Appeal held that the suit was not barred for lapse of time. Unlike *Leaf v International Galleries*, the misrepresentation here was negligent, and where the misrepresentation is negligent or fraudulent, the time should be counted from the date of discovery of the misrepresentation, rather than the date of the misrepresentation.

The second circumstance barring rescission is a sale to a bona fide third party. If the contract for which rescission is sought relates to the sale of goods, and if a third party has bought the goods for good consideration and without notice of the misrepresentation, the court will not grant rescission, because it will not disturb the title of an innocent third party. Although this exception is per se reasonable, it has caused considerable difficulty for the courts. We will consider this in more detail in section 11.3.

The third circumstance barring rescission is somewhat opaquely called impossibility of *restitutio ad integrum*. If a contract is rescinded, the law ordinarily requires both parties to be restored to their original positions—*restitutio ad integrum*. If the parties cannot be restored to their original positions, *restitutio ad integrum* is said to be impossible, and rescission will ordinarily be barred. A typical example is where the subject

---

37. [1950] 2 KB 86 (CA).

38. On why the gallery might have believed the painting to be a Constable, and why that was not an unreasonable belief, see A Fernandez, 'An Object Lesson in Speculation: Multiple Views of the Cathedral in *Leaf v International Galleries*' (2008) 58 University of Toronto Law Journal 481.

39. [2015] EWCA Civ 745.

matter of the contract has been used up, altered, or destroyed. The courts are, however, somewhat reluctant to permit this ground to be invoked too liberally. The following illustration should demonstrate why.

> **Illustration 11.4**
>
> Lisa buys a microwave, intending to use it to speed-dry tea leaves to make a luxury green tea blend. The shop tells her that the model she has chosen can be run for up to six successive half-hour sessions at full power. When Lisa tries to do this, the microwave overheats and burns a key circuit, rendering it unusable.

If we take the bar of impossibility of *restitutio ad integrum* literally, rescission will be barred in this situation as the shop cannot be restored to its initial position (since that would require it to get back a functioning microwave, which is no longer possible). Yet it appears somewhat unreasonable, to put it mildly, to say that rescission is barred on these facts. In cases like this, courts often get around the bar by ordering the representee to make counter-restitution, by paying the representor for any retained benefit or deterioration attributable to the representee. In *Erlanger v New Sombrero Phosphate Co*,[40] the purchasers of a mine sought rescission of the contract of sale on the ground of misrepresentation. The mine had been used for some time, and a portion of its mineral content had been extracted. The court held that this did not bar rescission, and granted rescission subject to the buyer accounting to the seller for the profit it had made.

In *Salt v Stratstone Specialist Ltd*,[41] discussed earlier in this section, the Court of Appeal held that the courts should ordinarily favour awarding rescission as long as practical justice could be done by ordering counter-restitution. In that case, by the time the buyer of the car discovered the misrepresentation, the car had been driven 15,000 miles and been subject to depreciation. The Court of Appeal held that this would not by itself bar rescission, as practical justice could be done by ordering the payment of compensation for the use of the car and for depreciation.

This approach applies directly to a case like Problem 11. Because the students have been studying at the college for a while, *restitutio ad integrum* is not strictly possible. *Salt v Stratstone* suggests that in such a case the court will seek to do practical justice by granting rescission of the contract, subject to the students being required to pay some fair compensation for the use of the college's facilities and access to tuition.

Damages

Damages are also available for misrepresentation. Under s 2(1) of the Misrepresentation Act 1967, damages are available for all types of misrepresentation except innocent misrepresentation. Due to the wording of the statute, however, innocent misrepresentors are frequently also liable to pay damages. To understand why this happens, it is necessary to look briefly at the history of the law.

Before the Act was passed, a representee who had suffered loss as a result of misrepresentation could only sue in tort, not contract. If the misrepresentation was fraudulent,

40. (1878) 3 App Cas 1218.   41. [2015] EWCA Civ 745.

she could sue for deceit. If it was negligent, she could sue in negligence. Neither was easy. To succeed in deceit, the representee had to prove that the representor made it knowing it to be false, without belief in its truth, or not caring whether it was true or false.[42] In negligence, the representee had to prove either that there was a special relationship between her and the representor giving rise to a duty of care or that the representor had assumed liability for the consequences of the representation being false.[43] The measure of damages was lower in negligence. A claimant could recover all losses caused by the misrepresentation in deceit, but only foreseeable losses in negligence. If the misrepresentation was innocent, no damages could be claimed.

Although this position had its defenders, it came in for strong criticism. A particular point of critique was that fraud was difficult to prove, even where it was clear that there had been a gross misrepresentation.[44] The issue attracted the attention of the Law Reform Committee (the precursor to the Law Commission), which recommended reform of the law in their Tenth Report, titled *Innocent Misrepresentation*.[45] The recommendations were enacted through the Misrepresentation Act 1967.

The wording of s 2(1) reflects its roots in complaints about the difficulty of proving fraud. Instead of the hard-to-prove tests that underlay the tort of deceit, it creates a two-step approach to determining whether damages are recoverable. In the first step, the Act creates a general right to recover damages for *all* misrepresentations, fraudulent and non-fraudulent, in relation to losses for which the representor would have been liable were the misrepresentation fraudulent. In the second step, it creates a limited defence, under which the representor will not be liable if he can prove, first, that he 'had reasonable ground to believe' that the representation was true and, secondly, that he did in fact believe this up to the time the contract was made.

Compared with the law as it stood before the Act, s 2(1) makes two changes. First, it eliminates the distinction between negligent and fraudulent misrepresentation. Secondly, it reverses the burden of proof for negligent misrepresentation. The person claiming misrepresentation no longer has to show the existence of a duty of care or a breach of that duty. Once she shows that a misrepresentation has been made, it is for the representor to show that he had reasonable grounds to believe the representation was true. Cumulatively, this imposes a level of liability which was previously only triggered by fraud, on any representor who cannot prove reasonable grounds for believing the representation. If a false representation and inducement are shown, the courts will proceed as if the misrepresentation is fraudulent, unless the representor manages to prove that it is innocent.

Two cases illustrate the extent to which the Act has altered the rules on liability for misrepresentation. In *Howard Marine & Dredging Co Ltd v A Ogden & Sons Ltd*,[46] a company selling two barges made a representation about the barges' tonnage in the course of discussion with a prospective purchaser. The figure that the company had stated was, in fact, incorrect. The person making the representation had taken the capacity from a book called *Lloyd's Register*, which is usually very reliable. In this case, however,

---

42. *Derry v Peek* (1888) LR 14 App Cas 337 (HL).
43. *Hedley Byrne & Co v Heller & Partners* [1964] AC 465 (HL).
44. Law Reform Committee, *Tenth Report: Innocent Misrepresentation* (Cmnd 1782, 1961–2) para 17.
45. Ibid.   46. [1978] QB 574.

Lloyd's Register had reported incorrect figures. The ships' documents had the correct figures, but the seller did not check them. The court held that the seller was liable in damages. Because it had documents in its possession giving the correct figures, it had failed to show that it had reasonable grounds for its belief in the wrong figures.

In *Royscot Trust v Rogerson*,[47] a car dealer was in the process of selling a car to a purchaser on hire purchase. He negligently informed the finance company that he had taken a deposit of £1,600, on a purchase price of £8,000. In reality, he had taken a deposit of £1,200 on a purchase price of £7,600. Although the total amount lent by the finance company was the same, from the company's point of view the difference was significant because it did not usually lend if the purchaser's deposit was below 20 per cent. The misrepresentation therefore induced the contract. It was evident that the car dealer was liable in damages. The finance company, however, sought recovery of damages on the (much higher) deceit measure. The dealer argued that damages should follow the negligence measure, as he had been negligent rather than fraudulent. The court held that the wording of the statute was clear, and left no room to award different measures for negligent and fraudulent misrepresentation. Damages would therefore be recoverable on the deceit measure.

The cumulative result of these cases is that a person in the position of the seller in *Howard Marine*, who made an innocent misrepresentation, will be liable to pay damages as if the misrepresentation was fraudulent. This was not the intention behind the Act, but it is nevertheless a consequence of the manner in which s 2(1) was drafted. Returning to Problem 11, the effect will be that the college will be liable to pay compensation as if it had behaved fraudulently, even if it had not in fact behaved fraudulently. Given that some of its employees were aware of the IERA findings, it is unlikely to be able to demonstrate that it had reasonable grounds for believing the figures it gave.

Remedies against third parties

The Misrepresentation Act 1967 did not alter the remedies in tort, and it technically remains possible to sue in deceit for fraudulent misrepresentation, or in negligence for negligent misrepresentation, instead of suing under the Act. In practice, it seldom makes sense to do so in a contractual context, as s 2(1) gives the representee the same level of damages as deceit for a much lower burden of proof. The one context in which the remedies in tort are useful is where someone other than the contracting party is being sued.

Illustration 11.5

Joe runs a plumbing business through his company, Kepwell Plumbing Ltd. He decides to retire and offers his business to Piotr, who is attempting to establish himself as a plumber. He shows Piotr his accounts, which suggest that the company is turning a healthy profit.

Based on the accounts, Piotr contracts with Kepwell Plumbing Ltd to buy the plumbing business. He then discovers that the books understated the business's costs, and that it is a lot less profitable than the accounts suggested. By the time he realizes this, Kepwell Plumbing has paid the purchase price to Joe as a dividend, and has no assets left.

---

47. [1991] 2 QB 297.

Here, Piotr's contract is with the company, Kepwell Plumbing Ltd. However, the company has no assets left, so there is little point in suing it. If Piotr wants to recover any damages, he will have to sue Joe, the person who actually made the misrepresentation. Because he has no contract with Joe, he cannot rely on the Act. Instead, he will have to sue in the tort of deceit (for fraudulent misrepresentation) or in the tort of negligence (for negligent misrepresentation). Both pose difficulties, making recovery against third parties considerably more difficult than recovery under the Act. In *Foster v Action Aviation*,[48] discussed in section 11.2.1, the claimant had bought the aircraft from a company, which at the time of the suit had no assets. He therefore sought to sue the owner of the company, who had actually made the false statements. His action failed, because he was unable to prove dishonesty or recklessness to the standard required by the tort of deceit, and was also unable to establish that the owner assumed responsibility for the statement's veracity as an individual (as distinct from in his capacity as an officer of the company). The outcome of any action brought on the facts of Illustration 11.5 is likely to be similar. The easier route put in place by s 2(1) will not be available, because the Act does not apply to actions brought against third parties to the contract.[49]

11.3 Unilateral mistakes

The law of misrepresentation is not the only body of doctrine dealing with untrue statements or information asymmetries. English law also has a more specialized set of rules, the law of **unilateral mistake**. Unlike misrepresentation, unilateral mistake deals with situations where one party knew that the other party had got the facts wrong. It also—unlike misrepresentation—does not require the party with knowledge to have induced the misunderstanding. It is sufficient if she had *knowledge* of the misunderstanding. Also unlike misrepresentation, unilateral mistakes render the contract void. The contract is automatically treated as if it never was. The mistaken party does not need to elect to rescind it, and the court has no discretion to award damages in lieu.

Only two types of unilateral mistakes are recognized in law: unilateral mistakes as to identity and unilateral mistakes as to terms. In this section, we will consider each in turn.

11.3.1 Mistakes as to identity and the problem of identity theft

Mistake and misrepresentation

Consider the following fact situation:

> **Illustration 11.6**
>
> Daniel is selling his laptop on eBay. He receives a message from an eBay user called sarah-deals74, offering him 15 per cent above the 'Buy it Now' price if he will accept payment by cheque rather than PayPal. Sarahdeals74 has excellent feedback on eBay, so he agrees.
>
> →

48. [2014] EWCA Civ 1368.
49. The position of third parties more generally is discussed in Chapter 17.

→

He receives her cheque and posts the laptop to the address she provides. The cheque is dishonoured, and he discovers that he had been dealing not with sarahdeals74, but with an unknown fraudster who had hacked her account. This fraudster has in the meantime sold the laptop on to Thomas, who has bought it in good faith without any knowledge of the fraud.

It is clear that there has been a misrepresentation here, but the law of misrepresentation is unlikely to be of much use for two reasons. First, because the fraudster has disappeared, suing him for misrepresentation is not a practical remedy. Secondly, Daniel cannot seek to get his laptop back by rescinding the contract with the fraudster, as rescission will be barred on the ground that Thomas is a good faith purchaser for consideration.

In English law, a person affected by a case of this type could potentially have an alternative remedy under the law of *unilateral mistake as to identity*.[50] The law of mistake as to identity deals with situations where one party believes himself to be dealing with someone else, and the other party was aware of this mistake. Because it is a type of unilateral mistake, all it requires is for the other party to know of the misunderstanding and do nothing to correct it. Also unlike misrepresentation, unilateral mistake as to identity renders the contract void. The contract is automatically treated as if it never was. The mistaken party does not need to elect to rescind it, and the court has no discretion to award damages in lieu.

From the perspective of a claimant in the position of the original seller in Illustration 11.6, the law of mistake as to identity is a lot more useful than the law of misrepresentation. Because the contract with the fraudster is void rather than voidable, the fraudster never acquires title. Under a principle of English personal property law called the *nemo dat* rule, this means that anyone to whom he passes the property also never acquires title, even if they bought in good faith and without notice of the defective title. In sharp contrast to the law of misrepresentation, the third party is not protected and can be sued by the original seller because the goods in law still belong to the original seller.

Identity and attributes

The key difficulty with which this area of law has to deal is that of distinguishing between, on the one hand, cases where the identity of the party genuinely mattered to the transaction and, on the other hand, cases where the identity of the party did not matter. Consider the following illustration:

Illustration 11.7

As a joke, Tom decides to disguise himself as the Chancellor of the Exchequer. He goes to the campus supermarket in disguise. He is very convincing, and the person at checkout serves him in the belief that he is the Chancellor.

---

50. In English law, the term 'mistake' is applied to three very different doctrines: mistakes as to terms (dealt with in Chapter 7), common mistakes as to fact or law (dealt with in Chapter 10), and unilateral mistakes (dealt with here). All three deal with mistakes made by one or both parties, but their ingredients are very different and they are triggered by rather different events.

It is clear that the people on the checkout in this example are under a mistake as to the identity of the person they are serving. But it should be equally clear that that mistake should have no impact on the validity of the contract under which Tom buys his groceries at the campus supermarket.

This commonsense insight has been surprisingly difficult to translate into the law. Early cases drew a distinction between mistakes as to the *identity* of the other party and mistakes that merely related to the *attributes* of the other party. *Cundy v Lindsay*[51] illustrate the nature of this distinction. A fraudster placed an order for handkerchiefs with Lindsay. He signed his name Blenkarn, but did so in a way that made his signature look like that of Blenkiron & Co, a reputable firm that carried on its business on the same street. Lindsay sent the goods in a parcel addressed to Blenkiron, at the address provided by Blenkarn. Blenkarn then sold the goods on to Cundy and disappeared without paying Lindsay. Lindsay sued Cundy, arguing that Cundy had no title to the handkerchiefs.

The difficulty cases like this pose is that both Lindsay and Cundy were innocent victims of Blenkarn's fraud. Nevertheless one of them had to bear the cost, despite neither being at fault. The distinction between identity and attributes deals with this by looking at contractual intent. If Lindsay had genuinely intended to deal only with Blenkiron & Co, then the mistake was as to identity rendering the contract void. If, however, he was willing to deal with all-comers, then the main impact of Blenkarn's fraud would have been on his evaluation of the creditworthiness of a potential customer. This would be a mistake as to attributes, leaving the contract valid.

In *Cundy v Lindsay* itself, the court held the contract to be void for mistake, as Lindsay had only intended to deal with Blenkiron. The distinction was not, however, easy to apply, because the 'contractual intent' in practice proved hard to ascertain. The cases, in consequence, were not very consistent. In *Phillips v Brooks*,[52] a man called North went to Phillips's jewellery shop and selected a ring worth £450. He claimed to be Sir George Bullough, a well-known wealthy man, and said he would pay by cheque. The shopkeeper checked the address provided by North in the phone directory, found that it corresponded to Bullough's, and accepted a cheque. North then pawned the ring to Brooks Ltd, and disappeared. When the cheque was dishonoured, Phillips sued Brooks Ltd for the ring. The court held that the contract was not void for mistake, as Phillips contracted with the person who came into the shop. He may have believed that person to have been Bullough, but the contract was with the person before him.[53]

In *Lake v Simmons*,[54] in contrast, a woman called Esmé Ellison procured a necklace on approval from a jeweller. She said she was married to a man named Van der Borgh living at Stonelands, described in the judgment as 'a well-known residence'. In interwar society, most shopkeepers would have been unlikely to check the credit of someone at such a residence. Van der Borgh was in fact the occupant of Stonelands, but Ellison was only his mistress. The jeweller entered the necklace in his book as out on approval to 'P.F. Van der Borgh, Stonelands, Dawlish'. Ellison disappeared with the necklace. The jeweller sought to recover the cost from his insurers. To decide the claim, the court had to consider whether the contract with Ellison was valid. It held that it was not, as the mistake as to identity made it void.

---

51. (1878) 3 App Cas 459.   52. [1919] 2 KB 243.   53. Ibid, 246.
54. [1927] AC 487 (HL).

It is hard to see how the facts of the cases justified the different outcomes. Other cases reflected the same underlying problem. In *Ingram v Little*,[55] a buyer of a used car claimed (falsely) to be PGM Hutchinson of Stanstead House. The owners verified the address in the telephone directory and accepted a cheque. The buyer sold the car on and disappeared, and the cheque was dishonoured. In *Lewis v Averay*,[56] a buyer of a used car claimed (falsely) to be Richard Greene, a well-known actor. He showed the sellers a studio pass in the name of Richard Greene. The seller accepted a cheque on the basis of the documentation. The buyer sold the car on and disappeared, and the cheque was dishonoured. In *Ingram v Little*, the contract was held to be void for mistake (following *Lake v Simmons*), but in *Lewis v Averay* it was held to be valid (following *Phillips v Brooks*) as the seller intended to deal with the person in front of him.

Apart from the fact that the cases seemed inconsistent, it was also hard to see why misrepresentations which can be characterized as causing mistakes as to identity should be treated differently from other misrepresentations. For most misrepresentations, the law protects the rights of third party purchasers in good faith. Why should mistakes as to identity be any different? In 1966, the Law Reform Committee recommended that this distinction be abolished, with third party purchasers being protected in all cases. The report was not implemented.

Shogun Finance and the documentary/face-to-face distinction

In 2004, the issue of mistake as to identity came before the House of Lords in *Shogun Finance Ltd v Hudson*.[57] A crook sought to buy a car on hire purchase, using a stolen driving licence to impersonate a man named Patel. The car dealer faxed the information to the finance company, which ran credit checks on Patel and approved the transaction. The crook paid the deposit partly in cash and partly by cheque, and took the car away. The cheque eventually bounced. In the meantime, the crook sold the car to Hudson and disappeared. The finance company sued Hudson, arguing that he had no title as the contract between the finance company and the rogue was void for mistake as to identity.

The House of Lords held by a 3:2 majority that the contract was void. It did so by interpreting prior cases as being grounded in a distinction between face-to-face transactions, on the one hand, and documentary transactions on the other. In face-to-face transactions, the presumption is that the seller intends to deal with the person in front of him. As such, the contract is not void for mistake. If the transaction is documentary, however, the question is simply one of interpreting the document. Because a person is named on the document, it is presumed that the named person was intended to be the other party. Under the parol evidence rule, oral evidence cannot ordinarily be adduced to contradict the written document. As a result, the contract in such a case will usually be void for mistake as to identity. Because the contract in *Shogun Finance* was entered into between the finance company and the fraudster, it was a documentary contract rather than a face-to-face transaction. As such it was void for mistake.

Applying this to Illustration 11.6, the transaction between Daniel and the fraudster posing as sarahdeals74 is clearly a documentary transaction. This means that the courts will presume that Daniel intended to deal with sarahdeals74, and not the person he

---

55. [1961] 1 QB 31.   56. [1972] 1 QB 198.   57. [2004] 1 AC 919 (HL).

actually dealt with, thus making the contract void for mistake as to identity. Thomas therefore does not acquire good title, and will be liable to Daniel.

As this suggests, the test in *Shogun Finance* is somewhat clearer than the old identity/attributes distinction. Before we proceed to consider whether it represents a sensible response, one qualification should be noted. Documentary contracts are only void for mistake as to identity if the person named on the document (ie the person impersonated by the fraudster) is a real, existing person. In *Shogun Finance*, Patel was a real person whose identity had been stolen. Likewise, in *Cundy v Lindsay*,[58] Blenkiron & Co was a real business. *Shogun Finance* makes it clear that this is essential. Where the person being impersonated is fictitious, the defrauded party will be taken to have intended to contract with the fraudster and not the fictitious person named on the document. In *King's Norton Metal Co v Edridge, Merrett & Co Ltd*,[59] a man called Wallis procured goods from the claimants by pretending to be a member of a firm called Hallam & Co. He then sold the goods on to the defendants, leaving the claimants unpaid. Hallam & Co did not exist. The Court of Appeal held (in a judgment approved in *Shogun Finance*) that the fact that Hallam & Co was non-existent made the case different from *Cundy v Lindsay*. The claimants would be taken to have intended to deal with whoever was using the name 'Hallam & Co', and that is precisely what they did. There was therefore no mistake.[60]

Shogun Finance has been the subject of severe criticism. It has been criticized as being counter-intuitive—most people would have regarded the transaction in question as face-to-face rather than documentary.[61] It has also been pointed out that the decision fails to consider the issue noted by the Law Reform Committee, of why the original seller receives a higher degree of protection than an innocent purchaser in relation to this one type of dishonesty when he does not in others.[62] Two of the five judges on the panel hearing the case dissented for precisely these reasons.

An even stronger criticism, however, is that grounding mistake in a distinction between documentary and face-to-face transactions systematically favours certain types of businesses at the expense of other commercial and non-commercial actors. The main class of persons who the law now protects are the type of parties likely to enter into documentary transactions at a distance; namely, commercial sellers and financing companies. The vast majority of transactions involving ordinary individuals will be face-to-face transactions, in which the seller will not be protected. The result, as *Shogun Finance* itself illustrates, is that the law protects commercial sellers and financing companies—who are in a position to carry out identity checks and spot identity checks—at the expense of individual consumers and small businesses who lack the ability to carry out identity checks, even where they have bought in good faith. Such a position is obviously problematic, and does little to respond to the risks posed to third parties by identity theft. It is also at odds with the general policy of requiring financial companies to protect victims of identity theft. It is a matter of regret that a narrow

58. (1878) 3 App Cas 459.   59. (1897) 14 TLR 98.

60. See the speeches in *Shogun Finance v Hudson* [2003] UKHL 62, [135] (Lord Phillips), [189] (Lord Walker).

61. C MacMillan, 'Mistake as to Identity Clarified?' (2004) 120 LQR 369.

62. C Elliott, 'No Justice for Innocent Purchasers of Dishonestly Obtained Goods: *Shogun Finance v Hudson*' [2004] JBL 381.

majority of the House of Lords has made it unlikely that the position will change in the near future.

11.3.2 Unilateral mistakes as to terms

The second type of unilateral mistake that renders a contract void is a mistake as to a term of the contract. Consider the following illustration:

Illustration 11.8

Rob is browsing an online game shop, when he sees the latest instalment of *Civilization* for sale at a price of £0.49. The game has been widely advertised as retailing at £49.00. Rob immediately realizes that the shop has made a mistake, and decides to take advantage of it. He immediately places an order for the game.

Set aside, for a moment, the question of whether the display of the goods for sale on a website is an offer or an invitation to treat.[63] Should the fact that Rob knew the price was a mistake affect the contract's validity? The answer is that it does affect the contract's validity if four conditions are made out. First, one of the parties must positively believe that the terms are other than what was actually written or offered. Merely being unaware of the term does not constitute a mistake: there must be a positive belief that the terms are different from what they actually are.[64] Secondly, the mistake must relate to a term of the contract. A mistake on a matter connected with the contract which is not a term (eg a collateral warranty or a representation) does not give rise to an action in mistake.[65] Thirdly, the other party must know, or ought to have known, of the mistake.[66] Fourthly, the mistake must have caused the party to enter into the contract.

The classic case on unilateral mistake as to terms is *Hartog v Colin and Shields*.[67] Here, an offer to sell hare skins was mistakenly expressed in terms of a rate per pound of skins instead of a rate per skin. There were three skins to a pound. Singleton J held that the contract was void for mistake as the purchasers must have been aware of the mistake. Although the question has not yet come before a court in England, courts in other common law jurisdictions have applied this principle to transactions on websites where there was an obvious pricing mistake, as in Illustration 11.8.[68]

The limits of the doctrine can, however, be seen from the decision in *The Harriette N*.[69] In this case, two parties entered into an agreement to settle a dispute involving a shipping contract. The party which made the settlement offering had mistakenly believed that the cargo was discharged on 13 October, when it had in fact been

---

63. See the discussion in Chapter 2.

64. Cf *Pitt v Holt* [2013] UKSC 26, [108]–[109] (Lord Walker), distinguishing between mistakes and ignorance.

65. *Statoil ASA v Louis Dreyfus Energy Services LP (The Harriette N)* [2008] EWHC 2257 (Comm).

66. *OT Africa Line Ltd v Vickers plc* [1996] 1 Lloyd's Rep 700, 703 (Mance J).

67. [1939] 3 All ER 566.

68. See eg *Chwee Kin Keong v Digilandmall.com Pte Ltd* [2005] 1 SLR 502 (Singapore Court of Appeal).

69. *Statoil ASA v Louis Dreyfus Energy Services LP (The Harriette N)* [2008] EWHC 2257 (Comm).

discharged on 24 October. This affected its calculation of the settlement amount. The other party was aware of the mistake, but did not point it out and accepted the offer. It was held that the contract was not void for mistake, as the date of discharge was not a term of the contract. It was simply a background matter of fact, and unilateral mistakes as to background matters of fact did not render a contract void. This decision demonstrates not only the narrowness of the doctrine of unilateral mistake, but also that the courts are reluctant to widen it by analogy. Outside the area of terms and identity, the preference is to leave questions arising out of information asymmetry to the doctrine of misrepresentation.

11.4 Misleading selling practices

The rules we have been discussing thus far apply to all transactions, regardless of whether the parties are commercial transactors or consumers. Since 2014, the law of unfair commercial practices has also given consumers a separate set of statutory remedies if they encounter misleading selling practices.

The legal rules in relation to misleading selling practices were originally enacted in 2008, through the Consumer Protection from Unfair Trading Regulations 2008.[70] In 2014, the Regulations were amended on the recommendation of the Law Commission[71] to create a new set of civil remedies in favour of individuals affected by a violation of the Regulations.[72] The Regulations now provide an alternative to the common law rules on misrepresentation and mistake, and entirely replace the statutory remedy under the Misrepresentation Act 1967, in situations where they apply. Three requirements must be demonstrated before a consumer can avail himself of the civil remedies provided by the Regulations. First, the transaction must be of a type covered by the Regulations. Secondly, the consumer's complaint must arise out of a practice prohibited by the Regulations. Thirdly, the prohibited practice must have made a causal contribution to the consumer's decision to enter into the transaction in question. In this section, we will examine each of these in turn.

11.4.1 Transactions covered by the Regulations

The civil remedies provided by the Regulations apply in three different types of transactions between traders and consumers. The first are what are termed 'business to consumer contracts', which cover any contract for the sale or supply of a 'product'. The Regulations define 'product' very broadly, including goods, services (other than financial services regulated under the Financial Services and Markets Act 2000),[73]

70. SI 2008/1277.
71. Law Commission, *Consumer Redress for Misleading and Aggressive Practices* (Law Com No 332, 2012).
72. Until then, only government regulators had the power to take action if the provisions of the Regulations were violated.
73. See reg 27D(1). The logic underlying this exclusion is that the consumer should instead avail himself of the remedies for consumers available through the regulatory framework for financial services.

digital content, assured tenancies and holiday lets,[74] and even rights and obligations.[75] 'Product' is also defined to include agreements settling liabilities that a trader claims are owed by a consumer.[76]

In addition, the Regulations also apply to 'consumer to business contracts', that is to say, contracts under which a *consumer* sells goods to a trader (eg a contract under which an individual sells a used car to a car dealer), as well as to transactions involving a 'consumer payment'—a category that is intended to catch all transactions where a consumer makes a payment to a trader for the supply of a product (understood in the broad sense discussed in the previous paragraph).

11.4.2 **Prohibited practices**

The Regulations prohibit a wide range of practices, two of which are directly relevant to the topics we have discussed in this chapter;[77] namely, those that the Regulations term 'misleading actions'[78] and those they term 'misleading omissions'.[79]

Each of these terms is defined in exhaustive detail in the Regulations. Misleading actions, broadly speaking, cover practices which provide false information in relation to a broad list of matters.[80] The Regulations list 11 matters, including the 'main characteristics' of the product,[81] the need for service, replacement, or repair, and the extent of the trader's commitments.[82] Misleading actions also cover failures to comply with codes of conduct with which the trader has made a firm commitment to comply.[83]

A misleading omission is defined to include, amongst other things, practices which omit[84] or hide[85] material information, or provide material information in a manner which is 'unclear, unintelligible, ambiguous or untimely'.[86] Material information is defined broadly, to include all information which an average consumer might need to take an informed decision.[87] The Regulations go on to list a significant number of matters that will be treated as material in a contract for the purchase of goods, including matters such as the main characteristics of the product, its price, the identity of the trader, delivery charges, etc.[88]

In relation to both, although the Regulations use the terminology of 'practice', it is now established that conduct does not have to be systemic or systematic to fall foul of the Regulations. A single act which falls within the statutory definition of a misleading action or a misleading omission is sufficient for the purpose of the Regulations, even if it was the result of a clerical error and did not reflect the trader's usual practices.[89]

---

74. Reg 27C(2).   75. Reg 2(1).   76. Reg 2(1A) and (1B).

77.   Chapter 12 ('The limits of hard bargaining') deals with another category of practices prohibited by the Regulations, namely, aggressive selling practices.

78. Reg 5.   79. Reg 6.   80. Reg 5(2)(a).

81. Reg 5(4)(b). The term 'main characteristics' is defined to include 18 specific characteristics, enumerated in reg 5(5).

82. Reg 5(4).   83. Reg 5(3)(b).   84. Reg 6(1)(a).   85. Reg 6(1)(b).

86. Reg 6(1)(c).   87. . Reg 6(3).   88. Reg 6(4).

89. See the decision of the European Court of Justice (ECJ) in *Nemzeti Fogyasztóvédelmi Hatóság v UPC Magyarország* (Case C-388/13) of 16 April 2015. The Court of Appeal had previously held in *R v X Ltd* [2013] EWCA Crim 818, [2014] 1 WLR 591 that the Regulations were concerned with systems, rather than single failings to a single customer. Given that the ECJ has reached the opposite conclusion, the position taken by the Court of Appeal is now no longer likely to be followed.

11.4.3 **The 'significant factor' test**

Finally, the Regulations also impose a requirement of causation, in that the prohibited practice must be a 'significant factor' in the consumer's decision to make the payment or enter into the contract.[90] The recommendation that a causal requirement be retained came from the Law Commission. The rationale they provided is that the purpose of damages in private law is to compensate a person for harm, and a person has not been harmed by a misleading action or omission unless it has been a significant factor in the decision to contract or make the payment. To speak of a significant factor is to set the bar lower than a **but for test**. Nevertheless, it is arguably higher than the test for misrepresentation where the law only requires that the misrepresentation be *a* factor, with no requirement as to how significant it must be.

11.4.4 **Remedies**

The Regulations grant three remedies to consumers who are affected by a violation of these Regulations: a right to unwind the contract, a right to obtain a discount, and a right to claim damages. The first two of these are in the alternative, the third can be claimed in addition to either. The remedies are additional to those provided by ordinary rules of common law, and are not intended to replace them. However, there is a prohibition on double recovery, so that the consumer cannot recover under the Regulations as well as common law in respect of the same loss.[91]

Unwinding the contract involves, in a business-to-consumer contract, a right to reject the product supplied by the trader.[92] This right is subject to a long-stop of 90 days, and can also be lost if the product is incapable of rejection (eg if it relates to services that have been fully performed or to goods that have been used up). In a consumer-to-business contract, it entails a right to demand a return of the goods sold to the trader in the same condition as when they were sold (or, if this is impossible, to be paid compensation).[93] In either case, monetary payments that accompanied the sale of the product must be returned.

The right to a discount is decided according to four pre-set bands, of 25, 50, 75, and 100 per cent, depending on whether the prohibited practice is 'more than minor', 'significant', 'serious', or 'very serious'.[94] Seriousness, in turn, is assessed with reference to three factors: the behaviour of the person who engaged in the practice, its impact on the consumer, and the time that has elapsed between the action and the time the prohibited practice took place.[95]

The Regulations also include a right to damages, which includes damages for financial loss, as well as for categories of non-pecuniary loss, such as alarm, distress, and physical inconvenience or discomfort. This is subject to a requirement of foreseeability, and a defence of due diligence.

---

90. Reg 27A(6).   91. Reg 27L.   92. Reg 27K.   93. Reg 27G.   94. Reg 27I(4).
95. Reg 27I(5).

11.5 In conclusion: contract and the pre-contractual process

Let us now pull the strings together, and assess the strengths and limitations of the way in which English law deals with the problem of information asymmetry.

Two general trends can be noted here. First, the second half of the 20th century saw a shift in the law of misrepresentation, away from a focus on setting standards of conduct for representors towards a new focus on protecting representees who had been induced to enter into contracts by false statements. The result is that the law now imposes a relatively strict standard of liability on individuals who have made false statements: they will be liable even if they genuinely believed the statements to be true, as long as the other ingredients of misrepresentation are made out. This approach has in effect enabled the fusion, in a contractual context,[96] of the formerly independent actions of deceit and negligent misstatement, and extended the remedy to innocent misrepresentation. This fusion of principle is to be welcomed, even if the grant of damages on the deceit measure for innocent misrepresentation may be seen by some as having gone too far. That the law of mistake as to identity remains separate, and subject to a different set of rules, is an unfortunate exception to this trend, and *Shogun Finance v Hudson* must in this context be seen as a missed opportunity.

Secondly, in the past decade, a fundamental divide has opened up between the way in which English law approaches information asymmetries in consumer transactions and in all other transactions. As section 11.4 has shown, consumers receive a far higher degree of protection than non-consumers. The combination of the prohibition against misleading statements and misleading omissions, and the breadth of the definition of 'material' information, means that traders can neither rely on ambiguously worded statements nor on providing a narrow subset of information to their counterparty. The power of this approach can be seen if we return to Problem 11. Sarum College is almost certain to fall foul of the Consumer Protection from Unfair Trading Regulations 2008, because the information it suppressed is almost certain to be considered 'material' for the purposes of those Regulations.

The general rules of common law, in contrast, offer a lower degree of protection. In particular, the absence of a general duty to disclose material facts, coupled with the difficulty of ascertaining facts in the control of the other party, mean that the law of misrepresentation by itself will offer a far less efficacious remedy to the students in the problem at the head of this chapter.

To some extent, this highlights an emerging tension in English contract law, where an increasingly paternalistic and protective approach to consumers, which is largely statutory and usually associated with European harmonization, sits alongside more general principles that are still largely grounded in the idea that the law should impose relatively light-touch duties on parties negotiating contracts. Thus whilst there is an obligation not to provide untrue information, the law goes no further than that. If the parties want a guarantee that all material information has been disclosed, it is for them to obtain such a guarantee contractually.

---

96. Outside the contractual context, the remedies remain distinct.

Key points

- English law does not contain a general duty to disclose material facts when negotiating, save in very narrow circumstances.

- The main doctrine dealing with untrue statements made in contracting is misrepresentation. Misrepresentation occurs when a party makes a false statement, which induces the other party to enter into a contract.

- If the representation is ambiguous, making it unclear whether it is false, the court will give it a reasonable construction.

- Misrepresentation must relate to a matter of fact rather than opinion. Matters of opinion can, however, sometimes contain implied representations of fact.

- Misrepresentation can be fraudulent, negligent, or innocent. All three render a contract voidable, giving the innocent party the option to rescind it.

- Fraudulent or negligent misrepresentation also gives the innocent party the right to sue for damages. Although innocent misrepresentation does not give the right to sue for damages, the burden of proof is on the representor to prove that the misrepresentation was innocent.

- A narrower, and more focused, set of rules are contained in the law of unilateral mistake. These apply to mistakes as to identity and mistakes as to terms. They cover cases where one party made a mistake on one of these matters and the other party was aware of the mistake. Unilateral mistakes render contracts void, rather than merely voidable.

- A unilateral mistake as to identity only renders a contract void if it genuinely relates to the identity of the person, rather than their attributes (eg creditworthiness). In face-to-face transactions, the presumption is that mistakes relate to attributes. In documentary transactions at a distance, the presumption is that mistakes relate to identity.

- A unilateral mistake as to terms only renders a contract void if it relates to a term (and not a representation or some other matter that is not a term). It also requires a positive belief that the terms are different from what they actually are (and not mere ignorance of a term).

- A special statutory regime for consumers protects them against misleading commercial practices by sellers. This includes misleading actions as well as misleading omissions.

Assess your learning

You should be able to respond to each of the following points with a confident 'yes'. If you can't, then you should revisit the sections listed against that point.

Can you:

(a) *Outline* the key requirements of misrepresentation, and the types of statements to which it applies? (Sections 11.2.1 and 11.2.2)

(b) *Explain* the distinction between statements of fact and statements of opinion, and *identify* the circumstances under which a statement of opinion may contain an implied statement of fact? (Section 11.2.1)

(c) *Describe* the remedies of rescission and damages in relation to misrepresentation, including the bars to rescission, and *outline* the key consequences of the reversal of the burden of proof under the 1967 Act? (Section 11.2.3)

(d) *Explain* the distinction between void and voidable contracts, in relation to its effect on the rights of third parties? (Section 11.3.1)

(e) *Explain* the distinction between identity and attributes, and *describe* the significance of the distinction between documentary and face-to-face transactions in applying this distinction? (Section 11.3.1)

(f) *Outline* the circumstances in which a contract will be void for a unilateral mistake as to its terms? (Section 11.3.2)

(g) *Identify* the types of practices that are prohibited by the regulations on aggressive commercial practices? (Section 11.4)

In relation to each of the above, you should be able to:

(i)   identify and clearly explain the key rules and principles;

(ii) identify the key cases and statutes, and why they matter;

(iii) apply the principles and cases to specific real or hypothetical fact situations;

(iv) evaluate the limitations, if any, of the law as it currently stands.

Further reading

H Beale, 'Damages in Lieu of Rescission for Misrepresentation' (1995) 111 LQR 60.

I Brown and A Chandler, 'Deceit, Damages and the Misrepresentation Act 1967, s 2(1)' [1992] LMCLQ 40.

J Cartwright, *Misrepresentation, Mistake, and Non-Disclosure* (3rd edn, Sweet & Maxwell 2012).

A Chandler and J Devenney, 'Mistake as to Identity and the Threads of Objectivity' (2004) 1 JOR 7.

C Hare, 'Identity Mistakes: A Missed Opportunity' (2004) 67 MLR 993.

R Hooley, 'Damages and the Misrepresentation Act 1967' (1991) 107 LQR 547.

C Macmillan, 'Rogues, Swindlers and Cheats: The Development of Mistake of Identity in English Contract Law' (2005) 64 CLJ 711.

J Poole and J Devenney, 'Reforming Damages for Misrepresentation: The Case for Coherent Aims and Principles' [2007] JBL 269.

R Taylor, 'Expectation, Reliance and Misrepresentation' (1982) 45 MLR 139.

12

The limits of hard bargaining

Duress and undue influence

'Sign . . . or else'

Problem 12: setting the context

Consider the facts set out in the following scenario:

Joanne Heyton
Wilkinson and Partners
Brighton

Dear Joanne,

As you are aware, my husband, Charles Palmer, is the primary shareholder and Chief Executive Officer of Jarrow Steel Castings (JSC). JSC is wholly owned by our family and manufactures precision steel parts for use in high-performance machinery. Like many small companies, JSC suffers from a time-lag between its outgoing and incoming payments. We have to pay our suppliers for raw materials well before we receive payment for our products from our customers. Like many companies in this position, we bridge time gaps between incomings and outgoings through a working capital facility with a bank, in our case the City of Glasgow Bank. Having access to working capital finance is critical to our survival, as with many small and medium-sized companies. Our working capital facility agreement with the City of Glasgow Bank was scheduled to expire on 30 June this year. In April, we began negotiations with the bank to renew the facility for a further five years. The negotiations proceeded smoothly, and we were scheduled to sign a new agreement on 29 June.

On the morning of 29 June, Charles received a phone call from Ellen Armstrong, our relationship manager at the bank. Ellen told Charles that the bank had decided to increase the interest rate for the loan from 9 per cent to 14.5 per cent. She also said that I, Charles, and our son would have to issue personal guarantees for JSC's debts. When Charles protested, Ellen said that it was non-negotiable. Unless we agreed, the working capital facility would not be extended.

Working capital facilities take several weeks to negotiate, so it was practically impossible for us to find an alternative bank before the facility expired on 30 June. Without the facility, we would be unable to pay invoices as they fell due. The bank was aware of this. Under protest, Charles agreed to the increased interest rate. My son and I were extremely concerned about the implications of taking on liability. Charles told us that the company would fold overnight unless it obtained the facility, and there was no time to lose. Although we hold shares in the company, we leave its running to Charles. Relying entirely on his judgment and on the urgency of the matter, we agreed with some reluctance to give the personal guarantees. Due to the very short notice, there was no time to obtain independent advice on the implications of doing so.

I have now been reading horror stories in the press about people having guarantees invoked by banks, and I am desperately worried about the position I and my son are in (as well as Charles). I am contacting you to see if there is

→

> →
>
> anything we can do to get out of the guarantee, given the circumstances in which we signed it.
>
> Yours sincerely,
> Eilidh Palmer-Andrews

This letter sets out a scenario that is not uncommon in bargaining. A party to a transaction puts the other under pressure. Some of the persons on the other side end up signing it without having the time to understand its implications. Should the court take account of these circumstances? If so, in what way?

12.1 Introduction: the problem of coercion

The basis of contract lies in consent, and consent must be freely given. Consider the following illustration:

Illustration 12.1

As you are walking home late one night, you are suddenly confronted by a knife-wielding man, who says he will stab you unless you hand over your mobile phone. You immediately hand it over, and the man leaves.

On the face of it, the transaction between the parties has all the elements of a contract. There is an offer ('Give me your phone'), acceptance (the act of handing the phone over), consideration (the transfer of the phone in exchange for not being stabbed), and the requisite intention. Yet few, if any, would suggest that such a transaction should constitute a legally binding contract.

In legal terms, such a transaction is defective because one party did not freely consent.[1] Consent, to the extent it was given, was vitiated by the pressure to which one party was subjected. In Illustration 12.1, it is clear that one party has gone too far in applying pressure. But things are not always that clear-cut. Consider the situation in Problem 12. The bank's actions in that case certainly put the parties under pressure. But did its tactics go too far? Or was it simply part of the 'rough and tumble' of 'normal robust commercial bargaining', as the courts like to call it?[2] The commercial world assumes that people will bargain hard in their own interests. Hard bargaining is not seen as being a problem in and of itself. It becomes an issue when it crosses the line between tactics that are legally acceptable and pressure that is legally unacceptable. The primary task for legal doctrine is to find a basis on which to draw the line between these.

---

1. The transaction can also be called into question because of its illegality, as Chapter 14 discusses in greater detail.
2. *Adam Opel GmbH v Mitras Automotive (UK) Ltd* [2007] EWHC 3481 (QB), [26] (David Donaldson QC).

In English law as it currently stands, this 'line' is drawn in three different ways and in three different places. English law does not have one single doctrine of vitiated consent or unfair bargaining. Instead, it contains three different doctrines to deal with different ways in which a party's consent could be vitiated by excessive pressure: the doctrine of **duress** which has its origins in the common law, the doctrine of **undue influence** whose origins lie in equity, and rules on *prohibited practices* whose origins lie in the work of regulatory bodies.

Each of these doctrines takes a very different approach to the problem of hard bargaining. The focus of duress is on threats which illegitimately seek to coerce the will of the other party to the contract. Undue influence focuses on pressure which is not quite a threat, covering situations where one party has abused the trust and confidence which the other party has placed in them (although it is not confined to this type of situation). Rules on prohibited practices are sector-specific, and seek to identify and prohibit the most common types of unacceptable conduct one sees in bargaining in the relevant sector. Regardless of the specific doctrine that is applied, the legal response is similar: the party subject to pressure has the option to rescind the contract.

In this chapter, we will examine each of these doctrines in turn, beginning with the law of duress (section 12.2), followed by the law of undue influence (section 12.3), and a brief survey of prohibited practices in the formation of consumer contracts (section 12.4). We will conclude (section 12.5) by drawing the threads together in order to assess how successful English law is in dealing with the problem of excessively hard bargaining in contracting.

12.2 Overt threats in bargaining: the doctrine of duress

12.2.1 The nature of duress

The doctrine of duress is concerned with coercion through the use of threats. If you coerce a person to enter into a contract by making a threat that the law regards as illegitimate, the law will treat the contract as voidable. This means that the party who was threatened will have the option to either affirm the contract or to rescind it.

Until relatively recently, the only threats recognized as duress were physical threats, where one person sought to exert pressure on another by threatening them with violence ('*duress to the person*'). Illustration 12.1 is a classic example. In the latter half of the 20th century, however, the courts expanded the concept to also cover two other types of pressure. The first of these is *duress to goods*. Consider the following illustration:

> **Illustration 12.2**
>
> Your laptop's screen has started flickering. You take it into a shop. The engineer in the shop examines it, and says that the problem cannot be fixed. He then says that you will have to pay a £100 service charge for the tests he has carried out.
>
> You refuse, pointing out that he should have said there would be a charge before he started work. He grabs the laptop (on which you have important notes) and says that you will not get it back until you agree to pay him the charge.

What is threatened here is not harm to the person. It involves, instead, a threat to deny you access to your goods. Since the 1970s, the courts have consistently held that a contract can also be rendered voidable as a result of duress to goods—for example, threats to deny persons access to their goods, or to damage or cause harm to their goods.[3]

The other type of pressure that is now recognized as constituting duress is **economic duress**. Economic duress deals with the use of more subtle types of economic pressure which are neither threats to goods nor threats to property. Examples include threats to cancel a contract or to organize a boycott of a person's business. Of the various types of duress, economic duress is the most problematic because it deals with an area where it can be quite hard to draw a line between negotiating tactics that are legitimate, albeit aggressive, and behaviour which is duress. Consider the following illustration, setting out two examples of the sort of thing that might be said in the course of a commercial transaction.

Illustration 12.3

We know we're in breach. We've been three months late in delivering your machines. The good news is that the machines are ready and can be delivered within 24 hours. However, we'll only do so if you sign this document waiving all your claims in relation to any losses you've suffered to date. That's our offer. Take it or leave it. Of course you can sue us if you want. But can you really afford to see your losses mount? Or are you going to be sensible and cut them while you can?

Your behaviour is quite outrageous. You are far more confrontational and litigious than any of our other suppliers. You initiate litigation at the drop of a hat for trivial matters. Unless you agree to withdraw all your cases against us and start behaving in a more commercially reasonable way, we will have no choice but to have to stop considering you for any future contracts, and to inform all our contacts about how unreliable you are.

Both of these involve the application of commercial pressure. But should both render the contract voidable? Or is there a distinction between the two? On the face of it, the first statement appears to be a lot less defensible than the second. The party is in breach, is aware that it is in breach, and is saying that it will wilfully continue to refuse to perform unless the other party gives up claims in relation to what may be very significant losses. The second example, in contrast, appears to arise out of a genuine breakdown in a commercial relationship. In commercial terms, there is a clear distinction between the behaviour of the party making the 'threat' in the two cases. Should this distinction also be legally significant? Consider, as well, the situation in Problem 12. The pressure there does not come from a threat to breach a contract. It comes from a threatened refusal to contract. Should *this* difference have legal significance?

---

3. *Occidental Worldwide Investment v Skibs (The Siboen & The Sibotre)* [1976] 1 Lloyd's Rep 293.

Answering these questions is far from straightforward, and it has required the courts to reconsider the purposes and elements of the defence of duress in contract law. Duress today has three key elements: the *exercise of pressure* which is *illegitimate* and which *induces* another party to enter into a contract.[4]

The first element focuses on the impact of the pressure on the person who was *subject* to it. For pressure to constitute duress, it must have had a significant impact. Traditionally, this was summed up by saying that duress must entail 'compulsion of the will' or 'coercion of the will'. More recent cases, however, have tended to phrase the requirement differently (and less dramatically), preferring to say that the party must be left with *no practical choice* but to submit to the demand.

The second element of duress focuses on the *nature* of the coercive act. The usual way of summing this up is to say that the threat must be *illegitimate*. The mere fact that a person's will was coerced is in and of itself not sufficient. If the threat was a legitimate one, it does not matter that it was coercive. The person subject to the threat may have felt backed into a corner, or felt that they were left with no choice at all. None of this matters if the threat was legitimate. The contract will be valid notwithstanding the coercion.

The third element of duress focuses on the *link* between the threat and the defendant's decision to enter into the contract. There must be a *causal link* between the two. The precise nature of the causation requirement varies with the type of threat: where the threat is a serious one (eg a threat of causing bodily injury) the bar is set relatively low so that the causal link is made out if the threat is one factor among many inducing the decision to contract. Where the threat is less serious (eg a threatened breach of contract) the bar is set higher, and the party claiming duress must prove causation to a higher standard, known as the but for standard (discussed in detail in section 12.2.4).

There is likely to be overlap between these elements, particularly the first and third, and the ultimate finding will depend very heavily on the facts of each case.[5] Nevertheless, they indicate the approach that will need to be taken in establishing duress. They also demonstrate that duress is neither purely claimant-focused nor purely defendant-focused. Its elements require us to consider the defendant's conduct, the claimant's decision-making process, and the impact of the one on the other. In the remainder of this section, we will consider each of these elements, and how they fit together, in more detail.

12.2.2 **The impact of the threat**

For the doctrine of duress to operate, the threat must have been coercive. It must have affected the way in which a party saw its position, in effect leaving it to feel that it had little choice but to agree to the contract.

The courts have articulated this in two different ways. The first uses the language of 'coercion of the will' or 'compulsion of the will'. If one party has been coerced to

---

4. See the summary in *Carillon Construction v Felix (UK) Ltd* [2001] BLR 1. See also *DSND Subsea Ltd (formerly DSND Oceantech Ltd) v Petroleum Geo Services ASA* [2000] BLR 530, [113] (Dyson J).

5. *Adam Opel GmbH v Mitras Automotive (UK) Ltd* [2007] EWHC 3481 (QB), [26].

a degree that their will was overborne by the threat, then they have, in effect, been deprived of the free exercise of their will. This deprivation vitiates the party's consent, rendering the contract voidable at their instance.

The trouble with this formulation is that it does not accurately describe how threats affect decision-making. Threats do not deprive individuals of decision-making power. They simply place them in a situation where they are forced to choose an option they do not want, because they have little practical choice. As far back as the 17th century, English philosophers such as Thomas Hobbes pointed out that a person acting out of fear was still acting voluntarily: they are choosing to adopt a course of action that avoids the eventuation of the threat.[6]

Starting in the 1980s, academics influenced by legal realism, such as Professor Patrick Atiyah, began to criticize English law's reliance on the 'overborne will' as misplaced.[7] In *Lynch v DPP of Northern Ireland*,[8] a criminal appeal, the House of Lords suggested, obiter, that the language of 'overborne will' was an inaccurate description of the basis of duress in contract law. Duress 'deflects' the will without destroying it.[9] The reason contracts are voidable for duress is that the law does not accept the agreement's legal validity because of the pressure.[10] Subsequent cases on duress in contract law confirmed this approach. In *The Evia Luck*,[11] Lord Goff agreed that it was unhelpful to speak in terms of coercion of the will in contract.

Although the language of 'compulsion of the will' or 'coercion of the will' is still occasionally used,[12] the test is now more commonly articulated in terms of the *lack of a practical choice*.[13] Duress reflects the fact that a party has submitted to the inevitable.[14] If a party has a practical choice—'an alternative remedy which any and possibly some other reasonable persons in his circumstances would have pursued'—then she is not submitting to the inevitable.[15]

How, then, is this test actually applied in practical terms? In *Pao On v Lau Yiu Long*,[16] the Privy Council set out four factors that were relevant to assessing whether a person's consent was vitiated by duress:

> In determining whether there was a coercion of will such that there was no true consent, it is material to inquire whether the person alleged to have been coerced did or did not protest; whether, at the time he was allegedly coerced into making the contract, he did or did not have an alternative course open to him such as an adequate legal remedy; whether he was independently advised; and whether after entering the contract he took steps to avoid it.

---

6. T Hobbes, *Leviathan* (Richard Tuck ed, Cambridge University Press 1996) 146.

7. PS Atiyah, 'Economic Duress and the Overborne Will' (1982) 98 LQR 197.

8. [1975] AC 653 (HL).   9. Ibid, 695 (Lord Simon).   10. Ibid, 680 (Lord Wilberforce).

11. *Dimskal Shipping Co SA v International Transport Workers' Federation (The Evia Luck)* [1992] 2 AC 152 (HL).

12. See eg *R v Attorney-General for England and Wales* [2003] UKPC 22, [15] (Lord Hoffmann).

13. *DSDN Subsea Ltd v Petroleum Geo Services ASA* [2000] BLR 530, [131] (Dyson J).

14. *Universe Tankships Inc of Monrovia v International Transport Workers' Federation (The Universe Sentinel)* [1983] 1 AC 366, 400 (Lord Diplock).

15. *Huyton SA v Peter Cremer GmbH* [1999] CLC 230 (QB), 252 (Mance J).

16. [1980] AC 614 (PC).

Case in depth: *Pao On v Lau Yiu Long* [1980] AC 614 (PC)

Pao On arose out of a contract for the sale of shares. The claimants (Pao On and his family members) had agreed to buy 4.2 million shares in a company called Fu Chip from the defendants (Lau Yiu Long and his brother), at a price of $2.50 per share. The company had just been listed, and the defendants were anxious to ensure that the claimants did not cause the share price to decline precipitously through selling large proportions of their shares. The parties therefore agreed on a 'lock in' clause, under which the claimants agreed not to sell 2.5 million of their shares until 30 April 1974.

The claimants demanded a guarantee from Lau Yiu Long in exchange, so that they would not make a loss if the share price declined during the time that they were locked into their shareholding. The parties accordingly executed a subsidiary agreement. Instead of providing a guarantee, however, this agreement actually gave Lau Yiu Long the option to buy 2.5 million shares from the claimants at the issue price of $2.50 per share on 30 April 1974. Critically, this was not tied to a decline in the share price. This meant that even if the share price rose significantly, Pao On and his family would be contractually required to sell their shares to Lau Yiu Long at the issue price.

When the claimants realized what they had actually signed, they informed Lau Yiu Long that they would not complete their transaction unless the subsidiary agreement were to be replaced by a true indemnity. Because the subsidiary agreement had already been signed, in law this amounted to a threat by them to breach their contract unless its terms were altered. Lau Yiu Long technically had the option of suing the Paos for breach of contract. However, on the facts this option was unattractive. The deal had been announced, and if it fell through public confidence in the shares of Fu Chip would be adversely affected. The value of his own shares would come down. He therefore reluctantly agreed to cancel the subsidiary agreement and to replace it with a true guarantee, under which he and his brother indemnified the Paos against a fall in the share price for the shares they were locked into holding.

The share price fell far more than the parties had imagined possible, ending at 36 cents a share. The claimants invoked the indemnity. The defendants argued that the guarantee was unenforceable, because it was not supported by consideration and because it had been procured by a threat amounting to duress.

The Privy Council held that the contract had not been procured by duress. After setting out the four factors outlined above, Lord Scarman went on to hold that there was no coercion:

> [Lau] considered the matter thoroughly, chose to avoid litigation, and formed the opinion that the risk in giving the guarantee was more apparent than real ... In short, there was commercial pressure, but no coercion.

Also of relevance was the fact that Lau had at all times been advised by his lawyers, who had participated in the drafting of the guarantee, that the option of suing for damages was real, and that he had given no indication that he was signing the guarantee under protest. He had taken a calculated decision to take on a commercial risk in order to pacify his counterparties. The decision proved in hindsight to be an error of judgment, but that would not by itself render the contract voidable for duress.

Although *Pao On* used the language of 'coercion of the will', the factors are also relevant to the more modern approach of focusing on the lack of practical choice. Consider Problem 12. As the facts make clear, the parties did protest at the time of the alleged coercion, and they lacked an alternative practical course of action. Unlike in *Pao On*, where litigation was a viable option, the time constraints in this case mean that the alternative to not agreeing would have been the loss of their business. Equally, there was no time to take independent legal advice. Three of the four factors set out in *Pao On* are therefore made out, strongly suggesting that a sufficient degree of compulsion was present.

That is not, however, the end of the story. The element of compulsion is a necessary ingredient of duress, but it is not sufficient. The party claiming to have been subjected to duress must not only prove that pressure was applied, but also that the pressure was *illegitimate*. We will now examine this requirement in more detail.

12.2.3 **Illegitimacy**

The need to prove illegitimacy reflects the expansion of duress beyond threats to the person. A threat of bodily harm will almost always be illegitimate. This is not true of duress to goods or of economic duress. A threat to seize goods may sometimes be legitimate, as may a threat to breach a contract. A gas engineer who says that he will condemn a boiler unless he is paid to repair it is clearly exercising pressure over the other party. As long as the boiler is in fact in violation of the relevant standards, however, the pressure is not duress because it is legitimate.

The basic approach

In *R v Attorney-General for England and Wales*,[17] Lord Hoffmann discussed two ways in which legitimacy can be assessed. First, it can be assessed with reference to the nature of the *pressure* itself. Alternately, it can be assessed with reference to the nature of the *demand*. Consider the following illustration:

Illustration 12.4

> You wouldn't want your spouse to see these compromising photos of you, would you? Just sign this contract, and you'll never have to worry about those photos again.

Here, the act that is threatened is not illegitimate as such. Save in special circumstances, English law does not prohibit or restrict the ability of a person to communicate compromising information about another. What is illegitimate, rather, is the demand that the threat is used to make. For pressure to be illegitimate, either the threat or the demand must be illegitimate.

---

17. [2003] UKPC 22.

The facts of *R v Attorney-General for England and Wales* are a good illustration of the manner in which the courts go about determining whether threats or demands are illegitimate. The decision highlights another point; namely, that *any* illegitimate threat is capable of giving rise to duress. This is important, because not all threats can be easily slotted

---

Case in depth: *R v Attorney-General for England and Wales* [2003] UKPC 22

This case involved a dispute between the armed forces and a soldier ('R') who had served in the SAS in the Gulf War. R and his team had been sent behind enemy lines to try to cut communications. Unfortunately, they were detected by Iraqi troops. Three of the eight soldiers in the team died in the resulting fighting, one escaped, and the other four were captured and tortured. R was one of the latter group.

After the war ended, the soldier who escaped, as well as one of the commanding officers, published books about the operation, which were subsequently made into films. The films and books were widely seen in the SAS as being inaccurate and contrary to its traditions. To prevent this happening again, the SAS Regimental Association, with the support of the vast majority of members, asked the Ministry of Defence to procure binding contracts from all serving members to prevent 'unauthorized disclosure' in the future. The ministry accepted the recommendation. In 1996, R was given a confidentiality agreement to sign. He was told that if he refused, he would be treated as unsuitable for the SAS and returned to his original regiment. This was ordinarily only done for disciplinary reasons, and would have involved loss of pay and status. R was not allowed to seek legal advice. He signed the contract. Two weeks later, however, he left the regiment and moved to New Zealand. He then sought to publish a book about his service in the Gulf War. The Ministry of Defence applied for an injunction. R argued that the contract was vitiated by duress.

The High Court of New Zealand held that the contract was vitiated by duress. The relationship between the parties was such that R had in effect been ordered to sign the agreement. On appeal, the Court of Appeal reversed this decision, holding that the contract had not been procured by duress. Although the relationship between R and his superiors had elements of compulsion, he had not in fact been ordered to sign. That meant that he had an alternative; namely, accepting his removal from the SAS and his return to his regiment. He had therefore failed to establish duress.[18]

R appealed to the Privy Council. The Privy Council held that the contract was not vitiated by duress, but for different reasons from the Court of Appeal. Unlike the New Zealand Court of Appeal, it accepted that R had been placed under pressure, which left him with no practical alternative.[19] Nevertheless, the pressure was legitimate. The confidentiality agreements were introduced because the rise in unauthorized disclosures were threatening the effectiveness of the UK's Special Forces, and had the support of most serving members. Given that context, the ministry was 'reasonably entitled to regard anyone unwilling to accept the obligation of confidentiality as unsuitable for the SAS'.[20] The threat was therefore legitimate under both approaches to assessing legitimacy. The pressure was lawful, because the ministry had the power to return him to his regiment. Equally, the demand it was used to support was legitimate, because it was justifiable.[21]

---

18. *Attorney-General for England and Wales v R* [2002] 2 NZLR 91, 113 (Tipping J).
19. [2003] UKPC 22, [15].   20. Ibid, [17].   21. Ibid, [18].

into the categories of duress to the person, duress to goods, and economic duress. The threat here was neither duress to the person, nor economic duress, nor duress to goods. This is also the case in Illustration 12.4. The Privy Council's decision tells us that under such circumstances it does not matter that the threat does not fit into one of the three categories of duress. As long as the claimant can prove that the threat is illegitimate, and that the other two ingredients of duress are also satisfied, the contract will be voidable.

But cases are not always as straightforward as *R v Attorney-General*. Several of the early cases on illegitimacy involved industrial action, an area which has long divided judges. In *The Universe Sentinel*,[22] a trade union called the ITF was attempting to improve the pay and working conditions of crewmembers working on ships that flew flags of convenience.[23] If a ship met certain minimum standards the union had set, it issued the ship a 'blue certificate'. *The Universe Sentinel* had American owners but was registered in Liberia, and was therefore regarded as flying a flag of convenience. It did not hold a blue certificate. The trade union therefore 'blacked' the ship when it docked in England. This meant that no tug boat would service the ship, with the result that it could not sail. The owners entered into negotiations with the ITF, which demanded that they pay the ITF $80,000 to be given a blue certificate. The money included back pay for the crew of the ship, as well as a contribution of $6,480 to the ITF's welfare fund. The owners agreed to the demand, because that was the only way their ship would be able to leave port. After the ship had sailed, they sought to recover the money paid to the union on the basis that it had been paid under duress.

The back pay was protected by a statutory provision which legalized certain types of action taken during industrial disputes,[24] but the owners sought to recover the $6,480 paid to the welfare fund. The bench was divided on whether the ITF's demand for this sum was legitimate. The majority held that it was not. A trade union's actions were only legitimate if they related to the terms and conditions of employment. The welfare fund was a union initiative to support workers. It therefore had no connection with the terms and conditions of employment, and a demand for payment to the fund was illegitimate.[25] The minority, in contrast, held that the payment was legitimate. The welfare fund was for the benefit of seamen, and payments by employers to that fund were therefore clearly related to the terms and conditions of employment.[26]

The difference of views between the judges in the top court in *The Universe Sentinel* demonstrates how finely balanced questions of legitimacy can be. Although both *The Universe Sentinel* and *R v Attorney-General of England and Wales* related to non-commercial matters, the issue tends to be particularly acute in commercial cases. It is not

22. *Universe Tankships Inc of Monrovia v International Transport Workers' Federation (The Universe Sentinel)* [1983] 1 AC 366 (HL).
23. The term flag of convenience refers to a practice where a ship is registered in a country to which it has no real connection, simply because the laws of that country provide a more favourable regulatory framework.
24. See *NWL Ltd v Woods* [1979] 1 WLR 1294 (HL).
25. [1983] 1 AC 366, 389 (Lord Diplock).
26. Ibid, 403 (Lord Scarman), 409 (Lord Brandon).

uncommon in commercial cases for parties in a weaker bargaining position to be faced with 'take it or leave it' offers. Often, they may not be in a position to do anything but accept the offer. Problem 12 presents a good example. Are situations of this type duress? Should the courts be intervening to protect the party in the weaker position?

In general, the courts go to some lengths to ensure that the doctrine of duress does not affect legitimate commercial bargaining, even tough bargaining. Mere commercial pressure is not duress.[27] To constitute duress, the pressure must lack any commercial or similar justification.[28] In *DSND Subsea Ltd v Petroleum Geo Services ASA*,[29] Dyson J set out a number of factors that are relevant to assessing whether pressure is illegitimate:

> In determining whether there has been illegitimate pressure, the court takes into account a range of factors. These include whether there has been an actual or threatened breach of contract; whether the person allegedly exerting the pressure has acted in good or bad faith; whether the victim had any realistic practical alternative but to submit to the pressure; whether the victim protested at the time; and whether he confirmed and sought to rely on the contract. These are all relevant factors. Illegitimate pressure must be distinguished from the rough and tumble of the pressures of normal commercial bargaining.[30]

This paragraph should be read subject to two qualifications. First, the factors listed are indicative rather than exhaustive, and should not be taken as a precise test. They should, rather, be taken as indicative of the *type* of things to which the courts will look. Secondly, the factors should not be taken as a mathematical formula. The decision as to whether a line has been crossed will necessarily involve a value judgment.[31] The key point which emerges from Dyson J's judgment is that the value judgment will typically be exercised with reference to the standards implicit in commercial practice, rather than external standards of fairness or morality.

This means that the law of duress is sensitive not just to commercial needs generally, but also to accepted practices in the specific context in which the pressure was applied. Typically, three sorts of pressure tend to be the subject of claims of duress: first, pressure applied in the form of a *refusal* to contract if a demand is not met; secondly, pressure applied in the form of a threat to *breach* an existing contract if a demand is not met; and, thirdly, pressure applied in the form of a threat to take lawful but *disadvantageous action* if a demand is not met.

Refusals to contract

Problem 12 presents a good example of the first of these. Here, what is at stake is not just the nature of the demand, but also the bank's action in springing it on the borrower at the last minute. It is this that puts the borrower under pressure. Had the demand been made at an early stage, the borrower would have been free to walk away and find a loan elsewhere. At this late stage, however, the borrower has no practical choice but to assent to the demand. Nevertheless, the courts are reluctant to hold there

---

27. *Atlas Express Ltd v Kafco (Importers and Distributors) Ltd* [1989] 1 QB 833, 839 (Tucker J).
28. *Bank of India v Nirpal Singh Riat* [2014] EWHC 1775 (Ch), [56] (David Casement QC).
29. [2000] BLR 530.   30. Ibid, 131.
31. See *Adam Opel GmbH v Mitras Automotive (UK) Ltd* [2007] EWHC 3481 (QB), [26] (David Donaldson QC).

to have been duress in such cases. In *Bank of India v Riat*,[32] a company owned by Riat had taken a loan from the Bank of India. Riat had personally guaranteed the loan. He argued that the guarantee had been procured by duress. The Bank had demanded it at a time when it was too late for him to start negotiating with another bank, as he was under pressure to complete two transactions for which he needed the loan. The High Court held that there had been no pressure on the facts, but that even if there had been, the demand would have been legitimate. Until the loan agreement was signed, the Bank was fully entitled to make new demands and introduce new terms. A personal guarantee is commonly requested by banks lending to small companies, and the demand was therefore legitimate.[33]

Similarly, in *Bank of Scotland v Cohen*,[34] a company had exchanged contracts to purchase property, and had negotiated financing arrangements with the Bank of Scotland. Shortly before the completion date, the Bank demanded a personal guarantee from the directors and shareholders of the company, and said that it would reconsider the availability of the facility unless the guarantees were signed. The defendants reluctantly signed the guarantees. The bank also insisted that they sign confirmations that they had executed the guarantees of their own free will after obtaining legal advice. The court held, applying *Pao On*, that there was no duress because the bank's demand was not illegitimate. In addition, the bank was entitled to rely on the confirmation that the guarantee had been granted by the guarantors of their own free will.

The position taken by English courts is based on the view that every party is free to back out of a proposed contract at any time up to the 'moment of responsibility' when the contract is formed. If that is all a party is threatening to do, and if all it is demanding are more favourable terms, then it would require a very unusual combination of circumstances for the pressure to be considered illegitimate. The result is that it is rare for commercial pressure applied in the course of negotiating an ordinary commercial transaction to amount to duress. If the threat and the demand are legitimate in and of themselves, the courts will not treat it as having become illegitimate simply because they were made at a strategically late stage in the negotiating process.

Threats to breach contracts

The situation is very different when pressure is applied to force a *variation* of an existing contract by threatening to breach it. Consider the following illustration:

Illustration 12.5

Jarrow Steel Castings obtain much of their iron ore from a supplier called Continental Ore and Minerals. The supply agreement fixes a base price, and a band within which the price increases or decreases depending upon market conditions. Following extreme market volatility, Continental Ore demand an increase in the contract price that goes beyond the contractually agreed band. When Jarrow Steel refuse, Continental Ore tell them that it will no longer supply ore to them. Jarrow Steel are in the process of fulfilling a

→

---

32. [2014] EWHC 1775 (Ch).   33. Ibid, [70].   34. 16 January 2013, Ch (unreported).

> →
>
> large order, and will suffer significant losses if Continental stop their supplies. It is practically impossible for them to find an alternative supplier in time. They reluctantly agree to the increased rate.

Such a situation differs from the scenario set out in Problem 12. In Problem 12, pressure was applied by threatening not to enter into a contract. In Illustration 12.5, in contrast, the pressure applied is a threat to *breach* an existing valid contract. A threat to breach a contract is much likelier to be illegitimate than a threat to back out of an as-yet-unformed contract.

In *Atlas Express Ltd v Kafco (Importers and Distributors) Ltd*,[35] Atlas, a transport company, had contracted with Kafco, sellers of basketware, to transport basketware from Kafco's premises to Woolworth, a very large retailer. The parties' contract provided for a per-carton rate. Just before the goods were to be carried to Woolworth, Atlas tried to get Kafco to vary the rate to also include a minimum charge of £440 per trailer. When Kafco refused, Atlas said that they would refuse to load the basketware unless Kafco agreed to the variation. At this late stage, it was impossible for Kafco to find an alternative transporter and still get the goods to Woolworth on time. They reluctantly agreed to the new agreement, feeling that they were 'over a barrel' and had no choice. Once the goods were delivered, they refused to pay the additional amount. When Atlas sued, they defended themselves on the basis that the revised agreement was signed under duress. The High Court upheld the defence of duress. By threatening to breach their contract, Atlas was threatening to cause unlawful damage to the other party's economic interests. This went beyond mere commercial pressure, and was an illegitimate threat.[36]

The Canadian case of *Burin Peninsula Community Business Development Corp v Grandy*[37] is even more striking. Here, a financing corporation demanded a personal guarantee shortly before a transaction was scheduled to close. Unlike the English cases discussed earlier, however, the parties had already entered into a binding agreement as to the terms of the loan. It was just that the final documents had not been executed. The court held that the bank had exerted economic duress, because it had attempted to take advantage of the borrower's precarious financial position to vary the terms of a concluded and binding agreement by threatening to breach its obligations under it.

The fact that the demand is based on actual commercial exigencies, such as dealing with an unexpected cost, does not make it legitimate. In *B & S Contracts and Design Ltd v Victor Green Publications Ltd*,[38] a contract to build stands for a major international exhibition was affected by a strike. The trade union demanded a payment of £9,000. The contractors could not afford this, and told the exhibition organizers that they would be unable to carry out the work unless the organizers agreed to increase the contract price by £4,500. The organizers initially offered an advance instead of an increased payment, but the contractors insisted on the increase. The organizers

35. [1989] 1 QB 833.   36. Ibid, 841.
37. (2010) 327 DLR 4th 752 (Newfoundland and Labrador Court of Appeal).
38. [1984] ICR 419 (CA).

reluctantly agreed, as they would have been unable to find a substitute contractor at that late stage. They later sought to argue that the contract was vitiated by duress. The Court of Appeal agreed. In insisting on increasing the price, rather than accepting an advance, the contractors were trying to advance their own immediate economic interests at the claimants' expense. This made the threat illegitimate. Similarly, in *The Atlantic Baron*,[39] a shipbuilder demanded a 10 per cent increase in the contractually agreed price for a ship, threatening not to complete the ship unless the price was paid. The demand was a response to a 10 per cent devaluation of the US dollar, in which the price was expressed. The court held that the pressure constituted duress.[40]

The point underlying these decisions appears to be that the parties are free to *bilaterally* renegotiate a contract to deal with changed circumstances, and the courts will enforce this as long as the renegotiation is based on genuine agreement (as in *Williams v Roffey*). They will not, however, permit a party to use the threat of breach to *unilaterally* force the other party to accept terms against their will.

This also applies where the threat of breach is used not to force a renegotiation but to induce the other party to accept a disputed interpretation of a contract or a settlement of a disputed claim.[41] In *Carillion Construction Ltd v Felix (UK) Ltd*,[42] disputes had arisen between a contractor (Carillion) and a subcontractor (Felix) about Felix's performance on the subcontract. The disputes affected the amounts that were due under the contract. Felix demanded that Carillion agree to a particular settlement of their account, and said that it would withhold further performance unless Carillion conceded to Felix's account of how much was due to it. Carillion could not at that stage have found an alternative contractor, and gave in to Felix's demands under protest expressly stating that it was consenting under duress.[43] It subsequently sought to have the settlement set aside on the ground of duress. Dyson J in the High Court held that the contract was voidable for duress. The proper course of action for Felix would have been to refer the dispute to arbitration. It had no contractual entitlement to insist on settlement of the account at the stage at which it did, and no reasonable basis to believe that it did. Equally, it knew that Carillion could not have found an alternative contractor at that late stage. Consequently, its actions were illegitimate.

Threats of lawful acts

The principle we have just discussed has its limits, and it is important not to take it too far. It is common for contracts to be varied in the course of their performance in response to changing circumstances,[44] and there are circumstances in which pressure applied to renegotiate a contract will be taken to be legitimate. This is particularly true where the acts threatened are lawful. Merely telling the other party the true nature of their current liabilities, for example, will not constitute duress. In *Berntsen v National Westminster Bank*,[45] a bank informed borrowers in default that it would foreclose on

---

39. *North Ocean Shipping v Hyundai Construction (The Atlantic Baron)* [1979] QB 705.

40. Although relief was ultimately denied in that case for other reasons, as discussed in section 12.2.5.

41. See *Bonhams 1793 v Cavazzoni* [2014] EWHC 682 (QB).

42. [2001] BLR 1 (QB).   43. Ibid, [22].

44. See the discussion of *Williams v Roffey* in Chapter 3 ('Consideration').

45. [2012] WL 11908384.

certain properties unless they agreed to a refinancing agreement. Although it was acknowledged that this had put the borrowers under tremendous pressure, there was no duress as the bank had done no more than invite them to choose between refinancing existing liabilities or facing the consequences of default. Simply stating that you intend to enforce your contractual rights is certainly pressure, but it is not illegitimate.

This also appears to apply if the party did not actually have the rights it purported to enforce, but believed in good faith, and on the basis of a genuine and not unreasonable belief, that it did. In *CTN Cash and Carry Ltd v Gallaher Ltd*,[46] the defendants had contracted to sell cigarettes to the claimants and deliver them to the claimants' warehouse. They delivered the cases of cigarettes to the wrong warehouse, although also one belonging to the claimants. By the time the mistake was discovered, the cigarettes had been stolen. The defendants believed (incorrectly) that the goods were at the claimants' risk at the relevant time, and insisted on receiving payment. When the claimants refused to pay, the defendants threatened to revoke the claimants' credit facility. The claimants' business would have been jeopardized by the removal of credit. They had no alternative to dealing with the defendants, who were the sole distributors for all popular cigarette brands. They reluctantly paid. They then sought to recover the payment, arguing that it had been paid under duress.

The High Court and the Court of Appeal rejected the plea of duress. Three reasons were cited for doing so. First, the doctrine of duress was not intended to deal with inequality in bargaining power. The mere fact that the defendants used their superior bargaining position did not make their tactics duress. Secondly, the defendants were legally entitled to revoke the credit facility they owed to the claimants. Doing so was not a breach of contract. It was a lawful act. While lawful acts might be capable of constituting duress, they should only do so in rare cases. Thirdly, the defendants acted on the basis of a genuine, bona fide belief in their position. Commercial parties would often have disputes as to their rights and obligations under a contract, and it was important that any settlements they reached be legally protected. To do otherwise:

> would introduce a substantial and undesirable element of uncertainty in the commercial bargaining process. Moreover, it will often enable bona fide settled accounts to be reopened when parties to commercial dealings fall out.[47]

The Court of Appeal in *CTN Cash and Carry* was careful not to rule out the possibility that a threat of a lawful act might be duress in exceptional circumstances. *Progress Bulk Carriers v Tube City IMS*[48] is an example of one such circumstance. In this case, shipowners had agreed to charter a ship out to charterers. They committed a repudiatory breach of the charter by chartering the ship in question to different charterers. They conceded that they were in breach, and said that they would provide a different ship at a discount, but only if the charterers waived all their rights in respect of damages under the charter. The charterers faced substantial losses if they could not have their cargo carried, and they could not have found another ship easily at that late stage. They accepted the owners' terms under protest. Subsequently, they sued for damages and argued that their acceptance of the owners' terms was vitiated by duress. Crucially,

46. [1994] 4 All ER 714 (CA).   47. Ibid, 719 (Steyn LJ).
48. [2012] EWHC 273 (Comm), [2012] 1 CLC 365.

the owners' actions here were not a breach of contract. The contract had already been breached when they chartered the ship to someone else, and the pressure they applied took the form of a refusal to settle which they could lawfully do. Nevertheless, Cooke J held that their actions amounted to duress. Although their actions were not in themselves unlawful, they had to be seen in the light of their prior repudiatory breach, and that broader context meant that they were illegitimate.[49] But the facts of this case were exceptional. Although the owners were not threatening a breach, they were threatening to refuse to remedy their breach. This gave it features somewhat akin to a threat to breach. In the absence of such circumstances, the availability of duress in relation to lawful acts is likely to remain rare.

Before we leave the topic of legitimacy, it is vitally important to remember that the requirement that the threat or demand be illegitimate does not in any way replace the requirement that the party must have 'no practical choice' but to agree. The absence of a practical choice was an important factor in every single case considered in this section in which the claim of duress succeeded, including *Kafco*,[50] *B&S Contracts*,[51] and *Carillion Construction*.[52] The two requirements are in addition to each other, and both will need to be proven on the facts of any case.

12.2.4 Inducing the decision to contract

The final requirement which must be proven for an action of duress to succeed is that the pressure must induce the decision to contract. The extent to which duress must be a contributory factor depends on the type of duress. As far as duress to the person is concerned, the test is similar to that in misrepresentation. It is sufficient if the duress was a factor. It does not have to be the sole factor or even the primary factor. The leading case is the decision of the Privy Council in *Barton v Armstrong*.[53] Two shareholders in a company were in a dispute. This rapidly escalated to the point where one of them, Armstrong, began making serious threats of physical violence against Barton, including statements like 'You can employ as many bodyguards as you want. I will still fix you.' and 'Unless you sign this document I will get you killed.' Barton bought Armstrong out. In evidence, it was shown that he was partly motivated by the threats (which he took seriously) and partly by commercial reasons, in that he genuinely believed that he could make a success of the company if he bought Armstrong out. The Privy Council nevertheless held that he could rescind the contract for duress. Drawing an express parallel with misrepresentation, Lord Cross in the Privy Council held that it was sufficient if the threat was a factor in the decision to contract, even if it was not the only one.

This does not, however, apply to economic duress, where the position appears to be that causation must be established to the 'but for' standard. The 'but for' standard, also known as the '*sine qua non*' standard, requires the person claiming duress to demonstrate that he would not have entered into the contract but for the duress. It is not

49. Ibid, [42]–[43].
50. *Atlas Express Ltd v Kafco (Importers and Distributors) Ltd* [1989] 1 QB 833, 839 (Tucker J).
51. *B & S Contracts and Design Ltd v Victor Green Publications Ltd* [1984] ICR 419 (CA).
52. *Carillion Construction Ltd v Felix (UK) Ltd* [2001] BLR 1 (QB).
53. [1976] AC 104 (PC).

enough if the duress merely contributed to the decision as one factor among many. In *The Evia Luck*,[54] Lord Goff used the language of 'significant cause' to describe the link that must be made between the pressure and the inducement in cases of economic duress. In *Huyton SA v Peter Cremer GmbH*,[55] Mance J held that this meant at the very minimum a 'but for' test. The case arose out of a contract for the sale of wheat, where there was a dispute in relation to whether the documents tendered by the seller conformed to the requirements of the contract. Both parties claimed that the other had repudiated the contract. Cremer, the seller, initiated arbitration. Huyton said that it would only pay for the wheat if Cremer withdrew the arbitration and gave up the right to arbitrate. Cremer agreed to do so, but once payment was received it argued that its agreement was vitiated by duress. Mance J held that the agreement was not vitiated by duress. He held that it would not be appropriate to apply the test in *Barton* to economic duress, as threats to the person are inherently 'mala fide acts'.[56] A higher test was required.

> The minimum basic test of subjective causation in economic duress ought, it appears to me, to be a 'but-for' test. The illegitimate pressure must have been such as actually caused the making of the agreement, in the sense that it would not otherwise have been made either at all or, at least, in the terms in which it was made. In that sense, the pressure must have been decisive or clinching.[57]

Mance J further stressed that satisfying the 'but for' test would not be enough in and of itself: it would not substitute for the test of illegitimacy or the test of the absence of a practical choice. A party who only signed the contract due to the pressure, but who had a real choice not to sign, will not be able to claim for duress. All factors must be established.

12.2.5 Remedies for duress

Duress makes a contract voidable (not void). The remedy for duress is *rescission*: that is, the ability to have the contract annulled on the basis that it was vitiated by duress. Rescission is not automatic. It permits the victim of duress to set the contract aside by giving the other party notice. Once that is done, the contract is treated as if it never came into being. However, unlike a void contract, the contract remains valid until rescinded.

The right to rescind a contract is also not unconditional, and may be lost if one of three bars to rescission is triggered. First, it may be lost if the victim of the duress has affirmed the contract, either expressly or implicitly (eg by continuing to perform it even after the duress has ceased). Secondly, it may be lost for lapse of time. In *The Atlantic Baron*,[58] discussed in section 12.2.3, eight months had elapsed between the delivery and the date on which the claimant sought to rescind the transaction on the basis of duress. The court held that the right to rescind had been lost due to lapse of time. Finally, the ability to rescind a contract may be lost if counter-restitution is

---

54. *Dimskal Shipping Co SA v International Transport Workers' Federation (The Evia Luck)* [1992] 2 AC 152 (HL).
55. [1999] CLC 230 (QB).   56. Ibid, 252.   57. Ibid, 250.
58. *North Ocean Shipping v Hyundai Construction (The Atlantic Baron)* [1979] QB 705.

impossible. This bar is discussed in greater detail in Chapter 11 in the context of mis-representation. The principles applicable are identical, and the discussion will there-fore not be repeated here.[59]

Damages are not available in duress, unlike in misrepresentation. This means that if rescission is barred, the victim of duress will be left without a remedy.

12.3 Abusing confidence: the doctrine of undue influence

The focus of the doctrine of duress is on threats made by one of the parties. But pres-sure can also take more subtle forms. Consider the following statement:

> **Illustration 12.6**
>
> After everything I've done for you, I don't think it's unreasonable for me to ask you to sign this document. You owe it to me.

Although there are no threats as such, the person making this statement is clearly applying pressure on the other party to the contract. Depending on the context, and on the nature of the relationship between the parties, the pressure may well be even more effective than a threat.

The focus of the doctrine of undue influence is on pressure of this type; namely, pressure which is illegitimate but does not amount to a threat. Undue influence has its origins in equity, and was originally part of a broader jurisdiction exercised by courts of equity over fraud and trust. The traditional justification is that undue influence responds to conduct which is unconscionable, because it involves a dominant party taking unfair advantage of the influence they have over the other, or the trust and confidence that other person reposes in them. Equity saw this as being a species of fraud. The result is that unlike duress, the focus of undue influence is on the *exploitation* by a person of the ability to influence another. The key to establishing a claim in undue influence is demonstrating both that that ability exists and that it was exercised in a manner that is undue. Undue influence in this sense is not confined to contracts. It is also a ground for setting aside a range of transactions. A gift, for example, may also be rescinded if it was procured by undue influence.[60] The cases discussed in this section cover both contracts and gifts, as the principles applied in both types of cases are identical.[61]

---

59. For an application of the bar to duress, see *Halpern v Halpern* [2007] EWCA Civ 291, [2008] QB 195.

60. See eg *Hart v Burbidge & others* [2014] EWCA Civ 992.

61. Undue influence also applies to wills, but there are important differences between the doc-trine as applied to gifts and contracts and the doctrine as applied to wills particularly in relation to presumed undue influence which does not apply in relation to wills. A full discussion of these dif-ferences is beyond the scope of this book, and the cases relating to wills are therefore not discussed in this chapter.

In the 19th century, when the scope of duress was relatively narrow, undue influence was applied to very diverse types of illegitimate pressure falling short of a threat. In *Williams v Bayley*,[62] the claimant's son had forged his signature on bank bills. The bank told the claimant that they would prosecute his son unless the claimant agreed to take the son's debts upon himself. At that time, conviction would have led to the son's transportation to a penal colony. To prevent this, the claimant agreed to the bank's demand, including granting the bank a mortgage over a colliery he owned. The House of Lords held that the claimant was entitled to have the agreement set aside for undue influence.

Undue influence is no longer applied so broadly. The expansion of the scope of duress in the latter half of the 20th century has meant that undue influence has come to focus on a narrower set of cases. Specifically, undue influence in the modern context is more closely focused on the relationship between the parties, and on whether the stronger party abused or exploited her position within the relationship to gain some advantage. The starting point in any examination of undue influence is, therefore, now not so much on the *pressure* itself as it is on the nature of the *relationship* within which that pressure was exercised.

The heavy focus on the nature of the relationship is unique to the common law. Civil law jurisdictions focus more on the circumstances to which the weaker party was subject than to the relationship between the two. Dutch law, for example, recognizes a ground called 'abuse of circumstances' (*misbruik van omstandigheden*) which covers cases where one party induces another person to perform juridical acts even though he knew that the other person

> is under the influence of particular circumstances, like a state of emergency, dependency, thoughtlessness, an addiction, an abnormal mental condition or inexperience.[63]

One result of the position taken by English law is that most of the recent cases on undue influence have related to transactions taking place in an ordinary civil context, rather than in a commercial context. Cases involving intimate relations—and, in particular, spouses induced to offer security for their spouse's commercial debts—have formed a relatively large proportion of recent leading cases in the law of undue influence. While undue influence is still occasionally pleaded in commercial cases, it is very rarely successful. This means that in the context of Problem 12, undue influence will be most relevant to determining whether Charles put excessive pressure on his wife and son, rather than to whether the bank put excessive pressure on them all.

There are two routes to claiming undue influence. In the first, called *actual undue influence*, the party seeking to have the transaction set aside is required to prove that undue influence was exercised, and that that exercise caused the decision to contract. In the second, called *presumed undue influence*, the party seeking to have the transaction set aside must simply show that the transaction is not readily explicable, and that it took place in the context of a special relationship, or a relationship of trust and confidence. The courts will then presume that the transaction was procured by undue influence, unless the contrary is shown. Actual and presumed undue influence are also sometimes referred to as Class 1 and Class 2 undue influence.

---

62. (1866) LR 1 HL 200.   63. BW 3:44 lid 4.

In this section, we will begin by looking at actual undue influence (section 12.3.1), before moving on to study how the courts use an evidentiary presumption to address the difficulty of establishing actual undue influence (section 12.3.2). We will then look at the remedies for undue influence (section 12.3.3), before concluding by examining how the doctrine of undue influence operates in situations involving third parties (section 12.3.3).

12.3.1 **The elements of actual undue influence**

To successfully plead actual undue influence, the party who was subject to pressure must prove that its decision to contract was induced by undue influence. More specifically, four things must be proved. First, it must be shown that the dominant party had the ability to influence the other party. Secondly, it must be shown that that ability was exercised. Thirdly, it must be shown that that exercise of influence was undue (often termed the requirement of *unconscionability*). Fourthly, it must be shown that this exercise of influence induced the other party to enter into the impugned contract. The bar for establishing causation is not high. Undue influence is a response to the fact that the victim of the influence was deprived of the opportunity to make a choice by the dominant party's exercise of influence. Causation does not, therefore, have to be established to the 'but for' standard used in economic duress. As long as influence actually was exercised on the facts of a case and operated on the mind of the other party, the element of causation is satisfied.[64]

An important advantage of actual undue influence is that it is unnecessary to establish that the relationship between the parties was one of trust and confidence. All that needs to be established is that one party had the ability to influence the other, and exercised it. In *Morley v Loughnan*,[65] Loughnan was a travelling companion to Morley. Loughnan was also a member of a religious sect called the Plymouth Brotherhood and he converted Morley to that sect. Morley left his home and went to live with Loughnan. He had a fortune of £170,000 out of which he paid large sums of money to Loughnan, totalling over £140,000. After Morley's death, his executors sought to recover the money on the basis that it had been obtained by the actual exercise of undue influence. The action succeeded. Wright J held, on the evidence, that Morley was 'in a condition of subjection to an influence against which he was unable to contend, but to the true nature of which his mind became at times so far alive as to shew that the subjection was not wholly voluntary'.[66] The money was paid not out of Morley's free will but due to Loughnan's 'influence and domination'.[67] This was an 'abuse of personal influence and ascendency', and the money was therefore recoverable.

This case was exceptional both in the starkness of the facts and in the amount and quality of the evidence available. Evidence of this type is critical, and claims of actual undue influence only succeed where the claimant is able to demonstrate that the other party 'embarked on a course of conduct putting pressure' on them to agree,[68] or where there is evidence showing the exercise of pressure in other respects even if not specifically in relation to the impugned transaction.[69] It may also be discharged by proving

---

64. *UCB Corporate Services Ltd v Williams* [2002] EWCA Civ 555, [86].
65. [1893] 1 Ch 736.   66. Ibid, 755.   67. Ibid, 756.
68. See *CIBC Mortgages v Pitt* [1994] 1 AC 200 (HL), 205 (Lord Browne-Wilkinson).
69. *Re Craig (Deceased)* [1971] Ch 95, 121 (Ungoed-Thomas J).

that the party exercising undue influence acted fraudulently.[70] In *Annulment Funding Co Ltd v Cowney*,[71] the court found actual undue influence where the party did not understand the transaction, and was anxious and concerned by the fact that she did not, but nevertheless entered into it because of the pressure placed on her by the other party. In the absence of such circumstances, however, the ingredients of undue influence can be difficult to prove, and cases of actual undue influence are relatively rare.

12.3.2 Presuming undue influence

To deal with the difficulty of proving the actual exercise of influence, the courts in the course of the 19th and 20th centuries developed a very different approach to undue influence, called *presumed undue influence*. Presumed undue influence does not require a party to prove the four ingredients of active undue influence. Instead, it operates by looking to two aspects of the transaction: the nature of the relationship between the parties, and the nature of the transaction itself. The best way of understanding the relevance of these two aspects is to view them as representing two stages in the process by which the court decides whether or not to presume undue influence. In the first stage, the court examines the relationship between the parties. If the relationship between the parties was one of trust and confidence, the court will presume that it was of a type within which influence *could* be exercised. At this stage, however, the court makes no presumptions in relation to whether influence *was* exercised. In the second stage, the court looks at the nature of the transaction. If the transaction is not readily explicable with reference to ordinary motives, then the court will presume that the influence was exercised in an undue way—in other words, that the transaction was procured by undue influence.

The presumption so arrived at at the conclusion of the second stage is only evidential.[72] This means that it is rebuttable, but it is for the dominant party to rebut it. This is typically done by establishing that there was no abuse of trust. From the perspective of the person subjected to pressure, the effect of the presumption is to create a far simpler set of things to prove. This gives parties an easier way of establishing undue influence. The leading decision on presumed undue influence is the decision of the House of Lords in *Royal Bank of Scotland Plc v Etridge (No 2)*.[73] The nature of presumed undue influence, and the approach which the courts take to it, were however established in the earlier decision of the Court of Appeal in *Allcard v Skinner*,[74] which provides a good starting point for understanding the ingredients of presumed undue influence, as well as the logic underlying them.

Case in depth: *Allcard v Skinner* (1887) 36 Ch D 145

Allcard, the claimant, joined a religious order called the Sisters of the Poor as a novice. The defendant, Skinner, was the lady superior of the order and one of its founders. The order's rules required her to give up all her individual property, either to friends and relatives, or the

→

---

70. *UCB Corporate Services Ltd v Williams* [2002] EWCA Civ 555, [87].
71. [2010] EWCA Civ 711.
72. *Royal Bank of Scotland Plc v Etridge (No 2)* [2002] 2 AC 773 (HL), [16], [18] (Lord Nicholls).
73. [2002] 2 AC 773 (HL).   74. (1887) 36 Ch D 145.

→

poor, or to the order. If it were given to the order, it could not be reclaimed by the member on leaving. Allcard had been left considerable property by her father and she gave large amounts of this to the sisterhood.

In 1879, she left the sisterhood to convert to Catholicism (the Sisters of the Poor was an Anglican order). Most of the property she gave the sisterhood had been spent by that time, but some shares remained. Six years after leaving, she sued to recover the shares and some of the money she had paid (but not all). The basis of her action was that she had been induced to make over her property by Skinner's undue influence. Skinner's defence was that Allcard had joined the order of her own free will, and handed over the property pursuant to the rules which she agreed to accept on joining.

Kekewich J in the High Court found for Skinner. The evidence before him demonstrated that Allcard knew what she was doing, and there was no evidence of any influence exercised by Skinner over her decision.[75] Allcard appealed.

The Court of Appeal held that the transaction was affected by undue influence. There were two classes of cases that could be set aside in undue influence. The first was where the court was satisfied that the transaction was the result of influence expressly used by the other party for the purpose. The second was where the relations between the parties shortly before the execution of the transaction were such as to raise a presumption that one party had influence over the other.[76] The first depended on the principle 'that no one shall be allowed to retain any benefit arising from his own fraud or wrongful act'. The second, in contrast, rested on 'the ground of public policy, and to prevent the relations which existed between the parties and the influence arising therefrom being abused'.[77]

This transaction fell within the second class. Allcard was bound to 'render absolute submission' to Skinner because of the nature of the relationship between initiate and lady superior. In addition, the gift was 'so large as not to be reasonably accounted for on the ground of friendship, relationship, charity, or other ordinary motives on which ordinary men act'.[78] This meant that the burden was on Skinner to justify the gift. Although no influence had been brought to bear on Allcard beyond what 'inevitably resulted' from her spiritual discipline, this constituted a pressure which she could not resist.[79] In addition, she could not obtain independent advice as she had sworn not to consult persons outside the convent,[80] and as such could not 'freely exercise her own will' as to the transaction. The result was that she was not an entirely free agent.[81]

However, although she could have set the transactions aside in 1879 when she left the order, the six-year delay meant that her suit was now barred. Her action therefore failed, notwithstanding the undue influence.

The contours of the modern law of presumed undue influence remain as set out in *Allcard v Skinner*. First, the parties' relationship must be such as to create the possibility of abuse. In the modern context, this is typically either because of the power relations within the relationship or because it is a relationship of trust and confidence. Secondly, there must be something about the transaction that makes it not readily explicable on

75. Ibid, 165–8.   76. Ibid, 171 (Cotton LJ).   77. Ibid.   78. Ibid, 185 (Lindley LJ).
79. Ibid, 186 (Lindley LJ).   80. Ibid, 190 (Bowen LJ).   81. Ibid, 172 (Cotton LJ).

ordinary motives. The effect of the conjunction of these factors is to create a presumption, which the other party can rebut. The question of whether or not independent advice was obtained is often relevant to the process of rebutting the presumption, but it is not by itself conclusive.

The parties' relationship

Let us begin with the first of the elements of presumed undue influence: the nature of the relationship between the parties. The precise nature of this requirement has been the subject of some debate. Early cases drew a distinction between two sub-categories of type 2 undue influence: Class 2A and Class 2B. Under Class 2A, certain relationships were always treated as 'protected relationships'. Here, the court would always assume, and assume automatically, that the dominant party had the ability to influence the other party. This class includes the relations of solicitor and client, doctor and patient, spiritual advisor and follower, fiancé and fiancée, and parent and child. But it does not include many other common relations, such as that between husband and wife,[82] an adult child and her elderly parents,[83] or a bank and its customers.[84] Relations which do not fall under Class 2A must be brought under Class 2B to trigger the presumption of undue influence. Here, the party claiming to have been subject to undue influence will have to prove the de facto existence of a relationship of trust and confidence.[85]

This classification should not be taken too far. Its only significance is the light it sheds on the types of relationships that give rise to a presumption of the ability to exercise influence. It does not speak to the questions of whether that influence was exercised, or whether that exercise was undue. In *Royal Bank of Scotland Plc v Etridge (No 2)*,[86] the House of Lords expressed some scepticism about the broader utility of this classification. *Etridge*, like many recent cases on undue influence, arose out of a business loan, which was secured by a mortgage on the businessman's house. The house was jointly owned by the businessman and his wife, and the wife had consented to the mortgage. When the business failed and the bank sought to enforce its security, the wife contended that the contract had been procured by undue influence. In discussing the law, Lord Nicholls did not use the terminology of classification, although he accepted that undue influence encompassed cases in which there would need to be '[p]roof that the complainant placed trust and confidence in the other party'[87] as well as cases in which '[t]he complainant need not prove he actually reposed trust and confidence in the other party. It is sufficient for him to prove the existence of the type of relationship.'[88] Other judges were more openly critical of the 'wisdom of the practice which has grown up . . . of attempting to make classifications of cases of undue influence', which 'add mystery rather than illumination'.[89]

Given the narrowness of the class of protected relationships, in the majority of cases where a presumption of undue influence is sought to be established it will be necessary to demonstrate on the facts that a relationship of trust and confidence subsisted

---

82. *Midland Bank plc v Shephard* [1988] 3 All ER 17.
83. *Avon Finance Co Ltd v Bridger* [1985] 2 All ER 281.
84. *National Westminster Bank Ltd v Morgan* [1985] AC 686.
85. *Barclays Bank Plc v O'Brien* [1994] 1 AC 180 (HL).   86. [2002] 2 AC 773 (HL).
87. Ibid, [14].   88. Ibid, [18].   89. Ibid, [92] (Lord Clyde).

between the parties. This does not depend on the characteristics of only one party. Instead, it requires examining the relationship as a whole. The mere fact that one of the parties is vulnerable, physically frail, or suffers from cognitive impairment is not by itself enough to create a relationship of trust and confidence,[90] especially where they can be said to be confident and know their own mind.[91]

Strong hierarchies, coupled with institutional identification, are frequently sufficient to make a relationship one of trust and confidence. This was the case in *Allcard v Skinner*,[92] and it was also the case in *R v Attorney-General for England and Wales*,[93] discussed in section 12.2.3. In the latter case, the Privy Council was swayed by the combination of the military hierarchy, the culture of regimental pride, and R's admiration for his commanding officer. As in *Allcard*, these were seen as creating 'a relationship in which the army as an institution, or the commanding officer as an individual, were able to exercise influence over him'.[94]

The question is less straightforward where institutional identification and hierarchy are absent. Here, the courts tend to look at the extent to which one party relies on another in the conduct of their affairs. In *Lloyds Bank Ltd v Bundy*,[95] the court was faced with a transaction between a bank and a customer. The key question was whether the relationship was an ordinary commercial banking relationship or whether it had acquired an additional character of trust and confidence. On the facts, it was held that it had acquired that additional character. The Court of Appeal was swayed by the fact that Bundy had not just banked at the same branch for several years, but that he also placed a great deal of reliance in the manager of that bank for financial advice, and that the manager was aware of this reliance.

The primary reason for the decision was the nature and extent of the reliance reposed by Bundy in the manager, rather than in the fact that the relationship was one of banking. In *Watson v Huber*,[96] the claimant had relied heavily on her stepsister for her financial affairs, to the extent that she operated an account in their joint names. The court held that this was sufficient to create a relationship of trust and confidence. On the flipside, in the absence of such factors, a relationship between banker and customer will not be held to be one of trust and confidence.[97]

The marital relationship has proven a particularly difficult one to deal with. The nature of the marital relationship gives it a particular propensity to generate what the Irish High Court has called 'emotionally transmitted debt'[98] and, hence, to raise questions about the boundary between actions done out of love and those produced by undue influence. At one level, it is obvious that there is a strong bond between individuals who are married, or who are in a similar relationship. Yet it cannot from this be assumed that the relationship is one of influence. It is perfectly normal for spouses or partners to independently assess the merits of a particular course of action. Equally, it is also perfectly normal for spouses to undertake a course of

---

90. *Birmingham City Council v Beech* [2013] EWHC 518 (QB), upheld by the Court of Appeal in [2014] EWCA Civ 830.
91. *Gorjat v Gorjat* [2010] EWHC 1537 (Ch).   92. (1887) 36 Ch D 145.
93. [2003] UKPC 22.   94. Ibid, [24] (Lord Hoffmann).
95. [1975] QB 326 (CA).   96. [2005] All ER (D) 156 (Mar).
97. See eg *National Westminster Bank Ltd v Morgan* [1985] AC 686.
98. *Allied Irish Banks plc v Rostaff Property Development Ltd* [2017] IEHC 533, [6] (Barrett J).

action due to a genuine desire to support their spouse, rather than due to being under the influence of the spouse. As a result, the courts have tended to only hold marital relationships to be relationships of trust and confidence if there are specific factors pointing to one spouse having a high degree of influence over the other, or to one reposing a high degree of trust and reliance in the other.[99] On the flipside, the fact that they appreciate that they are taking a risk, and place no more trust than is normal in a family relationship, will weigh against the conclusion that the relationship was one of trust and confidence.[100] Either way, the marital relationship is by default not treated as one of trust and confidence, in the absence of specific factors to the contrary.

In addition to relationships of trust and confidence, in *Etridge* Lord Nicholls stated that undue influence could also apply to relationships of 'reliance, dependence or vulnerability on the one hand and ascendancy, domination or control on the other'.[101] The emphasis here is not so much on the trust one party reposes in the other as it is on the power which one party exercises over the other. *Macklin v Dowsett*[102] is a good example of this principle in action. Dowsett's house had been condemned by the local authorities. He was required to demolish it. He had been given permission to build another, but only if he started building it within five years. He lacked the financial resources to do this. He sold the land to the Macklins in exchange for money and a life tenancy. He used the money to pay off a mortgage debt, and consequently continued to lack the resources to build a new house. In 1999, a month before planning permission expired, the Macklins laid foundations for the house at a cost of £1,700. They also entered into an agreement with Dowsett, under which he granted them an option to require him to surrender his life tenancy if he had not completed the new house within three years. He was unable to do so, and the Macklins sought to evict him. The Court of Appeal found for Dowsett on the basis of undue influence. At the time the option agreement was entered into, Dowsett was close to losing his planning permission, and lacked the finances to start construction. The Macklins knew this, and sought to exploit his financial position. Given the financial disparities between the parties, and Dowsett's vulnerable position, the relationship was one of ascendancy and dependency at the material time.

The idea of ascendancy and dependency should not, however, be taken too far. A relationship will not be one of ascendancy and dependency simply because the parties were in an unequal position. It is, in particular, extremely unlikely that the *commercial* inequality of bargaining power will be seen as creating a relationship of ascendancy and dependency. To return to Problem 12, in the absence of an element of control, neither the inequality of bargaining power between the bank and Jarrow Steel, nor the bank's exploitation of it, will give rise to a presumption of influence. In contrast, the fact that Charles's wife and son rely on him to run the business, and almost always accept his commercial judgment without questioning it, would tend to suggest that

---

99. See eg *Barclays Bank plc v O'Brien* [1994] 1 AC 180 (HL).

100. See eg *Thompson v Foy* [2009] EWHC 1076 (Ch) (in the context of a mother–daughter relationship).

101. [2002] 2 AC 773 (HL), [11].   102. [2004] EWCA Civ 904.

the relationship between them is one of trust and confidence, thus giving rise to a presumption of influence as far as his dealings with them are concerned.

'Not readily explicable'

The mere existence of a relationship of trust and confidence (or ascendancy and dependency) is insufficient. There must also be something about the *transaction* in question that raises a presumption of undue influence. Until the 1990s, cases often used the terminology of 'manifest disadvantage' to describe this requirement, both in relation to actual undue influence[103] and in relation to presumed undue influence.[104] This language has since been rejected by the House of Lords. In relation to actual undue influence, the House of Lords held in *CIBC Mortgages plc v Pitt*[105] that there was no such requirement in cases of actual undue influence. Any transaction which was procured by undue influence was invalid, regardless of whether or not it was to the victim's disadvantage. In relation to presumed undue influence, in contrast, the language was rejected in *Royal Bank of Scotland Plc v Etridge (No 2)*[106] because it was held to be an inaccurate description of the relevant legal requirement. There may be very good reasons for a person to enter into a disadvantageous transaction. A wife who puts up surety for her husband's business is clearly entering into a disadvantageous transaction, but will often be doing so because she has an interest in her spouse's business succeeding.

Given this, the House of Lords in *Etridge* returned to a formulation remarkably close to that in *Allcard v Skinner*. In *Allcard*, the Court of Appeal had focused on whether the transaction could be 'reasonably accounted for' on ordinary motives. In *Etridge*, the House of Lords reformulated the test to state that the presumption will only apply if the transaction 'is not readily explicable' by ordinary motives or the relationship of the parties.[107] It must call for an explanation which is not forthcoming. In such a case, the burden shifts to the dominant party to show that he or she did not abuse the position of dominance.[108]

Since the decision in *Etridge*, the courts have shown an increased willingness to hold that a transaction was explicable with references to considerations other than undue influence. In *Turkey v Awadh*,[109] a father had entered into an agreement with his son and daughter-in-law, under which he took a long lease of property they owned. In return, he paid them money to enable them to clear a mortgage on the property and certain other debts which they owed. The Court of Appeal held that the presumption of undue influence did not apply, as the transaction did in fact have an easy explanation: the son and daughter-in-law would not have been able to pay off the mortgage in any other way. It is only where the transactions have involved significant proportions of the assets of the complainant with the complainant receiving nothing in return,[110] or where the transaction does not admit of any other independent reason, that the

---

103. *Bank of Credit and Commerce International SA v Aboody* [1990] 1 QB 923.
104. See eg *National Westminster Bank plc v Morgan* [1985] AC 686.
105. [1994] 1 AC 200 (HL), [26].   106. [2002] 2 AC 773 (HL).
107. Ibid, [21] (Lord Nicholls).   108. *Turkey v Awadh* [2005] EWCA Civ 382, [15] (Buxton LJ).
109. Ibid.   110. See eg *Watson v Huber* [2005] All ER (D) 156 (Mar).

courts have tended to be willing to hold that the transaction is not readily explicable, triggering the presumption of undue influence.[111]

Bringing this back to Problem 12, the upshot would appear to be that Charles will be unable to raise a presumption against the bank, because that transaction is readily explicable with reference to considerations other than undue influence. As far as the guarantees issued by Eilidh and their son go, however, the facts appear to be quite clear. As shareholders, they certainly had reasons for wanting the company to succeed. But the specific manner in which they issued the guarantees—without taking legal advice, and notwithstanding their concerns and uncertainty about what it meant for them—is not readily explicable save with reference to the confidence they placed in Charles. This will almost certainly be sufficient to raise a presumption of undue influence.

Rebutting the presumption

In order to rebut the presumption of undue influence, the dominant party will have to show that the complainant entered into the transaction freely, and in awareness of the risks. A classic way of doing this is by showing that the complainant received independent legal advice. In *Wadlow v Samuel*,[112] a settlement agreement was alleged to have been vitiated by undue influence. The Court of Appeal rejected the argument, in significant part on the basis that the complainant had sought and received independent legal advice.

The recognition of the importance of independent legal advice goes back to *Allcard v Skinner*, but it is not conclusive. A presumption of undue influence may be rebutted even if no independent advice was taken, and equally a court may hold that the presumption has not been rebutted even if independent legal advice was taken. But it is, nevertheless, an important factor.[113] Legal advice will not rebut a presumption of undue influence if the advisor was unaware of relevant circumstances, or if it did not meet the standard of advice from a competent or honest advisor acting in the complainant's interest.[114]

On the facts of Problem 12, it is hard to see how the presumption of undue influence, once raised, could be rebutted save with reference to independent legal advice. As a result, it is likely that the guarantees issued by Eilidh and her son will be held to have been procured by undue influence.

12.3.3 **Remedies and third parties**

A contract procured by undue influence is voidable. This means that the complainant has the option of affirming it or rescinding it. The usual remedy for undue influence, accordingly, is rescission. The contract must be affirmed or rescinded in its entirety. Partial rescission is not possible in English law.[115] The right to rescind may be lost through affirmation or the lapse of time, as happened in *Allcard v Skinner*. Where some

---

111. See eg *Smith v Cooper* [2010] EWCA Civ 722.   112. [2007] EWCA Civ 155.

113. See *Royal Bank of Scotland Plc v Etridge (No 2)* [2002] 2 AC 773 (HL), [20] (Lord Nicholls); *Curtis v Curtis* [2011] EWCA Civ 1602.

114. *Inche Noriah v Shaik Allie Bin Omar* [1929] AC 127 (PC).

115. See *TSB Bank plc v Camfield* [1995] 1 WLR 430.

benefits have been provided, the court may order counter-restitution. If exact counter-restitution is not possible, the court will typically make an order that restores the parties as nearly as possible to their original position. The details of these remedies are discussed in Chapter 11, and will not be repeated here.

Specific issues arise in relation to undue influence where third parties are involved. Consider, once again, Problem 12. Even if it can be shown that the consent of Charles Palmer's wife and son was procured through undue influence, the relief they will want to seek is not against Charles. It is against the bank. They will, in other words, seek relief not against the person exercising undue influence, but against a third party because it is a contract with that third party (in this case, the personal guarantee) that they seek to have set aside.

Situations of this sort are very common in practice, and a number of the cases we have referred to in this section, including *Royal Bank of Scotland Plc v Etridge*,[116] *CIBC Mortgages plc v Pitt*,[117] and *Annulment Funding Co Ltd v Cowney*,[118] involved relief that was sought against a third party, almost always a lender. The transactions in these cases, much like the transaction in Problem 12, involved a person agreeing, as a result of undue influence, to stand surety for the debts of another.

Under what circumstances, then, does undue influence affect the position of a third party lender? The traditional answer to this question was that a third party would only be affected by undue influence if it had actual or constructive notice of the exercise of undue influence.[119] In *Etridge*, however, the House of Lords criticized the language of constructive notice. The correct question to ask, they held, was whether there was something about the transaction that ought to have put the bank 'on inquiry' as to the presence of undue influence. In general, a bank will be put on inquiry if the transaction involves a person guaranteeing a loan to their spouse, or more broadly any guarantee arising out of a non-commercial relationship.

Once a bank is put on inquiry, it must take several steps. First, it must tell the surety to seek independent advice from a solicitor. It must then provide the solicitor with all relevant financial information relating to the facility and the borrower's indebtedness. If it has any reasons to specifically suspect undue influence (apart from being put on inquiry generally), it must inform the solicitor of that reason. The solicitor must give her advice at a face-to-face meeting with the surety, in the absence of the borrower. Finally, the bank must obtain written confirmation from the solicitor that the nature of the documents, the obligations they create, and their practical implications have been explained to the surety. A bank which follows these steps will be taken to have satisfied itself that the surety entered into the transaction of his own free will, rather than as a result of undue influence. The result is that the bank is protected even if it transpires that the contract was, in fact, induced by undue influence.

In Problem 12, it is apparent that the bank failed to require any of these steps to be taken, although it should have been put on inquiry under the rule in *Etridge*. This means that Eilidh and her son (but not Charles) are likely to be able to successfully contest the validity of the guarantees they issued, should they seek to do so.

---

116. [2002] 2 AC 773 (HL).   117. [1994] 1 AC 200 (HL), [26].
118. [2010] EWCA Civ 711.   119. *Barclays Bank v O'Brien* [1994] 1 AC 180.

Debates in context: a doctrine of unconscionability?

Neither duress nor undue influence deal squarely with the problems posed by inequality of bargaining power, or aggressive bargaining. Some sense of what is missing can be deduced by examining the position in the US, where the common law has developed a much broader doctrine of unconscionability. The decision of the US Court of Appeals for the DC Circuit in *Williams v Walker-Thomas Furniture Co*[120] illustrates the scope of this doctrine.

The Walker-Thomas Furniture Co was located in a poor, and predominantly African-American, part of Washington DC. It sold furniture on credit to residents of that area. Its credit was, however, subject to an unusual term. Until a purchaser had paid the purchase price on all furniture that he had purchased from it, none of the furniture was treated as having been paid off. In effect, missing an instalment on one item meant that the company could repossess everything it had sold to the purchaser. This is precisely what happened to Mrs Williams. Between 1957 and 1962, she had bought a number of items of furniture from the company. In 1962, she bought a stereo set from them. She had $164 outstanding at the time, which the purchase of the stereo set raised to $678. At the time, she had a monthly income of $218. When she missed an instalment, the company sought to repossess everything she had purchased between 1957 and 1962. It was entitled to do so under the contract. Nevertheless, the court held the contract to be unenforceable, because there was an element of unconscionability present at the time it was made. The unconscionability arose from a combination of the absence of meaningful choice on the part of Mrs Williams and the fact that the contract terms were unreasonably favourable to the company. Mrs Williams lacked a meaningful choice because the gross inequality of bargaining power, coupled with the fact that she did not have a reasonable chance to understand the contract's terms, meant that her consent was never given to all the terms. The terms were unreasonable because they were 'so extreme as to appear unconscionable according to the mores and business practices of the time and place'.

This decision weaves together elements of the formation process *and* the substance of the term complained of into a single doctrine. English law on duress and undue influence, as we have seen in this chapter, does not do this. In 1974, Lord Denning made a determined attempt to alter English law. In his decision in *Lloyds Bank v Bundy*,[121] he attempted to weld duress, undue influence, and equitable rules on the protection of weaker parties into a single doctrine of 'inequality of bargaining power'. Through this doctrine, he envisaged English law giving relief to a person

> who, without independent advice, enters into a contract or transfers property for a consideration which is grossly inadequate, when his bargaining power is grievously impaired by reason of his own needs or desires, or by his own ignorance or infirmity, coupled with undue influences or pressures brought to bear on him by or for the benefit of the other.

The other judges in the Court of Appeal, however, decided the case on narrower grounds. In 1985, the House of Lords definitively rejected Lord Denning's proposed approach in *National Westminster Bank plc v Morgan*.[122]

→

---

120. 350 F2d 445 (DC Circuit, 1965).   121. [1975] QB 326 (CA).
122. [1985] AC 686 (HL).

→

Underlying this rejection is the courts' reluctance to intervene too deeply in the bargaining process. This reluctance is clearly visible in the cases discussed in this chapter, and it reflects the same underlying perception as that discussed in Chapter 9 in the context of agreements to negotiate: namely, that bargaining is inherently an individualistic and competitive process, which it would be wrong to fetter. English law has, instead, preferred to rely on statutory rules restricting the ability of parties to rely on specific types of onerous clauses. A case such as *Williams*, were it to arise in England, would be decided not with reference to a broad doctrine of unconscionability, but with reference to the provisions of s 140A of the Consumer Credit Act 1974 which restricts certain types of onerous provisions in credit agreements. The rejection also reflects English law's suspicion of broader principles generally. Shortly after the decision in *Bundy*, Professor LS Sealy, a leading commentator on commercial contracts, argued that the doctrines which Lord Denning had sought to weld together were so different that it was impossible to identify a coherent set of common elements in them.[123]

Support for the narrower position has also come from commentators who adopt an economic approach. In an article deeply critical of Lord Denning's decision in *Bundy*, Professor Michael Trebilcock, a leading commentator in law and economics, argued that courts were not in fact in a position to be able to put transactions in the context of the relevant market. Lord Denning's decision would make them prone to see terms as unfair which, in their proper context, were both fair and necessary.[124] Richard Epstein, an American professor also broadly associated with the Law and Economics movement, argued that it made little sense to allow a party to avoid a contract which he had voluntarily accepted without fraud, mistake, or duress.[125]

Nevertheless, the position taken by Lord Denning is not without support. Professor Atiyah has pointed out that English law is based on drawing a sharp distinction between procedural unfairness and substantive unfairness, even though most cases will in reality involve a mixture of both.[126] A clause that may in the abstract seem substantively unfair may seem less so if one examines the bargaining process more closely, and vice versa.

Equally, there is a danger in an overreliance on statute. English statutes have had to periodically be updated to deal with issues that the original versions did not. But such updating cannot be guaranteed and, indeed, is becoming rarer. The strength of the US approach lies in the extent to which it recognizes the close interrelationship between the substantive and procedural aspects of contracts that are the outcome of inequality of bargaining power, and in the flexibility it gives the courts to rework the doctrine in response to changing conditions.

---

123. LS Sealy, 'Undue Influence and Inequality of Bargaining Power' (1975) 34 CLJ 21, 23.

124. M Trebilcock, 'The Doctrine of Inequality of Bargaining Power: Post-Benthamite Economics in the House of Lords (1976) 126 University of Toronto Law Journal 359.

125. R Epstein, 'Unconscionability: A Critical Reappraisal' (1975) 18 Journal of Law and Economics 293.

126. PS Atiyah, 'Contract and Fair Exchange' in PS Atiyah, *Essays on Contract* (Oxford University Press 1986).

12.4 **Regulating aggressive practices**

The rules we have been discussing thus far apply to all types of transactions. Since 2014, consumers have had a separate set of remedies in relation to *aggressive practices* by traders, under the Consumer Protection from Unfair Trading Regulations 2008.[127] The details of these Regulations, the types of transactions to which they apply, and the remedies they grant are discussed in Chapter 11, in section 11.4, and will not be repeated here. The focus of this section is on what constitutes an aggressive practice.

Under the Regulations, a commercial practice is aggressive if it meets two conditions. First, it must significantly impair (or be likely to significantly impair) 'the average consumer's freedom of choice or conduct', and do so 'through the use of harassment, coercion or undue influence'. Secondly, it must cause (or be likely to cause) the consumer to take a transactional decision that would otherwise not have been taken.[128]

'Undue influence' has a very different meaning in the Regulations when compared with the general law. The Regulations define it to mean:

> exploiting a position of power in relation to the consumer so as to apply pressure, even without using or threatening to use physical force, in a way which significantly limits the consumer's ability to make an informed decision.[129]

'Coercion' is not defined, beyond a statement that it includes the use of physical force. There is no definition of what is meant by 'harassment'.

Whether a practice is aggressive is to be determined by taking account of all its features and circumstances, and with reference to its factual context.[130] A range of factors are relevant to deciding whether a commercial practice used harassment, coercion, or undue influence. These include, amongst other things, its timing, nature, and persistence;[131] whether threatening or abusive language or behaviour was used;[132] whether the trader threatened to take actions which cannot legally be taken;[133] and whether the trader exploited specific misfortunes or circumstances of which he was aware, and which could have impaired the consumer's judgment.[134]

If an aggressive factor was a significant factor in a consumer's decision to enter into a contract, then the consumer has a statutory right to unwind the transaction, demand a discount, or obtain damages. The details of these remedies are discussed in Chapter 11, section 11.4.

The utility of this regime can easily be seen if we return to Illustration 12.2, involving the aggressive laptop repairman. The repairman's actions are likely to have amounted to duress to goods. However, they are even more likely to amount to 'coercion' within the meaning of the 2008 Regulations. From a consumer's point of view, proving this is far easier than proving the ingredients of duress, and the remedy it gives—in this case, the remedy to unwind the transaction—is likely to be far easier, and far more efficacious, than the equivalent common law remedy.

127. SI 2008/1277.   128. Reg 7(1).   129. Reg 7(3)(b).
130. Reg 7(1).   131. Reg 7(2)(a).   132. Reg 7(2)(b).
133. Reg 7(2)(e).   134. Reg 7(2)(c).

12.5 In conclusion: dealing with aggressive bargaining

Let us draw the threads together by returning to the problem with which this chapter began. What sort of outcome is it likely to produce, and what does that tell us about the law more generally?

We can begin by pointing to the features of the bank's conduct which the court will not take into account in determining whether JSC and the guarantors have a right to avoid the contract. The fact that the bank raised the issue at the last minute in a manner that left JSC with little choice—which, from a commercial perspective, lies at the heart of JSC's complaint—is largely irrelevant. The courts have in past cases stressed that a threat does not become illegitimate simply because it was made at a late stage, if it would have been legitimate at an earlier stage. Equally, a threat not to contract will only be held illegitimate in exceptional cases. JSC's past relationship with the bank, too, will not be of relevance in deciding whether the transaction is voidable. What matters is whether they placed trust and confidence in the bank or its employees, and this is unlikely to be the case in a purely commercial transaction such as that in Problem 12. The law is somewhat more responsive to the pressure placed by Charles Palmer on his wife and son. Yet here, too, the remedy is only practically available because of the failure of the bank to follow the process set out by the court in *Etridge*. Had that process been followed, no remedy would have lain notwithstanding the other pressures the borrowers were under.

English law's reluctance to intervene more heavily in regulating the process of negotiation reflects two underlying concerns. First, in a remedial sense, English law is relatively inflexible. The remedy for duress and undue influence is to rescind the contract entirely. There is no middle way. Civil law jurisdictions, in contrast, do give their courts the power to make orders short of rescission. In Dutch law, for example, a court has the option to modify the effects of the abuse of circumstances 'in order to undo its disadvantageous results' as an alternative to nullifying it.[135] Giving courts such a broad power is, however, quite contrary to the way in which English law approaches commercial transactions. While the remedy remains as inflexible as it currently is, the courts are unlikely to exercise it more broadly than they currently do. Secondly, the courts' reluctance to intervene more overtly in regulating bargaining reflects their view that commercial bargaining is best treated as an individualistic, self-interested process, where the responsibility to protect parties primarily vests with the parties.

On both these points, consumer contracts differ from commercial contracts. The courts do have the power to order remedies short of unwinding the transaction in a consumer contract—for example, a discount. Equally, the law intervenes more rigorously to regulate traders' commercial practices in respect of their customers in consumer contracts than in commercial contracts. This reflects a theme that is increasingly coming to the fore in English law; namely, a sharp divergence between its generally robustly individualistic approach to commercial transactions and its increasingly paternalistic approach to consumer transactions. This theme is discussed in greater detail in Chapter 13.

135. BW Art 3:54 lid 2.

Key points

- Excessive pressure can be a problem in contract negotiation. English law deals with this problem through three doctrines: duress, undue influence, and specific rules around aggressive practices.

- Duress and undue influence make a contract voidable (not void). The party affected by duress or undue influence (but not the other party) has the option of rescinding the contract.

- A contract is voidable for duress if one party induces the other to enter into the contract by making a threat which the law regards as illegitimate. Threats which the law regards as illegitimate include threats to the person or to property, as well as subtler forms of economic pressure.

- To determine whether a threat is illegitimate, the court will look both at the nature of the threat itself as well as the nature of the demand it was used to support. Courts are reluctant to treat ordinary commercial pressure as 'duress', although they may do so if the threat involved (for example) a breach of contract.

- There must be a causal link between the threat and the other party's decision to contract. If the threat involved physical violence, then it is enough if the threat was one factor amongst many that led the other party to agree to the contract. If the threat involved economic duress, the party claiming duress must show that he would not have agreed to the contract 'but for' the duress.

- The remedy for duress is rescission of the contract. Damages are not available for duress.

- Undue influence responds to the exploitation by one person of the ability to influence another. A party claiming undue influence must show that the other party had the ability to influence him, and exercised that ability in a way that was undue or unconscionable, inducing him to enter into the contract.

- Undue influence is difficult to prove. However, the courts will presume undue influence if: (a) there was a relationship between the parties of trust and confidence or of power; and (b) the transaction between the parties is not readily explicable.

- This presumption can be rebutted by showing that the transaction was entered into freely. This is usually done by demonstrating that the other party had independent advice.

- Undue influence can also affect contracts with third parties, if there was something about the transaction that put the third party on inquiry about the possibility of undue influence. In such a case, the third party must take steps to satisfy itself that the transaction was freely entered into.

- A special statutory regime for consumers protects them against aggressive commercial practices by sellers. This includes the use of harassment, coercion, or the exploitation of power.

Assess your learning

You should be able to respond to each of the following points with a confident 'yes'. If you can't, then you should revisit the sections listed against that point.

Can you:

(a) *Outline* the key requirements of duress, and the types of threats to which it applies? (Sections 12.2.1 and 12.2.2)

(b) *Explain* what makes a threat illegitimate, and *identify* the key factors that courts examine in determining whether a particular threat was illegitimate? (Section 12.2.3)

(c) *Understand* the different ways in which courts assess causation in relation to different types of duress? (Section 12.2.4)

(d) *Identify* the type of situations to which undue influence applies, and *outline* the key requirements of actual undue influence? (Section 12.3.1)

(e) *Explain* the effect of the presumption of undue influence, *outline* the factors that lead to the presumption being triggered, and *describe* the ways in which it can be rebutted? (Section 12.3.2)

(f) *Explain* how third parties are affected by undue influence, and *outline* the steps they must take to satisfy themselves that the transaction was freely entered into? (Section 12.3.3)

(g) *Identify* the types of practices that are prohibited by the regulations on aggressive commercial practices? (Section 12.4)

In relation to each of the above, you should be able to:

(i) identify and clearly explain the key rules and principles;

(ii) identify the key cases and statutes, and why they matter;

(iii) apply the principles and cases to specific real or hypothetical fact situations;

(iv) evaluate the limitations, if any, of the law as it currently stands.

Further reading

PS Atiyah, 'Contract and Fair Exchange' in PS Atiyah, *Essays on Contract* (Oxford University Press 1986).

R Auchmuty, 'The Rhetoric of Quality and the Problem of Heterosexuality' in L Mulcahy and S Wheeler (eds), *Feminist Perspectives on Contract Law* (Routledge 2005).

J Beatson, 'Duress as a Vitiating Factor in Contract' (1974) 33 CLJ 97.

D Capper, 'Undue Influence and Unconscionability: A Rationalisation' (1998) 114 LQR 479.

M Chen-Wishart, 'The *O'Brien* Principle and Substantive Unfairness' (1997) 56 CLJ 60.

N Enonchong, *Duress, Undue Influence, and Unconscionable Dealing* (2nd edn, Sweet & Maxwell 2012).

E Macdonald, 'Duress by Threatened Breach of Contract' [1989] JBL 460.

A Phang and H Tijo, 'The Uncertain Boundaries of Undue Influence' [2000] Conv 573.

SA Smith, 'Contracting Under Pressure: A Theory of Duress' (1997) 56 CLJ 343.

D Tiplady, 'The Judicial Control of Contractual Unfairness' (1983) 46 MLR 601.

Controlling contract terms

Exclusion clauses, penalties, and consumer protection

'Blessed are the meek'*

* Matthew 5:5.

Problem 13: setting the context

Consider the following scenario:

> Bernard Williams, a final year student at the University of Carmarthenshire, goes on a trip to the Gower Peninsula with his friends. They stay in a bed and breakfast. They are extremely dissatisfied with their accommodation. Bernard leaves a negative review on a popular Welsh travel reviews site.
>
> A month later, he is shocked to discover that the bed and breakfast has charged a sum of £1,000 to his credit card. When he contacts them, they point to the following clause in their terms and conditions, which he accepted when he made the booking:
>
> **13. Reviews:**
>
> (a) The customer agrees that he will contact the hotel with any complaints or concerns he may have in relation to the stay prior to leaving a negative review on any public forum, in print or online.
>
> (b) A negative review may only be left if the hotel has been given at least 28 days to resolve the complaint, and has failed to do so in that period.
>
> (c) The customer agrees that he will be liable to pay the hotel compensation of up to £1,000 for the harm to its reputation and loss of business if he leaves a negative review in breach of this clause. The customer consents to the hotel collecting this money through a charge to the payment card provided as security for his booking.

The term at issue in this scenario is problematic from the point of view of the affected party. This is partly because it is onerous, but also because the affected party had no realistic chance to negotiate the term. Nevertheless, in terms of the formation process, it was accepted by the party and forms part of the contract. Should its onerous character, or the fact that it could not have been negotiated, in any way affect its legal effect? If so, how, and to what extent?

13.1 Introduction: the limits of freedom of contract

Clauses such as the one at issue in Problem 13 are surprisingly common in contracting, and reflect an imbalance of bargaining power. One party prepares the terms, while the other has little or no opportunity to negotiate to alter them.

One way of dealing with this is to regulate the formation process itself, setting limits on how far one party can go in taking advantage of the other party's weaker position. As Chapters 11 and 12 have discussed in some detail, English law only does this in a limited way. Parties are not required to negotiate in good faith, nor is there a general principle against exploiting a superior bargaining position. Instead, English law protects the interests of weaker parties through rules which identify terms which the law considers to be particularly onerous, and limits their effect.

Such rules have long existed. Courts of equity historically had the jurisdiction to grant a party relief against the exercise of several types of contractual powers by the other party, including against the invocation of penal bonds or contractual powers of forfeiture. Statutes, too, often regulated specific types of clauses or contracts—for example, by imposing restrictions on the ability of railway companies to exclude liability for damage to goods caused by their negligence.

The modern law of contract, similarly, contains rules derived from common law and statute which restrict the ability of parties to a contract to rely on onerous terms. As is the case with much of English contract law, there is no general principle underlying these rules. There is no general rule applicable to all onerous terms, nor is there any general theoretical or doctrinal basis that the various restrictions imposed by law have in common. Instead, the rules setting limits to freedom of contract are particularistic, being addressed either to specific subject matters, types of terms, or parties. They do, nevertheless, share a common concern: namely, that weaker parties lack the ability to effectively protect themselves in the course of contracting, and that this can have material adverse effects not just on the parties themselves but also on the public interest.

As Chapter 1 discusses, Professors Adams and Brownsword suggested in the 1990s that this marked a significant shift in contract law. Contract law, in their account, had for much of the 20th century largely left it to the parties to protect their interests. If they failed to do so, the law would not do it for them. They termed this approach 'market individualism', on the basis that it gave a central role to the logic of free bargaining on a market, and did so in a manner that was highly individualistic.

In the 1970s, however, contract law began to take on a more paternalistic role. Parties with limited bargaining power, such as consumers and employees, received legal protection from the more egregious terms that might have been inserted into contracts if they were left solely to markets. In addition, the law also proactively began to insert terms into contracts that were designed to protect the interests of the weaker party, and which the weaker party could not have individually negotiated. They termed this a 'consumer-welfarist' approach, on the basis that it was individual consumers who were the intended beneficiaries of the majority of these rules.

In this chapter, we will examine the logic underlying the legal regulation of contract terms, and study a few examples of such regulation. There are a vast range of statutes and common law rules imposing limits on onerous contract terms, and it is impossible to cover them all in an introductory textbook. The aim of this chapter will, instead, be to give you an overview of the main *types* of rules that we find in the law, and the type of *circumstance* in which they tend to operate. We will begin by looking in section 13.2 at the role played by formal requirements, such as the requirement that contracts be in writing. We will then look, in section 13.3, at how the law regulates one of the types of terms that have historically been most problematic—namely, contract terms which seek to alter the liability that one party will have in the event of breach. Clauses of this type typically work by restricting the extent of a party's responsibility for defective performance, or by seeking to use financial consequences to deter a party from pursuing a particular course of conduct, as in Problem 13. In Section 13.4, we will move from studying legal regulation of particular types of *terms* to looking at how the law seeks, more broadly, to protect the interests of particular types of *transactors*. Our focus in this section will be on consumer contracts and, in particular, on the manner in which the law seeks to deal with the problem of **unfair terms** in consumer contracts.

13.2 **The requirement of writing**

One of the oldest ways of regulating contracts is by requiring them to meet certain requirements of form. Historically, many types of contracts had to be executed in a particular form. In the modern context, three such requirements survive. Some contracts are required to be made by deed,[1] some are required to be made in writing, and others are required to be evidenced in writing. This section describes a few such contracts and the rationale underlying the formal requirements.

The most commonly encountered requirements are those relating to disposition of interests in land, found in the Law of Property Act 1925 and the Law of Property (Miscellaneous Provisions) Act 1989. Under s 53 of the Law of Property Act 1925, a number of different types of agreements are required to either be in writing or be evidenced in writing. Conveyances of interests in land are subject to an even higher requirement: under s 52(1), they must be made by deed. Section 2(1) of the Law of Property (Miscellaneous Provisions) Act 1989 adds a further requirement; namely, that contracts for the sale or disposition of an interest in land must be made through a written instrument which incorporates all terms which the parties have expressly agreed. Similarly, s 4 of the Statute of Frauds 1677 requires guarantee agreements under which one person promises 'to answer for the debt, default or miscarriage of another person' to be in writing and signed by the guarantor or a person authorized by him.

The policy underlying the requirement that agreements be in writing, or follow a particular format, is to promote certainty, avoid evidential difficulty, and ensure that certain types of contracts are not entered into without full thought being given to their implications.[2] Nevertheless, such requirements can also have deleterious consequences, as *Yeoman's Row v Cobbe*[3] illustrates. Cobbe, a developer, entered into an oral development agreement with a company called Yeoman's Row to develop a property in London. He proceeded to obtain planning permission at considerable effort and expense. Because the property market was frothy at the time, the value of the property increased significantly during this period. Once Cobbe had obtained planning permission, the owners refused to proceed with the transaction, and found another developer who was willing to pay a higher price. Even though this was a breach of their agreement with Cobbe, he had no remedy for breach of contract. The agreement had not been reduced to writing, making it unenforceable under s 2 of the Law of Property (Miscellaneous Provisions) Act 1989.[4]

---

1. See Chapter 3 ('Consideration') for a discussion of deeds.
2. For a general discussion, see GHL Fridman, 'The Necessity for Writing in Contracts Within the Statute of Frauds' (1985) 35 University of Toronto Law Journal 43.
3. [2008] UKHL 55, [2008] 1 WLR 1752.
4. As Chapter 17, section 17.4.2, discusses in greater detail, Cobbe was able to obtain a remedy in *quantum meruit*, but the amount he received was a small fraction of what he would have received for breach of contract.

Pitts v Jones,[5] which is also discussed in Chapter 3, section 3.2.1, is a similar example arising out of the Statute of Frauds. Jones was the majority shareholder in a company, in which the claimants held minority stakes. Jones intended to sell his shares to a third party, WG Birch Ltd. The claimants were told they could sell their shares to Birch six months later, but not straight away. They were unhappy about the delay. To induce them to agree to the transaction, Jones gave them an oral undertaking that he would pay the price of their shares if Birch failed to do so. Birch became insolvent before paying. When the claimants sued Jones on his oral undertaking, it was held that the agreement between them and Jones was unenforceable. It was a contract of guarantee, and as such had to be in writing under the Statute of Frauds 1677.

These cases are clearly problematic. The difficulty with imposing formal requirements on commercial transactions is that they are frequently entered into by business people without legal advice. The requirements of the Statute of Frauds, or even of the Law of Property Act, are not common knowledge, and the result is that they often take business people by surprise. The Law Reform Committee, which recommended in 1952 that the requirement of the Statute of Frauds in relation to guarantees be retained, justified it on the basis that it was necessary to ensure that inexperienced people were not led into obligations which they did not understand.[6] But it is hard to see how the requirement of writing furthers this requirement. A guarantee buried in a complex 30-page document does nothing to make it clearer to 'inexperienced people' what their obligations are; yet it will be perfectly enforceable under the Statute of Frauds. The requirement that guarantees be signed is particularly problematic in an era where contracts are concluded over email. Although the courts try to take a commercially realistic approach—holding, for example, that the sender's name typed at the bottom of a single email can authenticate a contract contained in a chain of emails[7]—they cannot ignore the plain words of the statute.

A very different, and more justifiable, approach to formal requirements has been taken in more recent statutes. The requirements of form they impose are more nuanced, unlike the Law of Property Act or the Statute of Frauds, and expressly targeted at ensuring that the weaker party understands their rights and obligations under the contract, as well as their rights and obligations under the general law. The Consumer Credit Act 1974 provides a good example. Under s 61(1) of this Act, certain types of consumer credit agreements must be made in a prescribed form, contain all terms other than implied terms, be in a readily legible state, and be signed by both parties. The policy underlying these requirements is to ensure that the consumer is fully aware of her rights and duties under the agreement as well as under the Consumer Credit Act, the actual charge for the credit, and other matters which it is desirable that she have knowledge of.[8] Critically, because the policy is to protect consumers against exploitation, the failure to comply with the formal requirements only has a unidirectional effect. The agreement cannot be enforced *against the consumer* without the consent of the court.[9] The consumer's own ability to enforce the agreement, however, remains unaffected.

5. [2007] EWCA 1301, [2008] QB 706.
6. Law Reform Committee, *First Report: Statute of Frauds and Section 4 of the Sale of Goods Act 1893* (Cmd 8809, 1953).
7. *Golden Ocean Group Ltd v Salgaocar Mining Industries Pvt Ltd* [2012] EWCA Civ 265.
8. See s 60(1).   9. S 65(1).

Such an approach, which links the formal requirement very clearly to the underlying policy, and expressly seeks to minimize the likelihood of perverse outcomes such as those in *Pitts v Jones*, has much to commend itself. The increased use of such provisions in more recent statutes is, therefore, to be welcomed. Regrettably, it is at present unlikely that the more blunt-edged approaches taken in older statutes will be altered.

13.3 Liability clauses

One type of clause that is commonly seen in contracts is a clause seeking to vary the liability of the parties in the event of breach. A party may seek to restrict its liability in the event of breach—for example, by capping it at a particular figure or by excluding certain types of liability. Alternately, a party may seek to increase the liability of the other party, to ensure that it covers certain types of losses that might not by default fall within the scope of its responsibility or to fix the quantum of damages. Problem 13 is an example of the latter.

Both types of clauses—those that seek to vary a party's liability downwards and those that seek to vary its liability upwards—are subject to legal regulation. The former are the subject of rules relating to exclusion clauses, while the latter are the subject of the *rule against penalties*. In this section, we will begin by examining common law rules governing exclusion clauses (section 13.3.1), followed by statutory rules on exclusion clauses (section 13.3.2), ending with a discussion of the rule against penalties (section 13.3.3).

13.3.1 Exclusion clauses in the common law

> **Illustration 13.1**
>
> Sigrid is staging a performance of Wagner's Ring Cycle in Bayreuth. She orders a steel frame for the dragon from Jarrow Steel Castings in England. Due to a clerical error in the English firm's workshop, the frame is shipped to Beirut, Lebanon instead of Bayreuth, Germany. By the time the error is discovered and the frame located, it is too late to construct the dragon on time for the opening performance, and the first week's performances have to be cancelled, resulting in a very heavy loss. Sigrid discovers that the sale agreement with JSC contains the following clause:
>
> > Our liability for any defects in the work we are contracted to do under this agreement is limited to a full refund of the purchase price.

The clause in Illustration 13.1 is an exclusion clause. Unlike the clause in Problem 13, which seeks to enhance the liability of a party, this clause seeks to reduce the liability of a party.

Exclusion clauses are governed by rules that are in some respects similar to, and in other respects different from, the rules governing other types of clauses in contracts. As far as incorporation is concerned, the same rules apply to exclusion clauses as to any other clause. Many of the rules on incorporation (discussed in Chapter 6) were developed in the context of exclusion clauses, and when considering whether an exclusion clause was validly incorporated into a contract, the courts will apply the standard three-part test of looking at the timing of notice, the nature of the document in which notice was given, and the extent to which attention was drawn to the term.

The interpretation of exclusion clauses, however, presents a different picture. Although the approach described in *Investors Compensation Scheme v West Bromwich Building Society* is not inapplicable, exclusion clauses are subject to two additional rules that are not applied to any other type of clause. The first, the contra proferentem rule, states that an exclusion clause should be construed against the interests of the person seeking to rely on it. The second, referred to as the *Canada Steamship* rule (after the case in which it was first articulated), sets out three principles that the courts should apply in determining whether a contractual clause successfully excludes or limits liability for negligence.

Both doctrines were at one time given a very broad application by English courts, and were applied to confine exclusion clauses to fairly narrow bounds. In recent years, however, English courts have been somewhat more cautious and less expansive in applying these doctrines. An important factor behind this more cautious approach is the creation of statutory schemes regulating exclusion clauses, which has made it somewhat less necessary to rely on common law doctrines of construction. Nevertheless, both rules remain part of English law, and in this section we will look at each in turn.

The *contra proferentem* rule

The essence of the *contra proferentem* rule is simple. It provides that an ambiguous exclusion clause will be construed against the party seeking to rely on the exclusion of liability, and in favour of the party seeking to impose liability. Although the origins of this rule appear to lie in a policy against overly broad exclusions of liability, in the modern context it is purely a rule of interpretation. The underlying logic is, accordingly, that of contextual interpretation. Most parties are unlikely to have wanted to give up a right to claim compensation for breach. As such, when construing an ambiguous exclusion clause contextually, a sensible starting point is that a **reasonable addressee** would read the clause narrowly. However, this is only a starting point. If the matrix of fact suggests that a broader reading of the exclusion clause is the more appropriate one, then that is the one the court will adopt.

Cases decided up to the middle of the last century evidenced a judicial willingness to construe exclusion clauses narrowly even if that meant adopting a strained reading of the clause. In *Andrews Brothers (Bournemouth) Ltd v Singer & Co Ltd*,[10] a term in a contract for the sale of cars, described as 'new Singer cars', provided that 'all conditions, warranties and liabilities implied by statute, common law or otherwise are excluded'. One of the cars delivered was not a new car. When the seller sought to rely on the exclusion clause, the court held that the wording of the clause only applied to implied terms, not express terms, and the term breached here was an express term.

In *Houghton v Trafalgar Insurance Co Ltd*,[11] a clause in an insurance contract excluded liability for damage 'caused or arising whilst the car is conveying any load in excess

10. [1934] 1 KB 17.   11. [1954] 1 QB 247.

of that for which it was constructed'. The car had seating for five people, but was carrying six at the time of the accident. The court held that the exclusion clause was not applicable. The term 'load' was construed to apply only to a limit on the weight the car was carrying, not the number of passengers.

Similarly, in *Beck & Co v Szymanowski & Co*,[12] a contract for the sale of reels of cotton required the buyer to give notice of any defect in the goods within 14 days of their arrival. If no notice was given within that time, the contract provided that 'the goods delivered shall be deemed to be in all respects in accordance with the contract'. Eighteen months after delivery, the buyer discovered that the length of cotton on each reel was shorter than the 200 yards stipulated in the contract. The seller sought to rely on the exclusion clause, but the court held that the clause was not applicable. The clause spoke of liability for goods delivered. However, the court held that the damages that were actually being claimed were not in respect of goods delivered but in respect of goods which were not delivered. This put them outside the ambit of the exclusion clause.

None of these cases have been overruled, but more recent cases show somewhat less willingness to place a strained construction on exclusion clauses. In *Photo Production Ltd v Securicor Ltd*,[13] Lord Diplock summarized what he took to be the general principles underlying the judicial approach to construing exclusion clauses. The starting point must be that:

> Parties are free to agree to whatever exclusion or modification of all types of obligations as they please within the limits that the agreement must retain the legal characteristics of a contract.[14]

Courts are entitled to construe such clauses strictly, and with reference to **reasonableness**, particularly when it comes to the exclusion of duties imposed by implied terms:

> the court's view of the reasonableness of any departure from the implied obligations which would be involved in construing the express words of an exclusion clause in one sense that they are capable of bearing rather than another is a relevant consideration in deciding what meaning the words were intended to bear.[15]

But this only applies if the exclusion clause is genuinely capable of bearing two meanings. Courts should not resort to strained constructions for the sake of reading down an exclusion clause:

> In commercial contracts negotiated between business-men capable of looking after their own interests and of deciding how risks inherent in the performance of various kinds of contract can be most economically borne (generally by insurance), it is, in my view, wrong to place a strained construction upon words in an exclusion clause which are clear and fairly susceptible of one meaning . . .[16]

In *Whitecap Leisure Ltd v John H Rundle Ltd*,[17] the Court of Appeal held that older cases on *contra proferentem* must now be read in the light of the contextual approach to interpretation adopted in *Investors Compensation Scheme v West Bromwich Building Society*. It

12. [1924] AC 43.   13. [1980] 1 AC 827 (HL).   14. Ibid, 850.   15. Ibid, 850–1.
16. Ibid, 851.   17. [2008] EWCA Civ 429.

is only where the parties' objective intention cannot be ascertained from the clause's words read in the context of the document as a whole, and the surrounding matrix of fact, that the *contra proferentem* rule will apply. In all other cases, the courts should read the exclusion clause like any other clause.[18]

Contra proferentem, in other words, has not gone away, but the set of cases in which it is applicable has diminished. The decisions at first instance and on appeal in the case of *University of Keele v Price Waterhouse*[19] illustrate how the post-*Investors* approach to contextual interpretation significantly reduces the role that was formerly played by the *contra proferentem* rule.

Case in depth: *University of Keele v Price Waterhouse* [2004] EWCA Civ 583

Price Waterhouse, a firm of accountants, contacted the University of Keele in 1996 offering to assist them in adopting a 'Profit-Related Pay Scheme'. If this had been successfully adopted, it would have restructured salary payments in a way that saved considerable amounts of tax for the university as well as the staff.

The scheme failed due to Price Waterhouse's negligence. The Revenue's requirements for schemes of this type required 80 per cent of the workforce to participate. Price Waterhouse advised the university that this threshold had been met when, in fact, it had not. The university's auditors refused to sign off on the accounts, leading to the scheme being cancelled. In litigation, Price Waterhouse accepted that it had been negligent in advising the university that the threshold had been met. It had negligently misinterpreted the relevant statute. However, it sought to rely on the following exclusion clause in its contract with the university:

> Subject to the preceding paragraph we accept liability to pay damages in respect of loss or damage suffered by you as a direct result of our providing the Services. All other liability is expressly excluded, in particular consequential loss, failure to realise anticipated savings or benefits and a failure to obtain registration of the scheme.

Price Waterhouse argued that the losses were a 'failure to realise anticipated savings', and were therefore excluded by the clause. At first instance,[20] Hart J rejected this argument. The first half of the paragraph accepted liability for damages that were a direct result of Price Waterhouse's performance, while the second clause excluded liability for the form of loss that was likeliest to be a direct result. This meant the clause was self-contradictory. He accordingly construed the clause *contra proferentem*, and held that it did not apply, leaving Price Waterhouse liable.[21]

Price Waterhouse appealed. The Court of Appeal dismissed the appeal, but approached the construction of the exclusion clause very differently. Rather than apply the *contra proferentem* rule, Arden LJ adopted a contextual reading of the clause. Read as a whole, the use of the word 'other' in the second sentence made it clear that it was a residual category and, as such, only applied to losses not covered by the first sentence. This meant that the

→

---

18. Ibid, [20] (Moore-Bick LJ).   19. [2004] EWCA Civ 583.   20. [2003] EWHC 1595 (Ch).
21. Ibid, [77].

> →
> loss suffered by the university fell within the losses for which Price Waterhouse had expressly accepted liability, and not within the exclusion clause. Because the meaning of the clause was clear once it was properly construed, it was not necessary to apply the *contra proferentem* rule.[22]

The implications of this shift can be seen by returning to Illustration 13.1. Had the courts still been as willing to apply strained readings of exclusion clauses as they were earlier in the 20th century, it is likely that the clause would have been read down, even at the cost of a far-fetched reading, meaning that Sigrid would have been able to sue for breach of contract. In the current approach, however, this can no longer be taken as a given. The court's starting point, in each of these examples, will be on a contextual reading of the clause. It is only where the usual interpretation clause yields a possible multiplicity of meanings that the court will resort to the *contra proferentem* rule.

The *Canada Steamship* rule

A second possible issue arises where the loss has been caused by the negligence of one of the parties, as was the case in Illustration 13.1. In general terms, it does not matter whether a contract has been breached because of a party's fault, or in spite of the party having done everything in its power to perform its contractual obligations. Where exclusion clauses are concerned, however, the law tends to be less willing to give effect to clauses excluding liability where the party has been negligent. The leading case on this point is the decision of the Privy Council in *Canada Steamship v R*.[23] In this case, the Privy Council considered the approach that should be taken when deciding whether an exclusion clause was wide enough to cover loss caused by negligence. Lord Morton set out a three-stage test, which has been widely applied in subsequent cases. In the first stage, the court asks whether the clause in question has *expressly* excluded or limited liability for negligence. If it has, it will be given effect. If the clause does not expressly exclude liability for negligence, the court proceeds to the second stage. Here, it asks whether the clause is worded widely enough to cover negligence. If there is any doubt as to the clause's scope, the court should apply the *contra proferentem* rule. If the *contra proferentem* rule is satisfied, the court proceeds to the third stage. Here, it asks whether the clause could cover some liability *other* than negligence. If the party in breach cannot be liable on any ground other than negligence, the clause is effective to exclude liability for negligence. If the party in breach may be liable on grounds other than negligence, then the clause should generally be construed to only cover those grounds, and not negligence.

The first of these stages is relatively straightforward. It will obviously be satisfied if the exclusion clause expressly mentions 'negligence', but the courts have held that it will also be satisfied by other phrases having a similar meaning, such as 'act, omission, neglect or default'.[24] Where the words used in the exclusion clause are more generic,

22. [2004] EWCA Civ 583, [22]–[26].   23. [1952] AC 192 (PC).
24. *Monarch Airlines Ltd v London Luton Airport Ltd* [1997] CLC 698.

for example 'all losses' or 'any loss howsoever arising', however, it becomes necessary to proceed to the second and third stages. The general import of these stages is that generic words will not be construed as excluding liability for negligence if there was some other ground on which liability might have been based. If, however, negligence is the only basis of liability, then the words will be construed as excluding liability for negligence.[25] The enquiry into whether there is an alternative head of liability is a contextual enquiry, not a technical one. The focus is on looking at

> the facts and realities of the situation as they . . . presented themselves to the contracting parties at the time the contract was made, and ask to what potential liabilities . . . did the parties apply their minds.[26]

If a contextual interpretation suggests that negligence was intended to fall within the exclusion clause, then it will be held to fall within the exclusion clause on a contextual reading, rather than on a strained reading of the words as was not uncommon in the early days of the *Canada Steamship* rule.[27]

In relation to Illustration 13.1, the key question will therefore be whether the phrase 'work we are contracted to do' refers only to the steelwork, or to the entirety of JSC's obligations under the contract (including the dispatch of the goods). This will be answered with reference to the matrix of fact. Once that has been done, the court will move on to asking whether the clause covers liability for negligence. The words 'any defect' are generic. However, given the context, it is likely that they will be held to cover negligence. This is because a significant proportion of the defects that could arise in the manufacture of a steel frame will be attributable to negligence on the part of JSC. The clause is likely to be held to be sufficiently wide to cover the type of loss that is at issue.

13.3.2 Statutory regulation of exclusion clauses

In addition to common law rules, statute has also long restricted the ability of parties to exclude or limit their liability, particularly where negligence is involved. The oldest statutes tended to be very specific, covering particular clauses in particular types of transactions, and the approach they took was not uniform. The Carriers Act 1830, which applied to contracts entered into with public common carriers, prohibited exclusion clauses altogether in relation to certain types of loss.[28] In contrast, the Railway and Canal Traffic Act 1854 permitted parties to exclude liability for negligence if the clause in question was 'just and reasonable'.[29]

---

25. *Alderslade v Hendon Laundry Ltd* [1945] 1 KB 189, 192.

26. *Lamport & Holt Lines Ltd v Coubro & Scrutton (M & I) Ltd* [1982] 2 Lloyd's Rep 42, 50 (May LJ).

27. *Shell UK Ltd v Total UK Ltd* [2010] EWCA Civ 180.

28. Carriers Act 1830, ss 1, 4, restricted the ability of 'mail contractors, stage coach proprietors, or other public common carriers' to 'limit or in any way affect' their liability in respect of 'any injury to any articles and goods' carried by them, unless the value of the goods had not been declared by the consignor. They were, however, permitted to impose a higher charge for the risk of carrying valuable goods (s 2).

29. Railway and Canal Traffic Act 1854, s 7. The section only dealt with loss or injury 'occasioned by the neglect or default of such company or its servants'. The statute took a much more permissive approach to exclusion of liability where the party had not been negligent.

Things have since become more uniform. Currently, two statutes cover the vast majority of exclusion clauses: the Unfair Contract Terms Act (UCTA) 1977 and the Consumer Rights Act 2015. The 1977 Act applies to exclusion clauses in commercial contracts which seek to restrict or limit 'business liability'. Business liability is defined to cover 'liability for breaches of obligations or duties' which arise either from things which someone does in the course of a business or from the occupation of premises used for business purposes.[30] It does not, however, apply to exclusion clauses in contracts involving consumers. These are covered by a separate regime contained in the Consumer Rights Act 2015. This section focuses on the 1977 Act. The Consumer Rights Act is discussed in section 13.4.

The approach of the Act

Illustration 13.2

Consider the following examples, which indicate the sort of circumstances in which UCTA applies.

> Free Range Kids is a newly started early years activity centre based in Hevingham, Norfolk, which provides services to local schools. The owners are worried by press reports concerning the 'compensation culture' and the large awards of damages that are sometimes made for personal injury. They decide to insert a clause in their terms and conditions that excludes all liability for any injuries suffered by children in their charge.

> Wallshire Computing Services is a small business which supplies laptop computers and tablets to businesses. They are concerned about liability for computing devices whose screens have dead pixels (ie pixels which do not light up due to a manufacturing defect). They therefore insert a clause in their terms of sale which excludes liability for dead pixels.

UCTA restricts the validity of clauses such as these. It does so in two ways. Some types of exclusion clauses are prohibited altogether. There are two such prohibitions in UCTA. First, it is not possible for a business to exclude or restrict liability for causing death or personal injury through negligence.[31] For the purposes of UCTA, negligence is defined to cover two things: the breach of any duty to take reasonable care or exercise reasonable skill, whether imposed by common law or arising from the terms of the contract, and a type of statutory duty known as occupier's liability.[32] Secondly, it is not possible to restrict liability for breach of the warranty of title in transactions involving the passing of possession or ownership of goods.[33]

Other exclusion clauses are restricted by being subject to a test of reasonableness. In UCTA this includes clauses excluding or restricting liability for causing loss short of death or personal injury through negligence.[34] It also includes breaches of other

30. S 10.   31. S 2(1).   32. S 1.
33. Ss 6(1), 7(3A). See the discussion of this warranty in Chapter 8, section 8.2.2.   34. S 2(2).

implied terms in contracts where possession or ownership of goods is transferred.[35] Where reasonableness is at issue, the onus is on the person asserting that the term was reasonable to prove it.

As this discussion should suggest, the activity centre's planned exclusion clause in the first scenario in Illustration 13.2 is directly hit by UCTA's prohibition on exclusion or limitation of liability for personal injury. Any such clause will not be enforceable. The only option for a business in the position of Free Range Kids will be to obtain insurance against the risk. It cannot legally exclude liability for the risk.

As far as the second scenario in Illustration 13.2 is concerned, dead pixels will be covered by the implied term as to the quality and fitness for purpose of the goods. As such, liability can only be excluded if it satisfies the requirement of reasonableness.

'Written standard terms of business'

Before we move on to the test of reasonableness, it is important to note that in several cases, UCTA's restrictions only apply if the parties deal on written terms prepared by one of them. Clauses excluding or limiting liability for breach of contract, for example, are only subject to a test of reasonableness if the parties contracted on 'written standard terms of business' prepared by the party who seeks to rely on the exclusion clause.[36] If the contract was individually negotiated, a clause excluding liability for breach will be valid. There is no need to demonstrate that it is reasonable.

What, then, are standard terms of business? The answer appears to be that terms are standard if the party in question habitually contracts on those terms.[37] They must be used for all, or nearly all, the transactions entered into by that company.[38] If the company regularly uses a range of different terms in its contracts, then they are not likely to be treated as standard terms. But if it has only used other terms in a very small number of transactions, then the terms it regularly uses may be treated as standard terms.

What, then, happens if the parties start with terms that were one party's standard terms, but then negotiate away from those terms—for example, by varying them? In such a case, the court will look at how substantial the alterations were. If the difference between the contract that was originally offered (the standard terms) and the contract that was finally concluded is significant, then the court will treat the contract as not having been made on the party's standard terms.[39]

The test of reasonableness

The key test under UCTA is the test of reasonableness. The requirement of reasonableness is defined in s 11(2) of UCTA as meaning that:

> the term shall have been a fair and reasonable one to be included having regard to the circumstances which were, or ought reasonably to have been, known to or in the contemplation of the parties when the contract was made.

35. Ss 6(1A), 7(1A), (4).   36. S 3.
37. *Chester Grosvenor Hotel Co Ltd v Alfred McAlpine Management* (1991) 56 BLR 115.
38. *Yuanda (UK) Co Ltd v WW Gear Construction Ltd* [2010] EWHC 720 (TCC).
39. Ibid, [26] (Edwards-Stuart J).

Schedule 2 lists matters that are of relevance to determining whether a term is reasonable for the purpose of transactions dealing with the transfer of ownership or possession of goods by sale, hire purchase, or otherwise. In addition, where the exclusion clause in question is linked to a monetary cap on liability, s 11(4) provides that the assessment of reasonableness will depend on the resources available to the party in question and how far it was open to him to cover himself by insurance.

Whether a particular term is reasonable depends on the facts. It is difficult to extract any general principles from the case law, even at the level of simply trying to summarize the factors that courts take into account in determining reasonableness, and the courts have been at pains to stress the fact that individual decisions have very limited precedent value. The fact that a clause is similar to one that has previously been held unreasonable does not in itself signify very much. The clause must always be read in the context of the facts of the specific case. In *Phillips Products Ltd v Hyland*,[40] Slade LJ in the Court of Appeal said, in discussing the reasonableness of the restriction at issue in that case, that:

> It is important therefore that our conclusion on the particular facts of this case should not be treated as a binding precedent in other cases where similar clauses fall to be considered but the evidence of the surrounding circumstances may be very different.

The clause at issue in *Phillips Products Ltd v Hyland* was contained in a set of standard terms prepared by an industry association. The case arose out of the hire of a JCB excavator. Phillips were building extensions to their factory and hired a JCB excavator from Hampstead Plant Hire, together with a driver. The contracts (there were three in total) were on the basis of a standard form prepared by the Contractors Plant-Hire Association. While the excavator was being driven, Hyland, the driver, collided with part of the factory causing considerable damage. When Phillips sued, Hampstead sought to resist liability on the basis of a clause in the contract which said that Hyland was under the direction and control of Phillips when he was on site, and that Phillips (and not Hampstead) would be liable for any claims arising in connection with Hyland's operation of the excavator. The Court of Appeal held that the clause was unreasonable. They were influenced by the specific facts of this case, placing weight on the fact that Phillips had had to find an excavator in a hurry, and had little practical choice but to contract with Hampstead.

In *Thompson v T Lohan (Plant Hire) Ltd*,[41] however, faced with a very similar clause (prepared by the same industry association, but in a newer version of the contract) and very similar facts, the Court of Appeal held that the clause was reasonable. The main reason appears to have been that in this case the victim of the negligence was a third party—not the hirer, as was the case in *Phillips*. In *Phillips*, had the clause been valid, it would have left Phillips with significant uncompensated losses. In *Thompson v T Lohan*, in contrast, the only difference the validity or invalidity of the clause would have made was in relation to who would compensate the third party. There was no question of uncompensated loss.

As this suggests, decisions about reasonableness are very fact-specific. A better way of viewing the effect of the Act, therefore, is that it is not clauses that are reasonable

40. [1987] 1 WLR 659 (CA).   41. [1987] 1 WLR 649 (CA).

in and of themselves. It is, rather, the application of a clause to a particular set of facts that is being judged as reasonable or unreasonable. This is not precisely what UCTA says, but it appears to be how the courts have applied UCTA to date. In *George Mitchell (Chesterhall) Ltd v Finney Lock Seeds Ltd*,[42] Lord Bridge described the process as one in which the court

> must entertain a whole range of considerations, put them in the scales on one side or the other, and decide at the end of the day on which side the balance comes down.

The amount of objectivity that can be achieved in such a process is necessarily limited. Trial judges therefore have considerable discretion to make a decision on reasonableness:

> There will sometimes be room for a legitimate difference of judicial opinion as to what the answer should be, where it will be impossible to say that one view is demonstrably wrong and the other demonstrably right. It must follow, in my view, that, when asked to review such a decision on appeal, the appellate court should treat the original decision with the utmost respect and refrain from interference with it unless satisfied that it proceeded upon some erroneous principle or was plainly and obviously wrong.

The open-ended character of the test makes it very difficult to predict what the outcome of any particular case will be, but as far as the second scenario in Illustration 13.2 is concerned, it is very likely that a term excluding liability for dead pixels will be reasonable. A single dead pixel is not very visible, and several of the industry standards for quality certification of LCD screens tolerate a certain number of dead pixels in a screen.

13.3.3 Liquidated damages, contractual remedies, and the rule against penalties

The discussion thus far has not directly touched on the particular clause that is at issue in Problem 13. Unlike exclusion clauses, the clause in Problem 13 does not seek to limit the liability of the party advancing it. It seeks, instead, to enhance the liability of the other party. Is such a clause enforceable?

Section 13.4 discusses the extent to which consumer protection law restricts the terms that can be included in consumer contracts. In addition, however, English law also incorporates an old rule called the *rule against penalties*. The rule against penalties was in origin equitable, but it came to be adopted by the common law as far back as the 17th century. In the late 18th century the common law rule replaced the equitable rule entirely. It was in origin related to the equitable jurisdiction to relieve against forfeiture, but in the common law it became a rule applicable to damages clauses. Under the rule as it currently stands, clauses which impose penalties on parties who breach contracts are unenforceable.

The rule against penalties is often challenged by commentators on the ground of freedom of contract. The main practical problem with the rule against penalties, however, is that it runs up against a common commercial practice, namely, the use of **liquidated damages** clauses. Stripped to its essentials, a liquidated damages clause

---

42. [1983] 2 AC 803 (HL).

provides that if a party breaches a contract, or a particular provision of a contract, it will be required to pay the other party a predetermined sum. Such clauses are common, and they perform an important function. The law in relation to contract remedies has a number of limitations, especially when it comes to proving loss. Given this, an obvious option is for parties to design their own remedies by agreeing in advance on the amount payable by way of damages. Liquidated damages clauses are a common way of achieving this end. Consider the following example:

Illustration 13.3

The University of Carmarthenshire is in the process of constructing a new teaching building. It will be admitting more students from September of the following year. It therefore inserts a clause in the contract requiring that the building and the teaching rooms in it be ready for occupation and use before 31 August of that year.

Consider, now, what the consequences would be if this clause were to be breached. The university would, in principle, be able to bring an action for damages. But what would this really mean, in practice? What loss would the university be able to show that it had suffered? Liquidated damages clauses are designed to deal with precisely such circumstances. The idea behind a liquidated damages provision is that rather than having to deal with the problems of attempting to prove the extent of loss *after* breach has happened, the parties simply reach agreement *before* breach takes place on how much will be payable by way of damages should the contract be breached. In a contract such as the one in Illustration 13.3, this would typically take the form of a 'late fee' payable for each day of delay, but the parties are free to specify any remedy they choose.

It should be clear from the foregoing discussion that there are sound reasons to want to enforce liquidated damages clauses, while at the same time maintaining the jurisdiction of the courts to refuse to give effect to **penalty clauses**. We would want a clause designed to deal with the problem in Illustration 13.3 to be enforceable, but we would not want a clause of the type set out in Problem 13 to be enforceable. Coming up with a test that distinguishes reliably between the two, however, has been far from easy. Consider the following example:

Illustration 13.4

> LIMITED TIME PARKING!
>
> Overstayers will be charged a fixed amount of £150 for each hour of parking over the time limit.

How might we go about deciding whether a clause of this type is a liquidated damages clause or a penalty clause? The task of answering these questions has occupied the courts since as far back as the 19th century. Over the years between then and 2015, a particular approach to making the distinction had evolved piecemeal. In 2015, however, much of the old law was swept away by the decision of the Supreme Court in *Cavendish Square Holding BV v Talal El Makdessi*.[43] Before we consider the decision in this case, it is useful to first briefly examine the legal position as it stood immediately prior to the decision.

Until 2015, the scope of the rule against penalties had been checked by two doctrines, both restricting the types of clauses to which it applied. First, the rule against penalties only applied to payments triggered by *breach*. A primary obligation, no matter how onerous, could not be a penalty clause which provided for payment to be made on the happening of any event *other than* a breach would always be a contingent promise to pay and, thus, a primary obligation. As such it would never be hit by the rule on penalties, no matter how onerous its provisions.[44]

Secondly, the law drew a distinction between penalty clauses and liquidated damages clauses based on whether they were intended to deter the other party from breach (in which case they were penalty clauses), or were a genuine pre-estimate of the loss that was likely to be caused by a breach (in which case they were liquidated damages clauses). The question of which side of the line a particular clause lay was a question of construction. In *Dunlop Pneumatic Tyre Co Ltd v New Garage and Motor Co Ltd*,[45] the House of Lords set out four factors which were of assistance in the task of construction. First, a clause would be a penalty clause if the sum it stipulated was extravagant or unconscionable in comparison with the greatest loss that could have followed from the breach. Secondly, a clause would be a penalty if the breach consisted of a failure to pay money, and the clause stipulated the payment of a greater sum than that which should have been paid. Thirdly, there was a presumption that the clause was a penalty if it stipulated the same sum for serious breaches as well as for trifling events. Finally, a clause could be a liquidated damages clause even if precise pre-estimation was difficult.

The first of these was criticized by commentators who argued for an *expansion* of the rule on penalties. The distinction between a clause providing for payment on breach and a clause providing for payment on an event other than breach, they argued, was anomalous and hard to support on principle. With skilful drafting, many clauses could be reworded as being the latter rather than the former, thus effectively turning the rule against penalties into a rule against bad drafting. In 2012, the High Court of Australia abandoned the distinction, and expanded the rule against penalties to cover payments on breach as well as conditional promises to pay.[46] Several commentators argued that the English courts should follow its lead.

At the same time, the 'genuine pre-estimate' test was criticized by scholars who argued for a *narrowing* of the rule on penalties. They argued that the test was uncertain and eroded commercial certainty because the entire rule was outmoded and outdated, and against the principle of freedom of contract. They accordingly argued for its abolition.

In 2015, the rule against penalties came before the Supreme Court for the first time in over a century in *Cavendish Square Holding BV v Talal El Makdessi*.[47] Arguments were

---

43. [2015] UKSC 67.
44. See *Export Credits Guarantee Department v Universal Oil Products Co* [1983] 1 WLR 399 (HL).
45. [1915] AC 79 (HL).   46. *Andrews v ANZ Banking Group* [2012] HCA 12.
47. [2015] UKSC 67.

advanced both for the expansion of the rule and its abolition. In its decision, the Supreme Court moved the law firmly in the direction of narrowing the rule. It kept in place the qualification that the rule only applies to payments on breach and not to conditional promises to pay, rejecting the approach taken in Australia. When it came to the distinction between penalty clauses and liquidated damages clauses, however, the Supreme Court abandoned the *Dunlop* test which, it held, had led to many clauses being struck down when they should have been upheld. In its place, the Supreme Court laid down a new test which replaced the 'genuine pre-estimate' test with a much narrower principle:

> The correct test for a penalty is whether the sum or remedy stipulated as a consequence of a breach of contract is exorbitant or unconscionable when regard is had to the innocent party's interest in the performance of the contract.[48]

This is accompanied by a new presumption of enforceability:

> In a negotiated contract between properly advised parties of comparable bargaining power, the strong initial presumption must be that the parties themselves are the best judges of what is legitimate in a provision dealing with the consequences of breach.[49]

This means that the courts should, in general, uphold remedial clauses agreed to by the parties if two conditions are met. First, the innocent party must have a legitimate interest in the performance of the primary obligation in question. Secondly, the remedy set out in the clause must not impose a detriment on the party in breach which is out of proportion to that legitimate interest.[50]

The case involved two conjoined appeals. The first, *Cavendish v Makdessi*, related to a shareholders' agreement between the shareholders of a company called Team Y&R Holdings, including Makdessi and Cavendish. The agreement contained a 'protection of goodwill' clause. Under this, Makdessi was restrained from competing with TYRH. If he failed to comply with this obligation, he would be treated as a 'defaulting shareholder', and would lose his right to receive certain payments from Cavendish. He would also be required to sell his shares to Cavendish at net asset value (a lower valuation than the standard valuation, because it does not include goodwill). Makdessi undertook activities which Cavendish believed were in breach of his non-compete obligation, and they sought to invoke the 'defaulting shareholder' provision. Makdessi argued that these provisions were penalty clauses. The Supreme Court held that properly construed, the clause in question was a price adjustment clause, which adjusted the contract price depending on whether or not Makdessi competed with the company. As such, it was a primary obligation, and the rule against penalties was not applicable.[51] The court stressed that it based its conclusion on the substance of the clause rather than its form: a clause which was a 'disguised punishment' for breach would be contrary to the rule against penalties even if it were dressed up as a price adjustment clause. But, on the facts, there was no basis for the court to reach a conclusion that this clause was actually a penalty.[52] The court further held that the clause would, in

---

48. Ibid, [255] (Lord Hodge).   49. Ibid, [35] (Lords Neuberger and Sumption).
50. Ibid, [32] (Lords Neuberger and Sumption).   51. Ibid, [74].   52. Ibid, [77].

any event, have been justified by the legitimate interest of Cavendish in maintaining TYRH's goodwill, and would not have imposed a disproportionate obligation.

The second case, *ParkingEye Ltd v Beavis*, involved parking charges. Mr Beavis had overstayed in a car park which permitted free parking for up to two hours, but imposed a charge of £85 for overstaying. The Supreme Court held that the charge was not penal. The charge was motivated by two reasons: managing demand for parking spaces by deterring overstaying and providing ParkingEye with an income stream. Both objectives were reasonable, and created a legitimate interest for ParkingEye to impose the charge. The amount of £85 was not out of proportion to that legitimate interest.

The position that a charge is not a penalty merely because it aims at deterrence fits well with the purpose of liquidated damages clauses, even if it represents a fairly significant departure from the old rule. Returning to Illustration 13.3, the university in imposing a daily late fee is in part trying to cover the losses it will suffer, but struggle to prove, if the teaching building is delayed. But it is equally reminding the contractor of the costs to it of delay and, thereby, seeking to incentivize it to complete on time, and deter it from delay. This intertwining of deterrence and compensation is characteristic of liquidated damages clauses, and the willingness of the Supreme Court to recognize it is a definite step in the direction of recognizing the nuances of commercial practice in this area.

Equally, proportionality and legitimate interests are conceptually easier to work with than the old 'genuine pre-estimate' test, and the courts have tended to approach them broadly. In *Signia Wealth Ltd v Vector Trustees Ltd*,[53] the High Court upheld a clause providing for differential valuations on buyout depending on whether or not the entity being bought out was in breach, on the basis that these clauses had an important commercial function, and were not out of proportion with the parties' legitimate interests.[54] Similarly, in *Wright v Prudential Assurance Co Ltd*,[55] the High Court upheld a clause in a Company Voluntary Arrangement (a type of agreement which tries to restructure a company's obligations to avoid insolvency) which gave the company a discount on its rent, but provided that the discount would be retrospectively revoked if the CVA failed to avert insolvency. The landlords had a legitimate commercial interest in the CVA's success or failure, and their desire to be returned to their pre-CVA position if it failed was not exorbitant or unconscionable.

These cases suggest that the new rule will make it significantly easier to draft enforceable liquidated damages clauses. The distinction between primary obligations and penalties, in contrast, appears to continue to cause difficulty. In *Vivienne Westwood Ltd v Conduit Street Development Ltd*,[56] a commercial tenancy agreement provided that a tenant would lose a substantial discount on its rent if it breached any of its obligations under the lease. The tenant missed one instalment on its rent, and the landlord sought to revoke its discount on the basis that it had breached an obligation. The High Court held that the clause in question was a penalty clause, as it involved a consequence of breach rather than a primary obligation. In *Richards v IP Solutions Group Ltd*,[57] the High Court held that a 'bad leaver' clause, which provided that a shareholder-employee could be compelled to sell their shares at an aggregate price of £1 if they breached their

53. [2018] EWHC 1040 (Ch).   54. Ibid, [653].   55. [2018] EWHC 402 (Ch).
56. [2017] EWHC 350 (Ch).   57. [2016] EWHC 1835 (QB).

service agreement, was enforceable because it was a primary obligation. In *Edgeworth Capital (Luxembourg) Sarl v Ramblas Investments BV*,[58] the Court of Appeal similarly held that a clause in a financing agreement providing for the payment of a fee on default was a primary obligation and not a penalty, even though it far exceeded any loss the bank could suffer. Although the result in these cases can be defended on the ground of freedom of contract, it is difficult to avoid the conclusion that the difference between them lies more in the way in which the clauses were drafted than the substance of what they sought to achieve. It was precisely this consequence that led the High Court of Australia to abandon the primary obligation/penalty distinction, and it is unfortunate that the Supreme Court did not follow its lead.

Outside the commercial arena, *ParkingEye Ltd v Beavis* appears to represent a step back from paternalism. Early indications are that courts may be inclined to take a wide view of what constitutes a 'legitimate' interest and, hence, of the types of charges that will be recoverable. In the Scottish case of *Indigo Park Services UK Ltd v Watson*,[59] the court held that a parking company's legitimate interest in the efficient management of the car park justified imposing a higher charge than would be recoverable at common law. Although the case has little precedential value, it nevertheless indicates the likely direction of travel.

It is also unclear how 'proportionality' will be judged in the consumer context. Compare the position in Illustration 13.3 with that in Problem 13. It is evident that the B&B also has a legitimate interest in safeguarding its reputation by controlling unfair reviews posted about it on internet fora. It is also evident that that interest will involve deterring knee-jerk negative reviews, in addition to encouraging consumers to engage with its own processes for resolving consumer complaints. It remains unclear, however, if £1,000 is a proportionate sum to that interest.

Finally, note that statutory regulation may affect whether a clause is a penalty. In *First Personnel Services Ltd v Halfords Ltd*,[60] a clause provided for the payment of a rate of interest greatly in excess of the default rate prescribed under the Late Payment of Commercial Debts (Interest) Act 1998. The court held that the provision was penal, as there was no evidence to explain why such a rate was justified.

13.4 Protecting consumers

In addition to the rules of general applicability discussed in sections 13.2 and 13.3, English law has in recent years enacted a number of laws specifically to protect consumers. These represent a relatively new trend. Whilst the law has long sought to ameliorate some of the problems caused by the inequality of bargaining power, the law had previously sought to apply the same principles to consumer transactions as it did to commercial transactions. This position came in for criticism,[61] and in the 1970s a number of consumer-specific laws were enacted, under the influence of the Law Commission. The most important of these was the Consumer Credit Act 1974, which remains in force and imposes significant restrictions on terms in consumer lending contracts.

---

58. [2016] EWCA Civ 412.   59. 2017 GWD 40-610.
60. [2016] EWHC 3220 (Ch).
61. JA Jolowicz (ed), *The Division and Classification of the Law* (Butterworths 1970).

Currently, the most important consumer protection statute in contract law is the Consumer Rights Act 2015. The Consumer Rights Act was enacted to consolidate a patchwork of statutes—specifically, the consumer-facing provisions of UCTA, the Sale of Goods Act 1979, and the Supply of Goods and Services Act 1982, as well as the Unfair Terms in Consumer Contracts Regulations 1999, which were based on a European Union directive.[62] The changes created by the 2015 Act are far-reaching, giving consumer law its own set of remedies, implied terms, and control on unfair terms. These supplement older statutes such as the Consumer Credit Act 1974. Other rules such as the Consumer Protection from Unfair Trading Regulations 2008[63] have created consumer-specific alternatives to core common law doctrines such as misrepresentation, duress, and undue influence. Most of these are dealt with elsewhere in this book. This section focuses on one specific aspect of consumer law; namely, the control of unfair terms under Part 2 of the 2015 Act.

The impetus behind Part 2 of the 2015 Act was that the regimes created by UCTA and the 1999 Regulations overlapped quite substantially, but imposed very different requirements. The 1999 Regulations used a test of good faith, whereas UCTA used a test of reasonableness, and the criteria used in each were different. This made it difficult for companies seeking to comply with the statutes to figure out precisely what they were allowed to say and what they were not allowed to say in their contracts. The Law Commission, accordingly, recommended that the regimes be merged. Instead of merger, however, the change that was actually made was the restriction of UCTA to commercial contracts. Part 2 of the 2015 Act is substantially based on the Directive on Unfair Terms in Consumer Contracts,[64] as were the 1999 Regulations, but it extends them in a few ways. The most significant extension is that the directive and the 1999 Regulations only applied to terms which were not individually negotiated, and had been drafted in advance by the trader. The 2015 Act removes this restriction, and extends the regime to all terms, whether or not individually negotiated. Unlike UCTA, it is not confined to exclusion clauses and clauses seeking to restrict liability in other ways. The regime it creates applies both to contracts and to notices that non-contractually seek to vary rights or obligations as between a trader and consumer, or to exclude or restrict a trader's liability to a consumer. A classic example of such a notice would be a disclaimer stating that a trader has not assumed responsibility towards the consumer for the purpose of tort law.

If a term or notice is 'unfair' under the 2015 Act, it does not bind the consumer. This means that the trader cannot enforce it against the consumer. The consumer, however, is free to rely on the term if she chooses.[65] In addition, the Competition and Markets Authority as well as other named regulators have been given a wide range of enforcement and investigatory powers against traders under the Act.[66]

13.4.1 Defining consumer transactions

Section 61 of the 2015 Act defines consumer transactions as contracts between a trader and a consumer, other than a contract of employment or apprenticeship. 'Traders' and 'consumers' are defined with reference to the *purpose* for which they enter into

62. Directive 93/13/EC on Unfair Terms in Consumer Contracts.   63. SI 2008/1277.
64. Directive 93/13/EC.   65. S 62(1)–(3).   66. See s 70 and Schs 3 and 5.

a transaction. A trader is 'a person acting for purposes relating to that person's trade, business, craft or profession',[67] whereas a consumer is 'an individual acting for purposes that are wholly or mainly outside that individual's trade, business, craft or profession'.[68] Contrast the following illustrations:

Illustration 13.5

Claire Devaux owns a café in Oswestry. She requires a second coffee machine. As finances are tight, she buys a refurbished coffee machine from a specialist dealer. She is given a receipt, on the back of which terms and conditions are printed. She has no opportunity to negotiate better terms. The machine is not able to handle the volume of coffee she produces, and breaks down frequently. It stops working completely within six months of her purchase. When she contacts the dealership, they point to the following term on the receipt:

> The buyer acknowledges that the goods are sold as-is, and that the seller makes no warranty in relation to the condition of the product or its suitability for any purpose. Any express or implied condition, statement, or warranty, statutory or otherwise not stated herein is hereby excluded. The seller excludes all liability for any loss caused by the mechanical failure or breakdown of the goods, or by their unsuitability for the buyer's purpose.

Uncle Percival buys a coffee machine for his kitchen. He places the order online, checking a box saying he accepts the webstore's terms and conditions as he does so. The machine breaks down within a month of his purchase. When he contacts the store, they point to a term in the webstore's terms and conditions which says that they exclude all liability for mechanical failure or breakdown in terms substantially similar to those quoted above.

Claire in the first illustration here is a trader because she buys the coffee machine for the purpose of her café. She is acting in a commercial capacity. Uncle Percival, in contrast, is a consumer because he buys the coffee machine for purposes wholly unconnected with any trade, business, craft, or profession. He is acting in a purely personal capacity.

The difference between the words 'person' and 'individual' in the two definitions is also significant. 'Person' includes natural persons as well as juristic persons. 'Individuals', in contrast, are only natural persons. Companies are persons in law, but are not individuals. This means that only human beings can be consumers. A company, or other juristic person, cannot. The exclusion of companies from the categories of consumers represents a departure from the situation before 2015. Before the Consumer Rights Act, companies could be consumers for the purposes of UCTA,[69] even though they were not consumers under the Unfair Terms in Consumer Contracts

67. S 2(1).   68. S 2(2).
69. See *R&B Customs Brokers Co Ltd v United Dominions Trust Ltd* [1988] 1 WLR 321.

Regulations 1999. The 1999 Regulations were based on an EU directive, and it was a long-established principle in most civil law jurisdictions that only individuals could claim the protection of consumer legislation. This was not true of the common law, and the inequality of bargaining power that makes regulation of onerous terms necessary arguably affects small businesses at least as much as it affects consumers. The approach of UCTA therefore had much to commend it. However, as things stand, the additional protection available to consumers is only available to individuals, and not to companies acting outside their trade.

13.4.2 Unfairness

The heart of the regime created by the 2015 Act lies in its definition of unfairness. The statute imposes two requirements for a term or notice to be unfair: it must cause a 'significant imbalance' in the parties' rights and obligations to the detriment of the consumer and it must be 'contrary to the requirement of good faith'.[70] The Act further provides that fairness is to be determined with reference to two things. First, the assessment of fairness must take into account the subject matter of the contract or notice. Secondly, it must take into account the circumstances existing when the term was agreed (or, in the case of a notice, when the rights and obligations arose) as well as the broader context of the other terms of the contract between the parties.[71]

In keeping with the general trend in English law of distinguishing between substantive and procedural dimensions of imbalances of bargaining power,[72] English courts have interpreted 'good faith' as being a procedural concept, while 'significant imbalance' has been interpreted as having substantive implications. Recent judgments from the European Court of Justice have suggested, however, that 'good faith' also has some substantive implications. It remains to be seen whether English law will evolve in a more European direction, given the impending withdrawal of the UK from the European Union.

Some terms are dealt with specifically in the Act. Part 1 of Schedule 2 contains an 'indicative and non-exhaustive' list of 20 terms which 'may' be regarded as unfair (although a court is not required to do so).[73] Item 1 covers terms which have the 'object or effect of excluding or limiting the trader's liability' in the event the consumer dies or suffers personal injury due to the trader's acts or omissions. Item 2 covers terms which have the object or effect of 'inappropriately excluding or limiting the legal rights of the consumer . . . in the event of total or partial non-performance or inadequate performance by the trader of any of the contractual obligations'. Item 6 covers terms which have the object or effect 'of requiring a consumer who fails to fulfil his obligations under the contract to pay a disproportionately high sum in compensation'. Part 2 of Schedule 2 qualifies some of these in relation to certain specific types of transactions. The Act also declares that a term must be regarded as unfair if it has the effect

70. S 62(4) (contractual terms), s 62(6) (notices).
71. S 62(5) (contractual terms), s 62(7) (notices).
72. See the discussion in Chapter 12 ('The limits of hard bargaining'), section 12.3.3, 'Debates in context: a doctrine of unconscionability?'.
73. S 63(1).

of making the consumer bear the burden of proof in relation to whether a distance supplier or intermediary has complied with obligations under the Distance Marketing Directive.[74] Outside these specific instances, however, questions in relation to whether a term is unfair will fall to be decided with reference to whether the term causes a significant imbalance contrary to the requirement of good faith.

The implications of some of these to the scenarios set out in Problem 13 are obvious, and we will return to them later on in the course of this section. Before that, however, let us look in some more detail at the individual elements that must be made out to demonstrate that a particular term is unfair.

'Contrary to good faith'

The key elements of unfairness are the requirements of contrariness to good faith and 'significant imbalance'. The first of these, contrariness to good faith, was controversial when the directive was first transposed into English law. At that time, English law had not yet taken the first tentative steps towards a doctrine of good faith that it did in *Yam Seng v International Trade Corp*.[75] Good faith was seen as being totally alien to English law, on the strength of cases such as *Walford v Miles*.[76] Commentators predicted that the introduction of the requirement would cause problems for English law.[77]

The courts, however, faced little difficulty in dealing with the requirement. They did this by giving the requirement of good faith a procedural meaning, rather than a substantive one. In *DGFT v First National Bank*,[78] the House of Lords interpreted good faith as requiring open and fair dealing between the parties. To comply with this requirement, a trader would be required to express the terms of the transactions fully and clearly, without hidden pitfalls. He should give appropriate prominence to matters which might operate to the consumer's disadvantage. Equally, the trader must not take advantage, even unconsciously, of the consumer's weaker bargaining position.

DGFT v First National Bank related to an interest term in a consumer borrowing agreement. The Consumer Credit Act 1974 gives courts the power to extend the term and specify a schedule of instalments for repayment of a loan. The bank in this case had added a term to its loan agreements providing that borrowers would remain liable to pay interest at the contractual rate on the outstanding amount of the loan over and above the instalments which the court specified. The Director General of Fair Trading (DGFT), who at the time had the power to challenge practices in contravention of the directive,[79] brought an action arguing that this clause was unfair within the meaning of the 1999 Regulations. As the definition of unfairness under the 2015 Act is the same as that under the Regulations it replaced, the case remains the leading case on the meaning of unfairness.

The DGFT succeeded at first instance and in the Court of Appeal. The House of Lords, however, reversed the judgment, and held that the clause was not unfair. This was because it was neither contrary to the requirement of good faith nor did it cause

74. S 63(6).   75. [2013] EWHC 111 (QB). See the discussion in Chapter 8 ('Filling the gaps').
76. [1992] 2 AC 128 (HL). See the discussion in Chapter 9 ('Flexible terms').
77. See especially G Teubner, 'Legal Irritants: Good Faith in British Law or How Unifying Law Ends Up in New Divergences' (1998) 61 MLR 11.
78. [2002] 1 AC 481 (HL).
79. The power now vests in the Competition and Markets Authority.

a significant imbalance between the parties. The court's interpretation of significant imbalance is discussed in the next subsection. On good faith, the House of Lords held the requirement had been met because the obligation in relation to interest was clearly and unambiguously set out in the terms and conditions. It was not a hidden pitfall. Nothing on the facts suggested that it was an attempt to take advantage of the consumer's weaker bargaining position. The problem faced by the borrowers arose out of the fact that there was a regulatory gap in the Consumer Credit Act 1974. Borrowers were often unaware of the precise nature of the protection offered by that Act and its relationship to contractually agreed terms. The requirement of good faith did not impose an onus on lenders to resolve this. Lenders did not have to draw the provisions of the Consumer Credit Act to the attention of borrowers. No statute required them to do this. Their failure to do so was therefore not contrary to good faith.

The meaning of good faith has since received some further elaboration from the European Court of Justice (ECJ), which held in *Aziz v Caixa d'Estalvis de Catalunya, Tarragona i Manresa (Catalunyacaixa)*[80] that a court considering whether a term was contrary to good faith must also take into account whether the trader, had he been dealing fairly and equitably, could have assumed that the consumer would have agreed to the term in individual negotiations. In other words, it requires the court to create a counterfactual situation where the parties individually negotiated the contract, and ask how the consumer would have reacted to the term in the course of such negotiations. As Part 2 of the 2015 Act is based on an EU directive, decisions of the ECJ on the meaning of the directive prior to Brexit also have binding force in the UK. The 2015 Act, unlike the directive, also applies the test of unfairness to terms that were not individually negotiated, and the decision is unlikely to be applicable in relation to such terms. But where the impugned terms have not been individually negotiated (as they were not in *DGFT v First National Bank*), the decision of the ECJ would appear to have injected at least some substantive considerations into the process.

'Significant imbalance'

The courts have taken a similar approach to the requirement that the term cause a 'significant imbalance'. In *DGFT v First National Bank*,[81] the House of Lords emphasized that the law requires not merely an imbalance, but one that is significant. This, they held, means that the clause must be

> so weighted in favour of the supplier as to tilt the parties' rights and obligations significantly in his favour. This may be by the granting to the supplier of a beneficial option or discretion or power, or by the imposing on the consumer of a disadvantageous burden or risk or duty.[82]

This involves looking at the contract as a whole, rather than at individual clauses.[83] The High Court had held that the clause was unfair because the bank had not 'adequately considered the consumer's interests'. The effect of the ruling of the House of Lords was to clarify that the law on unfair terms does not require the trader to do this. What matters is that the contract is not tilted significantly in the trader's favour.

---

80. Case C-415/11 [2013] 3 CMLR 5.   81. [2002] 1 AC 481 (HL).
82. Ibid, [17] (Lord Bingham).   83. Ibid.

A clause imposing an additional rate of interest did not cause a significant imbalance in this sense.

Assessments of the 'significance' of an imbalance are nuanced, and depend quite heavily on the specific facts and the overall context of the transaction. In *OFT v Ashbourne Management Services*,[84] an action had been brought by the Office of Fair Trading (OFT), the successor to the DGFT, in relation to payment obligations contained in contracts for gym clubs to whom Ashbourne provided recruitment services. As part of those services, it recommended standard form membership agreements to the clubs. The OFT's action related to several terms of those agreements, one of which imposed a minimum membership period. The terms were challenged under the Consumer Credit Act, the Consumer Protection from Unfair Trading Regulations 2008, and the 1999 Regulations. The last of these remains relevant to the meaning of 'significant imbalance' under Part 2 of the Consumer Rights Act 2015. The High Court held that the assessment of significant imbalances and good faith must be made with reference to the typical or average consumer:

> Such a person is generally assumed to be reasonably well informed and reasonably observant and circumspect, and to read the relevant documents and to seek to understand what is being read. The standard is a variable one and must, I believe, take colour from the context. For example, consumers who are financially sophisticated may be expected to bring to bear a greater understanding of the meaning and implications of the terms of a contract than consumers who are vulnerable as a result of their naivety or credulity.[85]

On the facts, it held that the defendants' business model was

> designed and calculated to take advantage of the naivety and inexperience of the average consumer using gym clubs at the lower end of the market.[86]

Nevertheless, the term only caused a 'significant' imbalance when the minimum membership period exceeded 12 months. Agreements which imposed a minimum membership period of 24 or 36 months caused a significant imbalance. Those which imposed a minimum membership period of 12 months, or which provided for termination by 30 days' notice after 12 months, did not cause a significant imbalance and were not unfair.[87]

A composite test

In *DGFT v First National Bank*,[88] the House of Lords emphasized that the requirements of s 62 were cumulative. Both requirements, 'contrary to good faith' and 'significant imbalance', need to be established. It is not sufficient to just show one. In addition, the two are closely related, creating a 'composite test, covering both the making and the substance of the contract', which must be applied keeping in mind the objective which the directive was designed to promote.[89] This requires the court to consider, among other things, the effect of the contract with the term against the effect of the contract without the term, whether this would have surprised the consumer had it

---

84. [2011] EWHC 1237 (Ch).   85. Ibid, [128].   86. Ibid, [173].   87. Ibid, [174].
88. [2002] 1 AC 481 (HL).   89. Ibid, [17].

been drawn to his attention, whether the term was also found in freely negotiated commercial contracts, and whether it was of a type that would lead a lawyer to object to it in a commercial context.[90]

As this suggests, the actual application of the test is very context- and fact-sensitive. The decision of the Court of Appeal in *West v Ian Finlay*[91] is a good illustration of how the courts draw on the factual context of a case, as well as the surrounding commercial context, to apply the two requirements of contrariness to good faith and the creation of a significant imbalance as a composite test.

Case in depth: *West v Ian Finlay* [2014] EWCA Civ 316

The claim in this case arose out of a dispute between the Wests and their architects, Ian Finlay, in relation to renovation and improvement works carried out to the Wests' property in London. The contract between the parties contained the following clause:

> We confirm that we maintain professional indemnity insurance cover of £1,000,000.00 in respect of any one event. This will be the maximum limit of our liability to you arising out of this Agreement. Any such liability will expire after six years from conclusion of our appointment or (if earlier) practical completion of the construction of the Project. Our liability for loss or damage will be limited to the amount that it is reasonable for us to pay in relation to the contractual responsibilities of other consultants, contractors and specialists appointed by you.

The last sentence of this clause contains what is called a 'net contribution clause'. The purpose of a net contribution clause is to alter the liability of the parties at common law. At common law, and under the Civil Liability (Contribution) Act 1978, where more than one person is responsible for defects in construction work, they will frequently be jointly and severally liable for the loss caused by the defects. This means that the claimant can sue either of them, and the person sued will have to pay the full amount of the compensation due. A net contribution clause replaces this system with one of proportionate liability. This means that each party is only liable for the amount of loss that is attributable to their breach of duty. The words 'limited to the amount that it is reasonable for us to pay' were intended to achieve this effect.

The impact of a net contribution clause can be seen from its effect in this case. The works carried out on the Wests' property had significant defects. Very extensive remedial works were required to correct problems with damp and electrical problems. At common law, Finlay and the main contractor for the project, a company called Maurice Armour (Contracts) Ltd, would have been jointly and severally liable. The Wests could have sued either, and recovered the full amount from either. If the net contribution clause was enforceable, however, Finlay would not be liable for the entire loss, but only for that portion that it would be reasonable for him to bear. In this case, Armour had become insolvent, and the Wests were unlikely to recover anything from them. If they could not recover the full amount from Finlay, they would be left significantly out of pocket. The Wests therefore argued that the net contribution clause

→

→

was unfair, because it was contrary to good faith. On the facts, it was shown that Finlay had not explained the meaning or implications of the clause to the Wests.

The Court of Appeal identified a number of competing considerations on good faith. On the one hand, the Wests were not in a weak bargaining position and were perfectly capable of understanding the meaning of the net contribution clause had they read it. On the other hand, Finlay had not drawn the clause to their attention, even though the guidelines compiled by the professional body for architects (RIBA) suggested that good practice required them to do so. The clause itself was worded in a way that did not make its true impact clear. Its effect was to shift the risk of any contractor's insolvency away from Finlay and onto the Wests. The wording of the clause distracted the attention of the reader away from this consequence.[92]

Likewise, on the question of significant imbalance, there was nothing inherently objectionable or unreasonable about a provision that made Finlay liable only for losses that were Finlay's own responsibility. Clauses of this type were not unusual in commercial construction contracts. On the other hand, whilst an architect like Finlay could take insurance to protect itself, consumers like the Wests could not. The reduction of Finlay's liability would force the Wests to initiate multiple law suits against multiple persons to recover compensation, over and above shifting the risk of insolvency to them. This was a procedural disadvantage.[93]

Putting these together, the Court of Appeal came to the conclusion that the imbalance was not significant, because the clause was not unusual in a commercial context, and indeed was similar to a clause that was part of the standard RIBA form. The Wests also had the final say in appointing the contractor, and hence had the ability to ensure that only contractors who were financially stable were appointed.[94] Likewise, on good faith, although it would have been preferable for Finlay to have drawn the clause to the Wests' attention, his failure to do so did not by itself make his behaviour contrary to good faith, as the Wests were 'savvy' clients and the parties were therefore in at least an equal bargaining position.[95] As a result, the clause was not unfair.

Let us then apply these tests to Problem 13. It should be evident that the clause in question causes an imbalance in the parties' rights and duties, against the interests of the consumer. But is the imbalance significant? It is highly relevant that he is not restricted *absolutely* from posting negative reviews, but is simply required to give the B&B a chance to resolve his complaint before he posts a review. This, by itself, is unlikely to be objectionable, if we go by the reasoning in *OFT v Ashbourne Management Services*.[96] The bigger issue, however, will be the quantum of money that is payable in the event of breach. This would, on its face, appear to be squarely within what is termed 'a disproportionately high sum in compensation' in item 6 in Part 1 of Schedule 2 to the 2015 Act. As such, it would seem highly likely to be unfair for the purposes of the Act.

92. Ibid, [55]–[58].   93. Ibid, [49]–[52].   94. Ibid, [59].   95. Ibid, [60].
96. [2011] EWHC 1237 (Ch).

Core terms

Section 64(1) creates a specific exemption for terms that are **core terms**. This category includes two types of matters. First, it includes the terms which specify the main subject matter of the contract. Secondly, it includes any assessment of the 'appropriateness of the price payable under the contract by comparison with the goods, digital content or services supplied under it'. No term may be assessed for fairness to the extent that it touches on these two matters. They are excluded from the statutory framework governing unfair terms and, as a matter of law, they are incapable of being unfair. However, to qualify for this exception, the term must be 'transparent and prominent'.[97] To be transparent, it must be 'expressed in plain and intelligible language'.[98] To be prominent, it must be 'brought to the consumer's attention in such a way that an average consumer would be aware of the term'.[99]

Why does the law refuse to treat core terms as unfair? One way of looking at the problem is to draw a parallel with the principle that consideration must be sufficient but need not be adequate. Some consideration must be given, but the court will not examine whether the consideration that was given was proportionate to the benefit received. Core terms are concerned with the thing contracted for, and the price paid for it—the precise things that are the focus of consideration. Assessing the fairness of core terms will, on this reading, inevitably draw the court into judging the adequacy of consideration. The idea that courts should not enquire into the adequacy of the price vis-à-vis what it purchases is one that has deep roots in common law as well as in the civil law systems of continental Europe, as well as in contract theory going back to the early Thomists.

This appears to be the view taken by the ECJ in *Kásler v OTP Jelzálogbank Zrt*.[100] The dispute in *Kásler* related to a loan issued by a Hungarian bank in which outstanding amounts and payments were calculated in a foreign currency, the Swiss franc. The term that was challenged was one providing for the conversion rate between the Hungarian forint and the Swiss franc. In calculating the amount outstanding, the contract provided that the rate used would be the bank's buying rate. In calculating the instalments payable, however, the rate used was the bank's selling rate, which is usually higher. Kásler, a borrower, challenged the term on the basis that it was unfair. The bank defended it on the basis that it was a core term. The ECJ held that the term could not be defended on the head of the adequacy of the price, as that exception was 'limited to the adequacy of the price and the remuneration on one hand as against the services or goods supplied on the other'. This simply reflected the fact that 'no legal scale or criterion exists that can provide a framework for, and guide, such a review'.[101] The 'main subject matter' exclusion, similarly, only applies to terms that 'define the very essence of the contractual relationship'. These terms 'lay down the essential obligations of the contract and, as such, characterise it'.[102] Such a category would necessarily be narrow, and would not encompass ancillary terms.

The English courts, however, approached the problem from a very different starting point. In *OFT v Abbey National plc*,[103] the Supreme Court held that the purpose of the directive was to deal with unexpected terms that would have come as a surprise to

---

97. S 64(2).   98. S 64(3).   99. S 64(4).   100. Case C-26/13 [2014] Bus LR 664.
101. Ibid, [54]–[55].   102. Ibid, [49]–[50].   103. [2009] UKSC 6, [2010] 1 AC 696.

the consumer. Core terms—the thing contracted for and the price paid—were in their reading the terms on which a consumer will be focused at the time of contracting. The reason that the courts do not examine their fairness is that they are unlikely to take a reasonable consumer by surprise. The case related to bank overdraft charges levied on personal current account holders. The charges were levied at an amount which vastly exceeded the cost to the bank of dealing with an overdraft. A number of cases in county courts had been decided in favour of borrowers on the basis that these terms were unfair. The Supreme Court, however, held that the term was a core term. This was because the exception in relation to price applies not just to the 'essential price' but also to any monetary price or remuneration payable under the contract.

The decision in *Abbey National* was heavily criticized. Paul Davies, a leading comparativist and scholar of contract law, criticized the case for adopting a very literal reading of the relevant statutory provisions, while failing to take account of the purpose of the statute. Most reasonable consumers, he pointed out, would be surprised at being charged £40 for a £1 overdraft. He also argued that the case sat uneasily with the decision of the House of Lords in *DGFT v First National Bank plc*,[104] and that the Supreme Court's rejection of the distinction between core and ancillary terms was regrettable. The error of the Supreme Court, in his reading, was to see the statute as being about 'consumer choice' rather than 'consumer protection'.[105] Chris Willett, similarly, argued that the Supreme Court was overly influenced by an ethic of 'consumer self reliance' and 'trader self interest', when in reality the ethic underlying European consumer law was one that 'aims to *protect* consumers against the weaknesses that they suffer relative to traders'.[106] Simon Whittaker, also a comparativist contract scholar, argued that the approach taken in the Court of Appeal, which had focused on the point of view of the typical customer, was to be preferred to that taken in the Supreme Court.[107]

But the decision also has its defenders. Anu Arora, writing from the perspective of a banking regulation lawyer, argued that in the context of the banking industry, the Supreme Court's decision was based on a correct reading of the relevant principles. Although there might be a case for reviewing the level of charges imposed by banks, 'the fundamental legal principles of contract law and freedom of contract which allow or enable these charges to be levied on the customer must not be undermined'. Overdraft fees were part of the bundle of fees charged by banks for providing a bundle of services, and the Supreme Court was therefore correct to hold it to be a core term.[108]

Be that as it may, there are aspects of the decision in *Abbey National* which are not entirely reconcilable with the decision of the ECJ decision in *Kásler* (which came after *Abbey National* was decided). In particular, *Kásler* affirms the relevance of the core/ancillary distinction which the Supreme Court rejected in *Abbey National*. It also arguably

104. [2001] UKHL 52, [2002] 1 AC 481.
105. PS Davies, 'Bank Charges in the Supreme Court' (2010) 69 CLJ 21.
106. C Willett, 'General Clauses and the Competing Ethics of European Consumer Law in the UK' (2012) 71 CLJ 412, 413.
107. S Whittaker, 'Unfair Contract Terms, Unfair Prices and Bank Charges' (2011) 74 MLR 106.
108. A Arora, 'Unfair Contract Terms and Unauthorised Bank Charges: A Banking Lawyer's Perspective' [2012] JBL 44, 67–8.

adopts a narrower reading of the 'remuneration' exception, taking the view that not all monetary payments under a contract are remuneration. The ruling in *Kásler* has not as yet been considered by an English court, and it remains to be seen how it will influence the approach taken in this jurisdiction.

13.5 In conclusion: substantive fairness in contracting

Let us now draw the threads together, and assess how well English law deals with the issue of onerous terms in contracts. As we have seen in the course of this chapter, the general common law rules of contract law have increasingly withdrawn from the task of protecting persons in the position of Bernard in Problem 13. The role is, instead, increasingly played by statutory regulation. For Bernard, notwithstanding the long-established status of the rule against penalties, a far more efficacious remedy is likely to be that provided under the Consumer Rights Act 2015.

This reflects a broader underlying trend. In consumer contracts, English law has been growing increasingly protective although, as the decision in *Abbey National* has shown, the courts have not always kept up with the direction in which the law is moving outside the UK. In commercial transactions, however, the law remains grounded in an ethos of market individualism, with the parties expected to take responsibility for protecting their interests.

One consequence of this has been that English law tends to favour transaction-specific approaches over substantive rules in regulating contractual terms. Thus, as this chapter has shown, common law controls on exclusion clauses have increasingly come to be subsumed within the broader process of interpretation, rather than being free-standing rules which actively set limits on what parties can and cannot agree to. The fact-specific character of reasonableness under UCTA arguably reflects the same underlying reluctance to develop substantive limits on the parties' freedom to agree the contract terms they wish to.

Statutory regulation, in contrast, takes a more obviously substantive approach to fairness in commercial contracts as much as in consumer contracts. The Housing, Grants, Construction and Regeneration Act 1996 provides an excellent example. Construction contracts are complex, and subcontractors are often small businesses who are in a disadvantageous position vis-à-vis large contractors. The 1996 Act, therefore, sets out a number of very severe restrictions on contract terms, which were enacted with a view to protecting weaker commercial parties in the construction sector. Among other things, subcontractors have been given the right to stage payments for work carried out under a construction contract, and to suspend work on a contract if payment is not received on time. Provisions wherein a main contractor delays payment to a subcontractor until he himself is paid ('pay when paid' clauses) are not permitted. Clauses which require a named party to pay both parties' costs even if the named party wins ('*Tolent*' clauses) are also not valid. The Consumer Rights Act 2015, from this perspective, forms part of a broader set of statutory measures that are aimed at injecting a greater degree of substantive fairness into contracts characterized by a sharp inequality of the parties' relative bargaining positions.

Key points

- English law includes a number of statutory provisions and common law doctrines which restrict the terms to which parties are free to agree.

- Some contracts are required to be in writing, and some are in addition required to follow particular forms. Contracts dealing with interests in land and contracts of guarantee are the two most common examples.

- Clauses seeking to limit or exclude liability are subject to special rules. The *contra proferentem* rule interprets these clauses against the person seeking to rely on them (although this rule has been getting less broad). The *Canada Steamship* rule similarly reads down clauses excluding liability for negligence. Both of these are rules of interpretation, and parties can get around them by careful drafting.

- Exclusion clauses in commercial contracts are also restricted by the Unfair Contract Terms Act 1977, which prohibits certain types of exclusion clauses and subjects others to a test of reasonableness. Some of its provisions only apply to exclusion clauses contained in written standard terms of business.

- The validity of penalty clauses is also restricted by common law principles. Penalty clauses are only enforceable if the innocent party has a legitimate interest in the performance of the primary obligation in question, and if the detriment on the party in breach is not out of proportion to that legitimate interest. Penalty clauses which fail this test are not enforceable.

- Consumers receive a broader degree of protection via the Consumer Rights Act 2015. Under this Act, clauses which are contrary to good faith, and which cause a significant imbalance in the parties' rights to the detriment of the consumer, are considered unfair. Unfair terms cannot be enforced against the consumer. Core terms, however, are not unfair.

Assess your learning

You should be able to respond to each of the following points with a confident 'yes'. If you can't, then you should revisit the sections listed against that point.

Can you:

(a) *Outline* the circumstances in which the requirement of writing applies, and *identify* some of its drawbacks? (Section 13.2)

(b) *Explain* the scope of the *contra proferentem* rule and the *Canada Steamship* rule in relation to the interpretation of exclusion clauses? (Section 13.3.1)

(c) *Describe* the approach taken by the Unfair Contract Terms Act 1977 to the validity of exclusion clauses? (Section 13.3.2)

(d) *Identify* the tests used to determine the validity of penalty clauses, and *explain* the role of proportionality in this determination? (Section 13.3.3)

(e) *Explain* how the Consumer Protection Act 2015 defines 'unfair' clauses, *outline* the tests applied to determine whether a clause is unfair, and *describe* the consequences of a clause being deemed unfair? (Section 13.4)

In relation to each of the above, you should be able to:

(i) identify and clearly explain the key rules and principles;

(ii) identify the key cases and statutes, and why they matter;

(iii) apply the principles and cases to specific real or hypothetical fact situations;

(iv) evaluate the limitations, if any, of the law as it currently stands.

Further reading

H Beale, 'Legislative Control of Fairness: The Directive on Unfair Terms in Consumer Contracts' in J Beatson and D Friedmann (eds), *Good Faith and Fault in Contract Law* (Oxford University Press 1995).

R Bradgate, 'Unreasonable Standard Terms' (1997) 60 MLR 582.

H Collins, 'Good Faith in European Contract Law' (1994) 14 OJLS 229.

C Grunfeld, 'Law Reform (Enforcement of Contracts) Act, 1954' (1954) 17 MLR 451.

E Macdonald, 'The Emperor's Old Clauses: Unincorporated Clauses, Misleading Terms and the Unfair Terms in Consumer Contract Regulations' (1999) 58 CLJ 413.

J Morgan, 'Bank Charges and the Unfair Terms in Consumer Contracts Regulations 1999: The End of the Road for Consumers?' [2010] LMCLQ 208.

E Peel, 'Reasonable Exemption Clauses' (2001) 117 LQR 545.

KM Teevan, 'Seventeenth Century Evidentiary Concerns and the Statute of Frauds' (1983) 9 Adelaide Law Review 252.

C Willett, *Fairness in Consumer Contracts: The Case of Unfair Terms* (Ashgate 2007).

14

Protecting the public interest

The doctrine of illegality

'For the greater common good'

Problem 14: setting the context

Consider the following post on http://www.thestudentplace.co.uk, a (fictitious) online forum for students at UK universities:

> My commercial law essay was due ten days ago, and I bought it from an online coursework help site. I was really stressed. I'm on the 2:1/first borderline and I needed a first on this coursework which they said they could guarantee. I gave them the marking criteria and the essay topic, and they said they would get an Oxbridge graduate to write me a guaranteed first-class essay. They also guaranteed that it would be plagiarism-free.
>
> I paid £750 for the essay which would have been worth it if I got a first. What I got was rubbish. It was full of spelling and grammar mistakes and was missing key cases, forget about articles. I contacted the website to complain, and they apologized and said they would have a new essay written. They didn't. They kept saying they would send it to me, but the day before the essay was due I still hadn't received it.
>
> I went to see my tutor and made up a story about family problems and stress. I got a two-day extension. I wrote the essay in 48 hours and handed it in. It's OK, but it's a two-day job so I'm going to get a low 2:2 at best. Obviously, I'm really upset. I want to do something to the site. They aren't responding to my emails any more. Is there any chance I can get my money back at least?

The difficulty this anonymous student faces is that the contract was for a purpose which many would regard as somewhat beyond the pale—namely, passing off someone else's work as their own, with a view to getting a higher mark than they deserved. In legal terms, the contract was created to facilitate a fraud.

Should this ulterior purpose have any implications for the way in which contract law deals with the contract? Should the court enforce contracts of this type by, for example, granting damages if the contract is breached? Similarly, should parties to contracts of this type be able to get their money back if the contract falls apart?

14.1 Introduction: the problem of illegal behaviour

Contracts in relation to certain types of subject matter are prohibited. Parties may not, for example, enter into contracts to buy and sell transplantable organs under English law. This is because, as a matter of policy, the law holds that people should have access to organ transplants based on a medical assessment of their relative needs and the relative benefit to them of the transplant, rather than on their ability to pay. Likewise, contracts that contemplate certain types of acts are prohibited. A contract that contemplates the illegal smuggling of goods into the UK, for example, is prohibited on the basis of public policy.

These prohibitions reflect the need for the law to protect the public interest, and not just the private interests of the parties. Consider Problem 14. The performance or non-performance of the contract in question has implications not just for the parties' interests, but also the university at which the student studies and the broader public interest. The idea behind an academic degree, and its social value, depend on honest engagement by students with the requirements of their programme. Contracts which subvert those requirements arguably harm the public interest by striking at the foundations of an academic degree.

What happens, then, if parties enter into such a contract, notwithstanding the legal prohibition? In English law, contracts against the public interest are dealt with under the doctrine of *illegality*. The doctrine of illegality reflects a broader principle that applies across private law, that legal actions cannot be founded on illegal acts. This is often summed up in the Latin maxim, ***ex turpi causa non oritur actio*** ('no action arises from a base (or disreputable) cause'). This applies in tort and equity in addition to contract. In contract law, its implication is that contracts contrary to law or public policy are void.

In theory, this may seem both simple and obvious. It stands to reason that courts should not enforce contracts which contemplate illegal acts, or were entered into for an illegal purpose. But, in practice, the doctrine of illegality has caused considerable difficulties over the past two decades, and the Supreme Court had to consider its precise scope and extent on no less than four occasions between 2014 and 2016. Several of these cases saw the court deeply divided on what the law requires judges to do when faced with a contract that potentially violates public policy.

The reason for the difficulty is that in the real world it is often far from clear that justice would be done if the courts were to refuse to enforce the contract. Consider Illustration 14.1 and Illustration 14.2.

Illustration 14.1

A foreign academic has been invited to deliver a two-week course of lectures at the University of Carmarthenshire. She has young children, and is unable to find suitable childcare in the UK. She therefore asks a nanny to travel with her from her home country to look after the children during the two weeks. No work permit is sought.

Here, the contract between the academic and the nanny violates UK immigration rules and is therefore illegal. Yet if the idea of the contract being void were to be taken to the fullest extent, it would mean that the nanny has no right to be paid for her work and that the employer would benefit from free labour—even though, arguably, the nanny was less at fault than the employer.

It may also be unclear whether the rule of public policy in question actually requires the court to refuse to give effect to the contract:

Illustration 14.2

John Twickeham is building an extension onto his house. The builder notices that the extension will have a footprint that takes it over the limit of permitted development, making planning permission necessary. John tells the builder to forget about planning permission, as the council is unlikely to notice or enforce the planning rules.

Here, the contract between John and the builder contemplates a deliberate violation of planning law. Should that make the entire contract illegal so John cannot sue the builder for defective work, and the builder cannot sue John if he refuses to pay? Or should the court conclude that the penalties imposed by statute for violation of planning law are sufficient?

Consider, also, Problem 14. The student has suffered non-performance. Intervening on the student's side may, at one level, give effect to a contract that is arguably against public policy. At the same time, however, it is not obvious that letting the essay mill keep the money is a good outcome. They, too, have acted in a way that contravenes public policy. Why should the law permit them to be enriched by their conduct?

As these illustrations suggest, in practice it is not possible to simply declare that a contract is void because it violates public policy and stop there. The question is, rather, whether protecting the public interests at stake requires the court to deny the parties a remedy. The subject of the doctrine of illegality is, accordingly, better conceptualized as being about the *interface* between the law of contract (which, ordinarily, focuses on the private interests of the parties) and the broader, underlying domain of public policy (which, as its name suggests, focuses on protecting the public interest). The task of the doctrine of illegality is to determine what happens when a private contract potentially has a negative impact on the public interest. How negative must this impact be for it to affect the validity of the contract? And what consequences should follow from the prioritization of the public interest over a private interest?

The answer to this question has changed in recent years. Over the course of the 20th century, the courts developed a rule-based jurisprudence based on distinctions between different types of illegality and different ways in which illegality affected the remedy that was sought. These distinctions were not always easy to apply, however, and in 2016, the decision of the Supreme Court in *Patel v Mirza*[1] swept away much of the old law, and put in its place a new multifactoral approach. Following *Patel v Mirza*, a court faced with a potentially illegal contract must proceed by weighing three matters. First, the court must consider the policy underlying the prohibition which gives rise to the potential illegality. Thus, in relation to the illustrations above, it must consider what public ends the immigration rules and the rules on planning permission are intended to serve. Secondly, the court must consider any other matters of public policy which might be affected by a decision to deny relief. Will any other public policy be affected by holding that the nanny is not entitled to wages due to the violation of immigration rules, or that the builder is not entitled to payment because of the violation of planning laws? Thirdly, it must consider whether a denial of relief will be proportionate to the nature and degree of illegality involved.

Section 14.2.2 examines these factors in some detail, and how they are likely to be applied to determine when a party to a contract tainted by illegality will be entitled to relief. Because *Patel v Mirza* is so recent, the vast majority of the case law on illegality dates from before that case was decided. Section 14.2.1 therefore briefly discusses how the law approached illegality before *Patel v Mirza*, and precisely what *Patel v Mirza* changed. Section 14.3 then proceeds to consider what makes a contract illegal, focusing

---

1. [2016] UKSC 42.

on the sources and types of rules that could lead to a contract being deemed to be illegal or against public policy.

14.2 The impact of illegality on contracts

14.2.1 Illegality before *Patel v Mirza*

The moralistic approach

Illegality is usually invoked as a defence. The issue of illegality comes before a court when one party sues on a contract, either for damages or to unwind the contract and recover an advance paid to the other party. The defendant contends that the contract involved illegality. He argues that the claimant should be denied relief on the contract because of that illegality.

The fact that illegality comes before the court as a defence is relevant to understanding the nature of the rule, because it highlights why the choice before the court is frequently unpalatable.[2] On the one hand, public policy and the protection of the public interest militate against giving any relief to either party. On the other hand, because illegality is being raised as a defence, upholding the defence will often leave a party to the illegal activity holding a windfall. In Problem 14, for example, it could potentially leave the website in a position where it neither has to supply an essay nor refund the student's payment. In Illustration 14.2, it could leave the builder in a position where he neither has to build the extension nor refund John's money. Or it could leave John in a position where he has had an extension built but does not have to pay for it.

For much of the 19th century, the courts were willing to countenance such a result, because the approach they took to illegality was quite strongly moralistic. Losses were left to lie where they fell, because it was believed to be contrary to the integrity of the legal system for civil courts to in any way assist those whose conduct was criminal. In the 1725 decision of *Everet v Williams*,[3] a highwayman brought a bill in equity to enforce an agreement with another highwayman on the division of their plunder. The judges dismissed the action, hanged the highwaymen, and imposed a heavy fine on the solicitors. Few other cases had such dramatic outcomes, but the reasoning underlying the approach was the same: persons who had engaged in illegal conduct had forfeited the right to the assistance of the courts.[4]

The decision in *Apthorp v Nevill*[5] is a classic example of this approach in action. Major Dudley Apthorp had broken off his engagement to his fiancée because he was told she was already married. She successfully sued him for breach of his promise to marry (at that time, an actionable tort). Apthorp entered into an agreement with an agent of the defendants', a publishing firm, to publish a book setting out his side of the story against his former fiancée and others. When the publishers discovered that the contents were libellous, they refused to proceed. Apthorp sued for breach of contract, and to recover a sum he had paid to cover costs of publication. The defendants

---

2. Cf the remarks of Bingham LJ in *Saunders v Edwards* [1987] 1 WLR 1116, 1134.
3. Discussed in (1893) LQR 197.
4. *Holman v Johnson* (1775) 1 Cowp 341, 343 (Lord Mansfield).   5. (1907) 23 TLR 575.

counterclaimed to recover costs of preparing the proof. Pickford J dismissed both the claim and the counterclaim. Because the contract was entered into for an illegal purpose—printing a libel—and because the publishers' agent had known it was libellous, neither party would be allowed to bring an action against the other.

The rule-based approach

As the 20th century progressed, however, this strict approach became less sustainable. The rise of the regulatory state meant that illegality was increasingly about matters that are *mala prohibita* rather than *mala in se*. That is to say, rather than being about matters that were inherently illegal (eg fraud, theft, or murder), cases involving illegality were increasingly about acts that contravened government regulations on commerce without being inherently reprehensible. The paradigmatic pre-war cases on illegality related to contracts to commit frauds or to steal another's property. The typical wartime and post-war cases on illegality related to contracts which breached licensing rules, planning laws, or export controls. Where a contract is illegal because it contemplates theft, it is easy to take a moralistic view. Where it is illegal because it involves a technical breach of a licensing regulation, it is not clear that such an approach is appropriate.

The result was that the courts began to develop a rule-based, legalistic approach in place of the moralistic approach that characterized the earlier case law. The heart of the rule-based approach to illegality lay in a distinction between claims that are *founded* on illegal acts and those that *relate* to illegal acts but are not founded on them.

Whether a claim was founded on an illegal act depended on two factors. First, it depended on whether the illegality related to the formation or purpose of the contract, or merely to the manner in which it was performed. If the contract was illegal because the law prohibited contracts of that type (eg a contract to sell organs for transplant) then any claim that depended on that contract would fail. If the contract was not itself prohibited, but was formed for an unlawful purpose (eg a contract to trade in smuggled goods), or contemplated the commission of illegal acts in the course of performance (eg breaches of health and safety laws), then the claim would only be barred if the claimant had *participated* in the illegality to some extent. Participation was often a matter of fact. A claimant who was unaware of the illegality was not a participant in it. It also encompassed a notion known as '*locus poenitentiae*' under which a person who voluntarily withdrew from an illegal scheme could in some circumstances recover. In *Archbolds (Freightage) Ltd v Spanglett Ltd*,[6] the claimants contracted with the defendant carriers for the transport of a cargo of whisky to London. The vehicle on which the whisky was carried was unlicensed, but the claimants did not know this. When the whisky was stolen, the carriers sought to rely on a defence of illegality. The court held that the illegality defence was not available. The illegality here was in the way the agreement was performed, and the claimants had not participated in the illegality. In contrast, in *Ashmore, Benson, Pease & Co Ltd v AV Dawson Ltd*,[7] where a lorry had been loaded above the maximum permitted weight, the claimants had been present at the time of loading and were consequently held to have participated in the illegality.

6. [1961] 1 QB 374.   7. [1973] 1 WLR 828.

Secondly, the question of whether a claim was founded on an illegal act also depended on whether the action relied on a right which only existed because of the illegal contract, or whether it relied on a right which existed independently of the illegality. In *Bowmakers Ltd v Barnet Instruments Ltd*,[8] the parties had in 1944 entered into hire-purchase contracts for the sale of machine tools which Bowmakers owned. Under wartime regulations made in 1940, a government licence was required for the sale of used machine tools. Bowmakers had no such licence, and the contract was therefore illegal. In breach of the hire-purchase contracts, Barnet Instruments sold the machine tools to a third party. Bowmakers sued, and Barnet sought to defend themselves arguing that the hire-purchase agreements were illegal. The Court of Appeal held that Bowmakers' suit was based on its ownership of the tools rather than on the hire-purchase agreement. It was therefore entitled to succeed. This also applied if the contract was tangential to the purpose of the statute. In *St John Shipping Corp v Joseph Rank Ltd*,[9] the owners of a ship had overloaded it in breach of applicable statutory rules. The owners of the cargo refused to pay the full amount due. When the shipowners sued, they defended themselves by arguing that the claim was barred by illegality (in this case, the shipowners' breach of statutory rules on maximum loads). Devlin J held that the claim was not barred. Although the statute prohibited overloading, it did not void contracts of carriage simply because the carrier overloaded the ship.[10]

The limits of the rule-based approach

In the 1990s, the courts began to run into the limits of this approach, resulting in a series of decisions where differences that, as a matter of policy, ought to have been irrelevant nevertheless produced vastly different outcomes. The decision of the House of Lords in *Tinsley v Milligan*[11] (which *Patel v Mirza* overruled) epitomizes some of these difficulties. Tinsley and Milligan, who were both lovers and business partners, had purchased a house together but registered it solely in Tinsley's name. This was done to let Milligan fraudulently claim benefits to which she as a house owner was not in fact entitled. Tinsley and Milligan eventually fell out. Tinsley left the property and tried to evict Milligan. Milligan claimed that Tinsley held the property upon trust with the beneficial ownership vesting in both in equal shares. The question for the courts was whether the fraudulent purpose of the original transaction barred Milligan from claiming equal beneficial ownership. The House of Lords, by a 3:2 majority, held that Milligan's claim was not barred by illegality. Her right to a half-share arose from her contribution to the purchase price. Under the law of resulting trusts, her contribution was sufficient to give rise to a presumption of resulting trust. She did not therefore have to rely on the fraudulent arrangement between herself and Tinsley to establish title: she simply needed to rely on the presumption of resulting trust. Because she could establish her claim without needing to rely on the illegality, she was entitled to succeed.

The decision was controversial. In his dissent, Lord Goff pointed out that it would mean that terrorists or armed robbers who bought a base for their activities in a third party's name would also be entitled to relief.[12] Other problems also emerged in practice. In *Collier v Collier*,[13] the facts were very similar to *Tinsley v Milligan*, except that the parties

---

8. [1945] 1 KB 65 (CA).   9. [1957] 1 QB 267.   10. Ibid, 285.
11. [1994] 1 AC 340 (HL).   12. Ibid, 362.   13. [2002] BIPR 1057 (CA).

involved were a father and a daughter. Because there is no presumption of resulting trust in transactions between a father and daughter, the Court of Appeal held that the father's claim was barred by illegality. It is hard to see, however, how the different outcomes can be justified. The result was a growing sense that *Tinsley v Milligan* demonstrated the shortcomings of the rule-based approach, and that a fresh approach was needed.

14.2.2 *Patel v Mirza* and the 'range of factors' approach

The background to *Patel v Mirza*

In 2010, the Law Commission issued a report on the illegality defence,[14] in which it suggested that the law on illegality had become complex, uncertain, and arbitrary. It identified five policy goals which the illegality doctrine should serve if it were to function well. It should, first, further the purposes of the statutory rule in question. Secondly, it should promote consistency across different aspects of the legal system, such that civil law did not operate at cross-purposes with criminal law or regulatory law. Thirdly, it should prevent parties from profiting from their wrongdoing. Fourthly, it should aim to deter (rather than incentivize) illegal conduct. Finally, it should maintain the integrity of the legal system. The law did not do this well, instead producing arbitrary outcomes. *Tinsley v Milligan* was singled out for criticism, as preventing the court from engaging properly with the underlying policy questions.[15]

The Law Commission recommended that the courts develop the law along different lines. Instead of focusing on technical rules, the courts should adopt an instrumentalist approach. Illegality should be adjudicated and construed in the light of how the public policy in question affects the transaction that is affected by illegality, taking a range of factors into account.

Between the report of the Law Commission and the decision of the Supreme Court in *Patel v Mirza*, the issue of illegality came before the Supreme Court in three cases, where different benches issued decisions that seemed to send the law of illegality careening off in different directions. In *Hounga v Allen*,[16] a case involving racial discrimination against an immigrant who had overstayed her visa and was working illegally, the Supreme Court held that the correct approach was not to ask whether she needed to rely on the illegal contract, but to take a more flexible approach balancing the public policy underlying racial discrimination law against the public policy underlying immigration law. But this flexible approach was not followed by the Supreme Court in *Les Laboratoires Servier v Apotex Inc*,[17] a case decided only a few months later. The case related to agreements which involved patent infringement, where it was contended that the patent infringement made the agreements illegal. The Court of Appeal in that case rejected the illegality defence, applying a flexible approach. The Supreme Court unanimously upheld the rejection of the defence. However, Lord Sumption, speaking for three of the five judges, held that the Court of Appeal was wrong to follow a flexible approach rather than the rule-based approach. Lord Toulson, who delivered a separate concurring judgment, held that the Court of Appeal was correct to follow a

---

14. Law Commission, *The Illegality Defence* (Law Com No 320, 2010).
15. Ibid, 2.13–2.15.   16. [2014] UKSC 47, [2014] 1 WLR 2889.
17. [2014] UKSC 55, [2015] AC 430.

flexible approach. A few months later, in *Bilta (UK) Ltd v Nazir*,[18] the bench was again divided between those who favoured the rule-based approach and those who favoured a more flexible approach. As a result, when *Patel v Mirza* came up before the court some months later, a nine-judge bench was constituted to address and resolve the issue.

Case in depth: *Patel v Mirza* [2016] UKSC 42

Patel paid £620,000 to Mirza. The money was to be used to bet on the price of shares in the Royal Bank of Scotland. Both of them expected Mirza to be able to secure insider information from contacts within RBS, relating to a government announcement which would affect its share price. Because the transaction would have relied on insider information, it was illegal under s 52 of the Criminal Justice Act 1993 as a conspiracy to commit insider trading. As it happened, however, no announcement was made and the bets were not placed. Mirza retained the money and Patel sued to recover it. Mirza argued that the money was not recoverable, as it was paid under an illegal arrangement.

The High Court upheld the defence, and held that Patel's action was barred by illegality. To recover, he had to rely on the non-performance of the illegal contract. This meant that it was reliance on illegality within the meaning of *Tinsley v Milligan*. Patel appealed to the Court of Appeal, which held that the illegality defence did not apply. The majority did so on the basis of the *locus poenitentiae* exception (discussed in section 14.2.1), that a person who voluntarily withdrew from an illegal scheme could in some circumstances recover. Gloster LJ, in contrast, held that the time had come to reject the reliance doctrine, and to instead apply a more flexible approach as recommended by the Law Commission and as evidenced in *Hounga v Allen*.

The Supreme Court unanimously approved the rejection of the illegality defence. The panel was, however, sharply divided on the law. Six of the nine judges hearing the case held that illegality should be decided on the basis of a more flexible test rather than a rule-based approach. Lord Toulson, delivering a judgment on behalf of himself and four other judges, stressed the importance of this approach:

> The essential rationale of the illegality doctrine is that it would be contrary to the public interest to enforce a claim if to do so would be harmful to the integrity of the legal system . . . The public interest is best served by a principled and transparent assessment of the considerations identified, rather by than the application of a formal approach capable of producing results which may appear arbitrary, unjust or disproportionate.[19]

This involved weighing three specific factors; namely, the policy underlying the prohibition, other relevant policies, and the proportionality of denying a remedy to the illegality:

> In assessing whether the public interest would be harmed in that way, it is necessary a) to consider the underlying purpose of the prohibition which has been transgressed and whether that purpose will be enhanced by denial of the claim, b) to consider any other relevant public policy on which the denial of the claim may have an impact and c) to consider whether denial of the claim would be a proportionate response to the illegality, bearing in mind that punishment is a matter for the criminal courts.[20]

→

---

18. [2015] UKSC 23, [2016] AC 1.   19. [2016] UKSC 42, [120] (Lord Toulson).   20. Ibid.

→

Three judges dissented. Lord Mance said that the majority's approach might 'prove more problematic than has the troubled doctrine of ex turpi causa itself'.[21]

> In my opinion, what is called for is a limited approach to the effect of illegality, focused on the need to avoid inconsistency in the law, without depriving claimants of the opportunity to obtain damages for wrongs or to put themselves in the position in which they should have been. This will offer the opportunity of resolving such problems as have, rightly, been identified in the present law, without replacing it wholesale with an open and unsettled range of factors.[22]

Lord Sumption dissented in even stronger terms. The majority's decision, and the use of a 'range of factors' test on a case-by-case basis was in his view unprincipled:

> it loses sight of the reason why legal rights can ever be defeated on account of their illegal factual basis . . . Whatever rationale one adopts for the illegality principle, it is manifestly designed to vindicate the public interest as against the interests and legal rights of the parties . . . The operation of the principle cannot therefore depend on an evaluation of the equities as between the parties or the proportionality of its impact upon the claimant.[23]

Lord Neuberger concurred with the majority, but would have gone further in one respect: he would have set out a general rule that a claimant is entitled to the return of money that has been paid even if the underlying transaction is illegal. Whilst there would be narrow exceptions, the illegality of the transaction should not in general stop the court from undoing it by requiring parties to return money that the other had paid to them to further the transaction.[24] This extension was not, however, accepted by the majority.

Despite the strength of the dissents, the three factors identified by Lord Toulson (which he termed a 'trio of considerations'[25]) are now the correct starting point for any analysis of illegality: not as criteria to be mechanistically applied, but as elements in a consolidated and integrated approach. In the remainder of this section, we will consider what they mean, drawing on the section of the pre-*Patel* case law that took a more flexible approach.

Considering the underlying policy

In determining whether it would be contrary to the public interest to allow a particular claim which is allegedly tainted by illegality, the first consideration is 'the underlying purpose of the prohibition which has been transgressed'. Lord Toulson cited the decision of the Court of Appeal in *Hardy v Motor Insurers' Bureau*,[26] where the court was faced with a motor insurance claim where the driver had deliberately (and criminally) injured an individual. It is a principle of law that deliberate criminal conduct cannot be insured against. It was therefore argued by the Motor Insurers' Bureau that

---

21. Ibid, [192], quoting McLachlin J in *Hall v Herbert* [1993] 2 SCR 159 (Supreme Court of Canada).
22. Ibid, [192].   23. Ibid, [262].   24. Ibid, [146].   25. Ibid, [101].
26. [1954] 2 QB 745 (CA).

the *ex turpi causa* principle operated to bar recovery. The Court of Appeal rejected the defence and allowed the injured individual to recover. The purpose of the prohibition was to protect persons who were injured due to the actions of motorists. This purpose would not be advanced by permitting claims to be defeated on the basis of illegality. Likewise, if the law's purpose is to protect a weaker party, then that weaker party will not be barred from enforcing a contract that breaches the law. If a tenancy agreement breaches rental laws framed to protect a tenant, the landlord might be barred from enforcing the agreement but the tenant will usually not be.[27] In contrast, in *Gujra v Roath*,[28] Roath had hired Gujra to set fire to Roath's cars so that Roath could make an insurance claim on them. Gujra was arrested, and Roath in breach of their agreement refused to drop the charges against him. After his release from jail, Gujra sought to sue Roath. The High Court held that the illegality defence barred Gujra from recovering in contract or tort (for malicious prosecution). This was because the purpose of the relevant prohibition was to deter dishonest insurance claims, which would be defeated if a party could sue in respect of an inherent risk of the fraudulent enterprise.[29]

It is also likely that the type of relief sought will be relevant. An action to enforce an illegal contract, or to claim damages for its breach, is likelier to contravene the underlying policy than is an action to undo the contract and seek recovery of money paid under it. Similarly, an action for a non-contractual remedy, such as damages for fraud[30] or for *quantum meruit*,[31] is less likely to engage the policy underlying the prohibition than an action for damages for breach because they accept the contract's invalidity.

In *Mohamed v Alaga*,[32] the claimant, a translator, entered into an agreement with a firm of solicitors to introduce asylum claimants from Somalia to the firm, and to offer translation and interpreting services in connection with their claims. He was to be paid half the fees received by the firm from these clients. Fee-sharing arrangements of this type were unenforceable at the time.[33] The firm refused to pay, and he sued for the agreed share of the fees. In the alternative, he made a *quantum meruit* claim for the value of the translation and interpretation services he had rendered. Both claims were struck out at first instance. On appeal, the striking out of the contractual claim was upheld on the basis that the contract was void for illegality. The claimant had argued that the Solicitors' Practice Rules' prohibition on fee-sharing agreements was only imposed on solicitors, and not on other persons. Lord Bingham in the Court of Appeal held that the policy reasons underlying the prohibition would be defeated if a non-solicitor party could enlist the aid of a court to enforce prohibited agreements.[34] The *quantum meruit* claim, however, was restored, on the basis that what was sought to be recovered was entirely different from a fee-share, and therefore did not engage the public policy in question.[35]

In *Re Mahmoud and Ispahani*,[36] in contrast, the claimants were unable to maintain an action. That case involved a regulation made under the Defence of the Realm Acts which required all dealers in linseed oil to have a licence. The defendant fraudulently

---

27. *Kiriri Cotton Co v Dewani* [1960] AC 192.   28. [2018] EWHC 854 (QB), [2018] 1 WLR 3208.
29. Ibid, [30].   30. See Chapter 11 ('Untrue statements').
31. See Chapter 17 ('Non-compensatory remedies').   32. [2000] 1 WLR 1815 (CA).
33. The relevant rules were rules 3 and 7 of the Solicitors' Practice Rules 1990, which had statutory force under s 31 of the Solicitors Act 1974.
34. [2000] 1 WLR 1815 (CA), 1824.   35. Ibid, 1825.   36. [1921] 2 KB 716.

told the claimant that he had a licence, and entered into an agreement to purchase oil from the claimant. He then refused to accept delivery. When the claimant sued for breach, the court held that the action was barred for illegality. Permitting a suit for breach under the circumstances would 'reduce the legislation to an absurdity'.[37] It is quite likely, however, that an action for fraudulent misrepresentation would have succeeded. The plea was not taken in the case, and the Court of Appeal expressly stated that its decision did not preclude that possibility.[38] Following *Patel v Mirza*, it is likely that such an action would be successful.

Finally, in considering whether the underlying policy is engaged, the court will consider the impact on the underlying policy of leaving things as they stand, as opposed to granting the relief sought by the claimant. In *Kliers v Schmerler*,[39] the illegality arose out of the fact that the arrangements in question were entered into to commit mortgage fraud. The High Court acknowledged the importance of the public policy against fraud. Nevertheless, it granted the relief sought by the claimant, on the basis that leaving matters where they stood would continue the perpetration of the fraud. Granting the relief, in contrast, would assist the process of undoing and remedying the fraud.[40]

Considering other policies

The second consideration in determining whether allowing a claim under an illegal contract is contrary to the public interest is to take into account 'any other relevant public policies which may be rendered ineffective or less effective by denial of the claim'.[41] *Hounga v Allen*,[42] discussed briefly earlier in the chapter, is a classic example. Hounga, a Nigerian national, was offered a job as a home help in the UK with the Allens. She was told she would be sent to school and given an allowance of £50 a month. Her documents were falsified, and she entered the UK on a visitor's visa and began working illegally with the Allens. She was subjected to abuse, and after 18 months she was taken into care by her local authority. She sued the Allens for unfair dismissal and unpaid wages, as well as for the tort of unlawful racial discrimination. Her claim for unfair dismissal and unpaid wages were dismissed and not appealed. Her claim for unlawful discrimination, however, succeeded in the Supreme Court. On such a consideration, the balance favoured racial discrimination law. To hold otherwise would encourage employers to enter into illegal contracts of employment, as that would let them discriminate without legal consequences. In consequence, Hounga's action succeeded. In *Patel v Mirza*, Lord Toulson suggested that a claim for *quantum meruit* might similarly have been looked upon favourably by the Supreme Court.[43]

A similar approach was taken in *R (Best) v Chief Land Registrar*.[44] In 2012, Parliament amended the law to criminalize squatting, if the squatter had entered the building in question as a trespasser.[45] The question was whether this affected the right to acquire title by adverse possession. The court held that although ordinarily a criminal act could not be relied on to establish a claim, in this case the policy underlying the law on adverse possession was a strong one, and was not affected by the criminalization of

37. Ibid, 732 (Atkin LJ).   38. Ibid, 730 (Scrutton LJ).   39. [2018] EWHC 1350 (Ch).
40. Ibid, [100]. See also *Saeed v Ibrahim* [2018] EWHC 1804 (Ch), [91]–[95].
41. [2016] UKSC 42, [101] (Lord Toulson).   42. [2014] UKSC 47, [2014] 1 WLR 2889.
43. [2016] UKSC 42, [119].   44. [2015] EWCA Civ 17.
45. Legal Aid, Sentencing and Punishment of Offenders Act 2012, s 144.

squatting. The situation, it was held, would be different if the squatter had murdered the true owner of the property, or bribed a law enforcement official, but no such circumstances were present on the facts of the case.

Proportionality

The third, and most controversial, of the considerations formulated in *Patel v Mirza* is the criterion of proportionality—or, as Lord Toulson put it, 'the possibility of overkill unless the law is applied with a due sense of proportionality'.[46] Factors that might potentially be of relevance in determining whether a denial of relief was proportionate to the nature of the wrongdoing include 'the seriousness of the conduct, its centrality to the contract, whether it was intentional and whether there was marked disparity in the parties' respective culpability'.[47]

The majority's reliance on proportionality was a particular target of criticism by Lords Mance and Sumption. Proportionality, in Lord Sumption's reading:

> is far too vague and potentially far too wide to serve as the basis on which a person may be denied his legal rights. It converts a legal principle into an exercise of judicial discretion, in the process exhibiting all the vices of 'complexity, uncertainty, arbitrariness and lack of transparency' which Lord Toulson attributes to the present law. I would not deny that in the past the law of illegality has been a mess. The proper response of this court is not to leave the problem to case by case evaluation by the lower courts by reference to a potentially unlimited range of factors, but to address the problem by supplying a framework of principle which accommodates legitimate concerns about the present law. We would be doing no service to the coherent development of the law if we simply substituted a new mess for the old one.[48]

Despite the strength of this criticism, however, there is sound sense to proportionality. As articulated by Lord Toulson, proportionality is, in effect, a measure of salience. Whereas the first consideration looks at the *purpose* of the policy in question, proportionality is a measure of the *extent* to which the policy at issue is engaged by the facts of a particular case. In some cases, the illegality may be so peripheral to the core of the transaction, and have so tenuous a connection to the policy at stake, that it would be disproportionate to hold the entire transaction to be unenforceable for reason of that illegality. *St John Shipping Corp v Joseph Rank Ltd*,[49] discussed in section 14.2.1, arguably reflects precisely this principle in action. Similarly, in *Coral Leisure Group v Barnett*,[50] Barnett had been employed as a public relations executive to find customers for the defendant casino. In the course of pleadings, he stated that one of his tasks had involved finding prostitutes for customers. The question for the court was whether this meant that the contract was unenforceable as being against public policy. The Employment Appellate Tribunal held that it was not. On the pleaded case, procuring prostitutes was not part of his employment contract, nor was it part of his purpose in entering into the contract. The fact that he had committed some immoral or unlawful acts in the course of performing the contract did not make the entire contract unenforceable.

---

46. [2016] UKSC 42, [101].   47. Ibid, [107] (Lord Toulson).   48. Ibid, [265].
49. [1957] 1 QB 267.   50. [1981] ICR 503.

In *Shaw v Groom*,[51] similarly, a landlord had let a room to a tenant, and had provided her with a rent book. The book did not, however, contain all the information which it was legally required to have. Failing to provide a compliant rent book was, at the time, punishable with a fine. The tenant fell into arrears, and when the landlord sued she argued that the claim was barred by illegality because, by failing to provide her with a compliant rent book, the landlord had committed a criminal offence. The court held that the illegality defence did not apply. The true test was whether the law had intended to prevent landlords from recovering rent if they failed to provide a proper rent book. Nothing in the law suggested that the intent was so drastic.

Proportionality also requires the courts to consider the parties' relative blameworthiness. If both parties are equally to blame, or if the party raising the defence of illegality is more to blame, the court may hold that it would not be proportionate to deny the claimant a remedy.[52] In *Mohamed v Alaga*,[53] Lord Bingham explained why relative blameworthiness was potentially of relevance:

> It is furthermore in my judgment relevant that the parties are not in a situation in which their blameworthiness is equal. The defendant is a solicitors' firm and bound by the rules. It should reasonably be assumed to know what the rules are and to comply with them. If, in truth, it made the agreement as alleged, then it would seem very probable that it acted in knowing disregard of professional rules binding upon it. By contrast the plaintiff . . . was ignorant that there was any reason why the defendant should not make the agreement which he says was made. In other commercial fields, after all, such agreements are common.[54]

This remains true even if the claimant has received a criminal sentence as a result of the illegality. In *Robinson v Ness*,[55] the claimant had purchased long leases over five flats in a house. The defendants, who were his solicitors in the purchase, failed to advise him that planning permission had not been obtained for converting the house into flats. An enforcement notice was issued. The claimant tried to comply with it, but was unable to do so for reasons beyond his control. He was convicted of breaching the notice, and made subject to a confiscation order. He sued his solicitors for breach of contract and in the tort of negligence. The High Court held that notwithstanding his criminal conviction, it would be disproportionate to deny him relief on the basis of illegality as the fault lay overwhelmingly with the solicitors.[56]

Where the illegality arises from the transaction's impact on a third party—for example, a fraud on a third party—the fact that the third party chooses to adopt the transaction on discovering the fraud may militate against allowing the illegality defence to succeed.[57]

14.2.3 Assessing *Patel v Mirza*

The utility of the more flexible, 'range of factors' approach can be seen if we return to the facts of Problem 14. Prior to *Patel v Mirza*, the rights of the student would have turned, first, on analysing whether the contract was illegal in performance or in

51. [1970] 2 QB 504 (CA).
52. *Harb v HRH Prince Abdul Aziz* [2018] EWHC 508 (Ch), [229]–[230].
53. [2000] 1 WLR 1815 (CA).   54. Ibid, 1825.   55. [2017] EWHC 2305 (Ch).
56. Ibid, [179]–[181].   57. *Stoffel v Grondona* [2018] EWCA Civ 2301, [39].

formation or purpose; and, secondly, on whether the student would have to rely on the illegality in order to claim relief. On the first of these, the facts suggest quite clearly that the contract was formed for a fraudulent purpose, and that the student participated fully in the fraud. On the second, too, it is hard to see how the student would be able to plead their case without relying on the illegal contract. Given this, it is likely that the student will be unable to claim any relief.

The 'range of factors' approach will in all likelihood produce a similar outcome, but through a more coherent process of reasoning. A court will begin by asking what the purpose of the common law rule against enforcing contracts created for dishonest purposes is, and whether permitting the student to claim relief against the essay mill will further or hinder that purpose. It will then ask whether there are any countervailing policies in the law, concluding on the facts that there are none. It will then examine the proportionality of rejecting the two remedies the student may claim—damages for breach of contract or a refund of the money paid—in the light of the factors identified as being of relevance in *Patel v Mirza*; namely, the seriousness of the conduct, its centrality to the contract, whether it was intentional, and whether there was marked disparity in the parties' respective culpability. On the facts, the answer to all these questions is likely to be unfavourable to the student.

Although the outcome is similar to that produced by the pre-*Patel* case law, it should be evident that the questions the court asks in the 'range of factors' approach map more closely onto those that ought to be asked if the court is to take its role in advancing public policy seriously. It is, arguably, the disproportionate consequence of a denial of any remedy that lay behind the strained reasoning in cases like *Tinsley v Milligan*, and that also lay behind earlier judicial attempts to articulate alternative tests for illegality, drawing on concepts such as 'public conscience'.[58] *Patel* also provides a better conceptual grounding for the doctrine of severability, under which the illegal portion of a contract can be severed from the portion that is not illegal, with the latter given effect to by the courts. Severability reflects the fact that even where policy is engaged, it is not always equally salient. That is precisely what proportionality seeks to capture, and its express recognition in *Patel v Mirza* is clearly an improvement over the law as it stood before that case.

The utility of *Patel v Mirza* becomes even clearer if we consider Illustration 14.1, involving the rights of the nanny who is illegally employed. Here, on the pre-*Patel* case law it is hard to see how the nanny would be able to recover anything in relation to her employment. The contract was illegal at formation, which means that the question of whether the nanny participated in the illegality is not relevant. Equally, any action she brought would have to rely on the illegal work she did, thus putting her outside the rule in *Tinsley v Milligan*. Under the 'range of factors' approach, in contrast, the court will have to weigh the policy implicit in employment law—and, in particular, in minimum wage laws—against the policy implicit in immigration law, in a process analogous to that done with discrimination law in *Hounga v Allen*.[59] The court will also have to take into account the disparity between the parties in assessing proportionality, as Lord Bingham did in *Mohamed v Alaga*.[60] The result is that the nanny may well be

58. *Tinsley v Milligan* [1992] Ch 310 (CA), 319–23.
59. [2014] UKSC 47, [2014] 1 WLR 2889.   60. [2000] 1 WLR 1815 (CA).

able to recover, if not in contract then in *quantum meruit*. Such a result, it is submitted, is sensible, and avoids the problems that plagued the courts between the decision in *Tinsley v Milligan* and *Patel v Mirza*.

14.3 What makes a contract illegal?

The discussion thus far has focused on how illegality affects the ability of parties to enforce contracts. But what determines whether a contract violates public policy, thus making it illegal? What sort of effect must a contract have in order to be held to violate public policy? What criteria do we take into account? Those are the questions we will examine in this section.

14.3.1 Contracts to commit wrongs

Criminal wrongs

The first, and most obvious, source of illegality is where the contract contemplates the commission of a crime. The cases we have discussed in section 14.2 have largely related to this source of illegality, and there is little to add to the discussion in that section as far as criminal wrongs are concerned. Three points, all building on matters discussed in that section, should however be noted.

First, few statutes expressly prohibit contracts (although some do). More commonly, statutes prohibit conduct such as 'buying' without expressly discussing contracts. The issue of illegality arises because the contract entails conduct of the type that has been prohibited. Older writing on the topic sometimes draws a distinction between 'express' and 'implied' statutory prohibitions of contracts.[61] Underlying this was a concern about the disruptive consequences of being too willing to find that a statute impliedly prohibited a contract. In the modern law, this concern is largely dealt with through the courts' focus on the policy underlying the statute and, after *Patel v Mirza*, on proportionality, rather than on a distinction between express and implied prohibitions.

Secondly, illegality can, in principle, apply regardless of whether the criminality in question relates to performance, purpose, or formation, although the evaluative process is likely to be different in relation to each of these. The contracts in *Patel v Mirza*, and in several of the other cases examined in section 14.2, were specifically prohibited by statute. Parties are not allowed to enter into contracts of that particular type or for that particular purpose. Slightly different considerations arise where the contract itself is not specifically prohibited, but nevertheless involves doing acts which are prohibited. Examples of cases of this type include *St John Shipping v Joseph Rank*. After *Patel v Mirza*, cases of this type are subject to the same three-part approach as any other type of illegality. As section 14.2 has discussed, the manner in which the court applies the test in such cases will depend on a consolidated and cumulative evaluation of a range of factors. These include whether the innocent party knew of the illegality, the nature of the underlying policy and how strict the courts need to be to give effect to it, and the salience of those policy considerations to the case at hand given the nature of the relief sought.

---

61. See eg RA Buckley, 'Implied Statutory Prohibitions of Contracts' (1975) 38 MLR 535.

Thirdly, although most of those cases we have discussed thus far have related to regulatory offences, the very same considerations apply where the contract contemplates the performance of a common law crime rather than a statutory offence. A contract to commit a murder, for example, will be illegal even though murder is a common law offence rather than a statutory one.

Civil wrongs

The discussion thus far has concerned cases where the illegality consisted of a criminal act. Problem 14 does not, however, involve a crime. The wrong it involves is a civil wrong, not a criminal one. It involves, first, a breach of the academic conditions at the university where the student is enrolled and, secondly, conduct that is fraudulent. Does the law pertaining to illegality apply when the action is a civil wrong, rather than a crime?

It has long been recognized that illegality applies to fraud and dishonesty in precisely the same way as it does to criminal acts even if the fraud in question is not criminal. To the extent the scenario in Problem 14 is fraudulent, therefore, the law pertaining to illegality will apply, and the impact of the fraud on the contract's enforceability will fall to be analysed in accordance with the criteria set out in section 14.2. But the position in relation to other civil wrongs is less clear. Until 2014, it was not infrequently suggested that civil wrongs, such as torts, could in appropriate cases be treated similarly to criminal wrongs for the purpose of the illegality defence in contract.

There was some authority to support this contention, particularly for intentional torts, but it was thin. There were relatively few cases (outside the domain of fraud) where the illegality defence had been successfully invoked where the purported illegality related to a civil wrong. Most cases related to civil wrongs, such as libel, which were also capable of being criminal (as libel was at the time).[62]

In 2014, the status of civil wrongs was thrown into further doubt by the decision of the Supreme Court in *Les Laboratoires Servier v Apotex Inc*.[63] The illegality in that case was the infringement of a non-UK patent. This is unlawful, but it is a civil wrong remediable by compensation. It is not a crime. The Court of Appeal had held that although the illegality defence was in principle capable of being applied to civil wrongs, it would not be proportionate on the facts to do so. In the Supreme Court, the majority upheld the decision of the Court of Appeal, but disagreed with its reasoning. Lord Sumption, delivering the judgment for the majority, held that the main focus of illegality should be on matters that are criminal. Civil wrongs should only be covered if they are 'quasi-criminal', concerning the public interest in ways similar to criminal wrongs. Dishonesty was one such quasi-criminal civil wrong. Outside this narrow domain, however, illegality does not extend to civil wrongs generally. This was a consequence of the rationale underlying the *ex turpi causa* principle, which is 'concerned with claims founded on acts which are contrary to the public law of the state and engage the public interest'. Civil wrongs, in contrast, 'offend against interests which are essentially private, not public', making it unnecessary for the law to withhold its ordinary remedies.[64]

---

62. See eg *Shackell v Rosier* (1836) 2 Bing NC 634 (where the claimant had been convicted of criminal libel before the action was heard). In *Apthorp v Neville* (1907) 23 TLR 575, discussed in section 14.2.1, the claimant was subsequently prosecuted for, and convicted of, criminal libel: see 'Charge of Libel', *The Times*, 21 April 1909, p 4 col 2.

63. [2014] UKSC 55, [2015] AC 430.   64. Ibid, [25], [27].

Lord Toulson concurred in the result, but differed from Lord Sumption on the law. He acknowledged that the doctrine was not commonly applied in cases where the alleged illegality related to a merely civil wrong. Even so, he thought that this should not be a matter of a bright-line rule. The court should, instead, consider the issue on a case-by-case basis, keeping in mind that the issue was one of public policy, based on a group of reasons. The key question for the courts, therefore, should be whether the policy considerations that are in play merit applying the doctrine of illegality to a particular set of facts. In his view this, rather than a blanket exclusion of civil wrongs, was the preferred approach, and the Court of Appeal was correct to have decided the case on that basis.[65]

Lord Toulson delivered the decision of the majority in *Patel v Mirza*.[66] *Patel v Mirza* repudiated the strict rule-based approach favoured by the majority in *Les Laboratoires Servier v Apotex Inc*,[67] although it did not expressly overrule that case. Lord Toulson also did not specifically discuss the question of whether illegality applies to civil wrongs, as the issue did not arise for consideration.[68] Nevertheless, it is submitted that the adoption of the 'range of factors' approach in *Patel v Mirza* in preference to a rule-based approach does call into doubt the continued validity of the strict rule in relation to the exclusion of civil wrongs. It is far more in keeping with the general approach taken in *Patel v Mirza* to hold that all civil wrongs, and not just frauds, should be dealt with through a consideration of the three key considerations set out in the decision of the majority in *Patel v Mirza*, as the Court of Appeal did in *Les Laboratoires Servier v Apotex Inc*,[69] and as Lord Toulson would have done in the Supreme Court.

14.3.2 Other types of illegality

Illegality is not confined to civil and criminal wrongs. It also encompasses a range of other matters of public policy.

The courts are generally wary of extending public policy too far. In *Richardson v Mellish*,[70] Burrough J described public policy as 'a very unruly horse, and when once you get astride it you never know where it will carry you'.[71] This is not to say that they reject public policy entirely. To the contrary, the need for taking account of public policy in private law cases has long been recognized. Their concern, rather, is with the breadth and nebulousness of public policy *as a concept*. This makes public policy inherently an 'unstable and dangerous foundation' for decisions.[72] Judicial engagement with public policy must, accordingly, be tempered by careful consideration of doctrine rather than simply invoking the abstract concept.

The result is that outside the realm of statutory or common law illegality, public policy tends to be applied through specific categories or types of matters that are seen as engaging public policy. The categories are not closed, but courts are hesitant to engage too readily in a process of expansion or even extension of these categories.

---

65. Ibid, [57]–[60].   66. [2016] UKSC 42.   67. [2014] UKSC 55, [2015] AC 430.
68. [2016] UKSC 42, [120].   69. [2012] EWCA Civ 593, [2013] Bus LR 80.
70. (1824) 2 Bing 229.   71. Ibid, 252.
72. *Janson v Driefontein Consolidated Mines Ltd* [1902] AC 484, 500 (Lord Davey).

The editors of *Chitty on Contract* have suggested four broad categories: those injurious to good government, those injurious to marriage and morality, those which interfere with the proper working of the machinery of justice, and those economically against the public interest.[73] Each of these, in turn, consists of a number of specific grounds of public policy.

Good government

The 'injurious to good government' ground is largely concerned with matters such as bribery, the sale of public offices, and so on, where common law rules of public policy historically precluded transactions from being enforceable even if the transaction in question was not expressly criminalized. With the growth in broadly framed bribery statutes, and increased statutory and administrative regulation of the processes of government, most cases that were dealt with under this head are now likely to be instead treated as contracts to commit statutory wrongs.

Marriage and morality

The importance of the 'marriage and morality' ground, similarly, has declined somewhat with increasing social liberalism. Cohabitation agreements were, for example, seen as being against public policy, but it is unlikely that any court would do so today, and there are cases in which agreements have been enforced by the courts if consideration and contractual intent could be found.[74] Pre-nuptial agreements, in which a marrying couple agrees in advance on how their assets will be divided, were also formerly seen as contravening public policy. In *Radmacher v Granatino*,[75] the Supreme Court held that they were enforceable, subject to the family courts' ability to depart from them if they failed to make adequate provision for one of the parties. Older authorities on this topic should therefore be approached with care.

Machinery of justice

The ground of interfering with the machinery of justice had considerable relevance until recently. Perverting the course of justice is a criminal offence, and contracts to achieve that end will therefore also be illegal as contracts to commit a criminal wrong. In addition, however, two other types of contracts relate to this ground of public policy. First, clauses ousting the jurisdiction of the court are void as contrary to public policy. Today, this provision mainly applies to maintenance agreements, where it has been codified in statute.[76] Maintenance agreements are agreements made between spouses who are divorcing or separating, under which one spouse agrees to pay a certain sum of money to the other on a periodic basis. If such an agreement restricts the right of either party to apply to the court for maintenance—understood broadly as any order about financial arrangements—then that provision is void.

Secondly, agreements for champerty or maintenance in litigation are also void. Maintenance in litigation relates to paying to support litigation in which a person has no legitimate interest. Champerty occurs where a person pays to support litigation in exchange for a share in the final proceeds of the litigation. Earlier, agreements between

---

73. Para 16-006.   74. *Tanner v Tanner* [1975] 1 WLR 1346.
75. [2010] UKSC 42, [2011] 1 AC 534.   76. See the Matrimonial Causes Act 1973, s 34(1).

solicitors and clients were particularly strongly affected by these provisions. Since the entry into force of the Access to Justice Act 1999, however, the law permits solicitors to pay the costs of an action (this would earlier have been void), and it also permits them to charge a success fee (which would also earlier have been void). Champerty and maintenance remain relevant outside the area of civil litigation funding, but their domain of application is now quite small.

Freedom of trade

A restraint of trade involves a person restricting his future liberty in order to carry on trade with other persons not parties to the contract in such manner as he chooses. Agreements in restraint of trade are void and unenforceable at common law, unless it can be shown that the term in question was reasonable with reference to the parties and the public interest.

In *Esso Petroleum Co Ltd v Harper's Garage (Stourport)*,[77] it was held that a line must be drawn between contracts in restraint of trade and contracts which 'merely regulate the normal commercial relations between the parties'. Accordingly, the principle of restraint of trade will not apply to

> ordinary commercial contracts for the regulation and promotion of trade during the existence of the contract, provided that any prevention of work outside the contract, viewed as a whole, is directed towards the absorption of the parties' services and not their sterilisation.

It is also relevant that the clause in question is a standard clause in the industry—in general, contracts of a kind which have 'gained general commercial acceptance' and not traditionally been subject to the doctrine will not be void as being in restraint of trade in the absence of special features, though this is not an immutable rule.

The desire not to interfere in legitimate commercial transactions has been implicit in the law since at least the 19th-century decision of the House of Lords in *Nordenfelt v Maxim Nordenfelt Guns and Ammunition Co Ltd*.[78] Nordenfelt made heavy weaponry, including machine guns and ammunition. He held a number of patents. In 1888, he sold his business and his patents to the Maxim Nordenfelt company. As part of the sale, he agreed to a covenant that for a period of 25 years, he would not

> engage except on behalf of the company either directly or indirectly in the trade or business of a manufacturer of guns, gun mountings or carriages, gunpowder, explosives or ammunition, or in any business competing or liable to compete in any way with that for the time being carried on by the company.

Nordenfelt was paid a substantial sum of money, in excess of £200,000 which at the time was a very large sum. In the view of the quantum involved, the court held that the restriction was reasonable as between the parties.

Schroeder Music Publishing Co Ltd v Macaulay[79] illustrates the sort of contract which the modern doctrine of restraint of trade will operate to avoid. The case involved a young songwriter, who had contracted with Schroeder Music Publishing to work exclusively

---

77. [1968] AC 269.   78. [1894] AC 535.   79. [1974] 1 WLR 1308.

for them for five years. Schroeder Music Publishing acquired the copyright to all his existing works, and to any works he composed during the next five years. There was no obligation on Schroeder to actually publish or commercially use any of his compositions, and Macaulay could not himself use compositions which Schroeder chose not to use. It was held that given that Macaulay's royalties depended upon whether his compositions were used, and taking into account the overall context of the contract, it appeared that the contract was unduly restrictive, especially given the inequality of bargaining power as between the parties.

14.4 In conclusion: public interests and private interests

The heart of the illegality defence is the recognition that private contracts are not entirely private, and that the imperative of protecting the public interest is as much a part of the law of contract as it is of public law. The difficulty posed by the illegality defence, however, is that it is almost always pleaded by one of the parties to the contract, and typically in circumstances that would leave that party holding a windfall notwithstanding that party's participation in the illegal transaction.

As long as illegality was mostly a matter of acts that are *mala in se*—inherently illegal, or inherently repugnant—the courts were able to take a strictly moral perspective, and proceed on the basis that the claimant by his illegal conduct had rendered himself unfit for judicial assistance. As the scope of illegality widened to encompass a much broader range of activities and regulatory breaches, however, this became increasingly difficult to justify.

The shifts in the doctrinal structure of the illegality defence in recent years must be seen against this light. *Patel v Mirza*, in this context, represents a particularly welcome development. Notwithstanding the arguments about certainty, it gives courts and advocates a strong basis to be able to weigh the competing factors, and consider the precise relationship between the grant or denial of relief and the public interests which the law or policy in question was designed to advance. To that extent, it marks a clearer judicial awareness of the extent to which the domain of private contracts increasingly intersects with the domain of public regulation.

The application of the *Patel v Mirza* factors to Problem 14 makes this particularly clear. Instead of the more abstract questions that the rule-based approach would have asked in relation to whether the illegality related to 'purpose' or 'formation', the new approach asks a more direct and to-the-point set of questions. What is the policy underlying the legal system's rules against fraud, particularly in the context of university work? Will denying the student relief against the website further that policy? Will it hinder other policies that may be at issue—for example, a policy to deter individuals from creating websites that encourage fraud? Is the total denial of relief to the student a proportionate response to their attempt to purchase an essay? These questions capture in far better detail the questions that a court should ask in considering the impact of public policy, and rules designed to protect the public interest, on private contracts.

Key points

- Courts have the power to refuse to enforce contracts which contemplate illegal acts. A defendant in an action in contract can therefore raise illegality as a defence to the action.

- Illegality does not automatically lead to the court denying relief. Three factors are taken into account in deciding whether to grant relief to a party who seeks to enforce a contract involving illegality or violation of public policy: the policy underlying the policy, other policies that may be affected if the claimant is denied relief, and the proportionality of denying relief given the nature of the illegality.

- A range of considerations are taken into account in determining proportionality. These include the seriousness of the conduct, its centrality to the contract, whether it was intentional, and whether there was a marked disparity in the parties' respective culpability.

- Contracts are illegal if they involve the commission of criminal wrongs. Certain civil wrongs, such as fraud, can also give rise to a defence of illegality, but most civil wrongs will not do so unless they are also criminal.

- There are also certain common law grounds of illegality. These include agreements which are against good government, agreements against marriage and morality, agreements that interfere with the machinery of justice, and agreements in restraint of trade. The importance of these grounds has declined with the growth in statutes and regulatory frameworks dealing more specifically with the underlying issues of public policy.

Assess your learning

You should be able to respond to each of the following points with a confident 'yes'. If you can't, then you should revisit the sections listed against that point.

Can you:

(a) *Outline* the key ingredients of the illegality defence after *Patel v Mirza*? (Section 14.2.2)

(b) *Explain* the concept of proportionality, its role in illegality, and the manner in which it is applied by the courts? (Section 14.2.2)

(c) *Describe* when criminal and civil wrongs make a contract illegal? (Section 14.3.1)

(d) *Identify* the main common law grounds of illegality, and *outline* the ingredients of each? (Section 14.3.2)

In relation to each of the above, you should be able to:

(i) identify and clearly explain the key rules and principles;

(ii) identify the key cases and statutes, and why they matter;

(iii) apply the principles and cases to specific real or hypothetical fact situations;

(iv) evaluate the limitations, if any, of the law as it currently stands.

Further reading

RA Buckley, 'Implied Statutory Prohibition of Contracts' (1975) 38 MLR 535.

RA Buckley, 'Illegal Transactions: Chaos or Discretion?' (2000) 20 LS 155.

N Enonchong, 'Title Claims and Illegal Transactions' (1995) 111 LQR 135.

M Furmston, 'The Illegal Contracts Act 1970: An English View' (1972) 5 NZULR 151.

Law Commission, *The Illegality Defence* (Law Com No 189, 2009).

A Phang, 'Of Illegality and Presumptions: Australian Departures and Possible Approaches' (1996) 11 JCL 53.

Enforcing contracts

PART IV

Introduction

As lawyers, we have a natural tendency to focus on the coercive aspect of contracts, and the role of the law in keeping the parties to the terms of the transaction. In the real world of contracting, however, the reason why most contracts are performed is that the parties remain committed to the contract. Contracts are made to be kept, and they usually are. It is very rare for a contract to be broken.

Think about the complex web of contracts you rely upon in the course of a typical day. You will draw upon, amongst others, contracts with bus companies, taxi companies, electricity companies, water companies, supermarkets, mobile networks, Facebook, email providers, your landlord, and your university. An action as simple as watching a YouTube video on your mobile phone is only possible because of a vast network of contracts amongst internet service providers, Tier 1 and Tier 2 networks, content delivery networks, internet exchange points, packet clearing houses, hosting services, and the manufacturers and maintainers of the equipment on which all these run.

We are able to ignore the complex contractual underpinnings of everyday life precisely because the vast majority of contracts are performed the vast majority of the time. Contract law is only called upon to enforce contracts where the parties are behaving *atypically*, with at least one of them no longer fully committed to the transaction. It is only in this type of situation that breach occurs and enforcement becomes necessary.

Breaches happen for a range of reasons, but they almost always involve unplanned circumstances or unexpected incentives. A party may be trying to extricate itself from a contract because the deal is no longer as attractive as it originally was. Alternately, a party may be finding it genuinely difficult to discharge its obligations under a contract even though it wants to. Either way, however, its continued commitment to the contract has been strained by changed circumstances. Parties can try to provide for changed circumstances through flexible clauses in the original contract,[1]

---

1. See Chapter 9 ('Flexible terms').

or by attempting to renegotiate terms when problems arise.[2] But there is only so much they can do. It is where they fail that breach becomes likely, and the need for legal enforcement arises.

A survey of the case law suggests that legal remedies for breach of contract tend to be invoked in three broad types of situations. The first is a situation where one party has simply abandoned the transaction. There are a range of reasons why parties may do this. They may be acting cynically, adopting a 'so sue me' approach. Alternately, they may be commercially unable to perform the transaction, because they have run out of money or resources, or because the transaction has become more onerous due to changed circumstances. But whatever the reason, the effect is the same. One of the parties has ceased to perform the contract and has walked away, leaving the other party with little option but to bring an action for breach of contract.

The second type of situation occurs where a party has not abandoned the contract, but claims that its obligations do not extend as far as the other party says they do. A situation of this type may be the result of a party's deliberate use of 'creative compliance' to reduce the burden of a transaction to which it is no longer fully committed. Or it may be the result of a genuine disagreement on the question of who should bear the risk of an event that was not clearly allocated by the contract.[3] It is not always possible to distinguish genuine disagreements from cynical attempts to slough off a contractual duty. The effect on the contract in either case is that one party argues that the contract has been breached, while the other argues that it has not.

The third type of situation arises where one party argues that its obligations have come to an end. A range of motives can lie behind a situation of this type. The party may be acting in good faith, genuinely believing that they are entitled to abandon the contract. Or they may be trying to exploit a loophole to get out of a contract to which they are no longer committed. Once again, however, the effect is that one party is arguing that the other is in breach of contract, whereas the other is arguing that they are no longer required to perform.

Two issues arise for the law in such circumstances. The first is defining what constitutes breach— or, to put it differently, what a party must do to be held to have performed the contract adequately, and to have been discharged from their obligations under the contract. The second is defining the consequences of breach. What happens once a contract is breached? What are the remedies that are available to the party affected by the breach? These are the questions which this Part studies.

Chapter 15 begins the discussion by examining how English law defines breach, and what the immediate effect of breach is on the validity of the contract and the obligations of the parties under the contract. Chapter 16 looks at the primary remedy for breach available to an affected party in English law; namely, compensatory damages. Chapter 17 looks at a range of non-compensatory remedies that are also available at English law. Chapter 18 rounds off the discussion by examining how English law deals with the problem posed by contracts whose performance involves not just the parties to the contract, but also third parties who have not formally become party to the contract.

2. See the discussion in Chapter 5 ('Non-contractual promises').
3. The issue of unallocated risks is discussed more fully in Part II. See especially Chapters 8 ('Filling the gaps') and 10 ('Fundamental changes').

15

Breach of contract

Repudiation and the right to terminate

'But you promised!'

Problem 15: setting the context

Read the following (fictional) press clipping, and consider the legal issues it raises.

Future Hope runs out of hope

Future Hope, a charity which has won awards for its work with the long-term unemployed, is facing an uncertain future, as its ambitious partnership with Avonside University to create a new adult learning hub for the region heads for the rocks.

The Project Agreement was signed in December 2016. Under the agreement, Avonside University agreed to refurbish its former library building which Future Hope would use as its regional base. Academics from a range of Avonside's departments would work alongside Future Hope's staff to design innovative programmes which, it was hoped, would significantly boost the employability of the long-term unemployed. Underpinning it all was an expected exploratory contract with the Department for Business, Innovation and Skills (BIS), which Future Hope was confident it could procure.

Now, however, Avonside University appears to be heading towards pulling out of the project despite having signed a binding agreement to proceed. We understand that a meeting was held between the university and the architects who were charged with producing a new design for the library, at which the university strongly hinted that the project may not proceed. A spokesperson for Avonside University denied that the university had decided to pull out, but admitted that they were considering their options. 'The Project Agreement of December 2016 said that Future Hope would have executed a signed agreement with BIS by December 2018,' she said. 'We have passed that date without any agreement in sight. This means that we need to take a hard look at whether the adult learning hub project remains realistic.'

Future Hope, however, say that substantive agreement had been reached with BIS. The final signature has been delayed by the change of government and the appointment of a new minister for BIS after the 2017 General Election. Speaking to the *Avondale Courant*, Dame Judith Speight said, 'We've done the substance of what we said we would, and we hope the university will stick to its word. If not, we will carefully consider all legal options available to us.'

According to sources within Avonside University, who have requested anonymity, the withdrawal from this project is part of a strategic shift by the university, away from social engagement towards a greater focus on funded research with a view to improving its ranking on league tables. The adult learning hub does not fit that template, and is likely to become yet another casualty of the league table race.

Is Future Hope in breach, as the university alleges? If so, can the university use that as an excuse to pull out of this contract?

15.1 Introduction: commitment and breach

15.1.1 Defining breach

As the introduction to this Part has discussed, breach of contract is rare. Nevertheless, it does happen, as Problem 15 indicates. This creates several tasks for the law. The first of these, and the primary focus of this chapter, is to assess whether the contract has been breached, and if so whether the breach has brought the contract to an end.

Creating legal rules to define breach and deal with its consequences is far from straightforward. The court is being asked to sit in judgment over behaviour which may or may not be opportunistically motivated, in circumstances for which the parties have not explicitly planned, and about which the courts have at best imperfect and incomplete information. The shape of the law of breach can best be understood against the background of these difficulties. The legal doctrines in relation to **performance** and **breach** are, in essence, a way of *simplifying* the complexity of the situations that give rise to breach, whilst at the same time attempting to ensure that the legal approach remains commercially realistic.

English law takes a relatively simplistic approach to defining breach, which can be distilled into four core principles. The first is that a party's motives in breaching a contract are irrelevant. Whether a party behaved honestly or dishonestly, or in good faith or bad faith, does not in general matter. A party who wilfully breaches a contract, callously causing great loss to the other party, is treated no differently from a party who goes to great lengths to fulfil its part of a contract, but finds itself unable to do so despite its best efforts. The only question for the law is whether or not the party in question has done what the contract requires. Why it failed, and whether it tried to comply, are not legally relevant. Putting this in the context of Problem 15, it makes no difference to the law whether the university is genuinely concerned about the failure to sign a formal agreement with the government or whether it is simply trying to find an excuse to get out of a project it no longer wants.

Secondly, a party's motive in alleging breach is also irrelevant. In Problem 15, the university has not actually been affected by the breach, and appears to be trying to use it opportunistically to get out of a contract it no longer wants. Many leading cases in the law of breach have involved precisely this type of situation, where an opportunistic party is trying to exploit a technical breach not because of the breach itself, but because the market has moved in a direction that means they will now make a loss. Here, as before, the law pays no attention to the party's motives in making the allegation of breach. It is concerned solely with the question of whether the contract was in fact breached.

The third principle is that the contract is the only touchstone by which performance is judged. In legal terms, performance and breach are defined purely in terms of contractual duties. If a party does what the contract requires, when the contract requires, in relation to the things the contract requires, and to the standard the contract requires, the party has adequately performed the contract. If not, it is in breach. This is very different from the way in which commercial parties think about transactions. Commercial dissatisfaction with the way a contract has been performed is typically not about duties per se, but instead reflects a feeling that the outcome is poorer than had been expected, and that responsibility for that outcome can be pinned on one of the parties. The law in effect translates commercial disputes in relation to *outcomes and responsibility* into legal questions about *terms and duties*. Identical fact situations will produce different legal outcomes if the contract is worded differently.

The fourth principle is that compliance with the contract is strictly assessed. The fact that the breach was relatively minor is no excuse: if the contract was not complied with, the party who failed to comply is in breach. In *Arcos v Ronaasen*,[1] a seller had agreed to supply a buyer with wooden staves that were ½-inch thick. Some of the staves were ⅛-inch thicker. The court held that the seller was in breach, even though the staves were perfectly fit for the purpose for which they were supplied. In *Re Moore & Co v Landauer & Co*,[2] the contract provided for the sale of 3,100 tins of peaches packed in cases of 30. The peaches were supplied in cases of 24. The Court of Appeal held that the contract had been breached, even though the peaches themselves were supplied in good condition: the fact that they were not packed as agreed meant that the contract had not been complied with.[3] There are some exceptions in relation to *extremely* small breaches (discussed in section 15.2), but the general rule is that size does not matter.

15.1.2 **Responding to breach**

The strict approach which the English courts take to *defining* breach sits alongside a much more nuanced approach to determining how parties can *respond* to breach. Under English law, a party cannot respond to a breach by ceasing to perform their bit of the contract. The general rule is that the parties must continue performing the contract even if the other is in breach. This is because a breach does not automatically bring a contract to an end, and it does not excuse (or **discharge**, to use the legal term) the innocent party from their obligations under the contract. In most cases, the only remedy the law gives the innocent party is to bring an action seeking damages for the loss it has suffered as a result of the breach.[4]

An innocent party is only entitled to treat itself as discharged as a result of breach if it is a **repudiatory breach**, that is to say, so serious that it is in law treated as an effective abandonment or repudiation by the other party of its obligations under the contract. English law recognizes three, and only three, circumstances in which a breach is repudiatory. The first is where the contractual term that has been breached is an important term which goes to the root of the contract (a **condition** of the contract). The second is where the term is of intermediate importance (an **innominate term** or **intermediate term**), but is breached in a way which deprives the innocent party of substantially the whole benefit which the parties intended it to obtain under the contract. The third is where the other party, by words or conduct, indicates that it does not intend to perform a substantial portion of its obligations under the contract (**anticipatory breach**). Although we will examine the details of each of these categories in section 15.3, they are only triggered in a minority of cases. In most instances of breach, the contract remains fully binding on both parties even though it has been broken by one of the parties, and both parties are in law required to continue to perform it.

---

1. [1933] AC 470 (HL).   2. [1921] 2 KB 519 (CA).
3. Both cases are discussed in more detail in section 15.3.   4. See Chapter 16.

The combination of a strict approach to *defining* breach, a nuanced approach to determining the *consequences* of breach, and the ability to keep the contract alive *notwithstanding* breach give English law the flexibility to deal with breach pragmatically in a wide range of circumstances. We will begin this chapter by looking at how the courts approach the question of whether a contract has actually been breached on the facts of a case (section 15.2). We will then consider how the courts determine the legal consequences of breach, focusing in particular on the role played by the type of term which has been breached (section 15.3). We will conclude the chapter with some general observations on the way in which the law deals with the problem of breach (section 15.4).

15.2 Assessing performance

As Problem 15 should indicate, the question of whether a contract has been breached will almost always be contested. A party who is accused of being in breach will usually respond by arguing that it has properly performed the contract. The starting point in any case of breach, therefore, is to determine what the party is required to do under the contract and whether it has done it. In practice, this tends to revolve around three specific dimensions of the contract: the question of *what* must be done (section 15.2.1), the question of *when* it must be done (section 15.2.2), and the question of *whether* it was done (section 15.2.3).

15.2.1 Determining the scope of performance (The 'what' question)

The first of these is relatively straightforward. Whether a contract has been breached depends entirely on what the terms of the contract, properly construed, require the parties to do. Commercial goals, expectations, and understandings of the allocation of risk are not relevant to the question of whether a party is in breach, save to the extent that they affect the interpretation of the contract[5] or the implication of terms into it.[6] What matters is not what the parties wanted to achieve but what they put into their contract, even if the result is an allocation of risks the parties are unlikely to have intended.

Focusing on the contractual framework helps the courts avoid getting drawn into complex questions as to what the parties intended. However, on the flipside, it also means that a carelessly designed contract can have unexpected consequences. There are usually several ways in which an obligation can be worded, and parties have often discovered to their cost that the choice of one wording over another has far greater legal significance than they anticipated.[7] Of particular importance is the distinction between, first, a contractual duty to do an *act* and a contractual duty to achieve a *result*; and, secondly, between contractual duties that are *conditional* and those that are *unconditional*.

---

5. See Chapter 7 ('Interpreting the terms').   6. See Chapter 8 ('Filling the gaps').

7. See *Co-operative Wholesale Society Ltd v National Westminster Bank plc* [1995] 1 EGLR 97 for a particularly striking example.

The act/result distinction is both simple and fundamental. If the contract is structured in terms of a duty to do a set of things, then once you have done those things you are discharged, even if the intended result is not achieved. In contrast, if the contract is structured in terms of a duty to achieve a particular result, then you are in breach if that result is not achieved, even if you did everything that was humanly possible. The conditional/unconditional distinction is equally simple and particularly significant in allocating risks. A party's duties under a contract can be made conditional on something happening (eg the grant of planning permission or the successful conduct of a test study). In such a case, if that thing does not happen (if planning permission is not granted or the test is unsuccessful), the party is discharged from those duties. If a party's duties are unconditional, in contrast, they remain unaffected. In effect, that party bears the risk of the thing not happening.

Often, these distinctions are simply a matter of using a few words differently: 'approximately' instead of 'exactly';[8] or framing the obligation in terms of an obligation to 'use best endeavours' to achieve a result rather than a bare obligation to achieve that result; or implicitly or explicitly acknowledging that a certain risk is outside the responsibility of either party to manage by adding an 'if' condition. Consider the following illustration.

Illustration 15.1

John's smartphone stopped working after he tried to install a leaked build of an update to the phone's OS. He has several photos and other files on the phone which he does not want to lose. He sees an ad for a service called 'The Tech Guy', who promises to 'unbrick' phones and recover data.

In such a scenario, The Tech Guy's terms of service can be worded in a range of ways, with very different consequences. Thus, for example, a clause which says:

We will unbrick your phone and fully recover your data within 48 hours.

---

creates an obligation to achieve a result. If The Tech Guy fails to do so, he is in breach of contract, even if the data on the phone was, in fact, unrecoverable. In contrast, a clause which says:

If your phone is recoverable, we will make best efforts to unbrick it and recover your data within 48 hours.

---

8. *Louis Dreyfus & Cie v Parnaso Cia Naviera SA (The Dominator)* [1960] 2 QB 49 (CA).

imposes a far more limited obligation. It makes the obligations of The Tech Guy conditional on the data being recoverable. If the data turns out to be unrecoverable, The Tech Guy will not be in breach. Secondly, the obligation is qualified by the words 'make best efforts'. The effect of these words is to restrict the contractual obligation of The Tech Guy to doing certain acts (ie making best efforts), rather than achieving a result (ie recovering the data). He will not be in breach even if the data is ultimately not recovered from the phone, as long as he can show he has made 'best efforts' to do so.[9]

Dany Lions Ltd v Bristol Cars Ltd[10] is a good illustration of this principle in operation. Bristol Cars agreed to restore a vintage Bristol 405 saloon owned by Dany Lions Ltd. Part of the work involved converting the vehicle from manual transmission to automatic transmission. After Bristol Cars had commenced their work, they discovered that fitting an automatic gearbox would affect the proper functioning of the car, and did not carry out the work. In an action brought by Dany Lions for breach of contract, the High Court pointed out that in approaching the question, the starting point must be that:

> the Defendant agreed to adapt the automatic gearbox to suit this Bristol engine and match the transmission points as required. It did not agree to see if it could do that; it did not agree to consider whether it could do that: it agreed to do it.[11]

Bristol Cars' duty was therefore a duty to achieve a result (converting the car), and not merely a duty to do certain acts (examining the feasibility of converting the car). The obligation to achieve that result as set out in the contract was not conditional on technical feasibility. As a result, a failure to achieve the agreed result was a breach of contract. It is extremely unlikely that Bristol Cars intended to accept such a broad responsibility, but that was nevertheless the consequence of the way in which its obligations had been articulated in the exchange of emails on which the contract was based. What this case should highlight is the importance of careful contract design. If Bristol Cars had articulated its duties more carefully, or with greater precision, it would not have found itself shouldering responsibility for an unforeseen risk which was beyond its control.

15.2.2 Is performance due? (The 'when' question)

Conditions precedent and the order of performance

The next issue is the issue of *when* the parties are required to perform their respective obligations under their contract. This raises the question of the *order of performance*. In many contracts, the parties perform their obligations at more or less the same time. When you buy goods at a supermarket, for example, the supermarket's obligation to let you take the goods away and your obligation to pay for the goods arise and are discharged at the same time: the moment when you check the goods out at the till. This reflects a long-standing common law rule, now codified in statute,[12] which holds the seller's obligation of delivery and the buyer's obligation of payment to arise at the same time. Obligations of this type, which arise simultaneously and must be discharged together, are termed *concurrent obligations*.

---

9. See Chapter 9 ('Flexible terms').   10. [2013] EWHC 2997 (QB).
11. Ibid, [23].   12. See Sale of Goods Act 1979, s 28.

Concurrent obligations are familiar from the contracts we enter into in the course of everyday life. However, not all contractual obligations are concurrent. In more complex transactions, where performance is prolonged and not instantaneous, the order in which parties are required to perform their obligations can be more involved. In some situations, the performance by one party of a particular contractual obligation may constitute a **condition precedent** to the performance by the other party of all or a part of their obligations. Consider the following illustration:

Illustration 15.2

Avonside University proposes to refurbish its former library building to house its proposed Adult Learning Hub. It has engaged Wharram, Percy and Woldway, a local firm of architects, to draw up plans for the new interiors of the building. The agreement requires the university to provide the architects with a detailed summary of requirements, which sets out, amongst other things, the number and size of the teaching rooms and other spaces required. The architects are required to provide five copies of the draft plans at an initial planning meeting.

Here, it is obvious that the architects will be unable to produce draft plans until they receive the summary of requirements from the university. The duty to produce this summary is therefore a condition precedent to the architect's obligations. If the university does not provide it, the architects will not be in breach of contract for failing to draw up plans.

Conditions precedent can also involve a third party. Thus, for example, in the above illustration, obtaining planning permission will usually be a condition precedent to construction starting. Similarly, in Problem 15, getting ministerial support for the project is a condition precedent. Parties are free to agree on any conditions precedent they wish, and it is common for complex contracts to include detailed conditions precedent to each party's obligations.

It is also possible for the obligations of the parties to be *independent*. An independent obligation is one that is not dependent on whether or not the other parties have performed their obligations. Consider the following example.

Illustration 15.3

Avonside University's agreement with its architects requires them to provide certain safety equipment on the site. It also requires the architects to produce plans for the building in accordance with a fixed schedule.

Here, it should be obvious that the two obligations set out above are independent of each other. The university cannot refuse to provide safety equipment simply because the architects are late in producing their plans.

Although the basic principle is relatively simple, in practice it is not always obvious in which category a given set of obligations will fall. Consider the following example:

> **Illustration 15.4**
>
> Avonside University's agreement with its architects requires them to pay advances to the architects on certain dates. It also requires the architects to produce plans for the building in accordance with a fixed schedule.

Is the architect's obligation to deliver designs conditional on the owner's obligation to pay an advance, or is it an independent obligation? To answer such questions, the first port of call is always the contract. Where the contract does not provide an answer, the courts will look to the overall context of the contract in order to determine the order of performance. In *Trans Trust SPRL v Danubian Trading Co*,[13] the parties had entered into a contract for the sale of steel. The purchaser was required to produce a letter of credit (a type of payment instrument), but the contract did not say at what time the letter of credit had to be opened. It was, however, known to both parties that the seller would not be able to get a supply of steel unless credit was made available. Given that, the court held that the opening of the letter of credit had to be a condition precedent.

Entire obligations and severable obligations

Even if an obligation has been identified as being conditional on the performance by the other party of one or more obligations, a further question may arise as to the *extent* to which one party has to perform their obligations before the other must perform. Must the first party perform the obligation in question *fully*, or is it sufficient if they perform a *substantial part* of the relevant obligations? Questions of this type typically arise in relation to the obligation to make payment for goods and services which have not been properly produced or rendered. Consider the following examples.

> **Illustration 15.5**
>
> #### 'We've been stitched up': customers' fury as designer tailor disappears
>
> Customers of designer tailor Mark Stagson may be left out of pocket after receiving bills for clothes that are unlikely to ever be finished. The erratic Leeds-based tailor disappeared last week, leaving a large number of designer jackets unfinished. Customers with unfinished orders have now received bills for the costs of fabric and work done on their orders until Stagson disappeared.
>
> Stagson, whose whereabouts are currently unknown, has told each customer the current status of their order. From the letters, it seems that all garments have been fully cut, but may not have been sewn together. Stagson says that customers can collect the garments in their present state from his workshop once they have paid. The letter, of which the *Yorkshire Mercury* has seen a copy, also says that those who do not pay can expect to find themselves facing legal action.
>
> →

---

13. [1952] 2 QB 297 (CA).

> →
>
> *Comments*
>
> 1. **Luke Thompson** A complete nightmare! I'm told my jacket is in pieces, with lapels and sleeves not even sewn on. There is no way I am going to pay.
> 2. **Matthew Williams** I'd ordered a suit with customized buttons and matching cufflinks. My suit is ready, but he hasn't provided the matching cufflinks I'd ordered and possibly not even the buttons. I guess I'm one of the lucky ones, but I'm still quite put out and I don't know if I'll pay.
>
> . . .

In this illustration, there has clearly been a failure by Stagson to fully perform his obligations under the contract. The question is the impact of that failure on the other parties' obligations. Will Luke or Matthew be in breach of their obligations if they refuse to pay for the work done to date? Or can they argue that their obligation to pay has not yet fallen due, because the other party has not finished performing his obligations under the contract? The commonsense response which most people reach is that Luke will not have to pay, but that Matthew may. This more or less reflects the outcome that English law reaches. In legal terms, the answer to this question depends on whether the obligation in question is **entire** or **severable**. An obligation is 'entire' when the contract requires performance of that obligation to be fully completed before the obligation of the other party to pay falls due. If it is 'severable', however, completion of a substantial part (or of a specifically delineated part) of the obligation is sufficient to trigger the obligation to pay.

The obligation to make the jacket in the first comment in Illustration 15.5 above is a classic example of an entire obligation. Parties who have contracted for a jacket will not usually have intended to treat the obligation to produce a sleeve as being severable from the obligation to produce a lapel. This is because their concern is with the entirety of the performance, rather than the individual items of work that go to making up the whole. The obligation in the second comment in Illustration 15.5, in contrast, is likely to both be severable and to have been substantially performed. Whilst the parties may have contracted for both a suit and cufflinks there is nothing that intrinsically connects the two. If, therefore, the performance that has actually been rendered amounts to a substantial portion of the work due under the contract, the contract will have been substantially performed, and the obligation to pay will have fallen due. What is 'substantial' is usually a matter of fact, and depends on the structure of the parties' contract. A tailor who supplies a suit jacket without matching cufflinks is likely to have substantially performed the contract. A tailor who supplies the cufflinks without the jacket, in contrast, is unlikely to have substantially performed the contract.

Entire obligations

With this basic background, let us now consider the distinction in more detail, and study how it applies in more complex cases like Problem 15. The leading case on entire obligations is the 18th-century decision in *Cutter v Powell*.[14]

---

14. (1795) 6 TR 320, 101 ER 573.

Case in depth: *Cutter v Powell* (1795) 6 TR 320

Thomas Cutter was a sailor and shipwright who had been hired as second mate on a slaving ship which was sailing from Kingston, Jamaica back to Liverpool. The contract under which he was engaged provided that he was to be paid a wage at the end of the voyage. The obligation was worded in these terms:

> Ten days after the ship 'Governor Parry', myself master, arrives at Liverpool, I promise to pay to Mr. T. Cutter the sum of thirty guineas, provided he proceeds, continues and does his duty as second mate in the said ship from hence to the port of Liverpool.

The wage was high by the standards of the day. The usual voyage for sailors was £4 per month. The reason for this higher wage is not entirely clear. In arguments, it was suggested that this was because it was hard to find sailors in Jamaica, and very high wages were not uncommon. Professor Martin Dockray, a leading scholar of maritime law, has pointed out that records of other voyages show that Thomas Cutter was a carpenter and shipwright (although this fact was not mentioned in the arguments), who commanded much higher wages because their skills were of particular use given that ships then were made of wood.[15] As it happened, Cutter died around halfway through the voyage, having served 50 days of the 70 days the voyage ultimately took. His widow sought to recover a proportionate amount of the agreed wage.

The Court of King's Bench held that she could not recover, because the wording of the contract suggested that his obligations under the contract were entire. This meant that the obligation to pay his wages did not accrue until he had completed the voyage. Because he died halfway through the voyage, his right to receive wages had not yet accrued. The shipowners' refusal to pay his wages was in consequence not a breach of contract.

In so holding, the judges were anxious to ensure that they had given the words of the contract an interpretation in keeping with commercial practice. Lord Kenyon CJ began his decision by saying that he would be extremely sorry if the court 'should determine against what had been the received opinion in the mercantile world on contracts of this kind, because it is of great importance that the laws by which the contracts of so numerous and so useful a body of men as the sailors are supposed to be guided should not be overturned'.[16] However, the court had been unable to find an unambiguous commercial custom on the meaning of the term. As a result, the instrument had to be construed on its words alone. Taken as a written contract, the court held, 'it is entire, and as the defendant's promise depends on a condition precedent to be performed by the other party, the condition must be performed before the other party is entitled to receive any thing under it'.[17] Additionally, two of the judges—Lord Kenyon[18] and Grose J[19]—were also influenced by the fact that the sum payable was significantly higher than the normal monthly wages of sailors. The fact that the sum was high, and was set out in terms of an entire amount, suggested that the contract was 'a kind of insurance', under which Cutter was 'stipulated to receive the larger sum if the whole duty were performed, and nothing unless the whole of that duty were performed'.[20]

15. See M Dockray, '*Cutter v. Powell*: A Trip Outside the Text' (2001) 117 LQR 664, 671–3.
16. (1795) 6 TR 320, 324.   17. Ibid, 325 (Ashhurst J).
18. Ibid, 324.   19. Ibid, 326.   20. Ibid, 324 (Kenyon CJ).

Cutter v Powell was decided in 1795, over 220 years ago, in conditions that are radically different from those that prevail in modern contracting. It is unlikely that the case would be decided the same way if it were to arise today. Professor Dockray has suggested that the judges in *Cutter* may have misread the significance of the facts,[21] and the legal position has been substantially altered by later statutes. In modern terms *Cutter v Powell* is an instance of frustration rather than breach. As Chapter 10 discusses in more detail, a contract which requires personal performance is frustrated by the death of a party. Nevertheless, because *Cutter* was decided before the law of frustration had developed, the judgment was based on ordinary rules of performance and breach.

In *Sumpter v Hedges*,[22] a builder contracted with the owner of a plot of land to build two houses and a stable on the land. The price agreed was £565. The builder completed a portion of the work, to a value of about £333, but then ran out of money and abandoned the project. The owner then completed the work himself. The builder sued for the value of the work done. It was held that the builder's obligations were entire. Because the work had not been completed, the landowner's obligation to pay the builder had not yet accrued, and he was not liable to pay any part of the agreed sum. His refusal to pay was not therefore a breach of contract.[23]

Severable obligations and substantial performance

The obligations in *Cutter* and *Sumpter* were entire. If a contract is structured so as to make the parties' obligations severable, a party who has performed a substantial portion of her obligations can sue for payment, even if she fails to complete performance. The classic example of a severable obligation is a contract where payment is due as specific parts of the contract are performed, rather than in a lump sum. This rule is an old one. Even at the time *Cutter v Powell* was decided, a person whose wages were specified in monthly or daily terms was entitled to claim wages for the period he had actually served, even if he had not seen out the full duration.[24] But contracts that are to be performed in one go may also be severable. In *Ritchie v Atkinson*,[25] the parties entered into a contract to carry cargo at a stipulated rate per ton. The carrier only carried part of the cargo. It was held that he could recover the corresponding proportion of the freight, even though he was in breach, because the obligations under the contract were severable. He was liable to the shipper for breach for failing to carry the rest of the cargo, but the shipper was also in breach for refusing to pay for the cargo that had been carried.

Even if an obligation is severable, it is not sufficient for any degree of performance to have taken place. Performance must have been *substantial*. The importance of this point is illustrated by contrasting the decision in *Bolton v Mahadeva*[26]

---

21. M Dockray, '*Cutter v. Powell*: A Trip Outside the Text' (2001) 117 LQR 664, 670–5.

22. [1898] 1 QB 673 (CA).

23. The builder was, however, permitted to recover on *quantum meruit* for the value of the materials he had left on the land, which the landowner had used in completing the building. This aspect of the decision is discussed in greater detail in Chapter 16.

24. See *Taylor v Laird* (1856) 1 H & N 266; JL Barton, 'Contract and *Quantum Meruit*: The Antecedents of *Cutter v. Powell*' (1987) 8 Journal of Legal History 48, 49.

25. (1808) 10 East 29.   26. [1972] 1 WLR 1009 (CA).

with the decision in *H Dakin & Co v Lee*.[27] Bolton had been engaged by Mahadeva to install a hot-water and heating system in Mahadeva's home for a price of £560, and to also supply and fit a bathroom suite. The system was defectively installed, and as a result failed to provide as much warmth as it should. In addition, the boiler flue gave off fumes. The cost of remedying these defects was approximately £174. Mahadeva refused to pay anything. When Bolton sued, the court held that although Bolton's obligations under the contract were severable rather than entire, the defects were so significant that he had not substantially performed the contract. Mahadeva's obligation to pay had therefore not yet fallen due, and he was not in breach for refusing to pay.

In *Dakin v Lee*,[28] H Dakin & Co had agreed to carry out certain repairs to a house owned by Lee. The repairs did not comply with the agreed specifications on a few matters. None of these involved any danger to the house, and all were remediable. The Court of Appeal held that the builders were entitled to the contract price, subject to a deduction for the cost of remedying the defects in the work they had done.[29] There was a distinction between a situation where only part of an obligation had been fulfilled and one where the whole of the obligation had been completed but it had been done badly.[30] To hold otherwise would give one party an undeserved windfall:

> Take a contract for a lump sum to decorate a house; the contract provides that there shall be three coats of oil paint, but in one of the rooms only two coats of paint are put on. Can anybody seriously say that under these circumstances the building owner could go and occupy the house and take the benefit of all the decorations which had been done in the other rooms without paying a penny for all the work done by the builder, just because only two coats of paint had been put on in one room where there ought to have been three?[31]

On this basis, the main distinction between *Dakin v Lee* and *Bolton v Mahadeva* is that in *Dakin* the work was essentially complete, albeit with some defects. In *Bolton* (as in *Sumpter v Hedges*[32]), the customer was left with something that was so defective that it was not functional. As a result, the contract in the former case had been substantially performed, whereas the contract in the latter two cases had not been performed.

The role of interpretation

What makes a contract entire or severable? The answer seems to be that it is a matter of construction. In *Hoenig v Isaacs*,[33] Isaacs had employed Hoenig to redecorate and furnish Isaac's flat for £750. The contract provided for payment terms of 'net cash, as the work proceeds; and balance on completion'. When the work had been completed, Hoenig had received £300, and asked for the remaining amount. Isaacs said there were defects in the furniture, and only paid £100. The Court of Appeal

---

27. [1916] 1 KB 566 (CA).   28. Ibid.

29. The cost of remedying the defects in the work is a standard remedy for breach of contract. See Chapter 16 ('Compensatory remedies').

30. [1916] 1 KB 566, 579 (Lord Cozens-Hardy MR), 580 (Pickford LJ).

31. Ibid, 579 (Lord Cozens-Hardy MR).   32. [1898] 1 QB 673.

33. [1952] 2 All ER 176 (CA).

held that Hoenig could recover the remaining £350, less the cost of remedying his breach, which was estimated at around £55. Lord Denning stressed the importance of the terms:

> When a contract provides for a specific sum to be paid on completion of specified work, the courts lean against a construction of the contract which would deprive the contractor of any payment at all simply because there are some defects or omissions . . . It is, of course, always open to the parties by express words to make entire performance a condition precedent. A familiar instance is when the contract provides for progress payments to be made as the work proceeds, but for retention money to be held until completion.

This position was not new. The decision in *Cutter v Powell*[34] itself reflected a similar approach, and was based on the finding that that particular contract contained wording which appeared to make completion of the voyage a condition precedent to payment. In emphasizing the contract, *Cutter* definitively rejected the paternalistic[35] approach to mariners' contracts that was common in the Court of Admiralty, and continued to hold sway there even after *Cutter v Powell*. In *The Juliana*,[36] a case in Admiralty, a ship had been wrecked on the last leg of the voyage. The surviving mariners' contract provided that 'no officer or seaman should demand or be entitled to his wages, or any part thereof, until the arrival of the ship at the above-mentioned port of discharge, and her cargo delivered'. Lord Stowell held that the clause should be construed 'to signify only a postponement of the payment, not a privation of the title which the law had guaranteed to them'.[37] The obligations of seamen should not be construed using the same principles as owners' obligations, because seamen were not in the same position to read and understand contracts as owners:

> the common mariner is easy and careless, illiterate and unthinking; he has no such resources in his own intelligence and habits of business, as can enable him to take accurate measures of postponed payments.[38]

In consequence, judges in Admiralty should 'protect these illiterate and inexperienced persons against their ignorance and imprudence'.[39] *Cutter v Powell*, in contrast, is based on a much more robust understanding of freedom of contract which has little room for paternalistic considerations. The court in that case saw the problem as simply one of giving effect to the intention of the parties as recorded in their instrument.

The modern law follows *Cutter*. Courts do not decide issues in relation to whether obligations are entire on the basis of *external* standards of what would be fair or just. The only standards that are relevant are those set out in the parties' contract, construed in the light of the commercial background and usage. In *Cutter* itself, Grose J said that he had made personal enquiries to ascertain what the commercial understanding was,[40] and the report suggests that the court delayed the implementation of its final

---

34. (1795) 6 TR 320, 101 ER 573.
35. See the discussion of paternalism in Chapter 1 and the introduction to Part III.
36. (1822) 2 Dods 504, 165 ER 1560.   37. (1822) 2 Dods 504, 522.
38. Ibid, 509.   39. Ibid, 522.   40. (1795) 6 TR 320, 325.

decision until the end of that term in case 'some other information relative to the usage in cases of this kind should be laid before the Court'.[41]

The role of construction and practice was reiterated in *Smales v Lea*,[42] where the Court of Appeal was asked to decide whether the obligations in a surveyor's letter of retainer were entire or severable. Jackson LJ cited Lord Denning's ruling in *Hoenig* with approval, and explained the logic behind this position:

> In modern construction of contracts and contracts of retainer for professional services, it is relatively unusual for the client to have no obligation to make any payment unless and until the contractor or the professional firm has performed every single one of the obligations undertaken. It does, of course, happen in some cases, but in my judgment the case before this court is not such a case.[43]

The mere fact that the agreement imposes 'a coherent package of obligations' does not by itself make the obligations entire. What is needed is for the contract to 'go one stage further and say that every obligation must be performed before there is any entitlement to payment'.[44]

This accurately summarizes the modern position on entire obligations and substantial performance. The commercially sensible starting point is that the parties intended the obligations to be severable. This means that if parties want their obligations to be understood as being entire, the best way of ensuring that they are so treated is to expressly provide for it in their contract.

The role of statute

Statutes show a similar trend to the general principles discussed in preceding sections. There is no general statute on when contracts are to be construed as being entire and when they are to be construed as being severable, but there is a clear trend towards regarding obligations as severable rather than entire in statutes dealing with particular types of contracts. In relation to construction contracts, for example, the scope of *Sumpter v Hedges*[45] has been substantially restricted by s 109(1) of the Housing Grants, Construction and Regeneration Act 1996. Under this section, a party to a construction contract is entitled to 'payment by instalments, stage payments or other periodic payments for any work under the contract', unless the parties have agreed that the duration of the work is to be less than 45 days. The position in relation to wages for sailors, the subject of *Cutter v Powell*,[46] has been altered by the Merchant Shipping Acts[47] in relation to sailors who have been discharged. It has also been altered in relation to death by the subsequent development of the law of frustration in the Law Reform (Frustrated Contracts) Act 1943. The Apportionment Act 1870 provides for a range of other types of payments, such as rent, to be treated as accruing periodically, rather than after the performance of an entire obligation. This list is far from exhaustive, and other statutes have had a similar effect in relation to other types of contracts.

---

41. Ibid, 327.   42. [2011] EWCA Civ 1325.   43. Ibid, [43].
44. Ibid, [40].   45. [1898] 1 QB 673.   46. (1795) 6 TR 320, 101 ER 573.
47. Currently the Merchant Shipping Act 1995, see esp ss 30 and 38, restating provisions originally introduced by the Merchant Shipping Act 1894.

Practice in context: avoiding opportunism through drafting

The legal trend away from entire obligations is also reflected in contract drafting. It is very common for standard form contracts to provide for periodic payments, or to expressly make obligations independent or severable, or even to expressly deal with the issue of substantial performance. These are particularly common in the engineering and construction sectors, which incorporate devices such as periodic payments or staged payments tied to particular milestones (thus making that portion of the contractor's obligations severable from others), for the production of 'punchlists' of outstanding issues when the work has been substantially completed and for the retention of a portion of the overall sum until those issues have been addressed (thus creating a contractually agreed understanding of substantial performance). Clauses of this type are also common in a very wide range of long-term contracts, including employment contracts (eg through clauses prohibiting dismissal for minor violations of the terms of employment or permitting a period of sick leave), joint venture agreements, long-term supply agreements, and so on.

These trends give some context to the relative paucity of reported cases on substantial performance. The fact that relatively few cases have been decided on the basis of substantial performance does not mean that the doctrine has little practical significance, as some commentators have suggested.[48] It suggests, rather, that severability and substantial performance are so ubiquitous in modern contracting that most cases where they might have become an issue can be decided simply on the basis of construing and applying the terms of the contract. This receives support from Jackson LJ's judgment in *Smales v Lea*,[49] discussed earlier, where he noted that whilst services agreements could be structured to make the obligations entire, it was relatively unusual for parties to actually do so.

There is sound commercial sense behind this approach. The issue with treating obligations as entire is that it often lets one party get a benefit without having to pay for it, as indeed happened in *Sumpter*, where the landowner took the benefit of the work done by the builder without having to pay the builder. This may have been justified on the facts of *Sumpter* itself, where living with the status quo was not an option for the landowner, who could hardly be expected to put up with half-finished structures on his land. It was almost certainly justified on the facts of *Bolton v Mahadeva*, where the system that was actually supplied was for all effects and purposes non-functional. Nevertheless, if the courts are too willing to hold obligations to be entire, the result will be a rule which leaves significant room for opportunism and for windfalls that have no contractual justification.[50]

That this danger is not illusory is illustrated by *Regent ohG Aisestadt & Barig v Francesco of Jermyn Street Ltd*.[51] In that case, the parties had agreed a contract under which the plaintiffs would supply 62 suits and 48 jackets to the defendants. While the garments were

→

48. See eg R Stone and J Devenney, *The Modern Law of Contract* (11th edn, Routledge 2015), 249.
49. [2011] EWCA Civ 1325.
50. For a similar (and more critical) assessment of the potential impact of the entire obligation rule, see SJ Stoljar, 'The Great Case of *Cutter v Powell*' (1956) 34 Canadian Bar Review 288.
51. [1981] 3 All ER 327.

→

in production, relations between the defendants and the plaintiffs' agent in England suffered a serious breakdown, and the defendants attempted to cancel the order. Because the garments had already begun to be made, the plaintiffs refused to allow a cancellation, whereupon the defendants told them that they would refuse to accept any consignments. The plaintiffs sent the garments in four consignments as and when they were ready, all of which the defendants refused to accept. The last consignment was one suit short. When the plaintiffs sued for the price, the defendants argued that the obligations of the plaintiffs were entire; as a result, the fact that the last consignment was one suit short meant that their obligation to pay had not arisen. That would indeed have been the result had their argument been successful. As it happened, however, Mustill J rejected the defendants' argument, holding that the obligations were severable, and that they had been substantially performed. The defendants were therefore in breach, and were liable to the plaintiffs for the loss they had suffered.

As this case demonstrates, entire obligations leave far more room for opportunistic behaviour than severable obligations, largely because of the all-or-nothing consequences they entail. The propensity of entire obligations to be used opportunistically, and the disproportionate outcome that their broad application would produce, were the precise issues that worried Lord Cozens-Hardy MR in *Dakin v Lee*.[52] The approach which emerged in *Dakin v Lee, Hoenig v Isaacs*,[53] *Smales v Lea*,[54] and the statutes we examined earlier is at least in part a response to that concern. It combines a recognition that obligations may be entire (and, hence, exclude substantial performance) with a healthy scepticism about whether parties to a commercial contract would have actually intended to structure their obligations in that way. The result is an approach which restrains opportunism without lapsing into paternalism, and which continues to insulate the courts from being drawn into considering the parties' motives in alleging breach. Whatever the strength of the conceptual and theoretical arguments that have been advanced against it, this approach makes practical sense and fits well with commercial expectations.

15.2.3 Was the contract performed? (The 'whether' question)

The final issue in determining whether a contract has been breached is assessing whether a party has done what the contract required that party to do. This issue is a relatively simple one. English law requires the parties to comply strictly with the terms of the contract. If one of them does not do so, then she is in breach. This is often expressed by stating that performance must be *perfect* or, more accurately, that the parties must *strictly* comply with a contract. It is no defence to say that the breach was relatively small. The generality of this rule is, however, subject to two qualifications, the first relating to extremely trivial breaches (the '*de minimis* exception'), and the second to situations where one of the parties has tried to perform, but has had their performance rejected by the other party ('tender of performance').

52. [1916] 1 KB 566 (CA), 579.   53. [1952] 2 All ER 176 (CA).
54. [2011] EWCA Civ 1325.

The *de minimis* exception

The first exception to the general rule on strict compliance is based on the maxim *de minimis non curat lex* ('the law takes no account of trifles'), and is usually called the *de minimis* **rule**. The nature of this rule is best illustrated by the case of *Shipton, Anderson & Co v Weil Bros & Co*.[55] The parties in that case had contracted for the sale of 4,500 tons of wheat. The contract permitted a deviation of 10 per cent from the agreed weight.[56] This meant that the seller was allowed to supply 10 per cent more or less than the agreed quantity. The seller shipped 4,950 tons 55 lbs of wheat, which was 55 lbs more than the maximum amount that was contractually permissible. The buyer argued that the contract had been breached. The High Court held that it had not been breached, because the deviation was so small as to be trivial, and had no commercial significance:

> the excess quantity is trifling, so trifling that it is quite impossible to suppose that any business man would regard it as in any way affecting the substance of the contract or as making the contract any the more or any the less an advantageous contract to enter into.[57]

The *de minimis* rule is narrow. As David Campbell has pointed out, the excess quantity in this case amounted to a deviation of 0.000496 per cent.[58] Professor Campbell argues that the rule only covers variations of this order, which on the application of reasonable commercial judgment would be seen as truly microscopic.

The case law supports Professor Campbell's view. In *Margaronis Navigation Agency Ltd v Henry W Peabody & Co of London Ltd*,[59] the Court of Appeal was faced with a situation involving a shortfall of 12 tons out of 12,600, which amounts to a deviation of just under 0.1 per cent. The court held that the case was not covered by the *de minimis* rule. Diplock LJ held that the rule was only attracted if the contract had been performed 'within the margin of error which it is not commercially practicable to avoid'.[60] Pearson LJ, similarly, suggested that the *de minimis* rule in essence sought to ask 'whether the departure from the precise terms of the obligation is so trivial as to be negligible or whether it has some significance'.[61]

It is submitted that these statements accurately capture the narrow scope of the rule, and the rationale underlying it. The *de minimis* rule is one of interpretation, not of policy. It reflects an understanding of the limits of measurement, specifically, that perfectly precise measurements are hard to make, and that in assessing whether a party is in breach, the court must do so with reference to the standard of measurement that the parties are likely to have had in mind. This will depend both on the degree of precision that is commercially practicable and the impact of deviations on the substance of the contract. The *de minimis* rule only covers deviations that are microscopic with reference to these criteria. Any other deviation, no matter how small, will be considered a breach of contract.

55. [1912] 1 KB 574.
56. The exact wording of the clause was 'weight as per bill or bills of lading . . . say 4500 tons, 2 per cent. more or less; seller has the option of shipping a further 8 per cent. more or less on contract quantity'.
57. [1912] 1 KB 574, 576 (Lush J).
58. D Campbell, '*Arcos v Ronaasen* as a Relational Contract' in D Campbell, L Mulcahy, and S Wheeler (eds), *Changing Concepts of Contract: Essays in Honour of Ian Macneil* (Palgrave Macmillan 2013).
59. [1965] 2 QB 430 (CA).   60. Ibid, 448.   61. Ibid, 447.

Tender of performance

A second exception to the general rule of strict compliance arises when a party tries to perform, but is prevented from doing so by the other party. Where performance depends on the cooperation of the other party, a performance which is rejected by the other party (called a '*tender of performance*') is treated as equivalent to actual performance. The decision in *Regent ohG Aisestadt & Barig v Francesco of Jermyn Street Ltd*,[62] discussed in section 15.2.2, is an example of the tender of performance rule in action. The claimants did not actually perform their obligation to deliver the suits, because the defendants prevented them from doing so by refusing to accept the consignments. However, their tender of performance was sufficient.

What, then, constitutes a tender of performance? It requires one party to demonstrate that it is ready to perform its obligations under the contract, and make an unconditional offer to the other party to do so. The party claiming tender of performance does not actually have to have attempted to perform. It is sufficient if it has offered to perform the entirety of its obligations under the contract, and done so without imposing conditions not found in the contract.

The classic case on tender of performance is the decision of the Exchequer Chamber in *Startup v MacDonald*.[63] The parties in this case had entered into a contract under which Startup was to sell ten tons of oil to MacDonald, with delivery to be made during the last 14 days of March. Startup tendered delivery at 8.30 p.m. on the last possible day, a Saturday. MacDonald refused to accept the consignment because of the lateness of the hour. The law as it stood at that time permitted delivery at any time up to midnight on the last day, as long as there was enough time for the buyer to 'examine, weigh and receive' the goods. Startup was therefore not in breach by delivering the goods at a late hour. The court accordingly held that tender was equivalent to performance of its obligation to deliver and Startup was entitled to payment.

Startup was a case where the performance rejected involved the delivery of goods. Cases of this type are rare. Most modern cases where tender of performance is an issue relate to the refusal to accept payment. The rule, however, remains the same whether the tender is of payment, goods, or services.[64]

15.2.4 **Pulling it together: the character of strict compliance**

As the discussion in this section has shown, English law takes a strict, contract-centric approach towards performance. Parties are expected to do what the contract says, when the contract says. If the contract is worded in terms of a duty to achieve an outcome, then the party in question is expected to achieve that outcome. If the contract makes consent from a third party a condition precedent to one of the parties' obligations, then that consent must come before the obligation is triggered. If the contract requires one of the parties to perform its obligations perfectly before the other party

62. [1981] 3 All ER 327.
63. (1843) 6 Man & G 593, 134 ER 1029.
64. See eg *Afovos Shipping Co SA v Romano Pagnan and Pietro Pagnan* [1982] 1 WLR 848 (CA).

must do anything, then that is what must be done. Courts for the most part do not apply external standards of fairness when it comes to the question of determining whether a party was in breach.

What implications, then, does this discussion have for the position of the parties in Problem 15 at the start of this chapter? Putting the scenario within the framework of the law of breach suggests that Future Hope is in breach of its obligations in relation to the agreement with BIS, because it has failed to achieve the outcome it was supposed to within the time it was allotted. This breach does not, however, automatically mean that the university is off the hook. The impact of the breach on the university's obligations will, instead, depend on what the Project Agreement says about the order of performance, on whether the consent was a condition precedent to the university's obligations, and on whether Future Hope can argue that it has substantially performed its obligations by reaching substantive agreement with BIS. The answers to these questions will depend on the precise wording of the agreement, and on the background matrix of fact that goes into construing the agreement. The fact that the university is acting out of other motives is, however, of no relevance to the law.

15.3 The consequences of breach

15.3.1 Breach and repudiation

Breach does not automatically bring the contract to an end. The other parties are not discharged from their obligations under the contract, and have to continue to perform the remaining portions of the contract as normal despite the breach. The exception is where the breach is serious enough to be considered *repudiatory*. Here, and only here, the party not in breach has the legal option of terminating the contract.

To understand the logic behind this position, contrast the following two illustrations:

Illustration 15.6

Avonside University is hosting a week-long series of Chinese-themed events. It enters into a contract with Haden Carr Nursery to buy potted specimens of plum blossoms, orchids, chrysanthemums, and bamboo for the week. Due to a mix-up, the nursery supplies geraniums, tulips, roses, and sedge.

Illustration 15.7

Avonside University is constructing a new building for its law school, and has engaged Wharram, Percy and Woldway, a local firm of architects, to draw up plans for the building. The contract requires the architects to provide five copies of the draft plans at an initial planning meeting. At the meeting, the architects discover that they have accidentally only brought four copies rather than five.

In Illustration 15.6, it would make little sense to say that the university must perform its obligations under the contract by accepting and paying for plants it has not ordered, and then claiming damages for breach. The sensible outcome would, instead, be for the university to terminate the contract and refuse to accept the plants. In Illustration 15.7, in contrast, it would be commercially absurd to say that the entire building contract can be terminated because the architects brought the wrong number of copies to one meeting. The task for the law of contract, then, is to find a basis on which cases where termination for breach makes sense, like Illustration 15.6, can be distinguished from cases where termination for breach does not make sense, like Illustration 15.7.

Legal systems have had a surprising amount of difficulty in finding a sensible basis for making this distinction. As things stand, each of the major European legal systems takes a very different approach to determining when a breach gives the other party a right to terminate the contract.[65] In English law, the answer revolves around the question of whether the breach is repudiatory.

In the remainder of this section, we will study the nature and consequences of the distinction between repudiatory breaches and non-repudiatory breaches in some more detail. We will begin by examining how the type of term that was breached influences the question of whether the breach was repudiatory (sections 15.3.2 and 15.3.3), before studying how the law deals with situations where breach has not yet occurred but appears imminent, which are in law referred to as 'anticipatory breach' (section 15.3.4). We will conclude by examining the scope and limits of the right to terminate the contract following a repudiatory breach (section 15.3.5).

15.3.2 Classifying terms

Conditions, warranties, and innominate terms: the core of the distinction

In general terms, there are two ways in which we can distinguish between breaches which are repudiatory (and, hence, give the other party the right to terminate the contract), and breaches which are not. The first is to look at the seriousness of the *breach*. Does it have a major impact on the contract? The second is to look at the importance of the *term* that was breached. Was it one of the contract's more important terms, or was it a less important term?

Historically, English law focused only on the importance of the term. In the latter half of the 20th century, the law shifted so that it now considers a combination of both factors. The law operates through dividing contractual terms into three types or classes: **conditions** (comprising the most important terms of the contract), **warranties** (comprising the least important terms of the contract), and **innominate terms** (comprising terms of intermediate importance).

Conditions and warranties

The first two of these have been around for centuries. Conditions are essential, important, or major terms of a contract. They may be statements of fact or promises, and they may be express or implied, but the factor common to them is that they go to the

65. For an overview, see JM Smits, *Contract Law: A Comparative Introduction* (Edward Elgar 2014) 230–5.

root of a contract. Warranties, in contrast, are minor or subsidiary terms which are collateral to the main purpose of the contract. They, too, may be statements of fact or promises, and implied or express, but they are not essential terms of the contract in the way conditions are. Whether a term is a condition or a warranty is a matter of contractual interpretation, but there is a significant body of case law and statutory law on many types of contracts, which gives considerable guidance as to which types of terms are conditions and which types of terms are warranties.

Whether a term is a condition or warranty influences the remedy for breach. A breach of a condition gives the other party the right to terminate the contract, in addition to the right to sue for damages. A breach of a warranty, in contrast, never gives the right to terminate: the other party has to continue to perform its contractual obligations, and its only remedy is to sue the person in breach for damages.

Innominate terms

Until the 1960s, conditions and warranties were the only two classes of terms recognized in English law. All contractual terms were assigned to one of these two categories. The advantage to this binary approach was its certainty. Most common terms were classified as conditions or warranties by case law or statute. The result was that when a breach occurred, it was relatively straightforward for the parties to determine what their rights were. All they needed to do was look to the term that was breached, and determine whether it was a condition or warranty. The nature of the breach, and its impact on the innocent party, were irrelevant.

In the 1960s, however, the courts began recognizing a new category of term, called *innominate terms* or (less frequently) *intermediate terms*. Innominate terms sit between conditions and warranties. The essence of an innominate term is that it can be breached in either a minor way or a serious way. If the breach of an innominate term is minor, the injured party must continue to perform the contract, and only has the right to sue for damages. If it is breached in a more serious way, however, the injured party has the right both to sue for damages and to terminate the contract, just as with a condition. In *Hongkong Fir Shipping Co Ltd v Kawasaki Kisen Kaisha Ltd*,[66] which first recognized innominate terms as a definite category, Lord Diplock explained that this differential effect was a result of the character of an innominate term:

> Of such undertakings all that can be predicated is that some breaches will and others will not give rise to an event which will deprive the party not in default of substantially the whole benefit which it was intended that he should obtain from the contract; and the legal consequences of a breach of such an undertaking, unless provided for expressly in the contract, depend upon the nature of the event to which the breach gives rise and do not follow automatically from a prior classification of the undertaking as a 'condition' or a 'warranty'.[67]

The new category of innominate terms supplements the old categories of conditions and warranties, but does not replace them. It does, however, represent a different approach to assessing repudiation. Whereas the remedies for conditions and

66. [1962] 2 QB 26 (CA).   67. Ibid, 70.

warranties depend only on the importance of the *term*, the remedies for innominate terms depend on the seriousness of the *breach*. A breach of an innominate term will only give the innocent party the right to terminate the contract if the breach will deprive him 'of substantially the whole benefit which it was intended that he should obtain from the contract'.

Understanding the distinction

Why, then, did the courts introduce a new category of terms, and what role does it play in contract law? The answer is that the rigidity of the condition–warranty dichotomy meant that contracts could be terminated for very minor breaches if the breached clause was a condition. The result was that the law regularly facilitated opportunistic behaviour in ways that were hard to justify.

In *Arcos v Ronaasen*,[68] which was briefly discussed in section 15.1, the parties had contracted for the sale of wooden staves that were ½-inch thick. Some of the staves were very slightly thicker (by about ⅛-inch), but were perfectly fit for the purpose for which they were purchased; namely, making wooden barrels. Similarly, in *Re Moore & Co v Landauer & Co*,[69] tinned peaches were supplied in cases of 24 tins rather than cases of 30 tins as had been agreed. The court in both cases rightly found the respective suppliers to be in breach. The consequences that flowed from the breach were, however, more problematic. In both cases, because the term that was breached was a condition, the buyer was held entitled to terminate the contract and refuse to accept the goods. The reason this outcome is generally considered problematic is that the buyers in both cases had suffered no loss. The buyer in *Arcos* had wanted wooden staves to make barrels, and had received them—the extra thickness made no difference whatsoever. This is also true of *Moore v Landauer*: it is difficult to see how the buyer could in any way have been disadvantaged by the fact that the tins were packaged in crates of 24 rather than 30. The real reason behind the buyers' anxiety to terminate the contract in both cases was, rather, that market prices had fallen, with the result that they could now get the goods cheaper elsewhere. In alleging breach, they were not seeking to redress harm or loss they had suffered, because they had not suffered any harm. Instead, they were trying to exploit a minor breach to get out of something which in retrospect seemed a bad bargain. The category of innominate terms, then, is primarily an attempt by the courts to give themselves the flexibility to deal with remedies for breach in a more nuanced and context-sensitive manner than is possible under the rigid conditions/warranties dichotomy, without being drawn into either taking a paternalistic approach by applying an external standard of fairness to judge the contract, or attempting to decide what a party's motives were.

Their utility is illustrated by the decision in *Reardon Smith Line Ltd v Yngvar Hansen-Tangen*.[70] In this case, the parties had entered into a contract to charter a ship that was then under construction in Japan. In accordance with Japanese shipping practice, the ship was identified by the yard where it was to have been built, as 'Osaka 354'. Because of the ship's size, it was actually built at a different yard owned by a subsidiary of the contracted shipbuilder, and bore the actual number 'Oshima 004', although it continued to be referred to as 'Osaka 354' in all correspondence. The market for container

---

68. [1933] AC 470 (HL).   69. [1921] 2 KB 519 (CA).   70. [1976] 1 WLR 989 (HL).

ships is frothy, and can fluctuate quite significantly in response to economic pressures. When the ship was ready for delivery in 1974, market prices had collapsed due to the oil price shocks of the 1970s. As a result, the charterers were keen to get out of the contract. They argued that because the ship delivered bore a different number from the specification in the contract, there had been a breach of a condition, entitling them to terminate the charter. On the logic of *Arcos* and *Moore*, their argument should have succeeded. The House of Lords, however, unanimously rejected their argument. Lord Wilberforce, who delivered the leading judgment, said that *Hongkong Fir* had developed the law of contract 'along more rational lines' in placing emphasis on the 'nature and gravity of a breach or departure rather than in accepting rigid categories which do or do not automatically give a right to rescind'.[71] The preference should be to follow this approach.

15.3.3 **Applying the distinction**

How, then, do we determine in which of these three categories we place a term in a given case? There are three sources to which we need to look in order to classify a term: common law rules, statutory rules, and the parties' contract.

Common law classification

Let us begin with the first of these. In *Hongkong Fir Shipping Co Ltd v Kawasaki Kisen Kaisha Ltd*,[72] Diplock LJ suggested that the question to ask in classifying a term is simple. A term is a condition if its breach will always and inevitably 'deprive the party not in default of substantially the whole benefit which it was intended that he should obtain from the contract'. If its breach could deprive the party not in default of substantially the whole benefit in some cases but not others, the term is an innominate term.

This distinction was relatively easy to apply to the facts of *Hongkong Fir*, which involved the charter of a ship by Hongkong Fir to Kawasaki for a two-year period. When the ship was delivered, however, Hongkong Fir failed to provide an adequate crew, with the result that the ship's engines broke down. Kawasaki lost 20 weeks' use of the vessel, and sought to terminate the charter. Hongkong Fir admitted that it had breached its duty to provide a seaworthy vessel but denied that Kawasaki was entitled to terminate the charter. The Court of Appeal held that the duty to provide a seaworthy ship was an innominate term. Seaworthiness was a very broad concept and, in law, if a single nail was missing from a plank in the hull of a wooden ship, the seaworthiness clause would have been breached. It would be 'contrary to common sense' to suppose that the parties had intended the charterer to be able to terminate a charter because of a missing nail.[73] Because a seaworthiness clause was an innominate term, the relatively brief duration of the breach meant that it had not been breached in a manner that deprived Kawasaki of substantially the whole benefit of the contract. Kawasaki's claim was therefore limited to damages.

Outside the specific facts of *Hongkong Fir*, however, Lord Diplock's test is less straightforward to apply. If we were to take it at face value, it is hard to see when a term could *ever* be a condition. Virtually any contractual term imaginable is capable of being

---

71. Ibid, 998.   72. [1962] 2 QB 26 (CA).   73. Ibid, 64 (Upjohn LJ).

breached in more and less serious ways and, thus, should be held to be an innominate term on Lord Diplock's test. In practice, the courts have not been prepared to go that far. In *The Mihalis Angelos*,[74] the owners of a ship agreed to charter it to a charterer. The charter stated that the vessel was expected to be ready to load at Haiphong in what was then North Vietnam on about 1 July 1965. In point of fact, the owners had no reasonable basis on which to make this statement, as the vessel would not have been ready to load for at least a further couple of weeks from the beginning of July. The charterer purported to cancel the charter. The Court of Appeal held that he was entitled to do so. The 'readiness to load' clause was a condition, the breach of which entitled the charterer to terminate the charter. Although a literal application of Lord Diplock's test in *Hongkong Fir* would lead to this term being treated as an innominate term, terms such as to readiness to load had long been considered conditions, and it would be 'regrettable at this stage to disturb an established interpretation'.

The Mihalis Angelos suggests that English law continues to have more room for conditions than a bare reading of *Hongkong Fir* might suggest. The editors of *Chitty on Contract* have distilled the subsequent case law into a fourfold test, which is generally taken to be an accurate statement of the basis on which courts classify terms as being either conditions or innominate terms. A contractual term, they suggest, will be taken to be a condition in the following four circumstances. If none of them apply, it will be an innominate term.

(i)   if an applicable statute treats it as a condition;

(ii) if there are precedents which have categorised a term of that type as a condition (although precedents from before the 1960s should be approached with caution);

(iii) if the contract expressly or implicitly designates the term as a condition;

(iv) if the nature of the contract, the subject-matter, or the circumstances of the case lead to the conclusion that the parties must have intended that the innocent party would be discharged from further performance of his obligations if the term was not fully and precisely complied with.[75]

Statutory classification

Many statutes expressly declare particular types of terms to either be conditions, warranties, or innominate terms. The Consumer Rights Act 2015 (which classifies terms in consumer contracts), and the Sale of Goods Act 1979 and the Supply of Goods and Services Act 1982 (which classify terms in commercial contracts) are the most generally applicable examples. Statutes also sometimes give a right to terminate for breach of certain terms. Thus, for example, the Consumer Rights Act 2015 gives the consumer a right to reject goods which are not in conformity with the statutory terms. Similar, albeit less strong, rights exist in relation to commercial contracts under the Sale of Goods Act 1979.

Because the category of innominate terms is relatively new, many statutes do not expressly deal with them. The Sale of Goods Act 1979, for example, only classifies terms as being conditions or warranties. It makes no mention of innominate terms.

---

74. *Maredelanto Compania Naviera SA v Bergbau-Handel GmbH (The Mihalis Angelos)* [1971] 1 QB 164 (CA).

75. H Beale (ed), *Chitty on Contracts* (32nd edn, Sweet & Maxwell 2015) 13-040.

Nevertheless, the courts have shown a willingness to extend the class of innominate terms to contracts for the sale of goods, as long as the term in question is not expressly classed as a condition or a warranty by the statute.

In *The Hansa Nord*,[76] the parties had contracted for the sale of citrus pulp pellets, which were to be used as animal feed. The contract price was £100,000, and the contract provided that the goods were to be shipped 'in good condition'. On arrival, part of the goods was discovered to have major damage, while another part had minor damage. The market price had fallen in the meantime, and the buyer rejected the entire cargo, arguing that a condition had been breached. The seller resold the goods at auction, where the original buyer purchased them for £34,000 and used them for the originally intended purpose.

The Court of Appeal held that the relevant clause in the contract was an intermediate term and the consequences of the particular breach which had occurred were not sufficiently serious to have entitled the purchaser to terminate the contract, particularly given that the purchaser was able to use the goods for the intended purpose. Although the Sale of Goods Act only provided for conditions and warranties, its classification was not intended to be exhaustive.[77] A court could treat a term as an innominate term if it had not been statutorily described as a condition or a warranty, and it would usually be commercially sensible to do so:

> In my view, a court should not be over ready, unless required by statute or authority to do so, to construe a term in a contract as a 'condition' . . . In principle contracts are made to be performed and not to be avoided according to the whims of market fluctuation and where there is a free choice between two possible constructions I think the court should tend to prefer that construction which will ensure performance, and not encourage avoidance of contractual obligations.[78]

As this suggests, it is likelier than not that a court will treat a term not expressly classified by statute as an innominate term, rather than as a condition, unless there are some factors which suggest that it should be treated as a condition.

Contractual classification

Finally, it is open to the parties to contractually designate a particular term as a condition (or a warranty, or an innominate term). If the parties expressly state that a term is a condition of the contract, or if the contract expressly links the performance of a term to the right to terminate the contract, the courts will usually hold it to be a condition.[79] But the courts do not take a mechanistic or literal approach to the parties' contract. Merely using the word 'condition' in a contract does not indicate that a term is a condition. Instead, the classification of a term will always depend on the overall construction of the contract.

In *L Schuler AG v Wickman Machine Tool Sales Ltd*,[80] Schuler, a German company, appointed Wickman as its distributor in the UK. It was said to be a 'condition' that Wickman would visit six named customers once a week for the duration of the

---

76. *Cehave NV v Bremer Handelsgesellschaft mbH ('The Hansa Nord')* [1976] QB 44 (CA).
77. Ibid, 60 (Lord Denning MR).   78. Ibid, 71 (Roskill LJ).
79. See points (iii) and (iv) in the fourfold test discussed earlier.
80. [1974] AC 235 (HL).

contract. Wickman failed to carry out a small number of visits, and the claimants claimed the right to terminate for a breach of a condition. The House of Lords held that the contract could not be terminated on this basis alone. Although the obligation to make weekly visits was termed a 'condition', the outcome of treating it as a condition in law would be that Schuler would have the right to terminate the contract if Wickman failed to make 1 out of 1,400 visits. It was unlikely that the parties intended that the failure to make a small number of visits should have such drastic results. Although the parties were free to agree on such an outcome, it would have to be abundantly clear from the contract that that was indeed their intention.[81] The contract did not do so. As a result, Wickman's breach was simply the breach of an innominate term, which was not serious enough to give Schuler the right to terminate the agreement.

In *The Hansa Nord*, Roskill LJ pointed out that the ruling in *Schuler* meant that 'great care would have to be taken regarding the choice of language used' to turn a contractual obligation into a condition.[82] This is no bad thing. It would be unusual for commercial parties to intend even trivial breaches to give rise to the right to terminate a contract. It therefore makes more commercial sense to err on the side of caution when construing such clauses. This is particularly so where general practice in the relevant sector indicates that trivial breaches of that type of clause are not usually regarded as being repudiatory.[83] Although treating such clauses as always being conditions would achieve a high degree of certainty, the issue for the courts is not a simple choice between certainty and uncertainty, but finding the right balance between certainty and the undesirability of allowing termination for a trivial breach, where damages 'would clearly be an adequate remedy'.[84]

It is worth emphasizing that the issue is a matter of construction, to be resolved using ordinary principles of construction. It does not reflect a general policy of the law, or even a desire to protect the weaker party from termination. If, on a contextual reading, a right to terminate even for trivial breaches makes commercial sense, the courts will treat the clause as a condition. In *SimplySure Ltd v Personal Touch Financial Services Ltd*,[85] a contract between an insurance company and a reseller said that it was a 'condition' that the reseller would be aware of and abide by all rules set out by the Financial Conduct Authority, and acquaint itself with any new rules or regulations it issued. The Court of Appeal held that the clause should be construed as a true condition. Breaches of the FCA's rules could give rise to criminal liability and regulatory sanctions, making a wide power to terminate commercially sensible even if the specific breach was trivial.[86]

15.3.4 **Anticipatory breach**

Consider the following memo from the architects engaged by Avonside University, within the context of Problem 15:

---

81. Ibid, 251 (Lord Reid).   82. [1976] QB 44, 70.
83. *Spar Shipping AS v Grand China Logistics (Group) Co Ltd* [2016] EWCA Civ 982, [2017] 4 All ER 124, [63].
84. *Bunge Corp v Tradax Export SA* [1981] 1 WLR 711 (HL).
85. [2016] EWCA Civ 461.   86. Ibid, [28]–[32].

> **Illustration 15.8**
>
> Laura,
>
> I have had a conversation with the Pro-Vice-Chancellor (Estates) at Avonside University, who has hinted very strongly that they are likely to drop the contract, and have 'suggested' that we hold off on preparing plans for the site. I am irritated by this, as I imagine you all are. Preparing the plans would have been a very strong addition to our firm's profile. We need to have an internal meeting to discuss our strategy, and how we're going to respond. I am somewhat minded to push ahead with the plans anyway, given that they can't just unilaterally cancel the contract.
>
> Jim

The instances of breach that we have examined thus far relate to actual breaches of obligations that have fallen due. It may, however, also happen that a party makes it clear that it does not intend to perform a contract at a time when performance has not yet fallen due. Consider Illustration 15.8. If the university terminates the contract with its architects at a time when it is not entitled to terminate, what options will the architects have? Can they choose to bring the contract to an end even though the other party is not yet actually in breach, or must they continue to prepare plans and carry out site surveys, even though they know that the other party has no intention of performing?

In English law, situations of this type are covered by the law of *anticipatory breach*. Unlike actual breach, which relates to past or present obligations, anticipatory breach relates to future obligations that have not yet fallen due. It arises where one party repudiates or renounces the contract, by indicating that it will not perform its obligations when they fall due. Once this happens, the innocent party has the choice of *accepting* the renunciation and bringing the contract to an end, even though the breach has not yet occurred, or of *affirming* the contract and continuing to perform it.

Anticipatory breach reflects the commonsense notion that it makes little sense to compel the innocent party to 'render useless performance, which the repudiating buyer had indicated he no longer wanted'.[87] In *Hoechster v De La Tour*,[88] De La Tour had engaged Hoechster to act as his courier for three months, starting from 1 June. On 11 May, he told Hoechster that he no longer required his services. Hoechster sued for breach on 22 May. De La Tour argued that no breach would occur until 1 June, and Hoechster should remain ready and willing to perform until then. The court held that Hoechster could start an action for damages without waiting until 1 June:

> It seems strange that the defendant, after renouncing the contract, and absolutely declaring that he will never act under it, should be permitted to object that faith is given to his assertion, and that an opportunity is not left to him of changing his mind.[89]

---

87. *Fercometal SARL v Mediterranean Shipping Co SA* [1989] AC 788 (HL), 797 (Lord Ackner).
88. (1853) 2 E & B 678, 118 ER 922.   89. Ibid, (Lord Campbell CJ).

The central element of anticipatory breach is repudiation. Repudiation does not need to be express, but it must be clear and absolute. The party must, by words or conduct, indicate that it no longer intends to perform the contract. The import of the party's words and conduct are judged objectively, with reference to the conclusion a reasonable person would draw from them. A court may infer anticipatory breach from a party's acts, even if there was no express repudiation. This was the case in *Frost v Knight*.[90] Knight, a bachelor, promised to marry Ms Frost when Knight's father died. He then married someone else while his father was still alive. At that time, the breach of a promise to marry was actionable through a suit for damages.[91] The court held that Ms Frost could sue Knight, as his marriage to another person amounted to a renunciation of his promise.

Not every statement indicating that a party is unable or unwilling to perform its part of a contract will amount to a renunciation for the purposes of anticipatory breach. As with other breaches, the renunciation, too, must relate to a condition of the contract, or to a breach of an innominate term that deprives the other party of substantially the whole benefit which it was the intention of the parties that he should obtain under the contract. A statement which relates to a warranty, or to a minor breach of an innominate term, is not a renunciation of the contract.

Secondly, the renunciation must be unequivocal. This requirement has created problems where one party announces a future course of conduct which it mistakenly believes to be authorized by the contract. Consider, once again, the developments described in Illustration 15.8. The university declares that it considers the contract to be at an end, and believes that it is entitled to do so under the contract. Let us assume, for present purposes, that it is wrong. Can the architects treat the university as having unequivocally renounced the contract, and thus being in anticipatory breach?

The case law on this point is not entirely consistent, and is not easy to reconcile. In general, the starting point is that a party who has honestly misinterpreted an agreement does not renounce it by acting on that belief, as long as she remains open to correction and is willing to perform the contract according to its true meaning once that is established.[92] In practice, however, this is not an easy test to apply, particularly where the party in question sticks to its interpretation of the contract.

In *Federal Commerce and Navigation Co Ltd v Molena Alpha Inc*,[93] disputes arose between the owners and charterers of a ship as to whether the charterers were allowed to deduct some sums from the hire charges. The owners' lawyers advised them (wrongly, as it turned out) that they were in the right, and could as a result refuse to issue certain documents which the charterers needed to operate the ships. The owners told the charterers that these documents would not be issued. The charterers argued that this was a renunciation of the contract, and that the owners were therefore in anticipatory breach. The House of Lords upheld the charterers' argument, even though the owners honestly believed that the contract permitted them to act as they had. They placed great weight on the urgency of the charterers' need for the documents in question, and on the fact

90. (1872) LR 7 Exch 111.
91. This action was abolished by the Law Reform (Miscellaneous Provisions) Act 1970, s 1(1).
92. See *Ross T Smyth & Co Ltd v TD Bailey, Son & Co* [1940] 3 All ER 60; *Sweet & Maxwell Ltd v Universal News Services Ltd* [1964] 2 QB 699 (CA).
93. [1979] AC 757 (HL).

that any process to resolve the dispute whether through arbitration or litigation would not have been concluded in time for the vessels to leave port on schedule.[94]

In *Woodar Investment Development Ltd v Wimpey Construction (UK) Ltd*,[95] in contrast, the result was very different. Woodar had agreed to sell 14 acres of land in Surrey to Wimpey, with completion set to occur on the earlier of 21 February 1980 or two months after the grant of outline planning permission for development of the property. Woodar subsequently changed its mind about the purchase, and sought to invoke a clause giving them a right to rescind the contract in certain circumstances. Wimpey argued that those circumstances did not exist, with the result that Woodar had renounced the contract by purporting to rescind it, and were in anticipatory breach. The House of Lords agreed with Wimpey that Woodar did not have a right to rescind the contract, but held that it was not in anticipatory breach:

> it would be a regrettable development of the law of contract to hold that a party who bona fide relies on an express stipulation in a contract in order to rescind or terminate a contract should, by that fact alone, be treated as having repudiated his contractual obligations if he turns out to be mistaken as to his rights. Repudiation is a drastic conclusion which should only be held to arise in clear cases of a refusal, in a matter going to the root of the contract, to perform contractual obligations. To uphold Woodar's contentions in this case would represent an undesirable contention of the doctrine.[96]

A number of commentators have suggested that *Woodar* is not compatible with *Molena Alpha*, and that it is the approach in *Molena Alpha* that is to be preferred. This view was shared by two of the judges in *Woodar*, who dissented on the basis that the case was indistinguishable from *Molena Alpha*. This conclusion is not, however, as straightforward as it might appear to be, not least because the leading speeches in both cases were given by the same judge, Lord Wilberforce, who does not appear to have seen the positions he took as being incompatible. It has been suggested that the key difference between the two cases is that *Molena Alpha* involved a degree of urgency which *Woodar v Wimpey* did not. In the former case, the shipowners' refusal to issue the documents in question had an immediate, disproportionate effect on the ability of the charterers to enjoy the benefit of the contract. In the latter case, the effect was neither as immediate nor as drastic, with the result that it did not immediately go to the root of the contract.[97]

15.3.5 **The right of election**

If an actual or anticipatory repudiatory breach has occurred, the injured party has the option to terminate the contract for breach. This is an option, and not an obligation. The party may choose to *accept the repudiation*, by terminating the contract and suing for damages. Alternately, the party may choose to *affirm the contract*, perform or tender performance, and claim damages for breach if the other side does not perform. The choice of affirming or repudiating the contract must be made within a reasonable time

---

94. Ibid, 780 (Lord Wilberforce).   95. [1980] 1 WLR 277 (HL).
96. Ibid, 283 (Lord Wilberforce).
97. M Furmston, *Cheshire, Fifoot & Furmston's Law of Contract* (15th edn, Oxford University Press 2007) 684.

of the repudiatory breach.[98] Once the choice has been made, it is final. A party who has opted to accept the repudiation cannot subsequently change his mind and seek to affirm the contract. Likewise, a party who has elected to affirm a contract cannot subsequently decide to accept the repudiation. The act of affirmation amounts to a waiver of the right to terminate.

The exception to this general principle is a situation where the repudiatory breach continues after the date of the affirmation. Here, an injured party who initially elects not to terminate the contract may subsequently elect to treat the contract as at an end if the breach continues.[99] In *Johnson v Agnew*,[100] the Johnsons agreed to sell a house and land to Ms Agnew, who agreed to purchase the property. However, Agnew failed to complete on the agreed day. The Johnsons sued for specific performance, but the order took several months to be drawn up, during which time the bank to whom they had mortgaged their property took possession and sold. The vendors sought discharge of the order for specific performance and to recover damages in its place. The House of Lords held that they could do so, notwithstanding their earlier decision to claim specific performance (and, thus, to affirm the contract). **Election** works in substantially the same way whether the breach in question is actual or anticipatory, and we will therefore deal with both together in this section.

Accepting the repudiation

If the innocent party chooses to accept the repudiation of the contract, she must **communicate** that acceptance to the other party by making it clear to the other party that she is accepting the breach and terminating the contract. The acceptance must pertain to the entire contract, and not merely part of it. There is no hard-and-fast rule in relation to how the acceptance must be communicated. It does not have to follow any specific form, nor does it have to take the form of words. A party accepting a repudiatory breach does not have to give any details of what it believes to be the repudiatory act, and if details are given it is irrelevant whether those details are right or wrong as long as there was an actual repudiation to accept.[101] All that matters is that it 'clearly and unequivocally conveys to the repudiating party that that aggrieved party is treating the contract as at an end'.[102]

A party may therefore accept the repudiation 'by so acting as to make plain that in view of the wrongful action of the party who has repudiated, he claims to treat the contract as at an end'.[103] An overt act which is both unequivocal and inconsistent with the subsistence of the contract will usually be sufficient communication of the acceptance of the repudiation.[104] Nor does the communication need to come directly from the innocent party to the party in repudiation. It is sufficient if the election comes to the repudiating party's attention, even if it is through an unauthorized source.[105]

98. *White Rosebay Shipping SA v Hong Kong Chain Glory Shipping Ltd* [2013] EWHC 1355 (Comm).
99. See *Stocznia Gdanska SA v Latvian Shipping Co* [2002] EWCA Civ 889.
100. [1980] AC 367 (HL).
101. See *Maredelanto Compania Naviera SA v Bergbau-Handel GmbH (The Mihalis Angelos)* [1971] 1 QB 164 (CA), 204 (Megaw LJ).
102. *Vitol SA v Norelf Ltd (The Santa Clara)* [1996] AC 800 (HL), 811 (Lord Steyn).
103. *Heyman v Darwins* [1942] AC 356 (HL), 361 (Viscount Simon LC).
104. *Holland v Wiltshire* (1954) 90 CLR 409 (High Court of Australia).
105. See *Vitol SA v Norelf Ltd (The Santa Clara)* [1996] AC 800 (HL), 811 (Lord Steyn).

In *Vitol SA v Norelf Ltd*,[106] the House of Lords held that in certain cases, a failure to perform the contract may be sufficient communication by the innocent party of its acceptance of the repudiation. Lord Steyn gave the example of an employer who notifies a contractor that he is repudiating their contract, and tells the contractor not to bother turning up the next day. In such a case, the contractor conveys his acceptance of the repudiation by the simple fact of not turning up the next day. This basic principle also applies to other types of transactions. *Vitol SA* involved a contract for the sale of goods by Norelf to Vitol. While the goods were being loaded onto the ship, Vitol sent a telex to Norelf repudiating the contract and rejecting the cargo. Norelf made no reply, but also took no further steps to perform the contract. Norelf resold the goods at a loss, and sued Vitol for compensation. The House of Lords held that Norelf's failure to send any shipping documents to Vitol in the days after shipment would have clearly communicated their acceptance of Vitol's repudiation.[107] As a result, they had successfully accepted the repudiation, and could sue Vitol for breach.

Affirming the contract

The innocent party is not bound to accept a repudiatory breach, whether real or anticipatory. He may, instead, choose to keep the contract alive, by affirming the contract and performing his obligations under it. But this is a double-edged sword. A party who elects to affirm remains liable to perform his obligations under the contract, and cannot sue for breach of contract until the time of performance is due. Affirmation is therefore ordinarily only advisable where accepting the repudiation and suing for breach would, for some reason, fail to provide an adequate remedy.

The leading case on this point is the decision of the House of Lords in *White and Carter (Councils) Ltd v McGregor*.[108] The claimants in this case had agreed with the defendants' representatives to advertise the defendants' business for three years on plaques to be attached to litter bins. The defendants purported to cancel the contract on the same day. The claimants refused to accept the cancellation, manufactured plaques to be displayed on litter bins, and displayed them in accordance with the contract. The contract contained a clause that the whole amount would become payable in the event of non-payment of an instalment. The defendants refused to pay, and the claimants sued for the complete amount. The House of Lords held that the claimants were entitled to affirm the contract, perform their obligations under it, and claim the full contract price. An innocent party was under no obligation to accept a repudiatory breach, even if the result was wasteful. Several judges were influenced by the fact that the suit was framed not as an action to recover damages for breach of contract, but as an action in debt, which is much more claimant-friendly and subject to far fewer restrictions than an action for breach.[109] The principle they stated was, however, much broader and not restricted to suits framed as actions in debt.

White and Carter was controversial when it was decided, and it remains controversial today. And, in practice, the right to affirm is subject to several restrictions.

---

106. [1996] AC 800 (HL).   107. Ibid, 811–12.   108. [1962] AC 413 (HL).
109. The differences between an action in debt and an action for damages for breach are discussed in greater detail in Chapter 17.

The first restriction is that affirmation will not be available if it is inconsistent with the party's duty to **mitigate** its losses. The topic of mitigation is discussed in greater detail in Chapter 16, and we will therefore not spend time on this restriction in this chapter, beyond noting its existence. The second restriction on the ability to affirm is that it will not be available if performing the contract requires the *cooperation* of the other party. This was highlighted by the High Court in *Hounslow London Borough Council v Twickenham Garden Developments Ltd.*[110] That case involved a contract under which Hounslow LBC had engaged Twickenham Garden Developments to do some work at a site, and then repudiated the contract. In the course of discussing the restrictions on the right to affirm, Megarry J pointed out that performing the contract would require a high degree of active cooperation between the parties, because of the way the duties of the parties were structured under the contract, and because the obligations of the contractor related to the council's property. As such, it would be inappropriate to permit affirmation.

By far the more significant restriction, however, is the third. Consider the following illustration:

Illustration 15.9

Uncle Percival hires an expert craftsman to restore and refurbish an antique chess set he owns. Before the craftsman can start work, Uncle Percival receives a substantial offer from a third party who wishes to purchase the set as it is, unrefurbished and unrestored.

Here, it would make little sense to permit the restorer to insist on performance, given that she can be adequately compensated by bringing the contract to an end and paying her damages for the loss of profit. The third restriction on affirmation deals with precisely such situations. A person who has no 'legitimate interest, financial or otherwise, in performing the contract rather than claiming damages' will not be allowed to 'saddle the other party with an additional burden with no benefit to himself'.[111] In the modern context, this has evolved into an equitable principle that the courts will not allow a party to affirm a contract if the party was acting wholly unreasonably or perversely. In *The Alaskan Trader*,[112] a company called Bulk Oil had chartered a ship called *The Alaskan Trader* from Clea Shipping for a period of two years. After a year, the ship developed serious engine trouble. Bulk Oil said that it did not have any further use for *The Alaskan Trader*, as the repairs would take many months. Notwithstanding this, Clea Shipping repaired the vessel at a cost of $800,000 and kept it anchored for the remaining eight months of the charter, ready to sail with a full crew. They then sued Bulk Oil for the hire charges for the final eight-month period. The High Court held

---

110. [1971] Ch 233.

111. *White and Carter (Councils) Ltd v McGregor* [1962] AC 413 (HL), 431 (Lord Reid). Lord Reid's views were not shared by the other judges who decided the case, but it has nevertheless come to be accepted as part of the ratio in that case.

112. *Clea Shipping Corp v Bulk Oil International (The Alaskan Trader)* [1984] 1 All ER 129, [1983] 2 Lloyd's Rep 645 (QB).

that Clea Shipping had no legitimate claim for hire, and hence could not validly affirm the contract. The result was that it was left to its remedy in damages.

This exception should not be taken too far, however. In *Isabella Shipowner SA v Shagang Shipping Co Ltd*,[113] Cooke J held that it should only be applied where the innocent party has no legitimate interest in maintaining the contract, typically because damages are an adequate remedy, with the result that his insistence on affirming the contract and keeping it in effect can be described as 'wholly unreasonable', 'extremely unreasonable', or 'perverse'.[114] In that case, the charterers of a ship that had been chartered for five years sought to return it 94 days early. The early return took place in a difficult market, where the shipowner would have had difficulty finding a substitute charter, and where mitigation of loss through trading on the spot market was also difficult. Against this background, the court held that the shipowner was entitled to affirm the contract, and sue for the hire for the remaining days.

 Practice in context: termination clauses

The legal rules pertaining to breach of contract play a secondary role to that of the provisions of the contract. Parties can plan for breach, and they often do. Many contracts incorporate provisions to deal with non-performance, or inadequate performance, by one or both parties. A typical mobile phone contract between a consumer and a supplier will contain provisions dealing with the liability of the operator in the event of downtime. As a result, situations of actual downtime will typically be dealt with under the rules relating to contract terms rather than the rules pertaining to breach of contract. If you read through the terms and conditions governing just the electronic and digital services you use on a day-to-day basis, you will find that pretty much all of them contain provisions regulating what happens when one of the parties fails to do what they've contractually agreed to do.

A well-designed contract, particularly in relation to complex transactions, will go further, and contain provisions that unravel the contract when its performance is no longer possible. Event of default clauses and termination clauses are two examples that are particularly common in complex long-term transactions. Courts will in general give effect to termination clauses if they are properly drafted, on the basis that 'it is open to the parties to agree that, as regards a particular obligation, any breach shall entitle the party not in default to treat the contract as repudiated'.[115]

Care must, however, be taken in drafting termination clauses. As with other aspects of the law of breach of contract, the courts will not enforce termination clauses in ways that 'flout business commonsense'[116] unless it is unambiguously clear from the contract that the parties did in fact intend to produce those outcomes. *L Schuler AG v Wickman Machine Tool Sales Ltd*,[117] discussed in section 15.3.3, is an example. In *Rice v Great Yarmouth Borough Council*,[118] Rice had entered into two contracts with Great Yarmouth Borough Council, under which he agreed to manage the council's sporting facilities and parks respectively. Each contract contained the following termination clause:

→

---

113. [2012] EWHC 1077 (Comm).   114. Ibid, [44] (Cooke J).

115. *Bunge Corp v Tradax Export SA* [1981] 1 WLR 711 (HL), 715 (Lord Wilberforce).

116. *Antaios Compania Naviera SA v Salen Rederierna AB* [1985] AC 191 (HL), 201 (Lord Diplock).

117. [1974] AC 235 (HL).   118. [2003] TCLR 1 (CA).

→

> If the contractor . . . commits a breach of any of its obligations under the Contract; . . . the Council may, without prejudice to any accrued rights or remedies under the Contract, terminate the Contractor's employment under the Contract by notice in writing having immediate effect.

After eight months, the council terminated both contracts on the ground that a number of breaches had occurred. Rice claimed damages for wrongful termination. The council argued that the termination clause was deliberately phrased in wide terms, and should be read to mean what it said; namely, that any breach would give it the right to terminate the contract.

The Court of Appeal rejected the council's argument and held that Rice was entitled to damages. The termination provision had to be given a sensible commercial construction. The council's reading would 'visit the same draconian consequences upon any breach, however small, of any obligation, however small'. It could not have been the intention of the parties that any trivial breach could be a justification for termination. The parties must therefore be taken to have meant that only a repudiatory breach, or an accumulation of breaches that as a whole could be described as repudiatory, would trigger the right to terminate. The parties could always specifically provide that a term was so important that any breach would justify termination, but they had not done so. On the facts, although there had been a number of breaches, they were not serious enough to have deprived the council of substantially all the benefit of the contract, even when taken cumulatively. As a result, the council had breached the contract by purporting to terminate it, and Rice was entitled to damages for breach.

15.4 **In conclusion: performance, breach, and opportunism**

Let us now pull some of the threads together, and assess the strengths and limitations of the law. The law of breach of contract is a lot less intuitive than many other areas of contract law. Promises are intuitive, and the gut reactions we have to broken promises are also intuitive. The law of breach does not fit particularly well with this gut response. It is complex, and can often be counter-intuitive, particularly when we get to the details of topics like termination clauses, repudiation, and substantial performance.

Part of the reason the law in relation to breach is as complex as it is, is that—like the rules on gap filling examined in Chapter 8—it aims to deal with a broad range of behaviour and motives in a broad range of contexts on the basis of the language of the contractual instrument. As we have seen in this chapter, doing so in a way that also adequately restrains parties from opportunistically exploiting relatively minor breaches has proven to be challenging. The importance of restraining opportunism is particularly strong when it comes to the question of termination for breach. As we have seen, the remedy of termination, as opposed to damages, is particularly prone to being turned to opportunistic ends, which have little to do with the substance of the contract.

The law has reacted to this general trend by becoming more complex, in an attempt to give judges greater flexibility to deal with the issues that come before them in a more nuanced way. As we have seen in this chapter, the second half of the 20th century has seen a move away from the bright-line, binary divides that characterized the law of breach in the late 19th and early 20th centuries. Most of these developments have concerned doctrines which permit one of the parties to extricate themselves from a contract, whether by arguing that their obligations have not yet fallen due (as the entire obligation rule does), or by arguing that they have a right to terminate the contract for breach (as the rules around repudiatory breach do). In both cases, the result has been the creation of new categories and concepts which are a lot fuzzier, and to that extent less certain, but which also are less prone to producing problematic results. These developments have, cumulatively, gone a long way to letting English law deal pragmatically with the issues created by breach of contract, without getting drawn into the complex issues of motives and commitment that underlie the parties' choice to perform or breach.

That said, it is important not to overplay the role of the law of breach in dealing with the problem of commitment. Planning for non-performance or improper performance is an essential aspect of transactional planning, and many contracts will do so expressly. The legal rules governing breach of contract are only brought into play when the specific instance of non-performance goes beyond the range of circumstances for which the parties have provided. Breach of contract is an exceptional occurrence, and the involvement of the legal process in dealing with breach is even rarer. Even where contracts are broken, it is unusual for the outcome to turn on the legal rules governing breach of contract. The vast majority of breaches are, instead, tackled commercially. The strength of English contract law lies in the room it gives parties to design effective contracts, and to structure their substantive obligations in a way that matches their commercial intent. The legal process only comes into the frame when the parties' immediate interests, motives, or goals have diverged to such a great extent that they are no longer able to do so. The law of breach is no different.

Key points

- A contract is performed if the parties do what is required when it is required and in the manner in which it is required.

- The order of performance determines whether the parties have to perform their obligations under the contract at the same time, or whether one party's obligations are conditions precedent to the other party's obligations.

- If a party's obligations are entire, then it must perform all of its obligations before the other party's obligation to pay falls due. If its obligations are severable, then completion of a substantial part (or of a specifically delineated part) of the obligation is sufficient to trigger the other party's obligation to pay.

- Breach does not excuse the other party from performing its obligations unless the breach is repudiatory.

- Breaches of conditions are repudiatory, as are serious breaches of innominate terms. Minor breaches of innominate terms and breaches of warranties are not repudiatory.

- A party who is faced with a repudiatory breach has the option of accepting the repudiation and terminating the contract or affirming the contract. A party will not be able to affirm a contract if this is inconsistent with its duty to mitigate its losses.

- Anticipatory breach arises where a party repudiates or renounces its obligations under a contract before those obligations have fallen due. The innocent party has the option of accepting the repudiation or affirming the contract, much as with other repudiatory breaches.

- Parties can insert termination clauses into a contract to give them the right to terminate for other breaches, but such clauses will not necessarily be construed literally.

Assess your learning

You should be able to respond to each of the following points with a confident 'yes'. If you can't, then you should revisit the sections listed against that point.

Can you:

(a) *Identify* how courts determine whether a party has performed, and the impact of the precise wording of the contractual clause? (Sections 15.2.1 and 15.2.3)

(b) *Understand* the distinction between entire and severable obligations, and *explain* the manner in which the order of performance is determined? (Section 15.2.2)

(c) *Explain* the main types of contractual terms, *identify* the tests used to determine which type a given term belongs to, and *outline* the relationship between classification of terms and the remedy available to the claimant? (Sections 15.3.2 and 15.3.3)

(d) *Understand* the right of election in relation to repudiatory breach and anticipatory breach, including the restrictions on the ability to elect? (Sections 15.3.4 and 15.3.5)

In relation to each of the above, you should be able to:

(i) identify and clearly explain the key rules and principles;

(ii) identify the key cases and statutes, and why they matter;

(iii) apply the principles and cases to specific real or hypothetical fact situations;

(iv) evaluate the limitations, if any, of the law as it currently stands.

Further reading

W Bojczuk, 'When is a Condition Not a Condition?' [1987] JBL 353.

R Brownsword, 'Retrieving Reasons, Retrieving Rationality? A New Look at the Right to Withdraw for Breach of Contract' (1992) 5 JCL 83.

B Coote, 'Breach, Anticipatory Breach, or the Breach Anticipated?' (2007) 123 LQR 503.

FMB Reynolds, 'Warranty, Condition and Fundamental Term' (1963) 79 LQR 534.

FMB Reynolds, 'Discharge of Contract by Breach' (1981) 97 LQR 541.

E Tabachnik, 'Anticipatory Breach of Contract' (1972) 25 CLP 149.

G Treitel, 'Discharge from Performance of Contracts by Failure of Condition' (1979) 42 MLR 623.

T Weir, 'The Buyer's Right to Reject Defective Goods' (1976) 35 CLJ 33.

16

Compensatory remedies

Damages for breach of contract

'There are some things money can't buy, but not too many'

Problem 16: setting the context

Read the following letter, and think about the legal issues it raises.

The Arts Endowment Trust
Constable House, Maryport, Cumbria

Rodrigo Suarez
Gray, Wilson and Partners
Newcastle upon Tyne

Dear Rodrigo,

I am writing to brief you on the background to our ongoing dispute with the celebrity chef Reinhardt Weiss. As you will remember, we were given possession of the derelict Dolceratto pasta factory site in North Shields in 2016, with a view to turning it into a centre for the vibrant art scene that had begun to emerge in North Tyneside. Our plan was to create a set of shops and studios for local artists and craftspersons to make and sell their products. The plan had a huge response from the local creative community, with participants ranging from artisanal bakers to potters, artists, and stained-glass producers.

Because of the somewhat remote location of the site, we were anxious to secure a prestigious anchor tenant, who would attract people to the development because of their presence. That was Reinhardt Weiss's role. We signed an agreement with him, under which he agreed to open a restaurant and cooking centre and keep it running for a ten-year term. As he was an anchor tenant, we gave him a steeply discounted rent. This would have been Weiss's first restaurant outside the south-east, so it was a big coup for us and a major factor in making the development viable. The development, including Weiss's restaurant, opened in 2018.

Unfortunately, late last year, Weiss's lawyers wrote to us telling us that he intended to close his restaurant and pull out of the development. No reason was given. The restaurant did not open on 1 January this year, and has remained closed since. The effect on the development has been catastrophic. Visits are down by 30 per cent, and some shops have seen their income plummet by well over half. We ourselves are not losing very much money, as Weiss's rent was so heavily discounted, but it has drastically affected our hard-won reputation for competence. We are even more concerned about the devastating impact it appears almost certain to have on the creative community which this development was intended to nurture.

As we see it, Weiss has breached his contract without any excuse, and he knew perfectly well that his breach would devastate the business of the other artists in the development and harm our reputation. We would like your advice on what we can do to force him to make good the losses.

Yours sincerely,
Joanne Wrackleton

→

> →
> The fact situation above sets out a common scenario. One party finds itself in a worse position than it expected. It alleges that this was because the other party failed to comply with its contractual obligations. On a reasonable reading of the contract, it is apparent that the other party has, in fact, failed to comply with its obligations and is therefore in breach. What happens now? What consequences flow from the failure of a party to perform its obligations?

16.1 Introduction: the role of damages

From a lay perspective, 'enforcing' a contract means requiring the party in breach to perform the contract. In law, however, it usually means something different. Courts have the power to require the party in breach to perform, but they rarely exercise it. Instead, the default remedy for a breach of contract is an action for **damages**—compensation for breach. Consider the following illustration:

> ### Illustration 16.1
>
> Simonside Engineering Works have purchased a new diesel generator to provide power for some work they are carrying out on an off-grid site. One month into the work, they discover that due to a manufacturing defect, the generator is prone to overheating and abruptly shutting down, making it impossible for them to use it as a reliable source of electricity.

A layperson might think that enforcement in this situation will entail requiring the seller to repair or replace the defective goods. In law, however, the default remedy is compensation for the loss caused by the fact that the goods were defective. The supplier may voluntarily offer to repair or replace the goods, but the law will not require it.

Damages can be claimed in relation to every breach, and they are available as a matter of right. They are usually *compensatory* in character. Their objective is to compensate the innocent party for the loss that was caused to it by the breach. Although courts can grant monetary remedies for purposes other than compensation, they only do so in exceptional cases, as Chapter 17 discusses in greater detail. The default position remains that damages are compensatory.

In this chapter, we will begin by studying the basis on which damages are awarded and the different ways in which they can be calculated, as well as the interests which damages protect (section 16.2). We will then examine the various ways in which damages can be limited in law (section 16.3), before concluding with an evaluation of the role damages play in English contract law (section 16.4).

16.2 **Assessing damages**

16.2.1 **The purpose of damages**

Judges explain English law's preference for ordering compensation rather than actual performance by drawing a distinction between 'primary' and 'secondary' obligations. On this theory, the things the parties contractually agree to do are their primary obligations. If these primary obligations are breached, the law replaces them with secondary obligations requiring the payment of compensation.[1]

Compensatory damages are said to reflect the principle of putting the innocent party in the position they would have been in had the breach never occurred. The role of the law, in this understanding, is to vindicate the contractual rights of the innocent party. It discharges this role by undoing the effects of the breach and, thereby, correcting the wrong suffered by the victim of the breach.[2] In practice, however, English law stops well short of full compensation. Theodore Sedgwick, a 19th-century American commentator on the law of damages, suggested that a court awarding damages 'in fact, aims not at satisfaction, but at a division of the loss'.[3] This remains true of modern English contract law. The aim of the rules governing compensatory damages is not full compensation. It is finding a sensible way to determine which portion of the loss should be borne by the party in breach, and which should be borne by the innocent party. In practical terms, this means that a party who has suffered a breach of contract—such as the Arts Endowment Trust in Problem 16—cannot assume that it will be able to recover compensation for all its losses. There will almost always be some losses for which it will not be compensated, and which it will be left to bear.

Consider the types of loss at issue in the following illustration:

Illustration 16.2

The Starling Inspectors are a music band from Broadland. They have a concert scheduled in Norwich on 18 September. Their van has broken down, so they contact a local van hire company and order a van to take them to the concert, paying in advance. The van does not arrive. They are unable to get to their concert.

A number of consequences follow:

First, they are forced to refund the price of all tickets which have been sold, amounting to £4,800 in total.

Secondly, under the venue's policies, because they did not give seven days' notice of cancellation, they have to pay the full hire charge of £1,250.

→

---

1. The clearest statement of this theory was provided by Lord Diplock in *Photo Production Ltd v Securicor* [1980] AC 827 (HL).

2. D Pearce and R Halson, 'Damages for Breach of Contract: Compensation, Restitution and Vindication' (2008) 28 OJLS 73.

3. T Sedgwick, *A Treatise on the Measure of Damages* (John S Voorhies 1852) 38.

> Thirdly, they would have made a profit of £2,765 on the gig, which they have now lost. They had intended to use this to pay for a holiday for the members, which they will now not be able to take.
>
> Fourthly, they paid a non-refundable advance of £250 for the van.
>
> Fifthly, they have an angry and disappointed fanbase, who are threatening to boycott future concerts unless the band 'does something to make it up to them'.

As this suggests, a breach of contract can result in very different losses, ranging from reputational harm to money paid for services not received. Three sets of doctrines determine when and to what extent these are recoverable. The first relates to the way in which English law determines the quantum of loss that will be compensated through the award of damages. English law does not begin with a broad-ranging enquiry into the ways in which the innocent party has been harmed by breach. Instead, the quantum of loss is determined using a small number of approaches to measuring and estimating loss. These are discussed in sections 16.2.2–16.2.5.

Secondly, English law does not permit recovery for all *types* of harm. Whilst the innocent party will almost always be able to recover for harm to its economic interests, it is much harder to recover for harm to other types of interests, such as harm to reputation, as section 16.2.6 discusses.

Thirdly, English law incorporates three sets of doctrines which impose bounds on the *extent* of harm for which the party in breach will be responsible. First, the claimant will only be able to recover compensation for loss that was caused by the breach. Loss that would have been suffered anyway is not recoverable. Secondly, the claimant is expected to work to reduce (in legal terminology, '*mitigate*') the impact of the breach on her business. If she fails to do so, she will not be able to recover compensation for loss that could have been mitigated but was not. Thirdly, the claimant will not be able to recover compensation for loss that is too remote a consequence of the breach, such as loss that was not reasonably within the parties' contemplation at the time of contracting. These are discussed in section 16.3.

Fourthly, English law sets up a number of hurdles to recovery where some of the loss is suffered by persons who are not parties to the contract (in legal terminology, third parties). It is not uncommon for breach to do so. In Problem 16, for example, Weiss's breach adversely affects the position not just of the Arts Endowment Trust itself, but also of the other artists who have outlets in the development. Because the anchor tenant has pulled out, all of them are going to see significantly less turnover than they expected. The hurdles to recovery faced by third parties are discussed in more detail in Chapter 18.

16.2.2 Quantifying loss: measured and estimated damages

As we have seen above, the purpose of damages is to ensure that contracting parties will not suffer loss as a result of a breach of contract by a counterparty. How, then, might we translate this general sentiment into a concrete sum of money to be awarded to a party who has suffered a breach?

In some cases, the facts make it relatively simple to put a precise figure on the party's loss. In Illustration 16.2, for example, we know the precise amount of money the band has lost on the hire charges for the venue and the van. In other cases, however, it is not as simple. Problem 16 is an example. We do not know how much the Arts Endowment Trust has lost due to Weiss's breach, nor can we calculate their loss with any degree of precision. Most cases in contract law involve at least some losses which cannot be precisely measured, and must therefore be estimated.

The task of articulating an approach to estimation that is both consistent and fair has presented non-trivial challenges for the law. In *Morris-Garner v One Step (Support) Ltd*,[4] Lord Reed explained the basic approach taken by the courts when estimating damages:

> The court will have to select the method of measuring the loss which is the most apt in the circumstances to secure that the claimant is compensated for the loss which it has sustained. It may, for example, estimate the effect of the breach on the value of the business, or the effect on its profits, or the resultant management costs, or the loss of goodwill . . . The assessment of damages in such circumstances often involves what Lord Shaw described in *Watson, Laidlaw*[5] at pp 29–30 as 'the exercise of a sound imagination and the practice of the broad axe'.[6]

English law recognizes two basic methods of approaching this task: the **expectation interest** and the **reliance interest**. When damages are awarded according to the expectation interest, the court seeks to put the party in the position it would have been in had the contract been properly performed. Its task is to compare the position the innocent party finds itself in after the breach with the position it would have been in had the contract been kept. Based on this comparison, it will then award a sum of money equal to the difference. In Illustration 16.2, this would mean asking how much money the band would have had after the concert (had it taken place), comparing that with how much money they actually have, and awarding them the difference.

When damages are awarded according to the reliance interest, in contrast, the court seek to put the party in the position it would have been in had the contract never been formed. It compares the party's position subsequent to the breach with the position it would have been in had the contract never been entered into. In Illustration 16.2, this covers the money spent in making arrangements for the concert—for example, the hire charge for the venue, preparatory expenses such as printing posters, publicity, and so on.

Despite the differences between them, both expectation and reliance damages share a common objective: compensating the claimant for the loss suffered as a result of the breach. The courts in any given case will award whichever most clearly represents the loss.[7] As we will see in the course of this section, each approach is useful in different types of situation.

---

4. [2018] UKSC 20.
5. *Watson, Laidlaw & Co Ltd v Pott, Cassels & Williamson* (1914) 31 RPC 104 (HL).
6. *Morris-Garner v One Step (Support) Ltd* [2018] UKSC 20, [37].   7. Ibid, [36].

16.2.3 **The expectation interest**

The logic behind the expectation interest is simple. A person who contracts has a legitimate expectation that the other party will keep their word. Breach violates this expectation. The law therefore intervenes to uphold it by awarding compensation which puts the innocent party in the position he or she would have been in had the contract been performed.

The idea that contract damages should seek to protect the innocent party's expectation of performance is an old one. It is implicit in late mediaeval case law and can possibly be traced back even earlier. The first explicit statement of the rule, however, only came in 1848, in the case of *Robinson v Harman*.[8]

Case in depth: *Robinson v Harman* (1848) 1 Ex 850

Harman had agreed to grant Robinson a lease over a dwelling house. The rent agreed between the parties was substantially below the market rent. It turned out that Harman did not actually have the right to lease the house out. It had belonged to his father, and his father's will had created a trust over the house. Harman was one of the beneficiaries of the trust, but only the trustees had the power to grant a lease. Robinson sued for breach of contract.

Harman's main argument at first instance was that Robinson had known of the defect in title at the time of the agreement. However, due to the way in which the pleadings had been framed, Harman's evidence on this point was ruled inadmissible. This meant that the primary issue for the court to decide was the quantum of damages.

Robinson argued that he had suffered two types of loss. First, he argued that he had incurred legal expenses of 15*l* 12*s* 8*d* in 'preparing the agreement and lease, and investigating the title'.[9] In addition, he argued that he 'lost and was deprived of great gains and profits, which would otherwise have accrued to him'[10] because the house was worth a lot more than the agreed rent. He sought damages under both heads. Harman admitted liability to compensate Robinson for his legal expenses, but denied that he was liable to pay compensation to Robinson for the loss of the bargain. The judge at first instance agreed with Robinson, and awarded damages totalling £225. Harman appealed to the Exchequer Chamber.[11] The Exchequer Chamber upheld the decision at first instance. Many of the authorities that were cited to the Exchequer Chamber appeared to favour Harman's case, however, and the case's importance comes from the way in which the Exchequer Chamber distinguished them.

Establishing title was a complex affair in the first half of the 19th century. The Land Registry was not set up until 1862, and in its absence sellers were often subsequently discovered to have defective title. Two such cases, both relating to contracts for the sale of land, supported Harman's position.[12] Both had held that where the seller had defective title, the buyer could only recover compensation for the expenses he had incurred on the sale.[13] He could not

→

---

8. (1848) 1 Ex 850.   9. Ibid, 851.   10. Ibid, 850.

11. The court hierarchy was rather different in the 1840s, and appeal from assizes lay to the Exchequer Chamber by way of a rule *nisi*.

12. *Flureau v Thornhill* (1776) 2 W Bla 1078; *Walker v Moore* (1829) 10 B & C 416.

13. In modern terms, these would be reliance damages.

→

recover compensation for the loss of bargain. Harman's lawyers relied heavily on these cases, and argued that they precluded Robinson from recovering damages for anything more than his legal expenses.

The Exchequer Chamber unanimously rejected Harman's argument. The prior cases cited by Harman, in their view, did not represent the general common law rule. They represented, instead, an exception which only applied to contracts for the sale of property which failed for want of good title.[14] The general rule at common law was that the party in breach must place the innocent party in the position he would have been in had the contract been performed. Parke B's formulation of this rule has come to be seen as the classic statement on the scope and nature of expectation damages:

> The rule of the common law is, that where a party sustains a loss by reason of a breach of contract, he is, so far as money can do it, to be placed in the same situation, with respect to damages, as if the contract had been performed.[15]

As the case related to a lease rather than a sale of property, it was covered by the general rule. As a result, Robinson could recover damages for the loss of his bargain as well as for the costs incurred in preparing the agreement and investigating title.

This remains the position today, but it is not all there is to the law. Three aspects of the way the law of damages is applied in practice mean that the compensation actually awarded can be significantly less than the rhetoric of 'expectation damages' might suggest, and lend considerable support to the loss-sharing argument.

The first relates to evidence and, in particular, to the burden of proof and the standard of proof. Expectation damages are awarded to compensate the claimant for the loss caused to him by the breach of contract. The claimant must therefore prove that he has suffered loss. The standard of proof is the balance of probabilities. In other words, the claimant must prove that on the evidence before the court, it is likelier than not that the claimant *would* have made the profit for which he seeks to recover damages. It is not enough to simply show that the claimant *could* have made a profit. The result is that a claimant who cannot discharge this burden of proof will only recover nominal damages. As we will see in the course of this section, the case law is littered with examples of persons who failed to recover damages despite having suffered breach because they were unable to demonstrate on the balance of probabilities that they had suffered loss.

Secondly, the claimant must also adduce evidence that establishes the extent or quantum of loss, or enables the court to estimate loss that cannot be precisely quantified.[16] As this section discusses in more detail, there are a number of different ways in which loss can be quantified. There is no ready-set formula to determine which of these different ways of quantifying loss should be used in any given case. Judges have a

---

14. The exceptional status of contracts for the sale of land was affirmed in *Bain v Fothergill* (1874–5) LR 7 HL 158. Expectation damages remained unavailable for breaches due to inadequate title in such contracts until the rule was abolished by the Law of Property (Miscellaneous Provisions) Act 1989, s 3.

15. (1848) 1 Ex 850, 855.   16. *Morris-Garner v One Step (Support) Ltd* [2018] UKSC 20, [38].

fair bit of discretion in deciding which is most appropriate on the facts of a given case, and will often choose a lower measure over a higher measure.

Thirdly, the general rule in relation to damages is qualified by the principles of causation, mitigation, and remoteness. These will be considered in greater detail in section 16.3. In the remainder of this section, we will look at the various measures of damages in more detail.

The loss of profit measure

The **loss of profit** measure is conceptually the most straightforward. Illustration 16.2 discussed earlier provides a paradigmatic example. Had the contract been kept, the claimants would have made a profit of £2,765. Because it was breached, they have not. However, this can be remedied if the court orders the defendant to pay them £2,765 as compensation for the breach. Under the loss of profit measure, this is precisely what the court does.

The key issue in this approach is the quantum of damages, which is a question of fact. The claimant must prove her loss on the balance of probabilities, by adducing evidence to show that she would have made a profit equal to the amount claimed as damages. This is relatively straightforward if the claim relates to the profit which would have been made on the breached contract itself: for example, where a contractor is engaged to do some work, but is then dismissed in breach of contract. Here, the court begins with the contract price (ie the amount the contractor was to receive under the contract for the work). It then deducts the expenses the contractor would have incurred on performance (ie money the contractor would have had to spend on buying materials, paying workers or subcontractors, and so on). The money that remains will be the money that is awarded.

Cases like Illustration 16.2, however, present a slightly different situation. Here, the profit that was lost would not have been made on the breached contract itself, but on a different contract which the breached contract would have facilitated. The Starling Inspectors would obviously have made no profit on the contract to hire a van. The lost profit would, rather, have been made on other contracts whose performance the breach prevented. Here, a party seeking to recover loss of profit will have to directly prove the amount of the lost profit on the balance of probabilities. This is not always straightforward. As a result, the law also incorporates other ways of quantifying damages which do not look to lost profits directly, but focus instead on other aspects of the loss. In the remainder of this subsection, we will consider the most important of these measures.

The 'cost of cure' and 'difference in value' measures

Understanding the measures

Consider the following two scenarios:

Illustration 16.3

Uncle Percival hires a decorator to renew the damp-proofing in his living room, and to subsequently replaster and repaint the room. When the work is finished, he is dismayed to discover that the work has been poorly done, leaving an uneven finish and several damp spots.

Illustration 16.4

White Rose Hosting Services is a web host. Its servers are connected to the internet through a dedicated fibre-optic internet connection provided by Yorkshire Telecom. Due to a number of failings by Yorkshire Telecom, the quality of the connection deteriorated dramatically in September, leaving WRHS with less than half the contractually stipulated bandwidth. WRHS has contracted for surplus bandwidth to cope with spikes in web traffic. The reduction in the bandwidth does not therefore have a serious effect on the accessibility of the sites it hosted for its clients, although users would have noticed that the sites were slightly less responsive than usual.

Both illustrations involve contracts that have clearly been breached. In neither case, however, has the breach led to an obvious loss of profit. English law has developed two measures to deal with such cases; namely, the **cost of cure** measure and the **difference in value** measure.

As its name suggests, the cost of cure measure focuses on awarding a sum of money that enables the party to engage someone to cure the breach. In Illustration 16.3, this will mean awarding Uncle Percival the market rate for a decorator to fix the shoddy portions of the work. This measure is most useful where the nature of the breach makes it relatively straightforward to find someone or something on the market that can fix it. It is commonly used in cases involving construction work, the supply of machinery, and so on.

The difference in value measure, in contrast, focuses on awarding the claimant a sum of money equal to the difference in value between what was contracted for and what was actually provided. In Illustration 16.4 above, for example, the sum awarded on a difference in value measure would be the difference in price between the bandwidth contracted for and the bandwidth actually delivered. This measure is particularly useful where it is not feasible for the claimant to procure a cure on the market, for example diamond jewellery in which the stones have blemishes.

Choosing between the measures

In many cases, it will be quite clear from the facts which of these two measures is most appropriate. In other cases, however, the situation may be less clear. Consider the following scenario:

Illustration 16.5

The Twice Brewed Real Ale Society organizes an annual Oktoberfest centred around real ales. They contracted with Core Security to provide bouncers and other security staff. On the day of the event, Core Security provided fewer than half the number of staff they had contracted to provide.

Here, damages could be awarded either on the cost of cure measure (the amount it would have cost the Society to hire extra staff to replace those Core Security failed to provide), or on the difference in value measure (a pro rata reduction in the contract price to reflect the fact that fewer staff were provided). The two figures will rarely be identical. How, then, should the courts decide which of these two figures to award? In practice, courts are influenced by a reluctance to award excessive damages. Two considerations underlie this reluctance. The first is the desire to prevent waste. If the breach is slight, and the cost of cure great, it would be unreasonable for the claimant to insist on having it remedied because this would be wasteful. Secondly, the courts are also reluctant to give a claimant a windfall that is out of proportion to the loss. Once damages have been awarded on the cost of cure measure, the money is the claimant's to use as he or she pleases. It does not actually have to be used to cure the breach. As a result, if it appears that the claimant does not actually intend to use the money to remedy the breach, the courts may award damages on the difference of value measure rather than the cost of cure measure.

The US case of *Jacob & Youngs v Kent*[17] provides a good illustration of these principles in action. Kent was building a substantial mansion in New York State, and engaged Jacob & Youngs Inc to do the building work. The contract provided that the wrought iron pipes used in the plumbing:

> must be well galvanized, lap welded pipe of the grade known as 'standard pipe' of Reading manufacture.

The contractor used Cohoes pipe instead of Reading pipe. Kent argued that he was entitled to the cost of cure by way of damages. Because the plumbing was encased in the walls, curing breach would have required demolishing much of the completed structure. In evidence, it was shown that the oversight was unintentional, and that the two pipes were identical 'in quality, in appearance, in market value and in cost'. The court held that under the circumstances, the appropriate measure would be the difference in value, even though this meant that the claimant would in effect get nothing.

The English position is similar. In *Ruxley Electronics v Forsyth*,[18] the House of Lords cited Cardozo J's decision with approval,[19] and linked it to the nature and purpose of compensatory damages in contract:

> Damages are designed to compensate for an established loss and not to provide a gratuitous benefit to the aggrieved party from which it follows that the reasonableness of an award of damages is to be linked directly to the loss sustained. If it is unreasonable in a particular case to award the cost of reinstatement it must be because the loss sustained does not extend to the need to reinstate.[20]

The decision of Oliver J in the High Court in *Radford v De Froberville*[21] provides a good illustration of the type of factors that the courts look at in deciding whether it is 'unreasonable in a particular case to award the cost of reinstatement'.

17. *Jacob & Youngs Inc v Kent*, 230 NY 239 (1921).
18. [1996] AC 344 (HL). The facts of the case are discussed in greater detail in the next section.
19. Ibid, 366 (Lord Lloyd).   20. Ibid, 357 (Lord Jauncey).
21. [1977] 1 WLR 1262 (Ch).

Case in depth: *Radford v De Froberville* [1977] 1 WLR 1262 (Ch)

The claimants in this case owned land. Part was occupied by a house that had been subdivided into flats and was tenanted, and part was undeveloped. A portion of the undeveloped land was sold, with the contract requiring the purchaser to erect a fence on the boundary. The purchaser sold the land on without doing so, and the claimants sued for the cost of cure.

In court, the defendant's lawyers conceded that the contract had been breached, but argued that damages should only be awarded according to the difference in value. On the facts of the case, this would have resulted in an award of nominal damages as the presence or absence of the fence made no difference to the value of the land.

There was some authority in support of the defendant's position. In the earlier case of *Wigsell v School for the Indigent Blind*,[22] the defendants had purchased a plot from the claimants intending to build a school for the blind on it. The contract required them to build a wall around the plot. The defendants ultimately built neither the school nor the wall. The claimant sued for breach of contract, claiming the cost of building the wall.[23] The court in that case had held that on the facts, the damage suffered by the claimant was not the cost of erecting the wall, but the difference in the value of the land without the wall.

In *Radford* itself, however, Oliver J held that it was the cost of cure that was the appropriate measure, rather than the difference in value. In coming to this conclusion, and distinguishing *Wigsell*, Oliver J placed particular emphasis on three questions that he thought a judge should ask in deciding whether to award the cost of cure:

> First, am I satisfied on the evidence that the plaintiff has a genuine and serious intention of doing the work? Secondly, is the carrying out of the work on his own land a reasonable thing for the plaintiff to do? Thirdly, does it make any difference that the plaintiff is not personally in occupation of the land but desires to do the work for the benefit of his tenants?[24]

On the facts, he held that the answer to the first question was 'yes'. The evidence before him suggested that the claimant actually wanted the wall to be built (unlike *Wigsell*, where the evidence pointed in the opposite direction). This meant that the starting point should be the cost of cure:

> I am entirely satisfied that the plaintiff genuinely wants this work done and that he intends to expend any damages awarded on carrying it out. In my judgment, therefore, the damages ought to be measured by the cost of the work, unless there are some other considerations which point to a different measure.[25]

Likewise, it was entirely reasonable for the claimant to build a wall, as its absence was causing inconvenience in the form of weeds and trespassers. Nor did it matter that he did not occupy the property himself, and was not contractually obliged to his tenants to have the wall built. All that mattered was 'the genuineness of his intentions'.[26] Accordingly, the court held that it was appropriate on the facts to award the cost of cure.

---

22. (1882) 8 QBD 357.

23. The history of the litigation was somewhat complicated. Earlier proceedings in the case before the Exchequer Division are reported at (1880) 43 LT 218.

24. [1977] 1 WLR 1262, 1283.   25. Ibid, 1284.   26. Ibid, 1285.

Subjective and objective elements

As the decision in *Radford* suggests, the question of whether or not to award the cost of cure depends on both subjective and objective considerations. Courts will look at whether the claimant intended to actually remedy the breach (which necessarily entails examining his *subjective* intention), as well as whether this was *objectively* reasonable in the light of the effects of the breach.

In relation to subjective intention, the editors of *Chitty on Contract* have identified three types of circumstances in which courts will generally award damages on the cost of cure measure:

(i)   the claimant has actually had the work done; or

(ii) he undertakes to have it done . . .; or

(iii) he shows a 'sufficient intention' to have the work done if he receives damages on this basis: the claimant's subjective intention is relevant.[27]

In relation to objective reasonableness, the courts look to the effect of the breach and the cost of remedying it relative to the benefit. In *East Ham Corp v Bernard Sunley & Sons Ltd*,[28] the stone panelling on the outside of a newly constructed school fell down because it had been poorly fixed by the contractors. In an action by the owners of the school against the contractors for breach, the House of Lords held that given the circumstances, 'it could not be disputed that it was reasonable for the appellants to insist upon reinstatement'.[29] Likewise, in *Jones v Herxheimer*,[30] a tenant had left rented premises in very poor shape. The landlord had them redecorated, and sued the tenant for the cost of the redecoration. The Court of Appeal held that it would be appropriate to award the cost of cure, as the repairs 'were no more than was reasonably necessary to make the rooms fit for occupation or re-letting for residential purposes'.[31]

If, however, the cost of cure is out of proportion to the benefit that would be obtained from curing the breach, the court will typically refuse to award it. In *Harrison v Shepherd Homes Ltd*,[32] Shepherd Homes had built 'executive homes' on a former landfill site in Hartlepool. The nature of the site meant that complex piling work had to be undertaken to support the houses. The work was negligently carried out, and several houses suffered cracking. This did not render the houses unfit for occupation, but it made them unmortgageable and in some cases unsaleable. The houseowners sued for the cost of cure. In evidence, it was found that curing the breach would have required the partial demolition of the houses, followed by work that was so extensive that its cost would exceed the market value of the houses in their undamaged state. Ramsey J held that this would be unreasonable. The defects in the houses were only cosmetic, and the main loss suffered by the claimants (apart from the cost of remedying the cosmetic cracks) was 'that the investment in the house as the main asset for most of the claimants has become less valuable than the asset in which they invested'.[33] This was best remedied by awarding the difference in value.

---

27. Hugh Beale (ed), *Chitty on Contracts* (32nd edn, Sweet & Maxwell 2015) 26-036.

28. [1966] AC 406 (HL).   29. Ibid, 434 (Lord Cohen).   30. [1950] 2 KB 106 (CA).

31. Ibid, 117–18 (Jenkins LJ).

32. [2011] EWHC 1811 (TCC), upheld on appeal [2012] EWCA Civ 904.   33. Ibid, [277].

Similarly, in *Sunrock Aircraft Corp Ltd v Scandinavian Airlines System Denmark-Norway-Sweden*,[34] an aircraft lease agreement required the lessee to return the aircraft without 'scab patches' on the frame. Scab patches are a result of a particular way of repairing surface damage to the aircraft skin. The other way of carrying out repairs is a flush repair. By requiring that the aircraft be returned without scab patches, the lease had in effect stipulated that surface damage must be repaired through flush repairs. One of the leased planes was returned with two scab patches, and Sunrock sued SAS for the cost of replacing them with flush repairs. The Court of Appeal held that it would be unreasonable to award the cost of cure. Scab patches had no effect on the aircraft's performance or value, and it was found in evidence that it would have been 'extraordinary' not to find scab patches on aircraft of that age.[35] As a result, Sunrock could only recover damages on the basis of the difference in value which, in practice, meant that it could only recover nominal damages.[36]

Loss of amenity and disappointed expectations

The three measures we have just examined, namely loss of profit, difference in value, and cost of cure, are between them sufficient to provide for the vast majority of cases. Nevertheless, they are inadequate in a small number of cases, typically involving consumer contracts. Consider the following illustration:

> ### Illustration 16.6
>
> Simon Allan is a fan of the All Blacks, the New Zealand Rugby Team. He is having his bathroom redone, and he decides he wants the tiles on one wall arranged in a mosaic of the flag of New Zealand. When the work is finished, he is appalled to discover that the builders have put in a mosaic of the flag of Australia instead. He contacts the builders who apologize profusely, but refuse to fix it. Remedying the breach will require removing a shower and plumbing in addition to all the tiles, at a cost of £12,250. This is more than what the whole redecoration cost originally.

Here, a court is unlikely to hold that it would be reasonable to award the cost of cure, as the benefit is very slight compared to the cost. At the same time, the difference in value is likely to be zero, leaving Simon with only nominal damages. The courts appear to have little difficulty with such an outcome in commercial transactions. They have, however, tended to take a more generous approach to consumers, awarding damages under the sui generis head of '**loss of amenity**'.

The decisions of the House of Lords in *Farley v Skinner*[37] and *Ruxley Electronics v Forsyth*[38] are illustrative. *Ruxley Electronics* arose out of the breach of a contract to build a swimming pool. Ruxley had contracted to build a swimming pool for Forsyth to a

---

34. [2007] EWCA Civ 882, [2007] 2 Lloyd's Rep 612.   35. Ibid, [34] (Thomas LJ).
36. Ibid, [35].   37. [2001] UKHL 49, [2002] 2 AC 732.   38. [1996] AC 344 (HL).

depth of 7 ft 6 in.[39] The pool they actually built, however, was only 6 ft 9 in deep. Forsyth refused to pay. When Ruxley sued for the contract price, Forsyth counter-claimed for the cost of cure.

The cost of cure would have been £21,560, a substantial increase over the actual contract price of £17,797.40. The House of Lords took the view that the cost of cure would not be reasonable because, first, it was out of proportion to the benefit gained (thus failing the objective element of the test) and, secondly, because the evidence suggested that Forsyth had no intention of using the money to remedy the breach (thus failing the subjective element of the test). The difference in value measure, however, would have led to an award of nominal damages. The trial judge tried to deal with this by awarding £2,500 for 'loss of amenity', to compensate Forsyth for the fact that the contract was for the provision of a pleasurable amenity (a pool) and part of the pleasure had been lost.

The House of Lords held that this was the correct approach, but disagreed as to why. Lord Mustill suggested that in making such an award, the court was giving recognition to the idea of a 'consumer surplus', an economic concept going back to Alfred Marshall whose relevance to consumer contracts had previously been discussed by contract scholars.[40] The breach deprived the claimant of a portion of the consumer surplus he would have gained from proper performance. Damages should compensate the claimant for this loss. Lord Lloyd, in contrast, took the view that the idea of 'loss of amenity' was too restrictive. Although he stopped short of articulating a 'final answer', he made it clear that the better position would be to hold that the damages were awarded for 'disappointed expectations', rather than merely the loss of a part of a pleasurable amenity.

Subsequent decisions have generally applied the rule in *Ruxley* in the narrower loss of amenity form, rather than the broader 'disappointed expectations' form suggested by Lord Lloyd. In *Farley v Skinner*,[41] Farley was considering purchasing a large country estate near Gatwick airport. He engaged Skinner, a surveyor, to survey the property and instructed him to focus in particular on whether it was seriously affected by aircraft noise, as he did not want to buy a property on a flight path. Skinner reported that it was 'unlikely that the property will suffer greatly from such noise, although some planes will inevitably cross the area'. In point of fact, the property lay along a 'stacking' course, which aircraft took while waiting for a landing slot. This meant that it was very drastically affected by aircraft noise at certain times of the day.

Unlike *Ruxley Electronics v Forsyth*, where a cure was possible but was held to be unreasonable, the effects of the breach in this case were impossible to cure. It is hardly possible for two private parties to alter the noise levels emanating from Gatwick airport. The difference in value measure would, as in *Ruxley Electronics*, have resulted in

---

39. The original contract provided for the pool to be 6 ft 6 in deep at the deep end. On Forsyth's request, the contractors agreed to increase the depth to 7 ft 6 in free of charge. The question of whether this variation was a binding obligation supported by consideration, or a gratuitous promise which was not supported by consideration and hence was unenforceable, appears never to have been argued.

40. D Harris, A Ogus, and J Phillips, 'Contract Remedies and the Consumer Surplus' (1979) 95 LQR 581.

41. [2001] UKHL 49, [2002] 2 AC 732.

the award of nominal damages, as the price at which the house had been purchased was a fair value for a property affected by noise from overhead aircraft. The House of Lords held that the appropriate remedy was damages for loss of amenity. The trial judge had quantified this at £10,000 and whilst the House of Lords thought this figure was on the high side, it was not so excessive as to warrant interfering with it.

The loss of chance measure

The measures of loss we have studied thus far must be proven on the balance of probabilities. Whilst this rule functions perfectly well in most situations, there are cases in which it breaks down. Consider the following illustration:

Illustration 16.7

Florence Achieng is a professional photographer based in Liverpool. In September, Liverpool City Council issues a tender for an event photographer for all events in the course of the following year. Interested persons are required to submit a sealed bid, together with a portfolio of photographs, by 15 October. Florence intends to submit a bid, and approaches a local lab to prepare high-quality prints of some of her work. She tells them that it is for the tender, and they agree to deliver the prints by 7 October. It transpires that the lab has taken on too much work, and the prints are not ready on the 7th, and are only made available to Florence on the 17th. Because of the delay, Florence has been unable to submit the bid, and loses the chance to win the tender. She estimates that she would have made a profit of £10,250 had she won, and that because of the quality of her work, she stood at least a 60 per cent chance of success.

A case such as this poses a prima facie conceptual difficulty. The claimant has no realistic way of establishing that her bid would have won. She can prove that she put in a competitive bid, but not that it would have been successful. To leave the party without a remedy, however, would be commercially questionable. English law deals with situations of this type by giving judges the ability to award compensation for the **loss of chance** to make a profit.

Loss of chance damages are awarded where profit is contingent on the actions or decisions of a third party. The law requires judges to adopt a two-stage approach. In the first stage, the court asks whether the chance of making a profit was real rather than fanciful[42] (or, in an alternative formulation, substantial rather than speculative[43]). If the claimant can show on the balance of probabilities that it was, the court proceeds to the second stage, quantifying the damages.[44] Here, the court begins with the loss

---

42. *Les Laboratoires Servier v Apotex Inc* [2008] EWHC 2347 (Ch), [2009] FSR 3, [5] (Norris J).

43. *Allied Maples Group Ltd v Simmons & Simmons* [1995] 1 WLR 1602 (CA), 1614 (Stuart-Smith LJ).

44. Note that this does not mean that the chance of success must be more than 50 per cent. A 30 per cent chance of making a profit will be recoverable, as long as you can on the balance of probabilities establish that the 30 per cent chance was real and substantial, rather than fanciful or speculative. See eg *Dixon v Clement Jones Solicitors (a firm)* [2004] EWCA Civ 1005. See also *Allied Maples Group Ltd v Simmons & Simmons* [1995] 1 WLR 1602 (CA), discussed in more detail later in the chapter.

suffered by the claimant, which will typically be either the profit she failed to make as in Illustration 16.7, or a loss which she might have avoided. The court then proportionately discounts that figure to reflect the fact that while the claimant had a reasonable chance of winning the tender, it was far from certain that she actually would have succeeded. Thus in Illustration 16.7, the claimant would have made a profit of £10,250 had she won the tender. However, she only had a 60 per cent chance of winning the tender. The court will therefore award her 60 per cent of £10,250, which comes to £6,150. The assessment of the probability of success as 60, or 50, or 70 per cent, is not a matter of scientific precision, but depends rather on the judge's overall assessment of the facts.

This approach has been applied in a wide variety of situations. In *Chaplin v Hicks*,[45] the claimant had entered a contest organized by the defendant to be selected as an actress on an annual stipend. She placed very highly in the first round, and had qualified for the second round, a personal interview. A letter was sent to her inviting her to the interview, but it did not reach her until after the interview. The defendant refused to give her an opportunity to reschedule her interview, and she sued arguing that the defendant was in breach. Breach was conceded, and the case was argued solely on the issue of damages.[46] The defendant's lawyers argued that damages were incapable of assessment because of the number of contingencies involved. The Court of Appeal rejected this argument. What had been lost was a valuable right, which should be quantified in the ordinary way (which, in 1911, meant asking a jury to do so).[47]

Allied Maples Group Ltd v Simmons and Simmons[48] involved a commercial loss of chance claim which, unlike *Chaplin v Hicks*, related to the chance to avoid a loss, rather than the chance to make a profit. A firm of solicitors had agreed to provide professional services in relation to a corporate takeover. Early drafts of the takeover agreement included a warranty from the seller of the business that the company being taken over:

> has no existing or contingent liabilities in respect of any properties previously occupied by it or in which it owned or held any interest, including, without limitation, leasehold premises, assigned or otherwise disposed of.[49]

In the course of drafting, this clause was dropped and replaced with a narrower clause covering fewer liabilities. After the takeover was completed, a number of liabilities came to light which would have been covered by the first clause but not the second. AMG sued Simmons and Simmons, arguing that they were in breach of contract for failing to consider the effect of the change of language. Had they advised AMG of the consequences, AMG would have had a chance to renegotiate the clause with the

---

45. [1911] 2 KB 786 (CA).

46. It is unclear why the defendant did not raise the issue of whether a contract was formed at all (in particular, the issue of consideration), and the issue of whether the failure to reschedule the interview was a breach (see the reference in Vaughan Williams LJ's judgment at [1911] 2 KB 786, 790).

47. Ibid, 793 (Vaughan Williams LJ), 796 (Fletcher Moulton LJ). The fact that the issue of quantification was left to the jury, rather than to the judges, appears to have played a role in persuading the judges to hold as they did. See the section 'Practice in context: proof and loss of chance damages' later in this section.

48. [1995] 1 WLR 1602 (CA).   49. Ibid, 1606.

seller and obtain something closer to the level of protection afforded by the original warranty.

The case came to the Court of Appeal on a preliminary issue of liability. Two points were stressed in argument. First, it was argued that *Chaplin v Hicks* related to the loss of a right, whereas here there had been no right lost. Secondly, it was argued that to succeed on the balance of probabilities, the claimant must show that the chance of success would have been at least 50 per cent. The Court of Appeal rejected both points, and held that Simmons and Simmons were liable to AMG for the loss of a chance to avoid the loss they suffered. Although *Chaplin v Hicks* itself related to a 'valuable right', the principle in that case had broader applicability. There was 'no difference in principle between the chance of gaining a benefit and the chance of avoiding a liability'.[50] Equally, there was no reason in principle why the chance of success had to be 50 per cent. The only requirement was that it must be substantial, and it could be substantial without reaching the threshold of 50 per cent.[51]

 Practice in context: proof and loss of chance damages

The position of loss of chance damages is peculiar. If a court awards damages on the basis of a 30 per cent chance, it acknowledges the possibility that the claimant would have made no gain even if the contract had been properly performed. A court awarding loss of chance damages is therefore, in effect, implicitly conceding that in purely monetary terms, there is a distinct possibility that the claimant will be left better off as a result of the breach than he or she would have been if the contract was performed. In *Chaplin v Hicks*, this was justified on the basis that the legal harm was the loss of a valuable right, namely, the right to be considered in the second round, and that the loss of this right was a wrong regardless of whether or not the claimant would actually have won the second round. This does not, however, account for the outcome in *Allied Maples Group Ltd v Simmons and Simmons* or other more recent cases.

The Court of Appeal in *Chaplin v Hicks* laid particular weight on the fact that 'chance' and 'probability' are synonymous, and hence that a loss of chance was inherently linked to the probability of success.[52] The modern association of 'chance' with 'speculation' rather than 'probability' obscures this link, and makes the terminology of 'loss of chance' damages somewhat more confusing than it originally was. This link means that the award of damages for the loss of a chance does not in any way erode the ordinary requirement that a party seeking to recover damages must establish on the balance of probabilities that he would have made a profit of the amount claimed. Loss of chance damages are not a way of claiming for speculative loss, a fact which is expressly emphasized by the first stage in the two-stage process discussed earlier. A better way of thinking about this particular measure, and the type of loss it is designed to cover, is to regard the damages as being awarded for the loss of the opportunity to engage in a process, with the quantum of damages being linked both to the claimant's probability of success in the process and to the profits that would have been made had the claimant been successful.

→

50. Ibid, 1611 (Stuart-Smith LJ).   51. Ibid, 1612 (Stuart-Smith LJ).
52. [1911] 2 KB 786, 798 (Farwell LJ).

→

Thinking about loss of chance damages in this way makes it clear that a party claiming damages for the loss of a chance must still prove on the balance of probabilities, first, that he had a realistic chance of succeeding in the process in which he has been unable to participate and, secondly, that success in that process would have to led to him making a profit (or avoiding a loss). It also makes it clear that the party must be able to express both the likelihood and the profits that would have followed on success as quantifiable amounts. A claimant who fails to do so will be unable to recover anything.

The existence of this type of damages is, thus, best understood in pragmatic terms. Contracts are frequently entered into by persons in contexts similar to Illustration 16.7. If loss of chance damages were not available, parties to such contracts would in effect be left remediless in the event of breach. From a pragmatic point of view, therefore, the case for some form of remedy is strong, and loss of chance damages are the remedy which English courts have devised.

16.2.4 Wasted expenditure and the reliance interest

The various approaches to quantifying damages we have examined so far have all sought to put the claimant in the position in which he would have been had the contract been fully performed. But English law also incorporates a very different approach to quantifying damages, which seeks to put the claimant in the position in which he would have been had the contract never been formed. This is termed the *reliance interest*. Much as the focus of the expectation interest is on unrealized gain, the focus of the reliance interest is on *wasted expenditure* which the party 'incurred in reliance on his expectation that the defendant would perform his undertaking', and which has come to be wasted as a result of the defendant's breach.[53] Consider the following example:

Illustration 16.8

Reham Farby buys a used lorry from Trustus Autos, which she intends to use in her transport business. Trustus contractually warrant that the lorry 'fully complies with all relevant roadworthiness standards applicable to Heavy Goods Vehicles'. Because of the warranty, she does not have the vehicle's condition independently assessed prior to purchasing it.

Reham has the lorry repainted in her company's livery, and installs her company's standard equipment, including a radio control system, GPS, and a hydraulic lift to load and remove heavy items from the lorry. She then commissions a 'first use inspection', a safety check which HGVs must undergo before they can be used. The lorry fails the inspection. The inspector finds that the lorry falls so far short of current roadworthiness standards that it is unlikely to ever be able to be commercially usable.

53. H Beale (ed), *Chitty on Contracts* (32nd edn, Sweet & Maxwell 2015), 26-022.

A significant part of the loss which Reham has suffered as a result of the breach in this case is the money she has spent on installing equipment in the lorry, and in repainting it. This is not a loss which expectation damages can cover. It is precisely this type of loss that reliance damages seek to cover.

Recoverable expenditure

Broadly speaking, two types of wasted expenditure are recoverable through reliance damages. First, a party can recover expenditure incurred in the course of performing its part of the contract, or preparing to perform. In *Anglia Television Ltd v Reed*,[54] Anglia Television had engaged Robert Reed, an American actor, to play the leading role in a TV film they were producing. The agreement was struck over the phone on 30 August 1968. Reed agreed to travel to England for filming between 9 September and 11 October 1968. After the agreement was concluded, however, Reed discovered that he had already agreed to act in a play in the US on some of those days. On 3 September, Reed's agents acting on his behalf repudiated the contract. Anglia attempted to find a substitute, but were unable to do so. On 11 September, they accepted the repudiation and cancelled the film.[55] They then sued Reed for damages for breach of contract. On the facts, it would have been almost impossible for Anglia to establish on the balance of probabilities the precise quantum of profits they might have made. They therefore claimed instead for the expenditure they had wasted, including the fees they had paid the members of the production crew, much of which they could not recover. The Court of Appeal unanimously held that this expenditure was recoverable through reliance damages.

Wasted expenditure can also cover money which was not incurred in order to perform the contract. Consider Illustration 16.8 earlier. The money Reham spent on repainting and equipping the vehicle in that case was not spent to perform her obligations under the contract with Trustus. Her only obligation under that contract was to pay for the lorry. Nevertheless, it is an expenditure that has been wasted as a result of Trustus's breach, and is recoverable through reliance damages. In *Bunny v Hopkinson*,[56] a plot of land was sold to a purchaser, who built a number of houses on it. The seller turned out not to have good title to some of the land, and the purchaser was evicted from four of the houses. He sued for breach, and sought to recover not just a proportionate part of the original purchase price, but also the value of the houses he had lost. Sir John Romilly MR held that he could recover the amount he sought, as 'the measure of the damages upon these covenants includes the amount expended in converting the land into the purposes for which it was sold'.[57]

Similarly, in *Manson v Burningham*,[58] the claimant had purchased a typewriter which she had subsequently had repaired and overhauled at considerable expense.[59] As it transpired, the typewriter had been stolen and had to be returned to the original

---

54. [1972] 1 QB 60 (CA).

55. The legal rules in relation to repudiatory breach are discussed in Chapter 15 ('Breach of contract'). As you should recall from that chapter, an innocent party has the right to either choose to accept the repudiation and terminate the contract, or to affirm the contract and continue to perform its part of the bargain. Anglia Television in this case chose the former option, as it was entitled to do.

56. (1859) 27 Beav 565 (Ch).   57. Ibid, 567–8.   58. [1949] 2 KB 545 (CA).

59. The purchase price was £20, and the cost of repair was 11*l* 10*s*.

owner.[60] She sued the seller, claiming repayment of the purchase price as well as the sum spent on overhaul. The seller admitted liability for repaying the purchase price,[61] but argued that he was not liable for the amount spent on overhauling the machine. It was found in evidence that having the typewriter overhauled was 'the ordinary and natural' thing to do. The court held that the claimant could recover the money she had expended on the overhaul, as its wastage was an ordinary and natural consequence of the seller's breach.

The key issue in determining whether a particular wasted expense is whether, first, the *incurrence* of the expenditure and, secondly, the *wastage* of that expenditure was within the reasonable contemplation of the parties.[62] The time when the expenses were incurred is irrelevant as long as the expenses and their probable wastage were within the parties' reasonable contemplation.[63] The *accrual* of an expenditure does not have to follow from the formation of the contract. It is its *wastage* that needs to follow from the breach. This was the case in *Anglia Television v Reed* itself, where some of the production crew had already been engaged before the contract with Reed was formed. Reed accepted liability for breach, but argued that he should not be liable for fees payable to persons engaged before he contracted with Anglia, as those fees would have accrued even if he had never been engaged. The Court of Appeal rejected his argument, holding that Reed must have known that the expenses would be wasted if he broke his contract. As long as the wastage was within his reasonable contemplation, he would be liable.[64]

There is one important type of expenditure that is not recoverable through the reliance interest; namely, sums paid by the claimant to the defendant under the contract, such as the purchase price, or a deposit. The remedy of recovering the price is much more tightly circumscribed than the remedy of reliance damages, and requires not just a breach but what is called a total failure of consideration. The legal rules pertaining to this are discussed in Chapter 17.

Choosing between expectation and reliance interests

A party who has suffered a breach of contract is, in principle, free to claim either expectation damages or reliance damages. Cases and commentary often describe this as a 'right of election' vested in the claimant. It is, however, unclear whether this language is still appropriate. In *Morris-Garner v One Step (Support) Ltd*,[65] the Supreme Court rejected the language of election on the basis that it was for the court to decide what measure of damages was appropriate, which it would do by first identifying the loss, and then quantifying it in monetary terms. The court in that case was concerned with different ways of measuring expectation damages, rather than the choice between expectation and reliance damages. However, the underlying logic of the decision

---

60. Under the *nemo dat* principle, which is discussed in connection with the law of misrepresentation and mistake in Chapter 11 ('Untrue statements').
61. The term breached was the warranty as to title which is an implied term in contracts for the sale of goods. See the discussion in Chapter 8 ('Filling the gaps').
62. *Anglia Television Ltd v Reed* [1972] 1 QB 60 (CA).
63. See the discussion in *Lloyd v Stanbury* [1971] 1 WLR 535, 546–7. Older cases holding the contrary, such as *Hodges v Earl of Litchfield* (1835) 1 Bing (NC) 492, are no longer good law.
64. [1972] 1 QB 60, 64 (Lord Denning MR).   65. [2018] UKSC 20, [36] (Lord Reed).

arguably also applies to the latter, and several other courts, including the High Court of Australia[66] and the Commercial Court,[67] have also recently expressed scepticism about the suggestion that a claimant can 'elect' to claim either expectation or reliance damages. A claim for wasted expenditure, on this understanding, simply reflects a 'rebuttable presumption' that the value of the benefit a party expects to derive under a contract is at least equal to the amount it has spent.[68]

Either way, it is established law that the courts will not allow a party to recover on the reliance interest under certain circumstances. Two of these are of particular importance. The first is where doing so will let the party recover more than it would have done had the contract been properly performed. This limitation is of particular importance where the innocent party would not have made a profit under the breached contract. In such cases, the claimant will usually be allowed to recover no more than his expectation loss. This was the case in *PJ Spillings (Builders) Ltd v Bonus Flooring Ltd*.[69] PJ Spillings was a contractor on a building project, and had engaged Bonus as a subcontractor for part of the work. Spillings terminated its agreement with Bonus, in a manner that was held to constitute a breach of contract. Bonus sought to recover compensation on the reliance interest. In evidence, it was shown that Bonus would have made a loss on the contract if it had been fully performed by both sides. The High Court held that under these circumstances, reliance damages were not available as they would lead to the claimant recovering more than he would have made had the contract been performed.[70]

The second is where the expenditure would have been wasted even if the contract had been properly performed. In *C&P Haulage Co Ltd v Middleton*,[71] the claimant had installed equipment in the defendant's garage which he occupied under a licence. Under the terms of the licence, it became the defendant's property and had to be left on the premises on termination. The licence was terminable on one month's notice, but the defendant ejected the claimant from the premises without giving notice, in breach of contract. The claimant sued for breach, claiming the cost of the equipment and its installation as wasted expenses. The Court of Appeal held that the claimant could only recover nominal damages, because he would have been in the same position even if the contract had been terminated properly.

A final point to consider is whether it is possible to recover compensation for both expectation and reliance losses. The legal position is not entirely clear. On the one hand, there have been express statements in a number of cases to the effect that claimants must choose, and cannot recover both, including in *Anglia Television v Reed*. This question was directly at issue in *Cullinane v British 'Rema' Manufacturing Co Ltd*.[72] The claimant had purchased equipment from the defendants, which was warranted to produce six tonnes per hour. In reality, it produced considerably less, and the claimant

---

66. *Commonwealth of Australia v Amann Aviation Pty Ltd* (1992) 174 CLR 64.

67. *Omak Maritime Ltd v Mamola Challenger Shipping Co Ltd (The Mamola Challenger)* [2010] EWHC 2026 (Comm), [2011] 1 Lloyd's Rep 47.

68. *Royal Devon and Exeter NHS Foundation Trust v ATOS IT Services UK Ltd* [2017] EWHC 2197 (TCC), [58].

69. [2008] EWHC 1516 (QB). The rationale is considered in some detail in the Canadian case of *Bowlay Logging v Domtar* [1978] 4 WWR 105 (Supreme Court of British Columbia).

70. Ibid, [14]–[25].   71. [1983] 1 WLR 1461 (CA).   72. [1954] 1 QB 292 (CA).

sued. The claimant sought to recover the money spent installing the equipment, as well as the lost profit for the useful life of the machinery. The Court of Appeal held by a 2:1 majority (with a dissent from Morris LJ) that he could claim either the wasted expenditure or the lost profit, but not both.

The correctness of this approach has been questioned by a number of authors, who have pointed out that the courts have in fact permitted the recovery of both in a number of cases. *Robinson v Harman*[73] itself is arguably an example, given that the court in that case permitted recovery of the legal expenses (and, hence, reliance loss) as well as the lost profit.[74] A better understanding of the rule is that advanced by the editors of *Chitty on Contract*, who have suggested that the true legal position is one against double recovery: the claimant should not be allowed to recover his profits as well as the money he would have spent to make his profit. This means that a claimant who recovers reliance expenditure will not be able to recover his *gross* profit, but will in contrast be able to recover his *net* profit (ie his gross profit less both the cost of performance and reliance expenditure).[75]

Such a rule is more consistent with the cases than the much more sweeping statement in *Cullinane*, and arguably more accurately represents the true legal position. In the *Mamola Challenger*,[76] Teare J held that it was an error to regard reliance and expectation damages as 'two separate and independent claims which could not be "mixed"'.[77] Instead, both should be seen as reflecting the principle in *Robinson v Harman*, of compensating the party affected by a breach for the loss suffered as a result of the breach.[78] Returning to Illustration 16.8, then, it would appear that Reham would be able to recover both the wasted expenditure and any lost profit caused by her inability to use the lorry, as long as the lost profit is calculated by deducting not just the lorry's running expenses, but also the expenditure claimed as a reliance loss.

16.2.5 **The hypothetical bargain measure**

> **Illustration 16.9**
>
> Consider the following scenario:
>
> > Thelma is a software programmer. She writes a program to make websites more resistant to hacking. She releases the program online, without charge and under an open source licence. The licence specifies that the program cannot be incorporated into or bundled with any commercial product. It can only be bundled with free, open-source software. Six months later, she discovers that Prophet, a large multinational company, has incorporated her program into a commercial web server it produces.

---

73. (1848) 1 Ex 850.   74. See the discussion in section 16.2.1.
75. H Beale (ed), *Chitty on Contracts* (32nd edn, Sweet & Maxwell 2015) 26-029.
76. *Omak Maritime Ltd v Mamola Challenger Shipping Co Ltd (The Mamola Challenger)* [2010] EWHC 2026 (Comm), [2011] 1 Lloyd's Rep 47.
77. Ibid, [65].   78. Ibid, [42].

A software licence is a contract. Prophet's access to Thelma's program is subject to the terms of the licence, which constitutes the contract between them. It has breached the contract by using the program in a way that the licence prohibited. Yet it is hard to see what remedy Thelma can get. She did not charge for the software, and has therefore suffered no loss compensable under expectation interest. The expenses she incurred would have been incurred regardless of breach, so reliance interest is also of little or no assistance.

Cases like these are dealt with using a different measure of damages, called 'hypothetical bargain damages', or *Wrotham Park* damages after the case of *Wrotham Park Estate Co v Parkside Homes*[79] in which they were first awarded. In some cases where a defendant has breached a binding undertaking, the court will award the claimant damages computed not with reference to the pecuniary loss the breach has caused, but with reference to the amount which the claimant would have hypothetically charged the defendant to waive that undertaking.

Hypothetical bargain damages are a relatively new addition to the law's arsenal of remedies, and their scope and purpose were for a long time the subject of significant controversy. In *Morris-Garner v One Step (Support) Ltd*,[80] the Supreme Court settled most of these controversies, but in doing so substantially altered the legal position on when these damages are available, and why they are granted.

Hypothetical bargain damages are now awarded in two circumstances. First, they can be awarded at the court's discretion, in lieu of an injunction. This ground is now relatively uncontroversial, and is discussed in greater detail in Chapter 17 along with injunctions. The second—and, for our present purposes, more important—circumstance in which these damages are awarded is when the breach relates to a right which is itself a valuable asset, such that its breach will lead to an identifiable loss even if there is no pecuniary loss.[81]

Illustration 16.9 is an example of precisely such a right. Thelma seeks to control the way in which her program is resold. Although this right to control is obviously valuable, no pecuniary loss flows from its breach. Nevertheless, it is clear that she has lost something as a result of the breach. It is circumstances such as these that the second ground for the award of hypothetical bargain damages is intended to cover. In *Experience Hendrix LLC v PPX Enterprises Inc*,[82] the parties had entered into an agreement concerning PPX's rights to commercially exploit music recordings made by the rock musician Jimi Hendrix. The agreement restricted PPX from releasing certain recordings. In breach of this agreement, PPX released recordings which it was prohibited from releasing. Experience Hendrix would not have released the recordings itself, and therefore could not claim damages for loss of profit. It instead sought hypothetical bargain damages calculated with reference to the fee that it would have charged to release Experience Hendrix from the restriction. The Court of Appeal granted an injunction in relation to future releases, and also awarded hypothetical bargain damages in relation to the past, which would be calculated with reference to the royalties PPX itself charged on the records. Similarly, in *Force India Formula One Team Ltd*

79. [1974] 1 WLR 798.   80. [2018] UKSC 20.   81. Ibid, [92]–[93] (Lord Reed JSC).
82. [2003] EWCA Civ 323.

v Aerolab SRL,[83] the defendant had used confidential information belonging to the claimant. The claimant had suffered no loss as a result of the use of confidential information, but nevertheless sought hypothetical bargain damages, which the Court of Appeal awarded.

The circumstances in which hypothetical bargain damages are awarded should not, however, be stretched too far. In *Morris-Garner v One Step (Support) Ltd*,[84] the Supreme Court emphasized that the remedy is a narrow one, which will only be awarded in cases where

> the loss suffered by the claimant is appropriately measured by reference to the economic value of the right which has been breached, considered as an asset.[85]

The defendant in this case was a former director and 50 per cent owner of the claimant company. She had sold her shares in 2006 and entered into a deed with the claimant under which she agreed not to compete with the company for a three-year period. In breach of this agreement, she and her partner set up a company in 2007 whose business was in direct competition with the business of the claimant. The claimant sought hypothetical bargain damages, arguing that damages for loss of profit would be hard to prove. The Supreme Court held that hypothetical bargaining damages would not lie, as the case did not fall into the relatively narrow categories where these damages are available.

In doing so, the Supreme Court was reacting to the expansionary approach to hypothetical bargain damages taken in a series of cases. Some cases took the view that hypothetical bargain damages were restitutionary, and sought to deprive the defendant of a gain which the defendant had made at the claimant's expense.[86] In *One Step* itself, the Court of Appeal suggested that hypothetical bargain damages should be awarded wherever the court thought it just to do so.[87] Approaches such as these, the Supreme Court held, missed the point that the purposes of damages was compensatory, and that hypothetical bargain damages were in substance compensation for the claimant's loss. The court simply awarded damages on a different measure on the basis that the right in question was valuable in and of itself. This would only be true of a small number of rights, 'such as a right to control the use of land, intellectual property or confidential information'. Outside these categories, it was hard to see 'how a hypothetical release fee might be the measure of the claimant's loss'. In relation to a non-compete clause, as in *One Step*, the appropriate measure was the pecuniary loss resulting from the wrongful competition, not a hypothetical bargain measure.[88] The hypothetical release fee might, at best, be used in evidence if it was relevant to the assessment of damages—if, for example, it shed light on the quantum of loss of profit. But it could not itself be a quantification of the loss caused by breach.[89]

---

83. [2013] EWCA Civ 780, [2013] RPC 36. See also the decision at first instance in *Force India Formula One Team Ltd v 1 Malaysia Racing Team Sdn Bhd* [2012] EWHC 616 (Ch), [2012] RPC 29.
84. [2018] UKSC 20.   85. Ibid, [95] (Lord Reed JSC).
86. *Experience Hendrix LLC v PPX Enterprises Inc* [2003] EWCA Civ 323.
87. *One Step (Support) Ltd v Morris-Garner* [2014] EWHC 2213 (QB).
88. [2018] UKSC 20, [93]–[94].   89. Ibid, [94], [95].

16.2.6 **Economic and non-economic harm**

Thus far, we have primarily been discussing situations where the losses caused by breach are pecuniary, that is, economic or monetary in nature. But not all cases fit this template. One of the points about which the Arts Endowment Trust is particularly concerned in Problem 16 is the harm to its reputation. Harm to reputation is different from monetary diminution in the value of tangible assets, or the monetary cost of curing a breach, or the loss of a chance of making a monetary profit. The difference lies in the fact that the focus of the latter three is on things which, conceptually at least, are capable of being measured in money. Reputation, however, is not the sort of thing that is ordinarily bought or sold on a market, and has no obvious monetary value. Can the Arts Endowment Trust recover compensation for the harm to its reputation as easily as it can recover compensation for loss of rent?

In English law, the answer is that it cannot. The general rule is that damages for breach of contract are usually only awarded in relation to pecuniary loss. Non-pecuniary loss, such as harm to reputation, injured feelings, mental distress, and so on, are not the sort of losses or harms with which the law of contract is ordinarily concerned. The classic statement of this rule is the decision of the House of Lords in *Addis v Gramophone Co Ltd*.[90]

Addis was the manager of GCL's business in Calcutta. He was paid a weekly salary and a commission on sales. GCL's London headquarters decided to replace him with a man called Gilpin. The contract of employment gave them the right to fire Addis on six months' notice. In breach of the notice requirement, GCL terminated Addis immediately, and instructed Gilpin to enter the premises and take the business out of Addis's hands. GCL also contacted their Indian bankers directly and told them that Addis was no longer connected with them. The manner of Addis's dismissal had an adverse impact on his reputation, 'importing in the commercial community of Calcutta possible obloquy and permanent loss'.[91] Addis returned to London, and sued for breach of contract.

The case was tried before a civil jury, which awarded him compensation for lost salary and commission, but also for 'the abrupt and oppressive way in which the plaintiff's services were discontinued, and the loss he sustained from the discredit thus thrown upon him'. GCL appealed, and the case reached the House of Lords which held (with a powerful dissent from Lord Collins) that while Addis could recover compensation for lost salary and commission, English law did not permit the award of damages in contract for injured feelings, or even 'for the loss he may sustain from the fact that his having been dismissed of itself makes it more difficult for him to obtain fresh employment'.[92] Contract law awards damages because the terms of a contract have not been complied with. Whether the contract was breached in a civil and polite way or in a rude and nasty way is irrelevant for the purpose of contract damages:[93]

> Is [a] creditor or vendor . . . to have the sum he recovers lessened if he should be shewn to be harsh, grasping, or pitiless, or even insulting, in enforcing his demand, or lessened because the debtor has struggled to pay, has failed because of misfortune, and has been suave, gracious, and apologetic in his refusal? On the other hand, is that sum to

---

90. [1909] AC 488 (HL).   91. Ibid, 504.   92. Ibid, 491 (Lord Loreburn LC).
93. The court did, however, suggest that compensation for such an injury might be available in the tort of defamation. Ibid, 503 (Lord Shaw).

be increased if it should be shewn that the debtor could have paid readily without any embarrassment, but refused with expression of contempt and contumely, from a malicious desire to injure his creditor?[94]

Although this remains the general rule today,[95] subsequent cases have narrowed it both in relation to financial loss and non-pecuniary loss. In relation to financial loss, the House of Lords held in *Malik v BCCI*,[96] discussed in more detail in Chapter 8, that *Addis* did not apply to a breach of the implied term of trust and confidence. If this term was breached in a way that caused reputational damage to the employee, and if that breach made it difficult for the employee to find new employment, they could recover the resulting financial loss.

More pertinently, subsequent cases have also recognized two, relatively narrow, types of circumstances in which the courts will, exceptionally, award compensation for non-pecuniary loss. We have encountered one of these in *Ruxley Electronics* and *Farley v Skinner*. The second type of situation arises where the breach relates to the failure to provide pleasure or enjoyment, the provision of which was an important purpose of the contract. This exception is relatively new, and first began to be applied in the 1970s. Prior to that, the general view, based on 19th-century cases involving railway journeys,[97] was that damages for disappointment were not recoverable in an action for breach of contract. In *Jarvis v Swans Tours*,[98] however, the Court of Appeal reconsidered the older cases, and held that it would in some circumstances be appropriate to award damages for disappointment.

The claimant in *Jarvis* had booked a Swiss winter sports holiday with Swans Tours. The package was called 'Swans houseparty in Mörlialp', and promised several parties, a number of themed evenings, and several other amenities. Most of these were not provided or, if they were, were of a much lower quality than had been agreed. The key question for the court was the quantum of damages. The High Court awarded damages on the basis of difference in value. Because Jarvis had only received about half of what he contracted for, he was held entitled to damages equal to half the amount he had paid. On appeal, Lord Denning in the Court of Appeal held that the correct measure of damages was for the disappointment he suffered which, in this case, would be 'the loss of entertainment and enjoyment which he was promised, and which he did not get'.[99]

In *Watts v Morrow*,[100] Bingham LJ attempted to systematize the evolving case law by identifying two circumstances in which disappointment damages are available. First, they are available if 'the very object of the contract is to provide pleasure, relaxation, peace of mind, or freedom from molestation' but, due to the defendant's breach, 'the contrary result is procured instead'. Secondly, they are also recoverable 'for physical inconvenience and discomfort caused by the breach and mental suffering directly related to that inconvenience and discomfort'.[101] The current leading authority on this point is the decision of the House of Lords in *Farley v Skinner*.[102] The House of Lords in

94. Ibid, 496–7 (Lord Atkinson).

95. See *Johnson v Unisys Ltd* [2001] UKHL 13; *Edwards v Chesterfield Royal Hospital Foundation NHS Trust* [2011] UKSC 58.

96. [1998] AC 20 (HL).

97. See eg *Hamlin v Great Northern Railway Co* (1856) 1 H & N 408; *Hobbs v London & South Western Railway Co* (1875) LR 10 QB 111.

98. [1973] 1 QB 233 (CA).   99. Ibid, 238.   100. [1991] 1 WLR 1421 (CA).

101. Ibid, 1445.   102. [2001] UKHL 49, [2002] 2 AC 732.

this case accepted Bingham LJ's two categories, but clarified that the 'very object' test did not mean that the contract should be primarily or exclusively about pleasure. It was sufficient if one of the major or important purposes of the contract was the provision of 'pleasure, relaxation or peace of mind'.[103]

Although, on its face, these cases widen the ends to which damages will be awarded in English law, they only do so for consumers. It is difficult to find any non-consumer case in which such damages have been awarded, and the courts have expressly stated that these exceptions should not

> include any case where the object of the contract was not comfort or pleasure, or the relief of discomfort, but simply carrying on a commercial activity with a view to profit.[104]

The exception to the general rule in *Addis v Gramophone Co* is thus primarily a recognition that non-economic motives play a very significant role in consumer transactions, unlike commercial transactions. As a result, a merchant who provides a consumer with shoddy service will therefore be required to pay compensation even if no economic loss can be demonstrated.

16.3 Limiting damages: causation, remoteness, and mitigation

As we have seen, the law of contract remedies is about compensating the victim of breach for the harm done by the breach. It is not about punishing the party in breach. As we have also seen, the law of contract remedies is based on an approach to splitting losses, rather than simply transferring all the claimant's losses to the defendant. Whilst these two principles are implicit in the various approaches to computing damages, they also underlie three other aspects of the law of remedies which limit the amount of damages that will be awarded to a successful claimant. These are the rules pertaining to causation, mitigation, and remoteness.

16.3.1 Causation

Causation reflects the first of the two principles discussed above; namely, the idea that damages are a measure of loss rather than a token of disapproval. Because damages seek to protect a claimant from losses incurred as a result of a breach, the claimant can only seek recovery for losses that are *caused* by the breach. A loss is caused by a breach if it was a *direct and natural consequence* of the breach. A loss that would have been incurred even without the breach, or which is connected with the breach but is not a direct and natural consequence of the breach, is not recoverable in an action for damages.

The issue of causation is rarely litigated in contract cases. In most cases, it is clear from the facts whether or not a loss was caused by breach. Nevertheless, there are some cases where causation is relevant, even if the doctrine is not invoked as frequently as

---

103. Ibid, [79].   104. *Hayes v James and Charles Dodd* [1990] 2 All ER 815 (CA).

remoteness. In *Automotive Latch Systems Ltd v Honeywell International Inc*,[105] ALS had invented a new kind of latch for car doors. It engaged Honeywell to develop and manufacture the latch. The collaboration did not go well. Twenty-eight months into the agreement, the parties had not advanced beyond concept development. ALS terminated the agreement, arguing that Honeywell was in breach of its obligation to 'take all and any reasonable actions without unreasonable delay' to manufacture the latch at a competitive cost. It sued Honeywell for lost profits.

The High Court held that ALS was not entitled to terminate the agreement for breach, but even if it had been, it would not have been able to recover lost profits because it had failed to establish causation. The delay caused by the breach was around three months. The court found that changes to the design on which both parties had agreed would have caused a three-month delay even if the contract had been performed. Additionally, Honeywell had a discretionary right to terminate the agreement unilaterally if it determined that the agreement was no longer commercially viable. It was likely on the facts that Honeywell would have exercised this option. As a result, the profits would have been lost even if the agreement had not been breached, as the latch would have never proceeded to manufacturing.

Causation also tends to be of relevance where actions taken by a third party, or by the claimants themselves, contributed to the harm. The courts often distinguish between a breach which merely provided an *opportunity* for something to happen, and a breach which actually *caused* that thing to happen. In *Weld-Blundell v Stephens*,[106] Weld-Blundell had written a letter to Stephens, an accountant, in which he asked the defendant to investigate the affairs of a company in which he held shares. The letter made serious allegations against two officers of the company. Stephens accidentally left the letter in the office of a third party, who made a certified copy which he passed on to the officers in question. The officers sued Weld-Blundell for libel, and recovered substantial damages. Weld-Blundell then sued Stephens, arguing that Stephens had breached his contractual obligation of confidentiality by leaving the letter in a third party's premises, and was therefore liable for the loss suffered by Weld-Blundell. The House of Lords held that Weld-Blundell could only recover nominal damages. The loss had been caused by the actions of Weld-Blundell in choosing to write a defamatory letter, and the third party in copying the letter. While Stephens had breached the terms of his contract, his breach had merely provided an opportunity for the loss to happen, rather than actually causing it to happen.

Where the conduct of the claimant himself is at issue, the courts tend to look at the reasonableness of the claimant's action. If the claimant's action was reckless, the courts will typically hold that the defendant's breach merely provided an opportunity for the harm to happen, and did not cause it to happen. In *Lambert v Lewis*,[107] a coupling holding a trailer to a tractor broke. The trailer came off and crashed into a car, killing two of the car's occupants. In the trial, it was found that the coupling had a manufacturing defect which made it unfit for use on a public highway. Evidence showed that the owner of the trailer must have been aware of the defect, and that it made the coupling dangerous, for at least three months before the accident. The House of Lords held that this meant that although there had been a breach of the implied term of quality and fitness for purpose, the loss was caused by the owner's continued use of what he knew

---

105. [2008] EWHC 2171 (Comm).   106. [1920] AC 956.   107. [1982] 1 AC 225 (HL).

to be a dangerous coupling and not by the breach of warranty. As such, he could not recover substantial damages for breach of contract.[108]

16.3.2 **Mitigation**

Where a breach occurs, the injured party is expected to *mitigate* the loss caused by the defendant's breach. This means that he must take reasonable steps to minimize his loss, and must not take unreasonable steps that increase his loss. If he fails to do so, he will not be able to recover damages for the portion of his loss which he could have mitigated. The classic example is a contract for the sale of goods. If a seller fails to deliver goods, the buyer must take reasonable steps to buy substitute goods on the market. He will be unable to recover compensation for any losses which he would have avoided by buying substitute goods.

The doctrine of mitigation reflects the focus of contract remedies on dividing losses between claimant and defendant rather than transferring losses from claimant to defendant. Parties to contracts are expected to behave reasonably even when their counterparty is in breach. If you behave unreasonably by failing to cut your losses, you will be required to bear the losses you could have cut. In this sense, mitigation can be said to be an aspect of a broader principle of causation: it is the claimant's unreasonable behaviour that has caused the loss, not the defendant's breach.[109]

The key requirement in mitigation is taking reasonable steps. There is no clear-cut answer to what is reasonable, beyond that it encompasses the sort of things a person might do in the ordinary course of business.[110] Courts are primarily concerned with what is *objectively* reasonable for someone in that position. A claimant who does not take steps which it fears would 'attract unnecessary negative attention', or might damage their standing in their market, will not be held to have failed to mitigate if this position was objectively reasonable.[111] A claimant is also entitled to refuse to take steps which, although legally permissible, would 'violate the standard of morality' which should attach to a 'firm of standing', and might have an adverse effect on their credit.[112] Companies may take into account their duties to their shareholders and customers in determining what steps are reasonable to take.[113]

A claimant is not expected to engage in risky activities to mitigate his loss. In *Pilkington v Wood*,[114] Pilkington had bought a house in Hampshire from a man called Wilks. Wood had acted as his solicitor. When Pilkington subsequently tried to sell the house, he discovered that he did not have good title to the property and was unable to complete the sale. He sued Wood. Wood argued that Pilkington should have mitigated

---

108. For a commercial example, see *Schering Agrochemicals Ltd v Resibel NV SA v Electro Industrie Akoustiek* 1992 WL 1351400 (CA).

109. See *Thai Airways International Public Co Ltd v KI Holdings Co Ltd* [2015] EWHC 1250 (Comm), [33] (Leggatt J).

110. *British Westinghouse Electric and Manufacturing Co Ltd v Underground Electric Railways Co of London Ltd* [1912] AC 673 (HL).

111. See the discussion in *Deutsche Bank AG v Total Global Steel Ltd* [2012] EWHC 1201 (Comm), [155]–[159].

112. See *James Finlay and Co Ltd v NV Kwik Hoo Tong Handel Maatschappij* [1929] 1 KB 400 (CA).

113. *Banco de Portugal v Waterlow and Sons Ltd* [1932] AC 452 (HL), 471 (Viscount Sankey LC).

114. [1953] Ch 770.

his loss by suing Wilks for having conveyed a defective title. The court held that mitigation did not extend that far. Wilks had made it clear that he would resist any suit brought against him. Suing him would therefore start a complex and fiercely resisted proceeding with no guarantee of success. This went beyond what was reasonable, and was not required for the purpose of mitigation.

Claimants are entitled to recover the costs of mitigation as part of their damages. Correspondingly, the defendant is also entitled to benefit from any reduction in loss brought about by steps taken in mitigation, including steps which went beyond what was reasonably necessary. This is illustrated by the decision in *British Westinghouse Electric Co Ltd v Underground Electric Railways Co Ltd*.[115] British Westinghouse had supplied steam turbines to Underground Electric. The turbines were defective, leading them to use excessive steam. The railway company eventually replaced them with more efficient turbines made by a different company, and claimed damages for the excessive fuel used while operating the British Westinghouse turbines, as well as for the whole cost of replacing them. The House of Lords held that in buying new turbines, Underground Electric had gone beyond what they were required to do to mitigate their loss. Nevertheless, because they had actually done this, the expenses they had saved, and the additional profits they had gained, had to be taken into account in computing the amount they could recover. The savings exceeded the cost of the machines, with the result that they could not recover damages under that head.

Finally, you should note that the requirement of mitigation does not apply where a party faced with repudiatory breach has chosen to affirm the contract, and subsequently sues for the contract price. Here, the test of mitigation is replaced by a less onerous test of legitimate interest.

16.3.3 Remoteness

> ### Illustration 16.10
>
> Consider the following scenario:
>
> > John Twickenham is an art dealer based in York. While looking through a catalogue for an auction in Liverpool, he notices that several unattributed sketches are for sale. As an expert on Constable, he realizes that some of these are very likely to be lost Constable sketches, worth several times the auction value. He decides to attend the auction and bid for them.
> >
> > On the morning of the auction, he orders a taxi to the station from a taxi company he uses for all his business travel. He tells them he is going to catch a train so that he can attend an auction. Unfortunately, the taxi arrives late, and he misses his train. By the time he catches the next train and reaches Liverpool, the auction has already begun and he misses the lot on which he was planning to bid. Some months later, he reads an announcement that the sketches in question have been identified as being by Constable, and he has lost the opportunity to make a significant profit.

115. [1912] AC 673 (HL).

Should John be able to sue the taxi company for his lost profit? On the face of it, it appears clear that they were in breach, and that their breach caused him loss. But that is not the end of it. John's ability to recover damages is also restricted by the rules pertaining to **remoteness** of damage.

Remoteness is one of the most commonly invoked principles limiting the recovery of damages in contract. Put simply, it states that the innocent party cannot recover damages for loss that is too remote a consequence of the breach. Much of the case law on remoteness is concerned with determining what makes a particular harm too remote. English law currently incorporates two different approaches to determining when a harm is too remote a consequence of a breach to be recoverable. The first dates back to the 19th century, and was first articulated in the case of *Hadley v Baxendale*.[116] The second is much more recent, and first appeared in 2008 in *The Achilleas*.[117] Although some of the judges in *The Achilleas* appear to have intended the new test to replace the *Hadley v Baxendale* approach, as the law currently stands it simply supplements it in some cases.

Reasonable contemplation: the approach in *Hadley v Baxendale*

Let us begin with *Hadley v Baxendale*.

Case in depth: *Hadley v Baxendale* (1854) 9 Exch 341

Hadley ran a corn mill in Gloucester. A crank shaft in their mill broke. They engaged a transport business called Pickford & Co to carry the broken shaft to Greenwich, so that a new crank shaft could be made to the same specifications. The contract required the shaft to be delivered to Greenwich within two days of dispatch. Pickford actually took seven days to get it to the recipient. The mill could not be operated without the shaft, and had to be closed for five days longer than anticipated. Hadley sued Pickford, claiming the lost profit for the five days of closure.[118] Pickford argued in its defence that the damages were too remote. The case was initially heard by a jury, who awarded damages of £50 for loss of profit. Pickford appealed, arguing that the jury should have been directed not to award damages for loss of profit as it was too remote.

The Exchequer Court upheld Pickford's argument, and dismissed the claim for lost profit. Alderson B held that liability for breach of contract extended to two categories of loss. First, it included all losses that arose naturally from the breach, 'according to the usual course of things'.[119] Secondly, it included losses that the parties could be supposed to have had within their reasonable contemplation, at the time they made the contract, as probable results of breach.

Losses caused by factors particular to the specific case fell within the second category. The defendant would only be liable for such losses if they were known to him, for example if they

→

---

116. (1854) 9 Exch 341.

117. *Transfield Shipping Inc v Mercator Shipping Inc (The Achilleas)* [2008] UKHL 48, [2009] 1 AC 61.

118. The suit was brought against Baxendale, who was the manager of Pickford & Co, rather than against Pickford itself. This is because Pickford was an unincorporated association, and therefore lacked the capacity to be sued in its own name under the law as it stood at the time.

119. (1854) 9 Exch 341, 355.

→

had been communicated to him by the claimant. If the defendant was not aware of the special circumstances, he would only be liable for the types of loss that would arise in general cases not affected by special circumstances.[120]

Alderson B justified his ruling with reference to the opportunity to negotiate. If a party was aware that special circumstances existed, and that they might aggravate the loss suffered by the other party in the event of breach, he would have a chance to negotiate special terms in relation to the quantum of damages payable. It would be unjust to deprive the parties of this opportunity to negotiate. The law should therefore adopt a rule where the party would not be liable for loss caused by special circumstances unless he was aware of them.[121]

On the facts of the case, the closure of the mill was held to be a special circumstance, rather than a loss arising naturally according to the usual course of things. Pickford had no way of knowing that a delay might lead to the closure of the mill. It was not uncommon for millers to have a spare shaft, and if Hadley had had one Pickford's delay in delivery would have had no effect. Consequently, the loss was too remote and Pickford was not liable.

Although Alderson B's decision discusses two different categories, later cases have been reluctant to treat the categories as separate. In *The Heron II*,[122] Lord Reid took the view that *Hadley* had not intended to create two rules, or two different standards or tests. The essence of the *Hadley* approach, in his reading, was to ask whether a reasonable person having the information available to the defendant would have realized that the loss in question was likely to result from the breach of contract. Likewise, in *Kpohraror v Woolwich Building Society*,[123] Evans LJ said that the starting point in a remoteness inquiry was the shared knowledge of the parties, rather than a line of demarcation between 'natural' consequences and special circumstances. In *Jackson v Royal Bank of Scotland*,[124] Lord Hope similarly held that both limbs of *Hadley* were united by a common focus on what was in the contemplation of the parties at the time they made their contract.

This last qualification is crucial. Only the parties' knowledge when the contract was formed will be taken into account. If the defendant acquired knowledge of special circumstances *after* the contract was formed, that knowledge will have no bearing on the application of the remoteness rule. This is because, as Parts I and II have discussed, English contract law treats the moment when the contract formed is the 'moment of responsibility' when the parties' rights and obligations crystallize, and anything that happens after that moment is irrelevant to determining the scope of those rights and obligations.

In some sectors, this focus on matters within the contemplation of the parties at formation has led to rules of remarkable clarity. In a contract for the sale of goods, for example, it is now clearly established that if the seller fails to deliver the goods, the buyer can ordinarily only recover the difference between the contract price and the market price at the time of breach. If the buyer suffered a higher loss, for example if

---

120. Ibid, 355–6.   121. Ibid, 356.
122. *Koufos v C Czarnikow Ltd (The Heron II)* [1969] 1 AC 350 (HL), 385.
123. [1996] 4 All ER 119 (CA), 127–8.   124. [2005] UKHL 3, [2005] 1 WLR 377, 384–5.

he had intended to sell the goods at a large mark-up under a lucrative resale contract, that higher loss will usually be seen as too remote unless the defendant was aware of the resale contract.

Elsewhere, however, figuring out the precise implications of the rule has caused some difficulty, particularly in relation to the meaning of 'contemplation'. Is a matter only within the 'contemplation' of both parties if the defendant has been given notice of the special circumstances in question? Or is it sufficient if those circumstances are foreseeable? In *Victoria Laundry (Windsor) Ltd v Newman Industries Ltd*,[125] the Court of Appeal suggested that the correct test was one of reasonable foreseeability. What had to be foreseen was that the loss was a 'serious possibility', or a 'real danger'—something 'on the cards' or 'liable to result'.[126] *Victoria Laundry* related to a contract to supply a boiler to the claimants, who ran a laundry. The boiler's supply was delayed by five months because it was damaged when it was being dismantled for delivery. The claimants sued for the profits they had lost for those five months. Two types of losses were claimed, the first an amount of £16 per week for general loss of profit from their laundering business, and the second an amount of £262 per week for the profit that was lost under a very lucrative dyeing contract that they would have received from the government. The Court of Appeal held that the first sum was recoverable, but not the second. This was because the defendants knew that the claimants intended to use the boiler immediately, and thus that some profit would be lost if delivery was delayed. However, they did not know of the lucrative government contracts that were lost, and could not reasonably have foreseen their existence. As such, that loss was too remote.

The use of the language of 'reasonable foreseeability' was, however, criticized by the House of Lords in *The Heron II*. Reasonable foreseeability as a concept is frequently used in assessing remoteness in tort, and the House of Lords was anxious to maintain a distinction between remoteness in tort and contract.[127] Remoteness in contract should be stricter. The focus in contract should be on the likelihood of the result, and in particular on whether it was 'quite likely to happen'.[128] This does not mean that the precise *mechanism* by which that result eventuated must be within the parties' contemplation, but results of that *type and extent* should be within their contemplation. In *Parsons (Livestock) Ltd v Uttley Ingham & Co Ltd*,[129] poorly installed feed storage equipment led to an outbreak of E. coli among pigs at a farm, with several pigs dying. The defendants were held liable on the basis that illness and death of pigs would have been within the parties' contemplation as a likely result of breach, even if the specific vector, E. coli, would not.

Assumption of responsibility: the *Achilleas* approach

The application of the *Hadley* approach to individual cases was often problematic. A particular sticking point was the question of whether it was sufficient if loss of a particular type was within the parties' contemplation, or whether loss of a particular extent needed to be within their contemplation. The distinction between the two can be illustrated by revisiting Illustration 16.10. The taxi company knew that the claimant was a dealer in antiquities, and that he wanted a taxi to attend an auction. They

---

125. [1949] 2 KB 528 (CA).   126. Ibid, 539–40 (Asquith LJ).
127. [1969] 1 AC 350, 389 (Lord Reid).   128. Ibid, 390.   129. [1978] QB 791.

would, therefore, have had within their contemplation the likelihood that he would be buying goods for resale, and would therefore lose profit if he missed the auction. If our focus is only on the *type* of loss, this will mean that the taxi company is liable. If, in contrast, we focus on the *extent* of loss, then the taxi company is unlikely to be liable, as they are unlikely to have had a loss of such a large extent within their contemplation. Several cases had taken the view that what mattered was the type of loss, but the trouble was that this contradicted the outcome in *Victoria Laundry*, and could potentially lead to very extensive and unpredictable liability.

Partly as a response to this difficulty, Lord Hoffmann, supported by Lord Hope, put forward a new test for remoteness in *The Achilleas*.[130] The focus of this test, like the *Hadley* approach, is on the parties at the moment of formation. Unlike the *Hadley* approach, however, it does not ask what the parties had within their contemplation. Instead, it focuses on whether the defendant *assumed responsibility* for the loss in the contract.

The Achilleas arose out of the late return of a ship that had been chartered. Because it was late, the shipowner was unable to fulfil its obligations under the next charter, and had to renegotiate that contract. The renegotiation resulted in a very significant reduction of $1,364,584.37 in the charter fee. The claimant sought to recover this from the defendant as lost profit. The defendant argued that the loss was too remote. The only reason such a large loss had been suffered was because the claimant had agreed the next charter at a time when market rates were very high. The defendant could not have had this in contemplation at the time of contract. The loss that was foreseeable was the difference between the rate that the shipowner could have got on the market for the nine days of delay, and the rate the defendant actually paid the shipowner. This amounted to $158,301.17. The arbitrators, the High Court, and the Court of Appeal all found for the shipowner, holding that the loss was not too remote as loss of this type was foreseeable even if the full extent of the loss was not. This appears to have caused some consternation in the shipping community, which had taken the view that liability for late return of ships was not so extensive.

The House of Lords unanimously held that the loss was too remote. Three of the judges did so by holding that the loss was caused by extreme market volatility, which went beyond anything the parties could have had in their contemplation. Lords Hope and Hoffmann, however, chose to articulate a new rule, under which the key question was whether the defendant had accepted or assumed responsibility for loss of the type that had eventuated. Lord Hoffmann drew a distinction between assuming responsibility for the nine-day delay, which he thought the defendants clearly had done, and assuming responsibility for the entirety of the next charter, which they had not done.

The new approach was both praised and criticized. It was praised on the basis that it puts the focus of remoteness on the parties' agreement itself, rather than on the parties' contemplation at the time of contracting, and hence is more in keeping with the central role which contract law assigns to the parties' agreed terms. The criticism of the decision, however, is that it creates a novel test with little guidance on how it might be applied to specific cases. How, for example, might we approach Illustration 16.10 through such a test? On what basis do we decide for what the taxi company assumed responsibility?

---

130. *Transfield Shipping Inc v Mercator Shipping Inc (The Achilleas)* [2008] UKHL 48, [2009] 1 AC 61.

Subsequent cases were, therefore, cautious in adopting Lord Hoffmann's test. In *Supershield Ltd v Siemens Building Technologies FE Ltd*,[131] the Court of Appeal held that in most cases, the correct approach would be to begin with *Hadley*. If the commercial background to the contract suggested that the *Hadley* rule did not appropriately reflect the parties' expectations or intentions, the *Achilleas* test of *assumption of responsibility* might provide a better basis for judging remoteness. This would seem to fit with the decision in *The Achilleas* itself, where the seeming mismatch between the shipping community's expectations and the decisions of the lower courts is likely to have been a not-insignificant factor in the decision of the House of Lords.

16.4 In conclusion: the problem of remedying breach

Three general points emerge from the discussion in this chapter. The first point to note is the limited range of interests which contract remedies protect. The focus of contract remedies is on economic interests, such as losses of profits, wasted expenses, and reduced values. It is only in consumer transactions that broader interests appear to be recognized. But even in consumer transactions, the logic of the interests it recognizes remains deeply embedded in the logic of economic exchange. The recognized interests are largely confined to the sort of things consumers transact to obtain: enjoyment, amenity, and the 'consumer surplus'. Contract law takes little notice of other dimensions of social interaction, even though some of these are not infrequently present in contractual transactions. Equally, it takes little note of the fact that many transactions today present complex networks of contracts. By default, the rules on remoteness and the limitations on recovery for losses suffered by third parties tend to isolate each transaction, and to confine remedies to losses incurred in that transaction alone.

The implications of these limitations can be seen if we return to Problem 16. As the law stands, it is unlikely that the Arts Endowment Trust will be able to obtain a satisfactory remedy. The main harm they will suffer is the damage to their reputation, and to the attempt to nurture a community of artisans in the area they have targeted. Neither of these are interests that contract remedies protect. Given that the Trust does not appear to have suffered very much monetary harm, any remedy it can obtain will be limited. And, given the reluctance of the law to award compensation for third party losses, the true victims of the breach, the independent artisans, will have no right whatsoever to recover compensation. The result is that Weiss's breach will, in effect, go unremedied.

The second point to note is that despite these limitations, the law tends to deal with the interests it does protect by and large sensibly. When it comes to the monetary exchange-related interests that are the core concern of contract remedies, English law's approach to dividing losses for the most part works well. The rules that guide judges' discretion in choosing between the different expectation measures, and between expectation and reliance measures, work well. Subject to the qualifications noted in section 16.3, so do the rules on mitigation, remoteness, and causation. Of particular interest

---

131. [2010] EWCA Civ 7.

is the rise in recent decades of concepts related to the idea of a 'legitimate interest in performance' as a key tool in guiding the exercise of judicial discretion across different areas of contract remedies, including the choice between the cost of cure, difference in value, hypothetical bargain, and loss of amenity measures. The increased emphasis on this idea is not limited to contract remedies: it also occurs in other areas, such as in the *Cavendish* approach to liquidated damages discussed in Chapter 13. This notion appears to be emerging as a key tool in ensuring that losses are divided in a proportionate way, so that the defendant's liability bears a proportionate relationship to the harm to the claimant's interests.

The third, and final, point is that contract law gives parties a range of tools which they can deploy to tailor remedies to their needs, and the courts have been inclining towards increasing the latitude the law gives the parties, rather than decreasing it. This is closely related to the preference for solutions which flow from the parties' own agreement rather than solutions imposed by law, which suffuses much of the law in relation to interpretation (Chapter 7), implication of terms (Chapter 8), and flexible contracting (Chapter 9). The power and utility of this approach can be seen by returning to Problem 16. A better designed contract could have ameliorated all the problems which we have discussed in this section. A liquidated damages clauses fixing damages at an appropriate level, or a multipartite agreement including the other tenants, would have addressed the problems created by the limitations of the law as it currently exists.

That, in the ultimate analysis, is the key point to remember. English law gives the parties a good deal of freedom to design remedies, which you would be well advised to use when designing contracts. The default remedies provided by law will never be as good as the remedies you tailor to the needs of a specific transaction.

Key points

- If a contract is breached, the innocent party has a right to bring an action for damages.

- The primary purpose of damages is to compensate the innocent party for the loss caused by breach. A party who has suffered no loss will only receive nominal damages.

- Not all loss will be compensated. The innocent party will only be able to recover compensation for interests and types of harm protected by the law. In addition, the ability to recover is also limited by rules pertaining to causation, mitigation, and remoteness.

- Two types of interests are protected by compensatory damages. The expectation interest seeks to restore the innocent party to the position they would have been in had the contract been performed. The reliance interest seeks to restore the innocent party to the position they would have been in had the contract never been formed.

- Expectation damages can be calculated with reference to lost profit. Where this is difficult to measure, they are calculated with reference to the cost of curing the breach, or with reference to the difference in value between the performance contracted for and the performance that was actually rendered.

- A party may claim either cost of cure or difference in value, but the decision is for the courts, and they will not award the cost of cure if that would leave the claimant with a windfall.

- In consumer contracts, the courts may choose to award damages for loss of amenity or disappointed expectations instead of the cost of cure.

- Reliance damages are quantified with reference to wasted expenditure. A party can recover expenditure incurred in performing or preparing to perform the contract, as well as ordinary and natural expenditure incurred in reliance on the contract.

- Where a defendant has breached a binding undertaking, a court may award the claimant damages computed with reference to the amount which the claimant would have hypothetically charged the defendant to waive that undertaking.

- Damages will ordinarily only be awarded for pecuniary loss. In consumer transactions, however, damages can be awarded for disappointment and distress if the object of the contract was to procure pleasure or provide peace of mind.

- Damages are limited in three ways. Damages will not be available for loss that was not caused by the breach. They will also not be available for loss which the innocent party could have avoided or mitigated by taking reasonable steps. Finally, they will not available for loss that was too remote (usually judged with reference to types of loss that were within the reasonable contemplation of the parties at the time of breach).

Assess your learning

You should be able to respond to each of the following points with a confident 'yes'. If you can't, then you should revisit the sections listed against that point.

Can you:

(a) *Identify* the purpose and main approaches to quantifying expectation damages, including cost of cure, difference in value, loss of amenity, and loss of chance and, *explain* the circumstances in which each is available? (Section 16.2.3)

(b) *Identify* when reliance damages are available, how they are quantified, and the principles used to decide between them and expectation damages? (Section 16.2.4)

(c) *Identify* when hypothetical damages are available, and how they are quantified? (Section 16.2.4)

(d) *Identify* the issues raised by non-economic loss, and *describe* the circumstances under which a party can recover for such loss? (Section 16.2.6)

(e) *Explain* how causation, remoteness, and mitigation operate to limit the losses which a party can recover, and *identify* the tests for each? (Section 16.3)

In relation to each of the above, you should be able to:

(i) identify and clearly explain the key rules and principles;

(ii) identify the key cases and statutes, and why they matter;

(iii) apply the principles and cases to specific real or hypothetical fact situations;

(iv) evaluate the limitations, if any, of the law as it currently stands.

Further reading

M Bridge, 'Mitigation of Damages in Contract and the Meaning of Avoidable Loss' (1993) 109 LQR 175.

M Bridge, 'Expectation Damages and Uncertain Future Losses' in J Beatson and D Friedmann (eds), *Good Faith and Fault in Contract Law* (Clarendon Press 1995).

J Cartwright, 'Remoteness of Damage in Contract and Tort: A Reconsideration' (1996) 55 CLJ 488.

J Cartwright, 'Compensatory Damages: Some Central Issues of Assessment' in A Burrows and E Peel (eds), *Commercial Remedies: Current Issues and Problems* (Oxford University Press 2003).

N Enonchong, 'Breach of Contract and Damages for Mental Distress' (1996) 16 OJLS 617.

D Harris, D Campbell, and R Halson, *Remedies in Contract and Tort* (2nd edn, Cambridge University Press 2002).

D Harris, A Ogus, and J Phillips, 'Contract Remedies and the Consumer Surplus' (1979) 95 LQR 581.

E Peel, 'Remoteness Revisited' (2009) 125 LQR 6.

H Reece, 'Loss of Chances in the Law' (1996) 59 MLR 188.

S Rowan, 'Reflections on the Introduction of Punitive Damages for Breach of Contract' (2010) 30 OJLS 495.

Non-compensatory remedies

Specific performance, debt, and restitution

'When expectation fails'

Problem 17: setting the context

Read the following (fictional) news clipping, and think about the legal issues it raises.

Lowest in the pecking order? Customers cry fowl as hens face the chop

Customers of Ethical Hens have been left dismayed after the local business dramatically changed its customer promise.

Since 2010, Ethical Hens has sold its eggs to customers at a hefty premium. The extra funds were to be invested and used to provide for a slaughter-free retirement for its hens after their laying days. The business was heavily patronized by local animal lovers, who were egg-static at the idea of sourcing their eggs from a company that guaranteed that its hens would be allowed to live out their natural lives. Yesterday, however, customers discovered that they might have been shelling out for nothing after the business quietly announced a major change in its sales pitch. A revision to their website now says that they 'aim' to achieve a slaughter-free retirement for 'up to' a third of their hens.

Nobody from Ethical Hens could be reached for comment, but we understand that this change has been prompted by the poor performance of Ethical Hens' investments, whose returns have been far below the necessary levels for them to keep their promise of not slaughtering any of their laying hens.

In the meantime, customers have been scrambling to form an action group, which intends to seek legal advice as to whether action can be taken to compel Ethical Hens to stick to its promise. A key figure in the action group, who asked not to be named, said customers were 'furious at Ethical Hens' betrayal'.

'They made a contract with us,' he said, 'and we intend to hold them to it.'

What sort of damages might be available to the customers in this case? Will that be a satisfactory remedy? What sort of remedies will they actually be looking to get?

17.1 Introduction: the problem of enforcement

Damages are the default remedy for breach, but they are not always enough. Often, the interests at stake are not easily compensable by awarding a sum of money. Problem 17 presents a good example. Neither expectation nor reliance damages will give the customers of Ethical Hens an adequate remedy. Damages compensate parties for losses, and the customers will struggle to demonstrate any tangible loss flowing from the breach. The cost of cure cannot be awarded as the hens belong to Ethical Hens, meaning that the customers are not in a position to cure breach. Difference in value might, at best, lead to a refund of the excess they paid over the market value of ordinary eggs, but that does little to compensate them for the harm caused by the breach. The hypothetical bargain measure could, potentially, provide a remedy, but its availability remains unclear.[1]

---

1. See the discussion in Chapter 16, section 16.2.5.

English law also contains a range of other remedies for breach, which can broadly be classed as *non-compensatory remedies*. These seek to respond to breach in ways other than compensation. Some of these remedies are geared towards literal enforcement. Instead of accepting breach and seeking to ameliorate its effects by erecting ever more elaborate structures of compensatory damages, they require the party in breach to do what she has promised to do. In most civil law countries, literal enforcement is the default remedy. Damages are only granted if the defendant successfully establishes that they are a more appropriate remedy, or if literal enforcement is otherwise inappropriate. In English law, however, the availability of literal enforcement depends on the type of term that you seek to enforce. The starting point for non-monetary obligations is that breach is best remedied through the award of damages. Literal enforcement of such an obligation, through an order for **specific performance** or an **injunction**, is only awarded in exceptional circumstances (discussed in section 17.2). Obligations involving the payment of a definite sum of money, in contrast, are frequently literally enforced through the remedy of **debt** (section 17.3).

Literal performance is not the only non-compensatory remedy. In a small number of cases, the courts may award monetary remedies which are gain-based rather than compensatory. Like damages, these involve the payment of a sum of money. Unlike damages, however, the sum awarded is measured not with reference to the claimant's loss, but to the defendant's gain. **Gain-based remedies** are discussed in greater detail in section 17.4.

17.2 Literal enforcement

17.2.1 Specific performance

Specific performance would approach the problem faced by Ethical Hens' customers head-on, by requiring Ethical Hens to actually perform the contract. Nevertheless, as we will see in this section, specific performance is only available in a very narrow set of circumstances, where damages are not an adequate remedy, and where the order can be clearly stated and implemented without further judicial intervention (or 'constant superintendence'). These restrictions make it unlikely that specific performance will be awarded in most cases.

The basic test: the 'adequacy' of damages

Specific performance is an equitable remedy. As such, it is inherently discretionary. From an early stage, it was established that equity would only intervene if the claimant could not obtain a sufficient remedy at common law. The traditional formulation was that specific performance would not be awarded if damages were an adequate remedy.

The notion of adequacy reflects the role of damages in splitting losses. A court awarding damages is deciding which portion of the loss ought to be borne by the claimant, and which by the defendant. From that point of view, damages cease to be an 'adequate' remedy if the standard ways of quantifying damages require the claimant to bear losses which, in the circumstances, she ought not to bear.

This means that specific performance is rare. The perception amongst judges is that damages usually do a good job of splitting losses between the parties. Where they

NON-COMPENSATORY REMEDIES

do not, the response is to develop the law of damages. Specific performance is only awarded in cases where it is impossible to deal with some aspect of the harm through the law of damages, and where it would be inappropriate to leave that aspect of the harm unremedied.

In addition, specific performance will not be awarded if damages are an adequate remedy. Courts also consider the impact of an order of specific performance on the relative bargaining power of the parties. Lord Westbury LC expressed this concern vividly in *Isenberg v East India House Estate Co Ltd*,[2] holding that courts should not grant orders of specific performance if doing so would 'deliver over the defendants to the plaintiff bound hand and foot, in order to be made subject to any extortionate demand that he may by possibility make'. More recently, courts have emphasized that the courts should keep in mind that the purpose of contract remedies is not to punish wrongdoing, and that specific performance will be unjust if it allows the claimant to enrich himself at the defendant's expense.[3]

Specific performance will not be awarded if to do so will be oppressive. Contracts of employment or personal service, for example, are not ordinarily specifically enforced, because doing so would interfere with personal liberty.[4] It will also not be awarded if enforcement would require 'continuous superintendence' or 'constant supervision' by the court, for example if the court may end up having to repeatedly rule on whether the defendant is doing enough to comply with its order.[5] It will not be ordered if the term is open-ended or lacks precision, if a court cannot see 'what is the exact nature of the work of which it is asked to order the performance',[6] or if it cannot draw up an order that gives the defendant enough certainty to know 'exactly in fact what he has to do . . . so that in carrying out an order he can give his contractors the proper instructions'.[7]

Some cases have drawn a distinction between contracts to achieve particular results and contracts to carry out particular activities, holding that the latter will ordinarily not be specifically enforced because they will usually require continuous superintendence.[8] In *Ryan v Mutual Tontine Association*,[9] a tenant had the contractual right to the services of a porter who was to be constantly in attendance. The court held that specific performance of this obligation would require constant superintendence. In contrast, in *Posner v Scott-Lewis*,[10] where the lease provided that a porter would be engaged to perform a number of specified tasks, the court was willing to grant an order of specific performance.

When, then, is specific performance actually granted? One example is where the claimant requires performance, and cannot easily procure substitute performance on the market. Specific performance has been awarded in many cases relating to the sale

---

2. (1863) 3 De GJ & S 263.

3. *Co-operative Insurance Society Ltd v Argyll Stores Ltd* [1998] AC 1, 15 (Lord Hoffmann).

4. The rule has its origins in common law, but has now been codified in statute: see Trade Union and Labour Relations (Consolidation) Act 1992, s 236.

5. See *Co-operative Insurance Society Ltd v Argyll Stores Ltd* [1998] AC 1, 12 (Lord Hoffmann).

6. *Wolverhampton Corp v Emmons* [1901] 1 KB 515 (CA), 525 (Romer LJ).

7. *Morris v Redland Bricks Ltd* [1970] AC 652, 666 (Lord Upjohn).

8. See eg *Co-operative Insurance Society Ltd v Argyll Stores Ltd* [1998] AC 1, 14 (Lord Hoffmann).

9. [1893] 1 Ch 116 (CA).   10. [1987] 1 Ch 25.

of 'unique' goods, such as works of art or industrial machinery which is not readily available on a secondary market. Because every plot of land is taken to be unique, the courts will usually specifically enforce a contract to buy or sell land on the application of either the seller or the purchaser.[11] Specific performance may also be awarded if it is difficult to quantify damages—if, for example, a party would find it difficult to adduce sufficient evidence to prove its loss on the balance of probabilities, or if the circumstances of the case make the exact quantum of the loss uncertain, or subject to factors that cannot be easily assessed.

Both sets of factors came together in the case of *Thames Valley Power Ltd v Total Gas and Power Ltd*.[12] The defendant had agreed to supply gas to the claimant for 15 years from 1995. The price was to be calculated according to a formula which depended on the value of a number of indices. In 2005, the defendant refused to supply further gas to the claimant, who sued for breach. Christopher Clarke J granted an order of specific performance because no comparable long-term supply was available on the market (thus meaning that damages were not an adequate remedy). In addition, assessing damages would be virtually impossible. The exact nature of the claimant's loss would depend on the indices' movement over the coming five years, which could not be predicted.

Many of these considerations also apply to the customers of Ethical Hens. The hurdle they will face, however, is that of constant superintendence. It is hard to see how the court could order the company to keep the hens alive without having to engage in a process of constant superintendence, to ensure (for example) that the company is not engaging in a process of deliberate neglect as a way of reducing the hens' expected lifetime. This means that specific performance is unlikely to be awarded, even though damages are patently not an adequate remedy.

A broader approach?

In the 1960s, it appeared for a time, following the decision of the House of Lords in *Beswick v Beswick*,[13] that the courts were on the verge of adopting a more permissive approach to specific performance. Mr Beswick had sold his business to his nephew in consideration of the payment of an annuity to him and to his widow after his death. When he died, his nephew stopped paying the annuity. The widow sued for specific performance in her capacity as the administrator of Mr Beswick's estate. The House of Lords granted an order of specific performance. As the law then stood, Mrs Beswick had no direct right of action.[14] The estate could sue, but it had suffered no loss and could therefore only obtain nominal damages. None of the grounds on which specific performance would ordinarily be refused were made out. This meant that it was appropriate to grant an order of specific performance.

Although the House of Lords in *Beswick v Beswick* did not expressly liberalize the rules on specific performance, it appeared to take a very broad approach to specific performance. Lord Reid said that specific performance was the appropriate remedy

---

11. This is clearly a rather tenuous fiction—there are a number of circumstances in which plots of land are for all practical purposes interchangeable—but it is well entrenched in law.

12. [2005] EWHC 2208 (Comm).   13. [1968] AC 58 (HL).

14. For the current position, see Chapter 18 ('Privity and third parties').

because the result was 'just'.[15] Lord Pearce simply said it was 'the more appropriate remedy'.[16] Commentators took the view that the House of Lords had implicitly adopted an approach in which specific performance and damages were coordinate remedies, with the courts awarding whichever was more appropriate on the facts of a case. They would no longer treat damages as the primary remedy or keep specific performance narrowly confined to cases where damages failed to provide an adequate remedy.[17] There was a lot of academic enthusiasm for this approach, and the case was seen as heralding a new era in which specific performance would be generally available in all types of contracts, if it would 'do more perfect and complete justice'.[18]

Subsequent cases did not follow this broader approach, although there were some moves towards loosening the bars on specific performance.[19] Instead, the traditional view that specific performance is an exceptional remedy was reaffirmed by the House of Lords in *Co-operative Insurance Society Ltd v Argyll Stores Ltd*.[20] The history of the case, and the disagreements between the judges hearing it, serve as a good illustration of the issues which specific performance raises.

Case in depth: *Co-operative Insurance Society Ltd v Argyll Stores Ltd* [1998] AC 1 (HL)

Co-operative Insurance owned a large shopping centre in Sheffield. One of the units in the centre was a supermarket run by Argyll Stores. The supermarket was an 'anchor' tenant, intended to attract customers to the development and make the other shops viable. Its lease therefore had a covenant requiring it to keep the premises open for retail trade during the usual hours of business in the locality. The lease was supposed to run for 35 years from 1979.

In 1994, as part of a broader business review, Argyll Stores decided to close down the supermarket in question, along with 26 others, as it was making a loss. Co-operative Insurance pointed out that this was a breach of the lease, and asked them to continue to trade until an alternative tenant could be found. They explained that they were concerned about the effect of the anchor tenant's closure on the rest of the centre, and offered to discount the rent further if necessary. Argyll closed the shop down without responding to Co-operative Insurance's letter, and removed all the fittings and fixtures leaving the unit bare. Co-operative Insurance sued for breach of contract, seeking specific performance of the covenant to keep the centre open.

Maddocks J in the High Court refused to order specific performance. An order to carry on a business, he held, would be difficult to enforce because of the vagueness of the duty and the extent of supervision that would be required (in contrast to a one-off, well-defined duty like signing a conveyance). It would also be exercising too high a degree of control to order a business to be run at a loss. Finally, given that it would cost over £1 million to reopen the shop (as the fittings had been removed), an order of specific performance would be inappropriate.

→

---

15. [1968] AC 58 (HL), 77.   16. Ibid, 88.

17. See eg FH Lawson, *Remedies of English Law* (Butterworths 1980) 223–4.

18. *Rainbow Estates Ltd v Tokenhold Ltd* [1999] Ch 64, 72–3.

19. For a review of the cases, see A Burrows, 'Specific Performance at the Crossroads' (1984) 4 LS 102.

20. [1998] AC 1 (HL).

→

The Court of Appeal, by a 2:1 majority, reversed the High Court and ordered specific performance.[21] The majority, Leggatt and Roch LJJ, pointed out that Argyll Stores had voluntarily agreed to keep their shop open for a specific period, and there was 'no reason why they should not be held to their bargain'.[22] Secondly, it was held that Co-operative Insurance would have 'very considerable difficulty' in proving the quantum of the loss. Not only would damages fail to compensate them fully, the losses of the *other* tenants of the shopping centre would also be irrecoverable.[23] Finally, Argyll had 'acted with gross commercial cynicism, preferring to resist a claim for damages rather than keep an unambiguous promise', and it was entirely appropriate for 'a sense of fair dealing' to influence the grant of specific performance.[24] Nor, contrary to what the trial judge thought, were the obligations too vague to be enforced. An order of specific performance would need to do no more than 'simply repeat the terms of the covenants into which the defendants had entered'. It had not been suggested that the covenants were void for uncertainty.[25]

Millett LJ dissented, arguing that an order of specific performance would be oppressive. 'To compel a defendant . . . to carry on a business which he considers is not viable, or which for his own commercial reasons he has decided to close down, is to expose him to potentially large, unquantifiable and unlimited losses which may be out of all proportion to the loss which his breach of contract has caused to the plaintiff.'[26] He also suggested that there was a settled understanding on the basis of past practice that the only remedy for the breach of such a covenant would be an action for damages, and it would not be appropriate to interfere with this understanding.[27]

The House of Lords unanimously restored the order of the trial judge, holding that the appropriate remedy was an award of damages.[28] The difficulty of drawing the order with sufficient precision meant that the danger of constant superintendence was present. A clause could be too vague to be specifically enforceable without being void for uncertainty.[29] In addition, there was also a danger that the order would be oppressive, and would put the claimant in an unjustly favourable bargaining position. Argyll would suffer 'unquantifiable loss' if it were to be forced to continue trading. The Court of Appeal had been wrong to place emphasis on fair dealing, as both parties here were large commercial organizations with only financial interests. There was 'no element of personal breach of faith'.[30] Given all this, it would rarely if ever be appropriate to issue an order of specific performance to keep a business open, and the trial judge was correct to have refused to do so.

An important influence on the majority on the Court of Appeal in *Co-operative Insurance v Argyll* was the position of the other tenants. They were not parties to the agreement between Co-operative Insurance and Argyll, but they were nevertheless quite profoundly affected by Argyll's breach. Damages are generally only awarded for loss suffered by the parties themselves. Third parties can only recover under very limited circumstances (discussed in Chapter 18), which did not apply on the facts of *Co-operative Insurance v Argyll*.[31] The Court of Appeal held this to be a reason in favour

---

21. [1996] 1 Ch 286.   22. Ibid, 294 (Leggatt LJ).
23. Ibid, 295 (Leggatt LJ), 296 (Roch LJ).   24. Ibid, 295.   25. Ibid, 298 (Roch LJ).
26. Ibid, 304.   27. Ibid, 305.   28. [1998] AC 1 (HL).   29. Ibid, 14.
30. Ibid, 18.   31. See Chapter 18 ('Privity and third parties').

of granting specific performance. The House of Lords disagreed. Argyll had made no promise to its fellow tenants, and specific performance should not therefore be used to create one. The only remedy the other tenants had would be to seek a reduced rent in the next rent review under their leases.

Academic reaction to the decision was mixed. A number of commentators criticized the decision, influenced, in part, by the fact that Argyll's conduct had been quite noxious. It refused to negotiate with its landlord, gave less than a month's notice, and left without attempting to find someone to take over the lease.[32] Professor Tettenborn argued that the decision was 'an unfortunate failure to liberalise the rules of specific performance' which 'sits ill with the idea that it should be the function of courts to make sure, as far as possible, that contracts are performed`rather than broken'.[33] The decision, however, makes more sense if we look at it from the point of view of loss-splitting. A key theme running through the judgment of Lord Hoffmann in the House of Lords, and the dissent of Millett LJ in the Court of Appeal, is the importance of maintaining a sense of proportionality in specific performance as much as in damages. It was of fundamental importance, both insisted, that specific performance not be used to give one party an unjustifiable advantage over the other. Both placed great emphasis on the potentially unlimited losses that an order of specific performance would impose on Argyll, and on the absence of any justification for such an imposition.

The issues that troubled Lord Hoffmann and Millett LJ, namely ensuring that the remedial burden imposed on the defendant is not disproportionate to the claimant's loss, should be readily recognizable from the cases we have examined on the measure of damages, whether in relation to the grounds for refusing to award the full cost of cure or in relation to the limits of reliance damages. It should also be recognizable from the approach taken by the courts in relation to **mitigation** and **remoteness**. *Co-operative Insurance v Argyll*, therefore, demonstrates the extent to which this principle informs the law of remedies more generally, and not just the law of damages.

 Debates in context: expanding specific performance

Should specific performance be more widely available? A number of academic commentators from around the common law world have argued that it should be, writing from very different perspectives.

One argument, advanced by scholars in England and Canada, begins with the view that the law of contract has (or should have) a moral element, grounded in the importance of promise. Promises are important in and of themselves. As a result, parties to a contract have an entitlement to performance. Breach of contract is a civil wrong because it violates this entitlement. Private law's role should be to act as an instrument of corrective justice, and intervene to reverse this wrong. Damages do this, but only indirectly. They are substitutive, in that

→

---

32. See P Luxton, 'Are You Being Served? Enforcing Keep Open Covenants in Leases' [1998] Conv 396.

33. AM Tettenborn, 'Absolving the Undeserving: Shopping Centres, Specific Performance and the Law of Contract' [1998] Conv 23.

→

they seek to substitute money for this entitlement. Specific performance is a far better option because it absolutely and directly protects the entitlement. Professor Lionel Smith, a Canadian scholar who is one of the leading exponents of this approach, has pointed out that civil law countries do in fact treat specific performance as the default remedy, and that in doing so they take the contract far more seriously than the common law does.[34]

Professor Smith's perspective is grounded in ethical philosophy, in particular in the morality of promises and in Kantian notions of corrective justice. The traditional counter-argument to this has a more hard-nosed economic perspective. Contract law in this understanding is simply an instrument that is necessary to ensure that markets are able to function. The key issue in structuring contract remedies should be to assist economic efficiency. In some cases, economic efficiency is best achieved by permitting parties to breach uneconomic contracts. Retaining damages as the default remedy does this. A party who comes across a much more lucrative opportunity will be able to take that opportunity, which is good for the economy, by breaching the original contract. At the same time, the availability of damages means that the party affected by the breach of the original contract will not suffer heavy losses as a result of the breach.[35] Damages therefore make economic sense, but specific performance does not.

Professors David Campbell and Donald Harris, writing from an economically grounded perspective, have argued that damages as a remedy give the contractual relationship much more flexibility than specific performance. As a result, damages are far better at facilitating cooperative responses to unforeseen eventualities than specific performance. Professors Campbell and Harris term this 'joint maximisation'.[36] A party who has the right to specific performance has no incentive to negotiate. Damages, in contrast, give both parties an incentive to negotiate. The party who is required to pay damages has an incentive to negotiate to try and reduce the amount he has to pay, whereas the party who is affected by breach has an incentive to negotiate to try and obtain a more efficacious remedy than he would get through the standard measures of damages. This creates a zone of possible agreement within which the parties can work out creative solutions. From a commercial perspective, these are likely to be far superior and more useful to the parties than anything a court could devise.

But economics does not inevitably lead to the position that damages are the better remedy. Professor Alan Schwartz has argued that an economic analysis should lead to a preference for specific performance. Damages have a tendency to undercompensate the party who has suffered the breach, and will therefore often not provide adequate compensation. Where damages do provide adequate compensation, rational parties will voluntarily opt for damages over specific performance, simply because it is a more attractive option than getting performance from someone who does not want to perform. Parties know their situation better than the courts, and if a party sues for specific performance the courts should take it as a clear sign that damages are not an adequate remedy.[37]

→

34. L Smith, 'Understanding Specific Performance' in N Cohen and E McKendrick (eds), *Comparative Remedies for Breach of Contract* (Hart 2005).

35. RL Birmingham, 'Breach of Contract, Damage Measures, and Economic Efficiency' (1970) 24 Rutgers Law Review 273.

36. D Campbell and D Harris, 'Flexibility in Long-Term Contractual Relationships: The Role of Co-operation' (1993) 20 Journal of Law and Society 166.

37. A Schwartz, 'The Case for Specific Performance' (1979) 89 Yale Law Journal 271.

→

A more nuanced view has been put forward by Professor Ian Macneil,[38] the leading proponent of the relational theory of contract.[39] Professor Macneil argues that theories of efficient breach fail to take account of the fact that breach disrupts commercial relationships, which carries non-trivial costs. This means that it cannot be said that efficient breach is more economically efficient, and it could equally be argued that it creates a bias 'in favor of individual, uncooperative behavior as opposed to behavior requiring the cooperation of the parties'. Professor Macneil called for greater empirical research, and a more empirically grounded approach, to contract remedies. The current approach assumes that the remedy of damages facilitates particular outcomes, but the reality is that these are simply assumptions. In the absence of sociological research across a range of different commercial sectors, we simply do not know what sort of behaviour different types of rules facilitate.

The debate continues.

17.2.2 Injunctions

An order of specific performance is an order requiring a party to comply with its contractual obligations. A similar remedy is provided by *injunctions*, which are orders granted restraining parties from carrying out an action that would amount to a breach of contract. Consider the following email:

Illustration 17.1

From: CEO's office <big.cheese@flogurstuff.co.uk>

To: General Counsel <legal@flogurstuff.co.uk>

Subject: James Bowerson

Dear Will,

We have recently discovered that James Bowerson, until recently our Chief Technology Officer, is planning to start a competing online auction site. He has registered the domain www.sellyourstuff.co.uk, and is apparently in talks with investors for initial seed capital.

James signed our standard non-compete agreement when he left our company. His actions are a blatant violation of that agreement, and could seriously harm our business. Could you advise on our rights and what, if anything, we can do to stop him.

Best,

Petra Petrovicova

Chief Executive Officer

flogurstuff.co.uk

---

38. See especially IR Macneil, 'Efficient Breach of Contract: Circles in the Sky' (1982) 68 Virginia Law Review 947.

39. See Chapter 1, section 1.3.3 'Contemporary views on contract: bundles of rights or relationships?'.

Covenants such as the non-compete agreement referred to in this email are often called *negative covenants*, because they commit a party to refrain from doing something. In a situation such as the one in Illustration 17.1, where a negative covenant might potentially be broken, the innocent party will frequently want to stop the covenant from being broken, rather than having to sue for damages after breach has taken place. This is the remedy which injunctions provide.

In *Lumley v Wagner*,[40] the parties had entered into a contract under which Wagner agreed, for a period of three months, to sing at Lumley's theatre two nights a week and not to perform at any other theatre. She then agreed to sing at a different theatre, and refused to sing at Lumley's theatre. Lumley was held to be entitled to an injunction restraining Wagner from breaching her promise. More recently, in *Araci v Fallon*,[41] a jockey was injuncted from breaking his agreement with a horse-owner by riding a horse for a different stable.

An injunction, like specific performance, is an equitable remedy, and is therefore discretionary. Injunctions will not be granted if they will cause hardship or be oppressive to the defendant. This is particularly true if the harm is small, or could easily be compensated through the award of damages.[42] In *Page One Records v Britton*,[43] a pop group was trying, in breach of contract, to fire its manager and hire a different manager. The court refused to grant an injunction restraining breach, on the basis that the courts would not force the clients to retain a manager with whom they no longer wished to work. For similar reasons, an injunction will not be granted where it would impose so much financial hardship on an employee as to, in effect, compel him to work for the original employer.[44]

Similarly, injunctions will not be granted if the effect would be to grant specific performance of a contract that would not have been specifically performed. In *Warren v Mendy*,[45] Warren, a boxing manager, believed that Mendy, a rival manager, was attempting to persuade one of Warren's clients, Nigel Benn, to fire Warren and to appoint Mendy in his place. He sought an injunction against Mendy. The court held that an injunction would not be granted. The relationship between boxer and manager involved mutual trust and confidence. An injunction would not serve either party if the confidence no longer subsisted. Specific performance of such an agreement would not have been granted, and the effect of an injunction would have been indistinguishable from specific performance.

Injunctions will also not be granted if their effect would be against public policy, for example through enforcing an agreement in restraint of trade.

 Practice in context: team moves and springboard injunctions

Cases like *Lumley v Wagner* related to potential breaches of conduct by a single employee. A more recent trend is the 'team move' in which a group of employees leave an employer as a team, either to work for a competitor or to set up a competing business of their own. The

➡️

---

40. (1852) 2 De GM & G 604.   41. [2011] EWCA Civ 668.
42. See *Jaggard v Sawyer* [1995] 1 WLR 269.   43. [1967] 3 All ER 822.
44. *Sunrise Brokers LLP v Rodgers* [2014] EWHC 2633 (QB).   45. [1989] 1 WLR 853.

growth of team moves has led to the development (or, rather, the extension) of a new type of remedy, the springboard injunction or springboard order. The cases in relation to springboard injunctions provide an excellent overview of why injunctions are sometimes necessary, but also why the courts approach their grant with so much caution.

Springboard injunctions were originally developed in relation to misuse of confidential information, to ensure that the party in breach did not gain an unfair competitive advantage (or 'springboard') through their breach. They have since been widened to encompass a range of duties arising under employment contracts including implied duties of good faith and fiduciary loyalty, as well as express terms such as non-compete clauses. Nevertheless, their availability remains tightly circumscribed. There is a natural tension between, on the one hand, the employer's interest of trying to ensure that former employees do not use knowledge, confidential information, and contacts they acquired in the course of their employment for their personal benefit against the former employer's interests, and, on the other hand, the inherent right of an individual to work freely after a particular engagement has come to an end, and the public policy in favour of free competition.

The rules in relation to springboard injunctions reflect this tension. The case law imposes three sets of requirements on the grant of springboard injunctions, in an attempt to balance these competing interests and policies. First, springboard injunctions are only granted where the employees have gained a springboard, or unfair head start, by misusing confidential information or by breaching legal or contractual duties. The key question which the court asks is whether the employee's activities were in breach of his or her duty to serve their employer faithfully and honestly. Springboard injunctions have been granted where the employees breached the implied duty of good faith and fidelity owed by employees to employers or breached the fiduciary duty which certain classes of employee owe. They have, for example, been granted where employees solicited clients of their current employer while still working for it, where a senior employee solicited junior staff in his team,[46] and where a group of employees deliberately misled their employer as to their intentions.[47] They are also granted where the team move has involved the commission of a tort—for example, an unlawful means conspiracy,[48] and can be granted both against the employees and against third parties, for example a poaching employer.[49]

The other two requirements are relatively straightforward. The second is that the unfair advantage must cause, or create a risk of causing, serious economic loss to the previous employer, and the injunction must be necessary to prevent the parties from continuing to enjoy this unfair advantage.[50] Finally, springboard injunctions are granted only to prevent harm to the claimant, and not to punish the party in breach. In particular, the egregiousness of the defendant's conduct is wholly irrelevant to the grant of a springboard injunction. It is only the impact the unlawful advantage has on the claimant that matters.

---

46. *QBE Management Services (UK) Ltd v Dymoke* [2012] EWHC 80 (QB).
47. *Kynixa v Hynes* [2008] EWHC 1495 (QB).
48. *UBS Wealth Management UK Ltd v Vestra LLP* [2008] EWHC 1974 (QB).
49. *Tullet Prebon v BGC Brokers* [2011] EWCA Civ 131.
50. *UBS Wealth Management UK Ltd v Vestra LLP* [2008] EWHC 1974 (QB).

➔

> This last point is of particular importance, because it reiterates a cardinal principle of English law in relation to contractual remedies. Remedies are granted for the sole purpose of redressing the harm caused by breach. They are not a mark of disapproval of the defendant's conduct. Whether the defendant acted capriciously, maliciously, or innocently is irrelevant once the fact of breach has been established. This principle runs through all of the law of remedies and should be kept in mind when studying its rules. The morality or otherwise of the defendant's conduct is never at issue in determining what remedy the claimant will be given.

17.2.3 Damages in lieu

Under s 50 of the Senior Courts Act 1981, the courts have a statutory discretion to award **damages in lieu** of specific performance or an injunction. Damages in lieu are awarded where the claimant will sustain loss as a result of the refusal of an injunction, in order to compensate the claimant for that loss.[51] The jurisdiction to grant these damages is equitable in nature, and therefore depends on the claimant overcoming equitable defences such as acquiescence and estoppel.[52]

Damages in lieu are often assessed using the hypothetical bargain measure discussed in Chapter 16, as the case of *Wrotham Park Estate Co v Parkside Homes*[53] illustrates. Parkside Homes held land subject to a restrictive covenant in favour of Wrotham Park Estate, under which there were limitations on its ability to build on its land. It built in breach of that restrictive covenant. Wrotham Park Estate sued for an injunction. The injunction was refused based on a principle dating back to the 19th century under which injunctions will not ordinarily be granted where the work has been completed, unless it would result in serious damage.[54] However, the court exercised its discretion to award damages in lieu of the injunction. The judge held that these should be assessed with reference to the price which the claimant would have charged the defendant for a partial release from the covenant. On the facts, this was likely to have been a proportion of the defendant's profits. The court accordingly awarded a sum equal to 5 per cent of the defendant's profits.

The hypothetical bargain measure is, however, simply one way in which damages in lieu are assessed. In *Morris-Garner v One Step (Support) Ltd*,[55] the Supreme Court emphasized that damages in lieu can be quantified in a number of ways, and that the appropriate measure to use in any case is for the court to judge, based on what will 'give a fair equivalent for what is lost by the refusal of the injunction'.[56]

17.2.4 The role of statute

Certain statutes give parties to contracts a specific right to bring an action for specific performance, either as a discretionary remedy or a remedy available as a matter of

---

51. *Jaggard v Sawyer* [1995] 1 WLR 269, 276–7 (Sir Thomas Bingham MR).   52. Ibid, 287.
53. [1974] 1 WLR 798.   54. *Deere v Guest* (1836) 1 My & Cr 516.
55. [2018] UKSC 20.   56. Ibid, [95].

right. Section 52 of the Sale of Goods Act 1979 is an example of the former. Under this section, the court has the discretion to order specific performance in any contract for the delivery of specific or ascertained goods.

Section 52 arguably adds nothing to the general discretion to award specific performance. The Consumer Rights Act 2015, however, takes a very different approach. Although it does not use the terminology of specific performance, it creates a number of remedial rights which are functionally equivalent. If goods supplied under a consumer contract fail to adhere to the statutory rights set out in ss 9–11 and 13–16 of the Act,[57] the consumer has the right to require the trader to repair or replace the goods.[58] Similar rights apply to digital content.[59] In each case, the remedy of repair or replacement will not be available if it is impossible or would be disproportionate compared with other remedies. Whether the remedy is disproportionate depends on the value of the conforming goods, the significance of the lack of conformity, and the inconvenience to the consumer caused by the non-conformity (keeping in mind the purpose of the goods).[60]

Where the contract is for services rather than goods, and the services do not conform to any aspect of the contract (statutory or otherwise), then the consumer has the right to require repeat performance to make the performance conform.[61] The only ground on which repeat performance can be denied is impossibility. Disproportionality does not apply in relation to services.[62]

Given the newness of the Act, it is as yet impossible to say how these remedies will develop, but they represent a very significant shift in English law in favour of literal enforcement, even if only in the domain of consumer law.

17.2.5 Putting it together: enforcement or compensation?

Let us now summarize the discussion thus far. Despite the rhetoric of 'enforcing' contracts, the law only rarely actually grants an order of specific performance outside the consumer context. Several reasons can be attributed to this. The first relates to commercial freedom. Parties should be free, on this view, not only to make contracts but also to break them. The freedom to deal with whomsoever you choose also includes the freedom to change your mind. As long as you ensure that you properly compensate your counterparty, there is no compelling reason to restrict this freedom. It is fallacious to regard breach as a 'wrong': the wrong is causing loss, which damages are perfectly adequate to redress. Specific performance is appropriately confined to the minority of cases where the harm cannot be properly compensated through damages.

A second reason is that contract law does not protect all interests that might be at stake in a contract, or which might be affected by breach. Contract law's main concern is with the subset of interests that are properly regarded as commercial and, in relation to consumer contracts, with a small number of additional consumer interests connected with contracts entered into primarily for the purpose of obtaining a pleasurable

---

57. These are discussed in greater depth in Chapter 8.   58. S 19(3), (4).   59. S 43.
60. Ss 23, 43.   61. S 55.   62. S 55(3).

good or service. The law of damages does not protect interests beyond these, and it would disrupt this framework if the law of specific performance were to take a different approach.

A third reason is more pragmatic, and relates to Lord Westbury's warning about the propensity of specific performance to deliver the defendant over to the claimant 'bound hand and foot'. Breach of contract is often a consequence of parties failing to properly foresee or plan for all contingencies that might unfold in the course of a transaction, or having an overly optimistic view of the resources, costs, and time frame involved in performing a transaction. Specific performance in such circumstances is arguably an overly powerful remedy, which puts the claimant in a position to dictate terms to the defendant in ways that are not helpful to cooperative behaviour.

These considerations lie behind English law's restrictive approach to non-monetary remedies. Where, then, does this leave the parties in the two examples we have examined so far—the employers of James Bowerson in Illustration 17.1 and the customers of Ethical Hens in Problem 17? As far as the employers of Bowerson are concerned, specific performance will be unavailable, as the contract involved is one of personal service. However, if they can demonstrate that an injunction will not be oppressive, that it will not amount to an order of specific performance through the back door, and that the harm they would suffer is not small or easily compensable through damages, they may be able to claim an injunction restraining him from working for a competitor.

The outlook for the customers of Ethical Hens is not as optimistic. Although Ethical Hens is clearly in breach, it is unlikely that a court will grant an order of specific performance. Following the decision in *Co-operative Insurance v Argyll*, the sort of order required would appear to almost inevitably entail constant superintendence. It is also difficult to see how it could avoid the problem of making an order that is so sufficiently precise that Ethical Hens will know what they have to do to comply. Although damages are clearly not an adequate remedy, it is unlikely that they will succeed in obtaining specific performance.

Although the result seems unfair, it points to the fact that the law of contract is a limited instrument. Contract law is not designed to protect every conceivable interest, and it does not protect interests that cannot easily be fitted into a paradigm of exchange—as, for example, the 'consumer surplus' can. The interests at stake for the customers of Ethical Hens do not fit into the template of exchange, and their violation is therefore not remedied by contract law. From a pragmatic perspective, this reflects the position that contracts and contract law are the wrong sort of instrument for the goals the parties are trying to achieve.

A far more promising legal vehicle is provided by the law of trusts, which is designed to create enforceable obligations of precisely this type. A consideration of trust law and how it might be used in such situations is well beyond the scope of this book, but the point to take away is that in thinking about transactions, it is usually important to take a broader view of the legal instruments which the law makes available, and to consider the relative suitability of each, instead of simply starting with contracts.

17.3 **Debt**

> ### Illustration 17.2
>
> Consider this message you receive from a friend:
>
> > Hey, you know I had to interrupt my studies earlier this year because I fell ill? I had to go home to get better so I vacated my room in the house six months before the lease was up. My landlord is now saying I need to pay the rent for the full year, including the six months after I vacated the room. She says she can sue me in county court for a debt. Is this right? It seems unfair, as she can rent the room out to someone else, surely?? Thought you might know, as you're a law student!

Specific performance is not the only mode through which the terms of a contract can be directly enforced. If the term in question involves the payment of a definite sum of money due under a contract, then it can be enforced through a claim in debt. Unlike specific performance, debt is not a discretionary remedy (although the court has some discretion in relation to some types of consumer credit). It brings with it startling advantages. Unlike an action for damages, the claimant in debt does not have to mitigate his loss. Equally, the rules on remoteness do not apply. This is because the claimant is not seeking compensation for loss, but is seeking the direct enforcement of a contractual obligation to pay. What is being enforced here is not a secondary obligation, but the primary obligation itself.

These rules make sense when we are talking about a debt in the commonly understood sense of a contract where someone has borrowed money. Here, it is hard to see how the creditor could take steps to 'mitigate' the loss arising from late payment. However, the legal remedy of debt applies not just to debts in the everyday sense, but to any claim for a definite sum of money due under the contract. The effect of this can be seen from the decision in *White & Carter (Councils) Ltd v McGregor*,[63] which was discussed in some detail in Chapter 15 ('Breach of contract'). The defendants had contracted with the claimants to display advertisements on the claimants' bins. They sought to cancel the contract on the same day but the claimants refused to accept the repudiation, displayed the ads, and sued for the price. One of the defences raised by McGregor was that the claimants had failed to take reasonable steps to mitigate their loss. This was rejected by the House of Lords, on a 3:2 majority. Whilst the two dissenting judges would have rejected the claim on the basis of a failure to mitigate, the majority held otherwise, on the basis that the requirement of mitigation did not apply to a suit for the contract price. Instead of mitigation, the court held the claimant's rights to be limited by the less restrictive idea of a 'legitimate interest' in performance.

The *White and Carter* exception is applicable more broadly, including (arguably) to the type of situation discussed in Illustration 17.2. In *Reichman v Beveridge*,[64] the

63. [1962] AC 413.   64. [2006] EWCA Civ 1659.

defendants were tenants who had leased an office for a five-year term from the claimants. Three years into the lease, they quit the premises. The landlord sued in debt for the full rent for the unpaid term. The claimants sought to resist the suit, arguing that the landlord had failed to mitigate his loss. The Court of Appeal rejected their defence, holding that a landlord was under no requirement to mitigate where a lease had been terminated for breach.

Other common law jurisdictions have moved away from this rule, holding it to be anomalous. In *Vickers & Vickers v Stichtenoth Investments Pty Ltd*,[65] Bollen J in the Supreme Court of South Australia challenged its logical basis:

> Why should not a landlord faced with abandonment take steps to try to reduce his loss? Why should a vendor of tomatoes faced with a refusal to take delivery by his purchaser suffer if he does not sell if he can to another purchaser and yet a quiescent and immobile landlord not suffer if he fails to seek another tenant? Modern ideas say that there is no reason for this anomaly.[66]

It is submitted that Bollen J's comments have substance. It is hard to see how the absence of a requirement of mitigation in cases like *White & Carter* or *Reichman* can be sustained, but as things stand there is little sign that the English courts intend to revisit the correctness of the rule.

17.4 Gain-based remedies and the restitution interest

If literal enforcement is not awarded to the customers of Ethical Hens, could a possible remedy lie in ordering a different monetary remedy, which does not suffer from the weaknesses that an award of damages would have?

A fundamental principle of compensatory damages is that they are awarded to compensate the innocent party for the loss suffered in consequence of the breach. This has a strong justificatory basis in law, as Chapter 16 discusses, but it also has limitations in situations like that faced by the customers of Ethical Hens, where the harm they suffered is not of a type that an award of damages can compensate. Gain-based remedies, or *restitutionary remedies* as they are also known, are based on a radically different principle. Like compensatory damages, gain-based remedies require the party in breach to pay money to the innocent party. Unlike the law of damages, however, the amount that must be paid is measured not with reference to the claimant's *loss* but with reference to the defendant's *gain*.

Gain-based remedies are therefore fundamentally different from ordinary damages. Unlike expectation and reliance damages, gain-based remedies are not limited by mitigation or by remoteness. This is because mitigation and remoteness set bounds on the claimant's recoverable loss, rather than the defendant's gain. For the same reason, restitutionary remedies are also not subject to many other limits on the expectation or reliance interest. The principle that the claimant cannot be placed in a better position

---

65. (1989) 52 SASR 90.   66. Ibid, 100.

than he would have been in had the contract been performed, for example, does not apply to gain-based damages.

Although gain-based remedies represent a striking departure from the ordinary approach to contract damages, their existence is not in itself controversial. Since at least the 1930s, gain-based remedies have been seen as protecting the **restitution interest** which, along with the **expectation interest** and the reliance interest, is one of the three core interests protected by contract remedies. However, the scope of gain-based remedies has expanded dramatically in the past half-century. Underlying this expansion was the theoretical claim that gain-based remedies were a response to situations where a party was *unjustly enriched* by breaching a contract, and were awarded in order to reverse that enrichment. The idea of reversing unjust enrichment helped shed significant light on a number of problematic areas of law. Nevertheless, the expansion of gain-based remedies has raised serious theoretical and practical questions about their proper limits, and when they should be awarded.

English law recognizes three different ways of quantifying the defendant's gain for the purpose of granting gain-based remedies for breach of contract. The first, restitution for total failure of consideration, involves the return by the defendant of money paid to him by the claimant where the consideration for which the money was paid has completely failed. The second, *quantum meruit*, enables the claimant to claim the fair value of goods or services provided under a contract which has turned out to be void or which was terminated before payment was made. The third, the **account of profit** measure, requires the defendant to pay the claimant all or part of the profits that he has made as a result of the breach.

The first two of these go back centuries and are relatively uncontroversial. The third is more recent, and is closely associated with the theory that gain-based remedies are a response to unjust enrichment. In this section, we will examine each of these three in turn. You should note that the literature on unjust enrichment is a complex one, with its own very particular terminology (involving concepts such as 'quadration' and distinctions between 'restitution for unjust enrichment' and 'restitution for wrongs'). Full details of this terminology, and of the distinctions it seeks to make, can be found in specialized texts on restitution. This chapter focuses on the key principles that are of relevance to contract remedies.

17.4.1 **Recovering money paid**

> ### Illustration 17.3
>
> Aoife books a package holiday at a luxury beachfront hotel in Cyprus. She pays 50 per cent of the price up front as a deposit. Two days before she is to depart, she is told that the specific hotel she had booked her holiday in is overbooked, and that her reservation has been cancelled. She is offered alternative accommodation. Aoife refuses, and asks for her money back.

We quite commonly encounter situations like the one in Illustration 17.3. In such situations, demanding one's money back is a perfectly usual response. Yet while expectation and reliance damages do provide some measure of compensation, neither actually gives the victim of a breach the right to claim a refund, or to get their money back. In English law, getting your money back for breach is a tightly circumscribed remedy, which is only available when the claimant can demonstrate that there has been a *total failure of consideration*. In effect, this requires the claimant to show that she received no part of the benefit for which she contracted. In such a case, the defendant is taken to have been unjustly enriched by having received money from the claimant without providing the corresponding benefit that he had contractually agreed to provide.

Two distinctions are of fundamental importance to the availability of this remedy. The first is the distinction between a total failure of consideration and a failure that is merely partial. A partial failure of consideration is insufficient for the purpose of recovering money paid to the other party. In such a case, the party in breach will only be able to recover damages on the expectation or reliance interests. The second distinction is between a payment and a deposit. Payments are recoverable but deposits are ordinarily assumed to be intended to have been placed at risk and will therefore not normally be recoverable.

Total and partial failures of consideration

A total failure of consideration is one in which the claimant receives no part of what she has bargained for. If a claimant receives some of what she bargained for, but not all, the failure of consideration is only partial. The distinction turns on what the parties contracted for and is a matter of contract interpretation. Cases which, on their facts, might seem similar can come out differently depending on the precise thing for which the parties contracted. In *Rover International Ltd and others v Cannon Film Sales Ltd*,[67] a distribution contract was discovered to be void. The distribution company had at the time received and distributed a number of prints, but had not yet received any share of the gross receipts. The Court of Appeal held that there had been a total failure of consideration. The distribution company had contracted for the opportunity to earn a share of the income from the films, which it had never had. In contrast, in *Hyundai Heavy Industries Co Ltd v Papadopoulos*,[68] a shipbuilding contract was rescinded before the ship was built, but after it had been designed. The House of Lords held that there had not been a total failure of consideration, because the agreement was not simply a sale and resembled a building contract, which meant that part of the consideration had been received.[69]

It is important to note that the court is assessing whether the consideration for which the party bargained has failed. This is not the same as asking whether the party has received a benefit under the contract. A party may have received a collateral benefit without having actually received the main benefit contracted for. The most straightforward illustration is a contract for the sale of goods where the goods in question have had to be handed to a third party because the seller lacked title, as happened in *Manson v Burningham*.[70] Here, it is no defence to say that the claimant received a benefit because they had the use of the goods for a period of time. What the claimant contracted for was not the right to use the goods for a period of time. It was the right to

67. [1989] 1 WLR 912 (CA).   68. [1980] 1 WLR 1129 (HL).
69. Ibid, 1134 (Viscount Dilhorne).
70. [1949] 2 KB 545 (CA), discussed in Chapter 16, section 16.2.4. See also *Rowland v Divall* [1923] 2 KB 500.

acquire title to the goods, and that was not received. Similarly, it is also not a defence to show that the defendant has spent time and money attempting to perform the contract.[71] An attempt to perform is not the same as giving the claimant the consideration for which she has contracted.

There is a body of academic literature that has argued against the distinction between total and partial failures of consideration, suggesting that the remedy should also be available where the failure of consideration is only partial.[72] Any hardship to the defendant, it has been suggested, can be got around by requiring the claimant to pay for the partial benefit she has received. A substantially similar approach has been endorsed by the High Court of Australia.[73] In England, however, the courts have refused to follow this lead, and have expressly affirmed the requirement that the failure of consideration must be total.[74] It appears that any change to this position will have to come from the legislature.

The implications of this can be seen by returning to Problem 17. The customers of Ethical Hens have clearly received some benefit in exchange for their money; namely, the eggs. This means that the failure of consideration is at best partial, thus taking the case outwith the scope of restitution for failure of consideration. In the Australian approach, in contrast, the court would have been more willing to order restitution, subject if necessary to counter-restitution for the market value the eggs would have had without the added promise of a slaughter-free retirement for the hens.

Deposits

The ability to recover money paid does not usually depend on whether or not the breach was the fault of the payer. If, however, the money was paid as a deposit by the person in breach, then she will not be able to recover it unless the contract expressly provides to the contrary. This is because a deposit is ordinarily assumed to be provided by way of security, which means that it will be forfeited if the contract is not performed by the payer. This rule applies even if the contract expressly states that the deposit is an advance towards the purchase price.[75] A party in breach cannot recover deposits, even if the breach has led to a total failure of consideration. This rule, however, only applies where the money was paid as a deposit, rather than as a part-payment, and where the payer has failed to perform his part of the contract. If either of these conditions is not met, the deposit will be recoverable if there has been a total failure of consideration.

Returning, then, to Illustration 17.3, it should now be apparent that Aoife will be able to claim back the money she has paid. Because she has been deprived of the specific holiday she signed up to, she has not received any portion of the benefit for which she contracted. This means that there has been a total failure of consideration. Although the sum she paid has been termed a 'deposit', she will be able to recover the money as it was the other party who was in breach.

---

71. See *Fibrosa Spolka Akcyjna v Fairbairn Lawson Combe Barbour Ltd* [1943] AC 32, discussed in Chapter 10.

72. See esp A Burrows, *The Law of Restitution* (3rd edn, Oxford University Press 2010) 330–4.

73. *David Securities Pty Ltd v Commonwealth Bank of Australia* (1992) 66 ALJR 768 (High Court of Australia), 779–80.

74. *Stocznia Gdanska SA v Latvian SS Co, Latreefers Inc* [1998] 1 WLR 574 (HL).

75. *Howe v Smith* (1884) 27 Ch D 89 (CA).

17.4.2 *Quantum meruit* and *quantum valebat*

A second set of gain-based remedies are the closely related remedies of **quantum meruit** and **quantum valebat**. These remedies grant the value of goods or services provided by the claimant to the defendant. The logic underlying these remedies is that the defendant has been enriched at the claimant's expense by receiving the goods or services. If that enrichment is unjust, the law should intervene to reverse it by requiring the defendant to pay the claimant the value of the benefit provided to the defendant. For historical reasons, the remedy is called *quantum valebat* where the benefit took the form of goods and *quantum meruit* where it took the form of services. The principles governing the two are identical, and we will, for brevity, refer to both under the term *quantum meruit*.

Quantum meruit does not displace the rule that the ordinary remedy for unpaid work is an action for damages. As a result, the remedy of *quantum meruit* is subject to two sets of requirements.

Requirement 1: availability

The first set of requirements restrict the circumstances in which *quantum meruit* is available, confining it to three specific sets of circumstances.

First, *quantum meruit* is available where the defendant has committed a repudiatory breach of contract, which the claimant has accepted.[76] If the claimant has provided services or goods to the defendant before the termination which remain unremunerated, the claimant will be able to elect to either sue for expectation or reliance damages, or to sue on a *quantum meruit* for the value of the goods or services provided.

Secondly, *quantum meruit* is available if the contract under which the goods or services were provided is subsequently discovered to be void. Where the contract is not just void but also illegal, for example because it is contrary to public policy, the claimant will only be able to recover if he has not participated in the illegality—for example, if he withdrew from the transaction before any illegal activity took place[77] or if he was unaware of the illegality, and the claim can be made without relying on the illegal contract.[78]

Thirdly, *quantum meruit* is available where work was done anticipating a contract, but no contract was entered into. This often happens when parties carry out the work while continuing to negotiate over the terms. The case of *British Steel Corp v Cleveland Bridge and Engineering Co Ltd*,[79] considered in greater detail in Chapter 2, is a paradigmatic example. If, however, it appears that the work was carried out at the risk of the party performing the service—for example, the party agreed to provide the services for free or 'in the hope of [being] awarded a contract which it might or might not receive'[80]—the court will not ordinarily permit a recovery in *quantum meruit*.

76. See the discussion in Chapter 15 ('Breach of contract').
77. *Patel v Mirza* [2014] EWCA Civ 1047, [2015] 1 Ch 271.
78. *Mohamed v Alaga & Co* [2000] 1 WLR 1815 (CA), 1825 (Lord Bingham CJ).
79. [1984] 1 All ER 504.
80. *MSM Consulting Ltd v United Republic of Tanzania* [2009] EWHC 121 (QB), [174] (Christopher Clarke J).

Requirement 2: 'at the expense of'

In addition to having to fall within one of these three circumstances, claimants seeking a remedy of *quantum meruit* must also demonstrate that they satisfy a second set of requirements; namely, that the defendant was enriched at the claimant's expense. The rules in relation to what constitutes enrichment at another's expense are complex, and a full treatment must be left to treatises on the law of restitution. In general, however, in relation to *quantum meruit*, the defendant will be held to have been unjustly enriched at the claimant's expense in only two sets of circumstances.

The first is where the defendant actually requested the work that was done or the goods that were provided. This was the case in *Countrywide Communications Ltd v ICL Pathway Ltd*,[81] where Countrywide had carried out preliminary work as a public relations consultant. Preliminary work in the hope of being awarded a contract is usually non-remunerable, but on the facts of this case Countrywide had been given express assurances of a contract by ICL beyond what was normal in work of this type. As a result, it was held that they were entitled to recover on a *quantum meruit* on the basis that the work had been requested by ICL with the expectation of payment.

The second is where the defendant received an 'incontrovertible benefit' from the work. This is usually satisfied where the defendant was saved an expense that was legally or factually necessary, or where the defendant obtained a realized or realizable monetary benefit. In *Craven-Ellis v Canons Ltd*,[82] Craven-Ellis had been appointed as the managing director of the defendant company. The company's articles of association required all directors to hold qualifying shares in the company, which Craven-Ellis did not. His appointment was therefore void. Unaware of this, he worked as a managing director for an extended period of time. When the company refused to pay him, he sued on a *quantum meruit*. The Court of Appeal held that he could recover. The company would have had to engage someone to carry out the services which Craven-Ellis carried out, and they had therefore been enriched by having been saved expenses that were factually necessary.

Yeoman's Row v Cobbe[83] similarly related to services rendered under a void contract. Cobbe entered into an oral agreement with Yeoman's Row to develop a property in London. Because the agreement was not reduced to writing, it was void under s 2 of the Law of Property (Miscellaneous Provisions) Act 1989. Cobbe spent a lot of time and effort getting planning permission. Once planning permission was granted, Yeoman's Row sought more money, and ultimately refused to honour the contract. The House of Lords held that Cobbe was entitled to recover £150,000 on a *quantum meruit* for the professional services he had rendered in obtaining planning permission.

The role of the contract price

A claim for *quantum meruit* is treated as being entirely independent of the contract. This means that where a claim for *quantum meruit* arises in connection with a void contract, the claimant can be awarded a sum in excess of the price agreed in the contract, even if this means that he will be left in a better position than if the contract had been valid. In *Rover International Ltd v Cannon Film Sales Ltd*,[84] the Court of Appeal expressly

---

81. [2000] CLC 324 (QB).   82. [1936] 2 KB 403.
83. [2008] UKHL 55, [2008] 1 WLR 1752.   84. [1989] 1 WLR 912 (CA).

rejected the suggestion that the agreed price under a void contract could form a 'cap' or ceiling on the amount recoverable under a *quantum meruit*.

Does this principle also apply to *quantum meruit* in the context of a repudiatory breach of contract? The position in other jurisdictions, such as the US, is that it does.[85] There has been no authoritative decision on the point as yet in England, but there have been some suggestions that English courts might draw a distinction between void contracts, where the contract price will not act as a cap, and breached contracts, where it will. In *Taylor v Motability Finance Ltd*,[86] Cooke J in the High Court expressed the view that where the contract was valid, there could be 'no justification' for permitting recovery in excess of the contract limit. To do so would be to put the party in a better position than if the contract had been performed. The contract provided a guide to the 'value put on the services', to which regard must be had.

17.4.3 Extending gain-based remedies: the 'account of profits' measure

Quantum meruit and recovery for total failure of consideration are both well-established remedies which go back centuries to the early modern actions of *indebitatus assumpsit* and money had and received. Though the remedy is, in theory, measured with reference to the defendant's gain, it also has the effect of ameliorating the claimant's loss, and could with equal plausibility be said to represent an attempt to redress that loss. A purchaser seeking the return of the purchase price has suffered a monetary loss of a type which the law of damages does remedy. A person who has provided services without payment, and who therefore seeks a remedy through *quantum meruit*, has also suffered a loss of a type which the law of damages ordinarily remedies. If this were all there was to gain-based remedies, they could just as easily have been treated as simply representing another approach to quantifying damages, like reliance damages and expectation damages.

Developments that began in the 1970s have, however, considerably expanded the scope of gain-based remedies, by extending them into areas that do not involve such interests and attempting to retheorize certain types of compensation as 'restitution-ary'. Until the decision of the Supreme Court in *Morris-Garner v One Step (Support) Ltd*,[87] for example, the hypothetical bargain measure was often treated as a restitutionary remedy, based on the defendant's gain rather than the claimant's loss.[88] Following the Supreme Court's decision in *One Step*, the main type of restitutionary award for breach is the 'account of profits' measure.

An account of profits requires the defendant to make over to the claimant the entirety of the profit they have made through their breach. Although this remedy was long known in equity, it was traditionally not awarded for a breach of contract. The idea of depriving the defendant of the entirety of its gain has a deterrent or punitive

---

85. This proposition originated in the US case of *Boomer v Muir*, 24 P 2d 570 (1933), where the court awarded over ten times on a *quantum meruit* as much as was due under the contract. For a critical analysis of *Boomer*, see D Campbell, 'Better than Fuller: A Two Interests Model of Remedies for Breach of Contract' (2015) 78 MLR 296, 314–22.

86. [2004] EWHC 2619 (Comm), [26].   87. [2018] UKSC 20.

88. See eg *Experience Hendrix LLC v PPX Enterprises Inc* [2003] EWCA Civ 323.

dimension. This sits uneasily with the fact that contract remedies were traditionally assumed to be about compensating the victim rather than punishing the perpetrator.[89]

This is no longer true. In the case of *Attorney General v Blake*,[90] the House of Lords held that an account of profits could be awarded for breach of contract, for the express purpose of ensuring that the defendant made no profit from its breach. Such a remedy, however, is exceptional, and will only be awarded very rarely.

> ### Case in depth: *Attorney General v Blake* [2001] 1 AC 268 (HL)
>
> *Attorney General v Blake* involved an exceptional set of facts. George Blake, the defendant, was a double agent who had successfully embedded himself in the British intelligence services but was actually a spy for the Soviet Union. He was tried and sentenced to 42 years' imprisonment in 1961, but escaped from jail and fled to Moscow. In 1989, he wrote an autobiography which he published in Britain. The information in the book was by then no longer confidential, but under the terms of his former employment he was required to obtain the prior consent of the Crown to disclose information relating to the Secret Intelligence Service. He published the book without doing so, and the Attorney General sued him on behalf of the Crown, seeking to prevent him from earning royalties on the book.
>
> At first instance and in the Court of Appeal, the primary claim that was advanced related to breach of confidence. This claim, however, failed on the basis that the information disclosed was no longer secret or confidential. In the Court of Appeal, Lord Woolf MR suggested in his judgment that the claim might succeed if it were framed in terms of breach of contract.[91] This claim had not been advanced by the Attorney General either in the High Court or in the Court of Appeal. As a result of Lord Woolf's suggestion, however, by the time the case made it to the House of Lords breach of contract became one of the primary grounds of the claim.
>
> The House of Lords held that an account of profits was available for breach of contract. Lord Nicholls, delivering the leading judgment, said that there are cases where 'the just response to a breach of contract is that the wrongdoer should not be permitted to retain any profit from the breach'.[92] In such cases, an account of profits should in principle be available as a possible remedy:
>
> > When, exceptionally, a just response to a breach of contract so requires, the court should be able to grant the discretionary remedy of requiring a defendant to account to the plaintiff for the benefits he has received from his breach of contract. In the same way as a plaintiff's interest in performance of a contract may render it just and equitable for the court to make an order for specific performance or grant an injunction, so the plaintiff's interest in performance may make it just and equitable that the defendant should retain no benefit from his breach of contract.[93]
>
> The foundation of this remedy is that damages are not always a sufficient remedy for breach of contract. Much as this has given the courts the jurisdiction to grant specific performance, it
>
> →

89. For a classic statement of this position, see *Teacher v Calder* (1899) 1 F(HL) 39.
90. [2001] 1 AC 268 (HL).   91. [1998] Ch 439 (CA), 455–9.   92. [2001] 1 AC 268, 284.
93. Ibid, 284–5.

should also give them a jurisdiction to award an account of profits. Lord Nicholls was careful to stress that this would not be an ordinary remedy. It was only exceptionally that an account of profits would be the most appropriate remedy for breach of contract.[94] Nevertheless, the law should recognize its availability in those exceptional cases.

Lord Nicholls did not expressly set out what made a case sufficiently exceptional to justify the award of an account of profits, but he gave some suggestions as to things that would not justify such an order. An account of profits should *not* be ordered merely because the breach was 'cynical and deliberate', or because it let the party in breach enter into a more profitable transaction with a third party, or because the defendant failed to perform the contract because he had entered into a new and more profitable contract.[95] On the question of what sort of factors *would* point in favour of the grant of an account of profits, however, he was rather more vague.

> The court will have regard to all the circumstances, including the subject matter of the contract, the purpose of the contractual provision which has been breached, the circumstances in which the breach occurred, the consequences of the breach and the circumstances in which relief is being sought.[96]

This general statement does not take us very far. Two specific points that he did make, however, were that accounts of profits were grounded in the inadequacy of damages, and that it would be a useful general guide to ask whether the claimant 'had a legitimate interest in preventing the defendant's profit-making activity and, hence, in depriving him of his profit'.[97] On the facts of *Blake*, both these criteria were satisfied, with the result that an account of profits was ordered, thus requiring Blake to pay all his royalties to the Crown.

It is worth noting that the expansion effected in *Blake* would not have come about had the Court of Appeal not suggested it as a possible ground. It was not raised by the lawyers for the Crown, and to that extent, even more so than in other areas, it represents a purely judicial innovation, and one made in a way that does not sit very well with conventional accounts of the common law developing through a purely adversarial process.[98]

Nevertheless, subsequent cases have built upon both limbs stressed by Lord Nicholls; namely, the importance of making the remedy available and the importance of ensuring that it is an exceptional remedy. The remedy remains available, but it also remains confined to exceptional cases. The majority of cases discussing *Blake* have done so in the context of explaining why it would not be appropriate to award an account of profits on the facts of that case. Before getting into these cases, however, it is worth examining one of the few cases apart from *Blake* to award a full account of profits for breach of contract. This is the decision of the High Court in *Esso Petroleum Co Ltd v Niad Ltd*.[99]

94. Ibid, 285.   95. Ibid, 286.   96. Ibid, 285.   97. Ibid, 285.
98. In this context, see the critical comments of Richard Buxton LJ (writing in his personal capacity) in R Buxton, 'How the Common Law Gets Made: *Hedley Byrne* and Other Cautionary Tales' (2009) 125 LQR 60, 73–8.
99. [2001] WL 1476190 (Ch).

Case in depth: *Esso Petroleum Co Ltd v Niad Ltd* **[2001] WL 1476190 (Ch)**

Niad Ltd ran a petrol station in Leyburn, Yorkshire, under a solus agreement with Esso. Esso had a 'Pricewatch' scheme, which obliged retailers to adhere to a cap on petrol prices. This was done to make Esso petrol pumps more competitive. In return, Esso would give dealers the benefit of a price-support scheme, which gave dealers a special margin.

Niad signed a contract agreeing to adhere to this scheme. In breach of this undertaking, Niad then proceeded to repeatedly sell petrol in excess of the cap stipulated by Esso. When Esso discovered this, it brought an action for breach of contract. Given the nature of the breach, it would have been very difficult for Esso to prove that it had suffered loss. Consequently, they sought an account of profits, relying on the decision in *Blake*.

Morritt V-C in the High Court granted an account of profits, justifying this on four grounds. First, the difficulty of proving loss made damages an inadequate remedy, thus satisfying one of the criteria set out in *Blake*. Secondly, the entire Pricewatch scheme depended on dealers complying with their obligation to implement and maintain the recommended pump prices, which Niad had failed to do. Thirdly, when complaints had been made about Niad's non-compliance in the past, it had falsely given the appearance of complying without demur. Fourthly, Esso had a legitimate interest in preventing Niad from profiting from its breach.[100]

Morritt V-C also held that Esso could recover the excess money charged by Niad through a standard restitutionary remedy, although it would have to elect between this remedy and the *Blake* remedy. Niad had been enriched by charging pump prices above the cap, and this enrichment was unjust because it was a breach of contract. As such, Esso could claim a remedy that reversed Niad's unjust enrichment.

The decision in *Esso v Niad* caused some concern. Two lines of criticism have emerged. First, it has been pointed out that if an interest of the nature of Esso's interest in the profits is to be considered a 'legitimate interest' for the purpose of the rule in *Blake*, then it is difficult to see how the remedy of account of profits remains exceptional.[101] By Morritt V-C's reasoning, an account of profit will end up being available in *any* case where it is difficult to prove loss, and where the term breached is important. Secondly, it has been argued that *Esso v Niad* reflects a deeper problem with the decision in *Blake* itself, namely, the tendency for judges to create 'nebulous' and 'open-ended' exceptions to cater for very rare situations. Such exceptions are problematic, because they have a deleterious impact on the certainty and predictability that contract law needs if it is to provide a stable framework for commercial transactions.[102]

Whilst *Esso v Niad* has not been expressly overruled, subsequent cases indicate that the courts have returned to a more cautious approach to awarding account of profits

---

100. Ibid, [63].

101. J Beatson, 'Courts, Arbitrators and Restitutionary Liability for Breach of Contract' (2002) 118 LQR 377, 378.

102. R Ahdar, 'Contract Doctrine, Predictability and the Nebulous Exception' (2014) 73 CLJ 39.

for breach of contract. In *Morris-Garner v One Step (Support) Ltd*,[103] the Supreme Court emphasized that they were not an ordinary remedy:

> Common law damages for breach of contract cannot be awarded merely for the purpose of depriving the defendant of profits made as a result of the breach, other than in exceptional circumstances, following *Attorney General v Blake*.

This arguably does no more than take the qualifications set out by Lord Nicholls seriously, and place them within the broader context of contract remedies. Within this broader context, the mere fact that the defendant has profited from his breach is not by itself problematic, and should not therefore lead to the award of an account of profits. The purpose of contract remedies—and, indeed, of contract law—is not to prevent the defendant from making a profit by breaching her contract or even to prevent her from breaching the contract. It is to ensure that the claimant is not left holding a loss as a result of the defendant's breach.[104] This purpose is best served through a narrow reading of the decision in *Blake*.

Some commentators have taken the view that the availability of the remedy in *Blake* will simply remain a matter of judicial discretion. In *Vercoe v Rutland Fund Management Ltd*,[105] however, Sales J in the High Court suggested a different approach, drawing a parallel between the courts' discretion to award an account of profits under *Blake* and its more general remedial discretion to 'control the amount of damages to be awarded in a contract case', seen in cases like *Ruxley Electronics* (discussed in Chapter 16, section 16.2.3). What the court was doing in such cases, he said, was assessing the remedy to be awarded in a contract case:

> by reference to the strength of the claimant's interest in performance of a contractual obligation, judged on an objective basis and weighing that against countervailing legitimate interests of the defendant, to ensure that the remedy awarded is not oppressive and is properly proportionate to the wrong done to the claimant.[106]

When applied to the question of whether an account of profits should be awarded, this would lead the court to ask 'whether the claimant's interest in performance of the obligation in question . . . makes it just and equitable that the defendant should retain no benefit from his breach of that obligation'.[107]

Sales J's approach has much to commend it. It fits with the view that contract remedies are primarily about loss-splitting which, as we have seen, underlies the case law not only on damages but also on specific performance. It may well mean that the grant of the remedy of an account of profits will be very infrequent and, indeed, that *Blake* may remain a 'solitary beacon' for the foreseeable future.[108] This, too, fits with the restrictive approach to *Blake* endorsed by the Supreme Court in *One Step*. The editors of

---

103. [2018] UKSC 20, [95] (Lord Reed JSC).

104. Professor Campbell has argued that the position of 'breach but pay damages' is in many respects the best position the law could take in encouraging parties to cooperatively deal with problems that arise in the course of contracting. See D Campbell, 'A Relational Critique of the *Third Restatement of Restitution* §39' (2011) 68 Washington & Lee Law Review 1063.

105. [2010] EWHC 424 (Ch).   106. Ibid, [339].   107. Ibid.

108. This phrase was used in *Blake* itself to describe the decision in *Wrotham Park*. See *Attorney General v Blake* [2001] 1 AC 268, 283 (Lord Nicholls).

Chitty on Contract have suggested that the import of the cases after *Esso v Niad* is that an account of profits will only be awarded where the relationship of the defendant to the claimant is akin to a fiduciary relationship, which will make it rare in commercial contracts. Such a result, it is submitted, is entirely appropriate, given the sweeping character of the remedy of account of profits and its dramatic impact on the defendant. The law of contract should not be dragged into assessing the legitimacy or illegitimacy of profits made by the defendant, and it is both fitting and proper to foreclose readings of *Blake* which might have the potential to draw it down that path.

17.5 In conclusion: remedies beyond compensation

As the discussion in this chapter has demonstrated, English law takes sharply different approaches to monetary and non-monetary remedies. When the remedy sought is monetary, English courts have been willing to look beyond damages in the traditional sense. They have been willing to literally enforce contracts by expanding the scope of the action of debt, even though that robs the defendant of the protection otherwise afforded by mitigation and remoteness.

When it comes to non-monetary remedies, however, English law takes a much more limited view. In the first instance, it offers a much narrower range of remedies than do civil law systems. Outside certain types of consumer transactions, remedies that we may commonly associate with responding to breach, such as the repair or replacement of defective goods, are not granted by contract law at all. This is even truer of specific performance where, despite promising developments in the 1960s, the remedy remains very narrow and is rarely granted—a position that appears to have been entrenched for the foreseeable future following the decision in *Co-operative Insurance v Argyll*. Despite the plethora of non-monetary remedies available in English law, therefore, it is extremely unlikely that the customers of Ethical Hens will be able to claim any of them.

Commentators remain divided on the desirability of both these trends, as well as of outcomes such as those that would be the likely result of an action brought by claimants in the position of the customers of Ethical Hens. These divisions are rooted in fundamental differences as to the role of the law of contract and the remedies it affords, which are unlikely to fade with time. The key point to take away from this is the one made in Chapter 16—namely, the importance of careful drafting, and in particular of ensuring that contracts incorporate remedies that are appropriate to the specifics of the transaction. If parties desire broader remedies than the basic remedies guaranteed by law, they will need to draft their contracts in a manner that provides for them. The flexibility of English contract law gives parties plenty of tools to do so; but at the same time the reluctance of English courts to improve or enhance the parties' contract means that in the absence of such design, the parties may well be stuck with a very limited set of remedies which stop well short of protecting the interests the contract was intended to protect.

Key points

- English law recognizes remedies other than compensatory damages. The most important of these are literal enforcement of the contract and gain-based remedies.

- Literal enforcement takes the form of debt when the obligation in question involves the payment of money. For all other obligations, it takes the form of specific performance or an injunction.

- Debt is available as a matter of right where a party seeks to enforce a term involving the payment of a definite sum of money. Unlike damages, there is no duty to mitigate losses in an action of debt.

- Specific performance is not available as a matter of right. It is discretionary, and is an exceptional remedy. It will only be granted where damages are not an adequate remedy. There are a number of grounds on which specific performance will be refused even if damages are not an adequate remedy. These include cases where the courts would have to engage in constant supervision to ensure that the order of specific performance was being complied with.

- Injunctions can be sought to enforce negative covenants. They are also discretionary, and can be refused for reasons similar to specific performance. Courts can award damages in lieu of an injunction or specific performance.

- In a limited number of cases, a party can sue for a monetary amount measured with reference to the other party's gain, rather than its own loss. There are three such remedies: the ability to recover monies paid under a contract, the ability to sue for *quantum meruit* or *quantum valebat*, and the remedy of an account of profits.

- A party who has paid an advance under a contract can sue for the return of the advance if there has been a total failure of consideration.

- A party can sue in *quantum meruit* or *quantum valebat* to claim the fair market value of goods or services provided to the other party if there has been a repudiatory breach, or if they were provided under a void contract, or if they were provided in anticipation of a contract that did not materialize.

- An account of profits requires the party in breach to hand over all the profit it has made as a result of breach to the innocent party. This measure is very rarely awarded, and will require the claimant to have a strong interest in the performance of the obligation in question. It will not be awarded if it would be disproportionate or oppressive to the defendant.

Assess your learning

You should be able to respond to each of the following points with a confident 'yes'. If you can't, then you should revisit the sections listed against that point.

Can you:

(a) *Identify* the circumstances under which specific performance and injunctions will be granted, and the main grounds on which their grant can be refused? (Section 17.2)

(b) *Outline* the key features of the remedy of debt, and the advantages it has over damages? (Section 17.3)

(c) *Identify* the circumstances under which a party can recover money paid under a contract, and the circumstances under which a party can sue for *quantum meruit* rather than damages? (Sections 17.4.1 and 17.4.2)

(d) *Explain* the circumstances under which damages can be sought on the account of profits measure, and the main restrictions on the ability of the court to award it? (Section 17.4.3)

In relation to each of the above, you should be able to:

(i) identify and clearly explain the key rules and principles;

(ii) identify the key cases and statutes, and why they matter;

(iii) apply the principles and cases to specific real or hypothetical fact situations;

(iv) evaluate the limitations, if any, of the law as it currently stands.

Further reading

J Beatson, 'Courts, Arbitrators and Restitutionary Liability for Breach of Contract' (2002) 118 LQR 377.

D Campbell, 'The Extinguishing of Contract' (2004) 67 MLR 817.

D Campbell, 'Better than Fuller: A Two Interests Model of Remedies for Breach of Contract' (2015) 78 MLR 296.

R Cunnington, 'The Assessment of Gain-Based Damages for Breach of Contract' (2008) 71 MLR 559.

J Edelman, *Gain-Based Damages* (Hart 2002).

D Harris, 'Specific Performance—A Regular Remedy for Consumers' (2003) 119 LQR 541.

AT Kronman, 'Specific Performance' (1978) 45 University of Chicago Law Review 351.

A Phang, 'Specific Performance: Exploring the Roots of "Settled Practice"' (1998) 61 MLR 421.

J Tarrant, 'Total Failure of Consideration' (2006) 33 UWA Law Review 132.

G Virgo, 'Recent Developments in Restitution of Mistaken Payments' (1999) 58 CLJ 479.

18

Privity and third parties

Protecting the rights of non-parties

'Remember the stranger in your midst'

Problem 18: setting the context

Consider the following letter.

THE HEXHAMSHIRE COUNTY CRICKET CLUB
Hutton House, Corbridge, Hexhamshire

Petra Konvalinka
Northern Law Partners
Leeds

Dear Petra,

You will doubtless be aware of the unfortunate incident that has effectively ended the career of Louis Duckworth, formerly our captain and star bowler. I am writing to give you a bit more background on the case, so that you can advise us on our chances of recovering compensation.

Last autumn, Louis began suffering from wrist pain. He turned out to have suffered a serious injury to his tendons, which required careful and complex physiotherapy. We arranged for Louis to receive an intensive course of sports therapy from a practice called Sports Therapists Ltd, the country's foremost experts on wrist strains and injuries. All our players benefit from private medical insurance, paid for by the club. The cost of treatment was paid by the insurance company directly to Sports Therapists.

Unfortunately, the treatment went very badly, and it is now unlikely that Louis will ever bowl again. Examination by experts has revealed a catalogue of errors and incompetence by Sports Therapists and their team. Most seriously, they failed to carry out all the tests that had been agreed in the contract, or to have Louis's progress reviewed on a fortnightly basis by a specialist orthopaedic surgeon as the contract also required them to do.

Apart from ending Louis's career, this has caused our club a huge loss. Losing his contract is a big financial blow. In addition, Louis was our star player, and a significant proportion of our international fan-following was due to his personal talent and charisma. His departure will have a huge impact on our revenues.

Due to Sports Therapists' policies it was Louis who signed the actual contract with Sports Therapists, but they knew that it was our insurance that was paying for the treatment. Our physiotherapy team had the initial discussions with them, and the contract expressly recognizes the need to synchronize their treatment schedules with our training schedules. They would also have known that we had a strong interest in Louis's recovery. As we see it, Sports Therapists' mistakes constitute a breach of contract, and we feel very strongly that they

→

→

owe compensation to us as well as Louis. We would like your view on our legal
position before we take further action.

Yours sincerely,
Geoff Hutton
Club President

The issue the club faces is that it may not have been a party to the contract between the
therapists and their player. It was, however, directly affected by the breach, and it has suffered
loss as a result. Should the club be able to sue the therapists for failing to treat their player
properly?

18.1 Introduction: the problem of third party rights

When we study the law of contract, our focus is usually on the parties. We study how
the parties form contracts, how they provide consideration to each other, how gaps
they leave are filled, how their contractual framework is subject to regulation, the remedies one party has if the other party fails to keep to the contract, and so on.

In the real world, however, contracts frequently concern and affect persons who are
not formally parties to them. Persons who are not formally party to the contract are in
law referred to as **third parties**. It is quite common for third parties to have an interest
in contracts to which they are not party. Their interests may even be more closely at
stake than those of the parties themselves. Problem 18 presents a classic example. The
club has a strong interest in the proper discharge by the therapists of their treatment
obligations, but because it did not directly sign the contract with Sports Therapists Ltd,
it is a third party as far as that contract is concerned.

Virtually all legal systems have had to grapple with the issue of whether third parties
can claim rights under contracts. Most legal systems today answer the question in the
affirmative, albeit in a qualified way: a subset of non-parties are given a limited right
to enforce some terms under certain specific conditions. In civil law systems, such as
those of continental Europe and Scotland, the issue is dealt with under the heading
of *ius quaesitum tertio*, literally, 'rights acquired by a third party'. In English law, these
questions are not dealt with through a direct rule, but through a series of exceptions to
a doctrine known as **privity of contract**.

Stripped to its essentials, the doctrine of privity provides that a contract ordinarily
only affects persons who are party to it. Third parties are neither bound by the contract nor entitled to claim rights under the contract. This position is not without logic.
Parties create contracts by going through a process of offering, accepting, and providing consideration, while possessing the intention to create legal relations. A third party
who has not gone through this process has not accepted the contractual framework.
He is therefore not privy to the rights and obligations it creates, and should not be
allowed to sue (or be sued) under the contract.

Nevertheless, privity of contract is a relatively recent creation. Until the late 17th century, it was taken as a given that any person who had an interest in a contract could bring an action to enforce it or claim damages for its breach even if he was not a party: the rule of law was taken to be that 'he that hath the interest hath the action'. Starting in the late 19th century, however, the courts began to step away from this approach in favour of a stricter interpretation of privity. In 1861, the English courts definitively declared that third parties could not sue to enforce contracts,[1] a position they reiterated in 1915.[2] In the 1930s, the courts further consolidated the strict doctrine of privity by restricting the use of certain equitable doctrines which had until then provided a way of sidestepping privity.

The effect of the strict doctrine was, however, frequently undesirable, as section 18.2 discusses in greater detail. In response, the courts and Parliament developed a number of exceptions to privity, each of which gives third parties a right to sue on the contract in a certain type of situation. The most important of these is contained in a statute, the Contracts (Rights of Third Parties) Act 1999. This statute is primarily concerned with *third party beneficiaries*, and its main purpose is to give them a right to enforce contract terms. Under s 1 of the 1999 Act, a third party may enforce a term of a contract in two situations: first, if the contract contains an express term saying so and, secondly, if the term 'purports to confer a benefit on him' and there is nothing in the contract to suggest that the parties did not intend to give him a right to enforce the term.

Third parties, like the club in Problem 18, can only sue if they can bring their case within an exception to privity, and not otherwise. If a particular contract does not fall within the terms of the 1999 Act, or one of the other exceptions, the default position is that third parties to a contract can neither enforce its terms nor rely on them as a defence. This makes it important to begin by understanding how the doctrine of privity affects third parties, before considering the extent to which, and techniques through which, these problems can be mitigated. This chapter accordingly begins by discussing the types of situations where privity of contract historically created problems (section 18.2). It then discusses the main categories of exceptions to privity (sections 18.3 and 18.4), before moving on to considering a different approach to dealing with the rights of third parties; namely, giving the contracting parties themselves the right to sue on behalf of third parties (section 18.5). It concludes with an assessment of the extent to which privity continues to be problematic, and what this tells us about the strengths and limitations of contract law more generally (section 18.6).

18.2 Privity and its effects: understanding the context

The doctrine of privity is best understood as setting out three related principles in relation to the position of third parties, the first pertaining to third party *obligations*, ie the

---

1. See *Tweddle v Atkinson* (1861) 1 B & S 393, 121 ER 762 (QB).
2. See *Dunlop Pneumatic Tyre Co Ltd v Selfridge & Co Ltd* [1915] AC 847 (HL).

question of who can *be* sued under a contract; the second to third party *rights*, ie the persons who are entitled *to* sue under a contract; and the third to third party *exemptions*, ie the ability of third parties to benefit from exclusion clauses in their favour.

18.2.1 Privity and third party obligations

First, privity provides that a contract cannot impose obligations upon third parties. The only people a contract can bind, and the only people who can be sued under it, are those who are parties to it. This aspect of privity is uncontroversial. Consider the following illustration:

Illustration 18.1

Three housemates agree between themselves that henceforth doing the washing-up, and buying and paying for washing-up supplies, will be the responsibility of the fourth housemate.

Few would argue that this agreement should be binding on the fourth housemate. The reason would usually be that the fourth housemate did not agree to take on this responsibility. This is precisely the position that the doctrine of privity reflects, and the exceptions to the doctrine of privity have not altered it.

18.2.2 Privity and third party beneficiaries

The other two consequences of privity, in contrast, are more problematic, and it was these consequences that were the primary target of the Contracts (Rights of Third Parties) Act 1999. Privity in its classical form provided that the only persons who are entitled to sue for breach of contract are the parties to the contract themselves. Nobody else may bring an action under a contract, even if they have suffered loss as a result of its breach.

The results this rule produced were often hard to justify, particularly in situations involving third party beneficiaries. As the name suggests, these involve contracts whose main benefits flow to a third party. Consider the following scenario:

Illustration 18.2

Helen is having financial difficulties, and has fallen into arrears on her rent. Helen's friend Robert speaks to her landlord, and agrees that Robert will tutor the landlord's son in A-level English for six months. In exchange, the landlord agrees to waive Helen's arrears.

Although Robert is the party to the contract in this illustration, he derives none of the benefit under the contract. The benefits flow, instead, to Helen, who is not a party to the contract. What, then, happens if the landlord breaches the contract by demanding that Helen pay the arrears? Should Helen be able to raise the contract as a defence, even though she is not a party to it? Under the strict interpretation that held sway from the 1860s onwards, the answer would have been that Helen could not use the contract as a defence. In *Tweddle v Atkinson*,[3] the fathers of a married couple had entered into a contract under which both fathers would pay certain sums of money to the groom. The bride's father failed to pay and the groom sued. It was held that he had no right of action, because he was not a party to the contract. Although the contract had been made for his benefit, as a third party who had not provided any consideration he had no right of action if it was breached.

Commercial transactions were also frequently affected. In *Eley v Positive Government Security Life Assurance Co Ltd*,[4] the shareholders of a company had agreed as between themselves to appoint Eley as their solicitor.[5] Eley was not party to this agreement, but he knew of it and had possibly even drafted it himself. When the directors of the company began using other solicitors, Eley sued arguing that the directors' actions constituted a breach of contract. The High Court dismissed his action,[6] and the decision was upheld by the Court of Appeal. The contract in question, it was held, was only between the shareholders. As such, it did not give a third party such as Eley the right to sue for its breach.[7] Lord Cairns in the Court of Appeal acknowledged that Eley was aware of the contract and had seen the provision as 'making his employment safe against the company'. Nevertheless, the mere fact that he had relied upon it to protect his interests did not alter the fact that at law he was a stranger to the contract, and as such had no right to enforce it.[8]

18.2.3 **Privity and third party exemptions**

Privity also provided that a third party could not claim the benefit of an exemption clause limiting or excluding liability, even if the clause was drafted to cover the third party. In *Scruttons Ltd v Midland Silicones Ltd*,[9] a contract for carriage entered into between the owners of goods and the carriers limited liability for damage to goods to $500 (at the time, about £179). The carriers entered into a contract with stevedores, which also limited liability for damage to $500. The goods were damaged due to the stevedores' negligence. The loss was well in excess of $500 (it was estimated at around £593). The owners of the goods sued the stevedores for the full loss. The House of Lords held that the owners were entitled to claim the full loss. The limitation clause contained in the stevedoring contract did not bind the owners of the goods, because they were not parties to it. The limitation clause in the contract of carriage did bind the owners, but the stevedores could not claim its benefit because they were not parties to that clause. As a result, they had not limited their liability to the owners of the damaged goods and were liable for the full amount of the loss.

3. (1861) 1 B & S 393, 121 ER 762 (QB).   4. (1876) 1 Ex D 88 (CA).

5. The agreement in question was contained in the company's Articles of Association which, as a matter of company law, are treated as a contract between the company and its members, as well as between the members inter se. See *Rayfield v Hands* [1958] 2 WLR 851 (Ch), and Companies Act 2006, s 33(1).

6. See *Eley v Positive Government Security Life Assurance Co Ltd* (1875) 1 Ex D 20.

7. Ibid, 26 (Amphlett B).   8. (1876) 1 Ex D 88, 90 (Lord Cairns LC).

9. [1962] AC 446 (HL).

Outcomes like this were seen as problematic for two reasons. First, they left the person for whose sake the contract was made unable to sue for its breach. It is somewhat peculiar to say that a contract which was expressly made to protect the interests of a particular person cannot be relied upon or enforced by that person. Secondly, and more fundamentally, the result was that nobody could sue to recover damages for breach of contract. In law, an action for damages for breach of contract can ordinarily only be brought by a party to recover losses which that specific party has suffered. Parties cannot ordinarily claim damages for losses which they have not suffered.[10] In cases such as *Tweddle* and *Eley*, therefore, the law presents the parties with a double whammy. The party to the contract has not suffered any loss and, in consequence, cannot claim anything more than nominal damages. The person who has actually suffered loss, however, is not a party to the contract, and hence is barred by privity from claiming anything. The very thing that the contract sought to prevent has happened; but privity prevents anyone from getting a remedy.

18.2.4 Developing exceptions to privity

The response of the courts and Parliament to these problems was to create a number of exceptions to privity. These exceptions fall into two broad categories, both of which are potentially relevant to the facts of Problem 18 (and also speak to Problem 16 in Chapter 16). The first category of exceptions addresses the problem directly, by giving third parties the right to sue on a contract in certain cases. They seek, in other words, to establish a set of exceptions that permit people in the position of the husband in *Tweddle v Atkinson*,[11] or the solicitor in *Eley*,[12] to sue for breach even though they are not actually parties to the contract. The most important of these is the statutory exception contained in the Contracts (Rights of Third Parties) Act 1999, which was introduced in section 18.1. This is not the only such exception. There are also other older exceptions developed through case law and statute which give third parties the right to sue under certain circumstances, and the door to creating further exceptions remains open. Section 18.3 discusses the 1999 Act in greater detail, while section 18.4 covers some of the more important older routes around privity.

The second category of exceptions operates indirectly, by relaxing the requirements in relation to loss. Their effect is to give one of the parties the right to sue the other for loss suffered by a third party. They seek, in other words, to in some circumstances permit people in the position of the father in *Tweddle v Atkinson*, or the shareholders in *Eley*, to claim substantial damages for breach even though they have not themselves suffered any loss. These exceptions are discussed in section 18.5.

18.3 The Contracts (Rights of Third Parties) Act 1999

The most obvious way around the doctrine of privity is to permit third parties to enforce contracts even though they are not parties to them. In the years leading up to 1999, case law and statute began to recognize a small number of circumstances in

---

10. But see the discussion of the *Linden Gardens* line of cases in this chapter in section 18.5.
11. (1861) 1 B & S 393, 121 ER 762 (QB).
12. *Eley v Positive Government Security Life Assurance Co Ltd* (1876) 1 Ex D 88 (CA).

which third parties had such a right. In 1999, a new and far broader exception was introduced through the Contracts (Rights of Third Parties) Act 1999. Because the 1999 Act represents the easiest and least convoluted route around privity, we will begin by examining when it is triggered and what rights it gives third parties, before moving on to some of the other exceptions.

18.3.1 The approach of the Act

The starting point of the 1999 Act is the idea of freedom of contract. Rather than creating a policy-based statutory exception to privity, the Act works through permitting parties, if they so desire, to structure their contract in a way that lets third party beneficiaries enforce it; and by presuming in certain circumstances that the parties did so desire.

The roots of this approach lie in the fact that before the Act it was very difficult for parties to work around the doctrine of privity even if they wanted to. This was because of the way in which privity interacts with consideration. The logical solution to privity, if you are drafting a contract, is to make all beneficiaries parties to the contract. In practice, however, this was frequently not possible, because of the requirement that all parties provide consideration. The mutually reinforcing relationship between privity and consideration, and the way in which they affect the position of third party beneficiaries, is neatly illustrated by the reasoning of the judges in *Tweddle v Atkinson*.[13] Although the most commonly cited report of the judgments in that case is focused on consideration, other reports of the case suggest that some of the judges also discussed privity.[14] The relationship between the two, as it emerges from a comparison of the different reports in that case, was that the privity bar was a consequence of the lack of consideration. The son-in-law could not enforce the contract because he was not a party to the contract, and the reason he was not a party to the contract was that he had not provided consideration.[15] To provide consideration, he would have had to give something of value in exchange for the promise, which he had not done.[16]

The hurdle this relationship between privity and consideration created was a high one, as the decision in *Dunlop Pneumatic Tyre Co Ltd v Selfridge & Co Ltd*[17] illustrates. Dunlop sold tyres to retailers through its dealers. It did not want retailers engaging in a price war, or selling its tyres for low prices. So it required them to stick to a minimum selling price, and to insert a minimum price clause in their contracts with retailers. Selfridge was a retailer who had bought Dunlop tyres via a dealer. In breach of its agreement with the dealer, it sold the tyres for less than the minimum price. Dunlop sued Selfridge. The House of Lords held that it could not do so because there was no privity between it and Selfridge. On the facts, however, it is hard to see how privity could have been created in this case. Even if Dunlop could have been added as a party to the contract between Selfridge and the dealer, for the contract to be enforceable Dunlop

---

13. (1861) 1 B & S 393, 121 ER 762 (QB).

14. For an overview, see M Furmston and GJ Tolhurst, *Privity of Contract* (Oxford University Press 2015) 1.14–1.22.

15. See esp the report of Wightman J's and Crompton J's judgments in the Law Journal: (1861) 30 LJ (NS) 265, 267.

16. See the discussion in Chapter 3 ('Consideration').   17. [1915] AC 847 (HL).

would also have had to provide consideration. This would have required either giving token consideration such as a peppercorn, or by executing it as a deed, which does away with the requirement of consideration. A law that requires parties to engage in a commercially pointless ritual in order to make their contract enforceable is clearly falling a good way short of appropriately supporting the institution of contracting.

The 1999 Act is primarily directed at this problem. Its aim is neither to do away with privity altogether nor to create a binding legal rule governing third party rights. It seeks, instead, to make it easier for parties to build third party enforcement into their contracts if they want to. The exception it creates is based on the intention of the parties. A third party will have the right to enforce a contract if the contract suggests that parties intended to give him that right. He will then be able to sue for any remedy that he could have pursued had he been a party to the contract,[18] and to rely on any applicable exclusion or limitation clause in the contract.[19]

Unlike most other areas of contract, the parties' intentions on this issue are not assessed through the usual device of the objective test. Instead, the Act sets out two distinct ways in which such an intention can be inferred from the contract, which the Law Commission report as well as the explanatory notes to the Act referred to as the two limbs of its central proposal. The first limb is the most straightforward. Under s 1(1)(a) of the Act, a third party may enforce a term of the contract 'if the contract expressly provides that he may'. In other words, if a contract says expressly that a third party can enforce some or all of its terms, the Act permits the third party to do so.

The second limb is somewhat more complex, and involves two steps. In the first step, the court asks whether the term in question 'purports to confer a benefit' upon the third party (s 1(1)(b)). If it does, the effect is to create a presumption to the effect that the third party can enforce the term in question. This presumption can, however, be rebutted in the second step of the enquiry. To rebut the presumption, it will be necessary to prove that 'on a proper construction of the contract', the parties 'did not intend the term to be enforceable by the third party' (s 1(2)).

The effect of the presumption is to partially shift the burden of proof from the third party to the promisor (ie the party against whom the third party seeks to enforce her rights).[20] The burden of proof in the first stage is on the third party. She must prove that conferring the benefit was one of the purposes of the parties' bargain. Otherwise, she will not have any rights under the contract. The third party does not, however, need to prove that the parties intended to give her the right to enforce the term. The court will presume that they did unless the promisor proves that they did not.[21] Academic commentary written by members of the Law Commission in their personal capacity suggests that the presumption was intended to be rebutted only in exceptional cases.[22]

We will examine the second limb in greater detail in section 18.3.3. Before that, however, you should note two further consequences which flow from the fact that the Act bases the rights of third party beneficiaries on the parties' intentions, rather than an independent legal rule.

---

18. See s 1(5).   19. See s 1(6).   20. See s 1(7).
21. See *Nisshin Shipping Co Ltd v Cleaves & Co Ltd* [2003] EWHC 2602 (Comm), [23] (Colman J).
22. A Burrows, 'Reforming Privity of Contract: Law Commission Report No. 242' [1996] LMCLQ 467.

First, s 1(3) provides that the third party must be expressly identified in the contract, either by name, or as a member of a class, or as answering a particular description. There must, in other words, be some evidence that the parties were, first, thinking of third party beneficiaries when formulating their contract and, secondly, that they had in mind third parties of the same type as the one seeking to enforce the contract. The mere fact that a third party is benefited by the contract is not sufficient. Unless this element of identification is also present, the third party will be unable to enforce or rely on the contract. The Law Commission justified this on the basis that it was implicit in an approach based on the parties' intentions that 'third party rights cannot be conferred on someone who is *impliedly* in mind'. Doing so would give rise to 'unacceptable uncertainty'.[23] In practice, however, this has led to some types of third party beneficiaries being excluded from the operation of the Act, as we will see in section 18.3.3.

Secondly, because the Act is grounded purely in the parties' intention, the third party beneficiary does not have to rely on the term in question or even know of its existence to acquire a right of enforcement (although reliance is relevant for certain other purposes, as discussed later). In *Charity Commission v Framjee*,[24] a website had been set up by a trust to let visitors make electronic donations, via credit or debit cards, to charities of their choice. The court held that each donation created a contract between the trust and the donor, under which the trust contractually undertook to pass the donation on to the charity nominated by the donor. This contract was enforceable by the nominated charity as a third party beneficiary, even though the charities in question had not requested the website to collect the money. The basis of the finding was simply that 'the contract purported to confer a benefit on the nominated ultimate recipient, and there is nothing to indicate as a matter of construction that the parties did not intend it to be enforceable by the ultimate recipient'.[25]

The decision in *Precis (521) plc v William M Mercer Ltd*[26] is an even clearer example. This case involved an exclusion clause in favour of a third party (the defendant in the action). The third party had been unaware of the existence of the exclusion clause until after the litigation began, when the contract was revealed in the course of the evidentiary process. The court held that it could nevertheless claim the benefit of the clause under s 1(1)(b).

18.3.2 The benefit test

Consider the following illustration:

Illustration 18.3

Thomas is having a bicycle custom-built for him. He asks the shop to install a top-of-the-line gearing system on his bike made by Jarrow Steel Castings. After he takes delivery, he discovers that the shop has used a cheaper unbranded system.

---

23. Law Commission, *Privity of Contract: Contracts for the Benefit of Third Parties* (Law Com No 242, 1996) para 8.1.
24. [2014] EWHC 2507 (Ch), [2015] 1 WLR 16.   25. Ibid, [46] (Henderson J).
26. [2005] EWCA Civ 114, [2005] PNLR 28.

It is clear here that the shop has breached the contract with Thomas,[27] and that Thomas will be able to sue for compensation.[28] But should Jarrow Steel be able to argue that they are a third party beneficiary, and sue for the lost profit from the sale they did not make? On the face of it, the contract has the effect of conferring a benefit upon them. They are also expressly named in the contract, thus satisfying the requirement of s 1(3). Yet it would seem peculiar to say that they can maintain a third party action for breach of contract. Could it be said that the parties did not intend them to have this right? If so, on what basis? What distinguishes their situation from Helen's in Illustration 18.2, where giving her enforcement rights would appear appropriate? The purpose of the benefit test is to provide a coherent way of answering these questions.

The meaning of 'purport'

Section 1(1)(b) requires that the contract must not simply confer a benefit, but must 'purport' to do so. 'Purport' is not a term that has an established meaning in contract law. Existing principles of contract law offer little guidance on what it means to 'purport' to confer a benefit (as opposed to simply conferring a benefit). The Law Commission report on which the Act was based[29] also does not explain the meaning of this phrase or the 'proper construction' test in any more detail than the Act does. However, it includes 17 hypothetical situations to illustrate how the test will apply in different circumstances.[30] A common theme in these hypotheticals is the role of ordinary principles of interpretation, reading the contract 'in the light of the surrounding circumstances', informed by the 'background practice and understanding' of the relevant industry.[31] In relation to a contract for the sale of goods, for example, a person purchasing goods through a retailer or reseller will not ordinarily acquire the right to sue the manufacturer or an upstream seller, because it is well understood in the relevant industry that the purchaser's remedies lie against the seller only.[32]

Courts will not, however, always have enough evidence as to the existence of a sufficiently clear 'background practice and understanding'. The examples the Commission gave related to two specific industries, construction and the sale of goods, where there is usually a clear background understanding to be drawn upon. In the majority of sectors, settled understandings of this type are harder to establish. Here, the language of 'purporting to confer a benefit' does not indicate what sort of factors indicate that the third party should have a right to enforce the contract.

The test of intention

Early cases tended to take a very broad view of the scope of the Act, which effectively treated the term 'purports to confer a benefit' as being identical to 'confers a benefit'. In *Prudential Assurance Co Ltd v Ayres*,[33] Lindsay J in the High Court suggested that

---

27. See Chapter 15 ('Breach of contract').   28. See Chapter 16 ('Compensatory remedies').
29. Law Commission, *Privity of Contract: Contracts for the Benefit of Third Parties* (Law Com No 242, 1996).
30. Ibid, paras 7.28–7.44.   31. Ibid, para 7.18.   32. Ibid.
33. [2007] EWHC 775 (Ch), [2007] 3 All ER 946. Lindsay J's decision was overruled on appeal to the Court of Appeal (discussed later), but for reasons that did not touch upon his discussion of the meaning of s 1(1)(b).

any clause which 'had the effect of conferring a benefit' upon a third party would satisfy the test of purporting to confer a benefit, even if that was not 'the predominant purpose or intent behind the term'.[34] Subsequent cases, however, adopted a narrower approach, more closely focused on the parties' intention. The courts, under this approach, ask whether conferring the benefit upon the third party was one of the purposes for which the parties entered into the agreement, or whether it was merely an incidental effect of the parties' true purpose. This approach was first articulated by Christopher Clarke J in *Dolphin Maritime & Aviation Services Ltd v Sveriges Angfartygs Assurans Forening*:[35]

> A contract does not purport to confer a benefit on a third party simply because the position of that third party will be improved if the contract is performed. The reference in the section to the term purporting to 'confer' a benefit seems to me to connote that the language used by the parties shows that one of the purposes of their bargain (rather than one of its incidental effects if performed) was to benefit the third party.[36]

Christopher Clarke J's approach thus requires some form of intention in both stages. In the first stage, the court asks whether conferring the benefit in question on the third party in question was a purpose of the term in question (note: not *the* purpose, but simply *a* purpose). In the second stage, the court asks whether the parties intend to give the third party a legal right to enforce the benefit they conferred upon him, or whether they intended that he would have to rely on their continued commitment to give him the benefit without having a legal right to insist upon it.

Applying the test of intention

Subsequent cases have taken up Christopher Clarke J's approach. It was applied in *San Evans Maritime Inc v Aigaion Insurance Co SA*,[37] which involved a contract to insure a ship, the *St Efrem*. The ship had been partly insured by three Lloyd's syndicates, and partly by Aigaion Insurance. Aigaion's policy included a particular type of clause called a 'follow clause', under which Aigaion agreed to follow and be bound by any settlement of claims made by two of the Lloyd's syndicates. The owners of the ship brought a claim under the policy, which the Lloyd's syndicates accepted and settled. The settlement agreement contained the following clause:

> The settlement and release pursuant to the terms of this Agreement is made by each Under-writer for their respective participations in the Policy only and none of the Under-writers that are party to this Agreement participate in the capacity of a Leading Under-writer under the Policy and do not bind any other insurer providing hull and machinery cover in respect of the *St Efrem*.[38]

Aigaion was not a party to this settlement agreement, but they sought to argue that its effect was to release them from the obligation under the follow clause. Teare J in the

34. Ibid, [28].   35. [2009] EWHC 716 (Comm), [2009] 2 Lloyd's Rep 123.
36. Ibid, [74].   37. [2014] EWHC 163 (Comm), [2014] 2 Lloyd's Rep 265.
38. Ibid, [8].

High Court rejected this argument. Seen in the proper commercial context, he said, the purpose of the clause was not to confer a benefit on Aigaion. The purpose of the parties in inserting this clause, rather, was to protect themselves from any liability to Aigaion, given that they knew of the existence of the follow clause. Although it 'might improve the position of Aigaion', that was an incidental effect rather than the main purpose of the clause. As a result, Aigaion could not rely upon the 1999 Act to take advantage of this clause.[39]

Apart from reaffirming Christopher Clarke J's approach, *San Evans Maritime Inc v Aigaion Insurance Co SA* also indicates that the question of whether a benefit was conferred is, ultimately, a matter of construction. This is borne out by other cases involving contracts which were somewhat ambiguous as to whether a benefit was conferred on a third party. In *Broughton v Capital Quality Ltd*,[40] for example, the defendant was a regional quality centre, which was licensed to assess whether organizations met the Investors in People standard. The licence was granted under a licence agreement with a government-owned company called Investors in People UK. Amongst other things, the licence agreement provided in clause 4.6(f) that the centre would 'ensure assessments are allocated promptly, fairly and appropriately with minimum risk'. The centre carried out its assessments through third party assessors, who were registered with it but not guaranteed any work. The claimant, Jane Broughton, was a registered assessor, but grew dissatisfied with the way work was allocated to her. She argued that her treatment violated clause 4.6(f) of the licence agreement in relation to the fair allocation of assessments, and that she could sue for breach as a third party beneficiary. The High Court rejected her argument, holding that clause 4.6(f) did not purport to confer any benefit on assessors.[41] In so holding, the judge appears to have been influenced by the fact that in the overall scheme of the system, the centre did not 'commit itself to deliver anything to assessors'. All the transaction gave assessors was 'the hope that work will be provided'.[42] Giving a third party rights under the licence agreement would not have been compatible with this setup. In *Cavanagh v Secretary of State for Work and Pensions*,[43] in contrast, the court was faced with an employment contract that let employees voluntarily choose to have their trade union dues deducted from their pay and paid by their employer to the trade union. Their employer, the DWP, unilaterally ended this arrangement. The court held that the trade union could sue for breach of contract under the 1999 Act as a third party beneficiary. On a proper construction, it was obvious that the purpose of the provision was to benefit both the employees and the trade union. It therefore purported to confer a benefit on the union within the meaning of s 1(1)(b).[44]

As with any other issue of interpretation, the court will consider the full 'matrix of fact' in deciding whether or not the contract purported to confer a benefit on the third party. This is illustrated quite well by the decision of the Court of Appeal in *Prudential Assurance Co Ltd v Ayres*,[45] which reversed the decision of Lindsay J in the High Court, although not on the point of the meaning of s 1(1)(b).

39. Ibid, [40]–[41].   40. [2008] EWHC 3457 (QB).   41. Ibid, [28].
42. Ibid, [29].   43. [2016] EWHC 1136 (QB).
44. Ibid, [73].   45. [2008] EWCA Civ 52.

Case in depth: *Prudential Assurance Co Ltd v Ayres* [2008] EWCA Civ 52

The defendants, Ayres and Grew, were partners in a law firm. In their capacity as partners, they had leased premises for the law firm from Prudential Assurance. In 2001, the firm decided that it no longer required the premises. With Prudential's consent, it assigned the lease to a partnership firm called Altheimer & Gray.

As part of this process, Prudential required the defendants to guarantee Altheimer & Gray's lease payments. Prudential also entered into a supplemental deed with Altheimer & Gray, under which Altheimer & Gray's liability to Prudential was restricted to the assets of the partnership, and did not include the personal assets of the partners.[46] Clause 2.1 of the supplemental deed provided, in part that:

> any recovery by the Landlord against the Tenant or any previous tenant under the Lease for any such default shall be limited to assets of the Partnership.

Ayres and Grew were not parties to this agreement, but they were aware of it.

Altheimer & Gray became insolvent, leaving substantial amounts outstanding under the lease. Prudential sought to recover the outstanding amounts from Ayres and Grew under the guarantee. Ayres and Grew argued that they were a previous tenant for the purpose of clause 2.1 of the supplemental deed and, as a result, their liability under the guarantee was limited *pro tanto*. Although they were not parties to the supplemental deed, the language of clause 2.1 made it clear that it purported to confer a benefit upon them, thus making them a third party beneficiary under s 1(1)(b) of the 1999 Act.

Their argument succeeded at first instance. Lindsay J held that on a 'natural and grammatical reading', clause 2.1 referred to two kinds of recovery, one against Altheimer & Gray and one against previous tenants, and limited both to the value of Altheimer & Gray's partnership assets.[47] Ayres and Grew clearly fell within the scope of the phrase 'previous tenants', and the clause clearly operated to their benefit. As such, it purported to confer a benefit upon them for the purposes of s 1(1)(b). This meant that they were third party beneficiaries and could enforce the term.[48]

Prudential appealed to the Court of Appeal, which overruled Lindsay J's decision and held that clause 2.1 did not purport to confer a benefit on the defendants. The Court of Appeal was influenced by the fact that the defendants had not been made party to the supplemental deed. This, Moore-Bick LJ held, did not fit with the suggestion that the clause was intended to benefit them.

> It is not plausible, in my view, to suggest, as the respondents must, that although the Prudential and Altheimer & Gray intended to confer a benefit on the respondents by restricting the measure of the Prudential's right of recovery against them, they were content to rely on the uncertain effect of the Contracts (Rights of Third Parties) Act 1999 in order to do so.[49]

→

---

46. In English law, partners of a partnership firm are ordinarily personally liable for the entirety of the firm's liabilities. There are certain forms of partnerships—notably, limited partnerships and limited liability partnerships—to which this principle does not apply, but it applies to all partnerships simpliciter.

47. *Prudential Assurance Co Ltd v Ayres* [2007] EWHC 775 (Ch), [22] (Lindsay J).

48. Ibid, [27]–[29].   49. [2008] EWCA Civ 52, [35].

> →
>
> In other words, given the nature of the transaction, and the fact that it involved sophisticated commercial parties, the very fact that the defendants had not been made parties to the supplemental deed suggested that it was unlikely to have been intended to benefit them. The correct interpretation of the deed was, therefore, that it was only intended to restrict the liability of the partners of Altheimer & Gray under the lease, and not of the defendants under their guarantee. As such, it did not purport to confer any benefit upon the defendants, and the 1999 Act was inapplicable.

Let us now get back to the issue with which this subsection began. The question we asked was how we might sensibly distinguish Helen's situation in relation to the rent arrears (Illustration 18.2) from Jarrow Steel's position in relation to the custom-built bike (Illustration 18.3). Although both situations involve a benefit to a clearly identified third party, the test suggested by Christopher Clarke J in *Dolphin Maritime & Aviation Services Ltd v Sveriges Angfartygs Assurans Forening*[50] points to a crucial distinction between the two situations. In Helen's case, the contract between Robert and Helen's landlord was entered into for the purpose of benefitting Helen. This was not its sole purpose, of course. Helen's landlord doubtless had his own interests, and his son's interests, more in view in deciding to enter into the contract. Nevertheless, it was one of the purposes to which the contract was directed. The situation in relation to the custom-built bike discussed in Illustration 18.3 is entirely different. It is correct to say that the transaction would, if performed, have benefited Jarrow Steel. However, neither party entered into the transaction in order to benefit Jarrow Steel. The benefit is, rather, an incidental effect of the contract. The result is that the *Dolphin Maritime* approach provides us with a clear and relatively easily applied basis on which to explain why it makes sense for Helen to have rights as a third party beneficiary but not Jarrow Steel.

The situation with Louis Duckworth's injury is, however, a lot less clear. Prior case law suggests that in the absence of a written agreement which says otherwise, a contract for private medical treatment will ordinarily be taken to have been entered into between the medical professional and the patient.[51] The fact that the contract was signed by Duckworth, rather than the club, supports this conclusion. There is nothing obvious to say that the benefit to the club was one of the purposes for which Duckworth and the sports therapists contracted. The fact that Sports Therapists Ltd was aware of the club's interest is unlikely to be sufficient for the purposes of the *Dolphin Maritime* test (although it probably would have been under the test suggested by Lindsay J).

Similarly, although the club appears to have been expressly mentioned in the contract, the provisions requiring the treatment to be synchronized with the club's training schedules could equally be construed as being there for the player's benefit rather than the club's. Because the onus is on the third party to establish that the contract purported to confer a benefit on it, it is for the club to establish that benefitting it was

---

50. [2009] EWHC 716 (Comm), [2009] 2 Lloyd's Rep 123.

51. See esp *West Bromwich Albion Football Club Ltd v Mohammed El Safty* [2007] PIQR P7. Note that third party rights were not pleaded in this case, and hence do not form part of the judgment.

one of the purposes of the contract. In order to do so, it will need to show that something about the circumstances of the case, seen against the background of the 'matrix of fact', leads to the conclusion that benefitting it was indeed one of the purposes of the contract of treatment. It might, for example, argue that the fact that it took out the insurance and paid the premiums, as well as the nature of the coverage, suggests that this was not simply part of the package of benefits the club provided its players. Instead, it was also an attempt by the club to safeguard its own interests, including the risks that the illness and injury of its players posed to it. Yet whether factors such as these are sufficient for the purposes of the Act is open to question.[52]

If the 1999 Act does not help the club, might the other exceptions do so? We will turn to this question in section 18.4. Before that, however, we need to first consider the implications of one further requirement imposed by the Act; namely, the requirement that the contract expressly identify the third party beneficiary.

18.3.3 **The requirement of identification**

In addition to the requirements of purporting to confer a benefit and intending to confer the right to enforce, the Act also requires that the contract expressly identify the third party. This provision is strikingly permissive. It permits the parties to identify persons by name ('William Blackstone'), by class ('professors of law', 'residents of Chipping Norton', 'persons under six foot ten') or by description ('the Lord Chief Justice of England and Wales', 'the first person to correctly guess the number of beans in this jar'). It also permits them to create classes that include persons not yet in existence ('all children who may be born to my daughter', 'any companies founded now or in the future by Mark Zuckerberg').

At the same time, the Act imposes one important restriction; namely, that the identification must be express. The fact that the contract purports to confer a benefit upon the third party, and that the parties intended to give her the right to enforce the benefit, are not by themselves sufficient. If the third party is not also expressly identified in the contract, she does not acquire any right to enforce the term.

The Law Commission's report makes it very clear that this was a deliberate decision, which was taken with the view that it would increase certainty.[53] Their intention was to exclude the possibility of the Act being taken to confer third party rights 'on someone who is *impliedly* in mind'.[54] The identification must be an express term of the contract, rather than a term arrived at through implication.[55] The case of *Avraamides v Colwill*[56] presents a good illustration of the issues this can cause.

---

52. Note, however, that Duckworth would clearly be a third party beneficiary had the contract been entered into between the club and the sports therapists. Alleviating the effects of his injury was an express purpose of the contract, and that purpose is an obvious benefit to him. Once this is established, the onus is on the promisor to establish that the parties did not intend to benefit the third party. It is difficult to see how that could be established in this specific scenario, unless there was an express contractual term saying so.
53. Law Commission, *Privity of Contract: Contracts for the Benefit of Third Parties* (Law Com No 242, 1996) para 8.1.
54. Ibid.
55. On the distinction between express and implied terms, see Chapter 8 ('Filling the gaps').
56. [2006] EWCA Civ 1533.

Case in depth: *Themis Avraamides v Mark Colwill* **[2006] EWCA Civ 1533**

Themis Avraamides and his wife had engaged a company called Bathroom Trading Co (Putney) Ltd to carry out work refurbishing two bathrooms in their house. They were not satisfied with the work that was done and sought to sue for compensation. In the meantime, the controlling shareholder of Bathroom Trading Co (Putney) Ltd had sold his business to the defendants in this action, who carried on trading under the name 'Bathroom Trading Co'.

By the time the action was brought, the original company had been wound up, and no longer existed. The defendants had purchased the business but they were not the persons with whom the claimants had contracted. As such, there was no privity between them. The agreement under which the defendants had purchased the business, however, contained the following clause:

> The purchasers undertake to complete outstanding customer orders taking into account any deposits paid by customers as at 31 March 2003, and to pay in the normal course of time any liabilities properly incurred by the company as at 31 March 2003.

The claimants argued that their claim was a liability incurred by the company and hence was covered by this clause. This made them third party beneficiaries, giving them the right to sue to enforce the term under s 1(1)(b). Their argument succeeded at first instance, and the defendants appealed to the Court of Appeal.

The appeal succeeded. Waller LJ, delivering the judgment of the Court of Appeal, agreed that the liability to the claimants was covered by the clause. However, he held that the claimants could not claim the benefit of the Act because they had not been expressly identified. The clause spoke of 'liabilities properly incurred', but these words did not identify any third party or class of third parties,[57] and the Act did not permit the court to do so through interpretation or implication:

> section 1(3), by use of the word 'express', simply does not allow a process of construction or implication. I considered whether it would be possible for Mr Mills to rely on the fact that 'customers' are identified in the contract as beneficiaries of the first part of paragraph 3, even if liabilities in the second part includes persons other than customers. Could he submit that even though others are included within the liabilities under the second part, 'customers' as a class are identified and that is sufficient. The difficulty is that the section is concerned with the benefit conferred on a third party, and with the identification of that person. The benefit from the obligation to pay liabilities properly incurred would benefit third parties but of a large number of unidentified classes.[58]

The court recognized that the result was unfortunate. It was clearly the intention that the defendants should take over all liabilities of the former company, including its liability to the claimants. The effect of the decision was that the claimants' right was against a company which no longer existed, which meant that they would have to seek to persuade the liquidator of the company to sue the defendants for failing to discharge the liabilities they had agreed to discharge. It would be far simpler to let the claimants sue the defendants directly.[59] However, the wording of the Act made this impossible.

---

57. Ibid, [17].   58. Ibid, [19].   59. Ibid, [18].

Part of the reason this decision appears unfortunate is that many parties who lack an in-depth understanding of the law are unlikely to be aware of the existence of the doctrine of privity, let alone the requirements of the 1999 Act. As such, they are unlikely to design their contracts in a manner that conforms to the strict requirement of express identification. In insisting on strict requirements as to how contracts should be drafted, the law assumes that commercial parties will have a level of legal knowledge and legal advice which are simply not present in the small, everyday transactions that are the lifeblood of any commercial system, even if they are common in complex, high-value transactions.

In *Chudley v Clydesdale Bank*,[60] the Commercial Court sought to mitigate some of these problems, by suggesting that the courts can use principles of interpretation to treat a clause as expressly identifying a class of beneficiaries, even if on its face it does not appear to do so. *Chudley* related to a Letter of Instruction issued by a developer and signed by the bank, which required certain funds provided by third parties to be deposited in a 'segregated client account'. The third parties who provided the funds were not expressly identified in the letter. Nevertheless, the High Court held that as a matter of principle, it must be possible to have 'an express identification by a process of construction of the relevant term'.[61] The reference in the letter to a 'segregated client account', on the application of ordinary principles of interpretation, could be construed as identifying a class of third parties; namely, the providers of the funds that would be deposited in the segregated account. That was sufficient identification for the purpose of the Act.

As a matter of principle, the decision in *Chudley* seems obviously correct: the Act requires an express identification, and as long as the identification is traceable to an express term, the requirement would appear to have been met even if the identification only emerges on a contextual reading of the section. However, it is hard to reconcile it with the binding decision of the Court of Appeal in *Avraamides* in which, as discussed earlier, Waller LJ held that s 1(3) 'simply does not allow a process of construction or implication'. As such, the decision in *Avraamides* would appear to stand for the time being, notwithstanding the fact that the approach in *Chudley* is commercially far more sensible.

Once an express identification has been made in a contract, the more permissive approach takes over, and the law once again admits a role for construction. Once there is a mention of a class, for example, the question of who that class includes will be settled through contextual interpretation. In *Laemthong International Lines Co Ltd v Artis*,[62] goods had been received in port before the documents of title arrived. The master of the ship was instructed to release the goods even without the documents of title, against a letter of indemnity. The letter of indemnity said that the indemnity was granted to the carrier and his 'servants and agents'. As it happened, the ship was chartered on a voyage charter, which meant that it was crewed and controlled by the owner of the ship, rather than by the carrier. Disputes arose as a result of which the owners of the ship sought to invoke the indemnity. The question for the court was whether

---

60. [2017] EWHC 2177 (Comm).   61. Ibid, [181].

62. [2005] EWCA Civ 519. See also *Starlight Shipping Co v Allianz Marine & Aviation Versicherungs AG (The Alexandros T)* [2014] EWHC 3068 (Comm).

the owners of the ship could be called the 'agents' of the carrier. The High Court[63] as well as the Court of Appeal held that they were. Given the context of the case, the only way the carriers could have released the goods at the port of arrival was through the owners' servants, which made them the carriers' agents for the purpose of release.

Let us now return to Problem 18. The facts suggest that the club is expressly identified in the contract, in connection with the requirement that the treatment schedules be synchronized with the club's training schedules. Yet, as the decision of the Court of Appeal in *Avraamides v Colwill*[64] demonstrates, this is not by itself sufficient. Customers were identified as a class in the contract at issue in that case, but the identification was not in the context of the specific benefit that the claimants sought to enforce. Similarly, an express identification of the club in the context of a discussion of the treatment schedules is also unlikely to be sufficient if the benefit that the club seeks to rely on is the obligation to treat the player with due care and skill. For the purposes of s 1(3), the identification will need to be made in the context of that obligation.

18.3.4 Other aspects of the Act

In addition to the requirements of intention and identification, the Act sets out four further conditions to which the right of the third party is subject.

Condition 1: the other terms of the contract

First, s 1(4) makes it clear that the third parties' rights must be enforced 'subject to and in accordance with' any other relevant terms of the contract. Thus if the contract sets out conditions precedent to the obligations of the promisor, or makes them dependent on the obligations of some other party,[65] the third party's rights are subject to the same qualifications. A third party will not be in a better position than the parties to the contract themselves are.

Condition 2: the availability of defences and set-offs

Secondly, s 3 seeks to ensure that the promisor will have at least some of the rights of defence or set-off against the third party that he would have had against the party to whom the promise was made (called the 'promisee' in the Act). Under s 3, if a third party sues to enforce a term, the promisor will retain all defences and set-offs that he would have had against the promisee in such proceedings, as long as those defences either arise from the contract and are relevant to the term,[66] or are covered by an express term which says they will be available in proceedings brought by the third party.[67] In addition, the promisor will also have any defences or set-offs that he would have had against the third party herself had the third party been a party to the contract.[68]

Condition 3: excluding the Unfair Contract Terms Act 1977

Thirdly, third party beneficiaries cannot challenge exclusion clauses under s 2(2) of the Unfair Contract Terms Act 1977. This means that although the promisor cannot

---

63. [2004] EWHC 2738 (Comm).   64. [2006] EWCA Civ 1533.
65. See Chapter 15 ('Breach of contract').   66. See s 3(2).
67. See s 3(3).   68. See s 3(4).

impose unreasonable limits on his liability to the promisee for negligence, or to any other party, he can do so vis-à-vis a third party beneficiary.[69] The result is a peculiar duality, where unreasonable exclusion clauses in the third party's favour are invalid, but unreasonable exclusion clauses in the promisor's favour are valid. This was a deliberate policy decision rather than an accidental oversight.[70]

Condition 4: rescinding or varying the contract

Finally, the third party's rights are subject to the power of the parties to rescind or vary the contract. Parties to any contract have a general power to vary, rescind, or extinguish it, as long as they meet the legal requirements for doing so, and the Act does not fundamentally alter this position. Section 2 of the Act does, however, create an important restriction on the parties' ability to exercise this power. It requires the parties to obtain the third party's consent to changes which extinguish or alter any rights which are enforceable under the Act, if one of two things has happened.[71]

The first of these is triggered if the third party has assented to the term, and told the promisor, by words or conduct, that it has done so. In such a case, the third party's rights become irrevocable and the parties can no longer vary the contract in a way that alters or extinguishes the third party's rights without its consent.[72] The Act specifically provides that the postal rule does not apply, meaning that an assent communicated by post is only effective on receipt.[73] Equally, an assent which is only communicated to the promisee, or which is not communicated to anybody, has no legal effect. Case law under the Act suggests that there is no time frame within which assent must be communicated, but until it is communicated the rights remain revocable.[74]

The second route to irrevocability is triggered by reliance. If the third party has relied on the term, and the promisor knows it, the third party's rights become irrevocable.[75] The third party's rights also become irrevocable if the third party has relied on the term, and its reliance was reasonably foreseeable by the promisor.[76] 'Reliance' is not specifically defined in the Act, which means that it is likely to have the same meaning it has in other areas of contract law.

The requirement of consent is a *default rule* not a *mandatory rule*. Because the Act grounds third party rights in the parties' intention, rather than in a general legal policy in favour of third parties, the parties can contract out of these rules. If the contract gives the parties the power to alter the third party's rights without its consent, then they have that power, notwithstanding s 2.[77] Equally, if the contract sets out additional circumstances in which the third party's consent is required, then it is those circumstances that matter, not s 2.[78] Courts have a discretionary power to dispense with consent in certain cases, such as where the third party cannot be found,[79] or has become mentally incapable,[80] or where it is difficult to ascertain whether the third party has in fact relied upon the term in question.[81]

---

69. See s 7(2).

70. Law Commission, *Privity of Contract: Contracts for the Benefit of Third Parties* (Law Com No 242, 1996) paras 13.9–13.13.

71. S 2(1).   72. See ss 2(1)(a) and 2(2)(a).   73. S 2(2)(b).

74. See *Precis (521) plc v William M Mercer Ltd* [2005] EWCA Civ 114, [39] (Arden LJ).

75. S 2(1)(b).   76. S 2(1)(c).   77. S 2(3)(a).   78. S 2(3)(b).

79. S 2(4)(a).   80. S 2(4)(b).   81. S 2(5).

> ### " Debates in context: is the 1999 Act a change for the better?

Despite the problems which the doctrine of privity created before the 1999 Act (see section 18.2), the Act was not universally welcomed. A significant number of academics were deeply critical of the Act, either because they disagreed with the very premise of the Act or because they disagreed with specific provisions of the Act.

Many of the criticisms came from academics who thought that privity was by no means a bad thing. The practical problems it created were not a result of the doctrine of privity but of other doctrines, and reform efforts should be targeted at these other doctrines. Professor Brian Coote, a strong defender of the traditional rule on privity, argued that the real problem lay in the limitations of the law of damages when it came to third party losses. The law, in his view, failed to recognize that these losses were not actually third party losses but losses suffered by the party to the contract who had not received the performance that had been contracted for.[82] Professor Steven Smith, writing from a more theoretical perspective, similarly argued that the reason privity appears problematic is because of broader issues with the rules governing quantification of damages, whether in relation to the expectation interest, reliance interest, or the restitution interest.[83] A particular problem he identified was the rule that expectation damages are only available in relation to tangible, pecuniary losses. Courts, he argued, should always award substantive damages rather than nominal damages, even if it meant that they strayed into speculative territory. Similar problems afflicted reliance and restitutionary damages. It is these issues in contract law that need reform, rather than the third party rule. Were they to be properly addressed, the doctrine of privity would cease to be a problem.

A second, and more practical, critique came from scholars who argued that privity had been part of English law for such a long time that it was deeply embedded in commercial practice. Changing it had the potential to create commercial uncertainty, by widening the body of persons to whom a party might be liable for breach.[84] The construction industry provides a good example. Most construction projects involve very complex networks of contracts between principals, contractors, site managers, architects, subcontractors, suppliers, and so on. Under the traditional doctrine of privity, every participant knew that they would only be liable to persons with whom they had directly contracted, and only for losses that those persons had suffered. The breadth of the presumption created by the 1999 Act, it was felt, significantly unsettled this, by making everyone potentially liable for losses suffered by any third parties in this wider transactional network.

Although this objection was seen as having some force at the time, in practice it has turned out not to be a very significant issue. Most of the affected sectors use very detailed sets of standard terms. These are drafted by industry organizations and incorporated by reference into most contracts in that sector. These standard terms were swiftly amended to expressly

→

---

82. B Coote, 'The Performance Interest, *Panatown*, and the Problem of Loss' (2001) 117 LQR 81.

83. SA Smith, 'Contracts for the Benefit of Third Parties: In Defence of the Third Party Rule' (1997) 17 OJLS 643.

84. H Collins, *The Law of Contract* (4th edn, Cambridge University Press 2003) 317.

state that the contract was not intended to confer any rights on third parties under the 1999 Act, which effectively rebutted the statutory presumption. Much of the pressure for this came from insurance companies, who were concerned about the impact of the Act on the scope of the risks for which they provided cover.

Since then, commercial bodies have become much more receptive to the Act. The cautious approach which the courts adopted to the requirement that the contract 'purport' to confer a benefit,[85] as well as the restrictive approach to the requirement that the third party be identified,[86] helped confine the Act to commercially sensible limits.[87] This has so reassured industry associations that some standard terms have now begun to engage directly with the Act, and to use it to create enforceable third party rights. The 2011 version of the Joint Contracts Tribunal (JCT) Major Project Construction Contract, for example, now extensively uses the Contracts (Rights of Third Parties) Act 1999 to delineate which provisions are enforceable by third parties and which are not.

The JCT suite of contracts is used in over 70 per cent of construction contracts within the UK, and this is therefore a very significant development which suggests that the 1999 Act has come a long way towards achieving its objectives, notwithstanding the academic concerns that continue to be raised.

18.4 Other routes around privity

Before leaving the topic of third party rights, it is useful to get a broad sense of the other legal routes around the doctrine of privity. Several of these are very specialized and relate to particular types of contracts. Special principles, for example, apply to letters of credit, which are a multipartite payment instrument commonly used in international transactions for the commercial sale of goods. Similarly, transactions such as bailment and covenants that run with land, too, are governed by their own distinct sets of principles. A detailed discussion of these is well beyond the scope of this book, and may be found in more specialized treatises. In this section, we will consider two of the most important generally applicable routes around privity; namely, the exception created by agency and the exception created by the concept of a collateral contract. Whilst both of these are narrower than the 1999 Act, they nevertheless offer ways of designing contracts to get around the strict doctrine of privity.

In addition, in certain cases, third parties who find themselves unable to enforce a contractual term due to the operation of privity may have a right of action under some other area of law. The two most important of these are the law of tort and the law of trusts. A full discussion of these areas of law is well beyond the scope of this textbook, but their existence should be noted.

85. See section 18.3.2.   86. See section 18.3.3.
87. Although this has not been without cost. See the discussion of *Themis Avraamides v Mark Colwill* [2006] EWCA Civ 1533 in section 18.3.3.

18.4.1 **Agency**

The law of agency is complex, and this chapter can do no more than provide a very brief survey of the way in which it can be used to design contracts to avoid some of the restrictions imposed by the doctrine of privity. A contract of agency is one in which one person (the agent) is empowered to represent another person (the principal) and enter into binding legal transactions on their behalf. Not all relationships where one party acts as a middleman or a special advisor amount to agency—they can equally be independent contractors or advisors. The key distinction is that the principal has given (or 'conferred') authority to the agent to bind the principal.

This authority means that the principal is treated as a party to all agreements entered into by the agent, even if the principal has not himself formally signed the agreement or otherwise participated in the offer and acceptance process, and even if the counter-party is unaware that the agent is acting as an agent for some other person. Before the entry into force of the Contracts (Rights of Third Parties) Act 1999, agency was sometimes used as a way of getting around the requirement of privity.

The decision of the Privy Council in *The Eurymedon*[88] illustrates this. The facts were similar to *Scruttons Ltd v Midland Silicones Ltd*,[89] which you encountered in section 18.2.3, but it involved a contract expressly drafted to get around the ruling in *Scruttons* using the device of agency. In *Scruttons*, Lord Reid had said that agency could overcome privity if the contract made it clear that the carrier was contracting as an agent (in addition to on his own behalf), that he had authority to do so, that the limitation clause was intended to protect the stevedores, and that the stevedores as principals provided consideration.[90] Each of these elements was present, or could be inferred, in *The Eurymedon*. As a result, the Privy Council held that the stevedores were parties to the contract and could claim the benefit of the exclusion clause it contained.

The template provided by *The Eurymedon* is perfectly capable of being extended outside the realm of contracts for the carriage and unloading of goods. However, as the case demonstrates, it requires fairly complex drafting to create an agency and to ensure that some form of consideration moves from the principal. As such, it is generally likely to be less useful than the Contract (Rights of Third Parties) Act 1999 when it comes to designing new contracts. Nevertheless, in appropriate cases it may provide a way to create more narrowly focused third party rights than the much broader brush approach taken by the 1999 Act.

18.4.2 **Collateral contracts**

A second contractual route around privity is provided by the legal device of the collateral contract. Collateral contracts are discussed in more detail in the context of formation (Chapter 2),[91] and that discussion will not be repeated here. As their name

---

88. *New Zealand Shipping Co Ltd v AM Satterthwaite & Co Ltd (The Eurymedon)* [1975] AC 154 (PC).
89. [1962] AC 446 (HL).
90. Ibid, 474 (Lord Reid). The stevedores in that case had unsuccessfully pleaded that the contract was entered into by the carriers as their agent. Lord Reid, in this passage, highlighted the type of facts that would need to be successful for the plea to succeed.
91. See also KW Wedderburn, 'Collateral Contracts' (1959) 17 CLJ 58.

suggests, they sit alongside some other contract, and are typically made to support some aspect of that contract. What distinguishes collateral contracts is that the consideration for the collateral contract is the creation of some other contract. Thus in a three-party situation, such as Problem 18, a collateral contract would in essence take the form of the therapists providing some form of warranty or covenant to the club, in consideration of the club agreeing to ensure that Louis Duckworth entered into a treatment agreement with the therapists.

Collateral contracts were a popular route around privity before the 1999 Act. In some cases, the parties expressly entered into a collateral contract between the promisor and the third party. In other cases, the court found that such a contract had been implicitly created. *Shanklin Pier Ltd v Detel Products Ltd*[92] is a good example of the latter situation.

Shanklin Pier owned a pier on the Isle of Wight, and engaged painters to paint it. They had previously spoken to Detel who had told them that its paint would be suitable for the pier and would have a life of seven to ten years. They therefore instructed the painters to use Detel's paint. The paint turned out to be unsuitable. Shanklin sought to sue Detel. Detel argued that there was no privity between it and Shanklin. It had entered into a contract for the purchase of paint with the painters, not Shanklin. As such, it owed no contractual duty to Shanklin. McNair J rejected this argument, and held that Shanklin could sue Detel for breach of contract. There was, he held, a collateral contract between Shanklin and Detel, under which Detel warranted the paint's quality for seven years and Shanklin agreed to ensure that its contractors would buy paint from Detel. The privity argument therefore had no basis.[93]

In theory, collateral contracts offer a powerful route around privity. The advantage they have over the Contracts (Rights of Third Parties) Act 1999 is that, unlike the Act, they deal with the question of contractual chains or contractual networks head on. Rather than discuss the question of third party rights in terms of 'benefits', they ask whether, given the nature of the overall transaction, the parties intended there to be some sort of direct relationship between the promisor and the third party. In the context of the problem with which the chapter began, the courts would ask whether there was a direct agreement between the club and the sports therapists, under which the club agreed to procure a contract between the player and the therapists in return for a guarantee of treatment. A court engaged on such an enquiry would be able to look to the nature of the dealings and relationship between the club and the therapists, in a way that would simply not be possible in an enquiry under s 1 of the Contracts (Rights of Third Parties) Act 1999.

This is a far clearer and more direct way of dealing with the issues created by contractual networks than the Act. It has been used to very good effect in consumer transactions. An area in which their use was particularly productive was hire purchase, where the transaction was usually structured in terms of an express contract between the seller and the financier, and another between the financier and the buyer, but not between the seller and the buyer. Here, the courts frequently implied a collateral contract between the seller and buyer, as a way of giving the buyer the protection of the seller's warranties.[94]

---

92. [1951] 2 KB 854.   93. Ibid, 856.
94. See esp *Andrews v Hopkinson* [1957] 1 QB 229.

Express collateral contracts or collateral warranties also have a long history in commercial transactions, particularly in the construction sector, where industry standard terms often use them to expressly give third parties a right to enforce certain terms. They have continued to remain popular even after the Contracts (Rights of Third Parties) Act 1999, simply because there is much more case law (and, hence, greater certainty) on their scope and effect. Where there is no express collateral warranty, however, the courts have been very reluctant to *imply* them in commercial transactions. Their starting point appears to be the assumption that if the parties did not expressly signal their intention to deal with each other by entering into an express contract, then the courts should be slow to find an implied contract between them.[95]

This approach is substantially similar to that taken by the Court of Appeal in *Prudential Assurance Co Ltd v Ayres*.[96] As we saw in section 18.3, the court in that case was influenced by its view that it was unlikely that commercial parties who sought to create an enforceable obligation would have relied upon the uncertain effect of the Contracts (Rights of Third Parties) Act 1999. This is regrettable, because it assumes a level of legal understanding that most commercial transactions will never reach. Nevertheless, it appears unlikely that the courts' basic approach will change. The result is that in cases like Problem 18, and similar situations, the device of the implied collateral contract is unlikely to be of practical use despite the fact that it is far more suited to addressing the actual issue between the parties than the 1999 Act.

18.4.3 **Statutory exceptions**

As a final point, you should note that there are other statutory exceptions to privity. These exceptions are almost invariably focused on one specific type of transaction or contract. A significant proportion deal with insurance contracts, and give someone other than the policyholder a direct right to demand payment from the insurance company. In some cases, such as life insurance, this is a matter of necessity: otherwise, the proceeds from the policy would form part of the policyholder's estate and would more often than not end up being used to meet any debts she left, rather than going to her next of kin. In other cases, such as road traffic insurance, it is a matter of policy and convenience rather than necessity.

As is often the case with English statutes, these provisions are not collected in any one place, but are found in a bewildering range of statutes. Provisions in relation to the right of next of kin to recover under a life insurance policy, for example, are to be found in s 11 of the Married Women's Property Act 1882, read in the light of s 19(1) of the Family Law Reform Act 1969 and s 67(1) of the Adoption and Children Act 2002. Under ss 148(7) and 151 of the Road Traffic Act 1988, a person who is injured in a road traffic accident can make a claim against the insurer of the driver who caused the accident. The insurer has an obligation, subject to certain conditions, to indemnify the victim even though there is no contractual privity between them.

The most general statute in relation to insurance is the Third Parties (Rights against Insurers) Act 2010, which replaced an older statute from 1930, and came into effect in

---

95. See eg *Fuji Seal Europe v Catalytic Combustion Corp* [2005] EWHC 1659 (TCC).
96. [2008] EWCA Civ 52.

August 2016. This statute primarily applies in situations where the person who is liable has taken out insurance against that liability, but has since become insolvent. In such cases, the statute gives third parties a right to directly sue the insurer, even if liability has not been established. The insurer may defend the action either on the substantive issue of liability or on the issue of whether or not the risk or loss at issue is within the insurance policy. This statute has been of particular use in relation to suits brought by employees against former employers for workplace-related illnesses, which often do not manifest themselves for decades, by which time the employers are often long gone.

A second set of exceptions to privity relate to very specialized commercial instruments, such as negotiable instruments[97] and bills of lading,[98] whose details are best left to more specialized texts.

18.5 Recovery by the parties

Before we leave the topic of privity, there is a final issue that we should consider.

If persons in the position of the club in Problem 18 cannot sue under the contract as third parties, should the party to the contract, such as Louis Duckworth, be able to recover compensation on their behalf? Problem 18 involves a commercial contract. The position in relation to consumer contracts is a lot clearer, and therefore makes a good starting point. Consider the following illustration:

Illustration 18.4

Agatha sees an advertisement in the newspaper for a holiday event called: 'Santa's winter wonderland', promising reindeer, snow, and Lapland-themed events. She buys tickets for her daughter Fiona and granddaughter Lorraine. When Fiona and Lorraine turn up at the venue, they are deeply disappointed to find that the reindeer have not arrived from Scandinavia, that the 'snow' consists of very low-quality powdery artificial snow, and that the Lapland-themed events have been cancelled.

As Chapter 16, section 16.2.5, discusses, courts can award a party damages for disappointed expectation. However, there is a potential problem. Agatha, who is ultimately the contracting party, has suffered no loss. If damages are confined to the contracting party's loss, she will only get nominal damages. Such an outcome is hard to defend. People often buy goods, holidays, tickets to events, and other such things as presents for others. A substantial body of consumers will be left without a remedy if the law only awards compensation for loss suffered by the parties personally.

Accordingly, in the 1970s, English courts began to allow the recovery of compensation for harm suffered by third party consumers. One of the first cases of this type was *Jackson v Horizon Holidays Ltd*.[99] Julian Jackson, the claimant, booked a holiday in Sri

---

97. See Bills of Exchange Act 1882, s 38.
98. See Carriage of Goods by Sea Act 1992, s 2.   99. [1975] 1 WLR 1468 (CA).

Lanka with Horizon Holidays for himself, his wife, and his children. They were supposed to stay in a newly built luxury hotel called the Pegasus Reef Hotel. The opening of that hotel was delayed and Horizon Holidays rebooked him in an alternative hotel, called Brown's Beach Hotel. When Jackson and his family checked in, they found it to be in a very poor state, quite far removed from the luxury that was promised. On returning home, he sued. Horizon Holidays admitted breach, and the only question before the court was the quantum of damages. It was common ground that the decision in *Jarvis v Swans Tours*[100] applied, so that compensation was available not only for the difference in value but also for mental distress and disappointment. The trial judge held, however, that he could only award compensation for mental distress suffered by Jackson himself, and not for the disappointment and distress of his family. He could take into account the effect of his family's distress on Jackson, but damages for the family's distress and disappointment per se could not be awarded. The Court of Appeal reversed the trial judge, and held that damages could be awarded to cover everyone's loss. Lord Denning, who delivered the leading judgment, held that a contract such as this was distinctive because the father 'was making a contract himself for the benefit of the whole party', and in such circumstances 'the only way in which a just result can be achieved' is if the person making the contract was

> able to recover for the discomfort, vexation and upset which the whole party have suffered by reason of the breach of contract, recompensing them accordingly out of what he recovers.[101]

Jackson was not appealed further, but the issue came to the House of Lords some years later in the case of *Woodar Investment Development Ltd v Wimpey Construction UK Ltd*.[102] In *Woodar*, the House of Lords expressly disapproved of the rule articulated by Lord Denning. They accepted that the outcome of *Jackson* was correct on the facts, but they held that that case had misstated the law. Contrary to what Lord Denning had suggested, the general rule was that a party to a contract could *not* recover compensation for losses suffered by third parties. *Jackson* could be supported on the basis that contracts for family holidays, or for certain other types of group activities such as a group taxi, were a special class which deserved special treatment.[103] Other special cases included agents and trustees, both of whom had long been recognized as having the ability to recover damages on behalf of their principals or the beneficiaries of the trust. Similarly, there is also a long-standing exception to this rule, known as the *Albazero* exception,[104] under which a seller of goods can, on behalf of the buyer, recover damages from a carrier who has damaged the goods, even if by the time the damage occurs the seller no longer owns the goods (and, hence, has suffered no loss). But these are exceptions to the general rule, and in cases not covered by the exceptions no recovery is possible.

---

100. [1973] 1 QB 233 (CA).   101. [1975] 1 WLR 1468, 1473 (Lord Denning MR).
102. [1980] 1 WLR 277 (HL).   103. Ibid, 282 (Lord Wilberforce), 297 (Lord Keith).
104. *Albacruz (Cargo Owners) v Albazero (Owners) (The Albazero)* [1977] AC 774 (HL). The rule itself is much older: see *Dunlop v Lambert* (1839) 2 Cl & F 626. It is worth noting that the claimant in *The Albazero* itself was unsuccessful, as the case was held not to fall within the exception.

The observations in *Woodar* were obiter, as the case was decided on the ground that the defendant was not in breach.[105] Not all judges in *Woodar* were happy with the majority view, although none pushed their dissatisfaction to the point of dissent. Lord Scarman thought that the position called for review, and it was open to the House of Lords to find some way of ensuring that third party losses were properly compensated.[106]

A few years later, in *Forster v Silvermere Golf & Equestrian Centre Ltd*,[107] the High Court was even more critical of the rule, but held itself bound by precedent to follow it. Ms Foster entered into an agreement with the defendants to transfer a large property, consisting of 60 acres. Under the agreement, the defendants were to discharge a mortgage on the property, and build a house which she and her children would use rent-free, with her children acquiring the right after her death. Until the house was built, she was entitled to continue to live in a cottage which already existed on the property. In breach of contract, the defendant failed to construct a house on the property, and the claimant sued for damages.[108] Dillon J in the Chancery Decision held that the claimant could only recover damages for herself, as her children were not parties to the contract. She could have recovered damages on behalf of her children if she had entered into the contract as their trustee, but she had not done so. The decision, he thought was 'beyond question unjust',[109] but as the law stood no other outcome was possible.

Despite this criticism, the rule in *Woodard* remains the law. Subsequent cases have declined to alter the law in the direction Lord Scarman envisaged. They have, instead, focused on whether new exceptions need to be created, and what the scope of existing exceptions is. The vast majority related to construction contracts, for good reason. Large construction contracts involve a host of contractors, subcontractors, and sub-subcontractors. Not all of these parties have direct relations with each other. A subcontractor, for example, will have contractual relations with the main contractor, but not the owner of the site; and a sub-subcontractor will have contractual relations with the subcontractor, but not the main contractor. Equally, if the building is sold to a third party, the third party will not have contractual relations with the contractor, leaving it with no direct claim in contract if building defects are subsequently discovered. The result is that contracts of this type are particularly prone to raising issues around third party losses. The decision of the House of Lords in *Linden Gardens Trust v Lenesta Sludge Disposals Ltd*,[110] a case which involved two conjoined appeals, shows both how complex the legal issues this creates can be and how far the law can diverge from the often-cited position of protecting 'the reasonable expectations of honest men'.[111]

---

105. This aspect of the case is discussed in Chapter 15 ('Breach of contract'), section 15.3.4.
106. [1980] 1 WLR 277, 300–1 (Lord Scarman).
107. (1981) 42 P & CR 255 (Ch).
108. The claimant had previously sought to claim for specific performance, but failed.
109. (1981) 42 P & CR 255, 258.
110. [1994] 1 AC 85 (HL).
111. See J Steyn, 'Contract Law: Fulfilling the Reasonable Expectations of Honest Men' (1997) 113 LQR 433.

Case in depth: *Linden Gardens Trust v Lenesta Sludge Disposals Ltd* [1994] AC 85

The appeals and cross-appeals in *Linden Gardens* involved two sets of disputes with very similar facts, but with differences in how the claim was brought. Both disputes involved construction contracts which had been poorly executed. In the first, the contractor had been engaged to remove asbestos from a building but had left significant amounts unremoved. In the second, the contractor had been engaged to redevelop a building but did so very poorly.

The problem in both cases was that the building had since been sold to a third party, at the full market price. This led to a peculiar double-whammy. The original owners, who had contractual relations with the negligent contractor, were the logical persons to sue. But they had suffered no loss as the building sold for the full market value. The purchasers of the building had suffered loss but they did not have contractual relations with the contractor.[112] The parties to the two disputes adopted slightly different litigation strategies. The claimant in the first dispute (Linden Gardens Trust) sued the contractor directly without the involvement of the original owner. The claimant in the second dispute (St Martins Property Investments Ltd) also sued the contractor directly, but was joined by the original owner who also sued the contractor as a joint claimant.

The joint claim by the original owner in the second dispute proved to be fortuitous. The House of Lords unanimously held that the purchasers had no rights of action against the contractors, because they were not parties to the contract. The original owners, in contrast, could sue for damages on behalf of the purchasers, and would be able to recover substantial damages even though they had suffered no loss themselves. They were suing on behalf of the purchasers and were therefore legally required to pay over whatever compensation they received to the purchasers. Linden Gardens Trust, therefore, had no action against the asbestos-removal contractor, even though it had suffered a significant loss as a result of the contractor's breach. St Martins Property Investments, however, could recover compensation indirectly: the original owner would recover compensation for breach, and would pay the damages to St Martins Property Investments.

Two different sets of reasons were given by the House of Lords for holding that the original owner could recover substantial damages, despite not having suffered any loss. The majority justified their decision on relatively narrow grounds which amounted, in effect, to an incremental extension of the *Albazero* exception. The *Albazero* exception permits a seller of goods to recover damages on behalf of the buyer, if the goods are lost or damaged during transport due to a breach of contract by the carrier. The rationale behind this exception is that in contracts of carriage, the carrier generally knows that ownership in the goods is likely to pass to someone else during carriage. Consequently, the original party would as a matter of law be treated as having entered into the contract for the benefit of everyone who might acquire an interest in the goods. As such, he would be entitled to recover damages on behalf of those persons for losses they might sustain.

→

112. In both cases, the seller had entered into a contract with the buyer assigning their rights against the contractor to the buyer, but the assignments were invalid in both cases. The construction contracts had used a standard form which required the contractor to consent to any assignment, and the contractors in this case had not given their consent to the assignment.

Lord Browne-Wilkinson, with whom three of the four other judges agreed, held that this exception should be extended. In the case before the court, both the contractor in charge of the redevelopment and the original owner knew that the units in the building would ultimately be owned and/or occupied by third parties. It was therefore foreseeable that a breach could cause loss to a later owner. As such, it was proper 'to treat the parties as having entered into the contract on the footing that [the original owner] would be entitled to enforce contractual rights for the benefit of those who suffered from defective performance . . .'[113]

Lord Griffiths, while concurring in the outcome, thought that the underlying principle was much broader than the relatively narrow exception set out in Lord Browne-Wilkinson's decision. The contractors had owed a contractual duty to the original owners. They breached that duty. They were therefore liable in damages to the original owner. The ordinary measure of damages in such a case was the cost of cure. This is what they would have to pay.[114] Whether in actual fact the cure had been commissioned by the original owner or the ultimate purchaser was irrelevant: that was a matter raised *inter alios acta* as far as the contractor was concerned.[115]

Although some of the other judges said that they were 'attracted'[116] by or had 'much sympathy with'[117] the 'broader principle' set out by Lord Griffiths, it was ultimately Lord Browne-Wilkinson's 'narrower ground' that prevailed. The result is that under the *Linden Gardens* exception, damages can be recovered on behalf of the third party if three conditions are satisfied. First, the loss or damage must relate to property. Secondly, the contracting parties must have known, or had within their contemplation, the possibility that a third party would have, or acquire, interests in that property.[118] Thirdly, the third party must not have acquired any direct rights against the contractor, and it must have been foreseeable at the time of contracting that third party transferees would not acquire direct rights.

The importance of the third point was reiterated by the House of Lords in *Alfred McAlpine Construction Ltd v Panatown Ltd*.[119] The Unex group of companies was in the process of constructing a new office building in Hills Road, Cambridge, and appointed Alfred McAlpine as the contractors. The site was owned by one company within the group (UIPL), but for tax reasons the construction contract was entered into by a different group company (Panatown). In addition to the construction contract, McAlpine also executed a separate document, called a duty of care deed, in favour of UIPL and its successors in title. Under the deed, UIPL acquired a direct remedy against McAlpine if McAlpine 'failed to exercise reasonable skill, care and attention in respect of any matter within the scope of McAlpine's responsibilities'.[120] The purpose of the deed was likely

---

113. [1994] 1 AC 85, 115 (Lord Browne-Wilkinson).   114. Ibid, 96 (Lord Griffiths).
115. Ibid, 98 (Lord Griffiths).   116. Ibid, 96 (Lord Bridge).   117. Ibid, 95 (Lord Keith).
118. This will usually take the form of a transfer of the property to the third party, but the exception will also apply where there is no transfer of property involved. Courts have held that third parties can recover under the *Linden Gardens* exception even in circumstances where the third party already owned the property. The key requirement in such cases is awareness that the building 'was being constructed for the benefit' of the third party. See *Darlington Borough Council v Wiltshier Northern Ltd* [1995] 1 WLR 68 (CA), 75 (Dillon LJ).
119. [2001] 1 AC 518 (HL).   120. Ibid, 536.

to have been to create a warranty which could be passed on to future purchasers, rather than to protect UIPL itself,[121] and the right it gave was significantly narrower than the building contract, which had a far more detailed set of requirements. Nevertheless, the House of Lords by a 3:2 majority held that its effect was that Panatown could only recover nominal damages against McAlpine, as UIPL had acquired a direct right of action against McAlpine under the duty of care deed. It made no difference whether the problem was approached through Lord Browne-Wilkinson's 'narrow' approach or Lord Griffiths's 'broad' approach in *Linden Gardens*.

The *Linden Gardens* exception as it currently stands is technical rather than commercial. The decisions in respect of the first dispute in *Linden Gardens* and in *Panatown* are unlikely to represent what the parties commissioning the building works intended. Both cases saw a 'legal black hole', caused by the fact that the party with the action had not suffered any loss, while the party who had suffered loss had no right of action. The contractors in both cases could, in effect, breach the contract with impunity. And although the second dispute in *Linden Gardens* did end with full recovery, this was only because the litigation had been carried out in a way that met the legal requirements. It is clearly questionable whether the law ought to impose the requirements it currently does, but the point to take away is that it is possible to get around these requirements as long as enough attention is paid to them when preparing contractual documents and deciding litigation strategy. However, the narrow focus of the exception on cases involving property means that it is unlikely to be of much use to those in the position of the club.

18.6 In conclusion: dealing with contractual networks

As we have seen in the course of the chapter, despite being directly affected by the therapists' omissions in Problem 18, the club is unlikely to have any remedy against them. Similar points could be made in relation to some of the other problems examined in this book. Problem 16, involving a breach by a celebrity chef of his contract as an anchor tenant, presents a very similar issue. The chef's breach adversely affects the position not just of the owners of the development, but also of the other artists who have outlets in the development. Because the anchor tenant has pulled out, all of them will see significantly less turnover than they expected. Privity will, however, preclude them from recovering, as they are unlikely to be covered by the 1999 Act or any of the other exceptions to the doctrine.

How well, then, does English law deal with the problem of third party rights?

This question can be approached in two different ways. The first is to view the law as a toolkit which the parties can use to carefully plan their transactions and to design effective contract frameworks to support them. From this perspective, English law does very well. A general theme of the rules we have studied in this chapter is that their focus has not been as much on dealing directly with the question of third party rights, as it has been on giving the parties a set of tools by which they can themselves structure mechanisms for dealing with those rights. The Contracts (Rights of Third Parties) Act 1999, in particular, gives commercial parties the opportunity to design enforceable frameworks

---

121. See the discussion in the speech of Lord Millett, ibid, 593–5.

to give legal rights to third parties—an opportunity that was long absent—while also providing a set of tests to judge whether it is appropriate in a given case to treat the parties as implicitly having intended to give a third party beneficiary such a right. The Act errs on the side of caution, particularly when it comes to the question of identification, but as long as the parties are well advised, and have the resources to engage competent legally trained draftsmen, the Act provides an excellent framework for contract design.

When it comes to giving effect to implicit dimensions of contracting, the law does less well. This is in no small part due to the reluctance of the courts to read things into commercial contracts that are not expressly there and, in particular, to imply relations between commercial parties who have not themselves clearly and explicitly expressed their intention to enter into legal relations. This is not peculiar to third party rights, however. A theme to which this book has repeatedly returned is the reluctance of the English courts to go too far in the direction of a more relationally grounded approach, and its continuing emphasis on the importance of attempting to foresee, and provide for, as large a proportion as possible of the risks that may arise in the course of contracting. Such an approach has weaknesses, but English law is unlikely to adopt a radically different approach in the foreseeable future.

Key points

- The doctrine of privity states that only parties to a contract can sue or be sued under it. Third party beneficiaries only have a right to sue if they fall within one of the exceptions to privity. The most important of these are the exceptions recognized by the Contracts (Rights of Third Parties) Act 1999.

- Under the Act, third parties always have the right to enforce a contract if the contract expressly provides so.

- In addition, if the contract 'purports to confer a benefit' on the third party, the courts will presume that the third party has a right of enforcement. This presumption can be rebutted by showing that the parties did not intend to give the third party a right to enforce the contract.

- A contract will only 'purport' to confer a benefit if that was one of the purposes of the parties. Benefits which are only incidentally conferred are not covered.

- It is not necessary to show that the third party was aware of the benefit or that he relied on it.

- The third party must be expressly identified by name, class, or description in the contract. An implicit identification is insufficient.

- The promisor will have all defences and setoffs against the third party that she would have had against the promisee. The third party has a lesser right in relation to the ability to challenge exclusion clauses in the contract.

- The parties' ability to alter the contract to the third party's detriment is restricted where the promisor knows that the third party has relied on the term, or where the third party has informed the promisor that he has assented to the term.

- The pre-statute common law routes around privity continue to exist. These include agency, collateral contracts, and special exemptions created by other statutes.

- In certain, very limited, cases, the party to the contract can recover compensation on behalf of the third party. This primarily affects certain types of consumer transactions and commercial transactions involving property.

Assess your learning

You should be able to respond to each of the following points with a confident 'yes'. If you can't, then you should revisit the sections listed against that point.

Can you:

(a) *Outline* the key features of the doctrine of privity, and its impact on third parties? (Section 18.2)

(b) *Explain* the meaning of 'purport to confer a benefit', its importance under the Act, and how the presumption it creates can be rebutted? (Section 18.3.2)

(c) *Identify* the key elements of the requirement of identification, and the consequence of these requirements not being met? (Section 18.3.3)

(d) *Identify* the restrictions imposed by the Act on the third party's ability to challenge exclusion clauses in the contract, and on the ability of the parties to amend the contract against the third party's interests? (Section 18.3.4)

(e) *Understand* the issues raised by third party loss, and *describe* the circumstances under which a contracting party can recover on behalf of third parties? (Section 18.5)

In relation to each of the above, you should be able to:

(i) identify and clearly explain the key rules and principles;

(ii) identify the key cases and statutes, and why they matter;

(iii) apply the principles and cases to specific real or hypothetical fact situations;

(iv) evaluate the limitations, if any, of the law as it currently stands.

Further reading

J Adams and R Brownsword, 'Privity of Contract: That Pestilential Nuisance' (1993) 56 MLR 722.

AS Burrows, 'The Contracts (Rights of Third Parties) Act and its Implications for Commercial Contracts' [2000] LMCLQ 540.

B Coote, 'The Performance Interest, *Panatown*, and the Problem of Loss' (2001) 117 LQR 81.

M Furmston and G Tolhurst, *Privity of Contract* (Oxford University Press 2015).

P Kincaid (ed), *Privity: Private Justice or Public Regulation* (Ashgate 2001).

NE Palmer and G Tolhurst, 'Compensatory and Extra-Compensatory Damages: The Role of the *Albazero* in Modern Damages Claims' (1997) 12 JCL 1 (part 1), 97 (part 2).

T Roe, 'Contractual Intention under Section 1(1)(b) and 1(2) of the Contracts (Rights of Third Parties) Act 1999' (2000) 63 MLR 887.

Glossary

Acceptance A final, unqualified expression of assent to the conditions of the offer as put forward by the offeror. An acceptance must not propose new terms, or change any terms set out in the offer.

Accord and satisfaction The technical term for an agreement to discharge a debt on terms different from those originally agreed to by the parties. The new agreement must be supported by consideration to be valid.

Account of profits A gain-based remedy, only awarded in exceptional cases, where the defendant is required to pay the claimant the entire profit the defendant has made as a result of their breach of contract.

Affirmation The innocent party in a case of repudiatory or anticipatory breach affirms the contract if it elects not to accept the repudiation, but instead to keep the contract alive and sue for damages or specific performance.

Agreement to agree An agreement in which the parties have not agreed on some of the essential terms, but have merely noted that they expect to reach agreement on those terms. Agreements to agree are not legally valid.

Ambiguity A situation where a term in a contract is capable of having more than one meaning. If the ambiguity cannot be resolved through a contextual interpretation of the contract, the clause in question is unenforceable.

Anticipatory breach A situation where one party repudiates or renounces the contract, by indicating that it will not perform its obligations under the contract when they fall due. The innocent party has the option to terminate the contract, or to affirm it and insist on its performance.

Battle of the forms A battle of the forms occurs where each party tells the other that it intends to deal on its standard terms, and the parties do not reach express agreement on which set of terms governs the contract.

Breach of contract A situation where one party has failed to perform its obligations under the contract in the manner stipulated by the contract.

Bright-line rule A term used by academics to describe rules which set out clear and unambiguous standards, with no room for nuance or weighting. The rule that a void contract creates no legal obligations between the parties is an example of a bright-line rule.

Business efficacy A test for implying terms into contracts in fact, under which a term will be implied into the contract if it is necessary to give the contract the business efficacy which the parties intended it to have.

But for test A test used to determine whether one event caused another. The test is satisfied if it can be proved that the second event would not have occurred 'but for' the first.

Causation A legal doctrine which limits recoverable damages to loss which is a result of the breach of the legal duty in question. Causation is usually determined with reference to the 'but for' test.

Caveat emptor Literally, 'let the buyer beware'. A Latin phrase used to encapsulate a legal rule that the court will not intervene in a concluded contract to make it fairer to the buyer. Statutory implied terms and consumer protection law have limited the scope of this maxim in modern contract law.

Certainty The requirement that the terms of a contract must be clear, and not so vague or open-ended that it is incapable of enforcement. Terms which are insufficiently certain are not legally valid.

Collateral contract A contract that sits alongside the main contract, and is made to support it. Collateral contracts are exceptions to the doctrine of privity.

Common mistake A legal rule under a contract which was entered into under a mistake of fact or law is void *ab initio*. The rule is narrow, and only applies where the mistake relates to the existence of the subject matter or one of its essential qualities, and where the risk has not been contractually allocated.

Communication The requirement that certain steps taken by one party must be brought to the notice of the other party in order to have legal effect. There are several exceptions to the requirement of communication, most notably the postal rule.

Condition precedent A contractual term which one party must perform before some or all of the obligations of the other party fall due.

Conditions The most important terms of a contract. A breach of a condition is always repudiatory.

Consensus ad idem Literally, 'agreement as to the same thing'. A Latin phrase used to describe the key requirement of the offer and acceptance process, namely, that there must be a meeting of minds between the parties, so that they are in agreement as to the terms of the contract.

Consideration Something of value which one party gives the other in return for the promise. Consideration may be a detriment or a benefit (including, in some cases, a practical benefit). A contract is not valid unless it is supported by consideration.

Construction The process by which a court 'construes' the terms of a contract to determine what they mean, and how they require the parties to act in a particular situation.

Contra proferentem A principle of interpretation under which an exclusion clause is construed against the person seeking to rely on it, if the clause is capable of multiple interpretations.

Core term In consumer contracts, 'core terms' are an exception to the general rules on unfair terms. Core terms are terms which either specify the main subject matter of the contract, or which entail an assessment of the appropriateness of the price paid for goods or services. Core terms are never unfair.

Cost of cure A measure of expectation damages, which are awarded with reference to the cost of procuring substitute performance on the market (and, hence, of 'curing' the breach of contract).

Counter-offer A counter-offer is a statement made by an offeree, which responds to the offer by proposing new or different terms. A counter-offer is a new offer, which renders the original offer incapable of acceptance.

Customary implied terms Terms implied into a contract because they are part of standard usage or custom in the relevant field or market.

Damages A sum of money which the court orders a party in breach of a legal duty to pay to the innocent party to compensate the innocent party for the loss suffered as a result of the breach of that duty.

De minimis **rule** A legal rule under which extremely small or trivial deviations from the terms of a contract are not considered breaches.

Debt An action brought to recover a definite sum which is payable under a contract. Unlike damages, actions in debt are not subject to the rules on mitigation.

Deed An instrument executed in writing and signed by the party making it, which complies with certain formal requirements. A contract executed as a deed does not need to be supported by consideration.

Difference in value A measure of expectation damages, quantified with reference to the difference in the value of the performance contracted for, and the performance actually rendered. The quantum will typically be lower than the cost of cure.

Discharge A contract is discharged when the parties' rights and obligations under the contract come to an end. Contracts may be discharged by being performed, by a repudiation which the other party accepts, or by frustration.

Duress Illegitimate pressure or threats applied by one party to another to coerce the other party into contracting. Duress renders a contract voidable at the instance of the coerced person.

Economic duress The application of subtler forms of pressure (eg a threat to breach a contract) which do not involve threats to harm a person's property or person.

Election An option granted to the innocent party to choose between different remedies in the event of breach of contract.

Entire obligation Obligations are entire if the contract requires performance of that obligation to be fully completed before the obligations of the other party fall due.

Estoppel A legal rule under which a party is prevented from going back on something which that party has in the past asserted. Estoppel usually requires the other party to have relied on the representation or assurance in question.

Ex turpi causa A shortening of the Latin maxim *ex turpi causa non oritur actio* ('no action arises from a base (or disreputable) cause'). The maxim expresses the principle that a legal claim cannot be founded on an illegal act, and is the foundation for the doctrine of illegality in contract.

Exclusion clauses A clause which seeks to limit or eliminate a party's liability to the other for breach of contract.

Expectation interest The interest a person has in the proper performance of a contract. The expectation interest is one of the bases for deciding the quantum of compensation to be awarded for breach of contract.

Express terms Terms on which the parties have expressly agreed. Express terms may be oral, contained in a written contractual instrument, or incorporated by reference.

Failure of consideration A situation in which the claimant receives no part of what they have bargained for (a total failure of consideration) or only some of what they bargained for (a partial failure of consideration).

Frustration A legal rule under which a contract is discharged if changes after the contract is formed render it a thing 'radically different' from what the parties had contracted for. The doctrine is very narrow, and only applies in exceptional circumstances.

Gain-based remedy See Restitution.

Gratuitous promise A promise made without the other party providing any consideration for it. Gratuitous promises are not enforceable as contracts (although they may
in some cases give rise to estoppel).

Hypothetical bargain measure A gain-based remedy for breach of contract, under
which the quantum awarded is measured with reference to the amount the claimant would have charged the defendant to release the defendant from the obligation
which has been breached.

Implied terms Terms on which the parties have not expressly agreed, but which as a
matter of fact or law are deemed by the court to form part of the contract.

Incompleteness A contract is incomplete if one or more essential terms have not been
expressly agreed, and cannot be implied in law, custom, or fact. An incomplete contract is not legally enforceable.

Incorporation The process by which terms contained in another document are made
part of the parties' contract. Incorporation requires notice of the terms to be given
to the other party.

Injunction An equitable remedy which restrains parties from acting in a way that is a
breach of contract.

Innominate terms Terms of a contract which are neither as important as conditions
nor as unimportant as warranties. Whether a breach of an innominate term is repudiatory depends on the impact the breach has on the contract.

Instrument A term to describe a written document containing some or all of the terms
on which the parties have agreed to contract.

Intention to create legal relations An ingredient of a valid contract, which requires
the two parties to intend to be legally bound by their agreement (as distinct from an
agreement that was only intended to create a moral or commercial obligation rather
than a legal one).

Intermediate terms See **Innominate terms**.

Interpretation See **Construction**.

Invitation to treat An invitation to treat is a pre-contractual statement made by one
party to another, which is intended to form a basis for negotiations but is not an
offer. Typically, an invitation to treat will either be insufficiently certain to be an
offer or will not evidence an intention to be bound.

Knowledge Where a party either actually knew certain facts, or is as a matter of law
deemed to have known those facts.

Liquidated damages An attempt by the parties to agree in advance on the amount of
compensation that one party will pay the other in the event of breach. Liquidated
damages clauses are used most often in circumstances where the exact quantum of
loss will be hard to prove.

Loss of amenity A measure of expectation damages awarded in consumer contracts, where
the defendant's breach has prevented the consumer from obtaining the full benefit of
a pleasurable amenity, or avoiding discomfort, which was the purpose of the contract.

Loss of chance A measure of expectation damages for breach of contract, which is
used in cases where the claimant's ability to make a profit depended in part on the
actions of a third party (eg where the claimant was unable to put in a bid because of
the defendant's breach).

Loss of profit A measure of expectation damages for breach of contract, under which the claimant is awarded the profit they would have made on the contract, had it not been breached.

Matrix of fact A phrase used to describe the body of materials to which a court can look in deciding what the terms of a contract mean.

Mere puff An extravagant statement made in the course of pre-contractual discussions, typically a hyperbolic exaggeration, which was not intended to be taken seriously and would not have been taken seriously by a reasonable person.

Misrepresentation A situation where one party has made an untrue statement to the other party, which has induced the other party to enter into the contract. Misrepresentations may be innocent, fraudulent, or negligent, depending on the state of mind of the representor. Misrepresentation makes the contract voidable at the option of the representee.

Mistake An omnibus term sometimes used to encompass three distinct doctrines: common mistake, mutual mistake, and unilateral mistake.

Mitigation A legal doctrine which prevents a party from recovering compensation for loss that could have been avoided had the party taken reasonable steps to minimize their loss after the breach of contract.

Mutual mistake A legal rule under which a contract is void if the words the parties used to express their agreement were capable of having more than one meaning, each party intended a different meaning, and the ambiguity cannot be resolved through a contextual interpretation.

Nudum pactum Literally, 'naked promise'. A Latin phrase used to describe an agreement that is not supported by consideration.

Objective test The legal position that a party's intention is judged not with reference to what was actually in that party's mind, but with reference to what a reasonable person would have understood from the party's words and actions. Intention is almost always assessed objectively in contract law.

Offer An offer is a statement made by one party to another, proposing to contract on the basis of terms set out in the offer. The statement must evidence an intention to be bound, and the terms must be sufficiently certain.

Officious bystander A hypothetical figure used by courts in deciding whether to imply a term in fact. The figure is used to decide whether a term was left out by the parties because it was so obvious that it went without saying.

Parol evidence rule A rule under which oral evidence cannot be adduced to displace the evidence of the written contract.

Past consideration Anything provided by one party to the other before the contract was made. Past consideration cannot be good consideration, save in exceptional circumstances, because it was not provided in exchange for the promise.

Penalty clause A clause which seeks to penalize a party for breaching the contract by requiring the payment of an exorbitant or unconscionable sum for breach.

Peppercorn consideration A nominal consideration (eg a peppercorn), added to a contract for the sole purpose of making it enforceable.

Performance Doing what the contract requires, in accordance with its terms.

Postal rule An exception to the ordinary requirements in relation to how acceptance should be communicated. Under the postal rule, an acceptance will be taken to have been communicated to the other party as soon as it is posted, even if it is never received by the other party.

Presumption A presumption is a rule of evidence in which the law assumes that a particular requirement has been met, unless the contrary is proved. Most presumptions are rebuttable (meaning that a party can lead evidence to disprove the presumption), but some are irrebuttable.

Privity of contract A rule under which only the parties to the contract can sue for its breach. Third parties cannot sue, even if they have suffered loss. The scope of this doctrine has been severely restricted by statute.

Promissory estoppel A legal defence, under which a party can defend themselves on the basis that the other party made a clear and unequivocal promise or representation that they would not rely on the legal right which they sought to assert. A party seeking to invoke promissory estoppel must have relied on the promise or representation in question.

Proprietary estoppel A variant of estoppel which only applies to interests in land. A party can acquire an interest in land through proprietary estoppel if they have detrimentally relied on a promise of the grant of that interest, in circumstances which would make it unconscionable for that interest not to be granted.

Quantum meruit A remedy under which a claimant can sue for the value of services provided to the defendant, rather than suing for damages. The remedy is available where there has been a repudiatory breach, where the underlying contract is subsequently discovered to be void, or where work was carried out anticipating a contract which was never entered into.

Quantum valebat A remedy under which a claimant can sue for the value of goods provided to the defendant, rather than suing for damages. The remedy is available in the same circumstances as *quantum meruit*.

Reasonable addressee A hypothetical figure used by courts in the process of construing the terms of a contract. The terms are always construed with reference to how a reasonable addressee would understand them.

Reasonableness A legal test used in a range of common law and statutory contexts. In common law, reasonableness is assessed with reference to the standard of a hypothetical reasonable person. Statutes often set out more specific criteria that are to be taken into account in assessing reasonableness in the particular context covered by the statute.

Rectification An equitable remedy under which the courts can alter the words in a written contract, if the written words did not reflect the parties' intention.

Red hand rule A rule pertaining to incorporation, under which a higher degree of notice must be given of unusual or unexpected terms for them to be validly incorporated. The red hand rule does not apply to terms contained in the contractual instrument itself, and only applies to terms incorporated by notice.

Reliance A situation where a party has altered their behaviour or conduct on the basis of a promise or assurance made to them. Reliance is sometimes (but not always) required to be detrimental.

Reliance interest An approach to quantifying damages which seeks to restore the parties to the position in which they would have been had the contract never been formed. A party suing on the reliance interest will typically recover expenditure spent in reliance on the contract.

Remoteness A legal doctrine which limits recoverable damages to loss which was within the reasonable contemplation of the parties at the time of contracting, or for which the party in breach contractually assumed responsibility.

Representation A statement which one party makes to another in relation to a fact or to that party's present intention. Representations, unlike terms, are not contractually binding promises and do not give rise to an action for breach of contract (although a remedy may be available in misrepresentation).

Repudiatory breach A breach of contract by one party which gives the other party the option to terminate the contract. A repudiatory breach is either a breach of a condition, or a serious breach of an innominate term.

Rescission The process by which a party affected by a vitiating factor rendering a contract voidable elects to avoid a contract. Rescission is usually accomplished by giving the other party notice, but it may be barred if certain criteria are met.

Restitution A term for a set of legal remedies which aim to reverse an unjust enrichment which one party has gained at the expense of the other.

Restitution interest An approach to quantifying damages which is based not on the loss suffered by the innocent party, but on the gain made by the party in breach. The scope of the restitution interest is much more limited than the expectation or reliance interests.

Revocation The withdrawal of an offer before it is accepted. Revocation must be brought to the other party's attention to be effective.

Severable obligation Obligations are severable if completion of a substantial part (or of a specifically delineated part) of the obligation is sufficient to require the other party to perform their obligations under the contract.

Specific performance An equitable remedy which requires the party in breach to perform its obligations under the contract. The remedy will not be granted if damages are an adequate remedy.

Standard form contract A contract where the two parties contract on the basis of one party's standard terms of business.

Status quo ante The state of things in which the parties were before the contract was entered into.

Stranger to the contract A term used to describe a person who is not a party to the contract, but is affected by its terms.

Sufficiency The requirement that consideration must have some value in the eyes of the law, but not necessarily a value that is proportionate to the benefit provided by the promise (thus, 'consideration must be sufficient, but need not be adequate').

Terms The obligations which the parties have contractually undertaken in relation to each other. Terms may be express or implied.

Terms implied in fact A category of implied terms, which are read into the specific contract before the court because the facts of the case suggest that the term belongs there.

Terms implied in law A category of implied terms, which are read into all contracts of a particular type as a matter of statute or common law.

Third party beneficiary A term used to describe a person who is not a party to the contract, even though some or all of it is made for their benefit. Third party beneficiaries have a limited statutory right to enforce the contract, as an exception to the general rule of privity of contract.

Undue influence The exploitation by one person of their ability to influence another, in a manner that is unconscionable. Undue influence renders a contract voidable at the instance of the exploited person, and may be either actual or presumed.

Unfair term In consumer contracts, a term is unfair if it causes a significant imbalance in the parties' rights and obligations to the consumer's detriment, and does so in a manner which is contrary to the requirement of good faith. Core terms are never unfair.

Unilateral contract A contract which is made as an offer to the world, and which is intended to be accepted by completing performance. The offeror is bound as soon as the offeree begins performing, but the offeree is not bound until performance is complete.

Unilateral mistake A legal rule under which a contract is void if one of the parties contracted on the basis of a mistake either as to the identity of the other party, or as to the terms of the contract, of which the other party was aware.

Vagueness A situation where the meaning or effect of a term is too unclear or uncertain for the term to be enforceable.

Value In the eyes of the law, anything which has economic value of some sort, even if it is negligible, has 'value', and is therefore sufficient consideration.

Void A contract is void if it is deemed as a matter of law to have never come into being because of some vitiating factor. Common mistake and illegality are examples of vitiating factors which make contracts void. Also used in the form 'void *ab initio*' ('void from the beginning').

Voidable A contract is voidable if one of the parties has the option to rescind it because of some vitiating factor. Duress and misrepresentation are examples of vitiating factors which make contracts voidable. The courts have greater remedial discretion in relation to voidable contracts than void contracts.

Warranties The least important terms of a contract. A breach of a warranty is never repudiatory, and only gives the innocent party the right to sue for damages.

Index

D

CONTRACT **LAW**